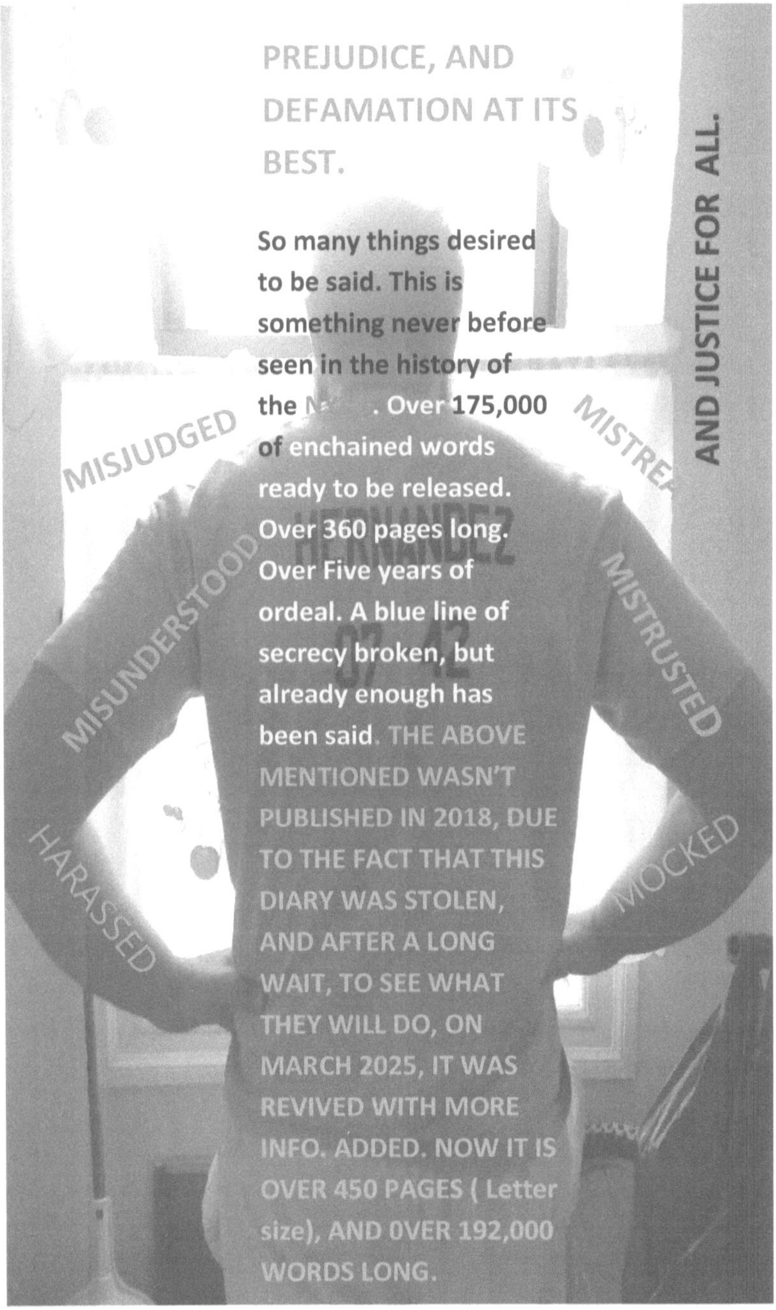

PREJUDICE, AND
DEFAMATION AT ITS
BEST.

So many things desired
to be said. This is
something never before
seen in the history of
the N . Over 175,000
of enchained words
ready to be released.
Over 360 pages long.
Over Five years of
ordeal. A blue line of
secrecy broken, but
already enough has
been said. THE ABOVE
MENTIONED WASN'T
PUBLISHED IN 2018, DUE
TO THE FACT THAT THIS
DIARY WAS STOLEN,
AND AFTER A LONG
WAIT, TO SEE WHAT
THEY WILL DO, ON
MARCH 2025, IT WAS
REVIVED WITH MORE
INFO. ADDED. NOW IT IS
OVER 450 PAGES (Letter
size), AND 0VER 192,000
WORDS LONG.

MISJUDGED

MISUNDERSTOOD

HARASSED

MISTRE

MISTRUSTED

MOCKED

AND JUSTICE FOR ALL.

Emmanuel Hernandez

MY TRUTH: (Illustrated Edition)

The Agony

Of a

NEW YORK CITY

police officer

Cover Design by Emmanuel Hernandez
Edited by Emmanuel Hernandez
Published by Emmanuel Hernandez
ISBN

DEDICATION

"You pushed me hard to make me fall, but the Lord helped me. The Lord is my strength and my song; He has become my salvation." (Psalm 118:13-14 HCSB)

First, I want to thank the Lord, God almighty for he was the only one who helped me thru the process. He only deserves glory forever and ever Amen.

In memory of those who had or have been wrongfully accused of anything. Of those who have hurt themselves, because they couldn't bear the injustice that were committed against them by the hand of an accuser(s) who does the work of the devil himself and who is the great accuser and the father of lies. Now you judge for yourself, which is worse? A false accuser or a murderer? A false accuser or a thief? Also, I want to encourage kids, adolescents, young adults, and people of all ages who are victims of bullies, to remember that all this will come to pass, and that if I made it, they could make it too. Just compare my tribulation to yours and look at me that by the grace of God, I am still alive to give you, my account.

I do cry like a baby every time I read on the Newspaper that a young person killed himself or herself because of bullying. For those who are struggling with bullying from peers, I want to advise them to remain strong. Have faith and courage which are the victuals that keep helping me move forward. I, myself was a victim of bullying from grown adults who knew better, and worse, I was infamously being labeled as being someone that I was not. It lasted for many years, and it is still happening today, but deep in my heart I know that one day all this will come to an end, because I still have faith in the judicial system of the United States of America. Look at me now, I am still alive and strong. Remember, everything will come to pass. And I want to cite Benito Suarez who once said that to respect other PEOPLE'S LIFE, is peace. NOW LETS SEE,

IF AFTER PUBLISHING THIS, I AM LEFT ALONE. FOR IT IS APRIL 2025, AND I HAVEN'T FOUND PEACE AND QUITE AND PRIVACY SINCE 2013.

HOWEVER; I DO WANT TO THANKS MY NEIGHBORS IN THE RESIDENCE I LIVE, AND THE BOARD OF NEIGHBORS, FOR SILENCING MY DOWNSTAIRS NEIGHBOR, WHO FOR, I BELIEVE 3 YEARS, OR SINCE THE DAY I MOVED IN TO MY APARTMENT, HAS BEEN YELLING, SCREAMING AND USING ALL TYPES OF WORDS AND REMARKS, IN AN ACT THAT I BELIEVE IT TO BE PURPOSELY PERPETRATED. THEY DID SO ON APRIL 2025.

MY FATHER WHO IS 90 OR CLOSE TO BE 90 YEARS OLD, THANK GOD, IS IN THE CARE OF TWO WOMEN AND A MAN EMPLOYEE. BEFORE THE ONE THAT IS WORKING NOW, FIVE WOMEN HOUSEKEEPER WORKED AND LIVED THERE. TO GO STREIGHT TO THE POINT, MY FATHER WAS MISSING MONEY, STAFF SUSPECTED AND WHY NOT ME ALSO? AFTER ALL THESE MESS, IN THE PRESENT TIME ON April 17, 2025, THE THREE STAFF AND MY UNKLE, THINK THAT I AM A THIEF. THEIR HARSH WORDS WHILE PLAYING DOMINO AND THEIR RUDE TREATMENT TOWARDS ME, SPEAK FOR ITSELF. NOW WILL CONVICE THEM THAT I WAS NEVER, THAT I AM NOT, AND WILL NEVER BE A THIEF SO HELP ME GOD? NOW IT IS TIME FOR ALL OF YOU TO DO YOUR PART OF CLEARING MY NAME, IF YOU TRULY BELIEVE IN JUSTICE.

"He was oppressed, and he was afflicted, yet he opened not his mouth; like a lamb that is led to the slaughter, and like a sheep that before its shearers is silent, so he opened not his mouth." (Isaiah 53:7 ESV)

"Remember the word that I said to you: 'A servant is not greater than his master.' If they persecuted me, they will also persecute you." (John 15:20 ESV)

"Whoever is slow to anger is better than the mighty, and he who rules his spirit than he who takes a city." (Proverb 16:32 ESV)

Throughout life, I learned that things are better to be written than be said. Whatever is written, carries a great deal of weight. However, what is simply said many times goes away with the winds after it has caused its momentary effects. Words can build, but it can also cause great destruction.

But when it is written, our naked eyes can see these words and even hear them within the inner voice of our mind. Words confirm and they take you back to those forgotten words that were once said. Written words can last a lifetime. But what is said can last seconds. Unless what is said is voice or video recorded, which in most cases, is illegal. But what is written is always legal and legitimate, and whomever does, regardless of whether it is true or a lie, the writer must be accountable for what he writes. **Emmanuel Hernandez**

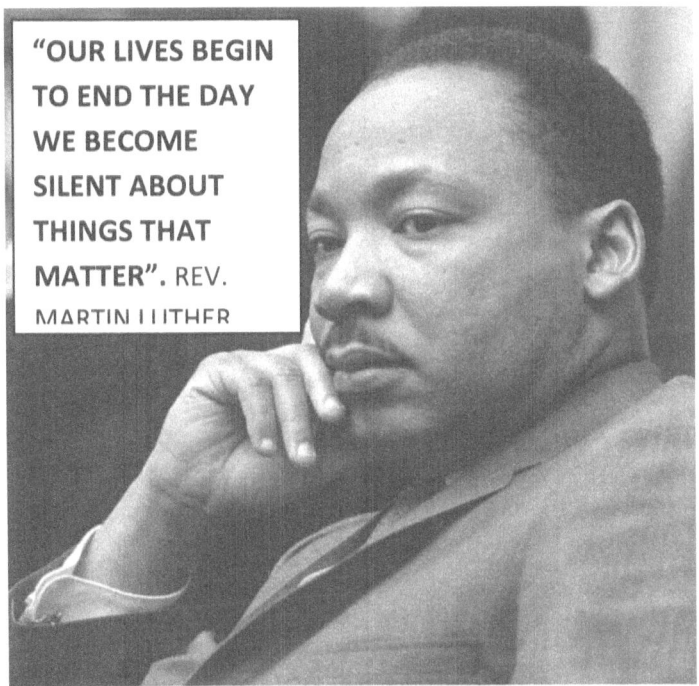

"OUR LIVES BEGIN TO END THE DAY WE BECOME SILENT ABOUT THINGS THAT MATTER". REV. MARTIN LUTHER

My Truth: The Agony of a New York City Police Officer.

Chapter 1

My Small Achievements

Hi. I am Police Officer EMMANUEL HERNANDEZ. I want to inform to whomever is concern, that by sharing my Diary with you, you will get inform of my great tribulation. My daily agony. How I had to bear and resist humiliation, insults, and harsh accusations. They have been slandering me every single day.

The right to privacy is one of the most valuable and precious possessions that one has, and I have been denied this right. I didn't know what to do then, and I don't know what to do now. Throughout my terrifying experiences, I found refuge in God, and in the process, the

Psalms encouraged me to keep on going because I could relate to the Psalmists' struggles while going through all my ongoing hardships. Something inside of me has moved me to write and now I believe that opening my diary to you is the only resort that I have because I don't know any other. But first I want to present and introduce to you my background history. I once heard somebody say that he is an open book, and that is what I am trying to be, to be as clear and transparent as the water is.

The great Rev. Martin Luther King Jr. who at the time was being maliciously persecuted unjustly by the founder of the FBI, J. Edgar Hoover, once said, "If a man has not discovered something that he will die for, he isn't fit to live." And I have discovered and seen how my good name has been stepped on, and how helpless I have been all these days. I do believe that it is worth fighting for the defense of one's dignity, one's wholeness and my reputation is no longer on the line for it is already damaged or better said, ruined. It is said, "To keep quiet is to consent to it", "Who says nothing, agrees", and "Silence is consent."

In a few words, not to speak is to speak and admit, and this is a huge mistake. Therefore, I feel obligated or obliged to break the silence. I don't know what repercussions this diary, my diary, will bring to me, but I do feel that publishing it is a must do. There are scars that last for a lifetime, but my open wounds are not healing. I am so hurt, and its publication is my last resort for I see no other alternative.

How can someone peacefully work in a place where everyone there believes, suspects and treats one as if one were a criminal?

First, I want to open my background to you. I was born in the Dominican Republic. At the age of 10, I immigrated to the United States of America. In the USA, I began school on the 5TH grade, which was a tough beginning in my education, for I didn't know how to read yet, and to be placed in a monolingual, only English class, was very tough, because of the language barrier and cultural shock. On the 6th grade, I was switched to bilingual class. I remained on bilingual education for the 7th and the 8th grade. Then I went to Park West High School where I completed my 9TH, 10th, 11th, and 12th grade, still on bilingual education.

I graduated from that troubling and problematic High School, where gangs and fights ruled the school. If you go to the search engine Google and type "Park West High School", you will find the New York Post article published on March 28, 1999, the year I graduated, and the article is titled: PARK WEST HS:' PREP SCHOOL FOR PRISON'; SEX, DRUGS & CRIME RAMPANT by Maria Alvarez. Read the article to confirm. I began my first job while still being a high school student, with the consent of my parents.

The first job I had was in a shoe and toys store on 34th street. My job assignment was to carry heavy boxes, store them upstairs and bring them down to the store and distribute them based on the need of the store, in addition to serving as security guard stairwell when the store required. Moreover, I worked for a year in a supermarket, at 72 street, in the kitchen area, peeling fruits and carrying cooked food from the basement up to the first floor, using the stairway multiple times a day, because the elevator was most of the time defective. One employee fell from the elevator, and sustained injuries. Later, I worked at the Au Bon Pain bakery store, the one on 50th street, for a while. I left the bakery job for the security guard. I worked for BURNS Security. First, I was assigned to Yeshiva University, in uptown Manhattan.

Then I was assigned to guard several offices in Wall Street, until finally, they had me working at reception for **Prudential Financial at One New York Plaza** (Picture above), close to the Twin Towers. All the time I did security I was attending LaGuardia Community College. In this multicultural college I met beautiful people of different nationalities, cultures, and of different ethnic backgrounds. I was delighted to be there, and form part of that colorful rainbow of different racial colors, languages and behaviors. There I met my best friend who is from Haiti. At LaGuardia, I obtained my associate's degree in liberal arts. At the same time, I proudly became a New York City Police Cadet.

Nevertheless, during my years at LaGuardia, I ended up doing two important internships. I was assigned to work as a volunteer at a Supreme Court Subdivision that handled complaints, Supreme Criminal Court: In the Court Dispute Referral Center. Responsibilities: Help complainants by referring them to the Supreme Court, Civil Court, Police Department, etc, depending on their problems, for several days. And for several days, I did another internship in Queens for City Council Member

Melinda Katz, who is now, at this present time, the Queens District Attorney.

She might not remember me, but I do remember her. I didn't get into conversation with her, but I did with her staff. I was limited in my conversation, because I was never used to speak English specially with native speakers, except with my teachers and professors. What I can say is that I was intimidated to talk in English with fluent speakers. However, I felt comfortable talking English with someone who had an accent just like me. For all I could observe during that brief period working in her office is that she is a hard-working woman, and I endorse her.

29th District

Melinda R. Katz (D)
Entered City Council January 2002
Represents: Forest Hills, Rego Park; parts of
Maspeth, Kew Gardens and Elmhurst
104-01 Metropolitan Avenue
Forest Hills, NY 11375
Phone: (718) 544-8800
Fax: (718) 544-4452

250 Broadway
New York, NY 10007
Phone: (212) 788-6981
Email: M29katz@council.nyc.ny.us

To be a public servant is equal to serving, and I am always delighted when I do serve others. Everywhere I go, I am always alert and willing to help anyone that I may get in contact with. For example, every time I take the subway station, and see someone, regardless of age, gender, race and nationality, carrying some luggage, a shopping cart, a baby carrier or carrying something heavy, and trying to go up or down the stairs, I always run to their need, and helped them. It is always a pleasure for me to do so, and I feel rewarded when they simply say, "Thank you."

I remember my days working at YM & YWHA, a Jewish recreational organization for the elderly and children of all ages and nationalities. In this place, I saw a man, whose company was hired to place rubber tiles at the gym facility this the organization. I saw just this man carrying those rubber tiles up to the gym. At that instance, I realized that he needed help, so I volunteered to help him carry those tiles right away. When we were done from sweating, he thanked me, and he took out a twenty-dollar bill to pay me for having helped him. I told him to keep it. He said that he would buy me food then, but I refused. Again, it was simply a pleasure for me to be a helping hand.

I remember the day when I bought an HP laptop at Staples 4320 Broadway Store #1573, New York, N.Y 1033. The moment that I bought it; I left the store. Then I went back to the store to ask for something else, and when the manager at the store saw me, she approached me. I noticed that she was very worried about something. She explained to me that the cashier that attended me, was missing $100 dollars from the cashier. The manager told me that the cashier is pregnant and that the cashier was going to get fired if she didn't find the missing amount. She believed that when she gave me my change, she accidentally gave me back a hundred dollars more than what I was supposed to have received.

Regularly, whenever I receive change due to any monetary transaction, such as when buying something, I am used not to counting the money I receive in return as change. So, I didn't know if she did, or if she didn't give me that extra $100 dollars, which now a day due to inflation, might be worth $200 dollars. As a result, acknowledging my lack of financial discipline, and that there was no way for me to find out whether she gave me in change, I gave her the benefit of the doubt. As result, I gave her the money back anyway, or a gave her that gift, because I didn't want her to be fired.

I WONDER HOW IS HER KID DOING SINCE THIS HAPPENED MANY YEARS AGO? The manager happily thanked me, and her gratitude was worth much more to me than a hundred dollars in gold. So, to be a public servant, and to be able to satisfy my desire of serving and helping others, have always been and still is a privilege to me. And one day, to have the authority to do so, and to have the vested power as a New York City police officer to expand more my ability of helping others as a public servant, was not just going to be a job, but a satisfaction, a pleasure, a dream come true. I know that many of you can relate and identify with me in regard to having a job you love doing.

After I graduated from LaGuardia Community College, and so obtaining my associate degree, I was more than being eligible to become a police officer. I had fulfilled all the requirements to become one, however; I didn't want to stop there. I ran in pursuit of my bachelor's degree. My decision to pursue my bachelor's degree right away, had nothing to do with just becoming a New York City Police Officer, but to fulfill, ahead of time, one of the main requirements to become a Captain, which is, that to be promoted to that rank, the candidate, must have a bachelor's degree. I had in mind to move up the ranks as soon I reached the opportunity, so I wanted to get it over with. In addition, by obtaining my bachelor's degree, I was going to be more positioned and academically prepared and more fluent in my English skill to better serve the NYPD, and the people of the community for whom I was going to be working for.

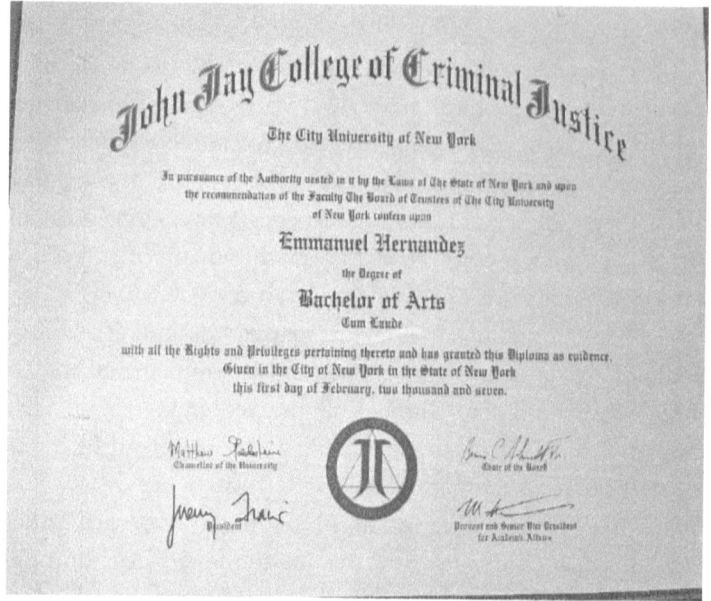

As a result of aspiring to become one of the finest one day, a New York City Police Officer, I went to John Jay College of Criminal Justice to obtain a bachelor's in criminal justice, which I did, with a minor in Literature, which also helped me fuel and nurture my inspiration and the desire to write. I graduated Cum Laude. I had accumulated 137 credits, when at the time, I think that the NYPD department only required 60 college credits to fulfill those requirements.

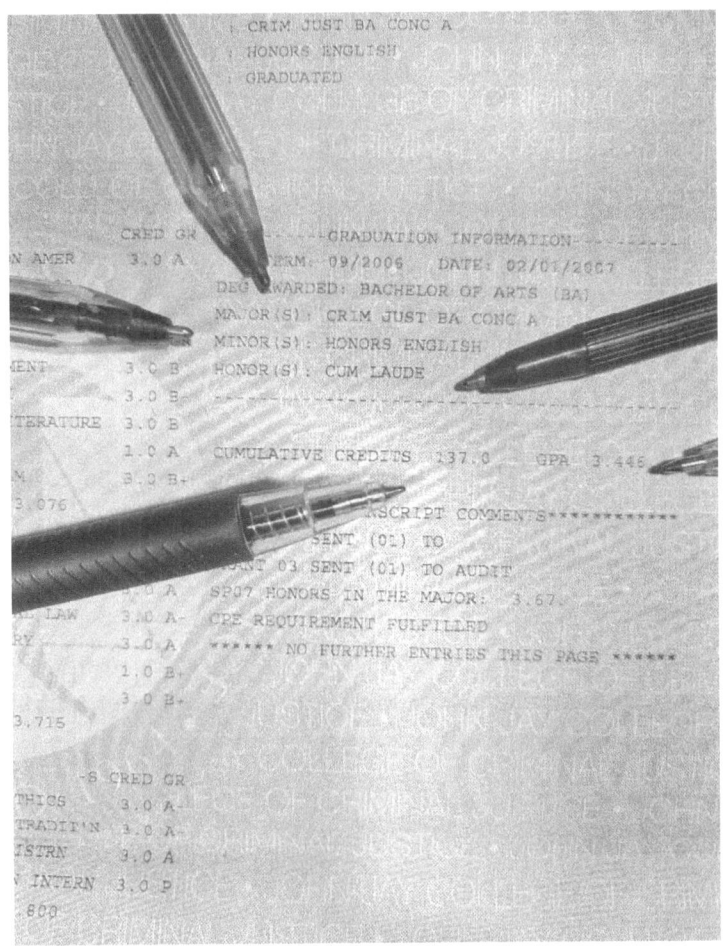

ONE THING I WANT TO EMPHASIZE AND PUT INTO CONTEXT IS THAT BY NATURE, I WAS ALWAYS A SLOW THINKING PERSON. I WAS SHY, AND IN ADDITION TO BEING SHY, I HAD TO FIGHT TRYING TO UNDERSTAND, TO ANSWER AND TO RESPOND TO A PERSON WHEN TRYING TO COMMUNICATE IN ENGLISH. THEREFORE, I RECORDED MY PROFESSORS DURING CLASS SECTION, AND WHEN I GOT HOME, I FORWARDED OR REWIND THEIR TEACHINGS. IT WAS DOUBLE WORK FOR ME, BECAUSE I AM A SLOW

WRITTER ALSO. SO, AT HOME, I PLAYED THE RECORDING AND TRIED TO TAKE NOTES AT MY OWN PACE. IT WAS DOUBLE THE WORK FOR ME; THEREFORE, I MANAGED TO KEEP A DECENT AVERAGE OR GRADE.

So, after working as a Police Cadet for the New York City Police Department for six years, in June of 2007, I graduated from the Police Cadet Corps. The following are pictures of my graduation with ex-police commissioner Raymond Kelly and my training Sergeant.

2007/06/16

A PHOTO OF ME WITH EX-POLICE COMMISSIONER RAYMOND KELLY.

2007/06/16

A PHOTO OF ME WITH SERGEANT MARLON LARIN, MY TRAINING SERGEANT AT THE TIME AND WHO IS NOW A DEPUTY INSPECTOR.

SO, I MANAGED TO COMPLETE AND TO GRADUATE FROM THE POLICE CADET PROGRAM. MANY BECOME POLICE CADET, BUT NOT ALL OF THEM DO GRADUATE FROM THE PROGRAM BEFORE BECOMING A NEW YORK CITY POLICE OFFICER.

On July 2007, I entered the Police Academy. At the academy, I still remember the day when another police recruit by the name of Gomez told me that the job was going to change who I am, since everyone in my police academy class knew that I was a man who fear God and do not curse or use inappropriate language by no mean. But this recruit told me that the job was going to make me curse, to watch and see, but the job never changed my personality.

This is something that I can assure you that during my pre-employment and pro-employment in the NYPD, my co-workers, colleagues and partners throughout my working years in the department and out of the department, can certify that I didn't use a cursing word in my vocabulary. So, on December 27, 2007, I finally and proudly became a New York City Police Officer. My family was so proud that I made it. It was a glorious day for me and my family.

I became part of the NYPD, the biggest police force in the country or as many say, "the most powerful law enforcement agency in the country." As a police officer, I performed my duties with courtesy, professionalism and respect and nobody can say the opposite. One day,

I overheard one officer say to other officers that I was dangerous. Simply, because as for me, wrongdoing is unacceptable, and if I got to witness any wrongdoing, they knew I wasn't going to stay quiet.

Overall, I was always accused of being judged mentally. I was sworn to protect and serve, and I honored my pledge everywhere I went, 24/7. During my regular daily commute, my method of transportation was and always is public transportation, using MTA buses and the subway train. While riding them, I was always on alert and ready to get myself involved or ready to engage in any situation that required police involvement to defend and protect.

After graduating from the police academy, I and almost all graduates were assigned to Instant Respond Team throughout the New York City Borough. I was assigned to Patrol Borough Brooklyn North (Instant Response Team). There, I did foot patrol, sometimes with a partner, but many times by myself. Then, after serving the Brooklyn community for six months, my partners and I were to be reassigned and transferred to our permanent command. When it was my turn to see my commanding officer in his office, he told me that I did a good job under his command.

Unfortunately, I was shy and timid. I don't know if to be shy and timid can be considered a curse. So, I made the unwise decision of telling him to send me anywhere he wants that might be close to home. So, I was transferred close to home, to Spanish Harlem, at the 25th Precinct, and wouldn't it be the case, this diary, would have never been written, wouldn't have existed.

At the 25thprecinct, I did what I was ordered to do. I followed the leadership and commands of my superiors, my senior officers, and the advice of my fellow officers that had less seniority time than me on the job. I was never a disciplinary problem because I had equal and mutual respect for each of them. I cannot think of any civilian complaints done against me by the agency **Civilian Complaint Review Board**, who supervises police abuses, corruption and misconduct against civilians.

On my police Annual performance evaluation, I had good ratings. I did my job with pride, enthusiasm and with a lot of motivation.

I was very productive when it came down to whatever it was that they wanted me to do. I was a happy man.

Every police officer, with more than two years on the job, are being evaluated yearly by a supervisor who rate the officers according to his or her achievements throughout the year. In regard to the yearly evaluations, the highest rating an officer can have been **5**, and almost no officer gets that. It is rare, and it is only given in unusual circumstances. The rating of **4.0** is considered way above average and only a few officers get this rating. When it comes to my yearly evaluations, the following are my overall evaluations for four straight consecutive years. IIn **2011** for the rating period **(12/16/2009-12/15/2010)** I was given a **4.0**,

In **2012** for the rating period **(12/15/2010-12/15/2011)** I was given a **4.0**,

In **2013** for the rating period **(12/16/2011- 12/15/2012)** I was given a **4.0**,

and in **2014** for the rating period **(12/16/2012-12/15/2013)** I was given a **4.0**.

So, for four straight consecutive years, I received a 4.0 on my evaluations, by which 4.0 is graded as HIGHLY COMPETENT. And again, I was never a disciplinary problem. The following are two of my yearly Performance Evaluations done by my supervisors.

Online Performance Evaluation System
Police Officer - Detective Specialist

RATEE

SURNAME	FIRST	M.I.	Appt Date
HERNANDEZ	EMMANUEL		7/9/2007

RATEE TAX NUMBER	RANK	COMMAND	DATE ASSIGNED TO COMMAND:	Borough
944269	PO	025	7/7/2008	MANHATTAN NORTH

TIMES SICK	DAYS LOST	PURPOSE	RECOMMENDATION
NLOD: 0	NLOD: 0	ANNUAL	CONTINUE IN PRESENT ASSIGNMENT
LOD: 0	LOD: 0		

Not chronic   Date of Primary Assignment: 7/7/2008   ☑ IF COMPLETED POLICE CADET PROGRAM

Primary Assignment: PATROL   Rating Period From: 12/16/2011 To: 12/15/2012

FORCE RECORD
☐ Checked if ratee's force record is current

RATER

SURNAME	FIRST	M.I.
GIBBS	IRA	R

RATER TAX NUMBER	RANK	COMMAND	DATE ASSIGNED TO COMMAND:
925348	SERGEANT	025	10/1/2008

PERFORMANCE AREAS		BEHAVIORAL DIMENSIONS	
Area	Rating	Dimension	Rating
1 Community Interaction	5	13 Police Ethics / Integrity	5
2 Apprehension/Intervention	5	14 Comprehension Skills	5
3 Victim/Prisoner Interaction	4	15 Communication Skills	4
4 Processing Arrests	5	16 Reasoning Ability	5
5 Vehicular Offenses/Accidents	4	17 Information Ordering	5
6 Handling Specific Offenses	4	18 Problem Recognition	4
7 Police Interaction/Notification	4	19 Visualization	5
8 Vehicle Operation/Maintenance	3	20 Spatial Orientation	5
9 Review and Maintenance	4	21 Memorization	5
10 Handling Special Cases	4	22 Judgement	5
11 Vouchering	5	23 Innovativeness	5
12 Report/Clerical Duties	4	24 Adaptability	5
		25 Drive/Initiative	5
		26 Interpersonal Skills	4
		27 Appearance/Professional Image	5
		28 Physical Fitness/Physical Activities	5

Overall Evaluation : 4
Annual Total of Quarterly Point: 57

26. Interpersonal Skills
OFFICER HERNANDEZ DEMONSTRATES THE ABILITY TO GET ALONG WITH PEERS,
SUPERVISORS AND THE COMMUNITY. SHE IS EXTREMELY TACTFUL IN SITUATIONS WHERE
A POTENTIAL FOR CONFLICT EXIXTS.

22. Judgement
PO HERNANDEZ' CONCLUSION ARE CONSISTENTLY SOUND AND VERY PRACTICAL. HE DOES
A GOOD JOB OF RECOGNIZING THE NEED FOR MORE INFORMATION TO AID IN DRAWING
CONCLUSIONS.

7. Police Interaction/Notification
P.O. HERNANDEZ IS VERY PROFICIENT IN DIRECTING POLICE ACTIONS DURING AN
EMERGENCY. HE ALWAYS ASSIST FELLOW OFFICERS INVOLVED IN COMMUNITY
INTERACTIONS AND DOES A TREMONDOUS JOB OF RELAYING INFORMATION TO OTHER
OFFICERS.

Recognitions Received:

n/a

Overall Rater's Comments:
OFFICER HERNANDEZ IS A VERY QUICK LEARNER, HE ACCOMPLISHES ALL ASSIGNMENTS
ON TIME AND HAS NEVER BEEN A DISCIPLINARY PROBLEM. HE CAN BE COUNTED ON TO
CARRY OUT DAY TO DAY ACTIVITIES. PO HERNANDEZ HAS A GREAT DEAL OF ARREST
THROUGHOUT HIS CAREER. HE IS A MODEL FOR ALL OFFICERS TO FOLLOW.

BY SIGNING THIS FORM, THE RATER AND REVIEWER CERTIFY THAT IN FORMULATING THIS PERFORMANCE
APPRAISAL. THEY HAVE REVIEWED AND CONSIDERED RATEE'S CPI, DEPARTMENT RECOGNITION, CCRB,
PERFORMANCE MONITORING RECORDS, EEO COMPLIANCE, AND ALL OTHER RECORDS OF PERFORMANCE
DOCUMENTATION FOR EVENTS IN THE IMMEDIATE RATING PERIOD. POSITIVE ACCOMPLISHMENTS SHOULD
BE NOTED.

REVIEWER

SURNAME	FIRST	M.I.	
YAGUCHI	NAOKI		
REVIEWER'S TAX NUMBER	RANK	COMMAND	DATE ASSIGNED TO COMMAND
937764	LIEUTENANT	025	8/21/2012

Overall Reviewer Comments:
P.O. Hernandez is a young and eager officer who is always willing to work. He is a team player whose
enthusiasm for the job has a positive effect on the rest of the platoon.

☒ ACCURATE AND COMPLETE, CONCUR ☐ SEE SEPARATE REVIEWER'S EVALUATION

THE RATER HAS SHOWN THIS EVALUATION TO RATEE AND FULLY DISCUSSED ITS CONTENTS,
INCLUDING RATEE'S RIGHTS AND RESPONSIBILITIES REGARDING EEO ISSUES.

☒ I WISH TO FINALIZE THIS EVALUATION ☐ I WISH TO APPEAL THIS EVALUATION

RATEE
SIGNATURE _____   Date _____

RATER
SIGNATURE _____   Date _____

Online Performance Evaluation System
Police Officer - Detective Specialist

RATEE

SURNAME	FIRST	M.I.		Appt Date
HERNANDEZ	EMMANUEL			7/9/2007

RATEE TAX NUMBER	RANK	COMMAND	DATE ASSIGNED TO COMMAND:	Borough
944269	PO	025	7/7/2008	MANHATTAN NORTH

TIMES SICK	DAYS LOST	PURPOSE	RECOMMENDATION
NLOD: 0	NLOD: 0	ANNUAL	CONTINUE IN PRESENT ASSIGNMENT
LOD: 0	LOD: 0		

Not chronic   Date of Primary Assignment: 7/7/2008   ✔ IF COMPLETED POLICE CADET PROGRAM

Primary Assignment: PATROL   Rating Period From: 12/16/2012 To: 12/15/2013

FORCE RECORD
Checked if ratee's force record is current

RATER

SURNAME	FIRST	M.I.
GIBBS	IRA	R

RATER TAX NUMBER	RANK	COMMAND	DATE ASSIGNED TO COMMAND:
925348	SERGEANT	025	10/1/2008

PERFORMANCE AREAS

BEHAVIORAL DIMENSIONS

Area	Rating	Dimension	Rating
1 Community Interaction	4	13 Police Ethics / Integrity	5
2 Apprehension/Intervention	5	14 Comprehension Skills	5
3 Victim/Prisoner Interaction	5	15 Communication Skills	4
4 Processing Arrests	5	16 Reasoning Ability	4
5 Vehicular Offenses/Accidents	4	17 Information Ordering	4
6 Handling Specific Offenses	4	18 Problem Recognition	4
7 Police Interaction/Notification	4	19 Visualization	4
8 Vehicle Operation/Maintenance	3	20 Spatial Orientation	4
9 Review and Maintenance	4	21 Memorization	5
10 Handling Special Cases	4	22 Judgement	4
11 Vouchering	5	23 Innovativeness	4
12 Report/Clerical Duties	3	24 Adaptability	4
		25 Drive/Initiative	5
		26 Interpersonal Skills	4
		27 Appearance/Professional Image	5
		28 Physical Fitness/Physical Activities	5

Overall Evaluation : 4
Annual Total of Quarterly Point: 51

17. Information Ordering
OFFICER HERNANDEZ IS A VETERAN OFFICER WHO IS ABLE TO PIECE TOGETHER
NARRATIVES OF WHAT SITUATIONS WHICH MAY HAVE OCCURRED. HE CAN DISCERN FROM
WHAT HAPPENDED IN A PARTICULAR ORDER WHICH LEADS TO THE PROPER ACTIONS
WHICH SHOULD BE TAKEN AS A RESPONDING OFFICER.

25. Drive/Initiative
OFFICER HERNANDEZ TAKES A PERSONAL INTEREST IN HIS DAILY ASSIGNMENTS. HE IS
EAGER TO HELP WITH DIFFICULT SITUATIONS, FURTHERMORE PO HERNANDEZ IS ABLE TO
SOLVE PROBLEMS WITH LITTLE OR NO SUPERVISION. HE IS WILLING TO GET INVLOVLED IN
SITUATIONS AND FOLLOW IT THROUGH.

28. Physical Fitness/Physical Activities
OFFICER HERNANDEZ KEEPS HIMSELF PHYSICALLY FIT WHICH ASSIST HIM IN
APPREHENDING SUSPECTS WHEN NEEDED. ALTHOUGH HE MAINTAINS THE PHYSICAL
ABILITY TO CONDUCT HIS JOB HE USES COMMUNICATIONS SKILLS AND REASONING
ABILITY TO ACHIEVE HIS GOALS AND ASSIGNMENTS.

Recognitions Received:

n/a

Overall Rater's Comments:
PO HERNANDEZ HAS BECOME ONE OF THE MORE ACTIVE OFFICERS ON THE FIRST PLATOON
DURING THIS RATING PERIOD. HE HAS STEADILY INCREASED HIS PRODUCTIVITY GOALS. HE
HANDLES THE BUSIEST SECTOR ON A NIGHTLY BASIS. HE IS VERY RELIABLE AND CARRIES
OUT DAILY ASSIGNMENTS WITHOUT COMPLAINING. OFFICER HERNANDEZ CONTINUES TO
BE PUNCTUAL, PROFESSIONAL AND RESPONSIBLE. PO HERNANDEZ IS VERY TRUSTWORTHY
AND CAN BE COUNTED ON THE ACCOMPLISH THE TASK AT HAND.

BY SIGNING THIS FORM, THE RATER AND REVIEWER CERTIFY THAT IN FORMULATING THIS PERFORMANCE
APPRAISAL, THEY HAVE REVIEWED AND CONSIDERED RATEE'S CPI, DEPARTMENT RECOGNITION, CCRB,
PERFORMANCE MONITORING RECORDS, EEO COMPLIANCE, AND ALL OTHER RECORDS OF PERFORMANCE
DOCUMENTATION FOR EVENTS IN THE IMMEDIATE RATING PERIOD. POSITIVE ACCOMPLISHMENTS SHOULD
BE NOTED.

REVIEWER

SURNAME	FIRST	M.I.	
ALLEN	TREVOR	R	
REVIEWER'S TAX NUMBER	RANK	COMMAND	DATE ASSIGNED TO COMMAND:
934383	LIEUTENANT	023	10/17/2013

Overall Reviewer Comments:
I concur with the supervisors evaluation of the subject officer.

☑ ACCURATE AND COMPLETE, CONCUR ☐ SEE SEPARATE REVIEWER'S EVALUATION

THE RATER HAS SHOWN THIS EVALUATION TO RATEE AND FULLY DISCUSSED ITS CONTENTS
INCLUDING RATEE'S RIGHTS AND RESPONSIBILITIES REGARDING EEO ISSUES.

☑ I WISH TO FINALIZE THIS EVALUATION ☐ I WISH TO APPEAL THIS EVALUATION

RATEE   Date _____
SIGNATURE _____

POLICE DEPARTMENT
CITY OF NEW YORK

March 15, 2012

From: Commanding Officer, 25 Precinct

To: Commanding Officer, Performance Analysis Section

Subject: **REQUEST FOR EVALUATIONS TO BE CHANGED**

1.   The following member of the service assigned to the 25th Precinct appealed their annual evaluation for the rating period ending on December 15, 2011 and the undersigned determined after careful examination of facts and circumstances to change the evaluation from a (3.0) competent to a (4.0) highly competent.

Rank	Name	Tax #	Command
PO	Hernandez, Emanuel	944269	025

2.   It is the request of the undersigned to have the above listed annual evaluation be removed from the database so that it can be prepared. Please feel free to contact Lieutenant Gloria Guilamo, the 25th Precinct Operations Coordinator, with any questions at (212) 860-6515.

3.   Submitted for your Information.

Nilda Hofmann
Deputy Inspector

YES, DEPUTY INSPECTOR NILDA HOFMANN WAS NEW AT THE PRECINCT COMMAND AND SHE DIDN'T KNOW ME VERY WELL, BUT SHE HAD TO GIVE US OUR ANNUAL EVALUATION FOR THE YEAR. UNFORTUNATELY, SHE GAVE ME A LOW GRADE. BUT UPON FURTHER INVESTIGATION, CAREFUL EXAMINATION, AND FACTS OF THE CIRCUMSTANCES, SHE RAISED MY PERFORMANCE SCORE FROM **3.0 COMPETENT** TO **4.0 HIGHLY COMPETENT**.

I did my job as if I were doing it for the Lord. My hours of work or, let's say, my nightshift tour was from 11:15 pm till 7:50 am, a total of 8 hours and 35 minutes a day, five days a week. I naturally, being a morning person, had to become a night person by adapting to the night shift. I had pride in what I did, because I loved my job, so much that I even volunteered to do overtime, besides the overtime that was mandate for me to do. Also, there were times that I volunteered to work extra hours without getting paid. I was what some calls, "an overtime machine."

So much was the overtime that I used to do that the Integrity Control Officer, who was the one to keep track of police officer's overtime, used to advise me to keep my overtime numbers down, because I was exceeding or about to exceed the maximum amount of overtime that an officer was allowed to do on a quarterly basis. This is how much time I wanted to spend doing what I loved to do. Going to work was like going to the amusement park every day, where every day, a new adventure awaited me. Such as the night when I worked with PO Monteith.

One day, as we were patrolling the street, we decided to stop at the intersection of East 126 Street and 2nd Avenue. There we saw an officer from the Triborough Bridge and Tunnel Authority trying to stop a man who was riding a motorcycle, but the motorcyclist managed to escape by riding his motorcycle recklessly on the sidewalk all the way down to 1st avenue. When we saw what was occurring, we went on hot pursuit of the motorist.

When we arrived at 1st avenue, there was a dead end to the street, so the motorist turned around and faced us. Then, he drove his motorcycle towards us and as we drove towards him, along the way, he threw his motorcycle at us. The impact from the collision between the motorcycle and the patrol car was so strong that my entire body went forward, but I didn't hit the windshield thanks to my seatbelt.

My partner sustained minor injuries, but before deciding to chase the perpetrator, I made sure that he was ok. When I realized that he was not seriously injured, I rushed out of the car and ran after the perpetrator who had left the scene on foot and had run to the Harlem River Drive. At Harlem River Drive, a livery car driver who seemed to have witnessed something, told me to get in. I did and I told him to drive forward for a canvass.

As he drove, I got to see the motorist jugging at the Harlem River Drive, looking back and forward, not knowing who was inside of the livery car that was next to him. Meanwhile, as I patiently thought of tactics beforehand in case he might have a firearm. When I saw that he got tired of jugging, I rushed out of the livery car, drew my weapon and he surrendered. I arrested the man.

There was another night when there was a pursuit of a man with a gun at another precinct or command. Then man climbed a fence of about 20 feet high and so I did, and two other officers. We walked into a dark territory where we needed to use our flashlight. We climbed the ceiling of a house in search of the armed suspect until I, with the use of my flashlight, managed to see, or let's say, spot the suspect at the corner of a house. I jumped, grabbed the man and arrested him. Then, the other two officers joined. Later, the three of us walked with the suspect to the fence. The fence was forced open so that we could get out. Since the incident happened outside of my precinct, another officer took the arrest.

These were just two examples of a regular day of work, besides the good desire to help the people of the community that I worked for, as a public servant that I was. But no matter the day, when I used to arrive home from work and on my days off, I couldn't wait to go back to work, even though we are police officers 24/7. I only **called out sick once (Two consecutive administrative sick day counts as one) in six (6) straight years**. But that unique call sick that I made, disqualified me from obtaining the famous pen that are awarded to those officers that for five straight years, hadn't call out sick. That was my goal, but unfortunately, one day, I got sick.

However, not everything is rainbow color. I remember the time when I was very proactive at work, and during this same time, I was overdoing my assignment by having more police activity done than what I was asked for. As a result, I was reprimanded many times by a few of my fellow officers, especially the senior officers, because according to them, I was trying to be a super cop, and I was going to make them look bad. But it is no work when you enjoy doing something that others consider work. Especially, when you are working for, and under the supervision of a wonderful man called Lieutenant Dwayne Lee. He is the epitome   of   how   a   supervisor   should   be,

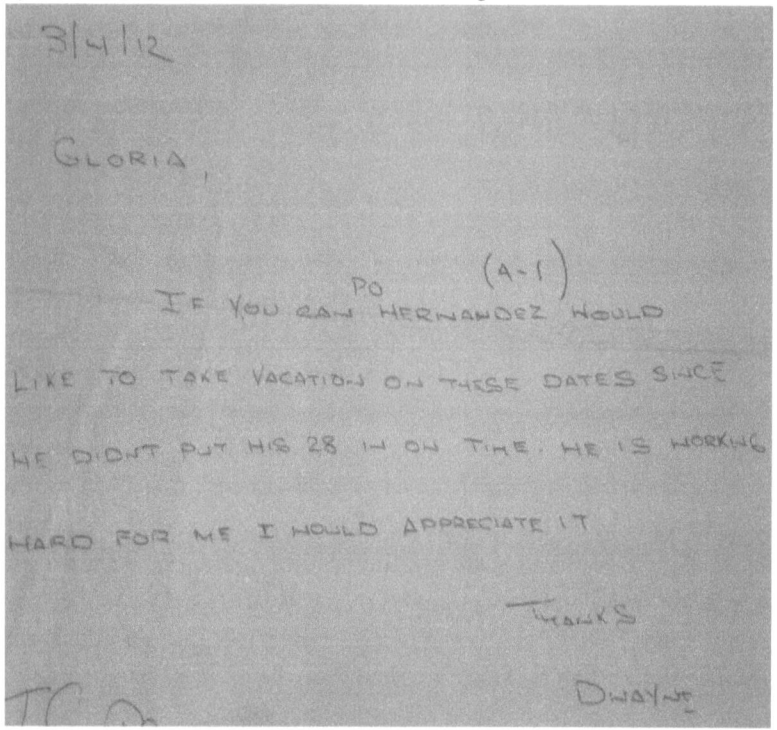

should manage themselves. I loved the man, and everyone at work loved him also.

It was a pleasure for me to make Lieutenant Lee look good before his superiors by me doing my job accordingly and with excellence. I remember the time when he wrote a note concerning me to the Administrative Lieutenant Galamo, because I was being denied a selected vacation week I had chosen, just because I didn't submit the required paperwork on time. And this is what Lt. Lee

wrote:

He was a great man. I looked out for him, and he looked out for me. But unfortunately, one afternoon, I was in the living room when I received a text message. It was Lieutenant Lee. He texted me to let me know that he was transferred. He thanked me for what I did for him. Now I confess to you that when I read his text message, I bitterly wept, literally I profoundly cried as I read through those lines and words, as tears were coming out of my eyes. I had a sense of loss, but also, I didn't know that since that moment, my life was going to change completely, and forever, BUT, for the worse.

Also, I want to emphasize that my relationship with the Manhattan District Attorney's office or Assistant District Attorneys were good and healthy, and I assisted them on all of their efforts of prosecuting those who broke the law and committed crimes. Underneath, there are two letters written to me by the Manhattan District Attorney's office.

DISTRICT ATTORNEY
OF THE
COUNTY OF NEW YORK
ONE HOGAN PLACE
New York, N. Y. 10013
(212) 335-9000

CYRUS R. VANCE, JR.
DISTRICT ATTORNEY

June 3, 2011

Officer Emmanuel Hernandez, Shield 2830
25th Precinct
120 East 119th St.
New York, NY 10035

Re: People vs. ▮▮▮▮▮▮▮ Indictment No. 4665/2010

Dear Officer Hernandez:

The defendant, ▮▮▮▮▮▮▮, pleaded guilty to the crime indicated below on May 2, 2011. Your efforts were very important to the successful prosecution of this case. I would like to thank you on behalf of this office and the citizens of our community.

Assistant District Attorney Karen Cherrington was in charge of the prosecution of this case. If you have any questions about this case, you may contact Assistant District Attorney Karen Cherrington at 335-4201.

Defendant Date of Birth NYSID No.	Crime	Sentence Date Term
▮▮▮▮▮▮▮ 9973136K	Sexual Abuse First Degree	6/1/2011 2 years in state prison

Thank you again for your contribution to this case.

Sincerely,

Cyrus R. Vance Jr.

Cyrus R. Vance, Jr.

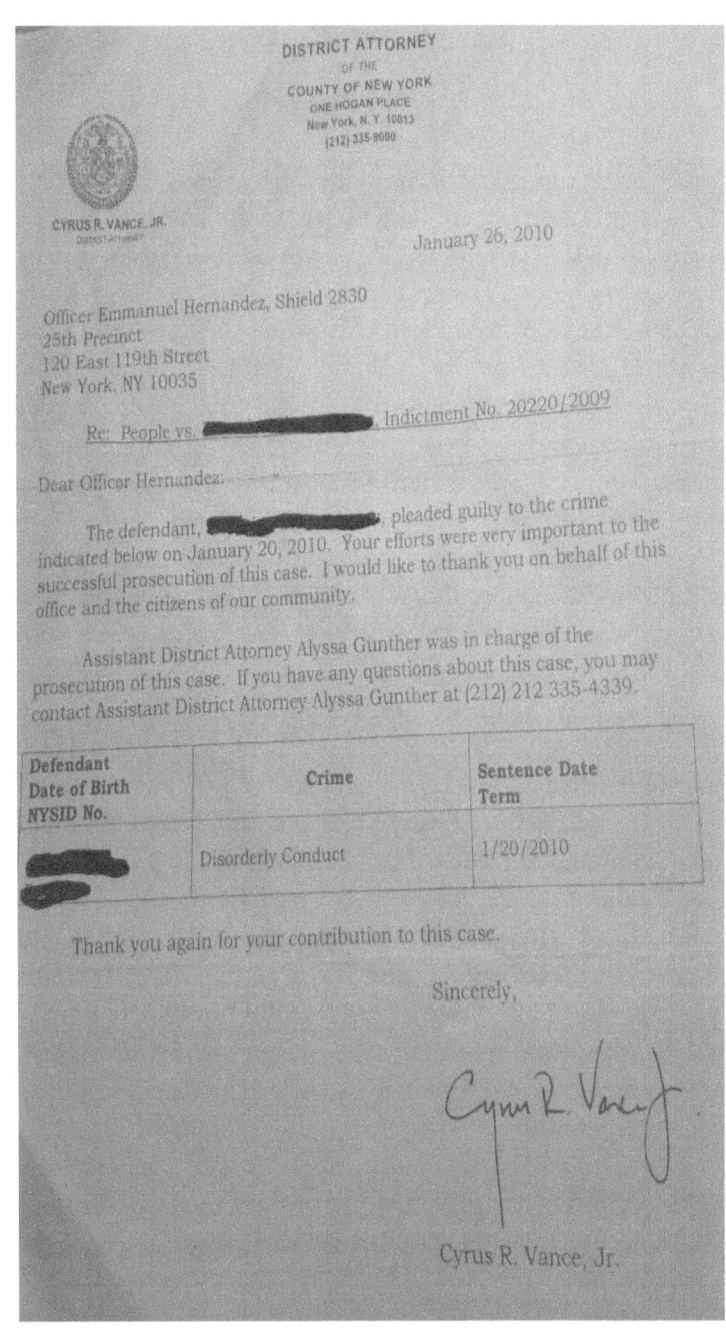

DISTRICT ATTORNEY
OF THE
COUNTY OF NEW YORK
ONE HOGAN PLACE
New York, N.Y. 10013
(212) 335-9000

CYRUS R. VANCE, JR.
District Attorney

January 26, 2010

Officer Emmanuel Hernandez, Shield 2830
25th Precinct
120 East 119th Street
New York, NY 10035

Re: People vs. ███████, Indictment No. 20220/2009

Dear Officer Hernandez:

The defendant, ███████, pleaded guilty to the crime indicated below on January 20, 2010. Your efforts were very important to the successful prosecution of this case. I would like to thank you on behalf of this office and the citizens of our community.

Assistant District Attorney Alyssa Gunther was in charge of the prosecution of this case. If you have any questions about this case, you may contact Assistant District Attorney Alyssa Gunther at (212) 212 335-4339.

Defendant Date of Birth NYSID No.	Crime	Sentence Date Term
███████	Disorderly Conduct	1/20/2010

Thank you again for your contribution to this case.

Sincerely,

Cyrus R. Vance, Jr.

33

Chapter 2

A Healthy Lifestyle

I was the happiest man in the world. I had everything. Everything was a dream come true. It was a pleasure for me to help the needy. I was a perfectly healthy man physically and mentally. I used to run in the park and ride my bicycle every week. I could easily do 15 pull ups and 50 pushups none stop. I religiously did my exercises for the purpose of being physically fit to defend the life and the well-being of my partners and of every civilian in situations where physical strength was needed, and to better protect and serve everyone. Also, to avoid comments such as the one made by a cop whose statement appeared in a New York Post article by Shawn Cohen, Aaron Feis and Bruce Golding.

The cop stated, "You see some of these officers out there: They are fat, they're sloppy, they're disgusting and they're not healthy." In addition, my theory is that the more physically fit a police officer is, the less likely is for the officer to have to resort to the use of deadly force as a mean to stop the threat. For example, an officer who can physically manage to take a bat out of a woman's hand, will never point his service gun and much less, shoot at that woman.

I used to have a very healthy eating habit. My favorite food were Sushi and Sardines. The same way that I took care of myself, I took care of others. As good as I treated myself, I treated others. Therefore, I always had in mind the CPR, which stands for Courtesy Professionalism and Respect. My greatest moment was spent in church, and one of my favorite hobbies was going to the movie theater and spending time in the park. I didn't drink alcohol nor smoke. One day I was asked why I was so happy. I was the pride of my family.

The search for God, was from the very beginning of my life. I went to a small bookstore to buy books and rent videos. I believe to have visited this library since 2003. Life with a Purpose is one of the books I bought in 2006.

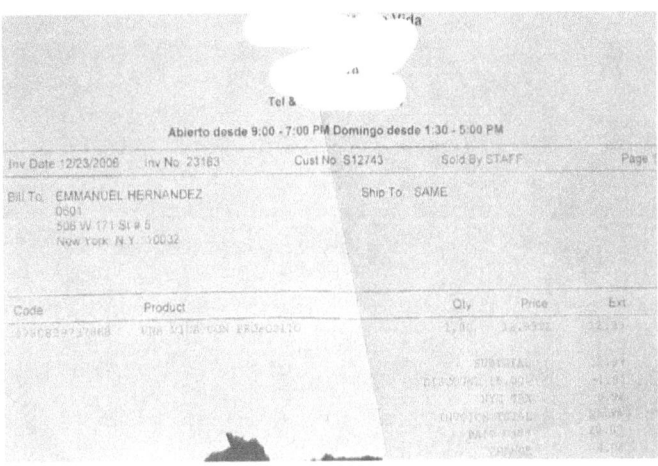

This is the moment where my former partner, PO Eddie Pinero, for the first time, placed a five-year bar on my uniform, marking my fifth-year anniversary in the police force as a police officer, for I had spent 6 years as a police cadet.

The following picture was taken on July 10, 2012. I was still celebrating my 5th year anniversary in the Police Department. As you can see, I had my hand up to show that I had five years on the job.

Wow, I was so happy, as can be reflected in the following picture, of my biological parents and me, as they were proud of me and I proud of them.

Back then in the Dominican Republic, when my mother was young, she aspired to be a police officer. But her mother and the woman with whom she grew up with forbid her from achieving her dream. Till this day, she still regrets her decision not to join the police force in the Dominican Republic. But she became more than happy when she learned that her youngest son, became not only a police officer, but one of the Finest, a New York City Police Officer.

As the years went by, each year was a better year for me, because I was getting to learn the job more. But suddenly, after working for more than 5 years as a police officer, everything began to change. Lieutenant Lee was gone, and Lieutenant Naoki Yaguchi took his place. At the beginning, everything was marching well between Lt. Yaguchi and me. I liked the man. He was younger than me and I respected him dearly. His accomplishments were impressive. Already in his twenties, he became a New York City Police Lieutenant and was attending Law school.

In the precinct, the officers used to say that he was a rising star **(Meaning that one day he was going to become chief of the police department, and a rising star because the chief's ranks are marked**

by stars, and the more stars they have on their necklace, the higher their ranks are). From 2000-2004 he attended the prestigious school **NYU (New York University)** where he obtained a **Bachelor of Arts (BA) in Politics**, in 2009-2013 he attended **New York Law School** where he obtained his Doctor of Law (JD) degree, and so becoming a lawyer. Now he is a **certified Attorney** in the State of Connecticut (2015-present) and in the State of New York (2014-Present).

He is a hardworking man, who also worked hard to make me fail. I had not only to face, but to resist this man who knows how to play politics, for as you can see, he spent four years of his life studying politics in a very prestigious school, NYU. (This explains why he buys a cake for each one of us on our birthday.

He is buying people's favor, and that's what politicians do). He bought me a cake in 2013 for my birthday, but the year after that he didn't buy me one. He bought cakes for other officers in private, as soon as he became the administrative Lieutenant, and he did it secretly as to not make me wonder why a cake was for them, and not for me. Also, he knows how to manipulate, bend and go around the law to screw up whoever gets on his way. I say "**resist**," because I didn't do anything to confront him and defend myself, because I feared the unknown. I just endured all the blows that he threw at me.

This is why, one day, with great mockery, he asked me how I was feeling, and I responded that I felt like "**Rocky**". But I don't know what I did to this man that he was so determined to destroy my career as a police officer. However, even though he used to swear and curse a lot, in the beginning, he appeared to be a good man. He used to ask me why I don't swear (don't use offensive or obscene language), and he used to mock me by telling the other officers that I didn't swear as if it was something unusual. He knew I was a Christian.

In addition, somehow, he found out how I and the rest of the officers liked Lt. Lee. So many times, he asked me if he was better than Lt. Lee. I wondered what his obsession was about comparing himself to Lt. Lee. Was it because his last name was Lee, and he thought that he was a Chinese man, since Chinese don't get along with Japanese and Lt. Yaguchi is Japanese. But Lt. Lee was a black man like in his fifties.

But I liked Lt. Yaguchi, and I did everything he commanded me to do. However, there is one thing that I can say about Lt. Yaguchi, that he is a very ambitious young man. I liked him and he seemed to like me. We joked and we laughed together. But suddenly, along the way, everything changed. He didn't treat me the same way that he used to. Unless, he pretended to have liked me at first. But suddenly, he changed and his dislike or hate towards me began to be manifested and it became very obvious, noticeable.

One day, I bought Lt. Yaguchi vitamin water, and I gave it to him at the Desk, in the precinct. When I handed it over to him, he told me that he liked the drink, and I said, "You see, we have the same taste." Immediately, and in front of everyone there, he angrily said to me, "No! We don't have the same taste." At that moment, I thought that because he is Japanese, he thought of himself better than me. But as time passed, **I realized that his bad attitude towards me had to do with something that happened in the precinct.**

In addition to that, like on three different occasions, Lt. Yaguchi had offered to take me home, since he had a car. I never had a car in the United States, and public transportation such as the train and the bus have always been my mean of transportation all of my life specially to commute from home to work and from work to home, which left me close to my destination.

I always had a good commute. But I wondered why he wanted to take me home, which I refused the favor, but he did take me home once. Was it to know me more and to find out where I lived? One behavior that I noticed of him was when he talked to me. He used to converse with me having his face down while his eyes were up looking at me, but without making enough eyes contact. I could sense that he was up to something, scheming something.

Knowing not what to do in such a hostile work environment, and before the matter escalated, one day I applied to work somewhere else. I had an interview. One way or the other Lt. Yaguchi found out about my interview, and when he saw me, he told me that if I got transferred to the work where I had applied, for me not to talk to him ever again. Despite everything, I was loyal to this man. Regarding the job he assigned us to do, I went the extra mile for him. I even stood after working hours without getting paid just to get his assignment completely done and to produce what he had expected to receive from me.

At the beginning, when my level of suspicion began to rise, I spoke to a very trustworthy member of my church, J…, about the issue, and I explained to him my concern, and how was my relationship with Lt. Yaguchi. He gave me some good advice. He told me not to worry, because I am a man of integrity. I followed his advice, and from that day on, I just ignored any negative behavior, and negative comments that were all planned and planted with the objective to influence and affect my emotions at my workplace. One day I asked Lt. Yaguchi if there was something wrong, if there was something that I should know about, and he told me that there was nothing wrong.

One night, I patrol with PO Christopher Gorman, who was my union PBA delegate, and he advised me to watch the movie "Frozen." Later in time, I watched the movie, and it had to do with betrayal. I watched the betrayal of Prince Hans on the sister of the Queen and the Queen herself. At the beginning of the movie, Prince Hans looked like a trustworthy man, I thought that he was going to be the good guy in the movie, the one who rescues the Queen, but it was the opposite, he was the evil one. He pretended to be someone that he was not. It is as if PO Gorman wanted me to watch the movie, so I may learn not to trust anyone, or better said, Lt. Yaguchi. On another night, PO Gorman told me that when you have an enemy, it is when you really need to be very close to him. He said, "Keep your friends close, and your enemy closer," and it explains why Lt. Yaguchi had volunteered to give me a ride home on several occasions.

However, it was completely confirmed to me that there was something going on when one night, as I stood close to the police car, I saw PO Angel Burgos approach me. He looked at me and said, "Hernández, it is not your fault, you were just at the wrong place and at the wrong time." When he told me that, everything began to make sense. There is a reason why I am treated the way that I am being treated. But till this day, I still regret why I didn't ask him what he meant by that. But

I guess it was too soon. But then, any opportunity for clarification was gone, because PO Burgos got promoted to Sergeant and transferred.

However, came the time when I began to be treated as a perpetrator, a convicted criminal, and such treatments were large, deep and profound. As a result, I was forced, compelled, obliged and pushed to type down a few or some of my abuses, abuses that I had to endure under such an oppressive hostile work environment. But before the martyrdom began, God had revealed it to me. But how can you effectively use information when you don't know what to do with it? The following is my Diary that marks the difficult moments of my miserable agony.

Now, if I were to type all the things that were done against me, the number of pages in this diary would have doubled or tripled. But I only typed when I had the time, and when I needed to unburden myself from all my distresses, because when I told someone about my circumstances, he or she looked at me with dismay and disbelief, and it grieved them to see me like this. So, I began to type down these words using my Microsoft Surface tablet's Microsoft Word, to type down my experiences and my daily struggles, which is the only mean and instrument that I have and use to calm down my affliction.

It is incredible to see how they have sorted out and looked at different methods of intimidation to break me, and throw me out of the NYPD, something that I have worked so hard to obtain and maintain. In the process, I have felt compelled or obligated to break or to suspend my relationships and interactions with friends and family, because I didn't want to drag them into this. As a result, I am now in the middle of a divorce. So, the following are just a few of the many things that I went through and that I am still enduring.

I was going to release my Diary for everyone to read in 2019, but one way or the other my plan was frustrated by the same people that follow me. There were saying things that I had written that had me thinking that they had stolen this Diary, which I had in a memory card. In that same memory card, I have a book that I had

41

written, but that I haven't published named, "<u>The Park of Love</u>." I was so passionate about writing, "<u>The Park of Love</u>," that I had postponed studying for my Sergeant exam, just to finish the book. A book that I began writing in 2004. I was so jealous of this book that with my savings, one day I bought a safety box to keep it safe from water and fire, which is fireproof and worse, from people. But it wasn't the case.

One day, Sergeant Lucic told me that I should be a writer. PO Rivera told me something about crossing over a wall, which I had written in my novel. There were enough signs that, one way or the other, they knew what I had written. My notebook was inside my closet, inside a gym bag locked by a luggage lock. Inside my Safety Box, there was something less valuable, like my savings and my memories cards.

I took the police Sergeant exam, but wasn't successful because I didn't study for it. I paid for the fast-track courses to prepare for it, but it wasn't enough, because I hadn't studied for it. So, all these years, I have been laying back on a seat covered by thorns, waiting for them to publish it. I have been hoping for that moment to come day in and day out, week after week, month after month and year after year.

I retired to the Dominican Republic, and every single day, since the day I set foot in this land, people have been harassing me, calling me all sorts of names, and their Gaslighting and false propaganda against me hasn't cease since 2013, and it is still happening now in 2025. Now I present to you my Diary, with ranks and names of the individuals that made my life a living hell, by violating my human rights my, my civil rights, my right to privacy, and my constitutional rights. If the individuals mentioned in this Diary deny these events, these accounts and allegations, the wrath of God will be upon them, and Devine Justice will follow them in this life and in the afterlife.

Chapter 3

This is how my Agony Begins

MARCH 2013

On **Monday, March 18, 2013,** at approximately 0735 hrs. or 7:35 AM, PO Maher asked me, "Bushy top are you stealing benches? Are you aware of the commandments, commandment number 11, 'You shall not steal benches?'"

On **Monday, March 25, 2013,** at approximately 7:35 am, I was getting dressed when all the sudden PO Gorman came into my aisle. His locker is there too. He laid his bag on the bench. Then he began to look for something. Then he asked me, "Hernandez, did you steal my Memo-Book?" I answered," I would rather die and go to heaven." How it hurts to be accused of something that I never did. This is an absurd behavior that keeps repeating.

In the morning, I had court, and I didn't talk to him. I greeted the officer next to him, but not him. The next day at the T/S, I decided to confront him. Next to Lt. Naoki Yaguchi, I told him that I was upset with him, because he is treating me as if I were a thief. He answered me the way I expected by saying, "You need to see a psychologist my friend," and he angrily walked away from me.

One day, it was just me and PO Fausto Gomez in the locker room, when he began to make the cat sound with his mouth, "Meow, meow, meow." For Hispanics, when a person tells the other person that he is a cat, what he means is that he is a thief. Therefore, he was making the cat's meow sound to imply that I am a thief, for there was no one else there, just me and him.

APRIL 2013

HEADQUARTERS SECURITY UNIT

DATE ___4/04/2013___

RANK _PO_ FULL NAME (L, F) _Hernandez, Emmanuel_ CMD _025 Pct_

TAX _947269_ SHIELD _2830_ DATE APPT. _07/8/2007_ D.O.B. _09/24/1981_ AGE _31_
(mm/dd/yyyy) (mm/dd/yyyy)

SOC. SEC. NO ▓▓▓▓ NAME OF IMMEDIATE SUPV. _SGT. Gibbs_

ADDRESS _930 Ogden Avenue Bx, NY10456 Apt 62_ CELL _(917)640-9317_

MAR. STATUS _Married_ RES. PCT. _044_ RES. CO. _Ins. Catalina_ HOME TEL _(917)962-9899_

CMD. TEL _(212)860-6511 T/s_ SQ./CHT. _A1_ TOUR PREFERRED _ANY_
6557 Desk.

DISCIPLINARY RECORD ___3 CD's in my entire career as a Police Officer.___

SUSPENDED FROM DUTY / PLACED ON MOD. ASSIGN.? _No_

CURRENTLY UNDER INVESTIGATION (FED. / STATE / CITY)? _No_

CHARGES & SPECS. PENDING? _No_ ON PROM. LIST? _No_

SCHOOLS ATTENDED / DEGREES _LaGuardia Community College (AA) Associate, John Jay College (BA) Criminal Justice
Liberal Arts_

REASON REQUESTING TRANSFER TO HQSU _To Explore different avenues within NYPD._

EXPERIENCE _Have done HQSU Details for years._

DEPT. QUALIFCIATIONS (SCOOTER, ETC.) _Rmp_

SPECIAL SKILLS (LANGUAGE, E.M.T., TECHNICAL, ETC.) _Bilingual (Spanish)_

MILITARY SERVICE: ACTIVE / RESERVE / VETERAN ETC. _No_

BRANCH / RANK _N/A_ UPCOMING DRILL DATES, ETC. _N/A_

VACATION SELECTION, JURY DUTY, ETC. _Vacation: 4/20-4/24/13, 4/28 - 5/2/2013, 5/20-5/24/13, 10/17-10/21/13_

HAVE YOU EVER BEEN DENIED ASSIGNMENT(S)? _No_

REASON(S): _N/A_

LIST ALL PREVIOUS COMMANDS, BEGINNING WITH THE MOST RECENT: _025 Pct Since_
PBBN.
July 2008, and Impact Response Team (IRT) in Brooklyn for six months.

*** IF SPACE IS INSUFFICIENT FOR ANY QUESTION, USE REVERSE SIDE ***

FORWARD COMPLETED APPLICATION WITH COPIES OF LAST THREE (3) PERFORMANCE EVALUATIONS
TO THE HEADQUARTERS SECURITY UNIT, POLICE HEADQUARTERS, ROOM 152G

On April, knowing that something beyond my control, something very bad was about to happen at the 25th precinct, I decided to submit my application to work somewhere else. To be transferred to Police Headquarter Security. They had vacant positions there. I was overqualified for the position, since I was assigned to do the same job several times a month. They met me there. They had no complaints against me there, because I had been doing that same assignment for years.

On **Friday, April 5, 2013,** at approximately 0730 hrs. or 7:30 am, I went to the locker room to get dressed. There I found a senior officer getting dressed. He was in the same aisle I was. He had his own bench. I dragged a different bench to seat there, but instead of seating, I rather laid my bag, my coat, my wallet, my I.D card and my smartphone on the bench, and I stepped out to use the bathroom. Then I returned to my aisle, and there I began to get dressed. The distance between his bench and my bench was about five feet. He looked as if he didn't want to talk to me.

Then he asked me how it was midnight, since I work at night. I told him that it is tiresome like always. Suddenly, he began looking for his wallet, but he couldn't find it. Then he said, " I hope to find it in my car, if not ...." But how was he going to lose his wallet when he had not left the aisle, nor had he left his belongings alone by itself because he was always there.

Then he looked at me as if he were suspecting me. When I walked down the stairways that I reached the first floor, I saw him again talking to someone. His face was flushed, and his head was all red. He was about to walk upstairs. I didn't know what to say. Now, he might think that I had stolen it, since it was just me and him in the locker room.

On **Saturday, April 6, 2013,** I arrested a person for disorderly conduct at 0026 hrs. or 12:06 pm. I placed him inside the RMP (police car), and I took him to the 25th precinct. Upon further investigation, we gave him two summonses, one for trespassing and the other one for disorderly conduct and then we let him go. We went back to patrol. At 0357 hrs. or 3:57 am we had our meal. We came out of the mealtime at 0457 hrs. or 4:57 am and we continued patrolling.

At the end of the tour, at 0735 hrs. or 7:35 am we decided to take our stuff out of the RMP (police car). When I picked up my bag, **I saw that underneath the bag, there was an almost brand-new blue**

45

Yankee hat. Right away, thinking about the plot that might be going on, I asked my partner PO Rivera, "What is this? What is this Yankee hat doing here?" He walked to my side, looked at it and said, "I don't know, just toss it out or something." I told him that the hat might belong to the guy we arrested. He told me that he would deal with it, and he placed it inside his bag. I told him to put it inside the property room or in the T/S, and he told me not to worry about it. Then we went to the locker room.

In the locker room, I helped him fix the locker of his ex-partner, PO Santiago, that had been turned upside down, because many of the officers in the precinct don't like him. Then I left the station house, but before leaving, I called him and reminded him to voucher the hat and he told me that he was going to voucher it tonight.

One night, we were at the muster room, and Lt. Yaguchi arrived for a roll call. He told us that there is a thief among us. As soon as he said that PO Banks jokingly asked Lt. Yaguchi, "Why are you looking at me like that as if I did it?" and many of us laughed. But is he serious that there is a thief among us?

These types of conduct or behavior towards me from my colleagues continue daily at work. Behavior that keeps repeating. I spoke to my brother in Christ, J..., about the matter and he told me that he believes in me. That I am a man with integrity, and just to keep ignoring them. I spoke to someone else that is close to me about the matter, and he told me the same thing, just to ignore them. So, I did so. Day in and day out I kept ignoring them. I stopped typing, and just let it be. But it is too much. So, in September, I decided to type again to cope with the stress of being indirectly suspected and accused of something that I don't know what it is.

SEPTEMBER 2013
September:

What should I do? If I ask them what is going on or tell them my concern there is a 90 % chance that they will answer, " What are you talking about?" or worse, they will give me the same answer that PO Gorman gave me, that I need to see a psychologist. How would you feel if you were in my situation? Well, I would feel embarrassed, and if I address or express to them my discomfort, the level of suspicion will rise for something that I have no knowledge of. However, now I am waiting, I am truly waiting for them to initiate the conversation in regard to such misunderstanding, such misconception of me that is based on I don't know what.

.... One day I called Lt. Yaguchi aside to discuss with him why my former partner, PO Eddie Pinero, was receiving certain unwanted tasks, and why Lt. Yaguchi failed to discuss and clarify certain misunderstandings with PO Pinero. He didn't ask my former partner what he had to say about the matter, but rather, he fully relied on what the other officers said. Lt. Yaguchi said to me, "His partners ratted him out."

It is very unjust and unfair on Lt. Yaguchi's behalf, because PO Pinero should have the right and the opportunity to defend himself. **Then, he told me that there are some things that he knows about an officer, but that he hadn't told that officer for fear of how he is going to react.** Because that is human behavior or nature to overreact when he feels confronted, but that he is trying to see whether there is a pattern on that person's behavior.

Was it an indirect statement towards me? Now I wish to tell him that there is no pattern because there was never a first time. And if he asks me, what am I talking about, I am ready to answer, "I first have to see if there is a pattern, and then, only then, I will ask," and I will leave him wandering. Or should I simply take my boss and my accusers aside and explain my concern to them? But I already did that with PO Gorman and looked at what happened.

47

On Monday, **September 20, 2013,** at 2332 hrs. or 11:32 pm, 28 minutes before my birthday, Lt. Yaguchi presented me a birthday cake that said, "Happy Birthday Emmanuel." My colleagues congratulated me.

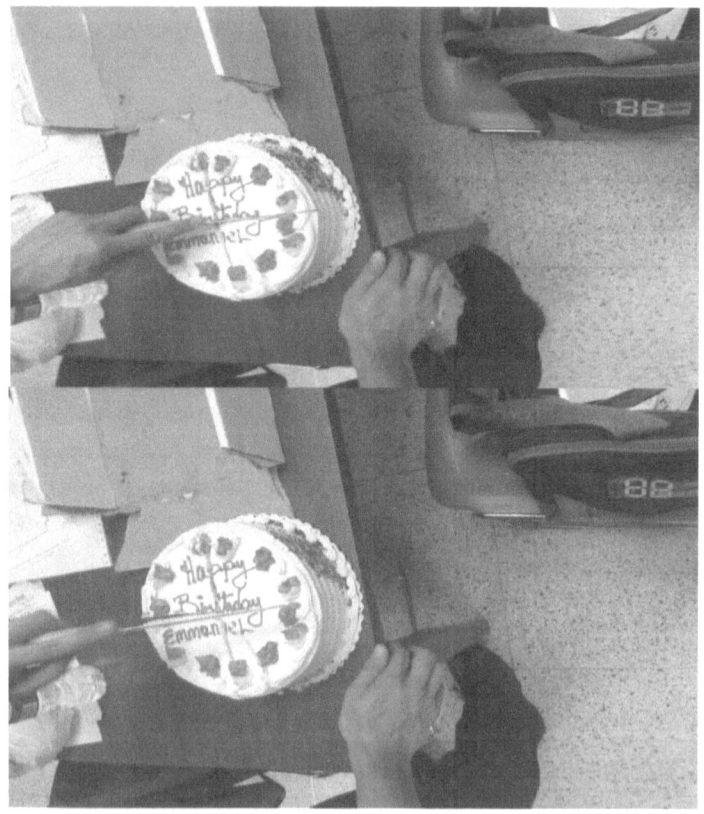

I took a picture of the cake as Lt. Yaguchi cut the cake with a knife as if cutting my life short. Here is the picture.

"The wicked plots against the righteous and gnashes his teeth at him…" (Psalms 37:12 ESV)

After the cake, I said the following in front of everyone at the muster room: "You guys cannot imagine how important every single one of you are to me regardless of rank. Now I see the smile on your faces, as a demonstration of how glad you guys are that I was born. I thank you for the cake, that even though he still doubts me, he still bought me a cake for my birthday, and that is called, professionalism." I continued, "'No matter what you take from me, you can't take away my dignity'." PO Banks said, "I think that I have heard that before." And I said, "Yes, it is from the Whitney Houston song. But remember guys, there is dignity in work, and all I want you to do is not to rob me of my good name." As William Shakespeare wrote in one of his nobles:

> **"Good name in man and woman, dear my lord,**
> **Is the immediate jewel of their souls:**
> **Who steals my purse steals trash; 'tis something, nothing**
>
> ...
>
> **But he that filches from me my good name**
> **Robs me of that which not enriches him,**
> **And makes me poor indeed." William Shakespeare**

Unfortunately, they are in the process of doing this at my workplace. They want to destroy my reputation and my good image. Also, they want to ruin my career by taking it away from me, which is equal to stealing, because by doing so, they will be depriving me of my job, which in exchange they will gain some things, and the list of the things that they will be able to obtain is long. They are selling me out indeed. All this sounds cruel, but it is happening.

OCTOBER 2013

On **Wednesday, October 2, 2013**, at approximately 2352 hrs. or 11:52 pm, we received a radio run for 242 East 116 Street. When we arrived, we went to the backyard of the building. From there, we saw an emotionally disturbed person threatening to jump from a two story high wall and in our presence, but he jumped to an adjacent two-second story Fire Scape, and he jumped back to the wall and he was about to fall, and he jumped back to the adjacent two-second story Fire Scape, almost losing his balance and then he climbed to the three story Fire Scape.

I couldn't just wait there and see, so I ran out of the building and rushed to the building next to it, which is where the Fire Scape is attached to. I ran up the stairs, and up to the roof top and climbed a small wall and reached the Fire Scape. Then, I began climbing down the Fire Scape and one part of the Fire Scape broke. Afterwards, I saw that PO Banks were behind me. I grabbed the aided at the two-story Fire Scape and with the help of PO Banks we managed to cuff him. Then I looked down to the backyard, and there I saw Lt. Yaguchi staring at me, and with a look of displeasure, he gave me a dirty look, he closed his eyes, and he looked the other way.

"Let not those rejoice over me who are wrongfully my foes and let not those wink the eye who hate me without cause." (Psalm 35:19 ESV)

Then I thought of how we were going to get him out. Immediately, I checked the closed windows, and I managed to open one. I took off my gun belt to fit in the apartment's bathroom window. I got inside the dark bathroom, not knowing if a deadly dog awaited me, and PO Banks helped me to get the aided inside through the window and then he got inside. As we took the aided out, we saw that the apartment was dark and empty. It seemed that nobody lived there.

Finally, we opened the door, and our brothers in blue received us. When I saw Lt. Yaguchi again, he didn't tell me anything. He just ignored me completely, as if whatever it is that he is holding against me, it is greater than any good I may do.

On **Sunday, October 13, 2013**, at approximately 2325 hrs. or 11:25 pm, Sgt. Gibbs was standing at the Desk staring at me and right next to him was Sgt. Young, who was also staring at me, while she was seated at the Desk. Sgt. Gibbs asked me, "Bushy top, what are you up to?" and I answered, "I am here ready for duty sir," and then he told me that I was assigned to a paid detail. Later, I Googled the meaning of "what are you up to," and its meaning is not a good one.

Again, most of the time, I don't want to type, I just want to forget about everything, but there is something in me that forces me to type. So, I use my fingers instead of my mouth, and my Microsoft Surface tablet instead of a person, to express myself. My tablet has become my therapist. So, I use it when I have the time, and most of the time, I don't use it, because I just want to ignore everything that is happening around me. But it is inevitable to just ignore it.

Chapter 4

The District Attorney Office Involvement

NOVEMBER 2013

Saturday, November 1, 2013, I heard the following comments about me: "You, you took too much time processing your collar", "But he hasn't even finish, he is still doing it", " You are too slow to go to the other squad", "No, I kicked him out of my squad", "Why don't you send him to take it to the Borough?", " No, not him, I don't trust him at all", " I hear you girl." Sargent Lucic talking to PO Gloria ….

I was patrolling the streets with my partner PO Rivera. He told me, "You know that our new platoon Lieutenant (Lt. King) always keeps the property room's door locked. When someone is going to do something in the property room, one needs to go and ask her first for the keys." He said it because this has never happened before. The door was always kept unlocked. **Now I have reasons to believe that the new Lieutenant was informed of the strange things happening in the precinct,** which are unknown to me. In addition to the negative rumors about me, which are the greatest falsehood of all time, and the sad part of it is that she might believe it too.

For my mealtime I went to the second floor. This time, finally, my partner didn't follow me upstairs like he always did these days. **I guess that he stopped doing so right from the moment that I sang to him the song, "Every breath you take, every move you make, every bond you break …," out of the music band 'The Police.'** It seems that he doesn't want to make it obvious anymore.

Finally, I went into the lounge, which at this time of the hour, we use the lounge to sleep. There, in the darkness of the room, I saw another police officer laying on the sofa staring at his smartphone. I saw him typing and texting something for less than half a minute and then he turned off his smartphone. I knew it because of the brightness of his smartphone's screen. A minute later, my partner arrived, and as soon as he arrived, the officer who was laying there turned on his smartphone again and he texted something like for ten seconds, which I knew because of the way that his fingers were moving on the screen of his smartphone.

Then, five seconds later, my partner began to use his smartphone. Quickly, my partner texted something and then he stopped using his smartphone. Immediately, the other officer there looked at his smartphone, as to read the text message that my partner had sent him, and then after reading the text, he stopped using it. **When I came out of meal, I told my partner, "How can you expect to catch a fish in a swimming pool," and he stared at me without altering or saying a word. Finally, I said, "I wish I wouldn't know.** This is why I am no longer being hooked at 1PP (1 Police Plaza= Police Headquarter), where I do security, because of how far this has gone."

This is why on **Thursday, October 24, 2013**, I texted PO Wilfred Nuñez, who always made the arrangements necessary to give me a good post every time I do 1PP (1 Police Plaza= Police Headquarter), but he never texted me back and I can imagine why. Now approaching the van, I saw another vehicle behind the van with the lights off. They were two of my fellow officers (PO Perez, PO Ramos). They were hiding back there. But why?

THIS IS A RECEIPT THAT SHOW THE OF A VISIT TO A LAWYER IN REGARD TO WHAT HAPPENED IN COURT. I BELIVE THIS IS MY SECOND VISIT.

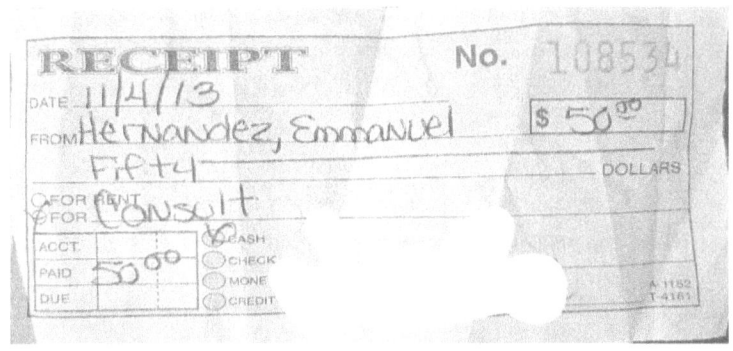

It was like on **Sunday, November 10, 2013,** that I was walking down the stairway after my meal was over, that I heard Sgt. Lucic yell out, "I don't trust TBTA at all." When I stepped outside with my partner, right when I opened the door of the RMP (police car), I told my partner PO Rivera, "You know what, I am going to do nothing. Zero summonses and zero arrest until I am told what is going on here." He asked, "Why you say that?" I answered, "Because I see something like a conspiracy taking place here. Everything started since Lt. Yaguchi first began working here.

It is like everything began with Lt. Yaguchi and it comes down to Sgt. Lucic, then Sgt. Gibbs, Elliot (Santiago), Gorman and it is becoming like an umbrella. It is spreading like a disease, and it is going down even as far as 1PP (1 Police Plaza= Police Headquarter). This is why I am going to bring zero."

Yes, everything began since the moment that Lt. Yaguchi set his foot at the 25th precinct. Then my partner PO Rivera said, "But you want to know what is going to happen after that?" I asked, "What?" And he said, "They will send you to psych, and they will tell you, 'Give me your gun and shield', and then you are going to say, 'Mammi'." Then I said, "You are right, Mammi." **(Before joining the NYPD, PO Rivera used to work for the EMS (Emergency Medical Service) unit. He is like 10 years older than PO Hernandez. Plenty of experience).**

This is **Wednesday, November 13, 2013**. It was a very tough day for me, not because of the job itself, but because of their distrust. Sgt. Gibbs stopped his RMP (police car) next to mines at the corner of East 125 Street and Lexington Avenue. He was signing our Memo-Books, which is how we cops name our Memorandum Pad, or let say, our Activity Log. My partner PO Rivera reminded the Sergeant that he is going to be on vacation next week. When Sgt. Gibbs heard that, he became disappointed. Then Sgt. Gibbs told us that Sgt. Young didn't want PO Elliot Santiago working with her at the T/S. Therefore, next week he was going to have me work with PO Santiago. I told him that I didn't mind. But I can imagine why he said that. Supervision. And the person who is indeed, truly not wanted at the T/S is no one else but me.

It was like on this same day, that PO Rivera asked me, "Do you believe that President Obama shouldn't be president?" and he continued, "No, not at all. I have a belief that those who are only able to become president are those who fought in the revolution. I mean, the descendants of those who fought for this country. Can you imagine someone from other country becoming president of the United States? Just because he was born here?"

I asked him, "Tell me, who else supports your point of view?", and he answered, "There is a radio station that does." I questioned him, "But do they say exactly what you are telling me right now?" He replied, "No, because they would have been taken off air right away." I told him, "Let me tell you that black African Americans fought for this country too, what you are talking about?" And he said, "Because they had no choice." I said, "But let me tell you that for them it was worse because they were slaves, mistreated and killed, so they do really deserve the presidency position. And even then, after slavery was abolished, mistreatments and the separate but equal law were still in place. Even in the 1960's and the 1970s racism was still part of America. I prefer being beaten then being demoralized." Yes, racism was alive and vivid. And he told me, "**But you are being demoralized every day**."

Wow, I truly felt that. What an insult. For some reason he said that. It has to do with what people are saying about me. Then he said, "Look, I believe that this president should truly be impeached, because of the job that he is doing now. Why not? What happens to cops that lie and steal, they get fired right? The same thing should be done with the president." What is going on here?

Almost at the end of our tour, a radio run came over about a security holding for shoplifting at Pathmark supermarket. I told my partner that I was willing to take the arrest if he didn't want it. He said that he was going to take it, because he didn't want me to take it, because I had so many things to do today. I had told him that I had court in the morning.

However, I told him that I was willing to take the arrest anyway. Also, I told him that PO Banks was looking for an arrest. When he learned that, he became excited, and he said, "So lets give it to him." I told him, "No, if he is going to take it, I rather take it because I do need an arrest." In the end, he managed to have the perpetrator not arrested by convincing the security guards at the location, and the security guards agreed to just make the perpetrator sign a no trespassing sheet, so she won't go back again. I was upset with him for not consulting with me first, before making that decision. But PO Banks showed up at the scene and arrested the perpetrator.

It is almost the end of the year and my union PBA delegate hasn't ask me if I want to order PBA cards (which are courtesy cards that are given to each police officer so they can give out to families and friends), but I saw him offering them to everyone in the precinct except me, as if I didn't deserve to have them.

After having worked the entire night for 8:35 hours, I went to Criminal Court in Manhattan. PO Maher strangely volunteered to give me a ride there. While taking me there, I noticed that every time we engaged in a conversation, he placed his hand in his jacket. Why? It wasn't cold inside of his vehicle. He told me that he was going to see Manhattan Assistant District Attorney Altman, about an arrest that I had made, but she didn't notify me. I was going to see a different Assistant District Attorney, ADA McDonald. He told me that he didn't remember the case at all. I told him the same. I didn't remember anything about the case either.

The night before, she, the Manhattan ADA (Assistant District Attorney), texted me asking me if I was working this week, but I didn't get to talk to her. PO Maher told me that it was she, the same Assistant District Attorney that he is going to see. Again, strangely PO Maher accompanied me to see my Assistant District Attorney, ADA McDonald, but she was not there. So, we went to see his Assistant District Attorney, ADA Altman. When we arrived there, she was so happy to see me. She received me with a great smile on her face, and with the same great smile, she told us that she was going to talk to us later. I told her that I didn't remember seeing her before, which she didn't expect to hear from me.

But upon further investigation, I found out that I met her eight months ago, on March 29, 2013, about the same case.

From there, PO Maher and I went to eat breakfast at Mama Café. As we were eating our food, I noticed that he was eating with one hand while keeping his other hand inside his jacket. But sometimes, he took the handout of his jacket's pocket, but rapidly placed it back again inside, especially when I was about to say something. Strange right? In addition, he asked me some awkward questions. He gave me reasons to believe that he was recording me all the way, but why did he need to record me? Then after breakfast, we went to see ADA McDonald. She assigned me to go and pick up a homeless witness. PO Maher volunteered to go with me. I found it unbelievable that PO Maher, who is an old timer, volunteered to go with me in search of a homeless witness.

When we came back with the homeless witness, the boyfriend of the witness who was accompanying her needed to use the bathroom. I told PO Maher that I was going to the bathroom and to keep his eyes on my bag, and to stay with the homeless witness. He agreed. When I returned, PO Maher told me that he just spoke with his Assistant District Attorney (Altman) and that now he was leaving. When I asked him about my bag, he told me that he didn't know where my bag was.

Then the homeless witness and her boyfriend began to argue with ADA MacDonald, and they began yelling. I asked PO Maher, "Why you tell me that you don't know where my bag is when I told you to hold it for me?" Then when he saw me in despair, he told me that it was inside ADA's (Altman) office. I rushed there and when I opened the door, there I saw Lt. Yaguchi sitting, talking to ADA Altman and my bag was on the other seat, right next to Lt. Yaguchi. I wondered if PO Maher had left it there on purpose so Lt. Yaguchi and ADA Altman may quickly search for my bag.

When they saw that I opened the door, the two of them stared at me. Lt. Yaguchi did not look pleased to see me, but I greeted him anyway. I grabbed my bag and stepped outside. I was waiting outside, because ADA Altman wanted to talk to me after she finished talking to Lt. Yaguchi. At 3:03 pm I had a missed call from Lt. Yaguchi. I suspected that they wanted me back in the office. When I went inside, Lt. Yaguchi told me that ADA Altman needed the original documents pertaining to the DWI (Driving While Intoxicated) case.

He ordered me, with a commanding tone of voice, and in front of ADA Altman, "Give me the number of your Combo so I may get it for you." I couldn't believe it. I asked him, "What do you mean by combo?" and he told me that he needed the combination of my lock, so he may go and look for the documents inside my locker. I felt so tired and besides being on the clock for more than 16 hours of work already, and counting, I couldn't believe what he was asking for. I became stupefied. Immediately, I not only gave him the combination of my lock, but I also gave him the combination of my second lock, so he may go and search my two lockers. I even wrote it down for him. As soon as I gave him the combination of my two locks, he hastened and left with the same serious face and without saying goodbye to me.

Then I looked at ADA Altman, and I noticed that she was no longer happy to see me. Her face looked neither happy nor sad. I wondered if Lt. Yaguchi had shared his belief (thief) about me with her. I wondered if he had asked her for advice concerning me, and it is the reason why he had asked me for the combination of my lock: To see if he can find something incriminating inside of my lockers. I couldn't believe it. ADA Altman gave me something to read (a transcript), about my previous grand jury testimony (8 months ago), which stated everything I had said on that day. But how was I able to read it and understand it when a thousand thoughts were coming to my head about Lt. Yaguchi's malice by telling me to give him the combination of my lock, and on whether ADA Altman now thinks that I am someone that I am not.

I remained, again, stupefied. What if they plant something in my lockers and then blame me for it. How many innocent people have gone to prison for crimes they have never committed? So, thinking of all the possibilities of what could happen to me, I didn't pay attention when I first read the transcript that ADA Altman gave me to read, especially when I noticed that she was staring at me as I read along those lines. A mind that doesn't have peace cannot concentrate. My mind was blocked.

Then I asked her if I could read it again, but she refused to let me read it again.

For sure, my interview with her was a disaster, because I was unable to understand what I was pretending to be reading, and I didn't even remember having ever testified in court about that case. Neither do I remember ever seeing her face before. What a pressure. At 6:54 pm, Lt. Yaguchi called me, and he told me that he couldn't find it.

I told him to try the other locker, and this is when he told me that the second combination lock that I gave him was not good. I gave him the combination again. Now I see why he called me. He couldn't find it, so I told him that I was going to get it myself the next day if he couldn't. What was the urgency?

"In arrogance the wicked hotly pursue the poor; let them be caught in the schemes that they have devised." (Psalm 10:2 ESV)

On **Saturday, November 16, 2013,** I worked with PO Elliot Santiago because my partner was on vacation. My Sergeant called PO Santiago on the cellphone to ask him if he wanted the arrest that sector Boy had. He told the Sergeant that he didn't want to take it, and PO Santiago asked me if I wanted to take it.

I told him that I would go to the precinct and from there I was going to decide on whether to take it or not. When we arrived at the station house (Precinct), the Sergeant was there and again, he asked PO Santiago if he was going to take the arrest, and PO Santiago said that he didn't want it, but I volunteered to take it. I told PO Santiago to go to the lounge and to relax there until I finish processing the arrest. I didn't need his help. So, he disappeared.

Then one of the officers who had finished doing his voucher, asked me what he had to do next after finishing the voucher. I told him that he needed to place it inside the property room, so he went to the property room and placed the voucher there. At approximately four seconds later, I heard a rough movement coming out of the T/S, and when I went to see, I saw PO Gorman walking out of the property room. His face was so red, like a red balloon that it was about to burst. He looked at me. He went from the T/S to the property room in a matter of seconds, just because he thought I was the one who had entered the property room.

Moments later, PO Gorman asked me for PO Santiago whereabouts, and I told him that he might be in the lounge. Approximately five minutes later, PO Santiago came down from the lounge. Then the Sergeant arrived, and he had a private conversation with PO Santiago on the stairwell. Then PO Santiago went to the T/S to talk to PO Gorman, and from there he didn't move until I finished processing the arrest. He kept his eyes on me all the time. The other Sergeant, who was at the Desk, told me that she already informed Sergeant Gibbs that I had given a DAT (Desk Appearance Ticket) to the prisoner. A DAT is a lieu of arrest, which means that instead of keeping the person arrested, he or she is let go on his own recognizance and he or she will show up to court on a later date.

When I went back to patrol with PO Santiago, he reminded me to make sure that I told Sgt. Gibbs that I gave the prisoner a DAT (Desk Appearance Ticket). What is their concern of informing Sgt. Gibbs that I gave the prisoner a DAT? It makes sense because if I had given a DAT to the prisoner, I would have had to stay with the prisoner, and they were concerned about letting me stay inside the precinct guarding the prisoner for long, because they don't want me around the precinct, because of you know what. PO Santiago told me that PO Banks approached him and asked him why he didn't take the arrest but had me taking it instead.

When we put ourselves out for meal, PO Santiago went upstairs to the lounge, but I decided to stay at the muster room, because I wanted to finish my overtime paperwork. PO Gorman was no longer at the T/S. Approximately twenty minutes later, I stood up from the table and when I turned around, I saw Sgt. Gibbs standing right next to the T/S. He was flipping the roll call pages, but in a way that he could keep his sight on me. I told him that I did so much court overtime, but I said it just to break the ice. Immediately, PO Gorman came down and he sat at the T/S.

I was standing right next to him waiting for PO Santiago to come down. Then PO Santiago came down, and when he approached us,

I yelled out, "Hey Papa Eliot," and everyone there including the Sergeant, PO Banks, PO Ahmed, PO Gorman, and the new Sergeant laughed. Then PO Gorman said to PO Santiago, "I believe the name is going to be a sticker." Subsequently, we walked out, and we grabbed our things out of the RMP (police car). As we did, PO Santiago didn't say a word to me. When we returned to the T/S, he asked PO Gorman, "Were you at the T/S the moment I was on meal?" and PO Gorman said, "No, but Sgt. Gibbs was here." I guess I know what he meant by that.

Then PO Gorman told me that Sgt. Lucic was transferred to the 107th precinct. I asked PO Gorman if he has a hook, so I may transfer somewhere else, and he told me with a big smile on his face, "You are never going to come out of the 25 my friend." As soon as he said that PO Santiago uttered to PO Gorman, "He seems to be having fun," and PO Gorman responded, "Yes, he seems to be having fun. But wait until he gets kicked."

On Monday, **November 18, 2013,** I was in court, in the police room, waiting to punch out and return to the 25th precinct. It was 17… hrs. or 5 … pm and when I was about to punch out, I saw PO Lolja walking in. He asked me if I was leaving now, and I told him that I was. We took the train together. Then when my stop came, I extended my arm to shake his hand, but he didn't, instead, he just tapped me twice on my shoulder.

On Wednesday, **November 20, 2013,** I went to 1PP (1 Police Plaza= Police Headquarter). At 1PP (1 Police Plaza= Police Headquarter), I was looking for my Headquarter Security friend, PO Wilfred Nuñez, but he was nowhere to be found. I remember that he didn't text me back the last time that I sent him a text message.

Now today it was proven what I had suspected. I went downstairs to go to my post, and accidentally I saw PO Wilfred Nuñez. He saw me, but he kept on walking. Having his smartphone in his left ear, he pretended he didn't see me. I was walking down to his left, and then I walked up to his right. Then shoulder to shoulder, I shouted out, "Hey Wilfred." He looked at me sideways and simultaneously he extended his left hand, and I extended my left hand, and we did a half handshake because of courtesy, for I know that he felt obliged to do so. Did he stop to say hi to me? No, because as he gave me half his hand, he slowed down his walking pace a little bit just to greet me, but as soon as he did, immediately, he kept on walking fast, while talking on his smartphone.

After being at 1PP (1 Police Plaza= Police Headquarter) for over twelve hours, PO Quiñones offered to give me a ride back to the 25th precinct. We arrived at the precinct at approximately 0825 hrs. or 8:25 am. I went to the Desk, and I waited there for PO Angel Lopez (The union PBA Delegate for the day tour) to finish using the copy machine so that I could use it after him, because I needed to make copies of my court sheet. As I was standing right in front of him,

I asked him, "Do you have allergies?" He answered, "No," and so I asked him, "So why is your face red and white? You look pale," and he said, "Probably because I just came from outside." Then I felt that someone was tapping my shoulder from behind. When I turned around, guess who it was? It was PO Santiago, and with a big smile on his face he asked me if I read the text message that he had sent me. He asked me why I didn't text him back when I read it. I told him that I was busy. Then I asked him what he was doing at the station house (precinct) late.

Seconds later, his smiling face turned into a very serious one, and right in front of me, he looked at PO Lopez, and when PO Lopez looked at him, PO Santiago moved his right index finger and placed it on his right, lower eye lid and he pressed it down, as if to remind him to keep his eyes on me. I became appalled because he did it right in front of me. My God, what is going on? I asked him, "Do you have a collar (arrest)? What are you still doing here?" and he answered, "I have to go to 1PP."

On Monday, **November 25, 2013,** we recovered a stolen vehicle in front of 240 east 119 street. My partner told me that he was going to the station house (precinct) and do the paperwork there. Meanwhile, as for me to stay guarding the vehicle in case the one who left it returns and drives away with it again. I had no problem with that, and so we did. Later, the tow truck came and picked up the vehicle, and I went back to the station house (precinct). There I saw my partner vouchering for the vehicle. I sat right next to him.

When I looked right at the door, I saw PAA Maria desperate to go home, but she couldn't leave because there was nobody there to cover for her. Then PO Begawan, PO Golden and PO Santiago stepped in, and they took PAA Maria's spot at the door. PAA Maria finally left. Meanwhile, PO Elliot Santiago was keeping his eyes on me. Then PO Golden, who saw me and my partner looking at the computer's monitor said, "Come on Hernandez, stop pretending to know that you can read," and immediately I asked her if she could help my partner with the voucher, but she didn't know.

At the time, it was approximately 0715 hrs. Or 7:15 am. Then came PO Nancy Ramos, the training officer, and she gave me the training sheet to sign. I signed it, and she turned the signing sheet and showed me the handout. It was about fire extinguishers. Then she said to me, "Look, there are fire extinguishers on each floor of the building. There are two on the second floor and...," immediately she was interrupted by my partner PO Rivera who said, "And that means, don't touch it," and PO Nancy Ramos laughing smacked the back of the head of PO Rivera and the two of them laughed, except me, because I knew well what it was all about.

Later, I signed out and left the station house (precinct). But before leaving, I saw PO Jackie ... who was right next to the T/S with Captain Marlon Larin. I shook Captain Larin's hand, signed out and when I was walking to the door's exit, I noticed that PO Perez remained by the Desk talking to Sgt. Lucic and Lt. Yaguchi. So, I stepped out of the station house (precinct). I went to the subway station at East 116 Street, and right before swiping my metro card, I sensed that I should call roll call and see if I had a court today. I called roll call and a person there confirmed to me that I had court today.

Unfortunately, I had to go back to the station house (Precinct). I called PO Rivera and told him that I had court today. He asked me where I was. I told him that I was walking back to the station house (precinct). As soon as I arrived, I saw PO Rivera looking at the roll call sheet. Then when he flipped a page, he looked at Lt. Yaguchi, who was a distance away, almost hiding against a door and PO Rivera gave the dumps up, either to Lt. Yaguchi, or/and to one of the supervisors who was standing near to or close to Lt. Yaguchi. There I saw PO Perez and Sgt. Lucic being watchful. Then PO Lucas walked up to me and with his massive body he asked me, "How may I help you sir?" and PO Nancy Ramos came, and she stood right next to PO Lucas. The two of them were facing me, and pretending to be playing around, I answered them, "I want to file a complaint against PO Lucas, shield number …," which I said it to break the ice.

Then I walked upstairs wondering why Sgt. Lucic didn't tell me that I had court today at the muster. When I arrived at the Department of Motor Vehicle traffic court at the Northern Manhattan Traffic Violations Bureau, right inside the entrance to the building, I saw Lt. Galamo there waiting for me. What a surprise. She asked me for my two Memo-Books (Memorandum Pad/Activity Log), and to see if I was in uniform, because if not, I was going to be given a Command Discipline, which we call, a CD.

Then she said something about me being the only one from the 25th precinct that is having a traffic court this morning. When I went upstairs, the Sergeant from the Internal Affairs Bureau told me that my court day was cancelled. This means that if I had missed court today, it wouldn't have been a big deal for the IAB (Internal Affairs Bureau) guys upstairs, but it would have been a big deal for Lt. Galamo who is the ICO (Integrity Control Officer). She would have given me a CD (Command Discipline) to not show up even though my court day was cancelled. She had probably received a tip from someone of interest in the stationhouse about me going there.

At night, I told my colleagues about it, and they told me that it was very strange because normally the ICO (Integrity Control Officer), never goes there, because the IAB (Internal Affairs Bureau) Sergeants are always there. But I wonder why she didn't wait for me on the second floor where the IAB (Internal Affairs Bureau) guys are, and she left the premise right away, soon after scratching (signing) my Memo-Book (Memorandum Pad/Activity Log), so in a way that she cut our conversation short, and she stepped out right away.

Then I went to Manhattan Criminal Court to see ADA (Assistant District Attorney) Deen. She wanted to see me, so I could identify the fingerprints of a defendant, so she may get a Bench Warrant against him. But meanwhile; she asked me what I was going to do after I was done with her. If I was going to hang out at the courthouse, I would eat breakfast. What type of question is that? Is she working for the ICO (Integrity Control Officer) now?"

Chapter 5

When your Union Representative Turns Against you

On Thursday, **November 28, 2013,** as I was working with PO
Rivera, he told me that he didn't know how PO Santiago many days had
off, when he doesn't do overtime to accumulate hours. However, I think
I know why. It could be that Lt. Yaguchi might have assigned him to do
some type of spy work overtime by assigning him to secretly monitor a
hidden camera and/or audio recording or to do some other investigative
work. Overtime that he must take in time instead of cash. Or it could be
that PO Santiago doesn't have the days off. He might be busy in the
private room doing the monitoring. This is why on various occasions, I
noticed that PO Santiago remained at the station house (precinct), every
time I and everyone else from our tour leave the precinct.

Then he told me how Lt. Yaguchi has inspired him to study and
move up, and that I should take the Sergeant Exam. "Do you see yourself
being a cop next year….?" he asked me. Then we went to a Job at East
116 Street and Lexington Avenue regarding a yellow taxi and a female
passenger who didn't want to pay. The passenger was inside the cab. Then
another police car, Sector Charlie arrived for no reason. PO Sovulj came
out of his RMP (police car) leaving PO Chan, who is his partner, inside
the RMP (police car).

Moments later, Sector Eddie drove by, and PO Gloria Byrd
exchanged some words with PO Rivera. The passenger came out of the
taxi and PO Sovulj told her to take everything out of the car. When she
stepped out of the car to charge her phone, PO Sovulj, again, asked her
if she had taken everything with her. She said that she already did. Since
I saw that PO Sovulj was so involved in a job that it was not his, I asked
him if he was looking for an arrest.

He said that only if it was going to be a DAT (Desk Appearance Ticket). Then as she was charging her phone, PO Sovulj was with me inside Domino pizza. My partner was going to check and see if her friend was at the apartment building information she gave us. He opened the door of the lobby, and he called us to go upstairs and when we did, we knocked at the door, but there was nobody there. So, we went downstairs, and after admitting that she didn't have a bank card with her, she cursed at my partner and then she took out her bank card and paid the taxi driver.

When we left, PO Rivera asked me if I had noticed that the woman was wearing an expensive purse and that inside her purse, he managed to see a document that said "ADA", which stands for Assistant District Attorney. He told me that it was the reason why he had asked her if she was a bus driver. He said that he had noticed something strange. He wondered and speculated as to how come Sector Charlie was going to our jobs as if they were following us. At approximately 0740 hrs. or 7:40 am, I was at work, walking up the stairs to go home, and behind me was PO Chan. He asked me if I had any plans for today, because it is Thanksgiving Day.

I said, "No, no plans for today." Then when reaching the fourth floor, at the door of the locker room, I told him, "I think I will buy myself a turkey sandwich," and exiting the locker room, was PO Gorman, and as he walked by me, he said, "And you are the Turkey," and he left without shaking my hand or uttering any other word, but he shook the hand of PO Chan and he wished him a Happy Thanksgiving day, and so did PO Chan to him.

But what did he meant by saying that I am the turkey? While getting dressed, PO Gambardelli was at the back talking to PO Maher. It was time to go home, but strangely, PO Gambardelli left, but not before passing through my aisle, and with a sad face he said, "Bye Hernandez," and I said, "Bye Gambo." Moments later, PO Maher passed by, and I found it suspicious that they didn't leave together. I said, "Hey Maher, come over here." He approached me without saying a word, he shook my hand, and he finally said, "Happy Thanksgiving," and I threw at him the small water cap that he had thrown at me.

When I went downstairs to sign out, I saw Lt. Gonzalez standing by the Desk. He was accompanied by PO Dominigildo (CC), who is Lt. Yaguchi's secretary. When Lt. Gonzales saw me, he called me 'Menudo,' and PO Dominigildo said, "No 'Chayanne.'" Moments later, I stood at the 124 room (The complaint room) to watch my partner PO Rivera do the Accident Report, and there was another officer with him. But all of a sudden, Lt. Gonzalez, just because he saw me standing by the 124 room's door (The complaint room), he went to look inside the 124 room (The complaint room), and when he did, he said, "What is going on here?", and he felt better when he saw that my partner was there finishing the police report.

My partner took notice of his rude behavior, and so that I won't think of such an event or to dissipate my thoughts due to the Lieutenant's actions, PO Rivera handed me over the finished report and told me to put it inside the basket, and he did so, so I won't feel that bad. Then, I decided to sign out at roll call, but I waited till PO Estrada finished signing out. When he was done, he took the roll call sheets with him, but I told him that I needed to sign out and he handed it over to me. I asked him to lend me his pen to sign out, but he completely ignored me by walking away without telling me anything. Feeling embarrassed, I asked someone who was seated at the T/S for a pen.

PO Gorman might have been assigned to Intel (a unit within the precinct. It stands for Intelligence), a unit that is under Lt. Gonzales' supervision, and which resource, might now be used to investigate me and to record the conversations that I have with PO Rivera who is, in so many occasions, asking me all type of compromising questions as he or they, expect a self-hanging answer, so that they may have me under their feet or at their mercy or lets say trapped within their claws.

Therefore, PO Rivera have been asking me a lot of controversial questions such as the day that he asked me how this president should be impeached, about religion, sexual orientation (Homosexuality), and so on. Also, he told me how Lt. Yaguchi was not having people submit 28's (A form that needs to be filled out every time an officer wants a day off, or wants to leave early from work, which will be deducted from the hours that the officer has accumulated, which if they don't, they will be stealing time). I know that didn't happen, but he or they wanted to know my response to such a comment and examine my reaction.

Friday, **November 29, 2013,** PO Christopher Gorman is the precinct's appointed union PBA delegate. He is a representative of the union, who is there to advocate on behalf of the police officers, whenever they get into trouble. The police officers' PBA (Patrolman Benevolent Association) cards are cards that are given to police officers, so they can give out to families and friends in case they get stopped by public servants. They show them their PBA cards and the public servants, in this case the police may decide whether to offer them courtesy or not. Two PBA cards and one calendar book are handed out to police officers for free every year. They will have to pay for any additional cards. So, every year, PBA cards are distributed to police officers by each precinct's union PBA delegate.

On this night, I was seated next to PO Gorman. I was looking at him distributing the PBA cards. He was calling out each officer one by one to give them their PBA cards, and one calendar book. When PO Matorelli saw me, he yelled out, "Mr. Hernández, where have you been?" I answered, "I have been hiding man." Then I saw that PO Gorman was ready to leave, so I asked him, "Where are my PBA cards. Why is it that I was never asked how many I want? How come?"

The reason why I asked was because the union's PBA delegates always ask the officers, in person, and many days in advance, before the day of the distribution of the cards, for they need to order them, how many do they want, because if they want more than two, they will have to pay for the extra ones. But I was never asked. Especially when I see him almost every time that I go to work, and his locker is close to mine. So, the answer that PO Gorman gave me was, "The sign was up, you come see your representative, I need to order cards."

I told him," Two cards are supposed to be given to me. And my book as well." Then he plainly and simply answered, "You don't get any. Rookies don't get any." Then PO Rivera received his and he told PO Gorman, "These are very nice. This is beautiful. Like so beautiful. Thank you so much man." PO Gorman replied, "No, thank you." I guess that he thanked PO Rivera for having to tolerate his partnership with me.

Then PO Gorman looked at me and said, "Did you paid yours?" I answered, "No man. I waited anxiously. No, I am joking, I was not waiting for it. One for you, one for my wallet and the other one for who? PO Gorman answered, "For nobody." Then I continued, "My PBA card. Where is my PBA card?" PO Gorman continued, "You don't get any." I asked him," Why?" He answered, "You have to be an actual active cop." I said, "Come on man." I continued insisting, "Where is my PBA card? I want my PBA card." He said, "You don't order them. You don't get them. That's how it works. You pay; you get. You don't pay; you don't get them." I answered, "Really!" He said, "Really... You don't get." I asked, "So I am not getting no PBA card?" He answered, "No. No order. No pay. You don't get."

I told him," There are two PBA cards that you don't have to pay for. They give it to you without paying. And the book. Itself. As well." He throws at me an invalid PBA card while saying, "Here, here is your card. Shut up." I responded, "What! Come on man," and he said, "Come on now. I don't want that crap." Then I said, ".... as worthless human being." I continued, "I didn't get mines, I haven't get mines."

Then PO Rivera, who I think was feeling sorry for the way that I was being treated said to me, "Lets get out of here." But I remained there. Then I said, "So I am going to leave without my PBA card then." Then PO Elliot Santiago said, "Give him the f***g PBA cards, Chris, please." Then PO Gorman said, "Stop bothering me." Then I left, empty handed.

When I was inside of the RMP (police car) with PO Rivera, I told him, "I don't know why he doesn't want to give me my PBA card. Come on man." Then PO Rivera said, "I am not going to defend you." Wow. Why did he say that he was not going to defend me as if PO Gorman did the right thing by treating me that way? Did I do something wrong to deserve such treatment?

"Vindicate me, O LORD, for I have walked in my integrity, and I have trusted in the LORD without wavering." (Psalm 26:1 ESV)

For a while, we remained quiet in the car. Then we went to a job, and after we were done with the job, that we were in the elevator, I said to PO Rivera, "Rivera, I hate when this happens. Unbelievable." He answered, "What did I do man? I am sorry man." Later, in the RMP (police car) I said, "Gorman, Gorman, Gorman," and PO Rivera reacted saying, "He is supposed to represent you, the delegate, he is the delegate." I answered, "I don't know man, sincerely," and PO Rivera continued, "I am going to run next time for delegate."

Then we drove to the precinct to get some money from PO Santiago who wanted food. When we arrived, he was waiting for us outside of the precinct. PO Santiago was angry at me. He walked to the other side of the police car to give the food money to PO Rivera. As PO Santiago walked back to the precinct, I saw a strange man dressing in business attires standing in front of the precinct's building and he was smoking.

By the time that PO Santiago came close to the man who was dressed in a suit, almost next to him, PO Santiago yelled out to me, "Come, have Gorman give you the cards, IAB (Internal Affairs Bureau, who investigate police corruption) is here." Since then, he treated me with antagonism. Immediately, after he said that my partner said to me, "Lets get out of here. You don't want to walk into the mouth of the lion."

When we brought him the food, PO Santiago said something loud enough to me, but I couldn't understand what he said, but he wanted to know why I yelled at him one time when he told me something that I didn't like, and not at Gorman when he refused to give me my PBA cards. I asked my partner why PO Santiago is upset with me. He told me that Gorman and Santiago were playing the same game with me. My feet have become cold on so many occasions.

Every time I go to the lounge for meal, that I lay on the sofa, I hear many of them peacefully snoring, while I remain awake, suffering quietly.

"Even though I walk through the valley of the shadow of death, I will fear no evil, for you are with me; your rod and your staff, they comfort me". (Psalm 23:4 ESV)

Chapter 6

When an Assistant District Attorney is Brainwashed

DECEMBER 2013

On **Tuesday, December 3, 2013,** when doing the mail run (The distribution of precincts' mails), somebody told me, "I like to see how you remain calm besides everything, besides all the chaos that is happening around you," and I answered, "God is in control my friend."

My partner and I went to a job at 2153 3rd Avenue. There we met with PO Mahoney and his partner. When we were in the elevator, PO Mahoney said, regarding the job, "Probably they are playing the robbery game with their friends." Almost everyone there looked at me when he said that, so I laughed, and when they saw me laugh, everyone there followed. When my partner and I went for a meal, the officers that were covering sector Boy were already in the lounge laying on the sofa. The lights were off, and I said, "You are doing a very bad job."

Later, my partner said, "I wonder what they were doing that they just went 98 (Resuming patrol, available)." He said so because their meal ended sooner than ours. Probably they were discussing on the mysterious 3rd or 2nd floor what I had said. At the end of my tour, over the police uniform I was wearing, I put on my civilian jacket to cover my uniform, and then I placed my gun belt inside my bag and left the station house (precinct) to go straight to criminal court.

In court, at the sign in the room or police room, I saw PO Sovulj. I greeted him. He greeted me back and he looked at my bag. He asked me if I had taken the train to get there, and I told him that I did. I took off my civilian jacket, and in his presence, I took my gun belt out of my bag, so he could see that what I had inside my bag was my gun belt. Then

I folded my jacket and placed it inside my bag. Then I went to see ADA (Assistant District Attorney) Altman.

While waiting to see Manhattan ADA (Assistant District Attorney) Altman in the waiting area, PO Sovulj and his partner PO Chan arrived. His partner walked to me, and he pressed his pointing finger on my chest to see if I was wearing my bullet proof vest, which I wasn't. Then he walked away with PO Sovulj.

Meanwhile, I was thinking about whether they had called Lt. Yaguchi to check my locker and see if there was another gun belt beside the one, I was wearing, and by the time that he might have checked, he would just find my bulletproof vest. This might be the reason why he sent them. To see if I was wearing a bullet proof vest besides the one that I had inside my locker, and therefore, PO Chan had to verify it by placing and pressing his own pointing finger against my chest.

Later in the day, Lt. Yaguchi called me, and he told me to go to 1PP (1 Police Plaza= Police Headquarter) and pick up a set of speakers for him and told me that he had submitted a 49 (a police form) for it already. When I went there to pick up the set of speakers, I saw that it was a box containing a pair of computer speakers. He told me that he needed it for the captain.

But as I was walking with the speaker at hand, I wondered if this set of speakers is going to be one of the instruments used to play the recorded conversations that I have been having and/or will have with my partner PO Rivera or with the other cops such as PO Lolja, while on patrol. I wondered if the thing that I was carrying with my hands was going to be one of the means ready to be used against me. I gave Lt. Yaguchi the box with the speakers inside and he told me not to do 1PP (1 Police Plaza= Police Headquarter) at 1900 hrs. or 7:00 pm, but to go there on my regular midnight shift, because he was going to send someone else there from the 4x12 shift/tour and that I was going to relieve him later when I begin my midnight tour.

At the end of the day, after working a 2315x1438 hrs. Shift or from 11:15 pm till 2:38 pm or lets say after having worked for 15 hours and 23 minutes, I went home, slept like for approximately 4 hours and then I went back to the station house (precinct) to prepare to go and do

1PP (1 Police Plaza= Police Headquarter) at approximately 2305 hrs. or 11:05 pm. When I arrived at the precinct, PO Gorman asked me, "Hey, what do you have in your bag? Are you not supposed to be at 1PP?" I felt so bad that I didn't know what to say. I can't catch or get a break.

I arrived to 1PP (1 Police Plaza= Police Headquarter) at 2350 hrs. or 11:50 pm and I was assigned to a foot post. I managed to see my old friend PO Wilfred Nuñez and he walked by me, on the opposite side of the street. He turned his face the opposite way to avoid looking in my direction, and not even seeing if there were cars coming by my side. How it hurts to see that. My old friend, the one who once rejoiced every time he saw me, now despises seeing me. It is a disgusting sight for him. However, I keep receiving strength from the Lord, he is keeping me strong.

Later, I walked by PO Rivera's post at 1PP (1 Police Plaza= Police Headquarter), which was at the opposite side of the street, and he placed two of his fingers under his eyes and then he removed them to point those same fingers at or towards me. He did it twice to let me know that I am being watched. However, I walked to the opposite side of the street, because I didn't want to compromise my old friend PO Nuñez, by forcing him to shake my hand. But as I walked by, my heart was rapidly beating. I entered Dunkin Doughnut, and there I did a Google search on my smartphone on how to travel to Mountain Sinai, not Mount Sinai hospital, but the actual Mount Sinai in the Middle East, because I was desperate to speak directly to God.

When I arrived at the precinct after doing 1PP (1 Police Plaza= Police Headquarter), I found PO Gorman getting dressed and PO Maher was on the other aisle with PO Gambardelli. I heard PO Gorman say, "Rob, rob, rob," when PO Maher said something about robbing PO Gambardelli's head. They sounded as if they were saying 'Rob, and robbing,' instead of 'Rub and rubbing,' but they were being cynical about it. They truly meant to say rob, and robbing because they are insinuating that a robbery had taken place at the 25th precinct and it seems that they are blaming me for it.

On Thursday, **December 5, 2013,** we had a job at Pathmark supermarket. As the man who harassed the security guard was crying, at approximately 0700 hrs. or 7:00 am, PO Gloria Byrd looked at me and said, "There is something on your face Hernandez that make people want to cry." When the tour was over, in the locker room, PO Maher opened a locker that is close to mine, on my aisle, and that belonged to some other cop. He started taking the uniforms out of that locker and he began to look at them. He invited PO Gambardelli to come and see. Then he began to show the police uniforms that were in that locker to PO Gambardelli.

They were like two feet away from me. As they were looking at the uniforms, I placed on my bench my gym bag, my dirty uniform and socks. It was approximately 0753 hrs. or 7:53 am, and before leaving with my bag, I said, "Until later guys," and PO Maher said, "…later," and then I repeated the same to PO Chan and PO Gambardelli who were together looking at something on the smartphone. But they didn't say anything to me.

When I signed out, there was PO Chan and my partner PO Rivera right next to me. Were they wondering what I had inside my gym bag? And why didn't the rest of the guys come down to sign out, but they remained upstairs? Where were PO Gambardelli, PO Maher, and why not, PO Gorman?

At the subway station, I realized that I had forgotten to submit my court and overtime sheet. I was going on my three days off, and if I waited until I returned to work to submit the paperwork, it was going to be very late, because it needed to be turned in, in a timely matter. As a result, I will receive a minor violation, which I already have two, and with this one, it will be three, and three minor violations is equal to a Command Discipline, which is a costly penalty. However, I didn't go back to the station house, because they might think that I returned for something. My presence there will have everyone in the precinct on high alert. This was a great and wonderful opportunity for those who hate me.

Tuesday, December 10, 2013, marked the beginning of my true misery. This is the day where my true agony begins. This is the day that my colleagues and I were assigned to testify in court regarding a DWI (Driving While Intoxicated) arrest. The prosecutor was Assistant District Attorney Altman.

I visited Manhattan ADA (Assistant District Attorney) Altman on November 13, 14, 25, December 3 and December 9 of this year 2013 about this case. During these visits, I remember the day when I told her (Altman, the Manhattan Assistant District Attorney) that I didn't remember anything pertaining to the case. In one of the days above, I remember that I was waiting outside the Manhattan ADA's (Assistant District Attorney's) office. I was waiting outside the office.

There, I was accompanied by PO Quinones and PO Maher who had already spoken to Manhattan ADA (Assistant District Attorney) Altman. They were pressuring me, telling me that I must remember what happened on the day of the arrest. While they were telling me that, I noticed that PO Quinones was sweating profusely. He was nervous. Even his father who is a police officer at the 23-precinct showed up. It seemed that he was there to support his son. His dad's visit exemplified and signaled the seriousness of the matter.

Then PO Maher told me that according to ADA (Assistant District Attorney) Altman, I was all over the place, and that she was considering whether to put me on the stand because if she did, I was going to be crucified by the defense attorney. But at the end of the day, she did. Probably to justify her end.

On our second visit to Manhattan ADA (Assistant District Attorney) Altman, I remembered that PO Maher had asked PO Quinones and me if we remembered when the defendant was trying to come out of the vehicle that he couldn't because he had his seat belt on him. We answered, "No". I thought about it and that was a question that threw me off. Previously, I had assisted other officers on DWI (Driving While Intoxicated) arrests, and I had made other DWI arrests myself. I never thought that I was going to be so certain about something that later turned out to be a total confusion for me. Since this day, total chaos knocked at my door and entered my life, and the peaceful life that I once enjoyed became totally chaotic.

At the beginning, I never paid heed at what PO Maher kept telling me by saying that I was going to make him do a lot of overtime. I never thought about what he meant by that, until it was too late, when I became fully aware of what was going on.

But why did he maintain his silence? Why did he keep quiet? Why did he keep it to himself? I don't know. All I know is that on one of the days listed above, I **was seated outside waiting for the Manhattan ADA (Assistant District Attorney), and I asked PO Maher why he didn't seat next to me, and he said to me that he didn't because he didn't want to associate with criminals. According to the NYPD Patrol Guide, police officers are not allowed to associate with someone "2. c. Reasonably believed to be engaged in, likely to engage in, or to have engaged in criminal activities." I knew that he was holding something against me, and it had nothing to do with this case, because it had been happening before this whole mess began.**

So, on this notorious day of December 10, 2013, when I arrived at court, there I saw PO Maher and Lt. Yagushi already there waiting. Lt. Yaguchi was looking at me very strangely, suspiciously, the same way that PO Maher did. They were uneased. I had the feeling and had the presentiment that there was something mayor going on, **but they didn't tell me what it was**. I was afraid. Then, Manhattan ADA (Assistant District Attorney) Altman took us to testify. She told me that she was just going to ask me about the vouchered bottle and that it was all. So, the three of us went to testify.

She took us into a small room. PO Maher and Lt. Yaguchi continued to look at me suspiciously. She called Lt. Yaguchi first to testify. Now it was just me and PO Maher alone in the small room. He just kept staring at me, with folded arms, and without pronouncing a word. At that moment, I thought that I was the one who they were incriminating against, because of the way that they were behaving in my presence. God knows that I didn't see myself coming out of court a free man. All I could think of at the time was about them considering me a thief and that they have already poisoned her by persuading and convincing the Manhattan Assistant District Attorney into thinking the same thing. I believed that charges were being brought against me for something that I didn't do, and that right at this moment they were testifying against me. There are no words to describe how nervous I was.

Then PO Maher broke the silence by telling me that the vehicle was turned on by a push of a button, and that there were no keys in the engine. At the time, I didn't know why he had to tell me that. My mind was not focused on the DWI (Driving While Intoxicated) case at all, but on their insidious motives and on what they were planning to do to me. Then Lt. Yaguchi came back from testifying and PO Maher and I were told that we were going to testify later. Lt. Yaguchi was very nervous, because he had said at the stand that the color of the liquor that the defendant had was clear, which it wasn't. He was sweating. Later, we walked out of court and ADA Altman said to me and to PO Maher that she was going to meet with us later. She walked away from me, PO Maher and Lt. Yaguchi, but Lt. Yaguchi told us to leave without him, and he hurried or chased after her to talk something in private with her.

As I walked with PO Maher to dinner, I noticed that he was not losing sight of me. I had the feeling that he was watching a future prisoner. Like when we keep our eyes on a prisoner to make sure that he or she doesn't escape. I used to keep my eyes on my prisoners, and now they keep their eyes on me, as if to prevent my escape. He walked in front of me and as we walked, he kept looking behind him to see me and then forward because he needed to see where he was walking to. And every time he did so, he didn't say a word. He was looking back and forward.

We sat in the diner. I got something to eat, and he got something for himself. We were silent most of the time. We exchanged some words and within what we spoke, every time I opened my mouth, he had to bring his hand inside his jacket, as if he were recording our conversation.

Then we headed to Manhattan ADA's (Assistant District Attorney's) office. Days before, he had told me not to trust the ADA's (Assistant District Attorney's) smile, and every time I see her, I think about that comment.

After waiting for a while, ADA (Assistant District Attorney) Altman walked to us and she told PO Maher that she didn't need him, that she only needed me to testify. While I was walking with her to the court room, by the elevator, she saw another young man who seemed to be another ADA (Assistant District Attorney). She invited him to witness the spectacle, the show of a man in route to his downfall. A man's path to his destruction, having no one to save him, because those who could have prevented it from happening, didn't do anything to stop it.

She preferred to crucify a young defenseless police officer, instead of her losing points for the case. I was there all alone, surrounded by powerful people, by wolves in sheep's clothing. There was no one to advise me. Whom could I ask what was going on when there was no one there I could trust. I was in great fear. I was seeing myself going all the way down the downward spiral. She didn't bother to extend, at least, her weakest hand to me. What a cold heart. But instead, she invited someone to the slaughter. In this case, she might be asking herself, why catch a small fish when you can catch a big fish? This is the scenario.

But yes, she used body language to communicate with him in the elevator, such as whispering, while I was pretending that I was neither seeing nor hearing. At that moment, I became convinced that there was something mayor going on. All the things that were going through my head and that were occupying my mind had to do with what was going on there. Am I going to be the defendant? I kept asking myself. Are they accusing me of robbery at the 25th precinct? My God what is going on? Then she placed me in the waiting room, all by myself. There I was so worried and alone.

I was waiting and waiting there all alone, and at the same time I was getting more anxious. Then I was told to go to the courtroom. I took the stand. There was the judge, and behind the judge, I expected to see the sign that says, "In God We Trust." There was the typographer, the prosecutor, the defense attorney, the jury and the audience. Right before them, I took the stand, and by taking the oath, I swore before God and man; to tell the truth and nothing but the truth so helps me God.

I took a seat. Manhattan ADA (Assistant District Attorney) Altman asked me questions pertaining to the bottle of liquor, and all those questions I answered. Then it was time for the defense attorney to cross-examine me. He asked me about what happened when I got to the scene, and what I had recovered from the defendant. My answers prompted the judge to get up in her seat, and immediately she (the Judge) walked to a corner, and she began talking to someone else. The typographer looked at me as if I were an alien. Manhattan ADA (Assistant District Attorney) Altman told the Judge, "Your honor" as if she were trying to prevent me from answering the defense attorney's questions and the ADA asked me, "He was already outside, right?" meaning the defendant, and I answered, ""No he was inside." I noticed how surprised everyone in the court room was, like looking at each other.

At this precise moment, even when I am typing this, my feet become cold, and I want to lay on bed. I wondered what I did wrong. I truly believed that I had seen the defendant inside the vehicle. I testified about what I believed to be true. But when the defense attorney asked me about the Lt.'s Operator, who was PO Maher, I didn't remember what he was doing.

When I was done testifying, I went outside the court room, to the waiting area. There, I began to think repeatedly about what happened on that day of the arrest, but especially, about what PO Maher was doing. Then after thinking and rethinking about what PO Maher did at the time of the arrest, my heart began to beat hard when I started to suspect whether PO Maher was outside the vehicle. I questioned myself, "Wait a second, was Maher outside the car holding the prisoner when I first got there?" Now the more I thought about him, the more I believed that he was inside the vehicle. Then I became confused, I didn't know whether he was inside the car or outside the car. I became very nervous.

In addition, Manhattan ADA (Assistant District Attorney) Altman had told me not to mention at the grand jury or at the stand that I found inside the defendant's packet, a zip lock of marijuana. But after she told me that, on the same day that I was going to testify, Lt. Yaguchi, probably not letting the Manhattan ADA (Assistant District Attorney) know or on the ADA's back, gave me the results of the marijuana lab test, which came back positive. He gave me the results, so I may use it at the stand. As a result, I mentioned my finding of a zip lock of marijuana, which the accused possessed. However, doing so seems to have infuriated ADA Altman. It seems to have served Lt. Yaguchi's purpose, for his goal is to have ADA (Assistant District Attorney) Altman against me. He wants her to hate me the same way he does.

As I waited outside the courtroom, I was seated, when I saw two men in uniform walking towards me. I believed that they were coming for me, but they didn't. When ADA Altman walked out of the courtroom, she asked me if I was ok. Then she asked me, "Do you want to tell me something?" In the inside, I was shaking, I was so confused, my mind was frozen, I couldn't speak, and I thought to myself that I have the right to remain silent, and that everything I say can be used against me, so answered, "No." But from that moment on, I felt that my life was no longer going to be the same. After working for 17 hours and 01 minutes that day, I walked out of the courthouse feeling all alone. While walking to the subway station, at 5:02 pm, I received a text message from Lt. Yaguchi that simply said, "Hi."

As soon as I read the text message, I realized that Lt. Yaguchi knew all along and was aware of the mistake that I was about to make, and did do in court. At that moment I felt mocked, and betrayed. I felt the stab wounds not behind my back, but in my heart. I wondered, what did I do to them for them to hate me so much to the extent of being willing to ruin my life? So, I walked into the subway station face down, hoping to never come out of the subway station again. But I did come out when the train came out of the subway and it arrived at my destination.

I came out of the number 4 train, and I walked down the stairs and out of the train system. Then I walked by the Yankee Stadium to go home. As I walked, tears began to come out of my eyes. I couldn't wait till I got home. I couldn't hold my tears; I couldn't sustain them. After passing by the Yankee Stadium, I walked through the small park in the area, and I began to cry there. I felt the weight of the whole world resting not only on my shoulder, but all over me. I looked up to the sky as I cried, and I began to think about my mother, my father, and my wife.

I couldn't believe that in a moment, my life was going to be so drastically changed. So much was my disgruntle state of mind that when

I arrived home, I looked at my wrist and my blue Ironman watch was gone. But I didn't care about my watch, I could care less about the watch, I was going to jail for having said the wrong thing in court. I was hurt and desperate. So much was my anxiety and desperation that I couldn't stay in my apartment, I had to go out to a place of refuge, and where else than church.

I headed to church and there I asked for G..., who is a trustworthy man who love God, and they gave me his cell-phone number. I called him, and he gave me the location of the church where he was. I met him there. He was playing a musical instrument there. When we walked out, I explained my situation to him. He told me not to be afraid and to trust in God. He gave me words of hope in that moment of distress. I told him to take care of my wife in case something happened, but he told me not to worry and that nothing was going to happen to me.

I went home and I called my wife to find out where she was. When she told me where, I couldn't wait for her to arrive home. I rushed out of my apartment and went out to meet her, for my desperation was drowning me. As I walked to meet with her, I saw her walking down the block and there I greeted her. I walked with her inside the building and then into the elevator. Inside the elevator, I told her that I was in serious trouble. We came out of the elevator and as soon as we entered our apartment, I explained to her what had happened to me. She was worried.

Later, when she sat down, I went to her, and I kneeled in front of her. I laid my head on her lap. Having my head on her lap, I began to cry, to cry silently, because I didn't want her to know that I was crying, unless she gets to see my tears all over my face or if my tears get too wet and penetrate her pants. I was taking away time from her studies, and she had finals to take. Moments later, I was preparing myself for the detectives to arrive and arrest me. I gave my wife all the cash I had saved at home and placed it in her hand for her to do whatever she pleased with the money. Money that I have earned with hard work and sleepless hours.

Every time I heard the elevator, I told my wife that it might be them, the detectives. I was expecting them to knock on my door. Every single time I heard the elevator door that opened on my floor, I rushed to the door and looked through the door's viewer or peephole to see if it was them. When I confirmed that it wasn't them, I went back to my seat and held my smartphone tight. I was expecting their call. I was feeling very tense. Right at 10:00 pm, I received a text message, but I didn't want to read it, because I knew that it was going to be bad news. Then I looked at who had text me, and it was Lt. Yaguchi who texted me, "Hi" "Are you up" I wondered if he was mocking me. If he was making fun of me, or in a few words to let me know that he now has me in his hands. I left it unanswered. I went to bed expecting the worst.

How could I sleep in peace that night? On my bed, I was thinking about my true misery that was about to begin, and about what would be done for me. Then I began to believe that Lt. Yaguchi and the Manhattan ADA (Assistant District Attorney) Altman knowingly and intentionally placed me in that position to have an excuse and a motive to open an investigation against me. Now they just found a way to pray on this vulnerable being. A man's word is one of the most valuable things he possesses, and they want to take the value and the worth of my words away from me by discrediting me.

In the morning of Wednesday, **December 11, 2013,** I kissed my wife on her forehead and said goodbye to her, while she was lying on bed. She told me not to worry and that everything was going to be fine. Desiring not to go out, I went to the station house (precinct) because I had to go to court and meet with Manhattan ADA (Assistant District Attorney) Altman again. In the precinct, I saw Lt. Yaguchi and he told me to wait for him, so we may go to court together.

As I was waiting for him outside his office, PO Pinero walked to me, and he taught me something about how to play the guitar. Then he went to Lt. Yaguchi's office. Lt. Yaguchi had his office door open. I could see them talking. Lt. Yaguchi glanced at me several times as he spoke to PO Pinero, which made me feel nervous, but I became more nervous or lets say, frightened, when I saw PO Pinero walking out of his office with a serious look on his face, and walking away, he wished me good luck in court. He didn't say goodbye nor shook my hand. As a result, my mouth became drier or drier than it was. Knowing not what to do, I decided to wait for the Lieutenant downstairs, for it is hard to remain still when nervousness takes dominion of oneself.

While waiting for him downstairs, I saw the officers and the Sergeant giving me some weird look. Among them was PO Angel Lopez who was by the T/S looking at me. Since he is the PBA union delegate for the day shift or tour, I thought that he was there because of me. At that moment, I wished to disappear. Then Lt. Yaguchi came down, but before we walked out of the station house (Precinct), PO Alexander asked him something about a cellphone. And Lt. Yaguchi told him that he had called IAB (Internal Affairs Bureau, investigate police corruption) already regarding the cellphone. Then I walked with Lt. Yaguchi to the train station.

While on the train, I wanted to express to him my concern, my worries, but every time I tried to tell him something, he placed his hand inside his jacket, the same way that PO Maher did every time I was about to tell him something, as if to record what I was about to say. But I did end up confessing to him my concern. I told him that I thought I made a mistake in court when I testified. He told me not to worry about it, and that he made a mistake too in his testimony when he said that there was a key in the engine when there was none. But he knows little that I have reasons to believe that he took advantage of this opportunity to apply and exercise his hate towards me.

As we walked to the courthouse, I saw a state, or a court police car parked in front of the courthouse. I thought that it was for them to place me there. I must admit that I feel so tormented every time I am typing this. When we arrived at court, the Manhattan Assistant District Attorney, ADA Altman, had us wait in the waiting area. But I could no longer bear my uncertainty, so I took the opportunity to go inside the ADA's (Assistant District Attorney) office and there I told her that I believed that I made a mistake at the grand jury when I testified. But she didn't want to hear it. She didn't want to hear what I had to say. But she still wanted me to take the stand at the grand jury one more time. I didn't understand what she was trying to do. Then I went back outside to the waiting area and there I waited seated.

Other cops came to seat close to us and they knew Lt. Yaguchi very well. I suspected them of being cops from IAB (Internal Affairs Bureau, investigate police corruption) who had been requested. I already knew that I was the target. Now there I was on the outside looking normal while a hurricane, a tornado, and an earthquake was taking place inside of me, especially a volcano that was about to burst or erupt, but it didn't wish to explode. All I was waiting for was for them to tell me to turn around and place my hands behind my back and then be handcuffed.

However, everyone there was making jokes. The legal aid I knew and who always greeted me every time he saw me, this time he walked by me, and he didn't say hello. Lt. Yaguchi was seated next to me. He then began to talk on the smartphone with someone, and I heard him when he said, "Yes, send the 61 (Complaint Report) to the 47th precinct …. To pick it up Sunday night. Because it left a bad taste on my mouth. I am letting you know what I am talking about." Right away I thought that since the 47 precinct is in the Bronx, and I live in the Bronx, they were going to be the ones who were going to pick me up Sunday night at my home. Of course, since my first day of work begins this Sunday night, I am going to be picked up before I go to work.

I guessed that I am in big trouble now. Then as soon as Lt. Yaguchi spat that poison, he departed from us, and he left me with PO Maher. At the end of the day, I didn't testify. With a big smile on her face, ADA Altman asked me if I was glad that I didn't testify. PO Maher was with me everywhere I went. As I moved, he moved. His eyes were always on me. Also, he told me that he was going to give me a ride back to the station house (Precinct). On our way to the station house (Precinct), he advised me not to say anything to the Desk Sergeant or Lieutenant in the precinct, and to go straight upstairs without saying anything, which I found it hard to believe. But I told him that I couldn't because I was doing a tour change.

When we arrived, when we walked right by the Desk, there was Lt. Gonzales staring at me with an angry look on his face. I heard him ask PO Maher, "What is he doing here?" and PO Maher answered, "He had court today." I walked up the stairs, having my face down because I am being treated as if I were a criminal. I left the station house (Precinct) feeling terribly bad for not knowing what my future holds nor what evil outcome awaits me.

Immediately, after I woke up in the morning of December 12, 2013, I went to visit my sister's apartment, which I hadn't visited for months. I went there to say goodbye, because soon I am going to be arrested. Very soon, I am going to be shown on the News, and I don't want the news to catch my family by surprise. So, I wanted to prepare them for the worse. I wanted to inform them that the cause of my arrest was because of a mistake I made in court. I told my sister and my brother-in-law not to worry about me, that I am going to be fine, because God is with me.

My sister took me to see my brother. I explained to him my situation and that I was the victim of a conspiracy. Then I went home and there I waited for my wife. As I waited for my wife's arrival, I was feeling very lonely, anxious and scared. And again, I was continuously looking at my smartphone. Also, I was on high alert and wanted to make sure who was coming out of the elevator every time I heard the elevator's door open by running, not walking, but running to the door to look outside through the peephole. This time, I wished that my wife be the one coming out of the elevator and not the detectives or the patrol car.

Finally, this time, I didn't hear when the elevator arrived on my floor, because I was far away from the door. But I heard the set of keys, and when the door of my apartment began to open. And when I heard those sounds, I felt relieved, because I knew that it was my wife. I was never in my life so happy to see her.

Chapter 7

My Cruelsome December

On Thursday, **December 12, 2013-Friday December 13, 2013,** I was waiting either for them to come and get me now, or they will wait until I get to work to take me into custody. So far, nobody has come to get me, and the time for me to go to work has come. I asked my wife to please pray for me, so I kneeled, and she prayed for me. I said goodbye to my wife and now I am going to work to face my destiny.

I went to the station house (Precinct) thinking that I might not be allowed to work there anymore or that I might be arrested right at the spot. When I arrived, on my way to the locker room, I was expecting to see my locker sealed with crime tape across it. But thank God it wasn't the case.

At the muster room (the place where the officers gather to receive their assignments), I noticed that the officers were quiet. The silence was unusual. Then PO Banks said, "Hi" to me at first. Then, when I sat, PO Banks and PO Jones turned their seats facing me. My lips and my mouth had no saliva and neither of them were wet. They were completely dry, probably due to my nervousness. But I tried my best not to expose myself and get them into thinking that I am nervous by maintaining my composure.

PO Banks took out a pack of gum. He took out one piece of gum for himself and he passed me his pack of gum, so I may take one. It truly made me feel that something very serious was happening. I took one gum and gave him back the pack of gum. In the muster room, I was accompanied by approximately seven cops. They were all quiet, as if they were at my funeral, because I was dying or inside of me, I was already dead.

Then PO Maher stood and walked away. When he came back, he told me that I was going to be working with PO Santiago for the night. Then they did roll call, which is where the supervisors give the officers their assignments, and a change of plan occurred. I was assigned to be the Lieutenant's Operator instead. The change confirmed my mind that I was in trouble.

Standing by the Desk were officers that I have never seen before. They were wearing civilian clothing. I believe that they were either from crime, narcotics or from some other units or department. I thought to myself that they were the ones assigned to take me handcuffed out of the precinct and then transport me to Central Booking (where they keep prisoners) or to court.

Then at the roll call, Lt. Allen ordered us to inspect our magazines and to make sure we were not missing any rounds or simply said bullets. Was I the cause for them to check how many bullets we have in case they might have to use them on me? So, being assigned to drive Lt. Allen, as I drove Lt. Allen, I was continuously squeezing the steering wheel of the vehicle. I was squeezing it very hard as I was wondering if he was going to turn me in any time soon, or if by the end of the day, or by the end of our tour or on our way back to the station house (Precinct). But fortunately, it wasn't the case.

In the morning, I had court at the Department of Motor Vehicle which is at the Northern Manhattan Traffic Violations Bureau, and guess what? PO Maher had traffic court with me also. Before going to traffic court, I asked PO Maher why he didn't go to traffic court in uniform like me, so that way, we may return to the station house (Precinct) together. But I was joking, because it is obvious that he was not going to do it, especially when he is an old timer with at least seventeen years on the job, but strangely, he agreed. Of him agreeing to it meant that instead of him going straight home after court was over, he preferred to go back to the station house (Precinct) with me and then get dressed.

All this without getting paid, just to be with me, which he didn't need to because he had the adequate clothing needed for traffic court, and didn't need to wear the uniform and waste his time by going back to the precinct. Who would do that unless there was something very important going on, which could be that nobody wants to see me by myself at the station house (Precinct).

It was almost time to go to traffic court. I noticed that everyone at the station house (Precinct) looked at me with a despised look on their faces. PO Nancy Ramos, the training officer, came in and she didn't say hi to me. She laid the plants that she had bought on top of the T/S. PO Maher asked her where she stole those, and she answered that she had bought it with her own money. Now I was feeling more than uncomfortable there, so much that PO Maher noticed it and he finally decided to go to the RMP (police vehicle), so he rushed me out of the station house (Precinct) due to the hostile work environment I was in.

We arrived at traffic court. We got there too early, so we waited in the RMP (Police car) a little longer, before heading into traffic court. So why the rush to get me out if the precinct when we were too early? Then PO Maher received a phone call, and it was Lt. Yaguchi, because I overheard Lt. Yaguchi's voice on the phone. Then PO Maher answered Lt. Yaguchi by giving him a yes or a no responds, as if he were answering a yes or no questionnaire. Then he hung up. Also, he didn't tell me that it was Lt. Yaguchi who had called.

I, myself, expected and suspected that I was not going to be allowed to testify again in traffic court, because of the erroneous and terrifying testimony that I gave in the criminal court case of **December 10, 2013**. And Guess what? When we arrived there, I was told that my court case was cancelled. I felt so embarrassed that I rapidly began to fill out the traffic court's attendance sheet paperwork, and while doing so, I was thinking that I was going to be arrested before Sunday or on Sunday, right before going to work. Probably now, right after court, while heading to the station house (Precinct) or at home or maybe my arresting officers were already waiting for me, seating right next to me, waiting just for me to walk out of the door. Feeling like a criminal and also feeling more than embarrassed and angry at the time due to all the bad things that are happening to me, I said goodbye to PO Maher. I left PO Maher behind, and from there, I walked to the station house (Precinct) all by myself.

When I arrived, I began to change clothing, and while doing so, I was wondering if I should now confront the whole issue with Lt. Yaguchi. When I was coming down the stairs, halfway through the stairwell, I had an internal debate within me or inside of me, on whether

I should confront this or not, but I couldn't remain steady. I went back to the locker room, and I opened my locker in case I forgot something, because I was going to have two days off. I checked and confirmed that I didn't miss anything, because as soon as I leave the door of the station house (Precinct), it won't be a good idea to go back again.

Then I closed my locker, and I went down the stairwell, still thinking about whether I should confront this again. Then, I made up my mind and decided to leave for good. Already outside, like a block away, I decided to go back to the station house (Precinct), but I believe that halfway there, I decided not to. Walking away again, I remember that I had with me my overtime court slip, and that if I submitted it late, I was going to end up getting a minor violation for it needs to be submitted in a timely matter or fashion, and since I already had two, one more was going to give me a Command Discipline. Therefore, I decided to go back after being a block away from the station house, and already there, I filled out my overtime court slip.

When I was done, I decided to go back upstairs, still undecided and wondering if I should put an end to all this. I was on the staircase debating what I should do or not do. At one point, my mind froze, and I was in the middle of two consciences, one that told me to leave for good, and another one that advised me to take care of it now and do what I must do. Whether it was time to do or not to do, it is human to be afraid of the unknown.

Then at that point, I thought that I might have probably left behind some piece of paper having some compromising notes written by me. In addition, I wanted to make sure, again, not to leave anything behind, since too many thoughts or an invasion of mass thoughts were entering my mind. As a result, I can tell that my brain was and is fully loaded and by doing what I am doing now, which is writing this, I expect to bring some ease or relief to my overloaded, and already exhausted brain.

So, I thought that I should go back to the locker room and search my pants and Jacket again to see if I can find any notes. Then I took the stairwell. I was sweating cold. Halfway there, I saw PO Maher walking up the stairs. Immediately, I felt that my enemy, whom I call Evil Maher, was ready to hunt me down. When he saw me, he asked me what I was still doing there, and with a brittle and rough voice I responded that I had finished submitting my overtime sheet. I had nothing else to say. Then I left with cold sweat.

When I walked out of the station house (Precinct), I took the bus which left me at 116 East Street and Lexington Avenue. I felt so bad. It is too much tension to bear.

On Friday, **December 13, 2013,** I visited a lawyer. As I waited in the waiting area, I felt much safer there, because there was someone whose job is to defend others. When I went to his office, I sat down, I couldn't say a word, I tried to talk, but I couldn't. I tried to contain myself from crying. But my tears came out without me having altered a word. My face was doing the talking as the muscles of my face were involuntarily moving. I couldn't keep them still, but I didn't care. I told him what happened to me on **December 10, 2013,** and it gave me great relief to know that I could talk to someone that I can finally trust. He comforted me by telling me not to worry.

But then, he mentioned something about my family putting money aside just in case. When he mentioned the words, "... putting money aside ...," these three words made me feel hopeless, because money is the least thing my family have, rather, I am the one who give them money out of the few dollars that I have managed to save in my NYPD career.

"Many are the afflictions of the righteous, but the LORD delivers him out of them all." (Psalm 34:19, ESV).

On Saturday, December 14, 2013, I was on the train on my way to Duane Reade. The one that is located at 86 East Street. At 1358 hours or 1:58 pm, inside the train, I began to experience for the first time in my life stomach ulcers. I believe that it is the result of thinking too much about what happened on **December 10, 2013** and on **December 11,** which was the day when Lt. Yaguchi intentionally seated next to me, and I overheard him say on his smartphone things that had double meaning, as to make me think that I was going to be picked up on Sunday. Also on **December 13**, when I felt the weight of all the accusations coming up against me.

On **Sunday, December 15, 2013,** at 0850 hrs. or 8:50 am. I have strong palpitations on my heart and sharp pain to the left side of my neck. I woke up thinking that I should go back to the station house (Precinct) and pick up my only and unique jacket suit that I have, and my small guitar, since I am going to be arrested tonight for saying the wrong thing in court. Also, they might not allow me to go back to the station house (Precinct) ever again. Probably, they might be waiting for me there. But I am more than determined to put an end to this nightmare. I am thinking about Lt. Gonzales, and I am still wondering why he asked PO Maher what I was doing there. Now I am desperate to know what they are going to do as soon as I get there.

The weather was very bad. The street pavements were slippery because of the rain and icy snow, but I was more than determined to go there no matter what. Then I got off at the train station and as I walked to the station house (Precinct), almost in front of the station house, there I saw a green suburban parked close to the precinct or lets say, almost in front of the precinct. I saw when the person who was inside the Suburban vehicle threw a PBA book on the windshield. When I arrived there, I told Sergeant Kim, who was at the Desk, that I was going upstairs to get my jacket suit. I went upstairs, opened my locker, took my suit, and my guitar.

Also, I took with me two or three of my A summonses that I found half or less than half written, because during the time that I was writing them, in the middle of writing them, I had to stop doing it, so either because I had to respond to an emergency that came over the radio, and so I had to rush to the scene, or did some misspelling and/or scratch on the summons that were hard to correct, unless I get a new summon, or something else more important than continuing writing the summon took place that I left the summon half done.

Unfortunately, I am a very, I really mean, a very slow writer. The partner that I had, PO Gomez, always rushed me and pushed me to write faster. He always grew desperate and impatient with my slow writing skill.

Unfortunately, again, due to laziness or negligence, I didn't take the time to void the summonses. I just threw them inside my messy locker, which in my circumstance, an officer would have just tear them apart and throw them away in the garbage, but my Lord is my witness, that I never dare and may God forbid me from doing such a thing, because summonses are official documents. Those summonses were written many years ago, during the time that I was learning the job.

So, I took them with me in case they search my locker and find them, and then be accused of something unmerited, especially when I heard rumors that officers are severely punish for getting rid of summonses. So, I grabbed the summonses and concealed them on my front waste, around by belt, by my stomach, sorry I don't know how to describe the place where I put them, and I am afraid to ask how that location in my body is called. Between my abs and my pants? But I did so in case I got searched by a detective downstairs.

Then I left the premises, probably never to return. After I walked out of the precinct, I was so disoriented that I went straight to church. There I told my pastor what I was up against. How I was being treated. He told me to trust in God.

On **Monday, December 16, 2013-Tuesday, December 17, 2013,** I arrived at my workplace. I was in the muster room when PO Banks greeted me. Later that night, PO Banks seemed to hate me. My partner PO Rivera responded to a job, and it was like PO Rivera and PO Banks seemed to despise my presence and sight. It seemed that they didn't want to be around me. I wondered why? I backed PO Banks on one of his Job and it seemed that my presence irritated him. He backed me on one of my jobs, and when we were coming out of the elevator, he made way for me by extending his left arm as a matador who was letting the bull pass. Then when he saw me padding down the aided, he furiously left.

Later that night, PO Rivera received a text message, and after that text message, he no longer wanted to talk to me. I drove back to the station house (Precinct) slowly, because I believed that they were already waiting for me there. Then we made a car stop, and it was PO Larry

Young who once worked at our precinct, but because of his conduct, was transferred somewhere else. I knew him, he knew me. He was wearing civilian clothing. But he drove by in his own vehicle to say hi. He was talking to my partner PO Rivera and in the middle of the conversation he said, "… liar, I punch him in the mouth even if I get suspended for 30 days." I know that he said it because of what happened on the **tenth of this month**. Nobody wanted to talk to me. Everyone in the precinct ignored me.

On **Tuesday, December 17, 2013-Wenesday, December 18, 2013,** I was sitting down with PO Rivera who was voiding an arrest and when he was done, that I was using the computer, Sgt. Lucic told PO Rivera to take me out, to go 98 (Available). I could notice how PO Rivera rushed me out of the precinct, probably because they didn't want me to look at a particular piece of information on the computer pertaining to a case open regarding me and against me.

On **Wednesday, December 18, 2013-Thursday, December 19, 2013,** when my partner entered the car, he was very thoughtful. I remember that I was looking for him in the locker room, but he wasn't there. Then I saw him in the muster room. There, I saw that his face was so pale that it resembled someone who had just seen a ghost.

When someone asked him for a pen to sign out, he told the guy to give it back to him when he was done with the pen. When we were in the RMP (Police car), he didn't say hi to me. Also, he remained quiet. He seemed not to have believed something that was just said to him, or it was something that he might have seen. He was acting strange, rare. He seemed to be disappointed in me.

When I went to the lounge, which is on the 2nd floor, for my meal, there was PO Gorman lying down on the sofa, watching a program on television. The program was about the correctional facility and how prisoners are being treated there. This was the first time that I saw PO Gorman taking his meal break at the lounge. He always goes to the dormitory, which is located on the 4th floor to get some sleep. But on this occasion, he decided to be in the lounge. Probably to enjoy seeing me watch the program, the program that teaches about life behind bars, or lets say, in prison. Yes, he enjoyed seeing me watch the future that awaits me. I laid down on the sofa wondering why they were doing that to me.

When I was going to sign out, I asked Officer Aquiles for a pen. As he passed me his pen, he said to me, "F…k you," and I asked him why. However, I signed out and I left.

On **Thursday, December 19, 2013-Friday, December 20, 2013,** there was some type of strange activity going on in the precinct. Nobody wanted to talk to me. Sgt. Gibbs's face looked sad and pale. The volume of his voice was low. It was like it hurt him to see me. He looked like he felt pain every time he saw me, and I felt the same way when I saw him looking at me like that. I asked him why he looked sad. He said that he was not feeling well, but I knew the reason for his down spirit. I have been undeservedly accused, therefore; he was not angry, but sad.

I went to have my meal at the lounge, which is on the 2nd floor. The television was on, and again, the program that was being shown on the television had to do with prisoners in a correction facility, and how they are treated there. They have put that program twice already. On the many years that I have been working in this precinct, this has been the second time that I see the television turned on this channel, and those two times were yesterday and today. It seems that they wanted me to watch it, so I can be intimidated at the future that awaits me.

In the police car (RMP), I said to PO Rivera, "I have been giving you guys so much time to find out, and you guys haven't done anything." I have asked myself so many times the question as to why they don't question me or inquire me in regard to what I don't know. Since the beginning, when I first began to hear rumors of false accusations against me, I wanted to call IAB (Internal Affairs Bureau, investigate police corruption), but everyone in the department would know. As result, it was going to make things worse, and if I do so now, things will become seriously complicated, for I don't know what type of monster is after me or with what type of evildoer I am dealing with or as my partner PO Rivera had said, "Open a can of worms."

Tuesday, December 24, 2013: I will spend Christmas by myself. Lt. Yaguchi sent me a text message at 9:29 a.m. that said, "Hi" I texted him back, "Hi Lt. are you working today?" He texted back, "Yes call u in a bit" "Is this about tonight" I don't know how and what words to use on my next text message to him, for all I know is that I want to meet him in person today to discuss what is going on. I want to know why I am being treated the way that I am being treated.

When I took the public transportation to go to the precinct and talk to him in person, on my way there, I changed my mind, because I knew that the moment I met him, he would begin recording me again. I didn't know what to do. I couldn't bear the pressure of my indecision anymore, so I went to the movie theater instead.

Walking out of the movie theater, and knowing that my job is on the line, tears began to come out of my eyes as I began to infer, "Mother, father, how I am now going to give you the life that I have always wanted to give you. Mother, what about the old car that you want to have before you pass away, and that I had offered to give you?"

On **Saturday, December 28, 2013,** PO Pinero told me that it was going to be his last night doing midnight. At that moment I felt lonelier, I lost a brother in Christ. After work, I went to talk to a friend, who is a good friend of my family, and his name is Carlos. I went to the small business that he is establishing by himself. I spoke with him about my situation, and how terrified I was because of what happened in court.

I told him about the day that I went to the station house (Precinct) thinking that I was going to be arrested. I told him that the purpose of me going there was to get my guitar and my suit jacket because I thought that I was going to be arrested, and that I was no longer going to be allowed to visit the precinct. I thought that it was going to be my last visit to the precinct.

Then when I told him that my coworkers thought that I was a thief, and that they were treating me as such, he laughed out loud, and so did I. I laughed out loud with him. Because the thought of me being a thief is so ridiculous, absurd, and funny that it made us laugh.

Today, **Monday, December 30, 2013,** I spent all day on the street feeling completely disoriented, not knowing what to do. So, I visited the same lawyer again to discuss my concern with him because I needed someone to talk to so badly about the matter.

Today, **Tuesday, December 31, 2013,** I noticed that my hair has been moving out of my head for it no longer wants to be part of me. There is a muscle/organ that is of the same size as my fist located at the center of my chest that is in constant suffering because it refuses to pay for the sins that other(s) have committed.

In the morning, PO Rivera greeted Lt. Yaguchi, "Happy New Year," and Lt. Yaguchi who had a malicious smile on his face said, "Not Yet." I didn't sleep all day. I have been tossing and turning.

It is 7:03 pm. I have neglected my body because of the job that I love, and that I am afraid to lose. My body, my entire body suffers because of this job. I have valued my job more than my own life, which I know is a sin. Now I do understand.

The true fortune is found in God. Those who enjoy good health, must acknowledge that it is by the grace of God, because our good health is a treasure itself, because without it, we can lose all our savings and material possessions just to maintain or treat our/and/or family health. I have erred. I have learned a lesson. I will leave everything in God's hands. He will oversee vindicating and of clearing my name because he is God. God, in you I trust, and I have faith that I will see your justice with my own eyes.

Chapter 8

JANUARY 2014 Events

It is now **Wednesday, January 1, 2014,** and my Sergeant didn't say Happy New Year to me when he saw me. All I could see was my partner receiving texts, which I know were texts of, "Happy New Year," from our colleagues that have forgotten to text me so, which last year they did. When I left work, I was so sad to be at home that I entered my apartment and there I began shivering. Not once or twice, but constantly. I lay on the bed, and I felt that my feet were icy cold. I laid and covered my dying body with two blankets.

At 8:25 pm on the television Channel, "Aliento de Vida," I received a message from the TV programing, "Tres Cada Dia," while I was typing this in the computer. The person in the program said, "Porque Dios quiere que uses tus talentos…" which in English means, "Because God wants you to use your talents…." Then he said that God talks to us in different forms/ways.

This is **Thursday, January 2, 2014 - Friday, January 3, 2014**. I am home desperately thinking about my situation. I haven't slept, and to know that I must go to work later tonight, makes me feel anguished and sick. I feel hopeless, but the only thing that is sustaining me is the fact that God knows the truth. Now I am thinking and re-thinking, so I have decided to go to church at approximately 8:00 pm. When I look at my phone, I see that I have a text message. At 8:02 pm, PO Rivera texted me, "U have 1PP tonight", "Wake up."

I didn't know that I had headquarter security detail at 1PP (1 Police Plaza= Police Headquarter). I put on the closest clothing I could reach for. I was supposed to be there at 7:00 pm and now they might give me a Command Discipline for being late, when every time that I go to work there, I arrive at least an hour early.

When I walked out of my apartment building, it was snowing very hard, and it was very windy. As I was jogging to the subway station, the snow was blowing hard on my face, and as continued jogging, at that instant, I cried out to the Lord. Meanwhile, tears were running down my cheeks, not because I was late, but because they have brought false accusations against me, and for not knowing what is going to be of my life. I arrived late, but fortunately they didn't give me a Command Discipline, because the supervisors there knew who I was, since I go there regularly without being late, and every time I go there, I give them what they expect of me.

Then I was inside the security booth silently thinking about the shameful and embarrassing life that I am leaving. I remained inside the booth thinking and re-thinking about my situation. Wow, you can't imagine how hurt I felt. As I was sitting there, tears were going down my cheeks again, and again, as I remained there seated, motionless, inside the cold, quiet booth, looking just at the snow outside. I was feeling so emotionally hurt. But there I remained seated in the same position, making very minimal body movement. I was there for approximately 10 hours, intact.

"I lift up my eyes to the hills. From where does my help come? My help comes from the LORD, who made heaven and earth." (Psalm 121:1-2 ESV)

On **Friday, January 3, 2014-Saturday, January 4, 2014** I and my partner responded to a job, and as we headed to the location, one of my fellow officers grabbed a bucket and he handed it over to the cop that was next to me while telling him, "You should take this, you paid for this," and then he turned his back on me. For how long should I put up or keep up with this?

In the morning, we went to the store. My partner didn't have enough cash with him, but I had enough, more than sufficient. I asked him if he wanted a coffee, but he refused to let me buy it for him. He came up with the excuse that he was going to buy his coffee somewhere else, but that he preferred to get his money first at the precinct.

At the end of the tour, I saw my brother in Christ, PO Pinero, but he didn't greet me. He spoke directly to my partner. He completely ignored me. How it hurts. When I was by the Desk, the Sergeant, who was often nice to me, now tried to avoid looking at me. Sgt. Kim, whom I had told that I was going upstairs to get my jacket that early Sunday, gave a despise look at me, which I believe had to do with that early Sunday morning visit to the command. My partner, who seemed to have noticed it, rushed me upstairs and as he did, he advised me not to go to the station house (Precinct) for my scheduled RDO (Regular Day Off) court. How it hurts that at the place that I once loved working, and that I felt was my second home, in the same place, I am now being mistreated and persecuted when I have done nothing wrong to deserve it.

I feel so disvalued, so devastated that at this moment I don't know what to do. I decided to fast, and after being done with my fasting at 10:00 pm, I still didn't want to eat. If it wouldn't be because of the faith and hope that I have in God, I would have starved myself until the one responsible for the wrongdoing, of what I am being blamed for, be caught, or confess to the crime, whatever the crime is. Whomever did what I am being blamed for, and have kept silent, he will not only be a criminal, but a monster. What type of evil person is he or she that after seeing an innocent man being blamed for something that he didn't do, and that he himself or she herself did, remains silent? This criminal must be a cop hater, because he or she is not thinking about the consequences that this would bring to his fellow officer, if whoever committed the crime is a cop. And if not a cop, he or she might be a wannabe cop by taking things that belong to cops like police equipment, if it is police equipment that is missing.

Oh, my fellow officers, you guys don't know how much I love every single one of you, and you guys think so low of me. What a cruel reality this is.

It is 10:42 pm and I still don't want to eat, but I must. I laid upside down on the floor crying for justice. Feeling like a mop on the floor for they have been mopping their dirty floor with me by tainting my name.

Until when my lord my God, until when do I have to keep looking at them straight in their eyes, because I have nothing to hide. There is no reason for me to feel embarrassed because I know I have done nothing wrong, but I feel bad, terrible because of what they are thinking of me. They are killing me with their false thoughts about me or lets say, their false thoughts about me are killing me. I am typing this because I must distract myself, but I really don't have the desire and the strength to keep on typing. All I want is to run and jump on the bed and cover my entire body with the bed sheet.

At one point I went to take the train, and two guys bumped into each other. Sometime in December I went to visit a pastor to explain to him my condition, regarding the possibility of me getting arrested for the **December 10, 2013,** incident. He referred me to a lawyer he knows, but just the consultation with that lawyer was going to be around $250 dollars. When I left the pastor's office, I considered that the consultation with that lawyer was too expensive. I walked around that lawyer's address, but I changed my mind and went home instead.

On **January 09, 2014,** I was on patrol with my partner. My partner began to write a parking summon. When he began doing it, he left it half done because he supposedly had to use the bathroom. I saw how he placed his hand on his stomach and told me to go. Minutes later, when he came back to the RMP (police car), and he told me to go back to the van that he was writing the summons too.

When we arrived, he began asking me questions about summonses, but as soon as he began with those bizarre questions, I realized that he was interrogating me. At that moment, I realized that he was being wiretapped either by IAB (Internal Affairs Bureau, investigate police corruption) and/or it was an internal thing being done by the command.

Scared, I began to answer his questions. I told him that he must void the summon that he left half written because the person is now inside the van. But he told me that he had observed it earlier and there was nobody there. Then he told me that we were not allowed to void it, that we must submit it and let the judge deal with it, let the judge determine what he or she is going to do with it. Then he asked me questions regarding the writing of summonses, such as what time I put on the summonses when I write them, I told him that I would write the time as soon as I began to write the summonses. He corrected me by telling me that the time that needs to be written in the summonses is the time in which the infraction happened. I was so nervous that I didn't care if he misunderstood me. I was not going to try to make him understand me. I was being recorded, and it was all I cared.

Then he asked me about the ticket fixing scandal, and if I knew anything about it. I answered that I didn't. He became astonished that I didn't know. But the reason why I told him is that I didn't know what had to do with their video/audio recording. I know they saw me hide the half-done A summonses on by abs or my belt that Sunday morning through a concealed tiny camera. If I had answered that I knew about the ticket fixing scandal, they were going to become more suspicious about me and they will think that I had done something wrong with the summonses, or lets say, some type of ticket fixing, which God is my witness that I have done no wrongdoing since the day I became a police cadet, till this day as a police officer.

Then we spoke about getting the motorists' information on the computer by the license plate when a vehicle is gone and then faxed the copy of the summons at the owner's address provided by the computer, and I told him that I didn't know. He was surprised, and he looked at me with disgust, because with all the fabricated questions he had asked me, I had answered them unsuccessfully. Now he might consider me the greatest liar ever, and so is whoever is listening to the recordings.

Then he said, "This is what happens when Gomez and Martorelli get people jammed up (in trouble). They laugh about it and say how stupid he is." As soon as he said that I was stone cold, my suspicion was confirmed, PO Martorelli and PO Gomez were behind all this.

It was obvious that PO Gomez, and PO Martorelli were listening to our conversation. PO Gomez and PO Martorelli might have held some resentment against me since the day I manhandled the two of them on a day that PO Gomez and PO Martorelli verbally abused me. Previously, PO Gomez was forced to take anger management therapy. Now they are taking advantage of this opportunity to make me pay. PO Gomez was the first partner I had when I began working at the 25th precinct. We separated because he told me that detectives have blood on their hands and that he wanted to be a detective. I never knew that he was going to shed mines. No wonder PO Rivera's mysterious visit to the bathroom. I didn't ask him why he said that I am swimming in dangerous territory.

When we arrived at the station house (precinct), there by the Desk, I could see PO Gomez and PO Martorelli laughing with joy. They were being greeted by other officers, which looked as if they were receiving a standing ovation for making a great discovery, which was attributed to the hateful look I was receiving from everyone there. In contrast, nobody wanted to say, "Hi" to me. Even the ICO (Integrity Control Officer) was looking at me and pretended that he didn't see me. I was so hurt. Then I saw PO Gomez place his gun on his head as if to be making fun of me. Then I heard PO Gorman say, "I pledge the 5th. "By saying so, he was referring to "The clause of the Fifth Amendment to the U.S Constitution barring the government from compelling criminal defendants to testify against themselves." (Black's Law Dictionary: West Group 2001). He said so while still playing around with PO Gomez.

The midnight crew was there also. Then out of nowhere came Captain Larin and he began to congratulate every single one of them except me. He turned his back on me. Later, he looked at me and said, "Oh, you are there, I didn't see you," and he greeted me. However, nobody else greeted me. I was just standing there like a dry tree. I was done with the court issue and a few hours later, I was dealing with another issue.

On **Friday, January 10, 2014** at approximately 2310 hrs. or 11:10 pm PO Gorman was surprised when he learned that I didn't do 1PP (1 Police Plaza = Police Headquarter), and far worse, when he learned that he was going to work with me that night, because my partner PO Rivera had decided to do 1PP (1 Police Plaza = Police Headquarter) for me.

The Sergeant too was expecting me to be at 1PP (1 Police Plaza= Police Headquarter) and was disappointed to know that I didn't. At 2340 hrs. or 11:40 pm, I was standing by the T/S and Sgt. Gibbs stood close to me. When he saw that a Sergeant from the 23 precinct and his PBMN Officer were standing right next to me, he decided to go somewhere else to do his duties. They didn't move; they just remained next to me quietly for as long as three minutes. Then the Sergeant from the 23-precinct lifted one of his arms to let his officer know to follow him and his officer did follow him. I called PO Gorman, and he told me that he was in the bathroom. When we went out, we remained quiet throughout the entire tour.

At approximately 0700 hrs. or 7:00 am Lt. Yaguchi asked me why I didn't do 1PP last night. I told him that I was too tired and had decided to give it to PO Rivera. I could see his furious look on his face, not only because of the news, but because he saw me by the Desk also. He looked at roll call (which are sheets detailing what every single officer are assigned to do) and after he did, he realized that I was working with PO Gorman, but PO Gorman had extended his meal time upstairs because according to him, he was in the bathroom, probably to lesser or to reduce the time that he had to spend working with me. As soon as Lt. Yaguchi finished looking at the roll call, he picked up his cellphone or smartphone and he stepped outside. Like in less than a minute, I saw PO Gorman coming out of the stairwell and he stood right next to me. Then came Lt. Yaguchi. He began to talk to us. PO Sovulj came in and he stood right in front of me. Later came PO Maher, and he stood right next to me also. I was literally surrounded by wolves.

Lt. Yaguchi remained there for more than I expected. Then I saw the captain who was behind the Desk talking with another Lieutenant. Then came PO Quinones and before Lt. Yaguchi went upstairs, with a smile on his face, he told PO Quinones that he would be upstairs. Then I saw Lt. Gonzales who had just arrived, and he began talking to Sgt. Rodriguez and Sgt. Rodriguez looked surprised at the news that Lt. Gonzales was sharing with him about something seen on a video. Then Lt. Gonzales turned around and when he realized that I was behind him, and as soon as he saw me, his face, reflected an angry expression on his face or lets say, he gave me a dirty look. He looked like a furious bull. Then Sgt. Rodriguez said that this was good for the new rookies to learn.

105

The officers from day tour were coming in to relieve us. None of them greeted me. Sgt. Kim who was at the Desk, didn't look at me not even for a second, but he seemed to hate me. I handed over the RMP (police vehicle) key to the Sergeant and with a very low tone of voice and without looking at me, he said, "Thank you". Then I saw the continuity of being followed again. Now PO Maher stood right next to me outside the muster room, while inside of the muster room, there was training going on where everyone was invited, except me and PO Maher, because he was busy watching me. I went inside without being invited because I was so embarrassed. There I saw everyone laughing and smiling as if there were some types of celebration, but what they were looking at was some type of pictures on the screen. At the same time, I was seeing their happiness on their faces, while I was standing there, suffering.

Meanwhile, when the training was over, that everyone was socializing, not even one of the day tour cops greeted me. Everyone seemed to look at me as if I were a criminal that nobody wants to associate with. At that moment, all I wanted to do was to go home, lay on my bed, and cry.

Sometime during the early week of **January 2014**, I heard PO Gloria Byrd tell PO Rivera, "I didn't talk to you because you were with" and suddenly when she saw me, she stopped talking to PO Rivera and she said to me, "Manolo," which was the name that everyone in the precinct gave me, because before Lt. Yaguchi was transferred to our precinct, I was very well liked. PO Rivera showed me on his smartphone a picture of a shot gun, and as soon as he did, he said to me, "Look, I am buying one, thank you."

I cannot move my tongue as I usually do. My tongue is sedated, but with a little effort, I can move it. Sorry, I have too much tension.

On **Friday night of January 17, 2014,** I went to the station house (Precinct) to change my combination lock because this passed morning, after I had finished my tour at 1PP (1 Police Plaza= Police Headquarter) that I went straight to the station house, I noticed that one of my lockers had been ransacked. On the same day of the night, I received a call from Lt. Yaguchi who asked me to do a day tour instead of a night tour. I decided to do it. I went to the grocery store and bought a new lock.

While I was inside the grocery store, a young man and a young woman abruptly entered the grocery store. They were around me, and as soon as I left the grocery store, they stepped out too. One of them was talking on the smartphone. They seemed to be undercover cops or Confidential Informants. I took a taxi to the station house (Precinct). When I arrived at the station house, my colleagues were so eagle and desirous to know what I was doing there because I was assigned to do a day tour. I told them that I was changing my lock, because I had noticed that in the morning, my locker had been ransacked. Then as I was leaving, they were looking at me strangely, and I left them wondering.

On **Saturday, January 18, 2014,** I did a day tour. My supervisors were Sgt. Kim and Sgt. Bennett. The two of them were very friendly to me, which I found to be very strange. Sgt. Kim told me that Sgt. Gibbs went out sick because of me. A few hours later, while I was processing an arrest that I had made of someone who was stealing, I overheard Sgt. Kim talking to another officer. I heard him tell the other officer, "They are just waiting to have something recorded, so he won't sue the city. It will take like a month for them to get rid of him." Then the officer asked him, "I am getting a detective shield right?" And then Sgt. Kim answered, "Yes, everyone is getting one."

"Rescue me, Lord, from evil men. Keep me safe from violent men who plan evil in their hearts. They stir up wars all day long. They make their tongues as sharp as a snake's bite; viper's venom is under their lips. Selah Protect me, Lord, from the clutches of the wicked. Keep me safe from violent men who plan to make me stumble. The proud hide a trap with ropes for me; they spread a net along the path and set snares for me. Selah" (Psalm 140:1-5 HCSB)

All this was going on around me while I was doing my paperwork. Now my focus was 25% on my paperwork and the remaining 75% of my concentration was spent on being highly attentive to what they were talking about, which wasn't good, because according to them, I am a criminal. A supposed thief who had just arrested a thief, a suspected thief who is processing the arrest of a thief, and a considered thief who is fingerprinting a thief. Oh, poor me, who has never stolen a thing in his life. How can a human being resist and bear all this undeserving amount of stress, pressure and humiliation that is being constantly provoked by the hostile work environment that I am in, and still haven't taken his own life?

Then when I was leaving, there was Lt. Gonzales next to the roll call. He made a cynical joke of me by calling me "Menudo." Then he asked me about my famous guitar. When he asked, I could notice the malicious and suspicious look on his face, so I told him that I was trying to learn how to play the guitar. Then he asked me why I was losing so much weight, and I told him that I was no longer drinking protein. He asked me if the protein was high in calories, and I told him that it wasn't, that it was just to gain mass, and he looked at Captain Larin, who was nearby, and I left.

Absolutely, they want to gather some type of information, so they could use it against me, so they may be able to legally fire me.

On **Sunday, January 19, 2014,** PO Rivera said, "Thank you" to the Sergeant, and the Sergeant said, "No, thank you." I gave $100 to an officer from the 40th precinct, because of a ticket that I gave him, for I didn't see his department issued plate that was on his windshield the moment that I gave him the summons.

When I left work in the morning when I arrived home, I received a call from my job. My Sergeant asked me if I had the RMP (police car) key. I told him that I might have left it on my gun belt. He asked me for my locker number, and I gave it to him. Then I went to the grocery store and bought a new lock, since they know my lock number, and decided to get a new one in case the wrong person decides to plant something inside my locker. But as I was buying it, I saw two undercover cops or informants, one was a young man and the other was a young woman. They were around my age. They were pretending to be buying something.

On **Monday, January 20, 2014,** I went out for breakfast and then I went home. At home, I dropped my exhausted, loaded, and overheated body on bed, and slept until my wife arrived. As soon she did, she woke me up by screaming at me, telling me that she was calling me all day to go to BJs as we had planned, and that when she comes home, she finds me sleeping. I couldn't get up from bed. My legs didn't want to move. I didn't want to get up. I told her that I would meet her there.

In the bus, my wife asked me who I like the most whether my father or my mother. I couldn't answer that question right away, because I wanted to cry. I don't easily cry, but a river of tears began to come out of my eyes, but I wasn't crying. I began to get rid of those tears before they got to my cheeks by using both of my hands. She seemed to have notice it, so she asked me, "What happened to you mother?" I said, "Nothing," but she continued asking, "What about your father, is he ok?" I answered, "Nothing is happening to them, I will tell you later," and she said, "No, tell me now. I am already anxious, tell me." Then I said, "I have always wanted to give my parents what they don't have.

I have wanted to supply them with everything they need. I am proud of my parents. I remember the day my mother asked me for a vehicle before she passed away, and I told her that I was going to give it to her. Now because of what I am going through, I don't think that I will be able to give her what she wants. I am not a fighter, but they want to take everything away from me, including the pride that my parents have for me."

On **Tuesday, January 21, 2014,** I was in bed all day long. I was feeling unwilling to do anything. My mind was already occupied with negative thoughts of what is happening to me. I didn't want to get up from bed. On Stars channel, in the morning I heard a message from Joyce Meyer about trusting God, not in the money that you may lose from one day to another. She talked about the Manna that God provided to the Israelites and didn't allowing them to keep for another day, because if not, it was going to get rotten, for he wanted them to trust him. She spoke about how we should fully depend on God, not on the Government, not on the money nor in the pension. Now I notice that my hands are shaking as I type this.

On **Wednesday, January 22, 2014,** I came out of church, and a young guy asked me for a quarter. I went to eat, and at the place that I was eating, a man like in his late thirties approached me, and he ate his food right next to me. When I went to the bus station, there was a young guy about my age waiting at the bus stop also. He was the only one waiting there in the very cold temperature.

My working place has turned into a hostile work environment, or lets say, my prison. I beg not to be there anymore. All I can say is that I am suffering there. I took these two weeks' vacation to escape from this cruel reality, but I didn't know that by taking these two weeks off, I was going to be trapped and confined to the four walls of my apartment, which is making this cruel reality more real and vivid. As a result, I have more time to think about my problems, and I can't control this negative thinking. I cannot escape the thought that I am being perceived and seen as a criminal by my colleagues, and according to what they think of me and the way that they are treating me.

At the subway station of East 161 Street, which is next to the Yankee Stadium, at the bus stop on bus thirteen, there were at least two young guys waiting for me. One of them followed me to take the bus, which is something that I didn't notice before. I remember that one time when one of them bumped into another one in a matter of confusion. One day, at East 125 Street, there was a guy with beard who was accompanied by another young woman. I shook my head to him, and as soon as I did, I overheard him say to her, "He knows." Another time at East 125 Street I saw a white man and a Hispanic man by the stairs, and I saw when the Hispanic man got into the train at the same time I did. Now, every day I see the same pattern where there is a young man always following me.

In the middle of my vacation day, I couldn't contain myself. I was home wearing my black sweater that has a hoodie, I placed the hoodie over my head, and I laid myself flat on the floor with my face facing the floor and there I wept. Another afternoon I lay on my knees and cried.

On **Sunday, January 26, 2014,** I officially told my wife that I was being followed. She said that I was crazy, and that if I kept thinking like that, they will take me to a psych ward. She said, "You just tell me that, but I bet you that you won't say that at your workplace, because you know well, they will send you to psych if you do."

It is **Monday, January 27, 2014**. It is incredible that I have no one to talk to at my workplace, including my partner PO Rivera, because I know that he is being wired. How terrible it feels.

Chapter 9

February 2014 Events

On **Friday, February 7, 2014,** I went to the station house (Precinct) to prepare to go and do 1PP (1 Police Plaza= Police Headquarter). There I saw a uniform pant hanging on a hanger and the hanger was hung on the outer part of my locker. I took the hanger and placed it on top of the bench. After working for 12:50 hours at 1PP (1 Police Plaza= Police Headquarter), I went back to the station house (Precinct) again. When I arrived, I found the pants hanging on the outer part of my locker again. I placed it back on top of the bench again. As I headed home, I began to think that I should have told Lt. Yaguchi about the pants hanging on the outer part of my locker.

One day, PO Banks, who was behind the Desk, asked me as he smiled, why I took the two-week vacation, to do what? I wondered if there was any malice hidden behind that question. But what he can't imagine is that I used my two vacation weeks to mourn. To mourn because of their abuse, to mourn about the unfair treatment that I am receiving and was about to receive by them.

I believe that it was on **Wednesday, February 12, 2014,** when me and my partner resumed patrol that we were walking back to the station house (Precinct), that one of the officers stopped him and I overheard my partner say to the other officer that Lt. Allen have his thing on the side. His "… underdogs …," which I believe are the people who are following me.

On **Saturday, February 8, 2014,** I heard PO Maher tell PO Gorman, "Now it is two storms. He should quit."

"Though an army encamp against me, my heart shall not fear; though war arise against me, yet I will be confident." (Psalm 27:3 ESV)

When I got home, my wife grabbed me and pushed me against the wall as she told me to stop it, to stop it, because she refused, she didn't want to hear what I was going through at work. Every time I fall asleep, and then wake up by opening my eyes, immediately I feel anguished. I really don't want to do anything. I am like in a spiritual coma. I will never forget **December 10, 2013.**

On **Monday, February 10, 2014,** I and PO Rivera went to the Shooting Range for shooting practice. Later, at the shooting range, he asked me if my mother did everything for me when I was a kid. Then I saw the fantastic four at the cafeteria of the Shooting Range. There were four officers seating next to us. As I listened to their conversation, one of them said, "He was shown like for 45 minutes walking on the video. I believe that he is from the 25th precinct. He has been working there for five years, and he didn't know what to do." And guess what? I do have five years' experience working at the 25th precinct.

Also, they kept mentioning the word "fire" multiple times as they spoke about cops getting fired. There were two men seated opposite to us staring at me. Inside the classroom, the instructor walked in talking about people who tell lies, and he also mentioned how there are criminals who become cops to steal. He looked angry, and he never looked at me as he spoke.

PO Rivera told me that he had two dreams. In one of them he saw a big yellow man walking thru, I believe he said a back yard or a building and jumped the barrier by lifting his leg. The yellow man was criminally trespassing private territory. Guess what? My skin color is olive, or lets say, yellowish.

The second dream he had was that he just finished smoking marijuana and that he had to do a Dole Test (Cops are randomly chosen to do a dole test to see if they have consumed any illegal drugs, which if the test becomes positive, the officer will ultimately get fired). He told me that he was very scared. When the train was about to get into the subway, he made the same sound using his throat.

At home I asked my wife how she was doing. She answered, "Yes, you ask me how I am doing just to come up with the same topic again."

Sunday, February 9, 2014, I believe that it was on this same date that I was waiting for the train at East 125 streets and Lexington Avenue. There I noticed that a guy was talking behind me to a lady. Then I heard her say, "I don't know what to think. They should bring it from level A to level C." Than the guy said, "This is so boring." All I wish to know is what do they want from me. On one occasion, there was a guy asking for money on the train. He said that he had lost his job, and not to look down on him. To please not to laugh at him.

Through all of this, I have lost my colleagues whom I love. There are times that through all my tensions and stresses, my tongue can't move. There were times when my legs didn't want to move at all. I don't want to get up from bed.

On **Friday, February 14, 2014,** I was doing patrol with PO Rivera when he told me that he wanted to show me a video about NYPD counterterrorism. He showed me the video as if to amaze me with how well protected the city is and the great security we have. Especially in the subway system with all the surveillance cameras. Probably he thought that I didn't know that. He thinks that I don't know the purpose behind him showing me the video.

I asked him if he got the video from YouTube, but he said that he got it from Netflix. Then he told me that the NYPD is working together with the FBI, and the CIA on the second floor of 1 Police Plaza. So, does this mean that the NYPD is working together with the FBI and the CIA to take me down? No wonder why I heard PO Maher tell PO Gorman the other day, "Now it is two storms. He should quit." But as the song "Burning Heart" by Survivor says, "In the warrior's code there's no surrender. Though his body says stop, his spirit cries never!" Because I have done nothing wrong. As simple as that.

What a Valentine Day this is. I was doing patrol with PO Rivera and in the middle of the street, a man like in his mid-forties stopped us. **He told us that he is a retired cop. He took out his ID and showed it to us. He told us that he is having a problem with his wife. She wanted him out of the apartment. He said that he lives on 119 streets between 2nd and 1st avenue and that his place is a bad place to live in, because there are bad people living in the area. He said that they can notice that he is a cop because of how he looks.**

Also, he was upset because he had gone to the 25th precinct to ask for a ride to 181 streets and Broadway, to the flower shop there to buy flowers for his wife, but they had denied him the ride. My partner told him that he couldn't take him there either because of inspection. Then my partner asked him why he needed to go to 181 street and Broadway when there is a flower shop right on 116 street? Immediately, he changed the topic because he didn't know what to respond.

Then he said that he has a lot of stories to tell about his time as a cop. He said that he could even write a book about it. Then he narrated to us a time when he was securing a crime scene with another officer. Later, it turned out that a gun was missing from the crime scene. Then they said that the other officer with whom he was with stole it and that they wanted him to wear a wire. He said that he refused to wear a wire in the beginning, and he called his wife, which they did allow him to call.

That he asked for a lawyer, but they told him that they were going to press the same charges on him if he did. Also, he said that the ADA (Assistant District Attorney) have their own squad team that go outside to do their own investigation. I could see his desperation on his face as he was giving us his narrative. He wanted to tell me something. He wanted to warn me about something, but he couldn't say anything more. Then he walked away without wanting to leave.

Enough said. If I get a lawyer or report their abuses, they will press charges on me. There is absolutely nothing I can do, even though I have done nothing to deserve to be charged. But even

though I am innocent, I will have to use all my savings to spend it on an attorney. Plus, the embarrassment of being in the press, the newspaper and on the news. What the man said was a warning or a threat. I really cannot move a finger on my defense. I can't defend myself. I must let everything be.

Then I looked at my partner and I asked him if he was wired, and he began to play around as if he did. Then he started talking about using codes such as "Omni" which means something else, not what it means. For example, what they meant by, "Omni" is drugs, and so and so. Then he told me about buying flowers for my wife. Later, he looked at one man who was holding in his hand a lot of flowers and he said, "Oh when you see that on this day a man buys a lot of flowers for his wife, it means that he is really in trouble with her. But when you see that he just buys one rose for her, it means that he is fine with her.

In the morning, I went to the same flower shop that the retired officer mentioned at 181 street and Broadway. When I came out of the bus to head over there, right at the corner, I saw a white man wearing a ski hood. He was drinking what appeared to be coffee or tea. Now it has been confirmed. They were expecting me there after the fact of what the retired cop told me. As soon as he saw me, he entered the flower shop. There, he pretended to be looking to buy flowers. I stood outside looking at the flowers that were outside. Then I saw when he was about to come out, but as soon as he saw that I was going inside, he went back inside.

Then, after being inside, he left, but immediately another white man entered the location and bought his roses. He was like he was in his late forties or mid-fifties. But he didn't spend time looking around at the different roses, no; he directly went and bought the first one he looked at. Then a Hispanic guy was there talking to one of the staff, but he didn't leave. He stood there. I made my payment and left. Then a white Hispanic woman at the bus stop didn't leave my sight or presence. She was wearing big sunglasses and at one point I heard a photograph taken from a smartphone. When I looked behind me, it was her, and there I was holding tight to the flowers.

On **Friday, February 14, 2014 - Saturday, February 15, 2014,** a taxi driver approached my RMP (police car) and he stated that someone had hit him on the face with his fist. When we followed the taxi driver that he pointed out to the guy who did it, I handcuffed the suspect right away. The victim was eager to prosecute. Later, at the station house (precinct), the complainant changed his mind, and he didn't want to press charges.

I was scared. I knew not what to do because I am being video/voice recorded everywhere I go, so much that when we brought the prisoner into the station house (precinct), I let PO Rivera search for the prisoner, because I knew the deal. When PO Rivera counted the defendant's money, he told Sgt. Gibbs that it was fifty-nine dollars, and Sgt. Gibbs asked loud enough, so that it may be well heard in the recordings, "Rivera you checked him? Good, fifty-nine dollars."

When I was writing the summons for disorderly conduct, I was so nervous that I didn't know what to write, because I knew that everything I write and do will be scrutinized. Therefore, I was afraid that they might find fault and fabricate things to make me look bad. I gave the prisoner the first copy of the summons, and I kept the original. Only the narration needed to be written. I was so disturbed by not knowing what to write on the narration that without saying anything, I passed the summons over to PO Rivera to see if he could write the narration for me. At the same time, I was hoping for him to do it quietly, which at first, he did, but when he finished the narration, he read it aloud to prove my incompetence. He wrote it on a piece of paper, which later I took home together with the summons, so there I could peacefully proofread it and make sure that he was not setting me up for failure.

On this day, we had multiple jobs related to intoxicated/drunk individuals. What a condition. More people than usual had gathered at East 125 Street and Lexington Avenue. There was a pedestrian struck. It was a young man who was struck by a yellow taxi. When we arrived, we noticed that the right-side front passenger mirror of the yellow taxi was gone. The pedestrian seemed to be an actor who was pretending to be drunk by not walking steadily. He had a black bag wide open and there were broken bottles of beer on the floor. What a perfect panorama. Then when I asked for his information, he told me, "Are you doing a 250 on me?" A 250 is a form that police officers carry with them and then fill out one of those when they stop and frisk somebody by documenting the persons they have stopped.

Then we had another job at East 125 Street and Lexington Avenue where there was a man bleeding from the nose. I don't know if that was a real event. However, the witnesses seemed to be actors because they were cursing loudly and laughing about what had happened to the victim who was punched on the nose. There was another scenario or lets say a show of a broken window at an apartment where a young Hispanic lady said that someone from outside threw a bottle that shattered the glass window of her apartment from the outside to the inside. Great, the net of the window was down, but it had a hole. There was no way that the bottle was going to go through the net and shatter the glass window. Somebody seemed to have spread the glass inside.

Later, as we spoke with her, she said that she didn't pass the psychological exam to join the department. Also, she explained to us that she had a deficiency in math, but that she had a bachelor and that she had smoked marijuana a few days ago. "Some of you cops use drugs, right?" she altered. Also, she said that she had a learning disability.

At home, I had a dream where I was taking pictures of a statue that was made of stone, and the statue was laying down. It looked like a Chinese statue. Then I saw myself surrounded by complete darkness, and there I began to see pairs of eyes looking at me. When I began taking pictures of those eyes with my camera, which every time I took a snapshot with my camera, the light of the camera's flashlight lights up the place, it showed and revealed to me whose eyes were those, and those eyes were the eyes of the wolves that were after me. Then I began to run away from them, while still taking snapshots with the camera, because it seemed that the light of the camera's flash kept them away for a moment. When they began getting closer and closer to me, I woke up.

After waking up, I began copying the narration at the back of the summonses, but the pen stopped writing. Then I began using another pen, but it was a Gel pen, and it was too messy, which messed up part of my sentence. Then I got another pen, and that pen was too light, but I finished those few lines with that pen and as a result, there were three to four sentences written with three different inks at the back of the summonses. And while I was writing those words, my hand was shaking, so I had to place my non-writing hand on top of my writing hand and press to ease the shake. After writing it, I had to rush to work.

On **Saturday, February 15, 2014-Sunday, February 16, 2014,** I was assigned to do the 28-precinct hub site (to transport prisoners from the 28th precincts to Manhattan Central Booking), which the last time I did it was several months ago. For example, in August, the officers from my precinct were supposed to do the 28-precinct hub site, but I was assigned to do it not even once. I had questioned myself as to why they didn't send me there, when before, I was always sent to do it at least twice during the month that the 25 precinct was assigned to do it.

But I guess I know why I was not sent to do the 28-precinct hub site, or to bring prisoners from the 25th precinct to the 28-hub site, or do the prisoners transport which I had done before. It has been a long time since I did the prisoner transport to Manhattan Central Booking. But on this day my suspicion was confirmed. I received a text message from Sgt. Gibbs who texted me, "Did you do 28-hub yet this month?" I texted, "No," and he texted me back, "Can you do it tonight?" and I responded, "Ok," and he finally wrote, "Thanks."

Being then at the muster room, I overheard Sgt. Lucic say, "… they are afraid that he will rob them." Sgt. Lucic's statement made me think that the 28 precinct officers were afraid to have me there, because they think that I will rob them. I believe that on this same day or on the previous day, when I asked Sgt. Gibbs for the key, he told me that he didn't have the key available, and when I turned around, there was PO Azcazubi, behind me laughing as he looked at me, and he was all by himself. He seemed to be one of my top accusers. So as soon as I saw him, and I was forced to say to myself in regard to him, "Are you possess or something?" But I do have to say something about this officer Azcazubi.

One-night, last year, after having worked nonstop and tirelessly all night long, on my break, I went to the lounge and there were officers lying on the sofa. One of them was snoring so hard that I decided to go to the locker room. There I took off my sweaty bullet proof vest, my gun belt, and I laid on the wooden bench in front of my locker. It was peaceful there. When I heard two police officers arrive, I seated on the bench to see who these officers were, and when I looked at one of the officers, it was PO Azcazubi, who had his locker at the end of my aisle.

He appeared to be surprised at something that happened with his locker. He yelled out something to the other officer who was many aisles away, and that officer told him that he didn't do it. However, the officer told him that it wasn't like the other day when they played around with him by hiding his hat. Then PO Azcazubi began to stare at me. I got up from the bench and left. From that moment on, everything began to change, and I began to be treated differently by everyone at the 25-precinct station house.

Before leaving the 28-precinct hub site, I asked the officers at the 25th precinct if they wanted a coffee or needed anything from outside before I left to the 28-hub site. Strangely, they didn't want anything, except PO Griffith who wanted coffee. She had been out for a while due to an injury she had sustained and therefore was not aware of what was happening at our command, especially of their false presumption of me, because they assume that I am no good. This is the first time after a very long time that somebody from the 25th precinct wanted something from my hand. Before the terrible suspicion that they had against me, they all wanted me to bring them something from outside. They didn't even care if I were to pay for their food. But now it is a no, no, as if my hands were dirty and corrupted.

I went to Dunkin Doughnuts and when I went back to the 25th precinct with the coffee, I wondered if they had already misinformed PO Griffith about me, and she might refuse to take the coffee from my hand. Well, I brought the coffee, and she thanked me for it, however, I placed it on top of the computer monitor, because as I expected, she didn't want to take it from my hand. I left thinking that they might have told her, and they might have advised her not to drink it because it comes from me.

When I arrived at the 28-precinct hub site, I noticed that the Desk Sergeant, who was seated, was surprised to see me there. He stared at me. I told him that I was the officer from the 25 precinct and that I was assigned to do the 28-hub site there. Then when I went to the room where they have the cells to keep the prisoners behind bars, the officer in charge of the 28-hub site asked me for my name, shield number and RMP (police vehicle) number. I gave them to him and when I walked out, I could see the Desk Sergeant standing straight, and still at the Desk as if he were in formation, and on high alert, because of my presence there. I stepped out of the precinct, and I waited inside the RMP (Police car) until they called me to do the prisoner's transport.

Meanwhile, as I was in the RMP (Police car), I could see people walking behind and in front of my police car continuously from 1200 am till 0200 am and they were on their phones and off their phone, by one and by two, and it was almost non-stop. I stopped seeing them because at 0200am, I decided to go inside the 28th precinct. When I went inside, there was another officer doing the 28-hub site. Now they were two young officers. One of them, Officer Hartidan, asked me for the officer who is from the 26 precinct and who is supposed to do the prisoners transport with me.

I told him that I didn't know where he was. Then he told me that I could wait another 15 minutes to do the transport. Also, he said, "You can wait here or in your RMP." I wondered why not downstairs in the lounge where everyone waits? I know why they don't want me to be out of their sight, because they think that I will rob them as Sgt. Lucic had said.

Moreover, he told me that he was going to look for him in the lounge. So why not send me to the lounge to look for him, while he stays in the Hub watching the prisoners? When he returned, he said that he didn't see the other officer there. Again, why didn't he simply send me out to look for the 26 precinct officer downstairs at the lounge? When is he supposed to remain there to receive prisoners and watch the prisoners from other commands that need to be sent over to Manhattan Central Booking?

But a moment later, the officer from the 26-precinct showed up. They didn't allow me to handcuff the prisoners, only they did. Placing the handcuffs on the prisoners at the hub was something that I used to do.

When the prisoners were in chains, PO Hartidan called the 26-precinct officer to the side, as for me not to hear, and he secretly told the 26-precinct officer something almost on his ear. Immediately, I knew it was about me, because I could see the 26-precinct officer's reaction on his face that was staring disappointedly at me as the other officer was whispering to him.

Before I forget, I want to mention that before being transferred as a Lieutenant to the 25 precinct, Lt. Yaguchi was a Sergeant at the 28th precinct. So, everyone at the 28 precinct knows him, and they will serve his purpose.

Then suddenly, we received two new prisoners, which made up a total of 13 prisoners so far for the night. So, we did the prisoners' transport. We took the prisoners down to Manhattan Central Booking and then we took them two by two to take their pictures. Then one of the prisoners said to me, "I make 2000 dollars a week on my job and now I am going to lose it because of this." I could see him moving his head from one side to the other as he showed regret and disappointment, and the money he mentioned is approximately the same amount of money I make every two weeks after taxes.

Then another prisoner said, "How can they put me in jail when I didn't do anything?" and he too kept moving his head the same way the other prisoner did. He didn't look at me in the eyes. I laid my hand on his shoulder wishing to tell him, "Don't worry about me." The statements made by these two prisoners gave me ground to believe that they were the same prisoners that came last to be transported, and that they might be undercover cops or they were working for another agency that investigate police officers or lets say they are Confidential Informants. Or they might have heard the rumors said by the 26-precinct officer and therefore they might be feeling pity for me.

Then, when I went to bring the warrant sheets upstairs to room 132, I left the other officer behind, so he could sign in the prisoners at Central Booking and hand them over to Correction. Moments later, I went back, and I heard one of the correction officers say, "Never going to win." Now as we drove back to the 28th precinct, I asked the officer if they might send us back to do another transport, and he said, "Don't worry, they are not going to send you back."

Now I could understand why he said that. He didn't say 'us' but he said 'you' because the problem is with me. When I went inside the 28th precinct to return to the chains, there I saw PO Chiodi standing by the Desk. I wondered what he was doing at the 28th precinct, when he worked at the 25th precinct. But before I stepped out of the door, PO Chiodi said to me, "Be good," and I responded, "I have always been good," and he replied, "Not all the time."

On the same night of **Sunday, February 16, 2014-Monday, February 17, 2014,** I texted Sgt. Gibbs, "28 hubs tonight?" He texted me back, "Do you want it?" I responded, "Ok" and he finally texted, "Ok with me." Then when Sgt. Gibbs was doing the roll call, he asked for volunteers who would like to do the 28-hub site, and immediately, PO Jones volunteered as if they had agreed beforehand, so I may not do it.

 I wanted to do the 28-hub site because I am tired of dealing with jobs that are probably made-up scenarios. Where I am being voice and/or video recorded just to see how I am doing my job and then show the recordings of how I handled the jobs to the public with highlights of the pros and the cons, so the people that are involved in these schemes may be rewarded. They seem to be experimenting with me as if I were a rat.

But what really bothers me is that my co-workers are aware that many, if not the majority, of these jobs, are made up scenarios, but they don't want to tell me anything about it, because they are literally waiting anxiously for me to do a mistake that may get me fired, but they need to find something that may help them justify my dismissal.

From underneath my locker, I took out my rug or small carpet, which I use to place my bare feet on top of it every time I get changed. "So, this is where you keep your praying rug?" PO Chiodi asked me. Why did he have to say that now when he always knows where I keep it? Did he say it for the records? I don't want to continue typing because these words are too heavy, and they hurt. All I want to do is to forget all about them. One day I heard someone say, "PEOPLE, IF YOU DIDN'T DO SOMETHING, WHY YOU SHOULD WORRY ABOUT IT?" True, but it is different when you are being harassed every single day for something that you didn't do. All types of harassment is a crime, period.

I believe that it was on **Saturday, February 15, 2014, or on Sunday, February 16, 2014,** that I saw PO Rivera on top of a wooden bench looking on top of his locker. He said that somebody stole the old boots he used since he was a rookie cop. Now I have three boots on top of my locker, and I wonder if he thinks that one of those is not mine.

On **Saturday, February 15, 2014,** in regard to all of these mess of having people follow me, I tried to share this experience with my wife, and her answer was, "Campesino Dominicano, lower your voice to me you crazy schizophrenic. I want my divorce even though I might have to eat shit. I cannot live with a psychopath. I will go to your workplace, and I will tell them that. I am going to talk to your family. I cannot be here in peace, not even for a moment.

You like to mortify me, your mortifier, you are making my life difficult. Begin looking for an apartment, I will stay here. I am losing a lot of blood because of you. I am going to have a heart attack," and she continued, "Shut up, I don't want to deal with you, you crazy schizophrenic." She proceeded, "Yes, they are following you because you are so important to them. And you call yourself a Christian?" One day I invited her to go out with me, and she stated, "Go out with you? I won't go out with you not even to the corner."

On **Sunday, February 16, 2014** – the officer that was driving PO Lolja drove by, and he stopped his RMP (police car) at East 125 Street and Lexington Avenue, right next to ours. From his RMP, PO Lolja said to me in a mocking matter, "Hernandez, why are you pressing your lips?" and immediately the driver drove away.

On **Monday, February 17, 2014,** in the Aliento Vision channel in TRES CADA DIA at 2:56 pm the person quoted Juan (John) 11 and he said, "Tu problema no terminara en fracaso," which in English means, "Your problem will not end in failure."

It was like on **Monday, February 17, 2014, or Tuesday, February 18, 2014,** that I was sleeping. Then I woke up and just laid on the bed, and at approximately 2:30 pm, I got out of the bedroom due to the improper sexual noise coming out of my next-door neighbor.

I walked out of the bedroom wondering why everything was going so wrong in my life that not even in my own apartment can I find peace. I went to the living room and immediately I turned on the television. As soon as I did, I saw that on the television's screen, which was on the Aliento Vision channel, was in black and it had white letters that said, "**Preparate, para ser el protagonista**", "**Del plan perfecto que Dios tiene para ti.**" Or "**Dios te invita, a ser el protagonista, del plan perfecto que tiene para ti.**" "Which Translated into English means, "**Prepare, to be the protagonist, of the perfect plan that God has for you**" Or "**God invites you, to be the protagonist, of the perfect plan that he has for you.**" As soon as I read that, I felt encouraged. There is no doubt that God has a plan for me.

On **Tuesday, February 18, 2014,** there was a group at the corner of East 125 Street and Lexington Avenue. They were not the common people that usually hang out there. They looked like a group of college kids taken from the New York film Academy to act as if they belonged-- were members of the Bloods gang, for one of them was wearing a red bandanna on his head.

I believe that it was on this same day that we were assigned to the station at the corner of East 125 Street and Lexington Avenue until 0200 hrs. or 2:00 am. It appeared that our supervisors assigned us there so we could respond to the actors and actresses that were acting or behaving in a certain way to gain our attention. They were provoking us just to see how we were going to respond and handle our jobs, while at the same time, again, they will be videoing/voice recording us. This is a 'kids playing around with cops' type of thing. There was a group of them playing around in the corner.

I felt so insulted and embarrassed to see how they were using us that I had to tell my partner that they were nothing more than actors. My

125

partner told me to look at one of them who is blood just because he was wearing a red bandanna, and I looked at him like: Are you kidding me? Then he told me to just ignore them. Then one of the guys who was part of the group came close to our RMP (Police car) and was trying to provoke us. He stood facing the front passenger side of the door and began staring at us. We completely ignored him, until he grew tired and walked away.

After having worked in the area for many years, I noticed the change. Again, they were not the same crowd that always gathered there, and it was not as crowded as it is now. As I told my partner that they were nothing more than college kids that were taken from the New York Film Academy to do this. However, where were the homeless people that normally gather there?

Then we received a radio run of a female trapped inside. Finally, we were moving out of that corner. When we arrived at the scene, there was already a senior officer accompanied by new police officers that recently graduated from the academy and that he was assigned to train. They were using the van. About five of the officers were outside the grocery store, where a man forgot to come out of the grocery store when the owner lowered the gate of the store, closing the store with him inside. The owner had left the premises. Then the owner was notified, and we had to wait until the owner arrived.

Meanwhile, as we waited outside, I was feeling surrounded by them. When they laughed, I had the idea that I was part of the reason why they were laughing, for they gave me or bestowed on me the reputation of something that is so embarrassing to even mention. All I have to say is that all this emotional stress is taking a toe on my body, which is aching, and hurting. I feel so alone, but so alone. The job is making me sick.

I feel that they have placed me inside a frying pan, where they are frying me at a very low temperature, at a very low pace, or low fire (bajo fuego lento). Many times, at home, I have found myself sleeping on the chair of my desk. How am I going to do my job, and give out my best performance, which is what I want, and what others expect of me, when at the same time I am being intimidated by the voice and video recorder that are set to be used against me? How can I do my job properly when every day I am being bombarded by their negative and destructive comments, opinion and behavior towards me?

The following is a brief look at what happened to me recently. I remember the day when Lt. Yaguchi was asked if he was a religious man, and the answer he gave was that he only believes in himself, while staring at me. One day, in February, PO Banks aggressively turned his seat around to avoid seeing me. He didn't greet me either. Lt. Yaguchi keeps telling me that I am losing weight. One day, the #4 train was not making local stops. It was going express to Burnside.

Then, when I was waiting for the #35 bus at Jerome Avenue, a man wearing a red jacket, and who was about 6'6 feet tall with a scar on his face, asked me how to get to Prospect and Tinton Avenue. He had one smartphone in his hand and then he took out a regular cellphone, which I found to be very suspicious. Many times, PO Rivera and I talk about his wife's illness, but sometimes I prefer to be sick, rather than going through all this ceaseless, dehumanizing treatment, day in and day out, day by day, every hour, every minute, and every second of this complex human life.

On **Wednesday, February 19, 2014,** I went to church. I took a moment to talk to G… about the unusual and inhumane treatments that I am receiving at my workplace. When I went to the Venezuelan eatery to eat my Cachapas, as I always do, I saw those young guys, who always follow me, getting inside the establishment. Also, there was someone who appeared to be a homeless man. He had a medical band on his right hand. I offered him food, but he didn't want any.

Behind me was a white man who is like in his fifties. Then he left and two young guys sat behind me. One of them had his green underwear completely showing. His jeans were more than halfway down, and he began to dance bachata. He was trying to attract my attention, for he was moving his behind right almost in front of my face. When I finished eating, the old homeless man approached me saying that he has pills for high blood pressure and diabetes. The two young guys who seemed to be undercover cops were behind, quietly observing what I was going to do. I knew that it was a test, so I stepped out.

In desperation, I went back to church and explained to G… what just happened, and how I was not left alone. He told me not to let them break me, because as he could see, they were doing it now.

On **Thursday, February 20, 2014,** I was inside the Laundromat and there I saw people looking inside the Laundromat, but as soon they saw me, they left right away.

On **Sunday, February 23, 2014,** I did a prisoner transport with PO Aquiles. Then another officer relieved PO Aquiles, so PO Aquiles may go back to the station house (precinct). Then I and the other officer went to Manhattan Central Booking to lodge in the prisoners. Then inside the RMP (police car), as he drove back to the station house (precinct), he was texting somebody. In one occasion, he placed his smartphone on top of the MDT (The small laptop that most police vehicle has), which was next to me. I got to see the text messages on the screen because they were positioned in plain view, as if he wanted me to look at it. As I read along, it said, "You can start your record now," and underneath that text it said, "How bad is it?" I looked at the time, and it was 5:24 pm.

After a long day of work, I had to continue dealing with all this nonsense. This is the first time I have seen this officer. He told me that he was transferred from the 20th precinct, and that they never told him the reason why. They just transferred him. What a mystery.

On **Tuesday, February 25, 2014,** at approximately 0630 hrs. or 6:30 am, PO Rivera told me that he was going to pick up PO Gorman who was driving Sgt. Gibbs, and that PO Gorman had texted him to know what he was doing. PO Gorman was then riding the RMP (police car) with us when he said to me, "We are cracking down on you." He continued, "Look, when you see four dollars inside the RMP (police car) you have to voucher it." Then PO Rivera began playing around by saying, "But if you see eight dollars you don't have to voucher it." I remained quiet. God will fight for me as I keep my silence. We were out to give summonses for improper turn. I wondered why he told me that. I am like a bird in the hands of a hunter.

In the morning of **Thursday, February 27, 2014,** I went to the gym at approximately 0700 hrs. or 7:00 am. As I was running on the treadmill, there was a guy behind me doing absolutely nothing. He was just standing there looking at his smartphone. Then when I went to the bathroom, where I was washing my face, there was a guy standing next to me looking at his smartphone. There is a big mirror there and he was facing the mirror that was reflecting me. Then I heard two snapshot pictures that he took with his smartphone. I wish they wouldn't make it so obvious.

Here I am suffering day and night, night and day. As I was going home, I noticed that they kept following me. They follow me everywhere I go, all the time. At my job, they keep treating me as if I were a rat with whom they can keep experimenting with. They are video/audio recording my every move, actions, and behavior, absolutely, every single step I take or make and every word I say.

They are entirely micromanaging me. I have no rest, not even on my way home nor on my way to work because they are on the train and on the bus. Not even when I get into my apartment building, nor in my own apartment, because from the inside of my apartment, I can hear sounds like footsteps of people walking on the rooftop of my apartment, because I live on the last floor building. While in bed, my mind can't stop thinking of all the things they are doing to me. I only find rest when I close my eyes, and I begin to dream. I want to do nothing. I feel lost. My God, why do I feel you so far from me?

On **February ..., 2014** I heard PO Banks tell PO Ahmed, "Good job partner," which reminded me of how bad I am doing my job, because I am not performing well, I am not doing my job at my best, because how can I do it when my partner is voice recording me every time, all the time that we are together. It is frustrating. Every time that we are assigned to a job, I must infer, "Oh my God, what now?" I really don't want to say anything, because I know that everything or anything I say will be scrutinized.

The voice recorder and the video recorder will be rewind and forwarded repeatedly just to highlight and find fault in me. Then they will interpret what I say or do or any action I take and find whatever is fit to be used against me. They will show the worst of me to the public. Having this in mind, what human being will be able to concentrate well on his job knowing that all these things are happening around him or her? As a result, my job performance is mediocre. This is the most horrendous moment in my entire life.

In **February /.... / 2014** my wife saw me laying on bed holding my notebook and a pen and she said, "I feel pity for you." Having a heavy burden in my heart, and knowing not what to do, I lay upside down on the floor and there I cried. Then I looked at the hot radiator to my left, and as I laid on the floor, I placed my left index finger on the side of the hot radiator and I kept it there for a few seconds, because I preferred the burning sensation of my finger being burned, rather than the burden and the pain that I am emotionally feeling inside of me.

At least my burned finger will temporarily help me with my emotional pain. But my burned finger wasn't strong enough to make me forget my internal pain.

Chapter10

March 2014 Events

In the morning of **Saturday, March 1, 2014,** or it was on the next day, that there was a sector Boy's job. It was a woman who lived in a shelter right at the location that we responded to. She was complaining about someone or some security guard at the Target store. She had a Target's shopping cart in front of the shelter. But she didn't exactly remember what had happened. So, she was looking at a small notebook she had with her. There she flipped those pages without saying anything at all. Then she began to say things pertaining to what she had written.

She had an orange sticker on her that said, "ADA," which of course, stands for Assistant District Attorney. She seemed not to remember anything that took place. I wondered if this was another scenario planned and organized by the Manhattan District Attorney's office, because of me, because when I testified in court on **December 10, 2013**, I couldn't remember the details of what happened on the day I made the DWI (Driving While Intoxicated) arrest, which was eight months previous to **December 10, 2013**, the day of my terrible testimony. This is simply a form of retaliation. As for now, I can't continue typing anymore about this because doing so saddens me.

On **Monday, March 3, 2014,** PO Rivera and I were assigned to do the T/S because PO Rivera asked for it. I found it strange. Meanwhile, I was behind the Desk when I noticed that PO Lolja and PO Gorman were observing my every move. I turned on the computer and when I was trying to use the mouse, the mouse wasn't working. Still, there was PO Gorman and PO Lolja staring at me. The other computer behind me was being used by the impact guys, and the Sergeant was using the other. So, I went to the T/S. Then PO Lolja ironically asked me why I was not helping PO Rivera, and I told him that there was no computer available.

Then he said, "But there is a mouse in the juvenile room, why don't you use that one?" Then the Sergeant told me to use him.

I was sitting down at the T/S and around me were Sgt. Lucic, PO C.C (Domigildo), PO Rivera, Sgt. Gibbs, PO Gomez and PO Martorelli. PO C.C. (Domigildo) asked PO Rivera where he was born. PO Rivera replied that he was born in Brazil, but he was playing around, so as he spoke, he made up words to pretend that he speaks Portuguese. Then Sgt. Lucic looked at me and said, "What about you Manolo, you were born and raised in the Dominican Republic right?"

I stood up from my seat and I told him that I was born in the Dominican Republic, but that I was raised here and there. I said that I came to the U.S on January 9, 1992. I told them that when I first came here, I was surprised to see all those new vehicles, and all the lights on the streets. That when I first came here, I ate a cereal brand Cheerios and that it made me sick. It made me go to the bathroom.

After I was done talking, it seemed that Sgt. Lucic became upset with me. Later, Sgt. Lucic gave a thumb up to PO Rivera and he ignored me. Then he greeted PO Rivera by telling him, "Good job on doing that 61 (Complaint report). It was well stated. I haven't seen such a good job since 1999. You should be a writer, because you are a creative thinker. You won't find many people that are good at that. Many will try to write something, but their minds become frozen. They don't know what to write." Then he looked at me and said, "You too are good Manolo." I answered, "What! Are you making fun of me Lucic?" and he said "No, it is true, you too are good."

Then he said, "You guys should be permanent T/S guys. You guys do a good job. But we need you guys out there, because you guys do a great job out there." There I wondered if he was saying that because they made a mistake by having me work inside, or a mistake was made as I worked inside, because they don't want me to work inside the precinct. Then he yelled out, "Good job Manolo on the 61, no I mean Alvin," just to undermine my effort.

Then PO Rivera looked at me seriously and he said to me, "Don't trust Albanians, Russians…." By him telling me that and knowing that Sgt. Lucic is Albanian, I tried to understand what I did to Sgt. Lucic that he is treating me that way. Later that morning, PO Gorman took out a pack of gum, and he took out a gum out of its pack, and he placed it in his mouth. Then he looked at the empty pack of gum, and he looked at me. He looked at the empty pack of gum again and he looked at me again, and he shook his head.

On **Wednesday, March 5, 2014,** I was at 1PP (1 Police Plaza= Police Headquarter). Oh PO Fuentes (Headquarter Security officer who used to be my friend before all this nonsense began). Now it is you. There you are driving the scooter, and here I am pressing the button of the barrier, so the barrier may come down and you may go through, go through none-stop not even to say hello to me. Every time you go through, you just give me a look and raise your hand, because it seems that it is the most you can do. This is the way or as far as you can go as to say hi to me. But at least you acknowledge that I am here, seating inside the booth, and don't just drive away without looking at me. Finally, thank you for your sense of compassion and pity to at least acknowledge me.

There you drive by, once, twice, for the third time and for the fourth time. You, whom every time you used to see me, you used to stop by to have a conversation with me, conversation that lasted for long minutes. You who once showed me through your smartphone the live video camera of your house. The perimeter and the angle of each camera that is installed in your house and what area those cameras are covering. You who invited me to go fishing, and to play football and basketball, and who at the same time, opened the album of your life to me, are now acting indifferently towards me. You trusted me that much, my friend, and I was so happy to know that you did so, and because you did, I was soon about to consider you one of my best friends.

But now every time you look at me, I know that you are thinking the worst of me, and it is hurting me. It hurts, because I am innocent. Here I am seating inside this cold booth. Tears are being held on my eyes, because I want my tears to remain there. I don't want them to fall. I don't want them to drop and run through my cheeks. No. This is the reason why I am keeping my eyes open steadily, because the moment that I blink, it will come out. There are like seven cameras installed on my left, capable of zooming in and neatly capturing whatever dot is placed on any paper lying on the table. If it captures that, it can easily capture any running tears on my face.

But I cannot contain it, I cannot hold it for too long from coming out of my eyes. But at least I manage to keep my face steady, only my lips move a little. But unfortunately, without blinking, it managed to come out, because my heart is aching. There is no way that a volcano that erupts can hold back its lava. So at least I manage to use my left-hand index finger, to wipe them out, while keeping my face straight and steady, so they won't say that I am crying.

At my meal, I went into the building and saw him coming out. I greeted him and he greeted me. He asked me if everything was ok. I told him that I was ok. Then he walked out of the building, and I headed to the bathroom. When I came out of the building, I saw that he was driving away. I got to raise my hand to him, and he stopped. He lowered the window. I told him that everything was not ok at all, but that everything is ok in Christ who strengthens me. But then in order not to force PO Fuentes to shake my hand, I placed my hand on his shoulder, and I said goodbye to him.

On Sunday, **March 9, 2014,** when I arrived at the station house (precinct), there was PO Gorman and PO Chiodi. PO Chiodi said, "This is a show," and I said, "This is the Gorman's show." We responded to a gun run at East 116 Street and 3rd Avenue. Then as we headed there, we stopped to talk to PO Gorman who had parked his RMP (police car) next to us, and from inside his RMP (police car), he said to us, "Sector Adam just gave the final for you." Then PO Rivera talked to us on how our precinct didn't have enough batteries for the radios, and PO Gorman ironically said that they had been stealing the batteries, and as soon as he said that he hastily drove away without saying anything else.

On **Monday, March 10, 2014,** I was in the precinct standing in front of the Desk when Sgt. Lucic said to me, "Hey Manolo, you look like you are going to rob a bank with that hat." I had to laugh at his comment. Even as I am typing this, I am smiling and laughing out loud because it is too much.

On **Tuesday, March 11, 2014,** I went to work out in the gym, as I normally do, just to keep myself strong, to be of good use to the department, and to better protect civilians, my co-workers, and myself.

When I went inside the gym, in the middle level of the gym, I saw a white man who was wearing a blue t-shirt. He was lifting weights. Then I went upstairs to run on the treadmill. When I was done that, I went to the middle level, on my way to the locker room, I saw the same man lifting weights. Then when I came out of the locker room that I went to the lower level to do my work out routine, I saw the same man rushing downstairs too. He began to work out close to the area that I was working out. He was approximately four feet away from me. I noticed that he was wearing a pair of Nike sneakers that were black and had the blue Nike check logo. When I was done, that I was leaving, he was leaving too.

On **Wednesday, March 12, 2014,** at 9:31 am, a thunder is heard close to my apartment that made my apartment shake a little bit, and the cars alarm began to sound. Later, I found out that it wasn't thunder, it was a gas explosion that occurred at 9:31 am, three blocks away from my precinct. According to Wikipedia, 8 people died, 70 people were injured, and 100 families were displaced. Two buildings have collapsed. It is a terrible day.

It was like on **January or February** that I said, "I quit, "and two thunders sounded very close to my apartment. It was so loud that my wife almost jumped out of her seat, and the cars alarm began to sound.

On **Thursday, March 13, 2014,** I was assigned to the building collapse gas explosion fixed post at East 115 street and Lexington Avenue.

On **Friday, March 14, 2014,** I walked out of my apartment building to go to the gym. At approximately a block away from where I live, I saw the same man that I saw in the gym, and this time, he was being accompanied by a woman. He is always wearing the same camo pants, and she was dressed in black. They took the same bus BX # 6 that took me to the gym.

When I came off the bus that I was walking to the gym, the two of them were behind me, walking to the gym as well. She was telling him, "She got on my face; she was like get off me." I entered the gym, and they did too. When I was running on the treadmill, she came by herself and used the treadmill that was in front of me. Then I went down to the lowest level of the gym to do more work out, and there he was by himself looking at me. Approximately, half an hour later, she came down and began to workout close to him.

On **Saturday, March 15, 2014,** I was assigned to the building collapse gas explosion and paid details and the guys, including PO Chiodi, turned their backs on me.

On **Sunday, March 16, 2014,** I was assigned to the building collapse gas explosion paid detail with PO Murray. When I was standing outside waiting for our assignment, Lt. Gonzalez didn't keep his eyes off me. He was constantly looking at me as a wolf who wanted to devour his prayer. Even when he was inside the THV truck, from the door's window he kept looking at me.

On **Monday, March 17, 2014,** I did the T/S after having worked long hours, and at the end I noticed that something had happened, but I didn't know what? Then I saw PO Fausto Gomez approach PO Chiodi's ear, and he said something to him.

On **Tuesday, March 18, 2014-Wednesday, March 19, 2014,** in the morning while on patrol, before going to do 1PP (1 Police Plaza= Police Headquarter) in the afternoon, I and PO Rivera saw a blind man walking with his stick. PO Rivera said that the man was following the stick before him, and I told him that it is the same case with everyone at the 25th precinct.

When I went to do 1PP (1 Police Plaza= Police Headquarter), I was assigned to a booth where I had to assist another officer. He seemed to be a very friendly officer. Then when the Sergeant drove by to scratch our Memo-Book (Memorandum Pad/Activity Log), the officer with whom I was working with asked the Sergeant why we were getting scratched (getting our Memo-Book signed by a supervisor) and being visited by our supervisors so often, and the Sergeant answered, "He is the one. We must keep an eye on him." Then the officer looked at me and he said, "Oh, I see."

When the Sergeant left, we began to talk about religion. He said that he is a good man, because he doesn't do bad things to others. Then he said, "… there are people that are, that are, you know, that are innocent but they are," and I finished the sentence for him by saying what he meant to say, "I know what you mean, that there are people who are innocent, but are accused of something that they didn't do," and he said, "You are right." Then he said, "It is cold, I talk to you later," and we departed.

We didn't talk again, because he had said enough. I know that he and the Sergeant intentionally said what they said, so I could hear and see what is going on and what is being done for me. So, I could wake up and do something about it. They want to help me. But how can I help myself when I am an inexperienced 32-year-old man who is neither book smart nor street smart? In Addition, I was already warned to do nothing by the retired officer that wanted to buy flowers for his wife on Valentine's Day, or else they will bring charges on me. I feel helpless.

It is **Thursday, March 20, 2014**. I don't know what it is going to be like of me. I don't know if when they are all smiling, friendly and laughing is because I am no longer in trouble and all the misunderstandings have been cleared up. Or it could be because my downfall is near, and they are rejoicing because of it, and they all will get detective shields for selling me out. I don't know if when they are angry with me, it is because they cannot find any fault in me. I don't know what to believe anymore.

When my partner is making jokes and is constantly talking to me, I wonder if it is because my success is close or my destruction is around the corner, and as a result, he is going to be promoted to detective the same way as the others. Then in the locker room, I heard PO Maher tell PO Gambardelli, loud enough so I could hear, "That's it, you are fire for the good of all of us." Then PO Gambardeli said, "And he doesn't have Deferred Comp." And guess what? I don't have a Deferred Comp.

On **Friday, March 21, 2014,** I was in the gym. When I went to the bathroom, a young man went into the bathroom too just to look at me and at himself in the mirror, and then he left. When I went to the lowest level of the gym, I saw another young man wearing camo pant. He was accompanied by the same guy who had gone to the bathroom to see what I was doing. Then a third guy met with them. They were working out close to me. Then at the same time I left, they left too by immediately stopping and abandoning what they were doing just to follow me to the bathroom. When I got into the bathroom, the same young guy was by himself in the bathroom also, keeping his eyes on me.

On **Sunday, March 23, 2018-Monday, March 24, 2014,** as I was on patrol with PO Rivera, I noticed that he was observing my every move. He wanted to know where my eyeballs moved. I moved my right arm and my pointing finger up and down as if I were testing the vital sign of his sight, and he was moving his eyeballs up and down accordingly, until he realized that I was doing it on purpose. I know that he knew well what I meant by doing that, because he didn't question it.

In the morning, while on patrol, PO Rivera and Lt. Yaguchi texted each other. Then PO Rivera told me to drive back to the station house (precinct) because Lt. Yaguchi wanted him to choose his IVD days. Then he told me that Lt. Yaguchi wanted me there too.

We arrived at approximately 0740 hrs. or 7:40 am and when we went into Lt. Yaguchi's office, we found him talking on the phone. There I saw PO Soto, who seems to be Lt. Yaguchi's secretary, and he was seating in the office that is prior to Lt. Yaguchi's office. He began to have a conversation with PO Rivera about some of the RMPs (police vehicles) that didn't have computers, but while talking to him, PO Soto was busy looking for something in his drawer and around his desk until he questioned himself, "Where is it? Someone robbed it already?" and he didn't look at me not even for a moment when he said that. Then we entered Lt. Yaguchi's office, and he gave us the calendar so we could pick up our IVD days.

Then PO Soto entered Lt. Yaguchi's office, and he asked Lt. Yaguchi for something, and when Lt. Yaguchi began to look for it, PO Soto asked him, "What happened? Someone robbed it already?" and then Lt. Yaguchi told him that he was going to give it to him some other time. PO Soto made the same statement twice already. Wasn't all this already planned? Was this act on behalf of PO Soto the reason why Lt. Yaguchi wanted me there?

Then I went to the THV truck for the details. They partnered me with PO Kroski. We were assigned to East 116 Street and Park Avenue. Before going there, I saw him talking to other cops and he was twisting his head sideways, as if showing disappointment for being assigned to work with me. Well, what I did was to let him stay inside the RMP (police car) all day, while I remained standing outside, until the end of the tour when he gave me a ride back to the station house (precinct). I worked from 11:15 pm till 4:30 pm.

At night, after having worked for 17 hours and 15 minutes straight, and having slept for only two to three hours, I went back to work to the station house (precinct). My partner was running out late. Meanwhile, at the Desk, Sgt. Lucic told me to teach PO Pedrosa how to do the properties and organize the written summonses.

When I got close to her, I saw that she was talking to PO Banks. I was waiting for her to finish talking to him and then tell her that I was assigned to teach her how to do the properties and the summonses. She was talking to PO Banks about working at midnight. Then he pointed at me and said, "The midnights are good, except for this fine officer that you see here next to me." I smiled out of embarrassment. Then I said, "And this super officer that is making collars right and left." Then Sgt. Gibbs angrily said, "No, I don't want to keep supervising, have Dominick teach her how to do the properties," and I felt as bad as I always do every time I go to work there.

Then when I and my partner PO Rivera went to the station house (precinct) for our meal at 0306 hrs. or 3:06 am, being already **March 25, 2014** in the morning, I saw that Sgt. Gibbs was complaining to Sgt. Lucic about something and when I heard Sgt. Gibbs say that he didn't know what to do, I told him, "Have patience Serg." Then smiling he said to me, "I have one eye on you Bushy Top (as he used to call me)," and I answered, "Oh, so you are an illuminati," and everyone who were around, including him, laughed.

Then, at the end of the tour, I asked PO Griffith for her pen to sign out, and she threw her pen at me, as if she didn't want to pass it to me hand to hand. Then when I finished signing out, she told me to leave it on the table. Probably, she wanted to keep her distance from me, and to just pass a pen to her might have been enough contact with me to create suspicion. But instead, I passed it to PO Rivera who needed to sign out too. Then he gave her the pen, which she took from his hand, and she said, "Yes, give it to me before it disappears."

On **Thursday, March 27, 2014,** we went to drop off a prisoner to the 28-precinct hub site. There the Desk Sergeant received me with surprise, and an unwelcome look on his face. He looked at the prisoner and then greeted my partner. When we lodged the prisoner inside, that we were leaving, the Sergeant only said goodbye to my partner.

In the afternoon, I went to 1PP (1 Police Plaza= Police Headquarter) to work for the 28th of the Month. When I went there at approximately 1745 hrs. or 5:45 pm, I scanned my police ID, and I began to write down my name on line 4 of the list. Then I overheard a Sergeant there say, "I don't know why they keep sending this guy here." I didn't get to see him, but he probably saw me coming into the building through the camera. Then I went to the 2nd floor to eat something. When I was done eating, I went back downstairs, and I waited for my name to be called. After waiting for a while to be assigned to a post, I saw that an officer walked by already with a post being assigned to him and that's when I realized that the Sergeant was calling out names. When I went there, I discovered that my name was called a long time ago, and that he was up to line 10, so many officers had already skipped me.

The post that I desired had been already taken, so they assigned me to a different post. When I arrived at my post, I saw that the officer who worked with me last week was going to work with me on this day also. When I extended my right hand to greet him, he gave me his left-hand fist with the excuse that he had sneezed and had used his right hand to cover his mouth. So, we greeted knuckles to knuckles. It was a bad day, and I felt so sad. Later, the Sergeant drove by, and he told me to keep my face up, because he didn't want to walk to my post and give me a Command Discipline. He said, "We have been trying to look out for you." I could have died there, and I would have said, "Thank You Lord". Only God knows how despised I feel.

1) During my two-week vacation I was like in a coma. I remained home, I didn't want to get up from bed.

2) I have lost a lot of weight.

3) "He is up to something" is what they are saying about me.

4) One day I was going down the stairwell and there I met Sgt. Jackson. I said to her, "Hi Serg," but she didn't utter a word to me. A few days before, after not seeing her for a long time, she greeted me

and showed me pictures of her children. But now, after I don't know what malicious mouths have spoken against me, she completely ignores me.

One day, as I was working with PO Rivera, out of nowhere I said, "Interesting." Immediately, putting a lot of interest, and looking around at what I was looking at, he asked me what I found interesting. So, I asked him, "Why do you find interesting what I find interesting?" but he didn't answer or said anything. Then in the locker room, PO Gorman said to me, "Interesting." This confirmed to me that our conversations are being monitored and that he is wired.

Now I must obey not only my boss, but every single cop there is. No matter if that cop came out of the academy yesterday. I am their prisoner. I have even neglected my own body. Here I am suffering, and with a red pen at hand, to shed my feelings on paper since they can't be seen.

Chapter 11

April 2014 Events

On **Thursday, April 3, 2014**, before doing 1PP (1 Police Plaza= Police Headquarter), I was at the 25 precinct, and there I saw a rookie cop. When leaving, I told him, "Excuse me sir" and I solute him also. Then I went to do 1PP (1 Police Plaza= Police Headquarter).

When I arrived there, that I was signing my name, the Sergeant there made fun of me as he raised his voice to say, "Hernandez, the Frank Forth and Park Row guy. Remember heads up, but I know, he is a veteran there." I so felt bad because I thought that they felt pity for me, that it is all I can do, to press buttons to lower and raise the barriers. I thought that he was going to assign me to work on that post, but that didn't happen, instead, I was assigned to a post that I disliked.

Then after I did 1PP (1 Police Plaza= Police Headquarter) in the morning, I went straight to court. After having worked a 12 hour and 50 minutes shift, I was very tired. There I met ADA … for the security holding case. Then when I testified, I said that the defendant's name was A … W…, and the ADA (Assistant district Attorney) said, "What is his first name again, would you like to refresh your memory?" I agreed and I took a piece of paper out of my pocket, and I said, "Sorry, it is W…" Then when I stepped out of the court with the ADA (Assistant District Attorney), as we walked, she began to make the throat sound again, the same sound that the guys at the 25th precinct are making. Behind us, there was a tall skinny man with one hand on his chin, as if he were examining me.

On **Saturday, April 5, 2014,** I went to the gym. Again, I saw all these unusual faces in the gym. When I was ready to go home, in the locker, where I placed my clothing, on top of it, I saw a gym belt, and this is when I realized that I haven't been left alone yet. It made me angry. My misery continues.

On **Tuesday, April 8, 2014,** I went to the gym at approximately 10:30 am. When I arrived at the gym, everything seemed to be ok. I went to the treadmill. I used the treadmill that was on the last line, and guess what? A white Hispanic man arrived wearing a red t-shirt and he went to use the treadmill to my far right. He began to take pictures with his smartphone, and I knew that because I could hear each snapshot he took with his smartphone.

In front of me, there were several empty treadmills. While using my treadmill, I already knew that someone was going to come and use the treadmill that was right next to me, and about four minutes later, that happened. A black man walked directly and used the treadmill that was right to my left, besides having all those other treadmills available. When I first saw him coming, I already knew that he was going to use that one. He was very interested in knowing what I was watching on my smartphone. When I was done running, I used the bathroom and then I went down the stairs to the lowest level to do my regular work out. I already knew well that they have already studied my work out routine. There I saw a woman wearing a camo tank top and at that moment I realized for whom she was working for.

When I began to do my work out, she walked close to my area of work out. Then, to my major surprise, guess who I saw in the gym? I got to see ex-cop Jonathan Wally, who once worked at the 34th precinct. He was arrested last year for improperly filing out taxes for others or lets say for tax fraud. He was arrested, lost his job, and his pension. I have known him since back then when I was a police cadet and worked at YHWA. I was informed of what had happened to him, because another cop, who was a police cadet also, told me about it. In addition, I was told that days before he got arrested, he had the feeling that there were people following him.

He was wearing a black sweater that had a white word written on it that said, "ill." I didn't greet him unless he greeted me. Did they release him just to observe my response when I got to see him? I don't know what else to think of right now.

When I was done, I went upstairs and when I went into the bathroom, I was again being followed. When I went to my locker, I saw a black gym belt on top of my locker once more, once more, because the same happened the last time that I worked out. When I first got there, I didn't see it, but when I went back to my locker to leave for good, I saw it. My wallet fell on the floor and my cards came out of my wallet. It was like when an ice cream or something that you are eating falls because somebody is staring at what you are eating, so that's probably why my wallet fell. What type of game are they playing with me? The van that they are using seem to be capable of carrying 6, 7 or 8 passengers, which are enough different faces to follow one man for a day without bringing suspicion. This is so wrong.

But the question that I do ask myself is, why haven't they placed a small, tiny camera at the location of interest, so at least they may know what is going on, and find out who is doing the things that I am being blamed for? The sad reality is that at this stage of my life, every day I feel threatened even by the simplest question that I am being asked at my workplace, and outside my workplace, including people in church, acquaintances and dear friends. I must review in my mind every word I say and see how he or she will react to my answers or to any statement I make no matter how small or big. I cannot be myself. And even when my partner is quiet, I don't know what he means by being quiet. For me not to talk?

Very often, since all of this began, many times that I am on patrol, I have become so accustomed to being holding the steering wheel tight, as I drive and even when I have the RMP (police car) parked. Squeezing hard, with all my strength, the steering wheel of the vehicle helps me restrain part of my anger and frustration for my inability and desperation to find a solution to this problem. Yes, lately, I have been squeezing the steering wheel of the police car so hard with both of my hands, for one way or the other I need to release some of the energy that is being produced by the anger that one feels when an injustice is being done. At the same time, as I do so, I am also wondering how to express to them what I feel, but I don't know how they will interpret my reaction.

But far even worse, when knowing that I am being recorded and that everything I say or do will be rewind, forwarded and played for their own convenience. They will make my words fit as they find them

145

convenient, and for certain, they will only show the public what they find convenient for them to show.

I truly don't want to interrupt their investigation, because I so wishfully desire, they find out what is going on, the truth, but it hurts a lot to know that I am the only target in their investigation for there is no one that I know of. Everyone is involved, everyone knows what is going on, and they are helping each other out on trying to find fault in me. The sad thing is that there is not much I can do, because they will be the ones funding my defense or any attorney I may have to get in the future, with the money I get paid for my hard work. If I do get a lawyer, and they halt me from working, how am I going to be able to afford and keep that attorney?

If I would have had money myself, I would have voiced and yelled out to the four corners of this world their abuses against me, but I am a poor man, without any connections, without a trade, but that of the job I do. Therefore, I must accept daily humiliation. I must learn to live with it. I am forbidden to say something, for there are too many. They have become my fearful masters, and I their slave.

On **Thursdays, April 10, 2014,** I went to the station house (precinct) to get dress for 1PP (1 Police Plaza= Police Headquarter). As soon as I arrived at the 25th precinct, at approximately 1515 hrs. or 3:15 pm, I saw PO Azcasubi, who is the officer who seems to have lost something or have been a victim of something that might have been taken from him. I say this because this is the same officer who looked at me strangely on that mysterious night when I was in the men's locker room.

However, this afternoon, he passed by my aisle. He greeted me and I greeted him back. Then he walked close to my aisle again, and he stopped somewhere close to me where I couldn't see him. He was over 7 feet away from me, just at the corner, at the end of my aisle to my right. He remained there where I couldn't see him. Then I heard someone who was cutting his nails, and it was him, because he was the only one there. I began to hear that sound continuously, as if he were doing it on purpose to let me know that he was watching me.

It makes sense to believe that he was trying to provoke me by doing so. Then, when I packed my bag and left the locker room, I greeted him goodbye. Coming down the stairs, I saw Lt. Yaguchi coming up the stairs, as I was expecting, and when he saw me, he greeted me saying, "Hey body I missed you. I know you have 1PP. How are you feeling?" At that moment I saw PO Clement coming down the stairs and she began to talk to Lt. Yaguchi. Now, knowing that he was being cynical about his question, I told him that I was not bad.

What a waste of resources. But I do still want to elaborate more on this. What if someone was playing again by hiding PO Azcasubi's stuff and when he or she realized the seriousness and the gravity of his or her actions, he or she decided to back up, and not come forward, because of fear of being punished? Or did PO Azcasubi, on a night out of drinking, lost his department properties, and thought that he was going to get fired for he is a rookie (a recently graduated police officer with less than two and half a year on the job) and could get fired for anything. Out of fear, he might have wanted to blame others for whatever it is that he lost.

In the many years of working at the 25th precinct, I never heard of someone stealing police equipment. But they have newly graduated police officers working at the 25th precinct. Could it be that one of them is a thief? All these possibilities exist. But the sad thing is that they are wasting time and money, and they will never, never, never find out who did the wrong thing, because the one who stole whatever it is that has been stolen, is helping them catch the supposed thief, which is not me.

When I finished work in the morning at 1PP (1 Police Plaza= Police Headquarter), I went to the station house (precinct). I arrived there at approximately 0835 hrs. or 8:35 am. When I was leaving, as I was walking down the stairs, I saw the same officer, PO Azcasubi, coming down the stairs and he was right behind me. I greeted him and he greeted me. I even opened the door for him. Then he said in a low tone of voice, "Dressing in black," which I was, because of the officer that lost his life. Then I went to the Desk and gave the Sergeant my overtime slip, which I knew was going to disappoint PO Azcasubi, who might be wondering what I was doing there. Then on my way to the subway station, that I was walking by East 124 Street and Lexington Avenue, I saw two man standing in front of the grocery store, and as I walked by, I overheard one of the man tell the other," He doesn't have anything because he didn't do anything," and I kept on walking.

Then I went to the office of Deferred Compensation. When I took the train home, when I got off the train, I decided to go to Metro pcs. When I entered there, I asked them about the new galaxy s5, and I saw when two men just entered the store and began looking at the smartphones there. One of them had a red book bag. Then I noticed that the staff there began to sneeze and cough, probably as a sign due to the presence of those two individuals that just entered the store to just wonder what I was doing there. Then I went home totally convinced that the game is not over yet. Again, what a waste of resources.

On **Saturday, April 12, 2014**, I went to work out in the gym. When I decided to leave that I went to my locker room, again I saw a black gym belt next to my locker, which wasn't there when I first got there.

On **Friday, April 18, 2014-Saturday, April 19, 2014,** I was feeling so uncomfortable at roll call that I heard that our mealtime was at 0200 hrs. Or 2:00 am instead of 0300 hrs. of 3:00 am. We responded to what appeared to be another made-up scenario at 125 East Street and Lexington Avenue. A man was assaulted inside the subway station. When we arrived there, that I came out of the RMP (police car), I said to a group of youngsters that were there, "And action," and as soon as I said that one of them repeated the same words I said. Seating on the stairwell of the subway station, was a man who I had arrested before, and I laid my hand on his shoulder to see if he was ok, and then I continued going down the stairs.

We found the victim bleeding from the back of his head, and we took him upstairs. He pointed at a person who was wearing a red sweater and who was walking away, and he said that he thought that he was the one who did it. We asked him if he was sure, and he said, "I think, I would say it was him." Then after all the distractions, I was forced to tell PO Rivera, "Rivera, if good people turn against good people, what is going to be left then?" He remained quiet and thoughtful, processing what I had said. Then we responded to a shot fired job, and when we got to the scene, there was one man standing there, and he told us that it was fireworks, and suddenly, two young guys arrived.

When we gave the final over the radio, my partner asked me if I had noticed how the street could be empty and all a sudden these guys appeared out of nowhere. He said that they even come out of the sewer manhole, and that they use the manhole cover as their hat, and I laughed because I knew well what he meant. He just gave me a perfect hint as to what is really going on.

On **Tuesday, April 15, 2014,** I had to go to 1PP (1 Police Plaza= Police Headquarter) to do the security detail. At East 125 street and Lexington Avenue at approximately 5:00 pm, I went inside a public bus, which took me to Madison Avenue, and from there I walked to Charlie's restaurant (A Japanese restaurant). Inside the bus, I was almost next to the bus driver when one of the passengers, who was on my right, had a smartphone on his ear and he said, "If you think that they are not watching you, you are bugging me. They are even watching you from your own phone." Then I got off the bus.

After working for over 12 hours at 1PP (1 Police Plaza= Police Headquarter), I went to court, and after court, I went to the station house (Precinct). When I came out of the precinct, I decided to walk along Madison Avenue to see if the bookstore there was open, but there was no one there, so I left. When I was walking to Charlie's restaurant again to buy some ice cream, at the corner of East 124 Street and Madison Avenue, I saw two men standing. As I passed by them, I overheard one of the men tell the other man, "He is just an innocent bystander."

On **Thursday, April 17, 2014**, I had to do 1PP (1 Police Plaza= Police Headquarter) again. I took the bus to Madison Avenue to go to Charlie's restaurant, but this time when I got right at the door of the bus, a guy who was outside of the bus, but next to the door, told me, "Don't do it. You are in hot water."

Then on my mealtime at 1PP (1 Police Plaza= Police Headquarter), I went to Dunkin Doughnuts and there an old man approached me, and he explained to me how different doctors were giving him different diagnosis by falsely claiming that he has diabetes. He said that four doctors told him that he had it, and four others said that he didn't have it. And I say that this was another made up scenario.

On **Saturday, April 19, 2014,** at approximately 8:00 pm, my wife and I came out of our apartment to go to church. We took the elevator, and as soon as we came out of the elevator, one guy wearing a camo pant immediately appeared from the stairwell that was next to the elevator, and he walked out of the building with us. Then my wife and I took the bus.

Seating at the back of the bus, there was a woman who looked at my wife in a strange way. So strange that after the woman came off the bus, my wife asked me, "Did you see how she looked at me?" When we came off the bus, at the corner of East 181 street and Amsterdam Avenue, there was a suspicious woman waiting for us.

As we walked, we talked about how I shouldn't get involved in doing certain things for the church, like what I did a day when someone became sick, that I was asked to go with her in the ambulance to the hospital. She said that I shouldn't have done it because my job is too complicated. Then when we walked close to the woman who seemed to have been waiting for us, and my wife said, "And God doesn't want you to lose your job," and I hoped that the woman didn't hear her last sentence, because she might think that we are hiding something.

Then the stranger began to walk close to us and while walking, she began to smoke. Then I placed my right-hand index finger on my lips to let my wife know to stop talking. But she became upset, and she said, "Why do you want me to keep my mouth shut?" But what she didn't know is that there were people getting close to us just to listen to our conversations. Then I walked away from her, because I didn't want her to continue to reprimand me. It was impossible to keep her from talking.

I went into the bakery store without the intention of buying anything, and then I walked out to church. We walked out of church at approximately 9:35 pm and while waiting for the bus, a young lady approached us. She stood next to us. She didn't take her eyes off her smartphone, and I knew well that she did so just to listen to our conversation. I saw the same minivan that my followers keep using. Then when our bus came, out of nowhere came two young guys between the ages of seventeen or eighteen. They went inside the bus ahead of us, and one of them was wearing the same camo pant.

However, there was another guy who was wearing a camo pant in front of me, next to the door. Now those two kids who were on my right began to be loud and started acting up.

Then I asked loud enough, so they may hear, "What unit is this that doesn't deal with their behavior?" As soon as I said that they calmed down. They became quiet and behaved normally ever since. The guy that was sitting close to the door looked at me and I looked back at him to let him know that I knew. Then I said, "This is a violation," because not even out of work I can be in peace. This is a complete violation of a person's constitutional right that is declared and given by the Constitution of the United States of America and of my civil rights. Have some respect for my wife, my family, my church, my life. Why do they have to behave like that in front of my loved ones? This is an aggression.

In addition, at the back of the bus, there was a man wearing a red sweater and he was with a kid who he called Joel. He was seating like four seats away from me. The man took out a blue plastic toy gun with an orange end, and it was thrown almost in front of me, like a foot away from me, so that I may look at it. Then one of the two young guys, picked it up and handed it over to the man. Then the man began to play around with the kid and the toy gun. I couldn't believe it. They were doing all this just to attract my attention. At one point, those two guys thought that I was coming out at one stop, before my stop, and they got up in their seat to walk out the door too, but they didn't, because they saw that I remained seated. Then at the next stop, at my stop, they got off the bus when they saw that I was coming off the bus too.

At the corner of 162 Street and Ogden Avenue, I saw a group of youngsters hanging out too. They seemed to be of the same age as those that are now hanging out at 125 East Street and Lexington Avenue, part of what I call, students from the New York Film Academy. They are making scenarios to see how I will react. When we arrived at our apartment, I began to explain to my wife what is going on, but she didn't want to listen to me because she thinks that I am crazy. Every time I talk to her about the matter, she walks away from me. She told me that I was not right, that I was wrong, while again, walking away from me. All of this is causing problems even in my marriage to the point that she doesn't want to give me children. Why, oh why do they want to cause me harm so bad?

I read on the New York Daily News about the NYPD spying unit on mosque, eavesdropping, which according to Black's Law Dictionary, West Group 2001, it is "The act of secretly listening to the private conversation of others without their consent," checking on people's daily habits and using other means which violate the constitution and the civil liberty of its residents. Also, on how they base their strategies on demographic units. So, I wonder why they are doing all of this to me?

On **Monday, April 21, 2014**, I was going to the gym, and when walking down the hill of the street where I live, I saw a guy seating down on the steps of the affordable housing building that is next to my building. The guy was wearing the sponge bob yellow t-shirt, and he had pink sox on, which for me was very suspicious. At the gym, I ran on the treadmill. When I was done running, I went to the bathroom, and through the big glass mirror of the bathroom, I saw a guy watching me. We made eyes contact. He looked at me and I looked at him.

When I was done working out, I decided to go to the bathroom again. There I saw a man who was washing his hands repeatedly. I told him that it is very important to wash his hand well because there are people that blow their nose with their hands, and they don't wash their hands. I told him that the same happens with people who don't wash their hands when they use the bathroom, and they go and use the workout machines. When I was done washing my hands and I was on my way out of the locker room, before exiting the locker room, there was a strong smell of marijuana. It was another made up scenario just to see my response or how I was going to react to it. It happened at 3:35 pm.

Later, when I came out of my apartment at approximately 7:00 pm to go to the movie theater, I saw the same guy wearing a red sweater and a camo jacket without sleeves. In the train I saw guys wearing red, sometimes red mixed with green. I arrived at the movie theater and the movie was shown in room # 1. I took a seat, and at 8:13 pm I decided to go to the bathroom before the movie began. As I walked out of the room, I noticed that an Asian guy who seemed to be Chinese, came out of the room while I did. I walked to the second floor to use the bathroom, and he followed me from behind as well, and in front of the bathroom, I saw a black man wearing a red sweater and he was accompanied by others.

I was watching the movie, Captain America. The movie had to do with trusting no one, there were eavesdropping everywhere, his place was bugged, he was suspected of something he didn't do, there were police cars, he stole a car, the police went on his chase, he was betrayed by his own law enforcement people, he had a female neighbor of whom he later found out was a spy, the light blue suburban that was parked in front of the person they kidnapped looked like the same suburban that was parked at the station house (precinct) the day that I went to pick up my suit. Then at the end of the movie, one of the characters in the movie said, "This is not the world of spies anymore, not even the world of heroes, this is the age of miracles, doctor. There is nothing more horrifying, than a miracle."

Also, I watched the Spider Man trailer where NYPD cars were used. When I left the movie theater that I went to the subway station, there I saw a young man who was wearing a red sweater and a green Jacket. So, I guess that the color of the day was green with red, or red alone. When I took the D train to go home, that I was seated, standing to my right was a young man wearing black Nike sneakers with red ribbon. Then when I came off the bus that I was walking to my building, I got to see a guy crossing the street towards me and he was wearing a yellow timberland booth with red ribbons. What a combination right.

Now I think that everything is based according to a demographic map, and they divide their units accordingly. The people that are following me must be part of that demographic unit, which is separated by many different demographic sections. This might be based on the community, how they look, what country they are coming from, their culture, race and traditions so that they may easily infiltrate without being looked like strangers. Also, to avoid the saying, "What is this guy doing here, he doesn't belong here." But what I really hate is when they misbehave to bring my attention, and this is happening almost every day at work, and out of work, and on my days off.

On **Tuesday, April 22, 2014,** before entering the gym, at 2:40 pm, I went to the grocery store. When I was paying for the water, a guy rushed inside, and he asked for a plastic bag. He was wearing a red sweater and a red hat that said "REBE" on the back. He was one of them.

Already in the gym, when I went to use the locker, the same locker that I always use, which is in the corner, I saw an open lock hanging on it, so I took another locker. When I went upstairs to run, there was another man in front of me wearing a black t-shirt that said, "Ice Scream" at the back, and he had his red sweater hanging on the machine that was next to him to his left.

When he was done, he came close to others who had either a red T-shirt or were wearing something red. While I was running on the treadmill, a woman came and she used the second machine to my right, just skipping one machine next to me, but later she changed to the machine that was right next to me, to my right, just to be closer next to me, probably because she wanted to know what I was watching on my smartphone. Then I saw another man wearing an Adidas pant that had red stripes.

When I went downstairs, I was expecting them to be at the same spot where I do my pull ups, because they already know my routine, and Bingo, there was a guy there doing pull ups and he was wearing red sneakers. Then, when he saw me standing, he asked me, by pointing at the pull-up bar, if I was going to use it. I told him that I was going to use it. Then I looked all the way back and I saw a middle-aged woman wearing red pants. Also, there was a young man who was wearing a Chicago Bulls hat, and a red sweater, and my suspicions had been confirmed. Then he walked away.

I saw another guy with long hair, and he was laughing out loud with another guy, which made me upset, because I believed that they were laughing at me. Then when he looked at me, I stared at him on the eyes, and he looked the other way with a serious face. Then he grabbed the green jacket he had laying on the side and he walked away with his companion. I walked out of the gym and when crossing the street, I saw another guy who was wearing a red T-shirt, and he was crossing the street. I have no break. I have seen so many people wearing red today that it is ridiculous, and it is not even Valentine's Day nor Christmas's day.

On **Wednesday, April 23, 2014,** at 0441 hrs. or 4:41 am a 10-30 (Robbery) job came over at 2196 5th avenue at the corner of East …. We responded there. It was a robbery with a gun that took place at the grocery store. Before the robbery, the grocery store's employee had the grocery store's door closed and locked, which they do after a certain hour, but they were serving customers through the window. However, on this day, the employee, who was the only one working that night at the grocery store, decided to unlock the closed door, and he walked out of the store, when he saw that a person threw the garbage bin to the floor, which was in front of the grocery store.

The camera captured the moment when the employee came out of the grocery store, and how he took his time to go back inside. He even bent down to pick up something before getting in, when someone came from around the corner wearing a mask, a green hoodie sweater, and gloves, and forced his way inside the grocery store by pulling out a gun and pointing the gun at the employee. He pushed the employee around while pointing the gun at him and he took him to the register, opened the register, took the money, and with a key (Not a combination safe) opened the safe.

Then he grabbed the employee and took him with him back to the door's entry. The employee looked outside the door to make sure that there were no cops coming, and when it was clear that there were none, the robber pushed the employee to the side and he left carrying a black bag. All this was seen on the camera. However, as for me, all of that didn't look real, or wasn't real. For the Detectives, the employee looked like an accomplice, because of the way in which the robber proceeded by not using excessive force. It looked like a scenario, as I do call it, or better said, a WWF wrestling match.

In addition, the way in which the robber came through the door, appeared as if the employee was waiting for him to come. The fake push of the employee here and there, and that the robber knew where the money was, rings the bell. The garbage bin was still lying on the floor. Then I asked the supposed victim if he was injured and he said that he didn't. Then Lt. Allen saw that I was very curious and suspicious about the events, especially when I placed my right hand to my chin and said "strange," and that it was more than one person involved. Then I stepped outside. As I was outside, Lt. Allen came out of the grocery store too and he asked me what I found suspicious. I told him that the robber wasn't aggressive enough. Then Lt. Allen went back inside the grocery store. Then suddenly, the employee needed medical attention due to pain in his right flank, because the robber had kicked him three times.

However, the employee was in his early twenties, and he was wearing a red hat, a red T-shirt or sweater, and red sneakers. The robber was wearing a green hoodie sweater, and one of the owners of the store, who showed up later, was wearing green sneakers. I knew right away and had come to realize what it was all about. Moreover, the other grocery store owner suspected and pointed at one customer who had just arrived and was wearing red. He was also wondering what had happened. The owner told me that he was the employee's friend. I told the detective about it. What a scenario. It seemed that they were watching me, as I was watching the camera.

When I arrived home at 0902 hrs. or 9:02 am, when I came out of the elevator, I saw someone coming out of my neighbor's apartment, the apartment to my left side when facing my door from outside, or to be more specific, from apartment #61, and guess what? The guy that just came out was taller than me, and he was wearing a red sweater, and a camo hat. Wow, I feel so violated. My privacy, and my rights seem to be going down the drain. It appears that they are doing a reality show with me.

156

On **Saturday, April 26, 2014,** PO Rivera and I received a radio-run job. When we arrived at the location, it was about a woman who had dropped her smartphone and cards at a business premise. The person who found them said that an unknown woman had drop it. I knew right away that this was another scenario, and it was done because the public distrust of NYPD officers is disappointing.

I and my partner PO Rivera vouchered the items. However, the following took place while we were doing the vouchers:

When we arrived at the precinct with the items, PO Rivera laid the items on the table, and he decided to go somewhere, I believe to the bathroom, but before living he told me, "Don't touch." Then Sgt. Gibbs came in with PO Maher and sat next to the properties, which made me believe that they were there because they distrust me. I swallowed hard my saliva and then went to the RMP (police car) to get my water bottle. When I went back, PO Rivera was already there

. Then I told Sgt. Gibbs about the meaning of his first name, Ira, in Spanish which means anger, Ire, and watchful. He seemed to have disliked my comment. Then we began talking about my faith, by which I told him that God is in control of everything. I asked him how his back was, which many months ago he had told me that he had back pain here and there, and he answered, "Oh, so you do remember that." His response made me feel so bad, because I knew what he meant by that, which dates to **December 10, 2013**. Then he told me, "So, are you going to preach for a living?" He killed me with that question. Who does he think I am? A man without feelings? Is he trying to warn me about my future disaster?

I took the subway home. When I came out of the train at 161 street, walking down the stairwell, I saw a Hispanic woman dressed in black and she was carrying a pink bag. It was approximately 0818 hrs. or 8:18 am. I noticed that she was walking behind me, because of the sound she was making with her throat. Then I stopped walking to wear my winter hat, and she passed me by. Another young man was behind her wearing a green jacket. When I was at the end of the stairwell, I saw that she kept walking and when she almost headed to the Manhattan bound train, she became confused for a moment and then she went out passing the turnstile. When I came out of the subway station, I got to see the same young man wearing the green jacket and he was across the street from the Yankee Stadium, in front of the park, while the dressed in black lady went to the bus stop side.

When I arrived at my apartment building, I realized that I had left my keys at work. On my way back to the precinct that I was getting close to the subway station, I saw the same young man wearing the green jacket, and he was crossing the street back to the subway station. When I reached the platform of the subway station, I saw people wearing the same camo pants, and the green and red colors.

I noticed that they were close to me. When I was walking out of the subway station on my way to the station house (precinct), I noticed that there were a lot of strange movements around me. When I arrived at the station house (precinct), I got to see Sgt. Bennett standing straight at the Desk and he was wearing his police hat as if he were in formation, in attention, or as if he was ready to solute someone. He was expecting me. Someone might have informed him of my arrival. He stood the same way that the Sergeant from the 28-precinct stood when I went there to do the 28-precinct hub site. Why was he wearing the police hat inside the precinct when we only do wear it when we are at roll call, when we are out on the street, or to address a very high-ranking officer. I am no high-ranking officer; I am simply a police officer. Then at the other end was Sgt. Kim.

On my way back to the subway station, I saw a woman wearing red pants. She was behind me as I waited for the number four train. I am so tired of typing and typing. I see no end to this. All they want is to hurt me. They truly want to hurt me in a way that I may never get up again.

On **Sunday, April 27, 2014,** I found a Glock magazine inside RMP (police car) 3333. My gun is a Glock, and we are to choose from three service weapon brands, a Sig Sauer, a Smith Wesson, or a Glock. So, to find a Glock magazine knowing that I carry a Glock gun really rings the bell. Right away, I left the magazine inside the RMP (police car) and I went inside the precinct and informed Lt. Allen about my finding. Later, PO Maher accompanied me to the RMP (police car) to retrieve the magazine. PO Maher told me not to worry about it, and then I went to the hospital to stay with PO Rivera.

At the hospital, I showed and handed over to PO Rivera a receipt of my trip to Dominican Republic, which contained all the information pertaining to the flight, the time and the resort that I was going to lodge in. I even read it to him so that those who were listening through him may know it too. When I arrived to the station house (precinct) with PO Rivera, after being assigned to a hospitalized prisoner at Bellevue hospital, I saw Sgt. Kim standing behind the Desk, again, like in attention or in formation, as I had seen Sgt. Bennett do the last time, and the same way that the 28 precinct Sergeant does every time I walk into the 28 precinct to do the 28 hub site. Then as he stood there in attention, he looked at me in disbelief as he shook his head side to side as if demonstrating his indignation for something that is unknown to me, and as he did so, he was saying, "That's not right, that's not right."

Due to the strange and unusual circumstances of the moment, PO Rivera seemed to have noticed Sgt. Kim's reaction, and he told me to go ahead first to the locker room and get changed. I think that he wanted to find out what wasn't right according to Sgt. Kim. Then in the locker room, I showed PO Rivera the small luggage I was going to use to travel to Puerto Plata, and I showed him that it was empty. This is the same small luggage I use to carry my police equipment every time I go to do headquarter security at 1PP (1 Police Plaza= Police Headquarter).

As I was walking away from the station house (precinct) with PO Rivera, and while dragging my luggage, I could see those who were following my footsteps altering their behavior. Before entering the subway station, we stopped outside and PO Rivera, as he raised his voice so my followers, who were around me, could hear, and know of the reason why I was carrying my small luggage, told me how much he dislikes boarding planes, and I told him how much I liked it. Then he said to me, "Listen, enjoy your vacation," and loud and clear I told him, "Thank you."

Why, I wonder, why they don't come to me and ask me about my life? About whom I am. I will gladly introduce myself and my family to them because I am an open book. I am as transparent and clear as the

159

water is. My conscience is clean. But I wonder why they act towards me as if I were a stranger, after being a police officer for more than six years, and after being a police cadet for six years, which in total, I have been working for the New York City Police Department (The NYPD) for more than 12 years, and they still don't know who I am?

Now they are hiring the old, and the young. Every adult and person of all ages, race, ethnicity, sexual orientation, religion, etc, to come after me, testing me in all areas of my life just to find fault in me to later hang me, when my heart is clean. What do they want from me? If they would like to spend a day or more in my apartment they only need to ask. But for God's sake, stop doing what you are doing. It is hurting me, it is horrifying, and it is so painful.

On **Monday, April 28, 2014,** in the morning, I went to the gym. Before entering the gym, I decided to go to the grocery store as I always do, and as soon as I did, immediately a young man wearing red colors went inside the grocery store. Then, one of the guys who was next to me, said to himself, "This is cruel and unusual punishment." I knew that he was referring to the treatment that I am receiving, and I do agree with him. Then I went home. Also, I went to eat breakfast at the Mambi restaurant, and when I was done eating, outside, in front of the restaurant, I observed a woman talking on the phone. Then I went to the Banco Popular bank.

As soon as I got there, a man wearing a red jersey came in. Then one of the bank's staff asked me if I would like to apply for a secured loan. I told her, "Ok". Then I wrote my name on the waiting list at 10:51 am and she wrote on the side, secured loan. Then I took a seat and waited. Then the man who was wearing the red jersey looked at me as he was waiting on the line to see the clerk. When he was done with his transaction, he looked at me again and left.

Almost a minute later, another Hispanic man walked in. He was wearing camo pants. He decided to write his name on the waiting list also. Then he unnecessarily sat right next to me, to my left. If there were many seats available to my left, why did he have to sit right next to me? He was carrying like a suitcase. I was wondering if the suitcase had a hole and from that hole, he was recording me.

There he took out a stack of money and he began counting it right next to me. I felt so bad, so uncomfortable, disgusted and disappointed that I decided to get up and walk to the line and I told the lady at the bank that I just wanted to withdraw $3,000 dollars. I couldn't wait, because indeed, I was waiting there even when I saw that they were not taking care of other customers. When the man wearing the camo pant saw that I got up, and that I was waiting online, he immediately got up too and he got on the line next to me. In the first place, I don't know why he wrote his name on the waiting list when he was not going to talk to a representative.

Then I left, and everywhere on the street, I saw all of these people wearing the colors red, green, and the camo type of clothing. I couldn't even take money out without the whole world knowing about it. Could it be that they are planning to rob me? If not, what about if the information about me about withdrawing money from the bank goes to the wrong person's ear? Where is my safety?

As I walked around wandering off aimlessly and directionless, I decided to call my barber, which I liked about eight times just to make sure that he had arrived at the barbershop and when I got there, he was not there. I became so disoriented that I didn't know where else to go. Then I decided to go to another barber, and on my way to the other barber, he called me to tell me that he was already there. He even took a taxi to get there. I went back there, and as I was having my hair cut, I could see through the glass wall of the barbershop, young guys walking by wearing red colors. I am so tired of this.

There I told my barber about a dream I had last week where I saw a black dog that wanted to bite me and the dog was looking at me with hateful eyes, but somebody was holding the dog by the lace. Then at the same time a white dog that looked like a wolf with white eyes was doing the same. This dog looked at me like he wanted to destroy me and devour me. I saw a lot of hate in this dog's eyes. But as somebody was holding the dog by a lace, I grabbed a garden fork and I plunged it into half of the dog's body, then I began to cut the dog's head with a sharp instrument.

After my barber was done cutting my hair, I went back home. I took a shower, and I slept all day until the next day.

On **Tuesday, April 29, 2014,** I went to work out in the morning, but before entering the gym, I went to the grocery store to buy myself a bottle of water. As soon as I entered the grocery store, I saw a young black man waiting there. He was wearing red, the same as the others. Then I heard a young lady, who was talking to him, telling him," I don't know why people go to other countries, except ours? ... South Africa..." I knew that she was talking in a way that I could hear. She already knew that I was going to travel and where I was going to.

I entered the gym, and when I went into the bathroom, I saw a black hoodie. When I saw it, my first reaction was to shake my head side to side and feel bad for all this nonsense injustice. After working out, I went to my apartment, and then I came out of my apartment to go to Duane Reade, the one that is located on 86 street, there I saw those wearing red and green colors again. When I came out of Duane Read, I took the six train to go downtown and there I stopped at Walgreens. In there, I asked for computer glasses, and the staff walked with me to the second floor, and he showed me the section where they have the glasses, and guess what? In that section I saw a young black male wearing red. He was walking around me as I was looking to buy white T-shirts for my trip. I bought two packages of white T-shirts and then I walked down the stairs. There I saw that he was not by himself.

Then I went to Paragon sports to buy my swimming gear, and there I could see that I was being watched too. When I came out of the store, I saw a Hispanic guy wearing a red t-shirt standing at the corner of the street, doing nothing, just standing there, and I could see why he was standing there. As I was waiting to take the number four train, I had the feeling that I was being watched there too. Suddenly, at approximately 1650 hrs. or 4:40 pm, the number four train arrived and opened its doors, and walking out of the train's door, like six feet away from me, I got to see no one more nor less than ADA Altman, the mother of my problems, the number one reason why I am going thru all the things that I am going thru. Not to forget that Lt. Yaguchi is the father of my problems. I didn't greet her, I just let her walk away, and I went inside the train.

Even there, I could sense that there was one, two or more people keeping their eyes on me. When I arrived home, I was feeling so mentally exhausted, drained and tired. I didn't even have enough strength to organize my luggage. As I was falling asleep, I told my wife that I was going to lay on bed for a moment. But she advised me that I should fix my luggage first, but I told her that I was feeling too tired to do so now. I was so tired that it became so hard for me to carry my body from my living room to my bedroom. So, in the living room, I got up my seat, went to my bedroom, and threw myself on the bed wearing whatever it was that I was wearing. Immediately, I was sleeping with the lights on.

When I woke up, a few minutes later, my saliva wetted my bed sheet. My body was aching, and I couldn't wait to go away. I told my wife that I was going to take my luggage the next day, and I went back to sleep.

On **Wednesday, April 30, 2014**, I woke up at two thirty in the morning to fix my luggage. I was going to travel alone because my wife couldn't travel because of work. But she never objects to my lone travel, because she trusts the man who sleeps every day next to her. She knows that I won't do the wrong thing because I love God. This is something that my co-workers can't visualize and consider for their hate towards me have blinded their own judgement, resulting in lack of trust in me.

I am feeling like inside of a box where I can't come out of, and to think that by going away to the Dominican Republic for my vacation was going to make everything come to halt or a pause, I was mistaking. At three something in the morning I came out of my apartment because I didn't want to miss my plane. It was raining, and as soon as I came down the hill of the block of where I live, that I was crossing the street, there I saw a black man wearing a red hoodie sweater. I knew that they were expecting me to come out of my apartment at this time of the hour because they already knew that I was going away, and that I was going to catch a plane. He walked past me and when I looked back, he looked behind him also. I just kept dragging my small luggage.

163

When I was waiting upstairs for the number four train, I learned that I had to wait another ten minutes, so since I had to take the A train anyway, I decided to go downstairs and take the D train to later transfer to the A train. Then after waiting there for a while, I decided to come out of the subway station, and I took a taxi instead. Already, there was a taxi waiting for me. The cab driver walked out of his car, and being loud he told me that he charges people sixty dollars to take them to the airport, but for me he was going to charge me fifty-five dollars. Inside the taxi, I told him that I was going to the Dominican Republic.

Then I saw him take his smartphone from the sun visor of his car, and then he touched I believe to be an application on the screen of his smartphone, and then he placed it back on the sun visor, which held and concealed most of the smartphone's body. Then I saw that the smartphone he had was connected to a camera through a USB cable, and that the camera was attached to the windshield pointing directly to the back passenger side seat, in this case, me. At that moment I realized that I was being framed and set for failure again. The language we spoke was Spanish.

As he drove, he began talking about the terrible things he used to do when he was a young man in the military. When he went overseas to Singapore, how he used to sleep with prostitutes and do other immoral, terrible and devastating things such as and to the extent of taking things from people. I was appalled, I didn't know what to say. How can a grown old man who looked like in his sixties be talking in such a way? As he did his nonstop talking, I didn't question him, I didn't give my opinion, I didn't show any emotions. I neither laughed nor smiled, nor showed nor demonstrated any type of anger nor outrage.

But I was angry at the system, at all of this set up, by hiring a man, or a cab driver to act as a former monster, an immoral, and demoralized ex pervert and ex thief to study my response and reaction. I wanted to throw myself out of the cab, but it was raining and to catch another cab at that time of the hour, especially when thinking that I was running late, was going to be difficult. I wanted to ask him if he was proud of the bad things he did when he was a young man. If he didn't feel any sense of shame for saying such things. If there was no remorse for those terrible things he did. But I was so tired to begin an argument with him. Not even on my way to the airport was I able to catch a break.

When we arrived at terminal eight, to my destination, the only thing I told him was that he had to look for God. Then reacting desperately, he said that he prays to God and that he had gone to Jerusalem, and that after his experience there, he stopped drinking alcohol and, he said that he prays for himself and his passengers all the time. So, I gave him the fifty-five dollars he charged me.

Then I walked into the airport, and there I was told that I had to pay twenty-five dollars for my small luggage, because it was too big to take it with me on the plane. Then the airport staff noticed that my small luggage was the type of luggage that can be separated into two smaller units, with one side turning into a book back, and under such conditions, I was going to be allowed to take with me the two small bags plus the extra gym bag that I was carrying with me. With a little effort I did that.

However, he then told me that since I had three bags, I needed to bring everything together and turn it into two bags because they don't aloud more than two bags by hand. Then I got to stock everything together making the smaller bag fit inside my gym bag, and after a hard time turning three bags into two bags, to avoid paying the extra cash, I went through the machine, and they told me that I couldn't take with me my sunscreen lotion, my deodorant my toothpaste, etc. I had to throw it away or pay the twenty-five dollars fee for the extra bag that I couldn't take with me. So, I chose option number two. Again, I had to take everything out of my bags, and I began to turn two bags into one big bag, plus my regular gym bag, and finally I paid the twenty-five dollars fee.

My first flight was going to Miami. The flight number was AA1345. When I boarded the plane, I was assigned to seat 30A which was next to the window. I believed that I could finally relax and enjoy my flight. However, two young ladies were behind me, and they began talking. One told the other that she had bought the tickets through Expedia, which I did. Then when the plane landed, one of them was trying to get up from her seat, and she said, "I feel handcuffed." What an irony, she mentioned handcuffs when part of my job is to handcuff people who commit crimes. She was trying to alert me that I was being watched, followed, and that she was one of them. Then she said, "You should have stay home."

In a few words, she was trying to let me know that all my movements and activities are monitored, and micromanaged, which I believe they themselves find to be too unjust. But I have the feeling that at the same time they are looking out for me. Then I went and waited for my next flight. Flight number AA935 to destination: Puerto Plata. Then we were told to board the plane, and as I boarded the plane, I managed to see two young tall black man wearing red and they were in the same lane I was in, which rose and confirmed my suspicion that they were still following me. I was assigned to seat number 26E. When I looked at my seat, I saw that my seat was in the middle, right between a man and a woman who were already seated. I told them to excuse me as I took a seat.

As soon as I sat down, the man who was seated to my left, and who had a headphone on his ear, headphone that carried a red wire, said something about four months. This small tip completely let me know that the two of them, he to my left and she to my right, were there to keep their eyes on me. I thank him for what he said, because indeed all this nonsense began like four months ago. Behind me were two men, and I saw that one of them was a white man and the other one I didn't bother to look. They were talking loudly there. In front of me was a young lady who was wearing red. She seemed to be the daughter of the woman who was seated to my right. The same as the two men who were behind me, it seemed that they were with the woman that was seated to my right as well. I felt that I was surrounded by wolves in sheep clothing.

Throughout the flight, I was tight because the man who was seated next to me had wide shoulders the same way I do, so we were almost rubbing shoulders. So, I kept doing my reading on my smartphone. Now, when the travel agent began to hand over the two handouts questionnaire to be answered, the man to my left began to fill it out his, right away, but the woman next to me didn't. Then when the man was done, the woman began to fill out hers. Meanwhile, the man opened his tablet, and he began to read from it. He even turned his body to the side to let me know that he was not going to look at the information that I was going to provide in the questionnaire, in case I decided to do mines now.

When I decided to answer the questions, I noticed that the woman next to me was doing hers and she had begun to move her body in awkward positions as if trying to see what I was writing, which made me feel very nervous. So, I decided to cover my information with the other sheet, in which as a result, I noticed that it made her feel upset because she could no longer see my information. After a while, I asked the two of them what flight number was this. I asked them if it was AA1345 and they told me that it wasn't, that it was flight AA935. Then the woman said, "Jesus," as if I were dumber than what I look like. Another thing is that I felt so pressured and uncomfortable writing my information that I left many questions unanswered and decided to finish it later when I got off the plane.

When we arrived, the man left without saying goodbye, and I told the woman, "Enjoy your vacation," and she thanked me. However, when I came out of the plane, I noticed that the woman that was seating next to me joined a group of people. Immediately, I decided to use the bathroom, and when I was using the toilet, another man entered the bathroom, and he used the toilet that was next to me on my left. When I was done, that I washed my hands and was about to walk out, the man who was using the toilet said to me, "Please, tell the lady that is wearing red sneakers that I will be right there," and I said to him, "Sure." When I came out, there was a lady waiting outside, but she was not wearing red sneakers, she was wearing a red t-shirt. When I told her that, she smiled at me, and I walked to my destination.

Now I believe that I am being considered a high flight risk person. But they didn't forbid me from traveling, because if they did, they were going to be forced to vomit, expose and unravel their evil motives against me. It was going to shed light to their obscure intent to track me and hunt me down. It would have put an end to all this madness.

It was like on the **month of March or April** that I did 1PP (1 Police Plaza= Police Headquarter) to get out of the turbulent situation that I am going thru at the 25th precinct. At 1PP (1 Police Plaza= Police Headquarter), I scanned my ID to go out and back to my post. There, I heard somebody say, "Hi" to me. When I looked to see who it was, it was my former Lieutenant back when I was a police cadet at the Manhattan North of Investigation located at the PSA 5 building. He greeted me and I greeted him back. He was working at 1PP (1 Police Plaza= Police Headquarter). He asked me if I was ok, if I liked where I was. Excited, I told him that everybody needs a change sometimes. But inside of me, I was inferring, "Help me, help me please." Then he went his way, and I went my way. Now I wonder if going to the 25 precinct is like entering the mouth of a lion, and going to 1PP (1 Police Plaza= Police Headquarter) is like entering the mouth of a Dragon. However, there is one word a police officer can't alter, and that word is the magic word, "Stress." But this is my penalty. I must pay for something that I don't know what it is. I must pay for something they suspect, not that I did.

Chapter 12

May 2014 Events

The next day, on **Thursday, May 1, 2014,** I went and bought my one-day pass at Wyndham resort because at the hotel where I was staying, "The Millennial," didn't have a buffet. Then when I finished eating at the Buffet that I stood up to leave, there I saw a young black man wearing a white Chicago Bulls hat with the bull drawn in red. He approached me. He looked at where I was sitting and then walked away from me. I walked away from the restaurant that is by the swimming pool. I greeted the security guard there.

It is **Saturday, May 3, 2014**. I am typing this with one hand because my left shoulder is being sustained by two t-shirts that I have bound together since yesterday I dislocated my left shoulder, while playing with the waves at the beach. I was playing with the waves and the sand on the beach shore. There, I was defying the waves of the beach for not being strong enough to dominate my body. But in the process of doing so, a magnificent wave crashed against my body, taking control of my entire body, and it threw me against the sand of the beach.

When that happened that I saw my left shoulder out of proportion, and that the bone on my left shoulder was showing more than usual, I held my left arm with my other hand, and I walked out of the beach. I saw two white young guys walking by and I lay on the sand in front of them so they may assist me. When they saw me on the ground, they began to look down to me and I told them in English to call the security guard that was several feet away, so he could come and help me. But all they did was to talk among themselves in another language. I pointed it out to the security guard, but still, they didn't understand what I was trying to say.

Then I tried to see if I could bring my dislocated shoulder to its former position by pressing my shoulder hard against the sand, but it was useless, no matter how much I tried to rotate it to different direction, the more painful it became, and did me no good. So, I told those guys to forget it and I stood up and walked to the security guard, while holding my left arm up with my right hand. I explained to him what had happened, and told him to pick up my sandals, as I walked to reception.

At reception, the staff began to look for someone that may take me to the nearest clinic. Once again, I laid on the floor trying to fix it by myself, before the doctor did it himself, which could be much more painful, but I was unable to correct it. I told them to hurry, because the sooner it is dealt with, the better it will be. Then someone from maintenance drove me to the clinic. As he drove me there, I began to look around to see if someone was following me. All I saw were people looking at me strangely, because obviously, I was holding my left arm up with my right hand.

When I arrived at the clinic, I was treated by a good doctor and after maneuvering my shoulder twice, he managed to adjust my shoulder. Then, when I was at the waiting room waiting for another appointment, a white man wearing a green polo shirt came. He was waiting in the waiting area. He was like in his late forties. Ever since, I left the clinic realizing that I was still being followed. But since this experience, I will never again defy and mess with Mother Nature.

I wonder why they are doing this to me. Treating me as if I were a criminal. I see no end to this. However, I am disregarding the pain that I feel on my shoulder because the anger that is inside of me is greater than my physical pain. What a vacation this is. Now I feel nostalgia, knowing that I am so close to my parents, Mami and Papi, but I am unable to go to them and hug them, and spend time with them as I did last year. But because of my followers, I can't. Besides, how can I look at them and pretend to be happy when at my job people don't trust me, they mistreat me and have brought false allegations and accusations against me. I really don't want them to see me in this condition of human decay. How my reputation has been reduced to dust. As the movie that I watched for a couple of minutes was Robert De Niro in one of his movies said that it takes a lifetime to build a reputation, and seconds to destroy it.

Oh, mother and father, how great was last April or May when I brought the two of you to the movie theater, and along with us was my cousin, who is in her forties, and who had never in her life visited a movie theater, and the Haitian man that I brought with us. I bought all of you besides the movie ticket, popcorn and drinks that I went by myself to buy, leaving all of you comfortably seated in the theater room, and I as your servant, went back to all of you to serve and hand over the popcorn and the drinks to the three of you. After that I took the three of you to a restaurant. What a joy it was for me to do all these things for all of you. To serve each one of you. Oh Uncle, how I wish to see you again. Oh, heavenly father, please control my tears. This is the only thing that I long for, but with these followers behind my back, I feel like a prisoner.

Now here I am, typing and typing, expressing my feelings through this means, because I cannot share and express my feelings with anyone, because if I do, I will end up being their servant. But as I can see, good things cannot last. But what I don't understand and would like to know is what are their motives and incentives behind all of this. Is it a promotion? A transfer to a desired unit, command or place? A rise in salary? Political reasons? Or a hunger for self-recognition? But I do have to say one thing. If they are doing what they are doing for any of these reasons, their motives are not pure nor sincere because all they want is to benefit from the hardships they are causing me, and not for the sake of justice to be served, and the deep desire to find the truth and nothing more than the truth.

Their lack of experience is enormous or humongous. They are a bunch of young faces trying to make the news and be portrayed as heroes. They think they know it all when in reality they don't know what they are doing, because they are being misled. I am so fully aware of their moves, and what they are doing, and guess what? Whoever has done the wrong thing is laughing on their faces right now, because as I can see, everyone knows what is going on including the criminal who committed the crime. They share their investigative information almost with everyone, and that is their first mistake.

But where are the experts. The men and women in their late forties and up that have years of experience, where are they? I am so tired of these wannabe youngsters who are praying on me and are desiring my downfall. They think that life is just a game. Right now, all I want to do is to take this Microsoft surface tablet, which I am using to type these words, and slam it on the floor. But that's not what God wants me to do; he wants me to pray for them because there is no virtual in them.

In this case, the blind is leading the blind. But there is one thing I will hate to hear, and that is people's rumors that could propagate everywhere. Rumors such as the youngest son of so and so, is a lying thief. That will truly break my mother and my father's heart. Especially my mother who suffers from high blood pressure and has a heart condition. How can I bring such dishonor to my family, when in the end, everything is a falsehood? And to think that it is what my mortifiers want is a shame. A massive portion of my life has been spent at work, working nights, and doing my best every day to be the best at work. Before, I wanted to be the best cop by focusing on fighting crime and on how to be a good public servant. But now I can't concentrate at work with all of this going on around me. Now I feel that I am the most mediocre police officer in the history of the New York City Police Department.

I am typing this on **Sunday, May 4, 2014,** while still having excruciating pain on my left shoulder. Every time I go to do 1PP (1 Police Plaza headquarter security), I feel that I am walking into a dragon's cave. As PO Rivera once told me, "…walking into the lion's mouth…" and this is how I always feel every time I go to the station house (precinct). But what can I do in regards? I work for the city and the NYPD. I belong to them, and I feel that I have no right to protest all the harm and mischief they are causing me. I must endure and tolerate. Day in, and day out, I am suffering for not knowing what my future holds. PO Rivera, who I once trusted, but whom I love as a friend, I can no longer trust, because I know very well that he is being wired.

He has turned against me because of all the controversial and sensitive questions he has been asking and keeps asking me. He is using all his wit, and years of experience, for he is ten years older than I, and his intelligence to find ways to legally do harm to me. But he is the only person at work that I have to trust a little bit, because I must have a little trust in somebody. It is like what happened with David that he had to find refuge on the enemy territory, because King Saul was seeking his life. There is no privacy in my life anymore. I am condemned for something that should have been avoided if they had done the right thing. ADA Altman knew well that I was not prepared to give my testimony, and still, she let me testify, and on top of that, she invited another ADA to witness the slaughter.

And you wonder how I feel? This is in addition to the false accusations they have brought against me dating back to or before **December 10, 2013**, which influenced the ADA's (Assistant District Attorney) decision to allow me to testify. In addition, it is the reason why my partners refused to talk to me about the case of **December 10, 2013,** which would have helped me clarify what happened on the night of the arrest, and as a result, I would have recalled the whole event. If I am being blamed for something serious that occurred in the precinct (before **December 10, 2013**), which I am not aware of, why didn't they conduct their investigation on the same day or night that it happened? If it was a robbery, why didn't they search for all the lockers in the precinct?

I wonder how many police officers have fallen victim of such malpractice and how many of them have resorted to destructive measure to escape from such inhumane treatment, such a pressure. "Give me freedom or give me death," a person once said. But I must accept, bear and endure all of this. In addition, an officer has no right to say that he is stressed, because that is the magic word for their gun and shield to be taken away from them, and as a result, they will be sent to a psych ward.

And I cannot hire a lawyer to clean all this mess, because the retired officer, in a few words, warned me not to do so. And hiring an attorney means that I will have to get a loan to pay for a lawyer that I cannot afford to pay. In addition, the city, the NYPD, and the District Attorney's office will hate me with a passion if I do so. Therefore, I have been threatened not to do so. Or probably, they are intentionally provoking me into getting a lawyer. In other words, they are pushing me hard, so I may get a lawyer, and the moment I do, they will crush me then.

I remember the day when PO Gorman told me that when one has an enemy, it is when one really needs to be close to him. So, I believe that this is the situation. They are treating me as if I were a bird that they are trying to catch. They are throwing at my footstep pieces of bread so I may go and eat.

Pieces of bread that are leading to them, going towards their direction, to the wide door of perdition, and at the end of the path or voyage, be their lovely hand wide open on the floor with plenty of pieces of bread of all desired flavors spread on their palm, waiting for this bird of me to step on it, or to land there, so that they may gently begin to close the hand, and all of a sudden, they will ultimately close the hand with all of their might, and then when having this little innocent birdy me captured inside their hand, hand that has turned now into a fist, they will slowly begin to squeeze the fist that is holding this bird of me trapped inside, and with joy and pleasure they will begin to slowly make the first tighter and tighter, and as they do, they will celebrate with dances and beers, drinks and cakes, while this poor bird of me, who is in agony, is yelling and screaming for help, but no one cares to listen to what he has to say.

They are just waiting for the moment, chance and opportunity that the traffic light may turn green, so they may be able to squeeze that fist with all of their strength, hate and fury, in order to make sure that all form of life may be squeezed out of that birdy me, leaving nothing more than the dry skin, que el bagazo, the skin of that deformed, unrecognizable piece of meat with feather. Poor me I should say. As for now, I am doing all the yelling and screaming, but all of this is being done inside of me.

One night at approximately 7:30 pm, I decided to go to the supermarket, the one that was close to the hotel. There was a suspicious man seating at the lobby area of the hotel. When I began walking out of the hotel to go to the supermarket, there I saw a black SUV (suburban) coming in. I greeted the person at the entrance, and I went across the street to the supermarket. When I was inside the supermarket, that I was buying a cheese, there approached me two tall black guys who seemed to have come from New York to spy on me. One of them was wearing a black tang top with the USA flag drawn on the front. They were behind my back pretending to buy something. Suddenly, a white American lady with black hair joined them.

I knew from where she was from because of her English accent. Now the three of them were behind me. They seemed not to know how to behave because they looked disoriented. When the man handed me over the cheese, I began to look around to see what else to buy. When I walked to the register to pay, a white man who was in there gave me a sudden look, and knowing not what to do, he turned around, went back to the entrance and grabbed a basket for his supposed groceries. I stepped out and outside I saw two to three SUVs there. One of the SUVs was black.

When walking into the hotel, I greeted the man at the entrance. Then I saw a black SUV coming out and on its front plate it said, "**Diplomatico**," which translated into English is," Diplomatic." Then I walked back into the hotel. I think that everyone there might be asking themselves questions as to what I am doing here alone, by myself. But what they don't know is that for a thoughtful person there is neither loneliness nor boredom. Now I think that I must fulfill my expedition and be brave enough and as daring as Christopher Columbus was. Now how can a soldier who is in the middle of a war take a vacation.

How can I be crossed handed when my adversaries are spending time, money, men power, efforts and other means necessary to destroy me, my future, my dream and my sane existence. However, God in his divine grace has granted me a weapon besides the bible. The Lord have equipped me with tools and these are: Pens, papers, a Microsoft Surface Pro tablet that I bought on March 11, 2013 for $999.00 at the Microsoft store located at 10 Columbus Circle (In case they think I stole it), and along with it, Microsoft word 2013, which I am using to type these bloody words.

Now my body is showing signs of decadency. My hair looks so debilitating, unhealthy, and it is falling. As the days go by, I see less hair on my head. It seems that very soon I will be bold headed. My face doesn't look that fresh anymore. I can see the two lines of worries that connect to the nose and mouth, one on the left and the other one on the right. I am looking so old and tired. But I must thank all of them for all of this. Because of them, I have become a waste, a total mess.

In the afternoon of **Wednesday, May 7, 2014,** I was waiting at the airport in Puerto Plata. I was going back home. Seating there, I saw my tormentors' right in front of me. One of them was wearing a green baseball hat, and the others were wearing something red. When passing my bag through the machine at the customs and border, in front of me I still saw those guys wearing red and green. One of them was wearing way below his hip, green pants which showed his green underwear to everyone. There was some major delay on my flight. I called the Desk to see if I could have the night off and I was told by Lt. Allen that I must report to work that night.

After the plane, I took the train. The train was delayed as well. Then I took a cab, but I had to pay $70.00 dollars, but instead of paying that amount, I went back to take the train. When I took the train, the last stop of the train was at Broadway and junction, so I took a cab home, and at home, I took a cab to work, and after work, I went home feeling overly tired. I slept for three hours and then I prepared for the dinner celebration dedicated to Captain Larin, who was being transferred to work somewhere else, to the 24 precinct Manhattan North Borough. Then at the dinner, Captain Larin said, "Help the kid, he will accomplish greater things than what I have accomplished." I wondered why he said that, and if I was the kid he was referring to.

Dear police officer Hernandez,
   I deeply apologize for omitting you from my list
of officers to thank for their hard work on the DWI
initiative. Even though your arrest was voided,
therefore being truly useless too me I still want to
thank you for all your hard work. Maybe next time
your efforts wont be wasted on a DWI arrest that was
really a pile of nothing and perhaps you could get the
supposed drunk to take a breath test so as to not
waste your time as well as the departments. Anywho
thanks for all your hard work.

                                    Yours Truly
                                    Cpt. Sarin
                                       25Pct

I remember the day when PO Maher and PO Gorman gave me the following letter that according to them was from Captain Larin to me.

I know that Captain Larin wouldn't have written me such a letter. But it reflects and projects how well I am at the 25th precinct.

On **Thursday, May 8, 2014,** I was assigned to do the 28-hub site. Walking the long hallway alone, I managed to hear people on my back say, "Lying, stupid." My mother called me to tell me that she needs money.

On **Saturday, May 10, 2014,** I was doing the 28-hub site prisoner transport. We were transporting 10 prisoners in the police van, plus in our police car, we transported a female prisoner. Inside the car, the female prisoner complained that her cuffs were too tight, so immediately, we corrected the problem.

Inside the car she told us that the cop had lied to her five times. Then she said that she was cold and that she had a jacket, but that the

177

officer didn't give it back to her. I went to talk to the arrest officer, and he told me that she didn't have a jacket with her. She lied. I went back to the car, and we drove away. We stopped next to the van, and I told PO Liu to tell the officer who was driving the van what had happened. PO Liu told the officer that she was screaming and that we had to stop to fix her cuffs. When she heard PO Liu's statement, she said, "I wasn't screaming officer. Tell it the way it is, I was not screaming." Then PO Liu said, "She was complaining about it," and she said, "There you go, tell it the way it is." At that moment I realized that she was pretending to be a prisoner. Back at the station house (25 precinct), PO Golden returned me the $10.00 contribution that I had given her to paint the female locker room.

Analyzing these events, the female prisoner complained that the cop had lied to her five times, that PO Liu was lying to the other officer by not describing the event as it happened, and that the officer that arrested her had not given her the jacket back to her, or lets say, stole it. It seems that this was a premeditated lying talk scenario because of what happened to me on **December 10, 2013,** and the jacket that was taken from her, might have to do with whatever they think I stole on the days before **December 10, 2013**. No wonder why the $10.00 contribution I made was returned to me.

On **Sunday, May 11, 2014,** when doing the 28-precinct hub site, one of the prisoners told the other prisoner loud enough so I could hear that every time one updates (Software) the Samsung phone, they are able to look at your information, every time one updates. But the strange thing is that I have a Samsung phone and the day before, I updated my smartphone's software.

I walked home after work. After arriving home at approximately 8:45 am, I went to the grocery store, and as soon as I entered the grocery store, that I bought two Perrier drinks and a gallon of water, there entered a white man wearing a red t-shirt and he stood next to me. The young woman that works there and who always treats me with a good sense of humor, when I was ready to pay for my groceries, she gave me a serious look and treated me with indifference, as if I were a stranger. She behaved very formally towards me. The white man who was to my right seemed to be staring at me, while I looked at whatever it was in front of me. Then I walked out of the store.

I had planned to send some money to my mother. However, I neither called her nor sent her the money, because I knew that they were going to check whom I was going to send the money to and find her address. No matter how urgently I wanted to send her the money, I couldn't because I didn't want them to do to my parents what they were doing to me. Not my family for God's sake. To violate my parents' freedom, and right to privacy the same way that they are violating mines, no señor, no sir. They have the spying unit all over me, they are eavesdropping (to secretly listen to a conversation) on my conversations, and checking my daily habits, no sir, I wish that to no one.

On **Monday, May 12, 2014,** I arrived to the 28th precinct to do the 28-hub site (prisoners transport) and the Desk Sergeant there received me by standing straight, in formation, in attention, or as if ready to solute someone. He was standing the same way that Sgt. Kim, and Sgt. Bennett once did by standing straight at the Desk. I don't know what message they are trying to convey or send to me by doing that.

I told the officer at the 28-hub site that I was going to wait inside of the RMP (police vehicle). I said it just to make him, and the Sergeant come to an ease, and to make them feel less pressured, because of my presence there. One of the prisoners there was a white young man. One Hispanic prisoner said that I will be arrested for arresting a white man. When I returned to the 25th precinct, I saw Lt. Yaguchi arrives at the Desk. He saw me, but he didn't greet me. Sgt. Kim didn't greet me neither. The two of them just ignored me. Sgt. Bennett looked very serious. Lt. Yaguchi exchanged limited conversation with Sgt. Gibbs, and Sgt. Gibbs looked serious too.

More than a year ago, the 25 precinct was a good place to work, but this is no longer the case. Very unusual events are taking place there that is terrorizing me. There is something happening or has happened in the precinct that they don't want me to know or to be aware of. In the locker room, I saw that PO Gorman, who was on vacation, cut his vacation short just to go to court in the morning, which is strange, because when a person is on vacation, they are not bothered with court. Then I saw that PO Gorman received a call. He was talking to a woman whom I think is his wife. Then he said, "He is out." That means that I am out of the job. Later, PO Lugo saw me standing by the T/S and immediately, as soon as he saw me, he began looking and prying around the T/S. He behaved and acted as if he was trying to protect from me the valuable things that were around the T/S, as if I were a thief.

I went home, and in the bus, I saw a black man wearing red and another black man wearing a camo green pant. I got off the bus and so did the two of them. I went to my apartment. Then I came out of my apartment building and took the bus to the Mambi restaurant. Meanwhile, while on the bus, there were people wearing red and green. When I arrived at the restaurant, one of the waitresses who is used to greet me every time she sees me, this time she didn't. She completely ignored me, but she instead greeted one of the two men who had just entered the restaurant with me, and she told him that it is been a long time since the last time she saw him.

Then a group of men arrived. I paid close attention to the one who was wearing green pants. I knew that they were there because of me, and so did the two men who entered the restaurant with me, but I was not sure about those two men, because they didn't wear or carried the colors. Then I left the restaurant and entered Rite Aid. I greeted the cashier who I knew back at college. I bought my Claritin and a shaving Foam Gillette, and when I grabbed the shaving Foam Gillette item, a man entered the store wearing a green t-shirt and he walked by me. He looked Hispanic.

Later, when I was paying at the cashier, I spoke to the cashier in Spanish, but then I looked to the side, and there was a white man behind me wearing what it seemed to be a green t-shirt. But I think that he was a different man, a white man. The cashier responded to me in English and was being very formal. Then she passed me the receipt, and the time on the receipt was 11:14 AM. I left feeling very sad. Then I went to the bus stop and there was a white woman waiting for the bus. Later came a man dressed in a suit. Then another white guy walked by. She took the same bus I took. Then inside the bus, I found a white woman who was wearing green. I arrived home knowing not what to do, but cry.

Here I am taking this daily mental and physical abuses, because their presence, their behavior and words are killing me from inside out. Those words, questions, answers, and statements are like physical punches to my body. Why do I have to keep bearing this daily mental stress, emotional distress? Emotional prison where I find no escape. I must keep on doing the walk of shame for something that I didn't do. But what am I being blamed for?

In the afternoon of **Wednesday, May 14, 2014**, I went to do the laundry, and when I was folding my dried clothing, a woman who was wearing a green jacket stood to my right and she began folding her clothing. Then she left, but minutes later she came back, and she asked to herself in Spanish, "I donde esta mi llave?" which translated into English is, "Where is my key?" while wondering around as she looked for her key, and then she left. Minutes later, another woman came by, and she found a small sock. She asked me if it was mine, and I told her, "No."

On **Thursday, May 15, 2014,** I went to work. PO Banks had a robbery arrest near the precinct. The perpetrator he arrested was wearing a green jacket, and a red book bag, and the purse that he had robbed was red. The victim was wearing red clothing. It was a well-planned scenario.

On this day, I was told to take Officer Jenkins' uniform, place it inside his locker, and to bring his civilian cloths over to St. Luke's Hospital, where he was being treated for injuries, he sustained after chasing an escaped prisoner. In addition, I was sent to do the narco run (to transport narcotics) to PBMN (Patrol Borough Manhattan North). After doing all that, I immediately went to the 28-hub site. Upon my arrival, I walked by the 28 precinct Desk, but the Sergeant was not there. So, I walked to the 28-hub site.

When I was done from giving my information to the officer, I turned around, and I saw the Desk Sergeant facing me, and looking angry at me. He asked me where I was. After I explained to him where I was, he angrily told me that I was going to transport a female prisoner to

181

Manhattan Central Booking, and after doing that, I was going to go back there and transport the other prisoners. And all he said, he said it with an attitude. It was obvious that he hated my presence there. Why not transport them at the same time, obviously, the female prisoner in our police car, and the other prisoners in the van, as it is always done. Why waste two hours of a trip when this can be done at the same time. We have done it before. But of course, during those two hours, he will not have me around the 28-precinct.

In addition, he rushed me out of the precinct, and police officer Napolitano (The officer assigned to do the transport with me), who is from the 23rd precinct, and who was talking to the other officers, had to rush and take the female prisoner out of the cell. In the RMP (police vehicle), while doing the transport, the officer asked me if I had done something wrong to the Sergeant, because of how he treated me. I told him that I hadn't done anything to him.

At MCB (Manhattan Central Booking), the other officers that did the transport of the other prisoners walked to me and told me what a bad Sergeant he is, and not to worry about him, because he was leaving to the day tour, as per the duty Captain, and that his last day was going to be on the 23rd of this month. When I arrived at the 25th precinct, Sgt. Lucic asked me how I was treated at the 28th precinct, and that I was his hero. I do wonder what I did to deserve this. What I did to him or to anyone. This confirms that there are some bad rumors about me.

Then I went to DMV traffic court at the Northern Manhattan Traffic Violations Bureau, and one of the DMV TVB (Traffic Violation Bureau) defense lawyers (or if not lawyers, they are the ones that advocate on behalf of those who have been summoned) told me, while staring at me on the eyes, or having his eyes fixed on me, that his IPAD or IPOD was stolen and he asked me what he most do to report it. He said that he knows who did it, and then he stared at the other defense lawyer on the eyes as well, and the other defense lawyer said, "Why do you look at me like that, I didn't do it."

But I do ask myself the same question too. Why did he look at me like that by opening his eyes wide open, and saying that he knows who did it? Then the other defense lawyer began with the famous cough again, the dry cough. This is indeed mentally draining or am I just being weak? Do I must keep bearing and carrying this weight that doesn't belong to me or is this just life? Should I just get used to this type of treatment? Or as somebody once told me that life isn't fair. But it really hurts so badly. It hurts a lot.

On **Friday, May 16, 2014,** I was at work with PO Rivera. He got inside the RMP (police car) and as I drove away, he began looking for his Memo-Book (Memorandum Pad/Activity Log) binder. He said that he was sure that he had placed it on the windshield. He looked at the back seat and inside the trunk, but he couldn't find it. Then he came back to the RMP (police car) and he told me that he had to go to the bathroom. I noticed that he was nervous, because he was continuously moving or shaking his legs. He felt the urge to use the bathroom, so we drove back to the station house (precinct).

Then he said that he might have left it on top of the RMP (police car). When we arrived, he looked again inside the trunk and there he found it. He no longer wanted to use the bathroom. The motive why he wanted to go to the bathroom might have to do with them recording our conversations since the RMP (police car) and/or he is being bugged. I saw red wires on the floor of the front passenger seat and two holes on the interior ceiling of the RMP (police car).

When I came out of work at 0821 hrs. or 8:21 am, I passed the turnstile of the subway station at East 116 Street and Lexington Avenue to take the # 6 train. But while I swiped my metro card that I went through the turnstile, while the train was stopping, as I was expecting, a young kid wearing a red sweater jumped the turnstile. I was certain that it was another scenario, and they wanted to know how I was going to respond. I didn't look directly at him when he did it. I looked at him sideways because I knew what was going on. Then the train opened the door, and I decided to enter the next wagon, different from the one that I expected the kid to enter, and it was like he followed me like a magnet, because he rushed to the same door that I was heading to, and we entered.

When I came out of the # 6 train that I took the # 4 train, inside the wagon, there was a man next to me, to my right, and he began to talk about Jesus Christ and that Jesus is coming. Then he talked about the football player Hernandez (which has the same last name that I have) that killed the man and how he was going to serve 15 years in prison. He talked about how he should repent. Then he said to stop being a hypocrite and repent. It seemed that he was making indirect accusations against me, but God sees everything, and he is my witness, my peace, so I looked at some pictures from the movie, "The Passion of Christ" that I had on my smartphone and I saw how my Lord was wrongfully accused and beaten to death.

Then I thought about how we as follower of Jesus Christ, must endure everything for the love of his name, and it gives me peace and comfort, because as the bible says, "...no servant is greater than his master." But my heart, my suffering heart is having some strange palpitation. Isn't this torture? Pure agony?

On **Friday, May 16, 2014, for Saturday, May 17, 2014,** Lt. Allen made a comment at roll call (where officers' assignments are given) about officers that come in to work, but don't want to do any work. That during their 8:35 hour shift they want to do nothing and then go home without having done anything. He compared that to collecting a welfare check.

Even though he didn't mention my name, I felt that he was referring to me, so I became so upset at his comment that I had to wonder how he wants me to be motivated to work when I am being treated unfairly by all of them. They are saying things about me that are not true, and they keep constantly harassing me. Many of the officers noticed my demeanor after he made that comment. PO Banks advised me to pay him no mind because Lt. Allen spent most of his time upstairs sleeping. Yeah right. I wonder if listening to my conversations upstairs. Then when I went inside the RMP (police car), already upset at Lt. Allen's comment, just because I and my partner didn't get the initiative summonses, I made a comment and my partner PO Rivera responded to my comment by saying, "I know you directed the comment at **us**."

After our meal, PO Rivera went to the bathroom, and I waited a moment inside the RMP (police car) finally all by myself. Then he came back to the RMP (police car). When he entered the RMP (police car), I asked him, "Did you go to the bathroom and did your thing?" I guess he realized what I meant. Then as I was driving PO Rivera, he pointed at one man who was wearing a black hat and he said to me, "That's not the color of the hat he is supposed to wear. He should be collared (arrested) for that," and I laughed because I knew well what he meant by that.

To change our conversation, and our mood, I told him that we should do twelve hours shift instead of the 8:35 hours work a day that we normally do, and his response was that if that were the case, he would end up shocking me. Also, when he asked me to pass him his Memo-Book (Memorandum Pad/Activity Log) binder, playing around, I grabbed it and held out of the window with my left hand as if I were going to drop it or toss it out of the window, and he said, " Yeah, you have been doing that all the time."

On my way home, walking up the hill, I saw three men seated on the bench and one of them was wearing red. Then on the route that I usually take to go up the hill every day, there was a pair of white shoes positioned parallel or opposite to the three man who were seated on the bench, and I continued walking. On one occasion, I heard PO Rivera tell someone, "… place the handcuffs on him and you will see how he will begin to sing opera."

On **Friday, May 16, 2014, for Saturday, May 17, 2014,** when I arrived at the station house, to feel better, I said to PO Chiodi in the locker room, "It is been a rainfall of blessing for me. Can you stop the rain from falling?"

On **Saturday, May 17, 2014, Sunday, May 18, 2014,** when I arrived at the station house (precinct), that I entered the muster room, I saw plenty of food on the table. Later I found out that Lt. Allen had bought it for us, because he felt sorry for what he said the previous day at the roll call. But I know that it was because of how I reacted or responded to his comment. What I had said, which made everyone concerned. No wonder everyone there was so friendly to me as well. PO Quinones, PO Gambardeli, PO Rivera and PO Banks were so friendly to me that they ate from the same small bottle of peanuts that I had bought.

Then we had a supposed GLA (Grand Larceny Auto) at 125 east street and 2nd avenue and the complainant was wearing a red sweater.

On **Sunday, May 18, 2014, for Monday, May 19, 2014,** I went to do the barriers, which were assigned to me on May 16, 2014. Five of us were assigned to one truck to pick up the barriers. One of them who seemed to be of Chinese descendant, was wearing a green t-shirt. It appeared that he was working for IAB (Internal Affairs Bureau). During the entire trip, and in the entire time that we were doing our work, we were all quiet, except for a few questions answered among us.

Later, on our meal, when we walked out for dinner, I saw PO Rivera talking to one of the officers who was from the 24th precinct. They were talking to one another, but when I got closer to them, they looked at me at the same time and immediately they stopped talking. After the barriers, I had to go to court, so I had my suit bag hanging on one of the metal barriers. Then at 0642 hrs. or 6:42 am, one of the officers who was wearing a camo book bag stood right next to my bag. PO Rivera, who was next to me, to my right, kept looking at him standing, and leaning on the metal barrier that was next to my bag. Then at approximately 0707 hrs. or 7:07 am, one of the officers who was wearing a red sweater stood next to me to my left as if to listen to our conversation. This is ridiculous.

When I got home, I slept all day because I was too tired. There is too much tension in my life.

On **Tuesday, May 20, 2014,** I paid a visit to the park, and while I was jogging there, almost at every corner of the park, there they were, on bicycles, wearing red and some wearing green, and some others were walking around and inside the park. Not even in the park could I find peace. This same day my mother called me asking me for money, and that she was not eating right. When I got home, my wife told me that I would die alone, and that she would not give me a child, because she doesn't want her child to have a father who thinks that everybody is following him.

On **Wednesday, May 21, 2014,** I went to the gym and there they were again. I ran on the treadmill and to my far right there was a woman wearing red and she was running as well. When I was done running, I went to the bathroom and there was a Hispanic guy wearing a red hat. He said to himself, "Getting fire on my day off." Being that this is my day off and by him making that statement, he made me angry and that's why I had to say, "This year might be good for you, but you never know about next year." Then he walked to me, and he washed his hands. Then I said, "It is like receiving slashes on my back."

Then I walked downstairs and there was a black man wearing full red doing the same workout I normally do, which are pushups and pull ups. There were men wearing green too. At approximately 1210 hrs. or 12:10 pm, I became so agitated that I had to make some nonsense, and when I did, immediately out of the group, one of them who was wearing red, decided to leave, so he walked upstairs. However, there I was fuming, because according to them, I am a suspect, but they are treating me as if I were a convict. Have I no right to be upset? Am I not a human being?

When I walked out of the gym, at the corner of the street, at the side of the grocery store, there were two women. One of them was wearing red and the other woman was wearing green, and when I walked by them, I said loud enough so they could hear, "That is not healthy." Then I walked to the nearby court house building that is located a block away from the gym, and I stood in front of it by the stairs, and by standing in the middle of the court house, and by staring at it, like for a minute or for a brief moment, I was hoping that they could get the message that whatever it is that they are doing to me is totally unconstitutional. Then I walked away hoping they understood what I meant by it. When I arrived at the building that is connected to my building, I went inside the elevator and when coming out on the first floor, there I saw a guy wearing green. Then I walked to take the next elevator to my apartment.

What a miserable life is the one that I am living. When I walk to my wife to tell her what is going on, what she tells me is that I need to see a psychologist. She says that I am suffering from delirium persecution, because I think that everybody is following me. She says that I am sick and that she is afraid of me. She tells me that I did nothing to them for them to follow me. I am so tired of all of this. Can't they see all the harm they are doing to me? When are they going to learn when to stop? It is causing me ulcers in my stomach. I am so exhausted. Do they want me dead, or they hope that I kill myself? I believe that all of them are setting me up for failure, preferring my death.

But what else can I say. Unfortunately, as a New York City Police Officer, as a city employee, as a public servant that I am, I don't govern myself, they govern me. They scrutinize everything I do, even in what direction my eyeballs move. But I cannot say anything. I cannot speak up. I cannot scream or cry out because according to them I must not have any feelings.

But all this suffering, and pain, I must bear and endure until God, and who else knows when. To know that I am not entitled to privacy really saddens me. By traveling by plane and going to the park, I thought that I was going to have some safe space, and to realize that, neither that, is it truly depressing. Where are my fundamental rights if I have any? I guess I have none, because they are overdoing it. I am under surveillance 24/7 and this is really consuming my life. I am being so violated. But I need to get paid.

On **Thursday, May 22, 2014, for Friday, May 23, 2014,** I went to work, living behind my wife who was complaining about me, because she cannot imagine what I am going through. She has no idea.

When I arrived at my workplace, there I saw PO Gorman looking on top of a locker and he said something about people taking stuff. I saw that there was a brown bench in front of my locker. He said that it was in the hallway, so he took it and brought it there. He said that it might belong in the female locker room, and he walked away. His head was as red as a red balloon. My partner PO Alvin Rivera arrived, and he greeted PO Gorman and PO Gomez, except me. Every time that we are on patrol that I hear him cough, I consider it to be a sign of something important that was altered or is about to be said for the records, since I am being recorded. On patrol, we remained quiet for a few hours. He spoke to me, but I didn't answer back.

At the end of the tour, he told me that I have been training him for hell. I do not know if he said that because I was making his job harder or because of those who are training him and preparing him to ask me political, controversial, and compromising questions, while expecting a conflicting, compromising, controversial, polemical, self-incriminating and destructive response or answer from me to destroy my career. In a few words, they only hope that I give them just a suicidal answer, which will be recorded, and later be shown to the public, which will give them legal ground and right to have me fired in dishonor and disgrace.

For example, he was blaming the rich, but I told him not to judge me because I am wealthy. We went to get coffee, and he told me that the woman that works in the bakery doesn't like him and that she always walks away every time she sees him. Then I told him that she walks away, because she dislikes seeing what PO Rivera is doing to PO Hernandez. When walking upstairs he said to himself, "Who should I collar now to make over time?" I knew he was referring to me. So, I told PO Rivera that the people there are afraid to speak up. He told me that the same happens at the 25th precinct, where people are afraid to speak up too, and that if they do, they will get changed to another tour. He said that they are in fear to speak up. No wonder why he said that Lt. Yaguchi has the power to do that and far more damage if it needs be.

Wow, I feel so, but so discouraged now that I am typing this on this **Thursday afternoon of May 28, 2014, at 3:07 pm**. The reason why I am typing this, three days after the day of the occurrence, is because on **May 25, 2014,** I made an arrest, and I ended up working 22 hours straight, non-stop. Then between **May 26, 2014, and May 27, 2014,** I worked 16:50 hours straight, non-stop, and now is the chance that I must type this out of the notes I take each day, which explains each of the events that take place daily, and that I am narrating almost daily. Thankfully, now I have the time for today is my day off. Also, today I am going to type down what happened on the **26th and the 27th of May**.

So, on **Sunday, May 25, 2014,** I was on patrol with PO Rivera when he made a comment about white woman being in Harlem and the possibility of them getting raped in Harlem. Right away, I knew that he made that malicious comment to hurt me, waiting to see if I came to agree with him or that I may say something negative to later crucify me. Such a comment made me so angry that I stopped talking to him. Then when we headed to the precinct for our meal, I slammed the door of the RMP (police car) hard, and furiously I greeted PO Jones.

"They lie to one another; they speak with flattering lips and deceptive hearts." (Psalm 12:2 HCSB)

"My heart races, my strength leaves me, and even the light of my eyes has faded. My loved ones and friends stand back from my affliction, and my relatives stand at a distance. Those who seek my life set traps, and those who want to harm me threaten to destroy me; they plot treachery all day long. I am like a deaf person; I do not hear. I am like a speechless person who does not open his mouth. I am like a man who does not hear and has no arguments in his mouth. I put my hope in You, Lord; You will answer, Lord my God. For I said, "'Don't let them rejoice over me — those who are arrogant toward me when I stumble." For I am about to fall, and my pain is constantly with me.'" (Psalm 38:10-17 HCSB)

By the time we arrived at the front Desk, PO Rivera told me that I had no magazine in my gun. I checked and saw that my gun had no magazine. Immediately, I skipped my meal and went in search of my magazine. I went to the places that I previously visited from the time I began my tour. I couldn't find it. Then I drove to 1PP (1 Police Plaza= Police Headquarter) and I couldn't find it there neither. Then we were told to go to the station house (precinct), and on our way there, we had a vehicle accident at 116 East Street. We responded to the location, and it was an intoxicated driver who had hit another vehicle. I ended up being an arresting officer.

At that point I was so disoriented because I couldn't find my magazine, and now I had to deal with this job. Surprisingly, Sgt. Hernandez arrived at the scene, and she handed me over to my magazine, which was found in the supervisor's RMP (police car). I was completely disoriented. Later, we went to the 28th precinct, and when I began doing my paperwork, PO Rivera and PO Quinones were standing right next to me as if they were supervising all my paperwork. I was looking for, almost begging for somebody else to take the arrest, but my supervisor, Sgt. Gibbs, told PO Rivera by phone that he would like me to take it. PO Ahmed and PO Rivera were volunteering to take it, but over the phone, our supervisor was telling PO Rivera that he preferred me to take it, so I had no other choice than to take it.

How was I able to concentrate when having the two of them, PO Rivera and PO Quinones, staring at what I was doing, and not only that, at the same time, I was being aware that I was being recorded. The defendant said something, and PO Rivera said, "Let him talk, the more he talks the more he buries himself to hell." I was terrified at his statement for those same harsh words he might be using when referring to me every time he talks to others concerning me. My focus was 75% on them and 25% on what I was doing on my arrest paperwork. How could I concentrate? They began to tell me, "…no, not that page, no, the other …" ect, etc. and I truly looked like a dummy who had never filled out those arrest paperwork forms before.

When I arrived at the station house (precinct), there were PO Quinones seated with me. He was trying to see faults and mistakes on my paperwork to later point out my incompetence, so those who are or will be listening to our recorded conversation, may know about it. PO Rivera went home without saying goodbye to me. I suspect that he is holding something against me. After long hours of vouchering and of dealing with the entire arrest process, I received a call from the Manhattan ADA (Assistant District Attorney). I was completely mentally and physically exhausted, and totally drained, because of all the things that are happening in my miserable life at work. The job that I once loved to do has now become my worst nightmare.

Just on that day of work I went through moments of panic, distress and frustration. I am living in agony. On that day I worked from **2315 hrs. till 2115 hrs. or lets say from 11:15 pm till 9: 15 pm the next day, which is a total of 22 hours straight**, none stop, because I didn't even get a chance to have my meal or break, because my mealtime was interrupted by my search for my missing magazine. In this job, meals are a privilege.

It was either **Friday, May 23, 2014, for Saturday, May 24, 2014, or on Saturday, May 24, 2014, for Sunday, May 25, 2014**. It was a very rough day for me. The heavy rain was coming down hard. I went to work, and when I arrived at the subway station at East 125 Street and Lexington Avenue, that I was waiting there for the # 6 train to take me to East 116 street, at approximately 10:55 pm, I decided not to wait for the # 6 train, so I rather walked to the precinct from East 125 street.

When I looked at the stairway to walk upstairs, I saw something that looked like a woman's bag in between the two stairways. I became so angry and confused because I knew that they had planted it there (since they know that I always stop there) just to see what I was going to do with it, for they suspect that I am a thief. So, I walked further down and took the other stairway up. When I reached the top platform, I did a clockwise move to see which exit I should take out of the four exits, because I took a different stairway. I was already upset.

When I arrived at the precinct, there was PO Arroyo and PO Gorman. However, PO Arroyo was wearing Camo pants like the one that my followers are wearing. Then PO Chiodi arrived. One of them said, "You better hide your umbrella," and PO Gorman replied, "Especially now," and PO Arroyo said, "Yes, there are thieves among us." I know they were directing those comments to me.

Later on, patrol, PO Gorman drove next to my RMP (police car) and I jokingly told him, "You look like you just woke up," and he said, "And what happened with the 511 (arrest for suspended license)? Were you afraid?" and he rapidly drove away laughing. He said that because there was a check point being conducted. I am afraid that he is right, thanks to all the things that are happening in my life. But I have no one to talk to, but God who is more than sufficient. God is giving me the strength, faith and confidence to bear and persevere. I cannot tell what I feel to any one of them, because I know that I am being recorded and being heard by many who are listening to every word that comes out of my mouth. I feel like having a gun pointed to my head, where the moment that I say the wrong thing, the trigger will be pulled, but as long as I have God on my side, everything will be ok, for I have wronged no one.

Knowing not what to do, and being in total despair, I called PO Fuentes to see if he had talked to his supervisors at 1PP Head Quarter Security Unit concerning me, so I could be transferred to work there permanently, but he didn't answer his phone. It might be because of all the false rumors and bad propagandas that are circulating and propagated concerning me, which might have landed on his ears and as a result, he no longer wants to talk to a person of such reputation or as PO Maher once said to me, "I don't want to associate with criminals." He never called me back. **According to the NYPD Patrol Guide, police officers are not allowed to associate with someone "2. c. Reasonably believed to be engaged in, likely to engage in, or to have engaged in criminal activities."**

I, in great desperation, went to 1PP (1 Police Plaza= Police Headquarter) and submitted my application to work there.

RANK _PO_ FULL NAME (L, F) _HERNANDEZ, EMMANUEL_   DATE _11/11/2014_

TAX _944269_ SHIELD _2830_ DATE APPT. _07/3/2007_ CMD. _025_

SOC. SEC. NO. _053-80-7664_ (mm/dd/yyyy)   D.O.B. _09/21/1981_ AGE _32_

     (mm/dd/yyyy) NAME OF IMMEDIATE SUPV. _SGT. GILES_

ADDRESS _930 Ogden Avenue, Bronx, NY 10452_   CELL _(917)640-9317_

MAR. STATUS _Married_ RES. PCT. _044_   RES. CO. _Ref. Ins. Huntington_ HOME TEL _(917)962-9899_

CMD. TEL _(212)860-6511 T/S_   SQ./CHT. _A1_   TOUR PREFERRED _ANY_

     6551 Desk
DISCIPLINARY RECORD _? CD's in MY entire career as Police Officer_

SUSPENDED FROM DUTY / PLACED ON MOD. ASSIGN.? _NO_

CURRENTLY UNDER INVESTIGATION (FED. / STATE / CITY)? _NO_

CHARGES & SPECS. PENDING? _NO_   ON PROM. LIST? _NO_

SCHOOLS ATTENDED / DEGREES _La Guardia Community College (AA) Associate, John Jay College (B.A,_
     liberal arts).   _(criminal justice)_

REASON REQUESTING TRANSFER TO HQSU _To explore different avenues in the NYPD._

EXPERIENCE _Have been doing HRSU details for years._

DEPT. QUALIFCIATIONS (SCOOTER, ETC.) _RMP_

SPECIAL SKILLS (LANGUAGE, E.M.T., TECHNICAL, ETC.) _Bilingual (Spanish)_

MILITARY SERVICE: ACTIVE / RESERVE / VETERAN ETC. _NO_

BRANCH / RANK _N/A_   UPCOMING DRILL DATES, ETC. _N/A_

VACATION SELECTION, JURY DUTY, ETC. _9/12/2014 - 9/16/2014._

HAVE YOU EVER BEEN DENIED ASSIGNMENT(S)? _No_

REASON(S): _N/A_

LIST ALL PREVIOUS COMMANDS, BEGINNING WITH THE MOST RECENT: _025 PCT Since_
July 2008, and Impact Response Team (IRT) PBBN in Brooklyn
for six months.

*** IF SPACE IS INSUFFICIENT FOR ANY QUESTION, USE REVERSE SIDE ***

FORWARD COMPLETED APPLICATION WITH COPIES OF LAST THREE (3) PERFORMANCE EVALUATIONS
TO THE HEADQUARTERS SECURITY UNIT, POLICE HEADQUARTERS, ROOM 152G

Last year, I was so desperate to get out of the 25 precinct that I
did the same by going and submitting my application to 1PP (1 Police

Plaza= Police Headquarter), because I could foresee what was coming and how dangerous it was going to turn out to be if I remained there. Unfortunately, they didn't pick me up. Also, I applied to be transferred to the 26th precinct, but nothing has come up.

Now, here I am standing, hoping that God may turn all my bad circumstances around and make it work for good, for his kingdom, his glory and for everyone to see that he is almighty God, who works in mysterious ways and who blesses those who he wants to richly bless abundantly, and he is my God. In the middle of all this is very hard to smile, but I trust in my God, for he is my rock.

"Cast your burden on the Lord, and He will sustain you; He will never allow the righteous to be shaken." (Psalm 55:22 HCSB)

On **Sunday, May 25, 2014,** my mother called me again to tell me how much she needs me to send her some money for her high blood pressure medications. I told her that I would send her the money.

In the afternoon of **Monday, May 26, 2014,** I was at work. I was assigned to a 4x12 detail. At his office, Lt. Yaguchi was supposedly accommodating me and PO Quinones by assigning us to work at a good location. Supposedly, he was looking out for us. Then PO Quinones made a joke while tapping his index finger several times on one of his ears. He was putting emphasis on the real reason why the two of us were accommodated as we worked together: That Lt. Yaguchi will be listening to our conversation.

At night, at approximately 2330 hrs. or 11:30 pm, PO Stephanski walked into the muster room, and he told me, "You are in deep sh…t" and PO Gorman said, "Especial Category." Nobody said anything else. Then Sgt. Hernandez told me to stay inside. For me to do whatever I want, and to go and rest since I did a double. Then, during the moment that I was doing the T/S (Tele-Switchboard), PO Maher stood quietly right next to me. He was staring at me in a very rude way, chewing his gum noticeably.

On **Tuesday, May 27, 2014,** I went to see Manhattan ADA McDonald (Assistant District Attorney) in regards to a case, and when I reached the seventh floor, I walked by ADA Altman's office holding my breath, hoping that she didn't see me. Then when I was done talking to ADA McDonald that I walked by ADA Altman's office again, I held my breath and when I was almost by the elevator, there I came almost face to face with the other Assistant District Attorney who has his desk next to ADA Altman and who had witnessed the mistakes I made on the DWI (Driving While Intoxicated) case. He looked at me and as soon he saw me, he lowered his head, and he walked past me without saying a word. It has been five months since that day, but for me, it feels like it happened yesterday. I cannot forget that moment. I am still deeply hurt from that terrible experience of **December 10, 2013.** To this day, I am still living with the consequences.

On **Tuesday, May 27, 2014,** my mother called me again. She was telling me to please send her some money. I told her that I would, and this time, I was going to. The next day on May 28, 2014, I went to Mateo Express, and I sent her $200 dollars, the money that I so longed to send her. I sent her the money at 17:59 hrs. or 5:59 pm. Finally, I did it, even though they will investigate and find out to whom I have sent the money to, I sent it, and even though my parents and my family's privacy might start to be violated, which I so dearly wanted to protect, I did send her the money. All I have to say is that I am sorry, dear mother, your privacy has just cost you $200 dollars, and this is what I wanted to prevent.

Then I went to Rite Aid and at 6:30 pm, I bought Claritin for my allergy, and when I did, immediately I saw someone wearing a camo shorts. He was just there to see what I was doing there or to see if I took something. This is very frustrating. Then I went to the Venezuelan eating place to buy a Cachapa. I ordered my food and suddenly, some youngsters came over and the place became crowded. Many of them were spying on me. So, I had to go somewhere else to eat my food, and where else than to the nearby park.

When I sat on a bench at the J. Hood Wright Park located at 174th street that I was staring at the beautiful view of the George Washington Bridge, I saw a young white woman arrive and she walked right by me as I was eating, probably just to see what I was doing there. Then she left. Also, a man came and left, and later two guys came over.

Then I went to church and there I saw a drunk church member. He had green on his shirt, and he was holding a smartphone that had a red cover. Immediately, I realized that it was part of another scenario. There was another church member who was overreacting to the drunk member's behavior, because he was interrupting the preacher. He was acting as if he was going to fight the drunk member. He was wearing red too, which made me conclude that it was part of another act. Then I saw another church member, N…, and he was wearing a green t-shirt, and there was another church member who was wearing a red t-shirt. I felt as if being surrounded by wolves, even inside the church. It is like one of the songs of Tupac Shakur that says, "All Eyes on Me."

Then I greeted G… and I told him that I wished to talk to him. He told me that he was going to practice (rehearse with musical instrument and the quire) now. So, I left having no one to talk to. But I returned to buy a sandwich and a drink to the intoxicated church member, and I paid for a taxi to take him home. Then I saw that G… finished the rehearsal. I swallowed my pride and shame, for I needed to talk to somebody. I walked to him, and I accompanied G… to the bus stop, but I wasn't able to express my frustration to him, because one of the church members was with us and he was wearing red too. He had never walked with us to the bus stop, but for some unknown reason, this time, he did.

On **Friday, May 30, 2014**, since PO Rivera had an arrest, I offered him a cup of coffee, but he said, "No" that he was ok. I insisted telling him that I will and he said, "No" again. Once more I told him that I was going to bring him the coffee, and finally he said, "Oh boy." Later that day, I saw Lt. Yaguchi who had The Grinch type of smile on his face, and he asked me how I felt, and I answered, "I feel like Rocky." Then he asked me, "Why, Is everything ok?" Two days later, a female was arrested, and she was wearing a t-shirt that had the picture of Rocky on it. Are you kidding me?

This is **Saturday, May 31, 2014**. I was at the 25 precincts when my Lieutenant told Sgt. Lucic, "You can be nice only once." I was assigned to do the 28-hub site. When I got there, there were few cops gathered and everyone there was quietly looking at me. When I transported the prisoners to MCB (Manhattan Central Booking), that I brought them to see the EMS-EMT (Emergency Medical Technician), the EMT who knows me there told me, "…the expedite … working 14 hours … they are looking to hang some people there. Ok, get out of here." Now I am really preoccupied. It seems that something evil, and unexpected is coming to me, which has to do with the ADA's (Assistant District Attorney) effort to bring charges me.

This is the point or the moment in my life that I wish I didn't have a family, so they won't see nor hear and suffer for what I am going through. There is no one, not one person standing up for me at work. Perhaps someone is, but not that I know of. It seems that the people that are following me have been hired by an institution or organization to do some kind of spy work on me. This gives the participants a sense of belonging to something big, new, unusual, and special, which also gives them a sense of self-worth and of social responsibility. They seem to use methods of identification and communication. They hire people of all ages, race, gender, culture, religion, sexual orientation and disability, including those with criminal records or criminal background.

But what really kills me is that my colleagues keep it to themselves. They have kept it secret by not informing me, because they expect me to fall victim to their demise. They prepare themselves for every scenario, and as for me, they expect me to fall, to fail, to hit myself hard on concrete. There is no compassion for me, but that of hate and malice, filled with hypocrisy. I can see that this tactic can lower crime drastically, because society is now involved, but when it is applied to an innocent man, it becomes a crime. I am clearly their target, and they have gone as far as to recruit members of my own church to serve their evil purpose.

Chapter 13

June 2014 Events

On **Monday, June 2, 2014,** things were going well at work, well, not so well because PO Byrd and PO Banks seemed to be not too happy to see me. PO Banks looked at me with a sad and pitiful face, but he greeted me anyway, but not with the same happy face and enthusiasm that he once did. PO Banks, I wish you had known the truth of my innocence. But I do have a small sense of hope that makes me believe that deep inside of you, you still believe in me. I know that you are feeling bad for me, because of all the atrocities they are making for me. PO Gloria Byrd doesn't even want to see me, and it makes me feel so bad.

Meanwhile, PO Rivera and I headed to a 53 (Vehicle Accident) at 122 street and 1st Avenue. After we were done with the job that we arrived at the station house (precinct), there was PO Jones staring at me, and finally he told me that somebody wanted to talk to me. When I saw who it was, it was the defendant of the DWI (Driving While Intoxicated) arrest I made on the 25th.

He had come back to pick up his properties and his pair of earrings. I went to the property room and found his property and I gave it to him. Immediately, I saw the 25 precinct Commanding Officer, Captain Thomas Harnisch. He was around the Desk, and suddenly, Lt. Yaguchi appeared in the picture. PO Rivera showed up. I became emotionally disturbed because of how come that all of them showed up at the same time. I believed that their presence there was because they don't trust me, and they knew that me and the defendant were meeting because the precinct is wired or lets say bugged, and all because of one man, me.

Then I took the owner of the vehicle with me to see his car, because he said that he had something in the car that I didn't find in the car. At the same time, I saw PO Rivera walking by us. Then PO Rivera stood next to me, for I knew that he was sent to see what was going on. At first, I wanted PO Rivera to go with him to destroy any suspicion, because I knew that it was going to create suspicion, but since PO Rivera was ready to go home, I didn't ask. But he came with us anyway. When the owner looked inside the car, he opened something that I didn't open when I searched for the car, and he got his documents out of the compartment that is located where one lays the arm to rest, as well as other belongings.

Then I went back to the station house (precinct) and there went PO Rivera with us. But still, I wanted PO Rivera there because I wanted him to be my witness. I was so disoriented by the lack of trust, so much that the Captain and Lt. Yaguchi had to be around, and PO Rivera had to follow me.

Then I observed that Lt. Yaguchi greeted PO Rivera with great enthusiasm, and he told PO Rivera to pick any date for CRV (easy overtime) that he would give it to him. It preoccupied me, because I didn't know what he had just done to harm me, for he has just been rewarded (paid) with easy overtime. I don't know what I did or have said that made PO Rivera gain favor on the eyes of Lt. Yaguchi. I cannot say anything because it could be dangerous. But great is my God who has allowed this to happen to me.

As part of my commute, I took the bus, I believe it was bus #6246, and seating in the bus on my way to the Mambi restaurant to eat my breakfast, at approximately 0935 hrs. or 9:35 am, there was a woman seating in front of me. She began to sing. I decided to pay attention to the song that she was singing. Then she stopped singing and in Spanish she said, "Si te preguntan algo, tu no tienes que contestarles," which translated into English is, "If they ask you something, you don't have to answer them." Wow, I believed that she was trying to communicate something to me. But she was not wearing anything red or green. Then I saw that out of her bag, she took out a big red container and she drank from it. Also, her smartphone cover was red. Then I was like, "I see."

Walking to the restaurant, I passed by a man who was talking to another man, and he said, "... un cellular. Pueden darle hasta veinte años por eso," which translated into English, "... a cellphone. They can give him even twenty years for that." When I arrived at the restaurant, the only thing I needed for them to do was to yell at me, "Surprise," because a few of them were there waiting for me, for I visit that restaurant very often and every time I go there,

I go at the same time. Many of them were wearing red T-shirts, and others Camo hat and pants. Now I wonder if people are intentionally saying things loud enough for me to hear whether to help me by keeping me informed of what is going on, or to make me fail and fall, by thinking that I will overreact to it nervously and confess to something that I didn't do, all by spitting poisonous words to my ears.

On **Tuesday, June 2, 2014-Wednesday, June 3, 2014,** I saw PO Banks doing his activity report with a sad look on his face. He was asked if he was ok, and he said that he had allergies. It broke my heart to see the way in which he was looking at me. PO Rivera and I went to the 711 store to buy coffee as usual.

When we entered the place, that we were getting our coffee, there were two men talking in their native language, which wasn't English nor Spanish. PO Rivera told me that they were the Pharisees, but I told him that it was he himself who was selling me out and was being paid with good overtime. Then lowering his tone of voice, he said, "Yaguchi," and he walked away from me.

Then we did a vertical, and when walking down the stairs, suddenly, he told me that the job doesn't care about me. He said that I can easily be replaced. That there are, I believe he said like 600 others waiting to take my position. He said that the job doesn't matter about me. That job can replace me with a heartbeat. That they have somebody to take my spot right away. That the only one who care about me is my family, because in my family, I am the only cop. But I wonder why he didn't say "us" or "we"? In a few words, what he meant was that I am replaceable, that I am just a number, and that the Department doesn't value me. In a few words, I am worth nothing to the NYPD.

Then he asked me about wine and if I drink wine, or the Malta drink and that the Malta has alcohol, and that wine has more alcohol level than the beer. Then I asked him if people think that I am drinking something containing alcohol just because they see me holding a bottle of mineral water Perrier mixed with grape juice. I can't believe this. They are really trying to get me in trouble. About Malta, I bought a Malta Alemana drink I believe it to be, "Lowenbrau Hamburg," for my wife who had text me to buy her one. She needed the drink because she was bleeding a lot and was feeling anemic. This proves that they are following every move.

It seems that PO Byrd doesn't want to talk to me. It was confirmed when PO Rivera told me that it looked like PO Byrd doesn't want to talk to us. Later, I saw PO Byrd and I called her aside. I asked her if she was ok, but she told me that she was fine, that she simply had allergies. The same answer that PO Banks gave me. Then as she walked away from me, she told me that I have wanted to steal her 1PP (1 Police Plaza= Police Headquarter) assignments.

Sgt. Gibbs is disappointed in me because of my lack of productivity. He told me, "…Do you want me to be changed to day tour? Do you want to get me fired?" I wondered why he used the word "fired", when they are the ones who want to get me fired. I told him, "I am just a wounded soldier in recuperation Serg," and he didn't say anything else, because he knows that it is the truth. Now here I am being a public exhibition or exhibited to the public. I am placed in an exhibition for them to see as if I were a thing or an animal. Again, I know that I am being recorded. But God is my witness, and he is far more than sufficient.

On **Wednesday, June 4, 2014,** I was in church. Suddenly, I saw A… wearing a green t-shirt and N… wearing a red t-shirt. Then A… gets into a conversation with me the same as N... I found it very strange that they initiated a conversation with me. Then when I was alone at church with G…, somebody knocked at the church's door, and it was the same guy that had accompanied us the last time we left the church. He told G… that A… was going to give him a ride home. But I asked G… to please stay that I will pay him a taxi, and he stayed.

It is **Thursday, June 5, 2014**. On this day, I went with my gym bag to do the laundry, and I left my uniform washing in the washing machine. Then I went to a dry cleaner nearby to dry clean my suit and as

I headed there, I heard a man talking on the phone and he said, "He is hot." I left my suit at the dry cleaner, and I returned to the laundromat.

Then I went home for a moment. Later, I went back to the laundromat and at the corner of 162 street and Ogden Avenue, I saw a man standing wearing a camo short, and the same minivan, the famous light blue minivan was close to him. Now I wonder when I am going to stop typing the unfortunate moments of my present life.

Friday, June 6, 2014- Saturday, June 7, 2014 -- My wife is always telling me how I am wasting all of my time typing, and I keep telling her to stop saying that, but she doesn't stop trying to discourage me from doing so. She keeps talking and talking, telling me that it is insane that she is not able to express herself even in her own home, because I keep telling her that somebody might be listening to us. That If we go outside, I keep telling her that somebody is watching us. She tells me, "You need to see a doctor."

At night I went to take the train and at exactly 10:47 pm, when a guy saw me, he jumped the turnstile to see what I was going to do. Later, he hung around me to see my response. While at work, I got to see PO Eddie Pinero, my former partner and brother in Christ. He was fixing the barriers when he saw me and PO Rivera inside the RMP (police car). He greeted us in a way as if he had disliked seeing us. He greeted us by extending his fist, a knuckle-to-knuckle greeting, and he sadly looked at me. He told PO Rivera how the midnight tour got hurt after he left, and he is right, I got seriously hurt since the time we stopped being partners. Later he said goodbye to us to limit our conversations.

Later, I went to the muster room to pick up my bag, which I had left behind at the station house (precinct), and when PO Pinero saw that I had taken my bag, he asked me if that was my bag. His question truly broke my heart. They have placed me in a Mafia type of situation or operation, where once you are in, there is no way out.

On **Thursday, June 12, 2014,** I went to court regarding a court case. I went to see ADA (Assistant District Attorney) McDonald who was assigned to the case. I noticed that ADA McDonald had two cellphones. One of them was a blackberry. The other Assistant District Attorney, with whom she worked on the case, had a blackberry as well, the same kind. She seemed to have been using it every time she spoke to me, which made me feel so nervous.

On our way to court to see the judge, that we were coming out of the building to go to the other building, ADA McDonald made a coughing sound right at the door, while I was carrying her box. I went to testify, while my heart was at all the time, beating hard. I couldn't think clearly. When I walked out of the court room after giving my testimony, I was terrified. But she walked towards me smiling, and her smile made me feel better. She smiled at me outside her office as well, and that smile made me feel much better, or was she smiling because she has me trapped?

On **June 15, 2014,** at approximately 0517 hrs. or 5:17 am, while on patrol, I called the T/S and PO Chiodi answered the phone. I said, "Hi, this is Officer Hernandez," and he said, "I don't believe you," and he abruptly hanged the phone on me. I called back at 0518 hrs. or 5:18 am and he answered it again, and this time he was ok. Is he now insinuating that I am a liar?

It was either on **Saturday, June 14, 2014, or Sunday, June 15, 2014,** that in the locker room PO Gorman told PO Arroyo that he had to go to 1PP (1 Police Plaza= Police Headquarter), to the 4th floor for negotiation and that he didn't know what it was for. Then PO Arroyo told him that it might be to negotiate charges. As soon as I heard that, I became nervous and frustrated, because I thought that it might have to do something with me.

On **Tuesday, June 17, 2014,** I had court. Last night, I had asked Sgt. Gibbs if I could do a day tour instead of a midnight tour because I had court, but he told me that I couldn't because he was short of manpower and he needed me. So, I had to go to work that night. I didn't want to go to work that night because I wanted to have my mind clear and rest by the time I go to testify.

After working that night for eight hours and some minutes, I was already concerned about testifying. I was worried. I was very concerned because I had the belief that they were building a case against me. That they were going to take advantage of every single opportunity to add more negatives to the stack of paperwork accumulated in their archives, which they might keep inside the storage bin of my destruction. Suddenly, I received a call from PO Gavillan. He asked me a question about the case, but I told him that we will talk about it when we meet.

One thing that impressed me the most is that when me and PO Gavillan went downstairs together, after we came out of the locker room, out of nowhere Lt. Yaguchi appeared, coming from upstairs to the Desk. As PO Gavillan and I were writing on the logbook where we were going, at that moment, I had flashback memory of **December 10, 2013**. Lt. Yaguchi was there waiting for an opportunity to tell something to PO Gavillan, in private. Then as we walked out of the precinct, suddenly, PO Gavillan told me that he had to go back inside to the station house (Precinct) because he forgot something. Now, there was me and Lt. Yaguchi standing by the exit door that is at the side of the precinct, looking at the RMPs (police cars) in the parking garage from behind the fence.

Then Lt. Yaguchi went back to the station house (precinct) and I followed him, because I had the feeling that he really wanted to tell PO Gavillan something, and it had something to do with me. Then PO Gavillan walked down the stairs, and he headed to the same side exit door and Lt. Yaguchi rushed to meet him. I decided to walk to them, and while I was walking towards them, there was PO Jones calling me out to fix my pants. PO Gavilllan was already outside talking to Lt. Yaguchi, while I jogged towards them to prevent or halt Lt. Yaguchi from executing or give birth to any devious plan against me, but there was PO Jones behind me yelling at me to fix my pant again, which he did to distract me and to stop me from getting any closer to them. So, I stopped fixing my pants.

As I walked outside, PO Jones walked after me as well, and he asked me why I had the edge of my pants under my socks, but why did he have to follow me when I had already fixed my pants? But I realized that he was following me, so I won't interfere with Lt. Yaguchi's plan, and PO Gavillan was being part of the scheme. Therefore, PO Jones tried to divert my attention. At the end, Lt. Yaguchi seemed to have finished telling PO Gavillan what he wanted him to know and what he wanted him to do. When Lt. Yaguchi saw that I was close to them, he immediately walked away from PO Gavillan and he walked to a near RMP (police car). At that moment, I realized that PO Gavillan was either wired or he was going to use his smartphone to record my conversation. I understood that our conversation is or was going to be heard by others.

When I was in the car with PO Gavillan, he used the coughing sound gesture. When we were having lunch, I observed that he was uncomfortable, and he was making the coughing sound gesture again. In one instance, he saw me looking at my Memo-Book (Memorandum Pad/Activity Log), and he seemed concerned because he asked me what I was reading. I told him that I did go to the hospital to interview the victim. Right away, he became concerned, and immediately he told me that we needed to go. He didn't even finish his lunch, but he took with him what was left of his food.

While walking in the courthouse, I told him that I didn't remember well the time when he made the statement about the man on the wheelchair doing it. Then we began looking for the paralegal guy until we finally found him. I felt so preoccupied to testify again. I really didn't want to testify. I felt that I was the defendant, not the witness. There was PO Gavillan recording me, there was ADA McDonald whose smile I didn't trust, and her Assistant District Attorney companion who didn't even say, "Hi" when she introduced him to me. He gave a detestable look at me, as if he abhorred me.

During the time that we were with the victim, ADA McDonald told us that we could return or go back there with the victim at 2:15 pm. The victim was handcuffed for violating parole. Then ADA McDonald took us to the Department of Investigation Unit where they have a jail cell, and there we momentarily placed the victim/prisoner. She told us that we were going to testify tomorrow, not today, and as a result, I felt immensely relieved. However, I wondered if they placed us there to investigate me. At that moment, I could imagine a small camera staring at me as they observed my behavior. I felt so pressured. I didn't want to talk because I couldn't talk. At that moment, I didn't doubt that even the victim, who was also a prisoner, was being wired. The possibilities and the mere idea of knowing that the place was being bugged, and that PO Gavillan and the victim/prisoner were being wired, was killing me softly.

As we waited, the victim/prisoner began to talk about life in prison. How people were getting stabbed and abused there. How they were doing drugs, and how they were only allowed to take a shower twice a week and so on. He was making me feel so uncomfortable. It felt as if he were telling me what I was going to go through when they put me in prison. I wondered if it was all part of their plan to have me terrorized.

At approximately five minutes earlier, we went ahead to meet with ADA McDonald at the time and place we had agreed to meet. We waited outside the courtroom and when the court officer saw us, he rushed us into the waiting room, because the jury was not supposed to see the victim handcuffed. I was told by ADA McDonald that I was not going to testify today. Then, when the defendant and the doctor were done testifying, I thought that we were done for the day, but then the court Sergeant called me out to testify. I was not expecting it. ADA McDonald had told me that I was not going to testify, and when I was told that it was my turn, my heart began to beat rapidly and hard.

After working a midnight tour, and later going to court, and having worked altogether approximately 16 hours straight, there was me walking into the courtroom, unprepared to testify in front of the jury. When I was inside the courtroom, the juries were seated to my left, and next to me was the typographer and further up was ADA McDonald and her partner, and further to my right, there was the defense attorney accompanied by the defendant and to my right, the judge. But what really scared me out was to see the paralegal guy seating among the audience, and two other suspicious women, which I believe them to be ADAs or to be working for the ADAs (Assistant District Attorney).

Those two women were like looking, at the same time, at some device or trying to record, hear and/or report what I was saying in order to find, highlight and point out any fault, error, and mistake I may do in my testimony, so they may then add the results to the prosecutorial file of PO Hernandez's case, which is being built against me. I was terrified.

When ADA McDonald began to ask me questions, I began to look behind her, right at the direction where the two women were, and at the paralegal guy. Later, the defense attorney asked me questions. Meanwhile, now, I am not only scared, but I was also completely terrified. All I can say is that when I was done from testifying, that I stood up and began to walk away from the Judge, the jury, the District Attorneys, the defense attorney, the parties involved (Victim/Defendant), the audience and all other participants including the court police and the typographer, as I, inside the courtroom began to walk away from them, I felt like a dead man walking.

When I arrived at the station house (precinct), I went with PO Gavillan to see Lt. Yaguchi, and when Lt. Yaguchi saw us, he said, "Yes," while having his phone on his ear as if desiring not to talk to us. Not knowing what to say or do, PO Gavillan said to me, "Lets go, we come back later." Later, when we were in front of the Desk waiting to leave, PO Gavillan said, "Bye," to the Sergeant and he left without saying good-bye to me.

Later at night, ADA McDonald texted me to see if I got the notification, because she might have me testify tomorrow. The moment I read the text, it angered me. All I can say is until when this torture will last.

The next day, on **Wednesday, June 18, 2014,** I went to court again. I decided to do a day tour. Then I went to the station house's (precinct) lounge and lay on the sofa for about two hours. I was watching the movie Die Hard on the television. Then I went to do 1PP (1 Police Plaza= Police Headquarter) at the Head Quarter Security Unit for a 12 hours and 50 minutes tour/shift.

At the end of my tour, PO Ahmed offered to give me a ride back to the station house (precinct). As he was driving me back, I knew well he was recording me, because he had begun to inquire me and ask me questions such as: Why did I want to transfer to 1PP? If I liked working on the 25th

precinct? How long does it take me to get from 1PP to the station house (precinct)? How long does the train take? If PO Rivera had gone away for his vacation, and some other questions that I felt were life threatening questions, which my exhausted mind and body felt obliged to answer.

To better understand the hours worked, I will incorporate the details of the many hours I worked on this day. On this day, I did a day tour from 7:05 am till 3:40 pm, which is 8 hours and 35 minutes. Then I rested, didn't sleep, for two hours and then I went to 1PP (1 Police Plaza= Police Headquarter) and **did a 12 hours and 50 minutes tour. In total, I worked for 21 hours and 25 minutes** in just one day. Plus, the 2 hours break in between that I took, plus the travel time, means that I have been awake for **more than 24 hours**. Then as PO Ahmed was giving me a ride home, he was asking me questions, which answer, I knew, could lead to negative outcomes. I felt as if I were being questioned in trial once more or was being interrogated by a detective.

When I arrived at the station house (precinct), I went to pay roll to make sure I didn't exceed the 120 hours per quarter overtime, because I didn't want to be punished for going over the limit and then be forbidden to do more overtime the following month. Being tremendously and overly exhausted for the over 24 hours without sleep, when I was seating down at the muster room, that I was doing my overtime calculations, there entered PO Soto, who seems to be Lt. Yaguchi's secretary, and who was complaining the other day about someone robbing something, when we were in Lt. Yaguchi's office the other day.

There was PO Moreno as well. He told PO Moreno, "I was afraid, I thought that it was you," and she moved her head as to deny it was her. Then he began to sing the music background song of Frank Sinatra's song called, "I did it my way," and he continued singing, "The time, the time is near…," and finally he changed his mood, and as he was leaving he said, "You cannot just throw lies like that," and the moment he said it, it was just me and him in the muster room.

Without doubt, he directed those words to me. My heart was already aching. So, when I was done, I went home wondering what I had wronged. What wrong have I done? Was he referring to the honest mistake I made on **December 10, 2013**?

"I am like a deaf person; I do not hear. I am like a speechless person who does not open his mouth. I am like a man who does not hear and has no arguments in his mouth." (Psalm 38:13-14 HCSB).

"Yahweh my God, I seek refuge in You; save me from all my pursuers and rescue me or they will tear me like a lion, ripping me apart with no one to rescue me. Yahweh my God, if I have done this, if there is injustice on my hands, if I have done harm to one at peace with me or have plundered my adversary without cause, may an enemy pursue and overtake me; may he trample me to the ground and leave my honor in the dust. Selah Rise up, Lord, in Your anger; lift Yourself up against the fury of my adversaries; awake for me; You have ordained a judgment. Let the assembly of peoples gather around You; take Your seat on high over it. The Lord judges the people; vindicate me, Lord, according to my righteousness and my integrity. Let the evil of the wicked come to an end, but establish the righteous. The One who examines the thoughts and emotions is a righteous God. My shield is with God, who saves the upright in heart." (Psalm 7:1-10 HCSB).

Right now, I am typing and today is Friday, June 20, 2014. Right now, I am in my bedroom lying on bed typing these words with the light off, because I am feeling frightened. As I am laying, I change positions to comfortably type.

When my wife entered our apartment, she went straight to our bedroom, and when she saw me laying here, I begged her to please seat on the bed, because I needed someone to talk to. I am feeling very anguished. But instead, she began to raise her voice to me, telling me that I needed help and that I needed to see a psychologist. That I was not on my right mind, and she cursed the day she married me.

Later at 6:41 pm, while I was doing the Laundry, ADA McDonald sent me a text message that said, "Hi. The jury found the defendant not guilty. Just wanted to let you know. Thanks." At that moment, I took it as a threat. I stopped folding my clothing. I felt that I was a failure. I believe that they are going to make me pay for it. Then I began to fold my clothes again.

When I got home, I lay on the floor, because that was how low I was feeling. But God gave me the strength to get up a moment later, to type these words, because I have no one else to talk to but God. People on the job say, "Don't bring your job home, leave it at work," but how can I leave my job at work when my life, and my future is being threatened by powerful people. I have the feeling that I am about to lose everything, including the hair of my head.

I am weary with my moaning; every night I flood my bed with tears; I drench my couch with my weeping. My eyes are swollen from grief; they grow old because of all my enemies." (Psalm 6:6-7 HCSB, ESV).

In my life, I am being attacked from many different angles. My only resting place is when I am inside my bedroom, when I turn off the light and lay on my bed, but not even there because negative thoughts begin to invade my mind. The only time that I can escape from all this is when I am dreaming. I consider their evil deeds to be a great distraction, not just a distraction, but also a great burden, but not just a burden, but a human spirit killing machine, and all this for what? What are they gaining from all this? A human sacrifice to their gods?

Now I wonder if they have applied this same due process to other officers and treated other officers with the same fugacity, and tenacity in which they are treating me. And if so, I wonder what have been the consequences or I should say, the outcome of such a practice? Have these officers attempted with their lives, or have they ended it. Or am I the only officer in the history of the NYPD that has gone and is still walking through this realm of hell?

But as one officer once told me, that in this Department, one cannot speak one's mind because if you do, your problem will worsen. Again, what is this excessive hostile work environment that I am working in and living in? They have placed me in a parole state of mind, for I don't know what my future holds. What tomorrow might bring. They hot-pursue me with so much hate. They hate me with passion.

In the morning of **Sunday, June 22, 2014,** PO Rivera told me that he felt as if he were living in a house of cards, where if one takes one card away from that house of cards, the whole house falls apart. Now I wonder if he was referring to the situation that I am in, not his. But God has given me the strength to carry on and fight my anxieties.

On **Monday, June 23, 2014,** PO Rivera and I had a job at East 123 street and 2nd avenue. The job was about a man who had expose himself to a group of guys. When we arrived at the scene, as soon as I saw that the one who did it was wearing green sneakers, I realized what it was all about. A simple scenario.

PO Rivera spoke to him in a very reasonable matter and in such reasonable matter, I told PO Rivera that he got the message. Another job came over where the complainant, who was wearing a green t-shirt, felt harassed by a drunken man who used profane words towards her. Green T-shirt, I got the point. The uneasy situations that I see myself in are distracting me from paying full attention to my duties. There is turmoil inside of me. How would I have liked to escape from this tumor of problems for at least a day, but so far, I see no end to this madness. But all I can in Christ who strengthens me.

On **Tuesday, June 24, 2014-Wedsnesdy, June 25, 2014,** Lt. Yaguchi approached me and PO Rivera, and with a big smile on his face, he shook my hand. As soon as he did, PO Rivera looked at him seriously. Then he asked PO Rivera, "What! Why are you so serious?" but PO Rivera didn't respond.

Later, patrol, PO Rivera continued asking the same controversial questions and he kept saying to himself, "It never fails," and when I asked him why he kept saying that he told me to forget about it. Then he said that people in this country should know English. He asked me what I thought of it. I told him that I would like to be multilingual so I may help people. He told me that the department doesn't want us to translate, because we are not certified.

Later, feeling frustrated, I asked him, "Do you want to hang me?" and he remained quiet, for he knew I was right. I knew that this simple question had caught his attention, because hours later, I clarified a misunderstanding to him and he asked me the same question that I had asked him, "Do you want to hang me?" It means that he didn't disregard my question at all. He was meditating on it, and he used it this time for me. Because, this is their goal, to have me hanged.

However, on this same day, I looked at the back light blue cover of my Memo-Book (Memorandum Pad/Activity Log), which I didn't bother to look at in the past and read. However, this time I decided to look at the words written on it. There, I read, discovered and learned the meaning of these two words: sustain and overturn. When I began reading the court testimony section, the more disappointed I became with me and those who wanted to see my downfall. How those who could have helped me didn't help me, and how poorly Manhattan ADA (Assistant District Attorney) Altman had prepared me for my court testimony.

As one can see, on number 12, underneath "THE TESTIMONY", it says, "… When an objection is made, wait for the judge's ruling ("sustained" or "overruled") before completing your answer. The ruling will tell you whether you are required to answer or not." Why didn't the ADA (Assistant District Attorney) tell me anything about it? Now, what truly hurts me is when I read the section that says, "PRIOR TO THE COURT APPEARANCE," where underneath it, on part number 2, it says, "**Review the case with other officers who were involved**." What really hurts me is that they, who were on the scene with me, didn't want to discuss the case with me.

Neither Lt. Yaguchi, PO Maher nor PO Quinones wanted to discuss the case with me. They completely abandoned me. They left me all alone, completely by myself, when they knew well of the importance of the case, and how I was going to get hurt if they didn't refresh my mind, but they didn't do anything to prevent it. They could have just simply reminded me of the event, but they didn't.

As I have tried to gather information as to what happened on the days before **December 10, 2013,** which was the most unfortunate day of my life, for on this date, I took the stand inside the court room and gave my self-devastating testimony. Days before **December 10, 2013**, ADA Altman had asked me about the previous jobs I had. In a few words, my resume. She wanted me to name them. In addition, she was asking me questions that were unrelated to and not pertaining to the case. She was like interviewing me, while having a second intention in mind, which made me nervous. At one point, she asked me how I obtained the alcohol bottle that I vouchered for. I told her that I didn't remember. She told me to go and speak to Lt. Yaguchi for clarification.

Back to the precinct, when I went to talk to Lt. Yaguchi about the case, and how I obtained the bottle, he told me just to say that he gave it to me. It was the only thing he told me about the case. I wondered why he didn't want to discuss the case with me. Why PO Quinones, who was my partner at the time of the arrest, told me that he didn't remember either. Why PO Maher, who was Lt. Yaguchi's driver at the time, and who was also at the scene, told me that he didn't remember either. Nobody wanted to tell me what happened.

They made me feel as if it was illegal to discuss the case with them, and that is why I didn't insist. However, days before **December 10, 2013**, I noticed that someone had ripped a piece of the back cover of my Memo-Book (Memorandum Pad/Activity Log). It is the one shown/illustrated below:

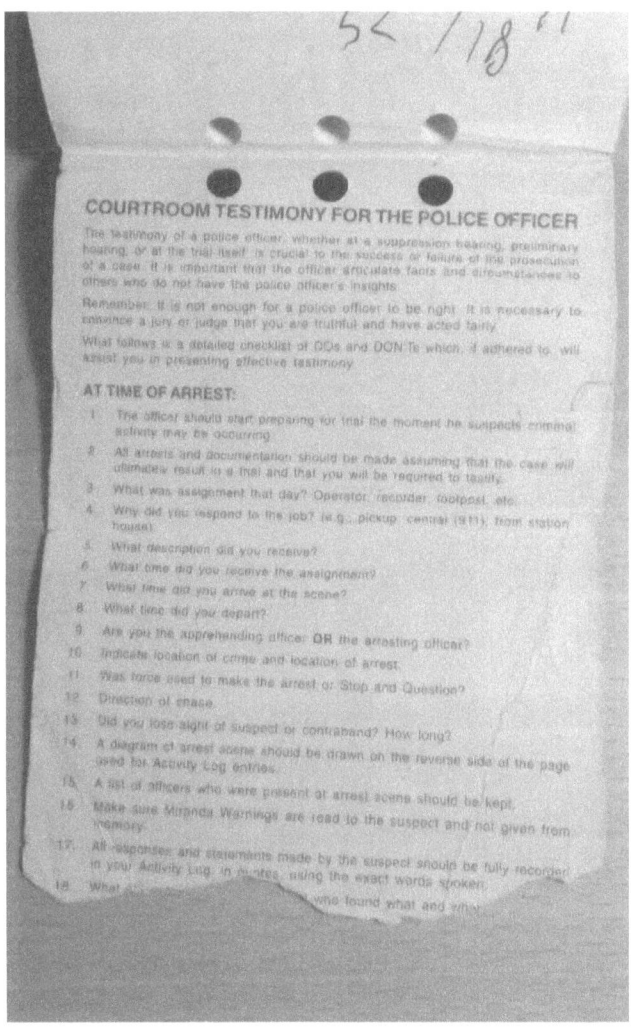

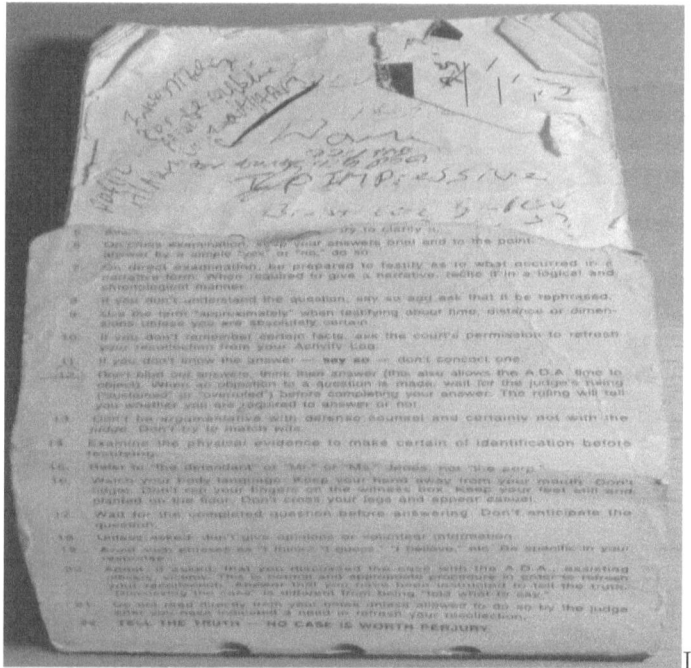

I have always wondered why an officer did tore that portion of my Memo-Book (Memorandum Pad or Activity Log). Why not the front? I mention an officer, because I only leave my Memo-Book behind among officers only, where there are other officers are around. My response was to ignore what he or she did to my Memo-Book, but I was still wondering why? Sorry that I am now going to repeat some of the things that I mentioned before, but the problem is that I find this information so annoying, but at the same time crucial.

Obviously, when our Memo-Book (Memorandum Pad/Activity Log) is fully written, we receive new ones. One day, out of curiosity, I decided to look at the back cover of a new and complete Memo-Book I had. At the back cover of my Memo-Book, I noticed that there were written words that were numerically numbered in chronological order. When I began reading line by line what was written on it, I never knew that there was so many crucial, useful and important information at the back cover of the Memo-Book. Nobody told me anything about it. If I had been aware of the important information hidden at the back of the Memo-Book, I would have been more effective and efficient when it comes down to the processing of the arrest paperwork and on the overall police paperwork, which as a result, I would have been much better prepared for court. The following is the complete back cover of one of my Memo-Book, and it explains why the unknown police officer, or any other higher rank officer did reap off that portion of my Memo-Book.

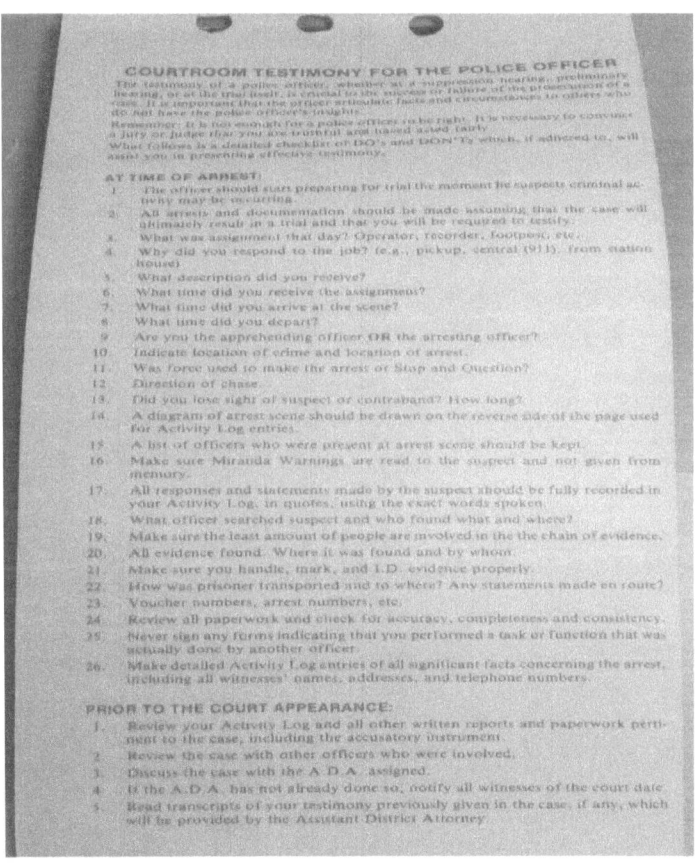

When I kept on reading that I paid close attention to the portion that they or he or she reaped off of my Memo-Book, as if there were some type of information in it that might in one way benefit me, and didn't want me to read, I became astonished, and I felt highly betrayed by my colleagues when I read the portion of **PRIOR TO THE COURT APPEARANCE** as shown below, and is highlighted:

18. What officer searched suspect and who found what and where?

19. Make sure the least amount of people are involved in the the chain of evidence.

20. All evidence found. Where it was found and by whom.

21. Make sure you handle, mark, and I.D. evidence properly.

22. How was prisoner transported and to where? Any statements made en route?

23. Voucher numbers, arrest numbers, etc.

24. Review all paperwork and check for accuracy, completeness and consistency.

25. Never sign any forms indicating that you performed a task or function that was actually done by another officer.

26. Make detailed Activity Log entries of all significant facts concerning the arrest, including all witnesses' names, addresses, and telephone numbers.

PRIOR TO THE COURT APPEARANCE:

1. Review your Activity Log and all other written reports and paperwork pertinent to the case, including the accusatory instrument.

2. Review the case with other officers who were involved.

3. Discuss the case with the A.D.A. assigned.

4. If the A.D.A. has not already done so, notify all witnesses of the court date.

5. Read transcripts of your testimony previously given in the case, if any, which will be provided by the Assistant District Attorney.

As we can see on the illustration, the #2 says, **"Review the case with other officers who were involved."** This is something that none of them were willing to do. In a few words, they didn't want to discuss the case with me. Or let say, they hid the information from me, for they wanted me to err on my court's testimony of **December 10, 2013**. At one point, PO Maher told me that Manhattan ADA (Assistant District Attorney) Altman was considering whether to put me on the stand to testify, because I was all over the place. He told me that she said that I would be crucified by the defense attorney if she had me testify. But still, nobody wanted to refresh my memory. It is as if they didn't want me to remember.

The # 5, which I also highlighted, says, "**Read transcripts of your testimony previously given in the case, if any, which will be provided by the Assistant District Attorney.**" As I had previously explained, in regards to what happened on my first meeting with ADA Altman on **November 13, 2013** (not taking to account the first day I met her when I made the arrest), which was the day when I first saw her with Lt. Yaguchi, and it was the moment when Lt. Yaguchi had ask me in front of her for the combination of my lock. At that instance, Lt. Yaguchi left to search for my lockers, and I was left alone with ADA Altman, which made me very nervous. Then she gave me the **transcript** to read. The transcript is a copy of the court statements I made many months ago.

At that moment I didn't know what I was reading, because what about if somebody or Lt. Yaguchi planted something in my lockers and then I was going to be blamed for it. As I read along the lines of the transcript, I noticed that she was staring at me, as I thought of what Lt. Yaguchi might have told her about me, and how he might have poisoned her mind against me. At the same time, I was thinking of Lt. Yaguchi, and of what he might be doing searching for my lockers. Again, what about if someone planted something inside my lockers and then I will be blamed for it. Also, I was thinking about the countless people that have been falsely and wrongfully accused, jailed, and imprisoned for things they didn't do.

I read the **transcript** once, but I was pretending to be reading it at the time. **Then I asked her if I could read it again, and she refused to let me read it one more time.** I couldn't understand why, until later in time, when I read the back portion of my Memo-Book (Memorandum

219

Pad/Activity Log) on the **PRIOR TO THE COURT APPEARANCE # 5**, that I realized that she had to let me read it for an indefinite time or countless time. This was the moment when I realized that it was all part of a set up. They set me up for failure. In a few words, she and Lt. Yaguchi framed me.

Now that I look at the whole picture, I can see that they have my blood on their hands. They needed to have a reason to investigate me. They needed a motive to have people follow me, and this was their opportunity. Therefore, nobody wanted to tell me anything pertaining to the event that occurred on the day of the arrest, and so to the extent that Lt. Yaguchi didn't want me to recall how he gave me the bottle of liquor by limiting the review of what happened by simply telling me, "Just tell them that I gave it to you."

"For without cause they hid their net for me; without cause they dug a pit for my life. Let destruction come upon him when he does not know it! And let the net that he hid ensnare him; let him fall into it ..." (Psalm 35:7-8 ESV).

But who is not prone to make mistakes when undergoing, every single day, through this tremendous amount of pressure daily. I have stopped countless number of vehicles, and how many times at DMV traffic court have police officers said that they don't recall? They even had to place IAB (Internal Affairs Bureau, investigate police corruption) Sergeants to work at the Department of Motor Vehicle traffic court at the Northern Manhattan Traffic Violations Bureau or on all Department of Motor Vehicle Traffic courts, because there were so many police officers saying that they don't recall. Even in Criminal Court in general police officers have the right to say that they don't recall.

So why did they put me against the wall just because I didn't recall an event? Why? Didn't Lt. Yaguchi say at the stand that the color of the liquor inside the bottle was clear when indeed it wasn't? Why did he say that the key was in the engine when the vehicle functioned without a key? He made mistakes, according to him. He himself told me this when

220

I told him that I thought I made a mistake on my court's testimony. So why am I being judged for something I thought I remembered?

"I said, "'I will guard my ways so that I may not sin with my tongue; I will guard my mouth with a muzzle as long as the wicked are in my presence.'" I was speechless and quiet; I kept silent, even from speaking good, and my pain intensified. My heart grew hot within me; as I mused, a fire burned; then I spoke with my tongue:" (Psalm 39:1-3 HCSB)

However, I do now remember why I took that arrest in the first place. On the day of the arrest, I didn't need to take the arrest because I already had one for the month. But PO Quinones needed one for the month and one of us had to take the arrest. But I was moved by compassion because he had his eyes very red due to allergies, so I volunteered to take it then, because if I didn't, he would be mandated or obligated to take it, because he needed an arrest for the month. But on court day, he turned his back on me by refusing to share with me what he knew and happened on that day, which was approximately eight months away from **December 10, 2013**.

"God of my praise, do not be silent. For wicked and deceitful mouths open against me; they speak against me with lying tongues. They surround me with hateful words and attack me without cause. In return for my love they accuse me, but I continue to pray. They repay me evil for good, and hatred for my love." (Psalm 109:1-5 HCSB)

I repeat it again, I remember the day when Manhattan ADA (Assistant District Attorney) Altman assigned me to get a copy of the prisoner pedigree from the 28 precinct, and the 25 precinct, and she told me to go and ask Lt. Yaguchi about the moment that he gave me the bottle of liquor to voucher, so I may remember. When I went to the 28th precinct that I picked up a copy of the pedigree from there, then I went to the 25th precinct to get the other pedigree. Then I went to Lt. Yaguchi's office, and I asked him to refresh my mind about the moment when he gave me the bottle of liquor to voucher, because I couldn't remember. He said, "Just tell them that I gave it to you."

At that moment, after spending approximately 10 seconds in his office, I left his office. Because of the response he gave me, the way he reacted towards my question, and his face expression, made me feel in a way as if the question that I just asked him was improper, that I was not supposed to have asked him that question. His face was so serious, as if he had hated to see me. He spoke to me while staring at the computer monitor. His whole demeanor said it all. From that moment, we never spoke again about the case. It was the only conversation we had about the case, besides the day that he gave me the lab result for the marijuana test.

The same with PO Maher, who had told me that he had to say the same things that his boss says in court, and that he didn't remember the case. Then one day that I was with PO Quinones and PO Maher in court, PO Quinones told me that he didn't remember too. On that day in court, I observed that PO Quinone was sweating profusely. PO Quinones told me that I must remember.

Then PO Maher asked me and PO Quinones if we remembered when the defendant had his seat belt on that he tried to get out of the car, but he couldn't because he had his seat belt on. What he said threw me off. I told him that I didn't remember that, and PO Quinones said that he didn't remember that either. PO Quinones didn't even remember the moment when we first arrived at the scene, and what had happened, which would have changed the whole outcome, I would have remembered, but it seems that they didn't want me to remember for a reason, and it had to do with Lt. Yaguchi. PO Quinones and PO Maher said nothing more about the case. I was all alone. Only God who sees everything knows.

Later, my misfortune came on **December 10, 2013**, a date that I will never forget. And now on June 25, 2014 that I read the section of the back cover of my Memo-Book (Memorandum Pad/Activity Log) that explains and clarifies to me that I should have and could have and had the right to review the case with the officers that were involved, is what makes me sick, and very angry. I have come to realize that I was set up for failure.

But how could I have perceived so much malice and hate behind that smile? But so great is his unlimited ambition. It is limitless, and what I mean by that is that he doesn't care if the person who he is harming is guilty or not, he just dislikes the guy. But God is good, all the time, and all the time, God is good, and he is in control of everything including my life.

"They hid their net for me without cause; they dug a pit for me without cause." (Psalms 35:7 HCSB)

On **Thursday, June 26, 2014,** PO Rivera and I went to back up Lt. Allen who had a car stopped on Second Avenue. When we arrived, Lt. Allen asked me for how long I had been working at the 25th precinct. PO Rivera answered for me saying, "Enough time." I wondered why he answered me. I became very suspicious. I told him that in July I will have five years to come on the 25th precinct. Then Lt. Allen confessed to us that there is a black cloud at the 25th precinct.

Later, when I arrived home, when I gave thought to the question he had asked me, I realized that I have not five, but six years working at the 25th precinct. I mistakenly gave him the wrong answer, but it is not easy to give out clear and accurate answers to a simple question when one's mind is restless. The tension that I am enduring is 24/7, and it is without doubt reducing my IQ levels. Even when I went to sign out, there I saw Lt. Yaguchi standing by the Desk.

I greeted him, and he greeted me back by just moving his head. It was obvious that he was not happy to see me. As I was signing out, Lt. Yaguchi had his back facing me and at the T/S, I asked the T/S operator to lend me his pen, which he did. When I signed out, PO Maher came out from the stairwells, signed out, and the person at the T/S asked me for his pen. I frisked my packet, and I couldn't feel it. Then I called PO Maher who was walking away, because I thought he had the pen, but he didn't have it.

However, I found out that I had it because the T/S operator pointed to my packet and the pen was popping out of my packet. Then PO Maher said that I was accusing him of taking it when he didn't take it. Now I wonder what is wrong with me. Am I losing my head? Because I don't even remember when I placed that pen inside my packet, but I see why, I simply wasn't paying attention to my actions, but at my surroundings. Besides, I have one of the same pen that I bought at East 125 Street and 2nd Avenue for .50 cents one night when I worked with PO Martorelli. And it is the pen that PO Rivera called a cheap pen when he tried to write with it.

Then as soon as PO Maher said that Lt. Yaguchi turned his face around and I could see half his body side way, as I saw a smile on his face as if he had liked what he just heard and would love to use against me. I am under a suspicious state of mind all around, everywhere I go and everywhere I turn.

I have been living with this false accusation sticker for a long time now. I see no end to this, and besides that, they are meticulously looking closely at all my conversations and at everything I say and do. Lt. Yaguchi is clever, astute, very well disciplined and he is a very determined individual. He has become a lawyer, and he seems to be using all his wit, all his law school experience and preparation, and is applying all that he has learned towards me and against me. I see no open doors. No escape.

He is my boss, and he has a very influential position or seat within the 25th precinct as head of the administration. He is the Administrative Lieutenant. So, if he sees that I make any move to defend myself, he will truly hurt me, he will crush me, he will hurt me bad. It is as if he has his gun pointed at my head and is telling me to freeze and not move or else.

I cannot go and seek help somewhere because he will know, he seems to know all my moves thanks to those who are following me. I know that not even my smartphone is safe, because they seem to be able to manage and look at everything I do with my smartphone. Lt. Yaguchi is using his charisma to gain the favor of almost everyone in the precinct or outside the precinct. Of course, he is a lawyer, and law and politics go hand in hand. As the Administrative Lieutenant, he decides who gets the best overtime details, and who will get the worse assignments.

(PO Elliot Santiago, an old timer who had worked at the 25th precinct for many years decided to transfer to another precinct because Lt. Yaguchi was already stepping on his tail. This might explain why PO Eddie Pinero decided to vest out of the job early, needing just 2 more years to retire and receive his full pension, but he left instead, probably to no longer endure two more years under Lt. Yaguchi's regime. He and Lt. Yaguchi already had many inconveniences.

Lt. Yaguchi seems to have poisoned the mind of everyone in the precinct concerning me. He has turned them against me, including my closest co-worker, my partner, PO Rivera. Well again, he is the boss in charge of handing over the overtime details, so he is the one to decide whom he is going to give it to. However, he gives me the 1PP (1 Police Plaza= Police Headquarter) overtime because very few people like to do it, so for June, I signed up to do 1PP (1 Police Plaza= Police Headquarter) 7 times.

This means that every day I did 1PP (1 Police Plaza= Police Headquarter), I had to work there for 12 hours and 50 minutes each day, which for me was worth it, because I rather do that, than to work 8 and a half miserable hours and minutes at the 25th precinct. I mention minutes because every second and minute that I have my foot set at the premise of the 25th precinct, dearly counts. In addition, Lt. Yaguchi counts with the support of the Manhattan ADA (Assistant District Attorney), and who knows, the Manhattan DA (District Attorney) himself. The Commanding Officer of the precinct hasn't shown much, I don't know if he is for Lt. Yaguchi, against Lt. Yaguchi's actions, or he just doesn't care. All I know is that I can only count on one being, God, and he is all I need.

But I want to know, I need to know, what cause or initiated all this investigation? Who triggered it? What spark has caused all this unstoppable flame, this ceaseless fire in my life that has been burning my mind every single day, hour, minute, second, mini-second, and that keeps occurring 24/7. Even when I am laying down on bed, I can't stop thinking about what they are doing to me. Even when I am dreaming, sometimes I dream about all this ordeal, or I should say nightmare.

But I know that all of this started by a man who doesn't care about another man's life and suffering, and is willing to play, and destroy that man's life, and if possible, kill that man, but knowing that killing a physical body is illegal, at least his spirit, his hope and future dreams. All this by turning everybody against me, even my closest friends. Their silence is killing me. Their silence let me know that they are up to something. For how long am I going to be able to maintain my sanity? Now it seems that they have added **orange** and the **dark blue** colors to their list. Now it is a total of **five colors** that my followers are using. But I am sure about something. I am certain that my problems are not bigger than God.

The next thing is that I went out with my dear friend who is from Haiti, whom I call Sebastiano, and we entered a restaurant. They assigned us to a table, and we sat and ate there. But as we were there, I heard two people talking. One told the other that he was 'fired'. Later she said, "He cannot imagine that we are here for him." Then when I left to take the train, I saw a guy walking towards me from the opposite direction and as he walked by me, he gave me the finger, the middle finger, as he walked past me. He did it without looking at me. Then in the train, I heard one young man say to the other, "… Being bugged everywhere. First him and now his family. I would rather live in a shelter."

At home, I went to bed. In the middle of the night, my wife asked me if I was not using my bed sheet, so she may use it, because the room was too cold, and it was so cold that the one she had wasn't enough. I told her that she could have mines, because I didn't want to use any. Of course, I was not feeling cold, my body's temperature was hot, because I couldn't stop thinking about them and what they were doing to me. My blood was boiling in anger. I am so angry that I cannot sleep well.

Chapter 14

July 2014 Events

On **Wednesday, July 2, 2014,** right after doing 1PP (1 Police Plaza= Police Headquarter) and having worked there for 12 hours and 50 minutes, I went to court to see Manhattan ADA (Assistant District Attorney) McDonald. When I got there, she told me to take the property (the evidence) back to 1PP (1 Police Plaza= Police Headquarter). Then she asked me if I was not going to ask her about the case, and I asked her what happened. She told me that it had nothing to do with us, but that it was hard to prove him guilty, because he was claiming self-defense.

Then I went and returned the property at 1PP (1 Police Plaza= Police Headquarter). When I finished, I went back to her and handed over the receipt. From her office's open door, I managed to see PO Quinones seated facing her desk. He had his back facing me. As I spoke to her, he didn't turn to see me not even for a second. Of course, he knew it was me because I have a thick accent and a voice that is unique at the 25th precinct.

Then the ADA (Assistant District Attorney) McDonald greeted me goodbye while saying, "I talk to you soon" and those last words caught my attention. "I talk to you soon," is for the charges that she is going to bring against me for I don't know what? And was PO Quinones there to contribute something in the conspiracy that is being built against me, or was he just simply there to unofficially talk bad about me? When I arrived home, I received a call from PAA Washington asking me if I wanted to do the barriers the following day. I so happily volunteered.

On **Thursday, July 3, 2014,** I went to the station house (precinct) to get my gloves and my bible. When I arrived there, I saw Lt. Gonzales and Lt. Yaguchi behind the Desk. Lt. Gonzales began playing with me by calling me "Menudo," which was a music band from the 70s and the 80s.

Then I went to do the paid details at the Barriers Section. I volunteered to do the barriers to escape the 25th precinct and to avoid doing patrol, because I am so tired of being tested. On this day, I was doing the barriers with PO Lopez and three others. While inside the truck, one of them said, "… Menudo…, …Ricky Martin …," and at one point one of the officers said, "I don't see him taking that property." This is when I came to realize that they are communicating with Lt. Gonzales, who is always calling me Menudo. At that point I realized that they are accomplices. That I was being recorded by them, and that I am being blamed for taking something.

On **Saturday, July 5, 2014,** I was assigned to do the Crime Reduction detail. I was at the muster room with PO Rivera and PO Domagildo (I don't know how to spell her name) whose nick name is 'CC'. Lt. Yaguchi began to give us our assignments. He assigned me to work with PO Rivera, and as soon as he said so, PO Domagildo (I don't know how to spell her name) made the throat sound once, but she had no response, so she did the throat sound one more time, and finally PO Rivera did the same throat sound as if to communicate to her that he got the message. Or let say, "Roger that", "Copy", which equals to our radio code 10-4.

On **Wednesday, July 9, 2014,** after doing 1PP (1 Police Plaza= Police Headquarter), I went to my sister's apartment. I had like five or six months before I didn't visit her. We spoke about my older sister who just had surgery. Also, I told her that there were people following me everywhere I go, and that I don't know who these people are. She became upset with me, and she told me that I needed help. She thinks that I am paranoid or schizophrenic. However, I had ground to believe that the NYPD, the Manhattan District Attorney's office, the private investigators or/and God knows who else have them following me.

My question is, who are these people that follow me? What type of background do they have? Who are they? Are they former criminals? Are some of them soon to be criminals? Are some of them psychopath, social path, people with mental illness you name it. The bottom line is that I don't want my family to be exposed to the public like that, and I am willing to sacrifice not seeing them anymore to protect their privacy and safety.

My parents' 50 years marriage anniversary was going to be celebrated on **Saturday July 19, 2014,** and my sister texted me the invitation. They got married in 1964. But how could I go to the

celebration by having these entire strangers following me. Then they will know who my family are, and they will begin to talk about them as if this were a reality show. I would hate to have my parents, of whom I am so proud of, and them who are so proud of me, to be scrutinized in public   view,   and   in   the   view   of   those   who

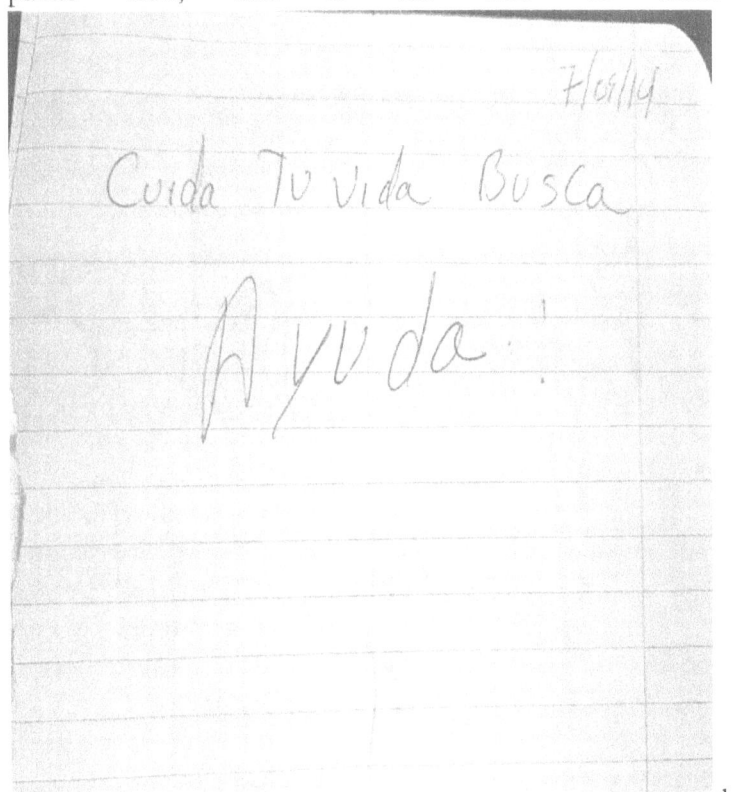

think the worst of me.

They are already messing up with me, and to do the same to my family. Please leave my family alone, out of it. I am fuming. I am so infuriated.

IT IS NOT MY HANDWRITING, EXCEPT FOR THE DATE. IT IS EITHER MY WIFE'S OR MY SISTER'S HANDWRITING. I POSTED THIS PHOTOGRAPH HERE ON March 2025; THEREFORE, I DON'T REMEMBER WHOSE HANDWRITING IS THIS.

On **Thursday, July 10, 2014,** I began working at 1PP (1 Police Plaza= Police Headquarter) **at 1900 hrs. or 7:00 pm till Friday, July 11 until 0750 hrs. or 7:50 am.** When I went to my post that I was seating inside my booth, I could see the Headquarter officer arrive to his post. He was wearing his hat and his dark glasses. Then I saw that he got inside his booth and sat on his chair. He remained seated, but he didn't take off his hat nor his dark glasses. This was odd behavior.

I faced him. Normally when an officer gets inside the booth, he or she immediately takes off his or her hat. I made it obvious to him that I was facing him, or looking at him, or lets say, staring at him. The first thought that came to my mind was that the dark glasses might have a camera and that they were observing me through those dark glasses. But why should I be concerned about him having a camera on his glasses when the Headquarter security office already have a camera facing me? But I stared at him purposely.

The Minutes went by, and he seemed to be getting tired, so he positioned his glasses to his forehead. He was looking in my direction, but not at me, and then in the opposite direction. He might have done it so I may see that his eyes were not looking at me. When the bus came, he positioned the glasses back to his eyes, and he stepped out. He gave me the thumb up and got inside his booth again and he kept the glasses on. Then, he seemed to be tired, and he took off his glasses.

But another Headquarter officer came and relieved him, either for meal or for a personal. Before leaving the officer, he walked out of his booth with his hat on and left his sunglasses. As he walked away, I was tempted to tell him that he had left his glasses, but I didn't. I wondered why he had left it behind when the light of the day remained the same since he came to his post. But then I looked back at his booth, and there I saw the sunglasses, on the window facing me. As usual, I felt like a chimpanzee inside a laboratorial cell, where everyone is studying my behavior. I feel the same way everywhere I go, for I know that everyone's eyes are on me.

In the morning, after doing 1PP (1 Police Plaza= Police Headquarter) for 12 hours and 50 minutes, I went to DMV (Department of Motor Vehicle) at the Northern Manhattan Traffic Violations Bureau traffic court already feeling mentally and physically exhausted, or better said, completely drained. I normally volunteer to do 1PP (1 Police Plaza= Police Headquarter), even though those are long hours of work, but it is much less stressful. I don't have to deal with people targeting and plotting against me to do me harm. At least there I feel safer, besides the glasses.

So, this morning I went to the traffic court, and as soon as I got there, I was told to go to a room. When I arrived at the hearing room, another traffic judge or clerk took me and those who I had given the summonses to, to another room. One of the people that I gave the summons to have a bag containing green, and there I realized that this was a setup too. In addition to that, he made a famous throat sound. Besides my exhausted body, I was feeling my hands shake. I could sense that the entire world was watching me. At the end, all I did was to read out my testimony without paying attention to what I was reading, and without taking my sight off those written words. I could see my handshake, and my voice was not the same, it changed too.

On **Saturday, July 12, 2014,** I was going to meet with my friend Sa… in front of the church to ride our bicycles together. Oh Sa… my friend, my brother in Christ, how you lower yourself by calling me and inviting me to go out with you with all the bad propaganda that are circulating against me. So, I rode my bicycle to church to meet with Sa….

When I got there, I saw a white man waiting in a red suburban and he was parked right in front of the church. He was wearing green. There I realized that I can't catch a break. I went to the restaurant for some juice and something to eat for ourselves. We ate it inside the park.

While in the park, I saw strange people walking by us. By then, I couldn't even trust Sa…, because he had some orange on his sneakers.

We went across George Washington Bridge, and we rode our bicycle inside the park. By the time that we stopped to look at the view of the George Washington Bridge, two men approached us, one wearing orange and the other one was wearing green. They asked Sa… to take a picture of them two, having on their background the view of the George Washington Bridge. Then I inferred by asking myself, "Until when they will continue doing this to me?" It seems that they are making a reality show out of me, and these are the participants. Indeed, they have to be doing a reality show with me.

Later that day, I happily went with my wife to visit my sister's apartment. From the hallway, I was hearing the old song that my father likes to hear, so I smiled as we walked there. When my brother-in-law opened the door, I found out that my parents were not there, so we left. Now I was at the bus stop on M… avenue with my wife waiting for the bus to come after having visited my sister's apartment, and in front of us, there was a black man outside the car, and he was wearing a green t-shirt.

Inside the car, at the driver's side, there was a black man wearing an orange t-shirt. Later, we took the #6 bus to the Yankee Stadium, and then we entered the subway station. At 8:30 pm, I was with my wife waiting for the D train. There I saw a young Hispanic man wearing a red hat, red t-shirt and a camo pant. He was being accompanied by a black female who was wearing a green dress. A white man walked by me, and he stood next to the other two. He was looking at me. He was wearing a red hat, dark glasses, and he had a green book back.

On our way back, inside the train, there was one man wearing a camo hat and the other one a red hat. One of them stood on one side of the door, and the other one on the opposite side of the door. Seating behind us, was a Mexican man wearing the color of the day, and he was trying to listen to our conversation. When we came out of the Subway Station, I warned my wife about those who were wearing orange and she became angry at me, because according to her, it was all in my head. She said that I was being schizophrenic, and she began to say it out loud, while I kept telling her to lower her voice. Then she said that she will not go out with me anymore. Even when we arrived home, we continued to argue about it.

On **Sunday, July 13, 2014-Monday, July 14, 2014,** when I first arrived at the station house (precinct) that I entered the locker room, on the bench that was next to my locker, there was a white Apple charger. Wow, they were trying to see if I fell for it. They are so desperately seeking an opportunity to arrest me. How good should I feel about all this?

Then I saw PO Rivera, and he told me that Lt. Gonzales had given him two court notifications to bring to the roll call and that he slides it under the door. He told me that one of the notifications had my name on it, but that Lt. Gonzales had told him to do it anyway, because he didn't want me to do overtime. He said that the Lieutenant did it on purpose.

When I was on patrol, many of the streets were occupied by pedestrians who were not only minorities, but also white men and white women who were walking around wearing these Five Main Colors: **The Dark Orange**, **the Dark Blue**, **the Camo**, **the Green**, and **the Red Colors**. It seems that the reason why they have added those other colors was because the colors that they were first using were beginning to be too obvious. Also, I suspect that the **Plane Black color** was added too, because this morning I saw different men wearing black t-shirts. This reminds me of my friend Ru…, who with his friend, during the time that we were going to the gym, wore plain black t-shirts. One day, I remember asking them why, but they never gave me an answer.

About the colors, they either combine them or they just wear one of the above colors. If they don't wear the colors, they carry them. By this, it seems that they have added another group to follow me, or they have brought groups from other geographical areas, because the case that they are trying to build against me is very important to them or let say, it is of a higher priority. As a result, they are making my persecution more intense and severe. They want to follow me more closely, either, because they might think that I don't know what is going on or because they know that I know I am being followed, and if so, they want to psychologically put pressure on me, by making me tense, more stressed and making me lose my head. I wonder if all of them are there to help me, or to take me down. Absolutely, I don't want to visit or talk on the phone with my family members because I don't want to bring this evil on them. I stay away from them, because I love them.

In the middle of the night, a different Captain scratched our Memo-Book (Memorandum Pad/Activity Log). When we left, my partner PO Rivera told me how Sergeant Gibbs disliked that, Captain. He said that our Sergeant is passive-aggressive with him, in such a way that the Sergeant does whatever the captain tells him to do, but in an aggressive way. He gave me an example as to when the captain asked Sergeant Gibbs to look for someone upstairs that he did go, but on his way there, he was slamming the doors behind him. I knew well that he was comparing him to me. Because one day, when coming out of the RMP (police car), I slammed hard the door of the RMP (police car), and this was when later I found out that my gun's magazine was missing.

At 0830 hrs. or 8:30 am, I was still waiting for roll call to open its door because I wanted to get my court notification, but there was no one there yet. Lt. Yaguchi wasn't in his office neither. So, I left with PO Rivera and in front of the station house (precinct), I told him that I didn't know if I should wait, even though I wasn't going to get paid for the wait, or if I should just go home. One of the reasons why I had to leave was because my wife's mother was going to be home by herself, and she had to leave at 10:00 am, but she didn't have the keys to lock the door. Previously, I had told PO Rivera that, and he told me to go home and finish my business.

We stopped in front of the precinct, because he was not going to walk with me to the subway station; he was going to walk the other way. I don't know what type of evil plan they are fabricating against me. I don't know whether I should trust PO Rivera, or not. I was still there wondering what I should do, until desperately, PO Rivera said to me, "Listen, you must protect yourself man. There are a lot of wolves in there." Enough said. After he said that, I went home, no longer doubting whether to leave or not to leave.

Walking to the subway station, in the subway station, out of the subway station, on the bus, and walking to my building, there they were.

When walking to my building, I threw away a green bottle of Perrier containing Perrier water and grape juice, which they might think is alcohol. I threw it away in the garbage bin, still containing a small portion of the drink. I knew that they were going to look in the garbage bin to see if it contained some type of alcohol.

When I got home, I saw my wife's mother. Then, when my wife's mother was leaving, I saw that she had a red umbrella, and a blue purse with her. At that moment, I wondered if she was hired by them, for by the time that I and my wife were not there, she could let them get inside my apartment to search for it. At this moment, I trust no one.

"Cursing, deceit, and violence fill his mouth; trouble and malice are under his tongue. He waits in ambush near the villages; he kills the innocent in secret places. His eyes are on the lookout for the helpless; he lurks in secret like a lion in a thicket. He lurks in order to seize the afflicted; he seizes the afflicted and drags him in his net. So he is oppressed and beaten down; the helpless fall because of his strength. He says to himself, "'God has forgotten; He hides His face and will never see.'" Rise up, Lord God! Lift up Your hand. Do not forget the afflicted." (Psalm 10:7-12 HCSB)

"How long will you threaten a man? Will all of you attack as if he were a leaning wall or a tottering stone fence? They only plan to bring him down from his high position. They take pleasure in lying; they bless with their mouths, but they curse inwardly. Selah Rest in God alone, my soul, for my hope comes from Him. He alone is my rock and my salvation, my stronghold; I will not be shaken." (Psalm 62:3-6 HCSB)

On **Tuesday, July 15, 2014-Wednesday, July 16, 2014,** I arrived at the station house (precinct). I noticed that when Sergeant Gibbs, who was at the Desk, saw me, he didn't greet me, but when I grabbed the key of the RMP (police car), he said with an attitude of suspicion, "Hold it, hold it, hold it. What RMP (police car) do you have there?" He wasn't happy to see me at all.

When on patrol, Sgt. Lucic scratched my Memo-Book (Memorandum Pad/Activity Log). He didn't greet me either, which he used to every time he saw me. I told PO Rivera that there is truly a black cloud at the precinct, as Lt. Allen had said. On one occasion, when I was driving, I stopped at the light, and mistakenly I used the word 'rewind' instead of 'reverse' when trying to refer to the car's reverse. As soon as I said that word, I looked at PO Rivera's face, and his face looked as if he were amazed, appalled, and his neck looked stiff, for he contracted the lower part of his mouth and chin that connects to the neck. I guess I shouldn't have said that, because I don't want them to suspect that I know that they are recording every single conversation that I am having with him.

When I arrived at the station house (precinct) from patrol, PO Nancy Ramos called me and PO Rivera to go to the muster room for training. When we got there, it was just me and PO Rivera there. She showed us a video about perjury. When I went upstairs to the locker room, there I saw PO Chiodi, PO Gorman and PO Arroyo. PO Arroyo was wearing a thick red watch, while still wearing his uniform. By the color of the watch, he was letting others know that he belongs to the same team, the team of the Reds.

When he was done from getting change, I saw that he was wearing red and black clothing. PO Chiodi was ready to go and see the Manhattan Assistant District Attorney. PO Gorman told PO Chiodi that he was going to go there to add more things to the 'Especial Folder', which I believe is the case that they are trying to build against me. Then PO Chiodi said that his name will be well known for a week. I wondered what name. Then he said that he hopes that he doesn't retaliate against him. He continued, "I believe that I have died in the inside" (on a biblical perspective). Then he asked me if what I give to church is called a 'tithe' and how did I spell that. He seemed to be making fun of me. He appeared to be getting ready to do something against me, to harm me, for now they are doing whatever they can to inflict fear on me.

As PO Rivera and I were walking away from the station house (precinct), I saw when PO Estrada walked by us, next to us, and he continued walking away from us without saying a word to us. He should have greeted us at least, but he didn't.

On **Wednesday, July 16, 2014 –Thursday, July 17, 2014,** I met with PO Rivera at 1PP (1 Police Plaza= Police Headquarter). There, the Sergeant said that there are members of the press on the second floor. I wondered if they were there because of me. Then I saw a poster sign by the Headquarter Security office's door that said, "Eye on Every Block Program." "Uniform members share intelligence with uniform members," and somewhere along the lines it said, "Watch List." There, I wondered if the "Eye on Every Block Program" has anything to do with the people that are following me, and are participating on the scenarios that are being done to see how cops will respond and behave on each of the case presented, having me, of course, as their main focus for they are paying close attention to me.

Also, when I read, "Uniform members share intelligence with uniform members," I wondered if that is what my fellow officers are doing against me. And the famous "Watch list" might mean that I am on their watch list. This might be the reason why they are following me.

It was a cloudy day. There was lightning and thunder like the day before. On my break, I went to visit PO Rivera who was inside his booth, and I asked him about what is happening on the 25th precinct. PO Rivera said to me that the gods are angry. I told him to behave. Then outside, as soon as we stepped out, it began to rain and when he got inside his booth, I touched PO Rivera on his hand, and I told him that the sky was crying for me. As I walked away, he told me that it was because God is angry at me, and from a walking distance I said to him, "No, it is because of what you guys are doing to me." When I got to my post, I saw that there was a black charger. By the time I found it, the officer who had relieved me was already gone.

When I went to the meal, I met with PO Rivera, and he asked me if I could lend him my charger. I told him that I would. He asked me if I could send it to him with the guy who relieved me. I told him that I would. I sent him my charger. I went to the Headquarter officer and he lent me his white charger, which I gave it back to him at approximately

0156 hrs. or 1:56 am. Then I went to take my second meal, and after my meal, I picked up my charger. Then I wondered if that charger was planted there on purpose, once again, they are setting traps for me.

Later, we left 1PP (1 Police Plaza= Police Headquarter). On our way back to the precinct, we stood inside the subway station to wait for the train. As we were standing there, a young man wearing a camo short stood by our left, and another young man soon arrived wearing a camo short, and he stood by our right-hand side. Immediately, I noticed how PO Rivera became uneasy and impatient. He became so nervous that he began to hastily walk away further up without telling me anything. I followed him, and further up the train came.

I got onto the train, and when I turned around to look at PO Rivera, the train's door closed, and PO Rivera remained outside the train, so I waved goodbye to him with my hand. I know why he didn't get onto the train with me and allowed the train door to close before him. He didn't want to be followed by being with me. Also, I saw a man in his 60's with his dog, and his dog was right next to me. I wondered if it was already planned just to see if the dog could sniff and detect some type of drug on me.

By the time I arrived at the station house (precinct), there was PO Chiodi and PO Gorman in the locker room. I wondered what they were doing there at this time of the hour, because our tour normally ends at 7:50 am. The time was approximately 0840 hrs. or 8:40 am. Were they there because of me? Then I saw that a letter was attached to one of my lockers. It said, "If this locker is not properly identified by 7/21/2014 the lock will be cut and contents within vouchered," and underneath it is circled with a pen the following: Transferred/No Longer Assigned Here. Remove Your Property and Lock Will Be Cut On: 7/21/2014. It was the following letter:

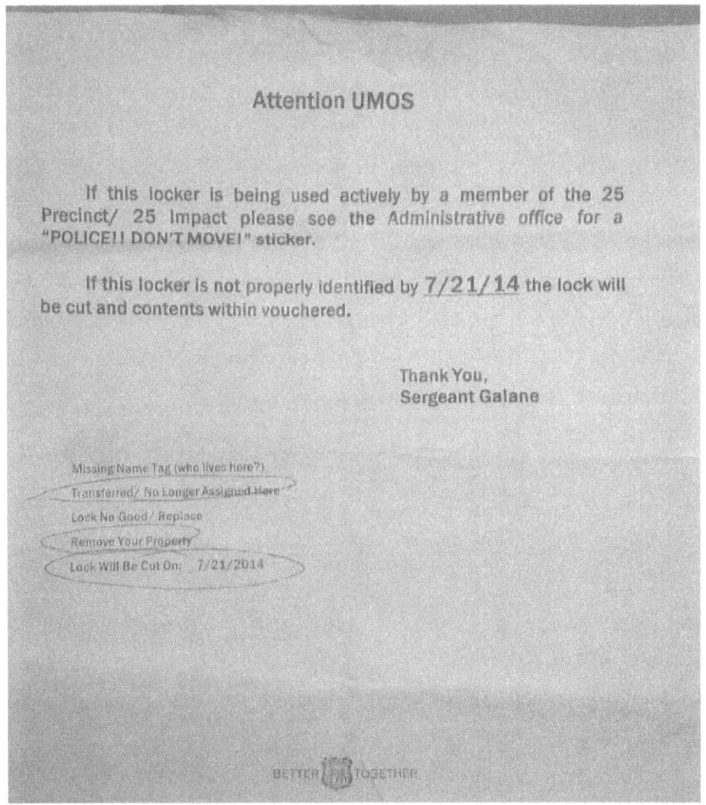

Why are they so obsessed with the lockers? Then PO Chiodi said that I have more than two lockers. That I have like 7 lockers and that somebody is in trouble. He asked me if I was going to call IAB (Internal Affairs Bureau, investigate police corruption), and he advised me that I should talk to my union PBA delegate and that he is here. My union PBA delegate who is PO Gorman, didn't say anything in regards, and they left after spitting poison on me.

There I wondered why PO Gorman doesn't do the job that he is mandated to do as a union PBA delegate. Why doesn't he inform me, advise me, and council me about all the things that are happening around me? Why did he take the job as a union PBA delegate representative when he is not going to represent his officers properly, but rather, he betrays the job that he has been commended to do. Now I know why our previous delegate, PO Kennedy, didn't want to transfer or delegate her position as union PBA delegate to PO Gorman before she retired.

Why did she want someone else to have the position of union PBA delegate? PO Gorman had said to me that the reason why she wanted another officer to have it was because she used to go out drinking with that person. But now, at this present time, I see why. Even PO Young once got into a heated argument or dispute with him for not representing him the right way. Now I see why. He is only interested in collecting that extra paycheck with minimal effort or with no effort at all. So instead of representing me, what he does is harass me the same way that the other officers do. If he can do me no good, at least don't do me harm.

My opinion of him is that during the time that I worked with him, his favorite moment was to park his vehicle on a safe spot and fall asleep there. I remember one time that I worked with PO Pinero that PO Pinero and I took our mealtime. When PO Gorman learned that we went out of patrol for meal, he stormed into the station house (precinct) furiously and in front of the Desk, he insulted me by releasing all the things that I never knew he held against me, just because according to him, we took his mealtime or let say, his sleeping hour time. He insulted me so badly that at the end of the day, he felt obliged to apologize to me.

When it comes down to productivity and work achievements, his record speaks for itself. But now, at this present time, he seems to have found an opening, a green light, an opportunity to destroy my life and my career. Now it seems that he has found an opportunity for career advancement and a shot for promotion. He and they have found a golden egg which is me. Besides all the promotions ahead if they make me fall, for PO Gorman, it will be a chance of a lifetime to be promoted to Detective. Since I am an easy prey, he just needs to attack me verbally, ignore my situation, and in a way facilitate, contribute and assist those who seek my downfall, and at the end, get rid of this easy prey. Now I am like a sheep who is waiting to be slaughtered. Now whatever it is that PO Gorman is doing, I find it to be very unethical, unprofessional, discriminatory, absurd, and goes against his own principles.

Also, I wonder why there is a locker outside the locker room. Probably they are trying to see if somebody opens it, since there might be a camera outside recording everything. I went to the 3rd floor, and I found Lt. Yaguchi talking to the woman in charge of payroll. When I went to roll call, I saw PAA Washington and another PAA who is working with her. For my surprise, PAA Washington was wearing an orange t-shirt and her partner a black one. Then I went to see Lt. Yaguchi, and I waited behind him, without him knowing, and when he turned around that he looked at me, he turned his back on me again without greeting me. Then after he finished talking to Payroll, he took me to his office, and in private, he greeted me, as if he didn't want others to see him greeting me and see what a hypocrite he is.

When I was walking down the stairs, I saw a young lady walking up the stairs from the first floor wearing a white t-shirt, and she had hanging on her left shoulder seemed to be a green t-shirt. I took the train and went to the Mambi restaurant. There, a guy wearing a blue T-shirt walked in to see what I was doing. When he left, another woman walked in wearing black dark glasses and a black t-shirt. It appeared to be that she was recording what I was doing. All I want to know is when enough is going to be enough. Enough is enough. I took the bus home and when I arrived, I saw that a big tree had fallen close to where I live. There were city parks employees cutting it down.

On **Thursday, July 17, 2014,** I began my 1345x2220 or 1:45 pm x 10:20 pm tour for the president detail. I had not eaten anything for almost all day. I was on foot post, standing there feeling fatigued, and mentally exhausted. I took a moment to buy something to eat, and when I returned to my post, I laid my food, which was inside a bag, on the floor to eat it later. As I was distracted by the people, a few minutes later, I looked at my bag, and I saw a dog already eating my food, great.

I was standing on the street feeling hungry and under the full-blown and full-bodied sun. There I saw Lt. Gonzales, whom I consider to be one of the main wolves or the 2nd wolf in command of the 25th precinct. He was lingering around like a wolf that slowly walks around its

Emmanuel Hernandez

prayer, and his presence there, each time, made me feel more and more tense and stressed.

At the beginning of the tour, he was in a bad mood, and later, I saw him, and I said hi to him, but he just looked at me and moved his head in response. By the time that we were done, I saw that he was in a good mood. Including, he was sharing his pack of gum with the other officers, except me. He looked as if he were celebrating something with them, while I was in a corner just looking at them. I was like an outsider.

There I was thinking whether his joy had anything to do with something that he just found out about me that would hurt me. My heart was beating so hard and rapidly. Inside the van, on our way back to the station house (precinct), I felt that my head was about to explode, due to the severe headache. I felt so much pressure on my head. Then I arrived at the station house (precinct), and took a nap there for a few minutes, before my next tour began.

My tour started at **2315 hours or 11:15 pm now Thursday, July 17, 2014, till 0750 hours or 7:50 am of Friday, July 18, 2014.** In the middle of the night, I told PO Rivera that I was having a headache. I stopped by Paladino Avenue for a moment, and at 1: 45 am, the Duty Captain parked his vehicle behind us, and he quietly walked towards us. I greeted the captain, and I told him that I had parked the vehicle there just for a moment. He told me that I shouldn't have parked the car there, because the location was considered a cooping prone location.

Then an EDP (Emotionally Disturbed Person) job was picked up by Sgt. Gibbs. The EDP was acting disorderly, and he was apprehended for such conduct. The Emotionally Disturbed Person was going to be taken to the hospital to be evaluated at the psych ward. But before, when I arrived at the scene, I noticed that the EDP was already searched, and his belongings were placed inside his **green** bandana. This is when I realized that this was simply another act or scenario. When he was being held against the RMP (police car) and facing the RMP (police car), with his upper body lying on the hood of the car, on one occasion I rested my hand on the hood of the car, and the EDP kissed my hand one time. I withdrew my hand right away in case he might try to bite it.

Then we escorted him to Harlem hospital. In the hospital, as he was sitting down on a chair, I noticed that he was wearing sneakers that had some **blue** on them. Also, he had a **blue** watch, which confirmed my suspicion. PO Rivera said to him, "Nice sneakers," and he continued saying, "Nice watch." This is the method that PO Rivera used to communicate to him that he already knows what is going on. As soon as the EDP heard that, he lowered his voice, looked straight, directly at PO Rivera by fixing his eyes on him, and he began to talk normal to him, as if he were no longer acting. I tried to catch what he was saying, but I was unable to understand him, because he had lowered his voice and was talking too fast. But suddenly, he changed his mood, and began acting up again, because the scenario must go on.

Then the EDP lowered his voice again and began to communicate some indirect truths. He was referring to someone, but he didn't name that mysterious person. He mentioned things such as a bicycle, and that he was just riding with him. The EDP said that the person was telling the truth, and that the person that he was referring to didn't do anything wrong. In the middle of the conversation, he looked at me straight on my eyes, and I stared at his eyes to the point that he began crying.

When I watched his tears drop, I realized that this time he was being for real. It was no longer part of the scenario. It was a revelation of what was hidden in his heart, and it was coming out of his heart. He was crying because of me and for me, because of the way that I am being treated. I know that deep inside his heart he knows the truth of my innocence. He could hardly keep to himself the words that he wishes to express, to better help me understand the situation that I am in. Because he sees a man that is being wrongfully accused of whatever it is that they are accusing me of. But his tears had said enough.

He continued saying some indirect truths, and PO Rivera began to interrupt him by saying, "Hey, hey, hey" in many occasions, as to try to prevent him from speaking up. PO Rivera told him that if he wanted, he would go back on his own time, and visit him without the uniform, but he kept talking. At one point, to distract us, PO Rivera began to snap his fingers with both of his hands, and at the same time, he began to hit an object to produce some noise with the intention of diverting my attention from the EDP by distracting me. Furthermore, to prevent him from talking. This time, PO Rivera was the one acting as an Emotionally Disturbed Person.

In the end, before leaving, I placed my hand on his shoulder, and he tried to kiss my hand again. Then in the RMP (police car), PO Rivera came up with an excuse as to why the EDP was acting that way. Now PO Rivera was trying to make me forget, so I won't think about the things that the EDP had said. He thinks that I didn't get the message, but I can't say anything, because I am in a dangerous zone, or better said, in a critical and insecure position. I am already condemned.

Moments later, there was a DWI (Driving While Intoxicated) arrest in our sector, which PO Ahmed volunteered to take. But Sgt. Gibbs approached me and asked me if I was not going to take it. I really didn't want to take it. I was scared to take it, because of what happened on **December 10, 2013**. He seemed upset that I didn't take it. But PO Ahmed volunteered to take it.

What is the big problem? I couldn't understand why he was upset if he was going to get credit for PO Ahmed's arrest anyway? Especially when he knows that I did a double and had court also. At that moment, my headache didn't want to stop. Then I began to think that what he wanted was for me to take the arrest having a second intention in mind. He seems not to wish me well. It appears that he is desperate to break me. When he saw me, he didn't look at me with good eyes. All I want to know is what I did now?

At one point, while on patrol, PO Rivera began to talk to me about Lt. Yaguchi's achievements. He informed me that Lt. Yaguchi just passed the captain's exam, and the Bar exam, which means that he is officially a lawyer. Also, he told me how Lt. Yaguchi always comes to work two hours early, and how he doesn't get paid for those extra hours. But how does he know that? Before, he had told me that even when Lt. Yaguchi is not physically at the 25th precinct, he is always there. I wondered what he meant by that. Of course, the precinct is bugged, wired, so it is not only when I come into physical contact with him that he is there.

When we were done with patrol, that I was driving, right before I drove the RMP (police car) back to the parking lot, I saw Lt. Yaguchi coming, and when I stopped the RMP (police car) at the entrance of the parking lot to greet Lt. Yaguchi, before getting into the parking lot, PO Rivera advised me to keep on driving into the parking lot, but I didn't. I stopped and when Lt. Yaguchi saw me, he showed an expression of disappointment on his face. He moved his eyeballs up as if to look at the sky, and then he looked at me. He shook my hand. He was holding a book in his hand, probably a book on strategies on how to bring a person like me down and crush him. But God is bigger than my problems.

PO Rivera kept telling me, "No regrets." He told me to enjoy my mini vacation with no regrets, and on different occasions, he kept telling me those same words. I asked him why he kept telling me that. But how can I enjoy my mini vacation when I use my vacation days to type.

PO Gambardelli opened his locker, and he began showing PO Rivera something that he had inside his locker. He was showing him some pictures, and PO Rivera was telling him how he kept his locker well organized. I walked there to see, and PO Gambardelli showed me pictures of his father. I told him that his father looked just like him. Then one of the officers said something about somebody stealing something. The officer said that they were breaking him, and this is when I heard PO Morovich saying that he was already broken, and that he couldn't wait for that moment. At home, while taking a shower, I kept thinking about those words. Why didn't they give out a name? Was it because the man they were referring to is me?

I have resolved not to go to my parents' 50 years wedding anniversary celebration. My mother called me 1 time on **July 13, 2014**, and I shorten my conversation with her, because I know, since they are following me the way they do, the same way my smartphone is being wiretapped. Then she called me **1 time** on **July 15, 2014**, but I didn't answer. On **July 17, 2014,** my mother called me **5 times**, but I didn't answer. Later my mother called me 1 more time and I didn't answer. On **July 18, 2014,** my mother called me **3 times**, but I refused to answer.

On **July 19, 2014,** my wife called my older sister and asked her about the celebration. My sister told my wife about the surgery she had, and that she was still recuperating from it. That my other sister lost her baby a day ago, due to the high level of stress in her life, causing the child to have a weak heart. She was devastated. I wondered if those unreturned calls were a contributing factor. In addition to that, my mother couldn't get up from her seat on her own. The celebration was cancelled. Later my mother **called me 1 more time**, and I couldn't hold it anymore, I answered her call, and being brief, I greeted her and told her that I couldn't visit her. We had a very short conversation, and I had to let her go.

To forget, I went to eat something outside. There my followers sat by me and one of them was right next to me. He was wearing a black T-shirt. Then I went to take train A on 177 Street, but the subway station was closed. I stopped there, and then two guys stopped there also, pretending to be disappointed that the A train was not working. Then I went to take the bus. My follower went inside the bus, and then as I walked to take the D train to go to the movie theater to watch the movie, "I Origins," I noticed that one of the persons who was in the bus, and who was wearing green, went to take the D train, and one guy wearing a black t-shirt and a camo hat stood on the second platform down to see where I walked to. I walked to the first lower platform. When the train arrived, he walked close to me, in addition to the man who was wearing red.

When I walked out of the movie theater room, and I was halfway away from the movie theater room on my way home, I saw a guy by himself seating on the stairs, as if he were waiting for me there. When I took the train home, the same happened.

On **Monday, July 21, 2014,** I went to the park for some peace and quiet, and to contemplate God's creation. There I took a seat on a bench, opened my book and I began reading. I was finally enjoying my moment, but not until a woman walked by and she was talking to another person when she said, "… going to use that against him." Her comment disturbed my peace, and I can't forget that statement.

This is **Tuesday, July 22, 2014,** and as I type this, I remember that around two weeks ago, PO Rivera was in the RMP (police car) with me, and he showed me a picture of a vehicle and how that vehicle looks like the one he has. But then he asked me if I remembered his vehicle.

Before **December 10, 2013**, ADA Altman had asked me the same question back then for the DWI (Driving While Intoxicated) case. If I remembered the color of the vehicle. This time, PO Rivera wanted to do the same, he wanted to put my memory to the test. I became so angry, because I couldn't remember, and knowing his intention I said to him that he is very clever. Immediately, I walked out of the RMP (police car) and I stood outside next to the RMP (police car).

I am so tired of witnessing how people keep playing with me. All I want is for them to leave me alone, but they are so eagle, blind and so determined to ruin my life. For them, I have such an easy high-value target. They keep squeezing me and oppressing me without room for compassion. I am so afraid to open my mouth and express my feelings, because if I do, I know that what I say will be misinterpreted, misunderstood, distorted and misused for their own benefit. They will distort my words. So, I can't spit out my enchained words, I must swallow them. I know that God will fight for me, while I keep my silence.

On **Wednesday, July 23, 2014,** I went to the gym, and inside the locker room, I saw a black pair of gloves on one of the benches, and there was nobody there. I couldn't believe that they were still testing me. On my way home I was still being followed. Then I went to the restaurant for something to eat, and inside of the restaurant, there was a guy wearing a green t-shirt. He had decided to stay and eat his food there with his friend. Neither of them seemed not to know Spanish. They sat close to me.

Then I went to take the train to watch a movie. I took train A to 59th street and on 59th street, I took the #1 train to stop on 72nd street, and from there I walked to the movie theater. But while I was inside the #1 train, heading to 72nd street, there was a man like in his mid-50's who out of his frustration began to express his feelings by raising his voice for everyone in the train to hear. He asked, "What is love?" He continued saying that we should stop hurting each other, and that every human being should have a little moment of peace. I believe that he was directing those comments to me and to those who are following me. He seemed to be frustrated seeing the way that I am being treated. How I am being followed everywhere I go at my job, and out of my job.

Then I went to the movie theater. The show time for the movie that I wanted to watch was cancelled. Then I went to see my dentist, and on my way to the dentist, I saw a white man who was wearing a white bandanna. He seemed to be recruiting a young Hispanic woman. As I walked by them, I heard her say, "That is not fare," and I thought to myself that it might be her response to the horrific idea of people following other people. After my visit to the dentist, I went and took the #1 train. Then I walked to Maoz food place and when I was there, a young guy who was wearing a blue T-shirt, sat in front of me. He seemed upset too. I don't blame him; I would have been upset too. This is not right. All this is absurd.

On **Thursday, July 24, 2014,** in the morning, after finally having finished patrol and being back to the station house (precinct), I wondered why they have placed those two black barriers at the station house (precinct). One barrier was placed next to the Desk, and the other one was placed right at the entrance. I was right next to the one at the entrance. PO Rivera was with me and PO Michael Margiotta was facing me. I said that the barrier looked like it didn't belong there, and PO Margiotta said that it was placed there because of me. I didn't say anything. After work, on my way home, that I took the number # 4 train, I saw a Mexican man wearing a black t-shirt with grey numbers that said, "24/7", which in my case, I am being watched 24/7.

Later that afternoon, I went to the station house (precinct) to prepare for 1PP (1 Police Plaza= Police Headquarter) and do a 7:00 pm till 7:50 am shift. At 1PP (1 Police Plaza= Police Headquarter), I was assigned to check point Able. There I thought that I was going to escape the scenarios at least for a moment, but it wasn't the case. There was a white guy wearing a blue t-shirt, and he had his phone facing me. He was trying to walk into the only NYPD personnel allowed area and I had to stop him. Also, there were a couple of people asking me where Pearl Street was, but I didn't know. There are three corners that don't have street names, but the 4th corner that was across the street, opposite where my post was said, 'Park Row'.

Later, one of them asked me for the 500 Pearl address and I directed her to another post that was at Pearl and Madison, so she could ask another officer there for directions. Then she asked me about SDNY, and I told her that the guard for that place was right opposite to her, across the street and to go and ask him. Then when I went for meal that I took a better look at the street signs, across the street, at another corner, I managed to see that on the side of the street name sign 'Park Row', it said 'Pearl' street, and when I took a better look at the street signs of the building across the street of my post, it said 500 Pearl. I felt so embarrassed.

In addition, a white man like in his late 50's, felled on the floor and when I got there, he was already getting up. He looked intoxicated. He asked me for an address. I walked over to the Marshall, because it happened on their side, but I asked him if he needed an ambulance. Later, being summertime, there was a man wearing a jacket, and he had a hoodie on his head. He was walking to the Marshall. As soon as I saw that he was wearing gloves that were white and orange colors, I realized that it was another game. When I went to the 2nd floor for my personal, I saw a 1PP (1 Police Plaza= Police Headquarter) Headquarter officer there, and he asked me, "A lot of things is going thru your head right?" He could see that I was not well.

When I finished my duty at 1PP (1 Police Plaza= Police Headquarter) that I took the train back to the station house (precinct), I took a seat, and everything seemed ok. Later, when I was seated, resting after a long night, when the train stopped at 86 East Street, where most of the people left the train, I saw a suspicious plastic bag underneath one of the seats, where there was no one sitting. The bag was there, unattended. It looked like it had something inside. At first, I believed that it was part of another scenario.

I looked around to see, but even though I suspected that there were a few people already participating in this (Because of the uniformed colors), I couldn't take the chance. I had to act even though the probability or possibility exists that it might be part of another scenario. So as soon as the train stopped at 125 East Street, I dealt with the bag and made sure that it was not an explosive. Later, I inspected it and took the bag out of the train. When I searched for it, and confirmed that it was not an explosive, I picked it up and placed it on top of the black subway garbage bin. I made sure it was safe.

When I arrived at the station house (precinct), I found it strange that only saw Sgt. Rodriguez was at the Desk writing, and PO Golden was busy doing something else. I went upstairs and left my stuff inside my locker. Later, I walked down the stairs, and I noticed that there were many cops already at the station house (precinct). Among them was Lt. Yaguchi, and Sgt. Jackson. They were behind the Desk. But what made me laugh was that standing, concealing or hiding by the door, probably looking through the small glass opening that the door has, prying to see with what I was going to leave the station house (precinct), was PO Alexander. But for his surprise and mines, I opened the door, because I needed to go to the Desk for something and that's how I discovered him.

Afterwards, I went home, having no one on whom I could lean on. If I tell my wife, she will get angry at me again. She will begin repeating the same discouraging sermons out loud and will end up saying that I need to see a doctor, that I am not well. It is almost 1500 hrs. or 3:00 pm and I haven't gotten any sleep, but here I am instead typing all this. I have been awake for how many hours? Do the math. Later, I received a text message from Lt. Yaguchi. He has me down for overtime on Saturday.

On **Saturday, July 26, 2014,** I noticed one of the many unusual treatments that I am receiving. PO Banks tried to avoid talking to me, also PO Ahmed. PO Jones and PO Chardonett talked to me because I talked to them first. I don't know how to deal with this situation in my workplace.

At the checkpoint (stopping vehicles randomly), when I was inside the RMP (police car) checking in the computer at the motorists' information, I noticed that PO Banks waited outside, as if waiting for me to come out. He went inside the vehicle the moment I stepped out of it. I wondered why he didn't go inside when I was inside. It was obvious that he was trying to avoid me.

On one occasion, while I was inside the RMP (police car), from the windshield, I saw PO Ahmed, PO Rivera and PO Banks secretly talking. When PO Rivera came back to the RMP (police car), he told me that he was feeling so good. Then he called me 'Goliath,' and that I could call him 'David'. Probably, because he is soon going to cut my head off, and for this reason, I am used to call him Judas. Now I wonder what happened.

Back home, when I spoke to my wife, she told me that my mother had called her, and that she told my mother that I was living a good life, just working and sleeping. But then my wife told me that she is living a tragedy with me. She said that she will not give me children to see me like this, and that I just keep wasting my time by writing down everything that is happening to me.

Monday—I stepped out of the elevator, and right before exiting the building's door, behind me, I saw a black young man wearing a black t-shirt, and outside, opposite to the building, I saw a man standing having his cellphone on his ear. As soon as he saw me, he changed position, as to alert someone of my exiting the building. In the Gym, there was a woman wearing a red t-shirt, and a black tight pant, the same colors. When I went to my locker, on top of it, I saw a black Beat earphone, with the red b letter, and a water bottle. I took the bus to the barbershop, and on my way, I saw many people wearing the black, green, red, blue and the camo colors, including a woman who was wearing a blue t-shirt.

For what should I hope for and thrive for when my future seems so dark. I went to school with the hope of becoming who I am now, a police officer. As a police officer, there are many things that I want to achieve, but the good things that I want to accomplish have been halted, because I have come under great attack. And what is even worse, they are stepping on my good name. Now, as I am typing, I feel terrified. I don't want to type anymore, but I cannot stop, I must continue typing. I have no one to talk to about this matter that has become the most horrific problem I have ever had in my entire life. But I know that my God hears my cries, and he sees what I am going thru, but it hurts.

I can't believe that all this is happening to me. All I wanted was to work and live a normal life, enjoy a simple life. But it seems that I am asking for too much. I keep hearing strange sounds, like footsteps coming from the rooftop of my apartment and I am wondering if they have people already spying on me from the rooftop. Oh Manhattan ADA (Assistant District Attorney) Altman, what have you done to me? Putting an innocent man's future on the line, by trying to ruin his life for the sake of a case that you wanted to win, when you knew well that I was not ready nor prepare to give out my testimony before God, the judge and the jury. You won the case, but still, your hate towards me hasn't ceased.

On **Tuesday, July 29, 2014,** I came out of my apartment and took the train to go to the shooting range. When I stepped out of the #4 train at East 125 Street, and waited for the #6 train, there I saw a white man wearing dark glasses, and right away I knew that he was spying on me. Later, I went into the train, and I no longer saw him, but the people who are following me around, were there wearing some of the magical colors, in this case, the blue, the black, and the green.

They are so much doing it, that inside the train, being worn out and out of my frustration, I began to squeeze the empty plastic bottle that I was holding. I did it multiple times, while making sufficient sound at every squeeze. When I arrived at Pelham Park, coming out of the wagon, I saw the same white man who was still wearing the dark glasses, and he was talking to another man. When I walked out of the subway station that I waited for the bus at the bus stop, I saw another white man approach me, and he was wearing a green t-shirt. He was right next to me. I became so frustrated that I took a taxi instead, just to run out of there. The taxi left me close to the shooting range.

Then, while I was walking to the shooting range, a police officer drove by me, and he stopped. He offered me a ride to the shooting range, which I accepted. He was wearing a blue T-shirt. When I was walking to the waiting line, there I saw PO Rivera walking to the line, and at the same time, PO Ahmed who was just coming from a different direction. It appeared to me that the two were just waiting there for me to arrive. However, there was PO Rivera wearing a blue shirt sleeve shirt, and PO Ahmed who was wearing a yellow greenish T-shirt. Most of PO Ahmed's conversations were directed to PO Rivera, as if he was trying to avoid having a conversation with me.

When the instructor arrived, I believed his name was PO Eastwick. The first thing he did was to talk about how there are cops who like to steal rounds (bullets), and how there are cops who become cops to steal. This was his introduction. During his lecture, he didn't look at my direction not even once, as if he was trying to avoid looking at me. When we were cleaning our gun, the same officer that gave me the ride was right behind me, cleaning his gun as well. I knew that PO Ahmed and PO Rivera had noticed it. In addition, I want to mention that one day, when doing the details for the building explosion at East 116 Street, one member of the ambulance approached me and two other officers that were with me and gave us each rugged green economy safety goggles to wear, and these came inside a clear plastic bag. The range has the same type of goggles for us to borrow.

Now walking to the shooting range, I showed PO Rivera the goggle, which was still inside the plastic bag, and it wasn't open yet. So, in front of PO Rivera, I opened it, and I threw the plastic bag away. I did it in front of him just to avoid any future confusion. At one point, I decided to go to the bathroom, and by the time that I arrived at the bathroom, the bathroom was empty. Then as I used the toilet, I heard a lot of officers arrive.

Back to the station house (precinct), I went to the lounge and lay on the sofa, and so did PO Rivera and PO Ahmed. Later, PO Ruffa walked inside the lounge. When it was 2304 hrs. or 11:04 pm, PO Ruffa made the famous throat sound loud enough. I knew that he did it intentionally, because he wanted to wake the two of them up, because our next tour was going to start at 2315 hrs. or 11:15 pm. So, as soon as I heard the throat sound, I said, "The alarm just sounded."

On **Tuesday, July 29, 2014-Wednesday, July 30, 2014,** at 0536 hrs. or 5:36 am a security holding job came over the radio. When I arrived at the station house (precinct) with the prisoner, PO Rivera helped me with the paperwork, before the day tour Lieutenant, whose name I don't recall, arrived. The day tour Lieutenant seems not to like me since the last time that he made me voucher for the items of a person that I arrested.

Then I transported the prisoner to Manhattan Central Booking with officer, I believe his last name is Dimflmaer, and he was wearing black sunglasses that on the side said, "Spy" and "+". I considered it to be a tip, so I may realize that he was spying on me, and that those glasses might be video/voice recording. I drove there, handed over the prisoner and then I went back to the precinct. The other officer drove me back. I finally got something to eat.

Back at the station house (precinct), I heard when the day tour Lieutenant spoke to Lt. Reid about the FBI and Internal Affairs getting involved in something, and about the Sergeants that were doing overtime etc. He was raising his voice loud enough as if he wanted me to hear, but PO Pedrosa tried to talk me out of it by trying to distract me, so I may not pay full attention to whatever the day tour Lieutenant was telling Lt. Reid.

She did it so consistently. They were behind the Desk. I became nervous. I felt like dying. The captain was around, and suddenly, Lt. Yaguchi, and the ICO (Integrity Control Officer) Sergeant, went with the Captain to the Captain's office. I saw strange people at the station house (precinct). Many of them were new faces. I was wearing my entire uniform: my gun belt, bulletproof vest, everything always, because my worn-out body wanted to take all those pounds off me, but I couldn't distract myself from trying to know more from them.

At first, it appeared that somebody had stolen a bike from the station house (precinct), because some officers rushed out of the station house (precinct), until they found out that it was one of their C.I.s (Confidential Informants) who had taken it legally. C.I.'s are people who give out information to detectives or to the Manhattan District Attorney's office about crimes that were committed, being committed or that are about to be committed. The Black's Law Dictionary defines an informant as the "One who informs against another; esp., one who confidentially supplies information to the police about a crime, sometimes in exchange for a reward or special treatment." (West Group 2001). I wonder if those who are following me are Confidential Informants.

Now, there I was at the station house (precinct) in great distress. Then I heard one of the officers say something about the Audio Section, and the moment I heard 'Audio Section', I became convinced of what I have always being suspecting, that the entire station house (precinct) is bugged, and that everything I say or do is being recorded. But I must endure all this and be strong.

When I got home, I took a shower, ate my food, and I threw myself on the bed. I didn't wake up until the next day. When I woke up, I began to think about the arrest I made, about what is happening back at the 25th precinct, and about all the turmoil that is happening there, around me and in me. All I can think of is that they are treating me as if I were a criminal. Even as I was talking to the Manhattan ADA (Assistant District Attorney) on the phone in regards to the arrest I made today, I believed that she was not the only one listening to me, but that there were more ADA's listening as well, in order to point out at every single mistake I might make, besides all the fun they are making of me. By the time I signed the affidavit, I had worked **28 hours** and **54 Minutes** straight.

Now I know that I am being perceived as the most incompetent police officer in the entire world, but not every officer in the world is going thru the same hell that I am walking thru. In addition, the arrest was simply another scenario, because the man was wearing a red t-shirt and a red hat. How can I focus on my job? From the moment that I am at the scene, I am thinking that it is another scenario. That I am being voice and video recorded, and that they are looking at different ways by trying to figure out how to cause me harm. It is like my mind is being divided here and there. Having 75% focused on my emotions, and their evil intents, which I must keep to myself, and besides always being on high alert.

In addition to the questions that keep raising in my head, and the other 25% of my attention is focused on what is happening in the job, and how I am doing my job. They are dedicated to looking at ways that may help them tarnish my reputation. They are abusing me psychologically.

On **Thursday, July 31, 2014, for Friday August 1, 2014,** I went to do 1PP (1 Police Plaza= Police Headquarter) from 7:00 pm till 7:50 am for a 12 hours and 50 minutes tour. When I was on my break, at approximately 10:34 pm, my wife called me and she told me that when she went to the bank, a man grabbed her butt. She told me that she reported the incident to the police and that they took her to East 123rd Street, to the Special Victims Unit.

When she told me that, I didn't ask her about the specific details of what happened, because I knew that my smartphone was being wiretapped. But I had in mind one important question. What was the perpetrator wearing? I could imagine what factor contributed to the crime. I am so angry, upset, and frustrated at what is going on. This is what I have been trying to avoid. This is the main reason why I don't get in touch with my family. I simply don't want to put them in harm's way. I have warned my wife, but she doesn't believe that there are people out to get me and look at what they just did to her. But I decided to wait until I got home to confirm.

Then I went to speak to my old friend, PO Wilfred Nuñez, who is an officer permanently assigned at 1PP (1 Police Plaza= Police Headquarter) as Headquarter security officer. He relieved another officer for meal/break. We spoke, but as I spoke to him, I had the notion that he was being wired. I told him that I felt like Rocky at the 25th precinct. He told me that there were three permanent spots or positions open and if I wished to get transferred there. He told me that he was going to talk to his Sergeant about me.

As we spoke, a stranger walked towards us wearing a black T-shirt, and he had long braids. The stranger told us that he could sense negative things. He practices Yoga and he is a numerologist. He asked me and PO Wilfred Nuñez for our date of birth, and he began talking about it. I knew very well that PO Wilfred Nuñez was already aware and familiar to the condition regarding the whole scenario thing. The stranger said that we go to court to testify against the unrighteous. He wanted my opinion, and I said that I had no comments, and his response to my short answer was that it was wise of me to have said so (It is more than clear that it had to do with the court case of **December 10, 2013**). I showed PO Wilfred Nuñez my other smartphone.

Back to my booth, inside the booth, in the silence, I couldn't stop thinking about what is going on in my life; except during the few minutes that I spent talking to PO Wilfred Nuñez or to the other Headquarter Security police officer. I spent almost all the time inside the booth, listening to nothing, not using my smartphone not even to listen to the radio, because there were a lot of thoughts already invading and occupying my mind. The mind doesn't rest if it is occupied.

At six in the morning, I decided to listen to the radio station. When I was done with changing in the bathroom, when I came out of the bathroom to go home, I saw someone with whom I had worked with at the Equipment Section back then when I was a police cadet. I believe that he is Chinese, and we call him Kenny. He still works in the Equipment Section. When he saw me, he told me that he had offered me coffee before, and that next time he would like to buy me coffee. He asked me when I was coming back to 1PP (1 Police Plaza= Police Headquarter), and I told him that since I was going to work next Tuesday for Wednesday, I will see him next Wednesday in the morning. He told me that he would buy me coffee then. I felt so glad when he told me that, that I wanted to cry. Oh, my Dear friend Kenny, you can't imagine what I been thru.

I remember one day that I visited the Equipment Section with PO Rivera. There was Kenny. Kenny told PO Rivera that I was a good man. That there were cadets who had worked there and were arrested for stealing things. There must be a reason why he told that to PO Rivera.

When I was on my way home, I knew that those who were following me could notice my anger towards them. I looked at them directly in their eyes, because what they are doing is not only bad, but it is a crime. Later that day, I took the bus to Mambi restaurant for breakfast. When I got inside the bus, I saw that the bus conductor was talking to an elderly woman who didn't know English. I translated it for her. I told the conductor where her stop was. Later, she told me that she had a memory problem. She said that sometimes she loses her memory, and that she just drank her medication for it (Again, it had to do with me not remembering the events in the court case of **December 10, 2013**).

Of course, they studied my commute, my habits, which didn't change. So, predicting what bus I was going to take, and at what time I was going to take it, they made this little scenario just to play with me, as if my life was a game. She was wearing red. In addition, she told me that she only had one good daughter, and that her other children were not good. Moreover, there was an elderly man who was wearing a green hat, and he had been trying to help her as well. The two were Hispanics. I was prone to believe that this was another scenario.

When I arrived at the restaurant, where I took a seat, there were my followers again. At the end, there were three of them sitting right next to each other wearing red T-shirts. When I left, I went to the bus stop that is in front of 656 west 178 street, and there I saw a man laying down with his eyes closed. He had an open box containing what appeared to be golden Jewelries. I found it to be so ridiculous that they came up with a scenario like this. Finally, I got home after a long and miserable day.

When I saw my wife, immediately, I wanted to know every single detail of what happened to her. I asked her: What was the perpetrator, who had grabbed her butt, wearing, and the first thing she told me was that he was wearing a green Polo shirt. Immediately, when I heard that, my frustration renewed, and it rose to the peak, again. She told me that she was afraid to walk there again. I am angry, I am fuming, I want to yell and scream, but I must bear, I must endure. There is nothing I can do. Wouldn't you have felt the same way if such a thing had happened to your wife? This has gone way too far.

Chapter 15

August 2014 Events

On **Saturday, August 2, 2014,** when I finished my tour, I decided to take my Cobra training equipment and place it inside my small luggage. I urged PO Rivera to take his Cobra training gear with him as well. At 0919 hrs. or 9:19 am, when I was going to take the train at East 116 street, that I went inside the subway station, and when I was about to swipe my metro card, there I saw one metro card standing and inserted at the swiping machine. I took it and placed it on top of the metro card dispenser machine. I knew what it was all about. It seems that they don't know what to do with me.

On **Sunday, August 3, 2014,** I arrived at the church. I went downstairs to the bible study class and there I saw the regular church members. One of them was wearing an orange shirt, another one was wearing a black shirt, many were wearing blue shirts, and another one a green jacket. Right to my left, there was one of them wearing a blue with white shirt. Trying to greet him, I offered him my hand, and he offered me his fist. I became so distressed that I had to say, "Not even in church," while moving my head. I who once participated openly and freely in the bible study class, have now become a silenced lamb.

At that moment, I considered them to be spies or Confidential Informants ready to do some kind of trick on me. For example, Man…, he was wearing a blue shirt and when I saw him in the bathroom, he didn't great me. My pastor didn't greet me with the same hug that he used to give me, but with a simple distant and firm handshake. She looked at me and pretended she didn't see me. I really want to know what is going on. Everybody has turned their back on me.

Later, where I was seating, one member of the church, who was seating behind me, told me how good the pastor looks being that he is 90 years old. I agreed with him. Then he told me that his memory is good, because without the memory, the body is nothing. I definitely know that he said that because of what happened back in court on **December 10,**

2013. The day that I couldn't remember well the details of the occurrence when I arrested the person. Now I know where this is going. Wherever I go, I can't find peace.

On **Monday, August 4, 2014,** I went to court to testify for an arrest that I had made. There I saw ADA (Assistant District Attorney) Connolly, who was assigned to the case. When she saw me, she didn't shake my hand, but she shook the witness' hand, who was next to me. She greeted him with amicability. She told me that my testimony was going to be very short.

When we headed to the courtroom, as we walked there, all I could hear was the throat sound being made by the nearby people. Now, how should I feel about it? Later, we had to go back in the afternoon, because there were no openings available to present the case. When we went back, ADA (Assistant District Attorney) Connolly reassigned the case to another ADA or to be introduced by this other ADA. I wondered why she didn't do it.

I testified. Then the new ADA (Assistant District Attorney) told me that I could leave without saying goodbye nor thanking me for coming. She said nothing at all. However, out of nowhere, a strange woman greeted us and shook our hand. She told us that we did well. I wondered who she was, but when we got to the elevator, the new ADA called out the strange woman by the name, I believe to be 'Supervisor Collins', and she was holding the elevator for her. At that moment, I discovered that she was their supervisor. I wondered why a supervisor was needed for this. And why did the ADA have to use the word 'supervisor.'

I went into a room, I believe is called "the police room," to punch out, and then I went to the bathroom. Inside the bathroom, I saw PO Estrada, who is from my precinct, the 25th precinct. I greeted him and he greeted me. I told him that I was leaving, and he asked me if I was going back to the station house (precinct). I told him that I wasn't, and he said to me that I was a smart boy for deciding not to go back there. My God, what is going on? I smiled at him and walked away. It reminded me of the day and moment when after I walked out of the 25th precinct to go home, that I was thinking of returning to the station house (precinct), that PO Rivera warned me not to go back there, because there were wolves there. I am in a very scary situation.

When I took the train, I could see my followers looking at me on the train. When the train was arriving at East 125 street, I could see them paying close attention to me. I knew that they were like hoping that I didn't come out of the train at that stop. When the train opened the door, I noticed that they were being attentive. Some stepped out of the train, but others remained inside, looking at what I was going to do next. They seemed concerned. While I remained standing there, and as I did, my eyes became watery, because deep in my heart, I was certain that they knew of my innocence, and that they were witnessing the cruel and gruesome treatment that was and is being administered towards me by the system, or let say, the city. I held my tears tight. I held my tears captive by making sure they didn't come out.

I went home, then I went to the gym, and on my way home that I was going to open the building's door, there I saw a red rosary hanging on the knob of the door. When I arrived home, again, I asked my wife about the person who had touched her. When she saw how furious I was when I said, "I knew it," she told me that I didn't care about her, but that all I care was about those who are following me.

Then I looked at a New York Daily News article, "Gunman shoots, pistol whips man in Bronx bodega," where a surveillance video showed that the gun man was wearing a red polo short and his hat appeared to be green, and those are the colors that the spies who are following me wear. Then on this same day I looked at another New York Daily News article, "Arrest in attack on Brooklyn teen…," and I was dismayed and appalled to see that one of the attackers was wearing an orange t-shirt. This is another criminal wearing the colors that my followers wear.

I am mortified; I don't know what to do. I see that I am in great danger, and so is my family. They seem to be hiring people with criminal records to do the job as well, but they don't care. They hire the good and the bad. I believe that my life and the life of my loved ones are in jeopardy, and there is nothing I can do. What I can say is that I feel helpless, but in

God I trust, and he is the one who is helping me move forward, to keep on going.

On **Tuesday, August 5, 2014,** I went for COBRA training in the morning. When I arrived, the training officer told me to seat in the front. Seating next to me was a female officer who was wearing red. She lent me a pen. She was looking at my handwriting. My right hand was shaking a little bit, because she was staring at my terrible handwriting, which was enough to make my handwriting even worse and messy. PO Rivera was seating behind me.

While I was talking to him, he began to make the throat sound as to let the others know that he was with them. Later, I turned to PO Rivera, and playing around I called him Judas, and as soon I did, he whispered to me, "Please, don't do it to yourself." As soon as he said that my offensive dropped to the floor, in other words, fell to the ground. When we went to Seven Eleven, one of the cashiers couldn't talk because she was mute, she couldn't speak. She showed me a poster sign where she had written something to show her gratitude. However, when I walked away, I heard her make the same throat sound, as a form of communication.

When we were done with COBRA training that we were inside the D train, PO Rivera began to talk to me about Lt. Yaguchi's virtual, discipline, and that Lt. Yaguchi is driven by the code of honor. Also, he told me that Lt. Yaguchi can do harm without compassion, and that when PO Elliot Santiago realized it, he ran away. He transferred to another precinct. Then I told PO Rivera, "And you are his disciple." Immediately, after I said that, he looked up and narrowed his eyes. When he saw that I was looking at him, he asked me for today's date, which he did to change the topic.

Before he walked out of the wagon at Atlantic Avenue, I shook his hand and I sang to him, "Here I go again by my own," and walking out of the wagon, he smiled at me. I took it from the White Snake song.

I arrived at the station house (precinct), placed my uniform inside my bag, and seeing PO Perez (whom I call Robin) there, I explained to him the reason why I was there. I arrived to 1PP (1 Police Plaza= Police

Headquarter), and I saw that Sgt. Calma was wearing a blue t-shirt, and Sgt. Rodriguez was wearing red. While waiting in the lobby, at approximately 1736 hrs. or 5:36 pm, I saw Sgt. Urit Booncome from the Equipment section.

I believe that he is Chinese descendant. He walked by me staring at his smartphone, as if trying to pretend that he didn't see me. He continued walking staring at his device, and he was so much into it, if not thinking about me, that at the turnstile, he forgot to scan his ID, and as a result, he bumped into the turnstile. Then he scanned his ID. I used to work with him at the Equipment Section back then when I was a police cadet. But it seems that he doesn't want to associate with a suspected criminal because **according to the NYPD Patrol Guide, police officers are not allowed to associate with someone "2. c. Reasonably believed to be engaged in, likely to engage in, or to have engaged in criminal activities."**

When I was inside my booth, Sgt. Rodriguez came by and scratched (sign) my Memo-Book (Memorandum Pad/Activity Log). I noticed that he was wearing a red wristband. Later, when I was waiting in the lobby to sign out, there I saw PO Monteith, who used to work with me at the 25th precinct, but he was later transferred from the 25th precinct to the Gun and License Division unit due to an on-duty injury he sustained.

He looked pale when he saw me, and he walked straight to his office pretending that he didn't see me. Later, he walked out of the office because he needed to, and since this time we were very close to each other, he greeted PO Chiodi who was with me, and then he greeted me. When I was changing the bathroom, there I saw Kenny, the person who works in the Equipment Section. He told me that he forgot the coffee, but to go with him to the Equipment Section at least to watch a movie there. I told him to leave it for Friday, because I was overly exhausted.

When I walked to the subway station, right on the first turnstile, laying on the floor, I saw a metro card. Why not think that they are still trying to test me. I was so tired and mad that by the time I reached the platform, I gave my followers a despise look. I so intentionally did it that one of them began to shake his head, he looked concern, and worried, as if he were inferring the same thing that PO Rivera had told me, "Please, don't do it to yourself." But while inside the train, I decided to forcefully change my mood, and I smiled instead, and as soon as I did, I saw their faces relax. It was a moment of great tension. But in my head, I was thinking of all the things they are doing to me. So much was my focus on them that when I looked at the stop of the train, we were already at 149 Street, when I was supposed to have stopped at 125 Street.

I walked out of the train at East 161 Street and went to the other platform that goes back to Manhattan. I came close to a woman that was wearing green and a Hispanic man who wearing black. They were talking in Spanish. I heard her tell the man that was with her how a man, after losing a good job he had, went home and killed himself. I regretted the moment that I approached them for information. I went back to the station house (precinct), and there I saw Lt. Yaguchi, who seemed not willing to give me the day off, besides not greeting me when he saw me. I went home and cried.

Later, when my wife arrived home, she saw me typing all this. I greeted her and she responded, "What Emmanuel?" She told me that what I was doing (typing) was consuming me, and that I was allowing my job to consume me too. About five minutes later, I saw her getting ready to go out. I asked her where she was going. She answered, "I am going out. I am not going to stay here with a crazy man."

Now I think I have the NYPD, the FBI, the CIA, the Manhattan District Attorney's office and the one who sleeps next to me, by my side, all of them against me. My family think that I have abandoned them, the members of my church greet me from a distance to avoid having any sort of interaction with me. All I have to say is that "Here I go again by my own." But my faith and the hope that I have in God have preserve me. I know that he is going to make something good out of it.

On **Tuesday, August 5, 2014,** from 1900hrs or 7:00pm-Wenesday, August 6, 2014, till 1950 hrs. or 7:50 am, I went to 1PP (1 Police Plaza= Police Headquarter). At approximately or between 8:13 pm and 8:28 pm, wearing my police uniform, I went to Rite Aids. There appeared to be a security guy dressed in civilian clothing watching what I was doing in the store. I greeted him to let him know that I was watching him, being watching me. Oh, come on, isn't this funny, a security guy keeping his eyes on a New York City police officer in uniform in case he steals a candy bar? Are you kidding me?

On **Wednesday, August 6, 2014- Thursday, August 7, 2014**, I believe that it was on this night that PO Sofoka Ahmed approached me from behind, and he laid his hand on my shoulder telling me to hang in there. Thank you, PO Ahmed, not only from the bottom of my heart, but from the center of my heart, thank you.

On **Thursday, August 7, 2014, from 1900 hrs. or 7:00 pm – till 0750 hrs. or 7:50 am of Friday, August 8, 2014,** I was doing 1PP (1 Police Plaza= Police Headquarter). As soon as I got there, I overheard a woman say that they should make it more obvious. The moment I arrived to 1PP (1 Police Plaza= Police Headquarter), I could see the cops staring at me. They were talking among themselves, and I could hear them say the word "Fire," and other negative things. I saw a Headquarter security officer approach another Headquarter security officer, and he began to secretly tell him something by covering his mouth with his hand, and while still looking at me. I went to the 2nd floor to eat my food, and as soon as I got there, there was one officer seating there. She made the annoying throat sound twice and loud enough.

I went to my post at Park Row and Worth. As I was there, I opened the barrier for my good friend PO Fuentes, who was driving the scooter, and when I did, he told me that he was going to come back later to talk to me. But he never did. I went to have my meal at a pizza restaurant and when I entered the establishment, I ordered a slice. When the slice was handed over to me, I was pouring some garlic on the pizza, I added more than usual. The pizza man told me that garlic is good for the heart, and I asked him, "For the broken heart too, right?" and we both laughed.

When I returned, the Headquarter officer told me that he was glad that I was back, and the officer who relieved me for meal told me the same exact words, and when I smiled, he said, "To hell." Then I looked at the booth's foggy glass, and somebody wrote on the foggy glass in big letters, "Help!" I wondered if it was written intentionally, because I remember that the last time, I did 1PP (1 Police Plaza= Police Headquarter), after having sign out, that I was walking out of the office, I whispered to them, "Help." I did it to see if they could hear my plea, and call for help, and out of compassion, transfer me to work there, because I no longer want to work at the 25th precinct. My heart aches every time I go to work there.

All I want to know is why nobody moves a finger to help me or at least intervene for me. Can't they see how needy I am? Can nobody foresee my great despair? Where are those who used to greet me at 1PP (1 Police Plaza= Police Headquarter)? Where are they? Haven't I done a good job every time I go to work at 1PP (1 Police Plaza= Police Headquarter)? If they know that I do, why don't they come to my rescue?

Another Headquarter officer relieved the one that was working with me. He walked to me, and he advised me that I should save some money. That I should put money aside in case of emergency. He told me to work for time too. What I found strange is that he told me that right as soon as he saw me, as if he were sent by someone to tell me so. He seemed to be warning me. Also, he told me and wondered what he would have been doing if he were not working there. Why did he say that?

When I headed back to the lobby of 1PP (1 Police Plaza= Police Headquarter) that I was waiting to sign out, I came to see PO Monteith, who raised he arm towards me as to greet me, but immediately, he went into his office. While standing there, I felt judged by the cops that were around me, waiting with me to sign out. While standing there, my good friend Kenny from the Equipment Section came by and he handed me over a bag containing a coffee, and a sandwich. Then he left. I ate it right in the lobby. Later, I saw him inside of the bathroom, and he said goodbye. From the bathroom, I went to the Equipment Section and said goodbye to him, and he said goodbye to me, and he pointed out at a cop who was in plain cloth. As he did, he told me to look, that he was from PSA 5, and that now he is working there with them.

It saddens me because he had asked me so many times to transfer to the Equipment Section and to work there with them because they had an opening. So many times, he had insisted, but I had refused, because I wanted to be out there fighting crime, and serve the community alike. I didn't know that his intention was to save me, but it is too late now, because somebody else has received the blessing, and he introduced him to me.

I went to the bathroom, and while being inside of the bathroom, I heard and saw people coming in and out of the bathroom. When I left the bathroom, a guy who was inside of the bathroom, walked behind me out of the bathroom and he followed me from behind, up until I exited the building. As soon as I exited the building, there was a white man wearing green and he had dark glasses. He walked by me to the point that I had to say, "This is too childish." I said it loud enough for him to hear.

I arrived at the station house (precinct) and Sgt. Bennett, who once used to greet me with amicability, didn't even say hi to me. I walked up to the locker room, and there I saw PO Perez, whom I call Robbin, and he was inside of the bathroom. I greeted him, and he greeted me without looking at me. Then I went to the third floor, and there I saw 'CC', whose name I believe is PO Domigildo, I don't know if I spell it right. She looked at me, but she didn't greet me. I walked out of the station house (precinct), and while heading home, the number of Confidential Informants or spies seemed to be increasing. While on bed, I had stomach ulcers, stomach pain and heart burn. I couldn't rest, I couldn't sleep well, because I was waking up like every hour.

"But I am a worm and not a man, scorned by men and despised by people. Everyone who sees me mocks me; they sneer and shake their heads: "He relies on the Lord; let Him rescue him; let the Lord deliver him, since He takes pleasure in him." You took me from the womb, making me secure while at my mother's breast. I was given over to You at birth; You have been my God from my mother's womb. Do not be far from me, because distress is near and there is no one to help. Many bulls surround me; strong ones of Bashan encircle me. They open their mouths against me — lions, mauling and roaring. I am poured out like water, and all my bones are disjointed; my heart is like wax, melting within me. My

strength is dried up like baked clay; my tongue sticks to the roof of my mouth. You put me into the dust of death. For dogs have surrounded me; a gang of evildoers has closed in on me; ..." (Psalm 22:6-16 HCSB).

On **Friday, August 8, 2014-Saturday, August 9, 2014,** when I was inside of the train on my way to work, a woman passenger, who was seated, took out a piece of paper where to write. She placed it on top of her bible. Then, in big letters, she wrote, "The blood of Jesus doesn't lie on trial," and she placed the written paper back inside her bag. **(As I am typing thi**s**, on Saturday August 9, 2014, at 9:35 pm, I was recently interrupted by someone outside of my apartment who just made a throat sound, and right away, the alarm of the rooftop began to sound. Now, I will continue typing**).

I arrived at work. My partner and I were assigned to work at the station house (precinct). I prepared the summonses and the narcotics to bring them to the PBMN (Patrol Borough Manhattan North). Lt. Allen was assigned to the Desk. As I was standing by the property room, I overheard Lt. Gonzales tell Lt. Allen, "Keep an eye on this guy." I wondered what guy other than me. When he said that, I looked at PO Rivera's serious face, as he was standing in front of the T/S, facing and staring at the nonfunctional elevator or broken elevator for no other reason than to meditate on what Lt. Gonzales had said to Lt. Allen. When I was ready to do the Narco Run, I was assigned to RMP (police car) 5424. When I was inspecting the RMP, at the back seat, I found a crack-pipe. I went inside of the station house (precinct), and I told PO Rivera to follow me. I took him to the RMP and showed him what I found. He vouchered for it, and I did the Narco Run. I wondered whether Lt. Allen and Lt. Gonzales had together conspired to assign me to that RMP (police car), already knowing what was inside of it or had planted the crack pipe to get me in trouble.

I don't feel safe working at the 25th precinct. I am not afraid of them doing their job right, but I am afraid of what they might be capable of doing. They can plant some drugs or stolen properties on me and later claim that I have taken them. But what can I do?

When I arrived at the PBMN (Patrol Borough Manhattan North), the officer there told me that the property's PTR number had been improperly scanned, so I had to go back to the station house (precinct) and do it again there. When we went back to the precinct, I had PO Rivera fix it, because I didn't want to have anything to do with it anymore.

As he was seated fixing it, he began to constantly shake, move both of his legs. It was obvious that he was nervous. Then he told me that he wanted to go to the bathroom. Finally, he confessed to me that when he gets nervous, he needs to use the bathroom, but by the time it was done, it was already too late to bring the property back to the Borough (PBMN).

Later, I was assigned to a hospitalized prisoner. Then PO Rivera came to do the prisoner transport with me to MCB (Manhattan Central Booking). I wondered why he was assigned to do the T/S? At first, he told me that PO Ahmed and PO Banks were supposed to do the transport. Then I realized that it was because they didn't want me near the T/S, after the messy transfer of the narcotics.

When we were at MCB (Manhattan Central Booking), we took our prisoners to a place called 'special,' which is where they keep unhealthy prisoners. There, two officers began to talk about a woman that was arrested for robbery, and how she ended up committing suicide. Then one of the prisoners inside the cell began to say, "Don't be afraid of man, as long as you have a clean conscious with God, everything will be fine." Then PO Rivera said, "That's too far." Then I looked inside the cell, and there was a man standing wearing green. At that moment, I realized that he was the one who said it, because he was the only one standing grabbing the bars of the cell, while the others were just inside laying down. Then, as I was leaving, I winked one of my eyes on him, and he just stared at me.

When we arrived at the station house (precinct), PO Ahmed offered me half of his toasted bread, which I ate right away. What a miserable life is the one that I am living. Later, when it was time to leave, I got dressed and I walked to PO Rivera's aisle. There I saw that he had his locker wide open, and his blue T-shirt was hanging there. I called him on the phone, and he was downstairs. When I went downstairs, I saw him at the T/S staring at the computer's screen. He was still wearing his uniform, except for the gun belt. Then he stood up and he walked away without letting me know what he was doing there, because we always left together.

But of course, what else than probably updating or adding more to the accusatory file of PO Hernandez. Where it seems that everyone wants to contribute something to the file, being that many can't be fully participant in the ongoing investigation, because they dream of being promoted to detectives or if not, at least be able to choose where they want to be transferred to. Everyone wants to be part of something, and in this case, part of this circle of secrecy or trust. But now I wonder what I have said this time that has triggered that excitement in him.

Now there they are, formulating in bad faith, a plan against me, no matter how wicked it might be, as a way to hurt me badly. This is the time where the downfall of a suspicious man is highly desired. As I can see, a suspicious man should be mistreated, a suspicious man must be always suspected, a suspicious man's reputation is to be destroyed, and his name is to be stepped on.

He is to be repudiated, looked down to, murmured, criticized, and for him many traps need to be set up, because he is to be worth less than a rat, for a rat is to be looked with disgust, be hated and if possible, killed. But this suspicious man is to be looked down to with disgust and be also hated, but since he is a suspicious man, he is to be condemned, tortured and framed to make him suffer. Even worse, he is to be publicly humiliated, embarrassed, and much worse, if he has always been a shy person, it will force his nature-loving personality to remain inside his home and wish to never come out again.

I am being played like a cat plays with his mouse, and when the mouse is finally trapped on the sticky glue, where he has no other choice than to wait for his executioner. But I lift and raise my head up, because I have done nothing wrong.

On **Saturday, August 9, 2014 – Sunday, August 10, 2014,** I went to work. I believe that PO Jones feels resented towards me, because he was the last person to have used the RMP (police car) where I found the crack pipe. He might receive a Command Discipline for failure to inspect the vehicle. Therefore, he is angry at me.

Later, we were on patrol, and Central (the radio dispatcher) seemed to have made a mistake, because she assigned us to a sector Boy job, but then sector Adam came over, well it was a confusion that is hard for me to explain right now. But PO Rivera said something to me in regards that I had to say, "I don't know man, I don't know." Then I said to PO Rivera, "You see, when I said that I didn't know, didn't mean that I didn't know," and as soon as I said that he began coughing, and doing the throat sound, which made me very nervous. As a result, I didn't want to continue talking, so I stopped. For as the Scripture says, **"Life and death are in the power of the tongue…"** (Proverbs 18:21 HCSB)

I wanted to clarify to him why I did say that. I felt anxious to see him so uncomfortable after I had said that. He acted as if I just committed a crime. What I wanted to tell him was that when I said that "I didn't know", didn't mean that "I didn't know", but I used it as an expression of sarcasm. I told him that I did know the mistake that Central (the radio dispatcher) had just made, but that I didn't know what was happening to her.

Such expression, I found it to be equal to those of, "Yea right", "Of course, go ahead," that are said in a sarcastic way, but the person's intention is quite the opposite. But how could I continue talking when he had given me a warning by making the throat sound communication, as if I had just committed a great, major crime. I wanted to make things clear to him, but I was afraid too.

We went to a job in housing at 2400 2nd avenue, and as we walked away, there were like two women walking by and I heard when one of them said, "Lying." Now they have label me a liar, when they don't know that I am more than willing to die for the truth. Later, we responded to an EDP (Emotionally Disturbed Person) job at 51 east 129 street. There was a senior woman who was wearing red, and she was waiting for us downstairs. She opened the door for us, and she took us upstairs to her son, who was misbehaving. Her son was wearing red too. He was handcuffed and we took him to the ambulance. Inside the ambulance, the

Emotionally Disturbed Person stared at me on my eyes, and he said, "Hernandez, I am sorry, I am sorry Hernandez."

Later in the hospital, seating down on a chair, he stared back at me, and he said to me again, "Hernandez, I am sorry Hernandez." I observed how he squeezed his mouth out of anger, and out of that anger, he tried not to cry. But what he couldn't hold were his tears that began falling from his eyes, as he stared at me. Then he said, "With you, I would comply Hernandez." Then he asked us if we wanted to know what was really going on, and this is when PO Rivera immediately stepped in. PO Rivera told him that we didn't want to know, that our job was just to take him to the hospital.

I couldn't believe what I just heard coming from PO Rivera, who is always so hospitable towards others, especially in scenarios like this, where he knows that he most performs at his best. As a result, PO Rivera walked away for a moment, and I told the EDP that he could tell me. He told me that he feels bad for his mother. For having yelled at her. Then as his tears began to drop out of his eyes again, he mentioned my name and he told me that he was sorry again. "Hernandez, I am sorry," he kept telling me. PO Rivera came over after his mysterious absence / disappearance and I told him that I was going to the bathroom.

When I came back from the bathroom, I heard PO Rivera talking to another EMT (Emergency Medical Technician) guy, and I heard when the EMT guy said "...Hernandez..." Then I heard PO Rivera say "...Hernandez..." too and this is when I stepped in, and I said that I couldn't believe that my name was so famous. As soon as I said that everyone began to laugh: The EMT guy, PO Rivera, and even the EDP (Emotionally Disturbed Person). Then before leaving, I placed my hand on the EDP's shoulder and told him not to worry that everything was going to be fine, just to go to his mother and apologize to her.

Later, we responded to Harlem hospital regarding a person who had fallen to his death. At the Hospital, we conducted an investigation, and in the middle of the conversation, I asked myself if his property had been vouchered. However, I avoided the question of asking them about the deceased's property, because then they were going to wonder why I was asking for his property. His ID (Identification Card) was on top of his body. He lived in an apartment building at 2407 on 2nd avenue. When we arrived at the building, we met with the detectives there. I told one of them that I had found a Mexico ID on the victim that confirmed that he lived on that address.

Later, the Sergeant arrived at the scene. We interviewed some of the people that knew him and then we went to the rooftop. Later the Detectives and the Sergeant wanted to know about the whereabouts of the victim's cellphone. They asked the people that lived with him if they knew where his cellphone was. They said that he took it with him. I knew that all this drama would have been prevented if I had raised the question at first, when we were in the hospital.

But I wanted to avoid any further misunderstanding about me. Now there was a major interest in knowing where his cellphone might be, and I knew that it had to do with me. In this case, if they don't find the cellphone, they will blame it on me, or at least, I am going to be their main suspect. This will be another element added to PO Hernandez's folder. As a result, I began to sweat profusely. I was very nervous. Then we went back to the hospital. In the hospital, I asked one of the hospital's staff if a cellphone was found on the decease and he said that he didn't know.

However, one of the medical staff, who is in charge of taking information, said that just his clothing was taken. At that moment, my body wanted to turn cold, but not until hospital police, by the name of Odispede Shield #1413 stepped in, and he told us that his property was vouchered, including his cellphone. He had the victim's Samsung smartphone written on his Memo-Book (Memorandum Pad/Activity Log). This news gave me great relief, and PO Rivera, whom I had been observing being tense, and nervous, came to an ease also. Then when walking out of the hospital, by one of the exit doors, there was one Hospital police seating by the door. When he saw me walking out with PO Rivera, he called me by my name and he said," Hernandez, take it easy," and he doesn't know how much I thank him for that.

Back at the station house (precinct), when PO Rivera and I walked out of the station house (precinct) to go home, I noticed that PO Gambardelli and PO Quinones were walking behind us. They were wearing civilian clothing, and they were also going to take the train. They walked with us to the subway station, and from there we departed. The three of them walked inside the subway station that heads southbound, downtown Manhattan, and I headed to the subway station that goes northbound to the Bronx. But before we separated, that we said goodbye, I sang to them, "Here I go again by my own," taken from the popular WhiteSnakes' song, and they laughed. I wondered if the three of them were going to see the Manhattan ADA (Assistant District Attorney) regarding new voice recorded evidence of me, to be used against me.

Then I arrived home, slept for an hour, and struggling to get up from bed, I went to the bathroom and took a shower. I got dressed, and then I headed to church. When I arrived at church, that I walked downstairs to the bible study section, there I saw one of my brothers in Christ preaching. Looking at me, he said to us that inside of the church, there are delinquents who dress in sheep's clothing. He explained how there are people walking around feeling afraid even of their own shadows. I saw much less people in the bible study class. I wondered if the numbers of attendees at the church have been affected by my bad reputation. A bad reputation that has been bestowed on me, a sticker label that has been placed behind my back, not because I misbehaved, but because of what they think of me.

When the bible class was over, that I walked to him to shake his hand and give him a hug as usual, he looked me, and he only shook my hand, while keeping his distance or maintaining his distance away from me as if I were a stranger. He made me feel as if I were no longer welcome in church. I wondered if I should continue going there, because it seems that my presence is negatively affecting the church. I have come to believe, based on how they are treating me, that for them I am a loss cause or simply a loss instead of a gain.

There, I can't even worship the way that I want nor in the same way that I used to, because they might be filming me, taking pictures of me and recording my voice. I no longer feel free to worship, because I can't concentrate. I cannot do it freely, the way that I wish to. They are looking for ways to harm me. They are hungry to obtain some information about me that may be useful to bring to the Manhattan ADA

(Assistant District Attorney) or to the NYPD. They are like reporters all over me. But in church, they will only hear me sing, because I can no longer stop singing to the Lord with my open heart.

"I am ridiculed by all my adversaries and even by my neighbors. I am dreaded by my acquaintances; those who see me in the street run from me. I am forgotten: gone from memory like a dead person — like broken pottery. I have heard the gossip of many; terror is on every side. When they conspired against me, they plotted to take my life. But I trust in You, Lord; I say, "You are my God." The course of my life is in Your power; deliver me from the power of my enemies and from my persecutors." (Psalms 31:11-15 HCSB).

"Let lying lips be quieted; they speak arrogantly against the righteous with pride and contempt." (Psalms 31:18 HCSB).

As I can imagine, they are trying to intersect or cut all types of communication I may have. Now it seems that I can't talk to my pastor, neither to members of the church, and even worse, not even to my family members. I cannot see a counselor or much less a doctor. I am forbidden to talk to my co-workers, because they are the ones trying to take me down, or let say, hunt me down. I can't talk absolutely to anyone. My life has become a disastrous martyrdom. Now, where can I ask for advice, and for companionship? There is no one I can turn to but to God. At this time, I can only talk to God. I have always wanted to live a quiet, normal, and simple life, but it seems that I cannot avoid getting everyone's attention.

I can't deny that what they are doing is truly effective. I give them credit for that. They are doing a tremendous job, but it is only effective against those who have committed a crime, but for those who haven't, all it does is to cause harm, mental harm, mental stress, emotional agony and anger, sadness and despair, anguish and physical decadency, and ultimately, high blood pressure, which is a contributing factor to the boiling hot blood body temperature that is fuming with anger, which is only caused when an injustice is being committed against one or someone else. My body is sickening for keeping all this to myself. By bearing all this alone. I want to cry out and say enough. But I am afraid to lose my job.

This reminds me way back when I attended John Jay College of Criminal Justice. As a student there, I read literature about slavery, such as those that were written by Frederick Douglass, and other contemporaneous authors. Also, during this time, I watched movies such as The Green Mile, and Amazing Grace, which portray the inhumane treatments, the monstrosities, and the injustices that were committed against humanity. As a result, when I read and watched those movies, I felt continuously irritated as I read along and watched along, and as a result, I couldn't hold and prevent my tears from falling.

On **Wednesday, August 13, 2014,** I went to Metro PCS located at West 125 street to disconnect one of my cellphones. When I got there, to my left, there was a man wearing red and green. I knew that he wanted to know what I was doing there, of course, he was eavesdropping.

It was 7:30 pm, and as I waited there, he was seated on a chair in front of the retailer, having his face down. Security at the location approached him and asked him if he was ok. He seemed not willing to answer back, but he rather took the Metro PCS landline telephone and placed it on his ear. He was still looking down, and he seemed disappointed. As if he didn't want me to do something stupid, which I believe he thought that I was about to do, but what was it? I don't know.

Am I not allowed to freely do whatever I want with my life as long as I don't break the law? What a Martyrdom. What the hell do they want from me? Later, that night I went to work - Wednesday **for Thursday** and as soon as I arrived at work, I saw PO Gorman with his face all red as if his head was about to explode. Everybody seemed to be in a bad mood, I guess because of me. What is it that they want me to do? Later, I bought a red pen that had black ink and PO Rivera questioned me as to why I bought a red pen, but I told him that it had black ink. Since that moment, he seemed to have suspected that I know what is going on.

After that, we were assigned to a job, and PO Rivera from inside the car warned me that the coming job was a test, and out of anger, he said something about Barabbas doing sector David and being put to the test. He said it with such anger, as if feeling frustrated about something that I don't know about. Barabbas was a criminal, who was freed in place of Jesus. So, was he insinuating that I am a criminal? I don't know what to do or what to say. I am being so targeted. I am under their radar. I am being examined under a microscope.

Later, in the morning we were assigned to a missing person, but it turned out to be a drunken person. A person wearing a blue t-shirt with a design at the back of two hands together in prayer position, approached us and told us where the drunken person was. As soon as I saw that he was wearing a blue T-shirt, I knew that it was a test. But it wasn't something new for me, because I have considered all the jobs to be part of a test or a scenario, since the moment that all of this began. Besides, PO Rivera had already alerted me of the test.

EMS arrived at the scene. I saw that the aided had a smartphone covered by a red cover, bingo. In addition, he was wearing a black polo shirt, which confirmed my suspicion. I am so angry and tired of all this. Later, the EMS guy and PO Rivera said something, and I asked them what happened. Everyone remained quiet. At that moment, I was thinking about what had happened to my wife by the hand of that green polo shirt person, but I reserved my anger for some other time. I tried not to let it consume me, especially when knowing that they are responsible for what happened to my wife. I didn't sign up for this job to play cat and mouse games.

Later, PO Rivera obtained the aided information and where he lives. As soon as he got that information, he wanted us to go there. I followed his lead. I wondered why he wanted to go to that address, when we never go to the house of a person who is found to be drunk and is getting EMS (Ambulance) assistance. We visited his place, and we spoke to someone there. Then we drove back, and as I was driving back, PO Rivera wanted me to stop for a moment. He came out of the vehicle and went into a grocery store. We have never visited that grocery store, and approximately half a minute later, he came out. I knew that it had to do with some type of information that he might have wanted to share with the others since he is being wired.

Then he came back into the car, and as I drove on Park Avenue to get to East 116 Street, a radio run came over about EMS (ambulance) requesting us back again to the scene. But immediately, PO Rivera took the opportunity to disregard that second notice by marking it 55 by EMS. As I was heading there, he told me not to go there, but to turn left to go to the station house (precinct). Why didn't he want us to go back there when we never leave a job half done? EMS requested us. They wanted us to return there again, so why did he disregard it? I was mute. I didn't know what was going on, but he knew best what to do, since this was a test. He knows what best decision to make, because he is already prepared for every scenario beforehand. In addition, he has more time than me on the job, and he is ten years older than I.

At the end of the tour, when handing over the car to PO Pedrosa, somebody said something about a perpetrator, and immediately, PO Rivera pointed at me. From the corner of my eyes, I saw when he did it. It is tough and hard to see how my own co-workers conspire to do me harm. But what he doesn't know is that I am allowing him to take the lead in this game that I refuse to play. But who do they think is better than me? Am I a stranger to the city? I have been working for the city for 13 years, 6 as a police cadet and 7 as a police officer, hello, isn't it enough time knowing me already? This is their test, this is their game, and I refuse to be part of it, I am tired of this. You have no idea how angry I am. I am so incensed and irritated.

On this same afternoon, I had to go to the park, and there I ran as hard as I could, because I had to release all of my anger, fury and frustration, because I was afraid that if I didn't, my wife would have found me dead frozen from a heart attack.

Today is **Thursday, August 14, 2014**. Right now, it is approximately 5:00 pm, and I have begun to type this even though I don't want to type. I don't want to do anything. All I want is to lay on bed until the hour to go to work comes and so continue with my next stage/phase of suffering. I don't want to type, because at this moment, it hurts me to type. I really don't want to, but I feel that I must, I must. This is the only means of communication that I have, and that I trust. This is the only means, way or method I have to express myself. Even though all I want is to lay on bed, I must go on.

This morning, when I arrived home from work, I approached my wife for support, but she moved away from me. She didn't want to talk to me at all. Before going out, I told her that she is an exemplar woman, but she said that I need help, and she walked away.

On **Thursday, August 14, 2014, for Friday, August 15, 2014,** Lt. Galamo spoke at roll call. As she spoke, she looked at PO Jones who was wearing a red t-shirt underneath his uniform. And she joked about the green and the red colors, and she said that today's color is white, as she played around with PO Jones for wearing a red t-shirt underneath. Also, she mentioned something about a **Pilot Program** that is taking place at the 25th precinct, since the 25 precinct was chosen for it.

Now, this is the first time, after trying to find out who these people are, that I discovered that a **Pilot Program** has been taking place here on the 25th precinct. As soon as Lt. Galamo said that PO Gomez, having a displeased and serious look on face, began to make the throat sound. It was obvious that he didn't want me to find out.

In the morning, after resuming patrol, and back to the station house (precinct), I saw PO Gorman leaving the station house (precinct), and he was wearing a Camo short. This same morning, I went to the Mambi restaurant to eat my breakfast. There, I sat down, and when I began eating my breakfast, one of the persons, who was wearing a white t-shirt (the color that Lt. Galamo mentioned), and a red hat, seated in front of me, and he was facing me. He grabbed his cellphone, and he began using it. He positioned his cellphone facing me as if he were video recording me. I ignored him. I couldn't even eat my breakfast in peace.

On **Friday, August 15, 2014, Saturday, August 16, 2014,** at the precinct, I began listing DAT's (Desk Appearance Ticket), because it had to go to the Borough together with the Narcotics. Almost next to me, there was a detective, who began making the throat sound as soon as I sat. PO Rivera approached me, and he asked me what I was doing.

I told him what I was doing, and he said to me that I didn't need to do it. I asked him if it wasn't always done every time, we do the Narco Run. He said that we didn't need to, because that could go with the mail. I became upset, because he was contradicting me. He was trying to portray me as a liar in front of the detective. I stopped doing it, brought it back to the Desk, and did nothing.

Then he came up and took it himself, and he began doing what I was doing, knowing well that it was going to be taken to the Borough together with the narcotics. So why didn't he want me to do it? He noticed how upset I was. I grabbed my bag, and decided to go outside, and as I headed outside, PO Quinones told me not to go too far, because everything was almost ready. I told him that PO Rivera was there, and Sgt. Gibbs heard everything.

As I waited for PO Rivera inside of the RMP (police car), PO Banks, who was Sgt. Gibbs driver for the night, walked out of the station house (precinct), and he stood right next to another RMP (police car), that was almost opposite to my RMP (police car). He was just there standing on guard, while facing and looking in my direction. He made it so obvious that I felt very uncomfortable.

A few minutes went by, and he hadn't moved from there. I turned on the radio and put a Christian radio station to relax. Then I decided to break the tension by walking to him, and I asked him if I could borrow his pen. He lent me his, and I walked back to my RMP (police car). As soon as PO Rivera came out of the station house (precinct), I walked to PO Banks, and I gave him back his pen. When he saw that PO Rivera was in the RMP (police car) with me, he walked back to the station house (precinct). Sgt. Gibbs might have sent PO Banks outside to keep his eyes on me, for they know well that it is too much, and they fear that I might attempt with my life.

Throughout our tour, PO Rivera kept slashing my back with his harsh words that were prepared and filled with bad intentions, to see if I fell. On one occasion, I told him that I should take my Memo-Book (Memorandum Pad/Activity Log) that has my name written on it, and throw it on the floor, so he could step on my name. His response was that he didn't need to, because I was already doing it to myself. For how long should I bear, and put up with this, by allowing him and all the others to keep on humiliating me, insulting me, and disrespecting my name and my reputation?

Before leaving, I saw PO Banks signing out and he was wearing a red T-shirt. Also, PO Jones signed out and he was wearing a green t-shirt. And PO Rivera walked out with me wearing his green pants.

At home, the janitor knocked at my door, and he was being accompanied by another man who was wearing a white t-shirt that said 'express' on it. The man was a white Hispanic man. He asked me if my fire escape was connected to the apartment next to me. I let them in, and the man who was with the janitor, opened the window of my living room, and he got into the fire escape for a moment. He came back immediately. I think that he was sent to my apartment, because they want to know what is going on inside of my apartment. This is why I allowed them in, so they can see that I have nothing to hide, and this way, see if they can finally end this diabolical game that is consuming and destroying my life little by little.

On **Saturday, August 16, 2014, for Sunday, August 17, 2014,** I went to work. My partner PO Rivera had an arrest. After PO Rivera processed the arrest, Sgt. Gibbs sent him and only him to pick up an officer and his prisoner. Sgt. Gibbs had me waiting inside the station house (precinct). I wondered why he didn't assign me to go and pick up the officer, since I was not processing the arrest. I was only assisting PO Rivera on whatever I could. He should have sent me.

I waited inside of the station house (precinct) until he came back, and when he did, we went back to patrol. While patrolling, we went to a job, and after that job, he told me that here (In Harlem) we must say 'hi' to black people. I asked him if he was crazy. I told him that we must say 'hi' to everybody regardless of race or nationality, and that if he wanted to continue working with me, he must stop making those types of comments or malicious jokes.

I went to the bank and then rushed to the station house (precinct), filled with anger. I grabbed my things out of the RMP (police car), and then I went inside of the precinct. I placed the RMP (police car) key on the Desk and I told Sgt. Gibbs that I was going to take lost time. With an attitude, he reprimanded me by telling me that I can't just come in and throw the key and say that I am going to take lost time without permission. I told him that I didn't throw the key. That I just laid the key on the Desk, but I still apologized to him. I asked him if I could take lost time, because I was not feeling well, and he granted it.

Finally, I wished him to enjoy his vacation. I went to the locker room and got changed. PO Morovich told me that **they love me**. Before I walked out of the precinct, PO Maher, who was at the T/S, wished me a good day, and PO Rivera as well. I wished them a good day also.

"In the cover of your presence you hide them from the plots of men; you store them in your shelter from the strife of tongues." (Psalm 31:20 ESV).

I got home early. At home, my wife asked me why I was home early, because her mother was there. I gave her no explanation, because she has always been trying to avoid listening to me, and to my problems, so why now? I got dressed to go to church, seated on my chair, and then I got undressed again. I laid on the bed for the rest of the day, missing church and dinner, because my appetite was gone.

Later, at approximately 0900 hrs. or 9:00 am in the morning, my wife told me that somebody had sent me a text message, and that she had read it. She told me that no matter what my problem is, God is with me, and she walked away. It was PO Rivera who texted me apologizing to me.

NYPD cops have been warned against using their personal cell phones to record video or take photos while on duty. August 17, 2014. New York Daily news.

On **Monday, August 18, 2014,** in the morning, I went to the gym and after the gym, I went for a nice sandwich at SUBWAY. In

SUBWAY, while eating my sandwich, a man came in begging. He was wearing the famous black T-shirt. He was a white Hispanic man. I told him to tell those who had sent him that I said, "No." He looked confused, like he didn't understand what I had said, and he asked me, "Who had sent me?" I said "Yes, tell those who had sent you that I said no," and he left saying that may God do the same to me. I didn't know what to say, but I cannot even eat a meal without being interrupted by them. If he, I believe, hadn't been sent by someone, I could have given him the second half of my sandwich.

On **Tuesday, August 19, 2014,** at approximately 2:30 am, while being on bed with my wife, I saw that she went to the bathroom. When she came back, she lay on the bed again. I asked her for a hug, while I lightly touch one of her arms, and angrily she responded, "Respect my space. Have I told you that I don't want to have anything to do with you. I said to respect my space." Immediately I removed my hand from her.

In the morning, I went to work out, and while I was working out, I saw my followers. I heard one of them say, "…Has no shame." But what do they want me to do? Then I went to the Laundromat to do my laundry. As I walked out of the elevator that I looked back to the other end of the building that is connected to the building to where I live in, there I got to see a man wearing a black t-shirt. He rapidly moved away as soon as he saw me. Then, when walking to the Laundromat, I saw a police officer seating inside the scooter. The scooter was parked on the sidewalk, at the corner of the block. I bypassed him as I was on my way to the laundromat carrying my laundry bags.

Inside the Laundromat, I saw a guy wearing a green t-shirt. He came from outside, and he was hanging out around the door of the Laundromat. Later, he sat close to me. I noticed that he had no legitimate purpose for being there. At approximately 12:00 pm, one female went inside, and she asked me for money. I told her that I was not going to give her any because I didn't know for what purpose she was going to use it. She told me that it was for the bus, but I refused to give it to her. Later, a man walked by, and he showed me a gold chain. I refused to even talk to him.

Moments later, a woman, who most of the time I see her hanging out around the block, walked in, and used the laundry's bathroom. Later, I went to look for my coins that were inside a zip lock bag, which I had laid on top of the washing machine, but when I went to look for it, it was no longer there. At that moment, I felt the same way that I am always feeling, invaded and attacked from all different angles, and every corner, by no other than my followers. Who are hired by city organization(s) that are unknown to me, and whose background I am afraid to imagine (people that are hanging out around the block). In addition to the officer inside the scooter, who is for sure, having his eyes fixed on me. I simply can't find rest not even on my days off.

Later, I went to the movie theater to watch "The Giver," and when I was seated watching the movie; one of the rules in the movie is not to 'lie'. The movie had to do with the 'lying' and not 'lying,' which made me wonder why I went to watch that movie. So, my followers may have more fun out of my misery, because of the big mistake that I was unable to prevent on **December 10, 2013**, which marked the beginning of my true misery? In the movie, the giver mentions the colors Red, Green, and Blue, which the receiver was able to see, and what is funny is that these are the colors that my followers are wearing or carrying. After the movie theater, I went to BJs, and there they followed me. They make it so obvious, and they don't even respect the fact that I am with my wife.

On **Wednesday, August 20, 2014-Thursday, August 21, 2014**, I did patrol with PO Rivera. He apologized to me at the beginning, and almost at the end of the tour, for what he did to me last week, when I lost time. We responded to an EDP (Emotionally Disturbed Person) job, and I asked the EDP what we could do for him, and he said that what he needed was a lawyer. I thought about what he said. I believe that he was trying to send me a message. That I should get myself a lawyer. But how can I when I have been advised and threatened not to.

Later, we responded to Harlem hospital for a past assault. In one opportunity, PO Rivera told a young woman who was accompanying the patient/victim something related to the detectives needing to talk to her. On one occasion, she said, "So… may snitch…", and later she said,

"Home is a bi…h." I wondered if she was trying to send me a message too. Besides being snitching on me, they are doing the same in my home. This means that my home is definitely, and absolutely not safe. It is being invaded, which I have been suspecting for so long.

Today is **Thursday, August 21, 2014**. I am solitarily confined to having any social interaction, besides the one I have at my job, in exception to my wife. I must have limited contact or interaction even with the members of the church attend to, which means that I must watch out even from my own shadow, and my family too, because I don't want to expose them to such public spectacle, where my name is being dishonored day in and day out.

Every single day, I must endure something new. No wonder why my good friend Rud… doesn't call me to work out with him anymore. In prison, there is solitary confinement, but at least they are by themselves, and are not being exposed to public shame, embarrassment, and humiliation. Where there are people murmuring about me behind my back, and right to and on my face. I am definitely not under house arrest, because I am allowed to go outside. But I am definitely under community arrest, social arrest.

I am being pointed at by accusatory fingers that are directed at me. People are looking down on me, to the point that they spit in front of them or to their sides, as I walk by. I feel like being part of a Zoo exhibition, where strange beasts are kept inside a cell for the public to watch with admiration. However, when they display me, they watch me with despise, because to them, I am despicable. From within their hearts, they detest me.

"But I am a worm and not a man, scorned by mankind and despised by the people. All who see me mock me; they make mouths at me; they wag their heads; "He trusts in the LORD; let him deliver him; let him rescue him, for he delights in him!"" (Psalm 22:6-8 ESV)

"I am ridiculed by all my adversaries and even by my neighbors. I am dreaded by my acquaintances; those who see me in the street run from me." (Psalm 31:11 HCSB)

Did I at any time say that I wanted to be in the spotlight? No. Did I sign up to be a celebrity or to be an entertainment for the public? No, for I value my fundamental rights to privacy more than money and recognition. I would rather pay to stay away from the public view. And much the less, to be a notorious figure.

As I can see, I have become a great burden to the city, but much more to the NYPD. I have come to believe that they will rather see me drop dead, than to see me alive, because with me dead, they will be able to close the unjust, cruel, and bloody case they have built, and are continuing to build against me. I am worth more to them dead than alive. They seem to have been fabricating cases and scenarios, and masterminding situations, to see me fall and fail. I am their main target, and I am growing impatient.

When I answer the job assignments, I don't only think about the job, but about the cameras that are being placed in different angles to see what my response will be, and on who is watching me. Also, I must watch out on who is playing tricks on me. I am just a 32-year-old inexperienced man, who in school, never learned, for it was never taught, how to deal with this problematic situation that for so long, and that at this moment, have been presented to me.

On **Thursday, August 21, 2014, for Friday, August 22, 2014,** at roll call, I was assigned to a hospitalized prisoner. As I was coming down the stairs of the 25th precinct, on my way to the hospital, I heard several shots fired in the vicinity of 119 east street and Lexington Avenue. I ran out of the precinct to find the shooter, all by myself.

On my way there, an unknown male indicated to me the second-floor window of a balcony located on the second-floor rear of 1900 Lexington Avenue, as to where the shots fire came. I did continue to 1900 Lexington Avenue. I went into the building, and I saw a black hat on the floor. Then I got into the elevator to go to the 2nd floor. When I walked to the other end of the balcony, I observed spent shell casings on the floor of the balcony where the unknown male had indicated.

Additional officers were present. I went into the staircase with other officers that were in front of me, and as we were going up the stairs, in the staircase, I saw that the officers that were in front of me didn't open the 3rd floor door, so I bypassed them and went up to the 4th floor, and I decided to open the door. Then I saw a male wearing black clothing enter an apartment, so as soon as I saw the person who was wearing black enter, I walked to that direction. As I walked there, two of the officers that were behind me walked past me and got in front of me. Sgt. Young was behind me. Then I stopped at the door to see if I could hear something.

At that moment, I just considered the person to be suspicious, but not too suspicious because the shooting had taken place many minutes ago, and whoever had done it was not going to hang around knowing that cops were around the area. Then I stopped in front of the door to try to see if I could hear something from that person's apartment. I don't remember if I used my flashlight first and knocked at the door before I heard the commotion, the noise coming from inside.

I used my flashlight to look, and I knocked on the door. Later, a young girl came out, and the door was closed behind her. Again, I knocked on the door and the door opened. I met a woman. I drew my gun and subsequently, I pointed my gun at the suspect, and he was arrested. He was a white Hispanic man.

However, after the perpetrator was arrested and I went to talk to one of the witnesses, I noticed that one of them was wearing an orange t-shirt. Knowing that the perpetrator was wearing black clothing, right away, I was able to identify the magic colors that were right on my face. When I asked the young lady, who was wearing an orange t-shirt, for her date of birth, she gave me 9/21/198..., which is the same exact month and day that I was born. At that moment, I was surprised to hear that this person also knew my date of birth.

My concluding verdict: It is another scenario where everything is being video/audio recorded. Well, she told me that she was pushing the perpetrator out, because she saw that he was running away from something, I think she said to the police. The second person was telling him to get out. As they spoke, I knew that it was a test, and that I was being video/audio recorded from all angles.

Right at that moment, I became frustrated, and I couldn't function the way that I had wanted to. Besides, where were the bullet holes? Were they shooting up to the sky? Yeah right. I asked them the same questions over, and over, because I wanted to make sure that I got the story right. So much was my frustration that I didn't want to take the arrest. Many of the officers that were around were amazed that I didn't want the arrest, because of the type of arrest it was. Who wants a scenario based fake arrest? I don't want, and I didn't want to be part of it at all. God forbid me. I am no actor; I am no clown. Besides, I have more than 112 hours of Overtime for the quarter, and I am not allowed to do more than 120 hours.

Later, Detective Morales wanted to interview me in his office. As he was seated there interviewing me, I wanted to walk away, for I felt that he was going to interview me having a second intention in mind. I observed when he placed his smartphone on an upward position to make sure to record me well. He told me that I must be committed to what I was going to say, because what I was going to say might be going to trial. I knew what trial. My trial, where I am going to be the defendant, because of their false allegations and accusations.

I told him that I heard several shots fired in the vicinity of 119th street and Lexington Avenue. I responded there and that an unknown male did indicate to me that the shots came from the balcony of the second floor in the rear of 1900 Lexington Avenue. I responded. I saw a hat on the floor. I then got on the elevator to go to the second floor. I did observe spent shell casings on the floor of the balcony where the unknown male had indicated. Additional officers were present. I went into the staircase, up to the fourth floor and then I saw a male wearing black clothing at the end of the balcony enter an apartment. Subsequently, a white Hispanic was arrested for forcibly entering an apartment where no one knew him.

When I finished telling him what happened, he asked me to read it, and at one point when I looked at what I was supposed to read, my mind froze, and he asked me if I was ok, because I was staring at the computer's screen, thinking that he was going to use this against me (The same happened when ADA Altman gave me the transcript for me to read).

I was not paying attention to the words that were on the computer screen, for as PO Rivera once told me that there are wolves at the 25th precinct. At that moment, I knew that the detective was one of them. I gave him a brainstorm or an outline of what happened, for the rest, I knew that he knew, for he was at the scene before. I expected that he had already conducted his investigation by interviewing the victims, Sgt. Jackson, and he has or will talk to Sgt. Young. Furthermore, he will look at the cameras, including the scenes that this **Pilot Program**'s cameras captured or is he not a Detective?

Sgt. Black gave me information written down on a piece of paper from a person who had witnessed everything, including the moment when the perpetrator got into the apartment. Of course, it was recorded. The information contains the apartment where that particular witness lives. I think it was apartment …. So, when I spoke to the detective, I went straight to the point. Even the detective had advised me to shorten what I had said. However, there is no better witness than the cameras itself.

Later, I was assigned to sector Eddie with PO Rivera. We kept silent until the job came over. After we resumed patrol, that we came out of the RMP (police car), and that we headed to the station house (precinct), PO Manny Encarnacion asked PO Rivera, "Are you still working with this?" as if I were a thing. Now, what did I do?

At approximately 0814 hrs. or 8:14 am in the subway station of east 125 street, while waiting for the number # 4 train, I saw a man wearing a green t-shirt and dark glasses. He got into the same wagon that I went in. Later, another man entered the train wagon wearing a black t-shirt, and he began to ask for money. When he was done, he stood right next to me, to my left. Then he asked me a question about where Grand Concourse was, and where was the D train. Definitely, they refuse to leave me alone.

As soon as I got home, that I tried to talk to my wife about what I am going through, immediately, she told me that I am crazy, and that she could foresee me losing my job and being hospitalized. She told me that I need help. That even in church they are noticing my behavior, because when she spoke to the pastor, our pastor told her that I was acting weird, strange, like looking around and checking outside the door. I am all alone. I have no one to come and lay his or her hand on my shoulder and tell me not to worry that everything will be fine.

On **Friday, August 22, 2014, for Saturday, August 23, 2014,** I went to work. Right at the muster room, I heard PO Gambardelli say, "… the final countdown…" I am highly preoccupied, and disturbed, because I think that he is referring to me and my final hours as a police officer. Then I saw PO Rivera talking to PO Sovulj, and PO Rivera was tapping on his wristwatch as he spoke to him. Later, I was assigned to work as the station house (precinct) security and PO Rivera was assigned to do the T/S as the T/S operator. Later, we were reassigned and Lt. Allen sent us to 125 East Street and Park Avenue to remove the homeless people that were sleeping on the sidewalk there.

When we were in the RMP (police car), PO Rivera told me that he hopes that nothing will change between us, regarding what he did to me last week. Later, we got into a conversation about the Miami police, and about New York City in the 1970's and the ruined and landmark buildings. Later, we talked about the park; he mentioned the Van Courtland Park that is on 207 street and Broadway. I asked him if that was the one that had a house that looked like some cattle, and he confirmed it. I told him that I do my running there sometimes.

As PO Rivera and I were leaving the station house, while walking through the waiting area, suddenly, I looked back and I saw that he made a malicious face gesture towards the Desk, probably as a gesture to let the others know that he had gained my trust once more.

As we walked to the subway station, when we were at East 117 street and Lexington Avenue, I saw a white Hispanic man who as he walked pass us having an angry look on his face, he made from his right hand a fist, which he seemed to be squeezing hard. At that moment, I feared for my life. I don't feel safe, because as I can see, everyone knows who I am, where I live, and worse, with whom I live with.

When I was waiting for the number # 4 train at East 125 Street, at approximately 0810 hrs. or 8:10 am, there I saw a white Hispanic man who was wearing a blue t-shirt, and one black man who was wearing a green t-shirt. The one who was wearing the green t-shirt, loud enough, as if for me to hear, told the other, "…lying…" So, there he was, I believe, referring to me.

He seemed to be so serious when he said it. I am being so judged over and over again, for the error of my past, error that others allowed me to make back then on **December 10, 2013**. If he was referring to me, I wonder why he or they don't rather use words such as 'mistaken' or 'wrong information' instead of using that evil, devilish, deceitful and distasteful word called "lie." Which is an action hated by God. Proverbs 6:16 says, "There are six things that the LORD hates, seven that are an abomination to him," and to tell 'lies' is one of them.

At that moment, when he used the word 'lying' my body turned cold, especially my feet. I got the chills sensation throughout my entire body, for they are reviving, and have kept alive the terrible mistake I made on that notorious and most infamous day of my life, **December 10, 2013**. This is the day that my life turned upside down. They keep accusing me repeatedly, and my mind is completely restless.

The person wearing the blue T-shirt went into the same wagon that I went into. As I walked home, I checked on the website about the Van Court Park and I discovered that it was not on 207 street and Broadway, but further up by 237 street and Broadway. He confused me there, because I thought that he was talking about Tryon Park, where one of the routes to get there is through 207 street and Broadway, and it has the cattle type of architecture, and it is right at the Cloisters. This was my confusion.

On **Saturday, August 23, 2014, for Sunday, August 24, 2014,** I was waiting inside of the locker room for PO Rivera to get change. I saw that he had a white detective card attached to the interior door of his locker, where he keeps the photos of his kids. Then as we waited inside the train, he began to tell me things, which I knew well, that behind his words was a malicious intent that was well wrapped and hidden, and well set to trap me, but it all depended on my response. And for that purpose, motive and intention, he wanted to ride the train with me. I am sure that it wasn't for luxury nor for decoration that he had the detective card attached to his locker's door interior.

At home, my wife said to me, "Hay Dios mío, tengo miedo, sácame de aquí. Super mal Emmanuel, super mal. Te lo digo desde ahora Emmanuel, vas a parar en un manicomio o te vas a morir. Te estoy dando un consejo grande Emmanuel, nadie va a vivir contigo en esta tierra bajo esta circunstancia Emmanuel. Yo voy a empezar mi escuela. Yo voy a buscar un estudio y yo me voy a ir de aquí tranquila Emmanuel. Busca ayuda Emmanuel en el nombre de Jesús Emmanuel. Tu no está bien Emmanuel. Admítelo, lo único que te puedo decir es que tu necesitas ayuda de inmediato… habla con Ni….." I asked her to stay, but she said, "No, no. ¿Para qué tú me sigas mortificando? Tu no me dejaste dormir, yo tengo que ir a la casa de mi madre a dormir. Yo empiezo la escuela, yo tengo que estudiar, yo estaba estudiando anoche, y tu vienes y me levantas Emmanuel. ¿Tú sabes la mortificación que yo voy a tener en Nursing School y trabajando? ¿Y venir a vivir esta tortura? Emmanuel te equivocaste conmigo. Dios me creo para que yo sea feliz. No para vivir en esta amargura. Lo ciento por ti. La única ayuda que yo te puedo dar es orar por ti … ya a mí me puede dar un ataque del Corazón, a mí me puede dar un derrame cerebral. Y tú vas a quedar a hi mismo viviendo. Tu mama te va a perder a ti, pero la mía me va a perder a mí. Y yo no quiero ver a mi mama sufriendo. A mí no me importa. No me quieren ver en la iglesia, si me critican no me importa."

Now I will translate the above mentioned.

At home, my wife said to me, "Oh my God, I am afraid, take me out of here. Super bad Emmanuel, super bad. Right now, I tell you Emmanuel, you will end up in a psych institution or you are going to die. I am giving you big advice Emmanuel, nobody in this earth is going to live with you under this circumstance Emmanuel. I am going to begin school. I am going to start looking for a studio and I will leave this place tranquil. Emmanuel. In the name of Jesus Emmanuel, seek help. You are not well Emmanuel. Admit it, the only thing I can tell you is that you need help immediately … talk to Ni…" I asked her to stay, but she said, "No, no. So, can you continue mortifying me? You didn't let me sleep; I must go to my mother's house to sleep. I begin school, I must study. Last night, I was studying, and you come and wake me up Emmanuel. Do you know the mortification that I am going to have at Nursing School and working? And come to live this torture? Emmanuel, you have mistaken me. God created me to be happy. Not to live in this bitterness. I am sorry for you. The only help I can give you is to pray for you … it can give me a heart attack; I can have a stroke. And you are going to be left here living. Your mother is not going to lose you, but mines is going to lose me. I don't want to see my mother suffering. I don't care. They don't want to see me at church, if they criticize me, I don't care.

On **Sunday, August 24, 2014, Monday, August 25, 2014,** when I arrived at the station house, I saw PO Maher seating at the muster room. He saw PO Quinones arrive, and he told PO Quinones that he was lying. It was about something that PO Quinones had said. At that moment, I came to believe that he was referring to me as a 'liar'. "You are lying," PO Maher emphasized to PO Quinones.

As I am typing this, I wonder what is going on, for I have been hearing the 'lying' word everywhere I go. Later, when I called the 28-hub site to do the prisoners transport, the person I spoke to told me that they had already assigned an officer from the 28th precinct to do it. This has never happened before. They always have two officers from different precincts do them. I am not blind. I know they don't want me there; therefore, they assigned their own officer to do it.

After I was done with the mail run, I went to the lounge and lay there. Then I went up to the locker room to get change, when suddenly, I heard PO Gambardelli coming, and as he was approaching, I heard him say, "He is so done." Then he saw me, and he greeted me. Then PO Pinero walked to the locker room and greeted me goodbye. He told me that he is praying for me. I know well why he is praying for me.

So, I went home, and I couldn't wait to be there. I arrived home, and I kept thinking about what PO Gambardelli had said, "He is so done." When I went to bed, I kept remembering those words. I kept meditating on those words, and those words were sinking me more and more into desperation. I felt like my life was over. I went to bed early in the afternoon, and later that night, my wife woke me up for dinner, but I told her that I didn't want to eat. All I wanted was to remain in bed.

On **Monday, August 25, 2014,** PO Pinero entered the locker room, and he told me that he was leaving. He was leaving the department; he was vesting out. He offered me his locker. He told me that there is no brotherhood in the precinct anymore. That the people in the community, and the media are against us, and that we only have each other.

I woke up early in the morning the next day, which is **Tuesday, August 26, 2014**. I didn't want to get up from bed. I didn't want to do anything at all. But I thought about God, and the hope that I have in him. I thought about the Holocaust survivors, and the hope they had by striving to survive. Then I went to the gym, and as soon as I got there, I saw a woman who was wearing orange talking to another gym staff. I heard her say, "Push", and she showed her action with her arms. There I knew that they were talking about the shot-fired event of 1900 Lexington Avenue, where the victims pushed the perpetrator. It was approximately 0650 hrs. or 6:50 am in the morning.

Later, I went downstairs and then I went upstairs to run on the treadmill. As I ran, at approximately 0705 hrs. or 7:05 am, a guy wearing a white t-shirt used the treadmill that was in front of me. He had the same hairdo that the perpetrator had. Long hair turned into braids tightened from the front to the back of his head. At that moment, I remembered when PO Rivera told me that the perpetrator has one brother. Later, when I walked by the entrance of the gym, where the cards are scanned to get into the gym, I heard one male staff saying that there were some noises inside, like putting someone against the wall, which is what happened on the shots fired scenario.

Here we go again, what I want to know is what did I do now? Do I have the right to defend myself before the world? Do I have the right to speak? But no, I must remain mute and let them think and say whatever they want to think and say about me, and I must take it. I must wait until I get home to express myself and my feelings through these words, and by this means, release all my frustration, pain and anger, because I have no one to talk to, absolutely no one, because my wife absolutely and definitely refuse to listen to me.

I cannot speak to anyone in church, because I believe that if I do, they will be debriefed. I cannot speak to an advisor, because they will be debriefed as well, and as a result; I will be sent to a psych ward, for I carry a gun with me. And when I go to the gym to try to escape from such madness, and to cope with the daily stress, this is what I find: criticism, humiliation, harassment and traps to see if I fall for it.

I was never a problem child, I was never a problem kid, I was never a problem juvenile, and I was never a problematic young adult, and much less I will be a problematic man now that I am in my adulthood. But now a problem has surge out of nothing, which has created a petty, meaningless and baseless suspicion. However, now in the present time, it has become the mother of all my problems. Because of the magnitude of this problem, I have been hated or pitied by everyone. And for my family, I have become a burden.

Now I wonder what wrong I have done by responding to the shots fired by myself, which I didn't have to respond, because I was assigned to do something else. I was assigned to be a hospitalized prisoner. However, I dropped everything that I was assigned to do, and ran down the stairs from the fourth floor, and out of the precinct by myself. I arrived at the scene by myself, simply because I care for the people's lives that I have sworn to protect. Believe me, many officers would have stuck to his or her assignment and could have cared less to go out of the precinct and run to the scene, because of shots fired.

Again, I responded to those shots fired because I care for the lives of the people that I have been assigned to serve and protect. This is why I didn't think twice to come out by myself and deal with the threat. I just didn't think that they were just shot fired, and continued walking as if nothing had happened, no, I rushed to the scene. I was the first one to arrive, and I went over the radio as soon as I got there.

Now why are they criticizing the work I did? What am I going to gain from doing the wrong thing? Do I want to go to hell? No way. Why don't they come directly to me and tell me what I did wrong? Don't they want me to see the mistakes I made, so I can learn from them? Why don't they punish me then? I guess I know why. Because their ultimate goal is to gather enough evidence of the mistakes I make to justify my firing. It is the unique reason why they don't want me to learn from my mistakes.

When I went downstairs, I heard people talking about lying. When I went to the lower level, I saw two white men working out, and another white man working out at the other end of the corner. It was plain, simple and clear that they were there because of me. All I must do is to repeat to myself, "Patience, patience, patience. No pain, no pain, no pain." I was so angry, and angry I was doing my work out. As I took a seat to rest, and to look at my smartphone, further up, I heard two men talking about 'lying'.

At approximately 0725 hrs. or 7:25 am, a music about being a 'liar' began play, and as the song was being played, the man who was talking to the other young man, while working out on a machine, told the young man, "How can you do this to this Gentleman?" He was referring to the song's lyric that was being played, which says, '...I am liar...'multiple times. I knew that the 'Gentleman' he was referring to was me.

At one point, I went to do dips, and I was waiting for a man to finish doing it first. When he was done, in a defiant matter, and with an angry attitude, he asked me what I was doing behind him, and not to get behind him. I ignored him and continued with my work out. When I was done, that I went upstairs, I went and apologized to the man. When I left the gym that I was walking home, I stopped by the courthouse nearby, and I said, "Oh God, remember that you are my God, and that it is too much for me." As I walked by the Yankee Stadium's sidewalk, that I crossed to the other side of the street, I saw a woman that had the same hairdo that the young man I arrested (handcuffed) at the shots fired, has.

I risked my life to save others, by looking after an unknown man suspected of carrying a gun, and being willing to be shot at and for what? To be treated like this? This is how we humans are, we focus on the errors that our fellow humans make rather than on the good things that he or she intended to do. I am sorry that I keep repeating this, but I still don't know the mistake I made, if there is any. It is not fair.

But all I know is that when I heard those shots fired, I went out of the station house by myself to respond to that location. I went there because I cared, I care about the life of others, and I was more than willing to go there by myself and put my life in harm's way for you. As I am typing this, I am even pressing hard on the keyboard. And about talking to Detective Morales that day, when I spoke to him, I was nervous and scared, because I suspected his motives. I wanted to go straight to the point, because it was common sense that he had interviewed everyone there.

But how am I going to do the wrong thing in a scenario? It doesn't make sense if I do. Moreover, they might have used someone that was on probation or had a criminal record for previous crimes committed, to be part of this scenario, and as I have suspected all along, many of those who are following me may have a criminal background. As I can see, everyone knows where I live, including them. The NYPD, the District Attorney's office, and the city, have no regards for my safety. They could care less about what happens to me. All they want is to create a bad image of me, because they are fully aware that they are committing atrocity against me. What are they doing? Again, I don't know what mistake I made by responding to the shots fire at 1900 Lexington Avenue. Was it that I spoke to the detective about it? Can anybody please tell me?

I have been counting on the public all this time, but now it seems that they are angry at me for no reason. Even at the church that I attend seems to have turned their back on me. Now I am a vulnerable prayer, and I don't know how many criminals are after my life, plotting to inflict harm on me now that they know everything about me. They are either waiting for the right moment to do me harm or waiting until I am no longer a police officer to do so. For how long have they been plotting against me? The authorities are recklessly disregarding my own safety. They are publicizing my personal life, and they are even going as far as to invade my own privacy, to the point that they want to know what I eat, and what I do inside of my own apartment.

I am afraid, but I must keep on going. I mostly persevere. I must endure all this suffering in my life. I don't have the will to continue, but God gives it to me, he is giving me the strength to carry on. The one thing I have to say is that I miss my family. I want to see them. How much do I long to see my parents, but I cannot. I can't, I don't want to bring them to this or make them part of this big, messy and horrific picture of dishonor. Right now, they might think that I don't love them, and that I don't miss them, but it is because I love them that I am doing this.

When a person gets arrested, he/she gets the privilege to get his/her head cover when they are around the press. Meanwhile, as for them, I am a suspect, but I am being treated like a criminal on parole, or let say, an officer on parole, without being found guilty. For how long must I bear all this? They are playing and doing whatever they want with me, when all I want is to live a simple and normal life. Now they are looking for ways to destroy my life. So far, they have damaged my image, my name and my dignity by considering me and portraying me as a lying thief that can't be trusted. Therefore, I must suffer the penalty of having people follow me everywhere I go. My future looks so obscure. For what should I thrive for, fight for and dream of when my good name is being crushed.

One time, I went to the Seven Eleven store, and the delivery man, who delivers the chips, asked the Seven Eleven staff how he is doing in school. When I heard that, I felt nostalgic, because it reminded me of the days when I was asked the same question by many, and how I, with a face full of joy, hope, dreams, and inspirations, answered them that school is great, because I could foresee a brilliant future ahead of me. Happy I was indeed. As for now, I am losing heart. I don't know where to go to, neither where to run to, but to God, who is more than enough.

Now, how can I wish to have children when they have damaged my reputation? A ruined reputation is what they have bestowed on me, when I have done nothing wrong. One of the wishes of a good man is to get married, have children and form a family, and to be able to provide for his family.

But how can I be an honorable and a respectable head of a household, an exemplar member of society, when they have damaged the reputation of the man I am, and they keep doing it as if it has been insufficient? How can my nephew, who I love very much as if he were my own son, go to school and proudly say to his teachers and his classmates that his uncle is a police officer, with the treatment that I am receiving? And what about if one of his bullying classmates, in front of his teachers and classmates, tells him that his uncle is so and so, who is going to heal or mend his broken and embarrassed heart?

On **Wednesday, August 27, 2014,** I woke up from bed very early in the morning. It was a good day to go out and work out, but I didn't go, because of the terrible and embarrassing experience that I had in the gym the last time I went there.

The guy in the gym who once greeted me, whenever I walk by, he ignores me. Even in the building where I live in, when the janitor sees me coming, he looks the other way. I definitely don't want to go out. But I have to because I need to buy new earphones because the one, I have is damaged. I must go out and get one because I cannot be without it. I must listen to something other than the negative rumors that are being said about me and around me that end up hurting me. So, I need to go out, no matter how much I don't want to and buy earphones. So, I went out of my building at 1336 hrs. or 1:36 pm and as soon as I came out, in front of the building, there was a man inside of his car wearing a red t-shirt.

Later, as I walked down the hill, I saw another man wearing a black t-shirt. He was standing across the street, and he was just standing there. Then as I kept walking down, in front of the affordable housing building that is next to my building, I saw a man wearing a black t-shirt, and red sandals. I kept on walking.

When I arrived at Best Buy, I saw strange people around me. A woman walked by me and she made the throat sound. Later, I went to the cashier to pay for it, and at 14:05 hrs. or 2:05 pm, the young man at the cashier treated me with such respect and dignity that he cannot imagine how good he made me feel during those few minutes that he interacted with me. I haven't received such treatment since the moment that I started being the target of the most famous law enforcement and criminal justice system in the world.

So far, I don't know if this judicial system is the most effective one, because of the injustice that they are committing against me. There was a time that I had a lot of respect for it, I had faith in it, in their capacity to bring justice and to solve any crime. Later, as I depended on it to solve the problem that they are accusing me of, I began to lose faith in the system. Now in the present time, I see no end to this, I have to say that I have completely lost faith in the system.

On **Wednesday, August 27, 2014-Thursday, August 28, 2014,** I don't want to leave my apartment to go to work. I don't want to get out of my apartment at all. I am tired of being hurt, humiliated, criticized, and to be called a 'liar' by the public. So before leaving my apartment, I will place my earphones on my ears and will raise the volume high, then I will walk out the door.

At work, when I was at the muster room, after Lt. Allen finished giving out the assignments, PO Gomez said out loud, "You shall not lie." I knew that he was referring to me. Later, I was assigned to do patrol. I didn't want to come out of the RMP (police car), because I was too embarrassed because I don't know why they are calling me a 'liar'. I want to know, but I cannot demand to know, because I know that I am in a very dangerous position.

Later, when I finished my tour that I signed out, I flipped the roll call sheet and I saw that PO Gorman, who is my union PBA delegate, has a union meeting. At that union meeting I was certain that they were going to have a conversation concerning me. When I read that, I became very concerned, and I didn't want to take public transportation. I didn't want to be exposed to the public. I wanted to hide. But I cannot, I must walk and swallow my shame even though I have nothing to be ashamed of. As I walked, I thought about my union PBA delegate PO Gorman, a man who hates me, and who is one of my primary accusers. He is the one who might be out to meet with the union and supposedly represent me for I don't know what. Why does no one come to me and tell me what is going on? As I can see, I am being misrepresented.

300

On **Thursday, August 28, 2014-Friday, August 29, 2014,** I did patrol. We responded to one job of a child neglect at 237 east 115 street, apt. ... There, we met with three women. We looked at the child and the child were fine. Later, the mother of the two females, while talking to us, she told me that her date of birth is 9/21..., but she didn't give me the year. At that moment, I realized that she was giving me a tip by giving me the month and the day without the year. The victim's birthday at the shots fired job the other day was 9/21/... I was born on 9/21 as well. It was absolutely no coincidence. They are throwing clues at me so that I may be careful.

On one occasion, I had my RMP (police car) parked, and PO Gomez parked his car next to it. At that moment, I hear PO Rivera say, "Fire," to PO Gomez. Before leaving, when we were by the stairs, PO Rivera told me that I could go ahead and leave because he needed to go back and get a summon pack. So, I left the station house (precinct) by myself. I do understand. With the negative image that they have bestowed on me, who would like to walk with me? There is a famous saying that says, "Tell me with whom you hang out with, and I will tell you who you are." I do understand your point of view, Mr. Rivera.

The NYPD and the DA's office seem to be going back and forward about the definition of aggravated harassment, on what to consider aggravated harassment or not. I wonder if this has anything to do with me being aggravated and harassed by them.

On **Friday, August 29, 2014-Saturday, August 30, 2014,** at work, when I was leaving the building with my bag, at the door, I saw PO Perez laughing with other officers regarding some gossip. I greeted him, but he didn't greet me.

When I was walking to the RMP (police car), I saw Sgt. Black talking to the officer that was with me at the shots fired job at 1900 Lexington Avenue. I heard Sgt. Black asking him if he had talked to .... because he didn't want him to get in trouble. I got closer to them and when I did, they stopped talking. I waited for PO Rivera inside the car.

Later, we respond to a job at 14 east 116 street. While we waited outside the building, PO Gomez said to PO Rivera, "sector Boy," while taking his handcuffs out of his handcuffs' pouch and he lifted his handcuffs and showed his handcuffs to PO Rivera.

Meanwhile, while we were on patrol, we went to back up housing cops and when we arrived, there were a group of young men. I heard one of them say, while walking towards me, "Basura," in Spanish, which in English means 'trash or garbage'. Later, I heard the same word, but this time In English. I noticed that the group for some reason despised not the police uniform, but the person who was wearing it, in this case, me, and it is because they might consider me a liar. Later, the day, when we had our RMP (police car) parked in a corner, we saw a man who began saying, 'POPO' with anger and out loud he began to say things against us. I asked PO Rivera why there is so much hate for the police. He told me that it is because they accuse cops of lying, and of fabricating things.

Here we go again. I wonder why they accuse me of such a terrible thing. I deserve an explanation. First, I have been suspected and accused of being a thief, and now of being a liar? No sir, under no circumstance will I aloud another false accusation against me. I am angry, I am furious, and frustrated. I fear for the safety and the reputation of my wife, my family, my brothers and sisters in Christ and of my friends, and this is why I prefer to be alone.

When I went to sign out, I saw that Lt. Yaguchi was wearing a grey t-shirt that has a Hispanic last name on the back. It looked like he was trying to gain the Hispanics' votes. He was playing politics. But there is no doubt about who Yaguchi is. He is a lawyer, and he is full of ambitions, and as a result, he is politically oriented. He is a smart and clever man, who has a lot of resources in his hand and at his disposal. When I signed out, I saw that PO Gorman had been assigned again to a union meeting. Lt. Yaguchi and Lt. Allen had their back on me. They didn't even say bye to me. When we walked out of the station house (precinct), I heard PO Rivera say loud enough, "See Yaa," which is said when a baseball ball has been batted out of the field and a homerun is made; what he probably meant was that they have made a homerun out of me, and to let the person who was close to us know that he was glad.

When I got home, I wondered what I did wrong. My wife told me that I was schizophrenic, because I was telling her that there were people following me, and she said that I needed help. She told me that she would start looking for a studio, and that after that, she will file for divorce. She told me that she was afraid that I would end up in a psych ward. I was telling her what was going on because I needed someone to talk to. If I am afraid, yes, I am afraid, I am afraid of the uncertainty, of the unknown, who wouldn't? But God keeps giving me the strength for I believe in him.

Now there are a few questions that I want to ask you: If somebody suspects that you are a thief, how would you react? How would you feel? How would you feel if people no longer trust you, and they doubt you because of something they think you might have done? What about if they doubt the words that come out of your mouth, because you are considered a liar? How will I find employment with such a damaged reputation? How am I going to gain public trust? How am I going to feel safe when riding on public transportation? Why shouldn't I think that at this very moment somebody is plotting to do me physical harm, because the mental harm, and internal damage to my body is already being done to me? What will be of my life after this?

On **Saturday, August 30, 2014-Sunday, August 31, 2014,** I patrolled with PO Rivera. There was a job at 1990 Lexington Avenue. When we got there, a woman talked to us. The brother of the female caller had leave. In the middle of the conversation, she told PO Rivera, "It is too much." There I understood that she was talking to PO Rivera not about her brother, but about me and my mistakes. On that job, there was no action taken, but to take a report. They seem to have canceled the scenario because of me. Because based on what appears, according to them, I might be making too many mistakes.

Later, we responded to a missing. The women who called us told me that the missing boy had tell her that he did try to commit suicide. She said that the boy was of my complexion, and that all he did was to go to Barnes and Noble. She said that he is a very smart boy, and that he has a lot of passwords. Later, inside the police car, I told PO Rivera, while he was talking to the Sergeant that the complainant told me that he did try to commit suicide. I told the Sergeant, and the Sergeant wanted us to go back to verify. It was like she couldn't rely on the words I said. The Sergeant wanted to confirm. So, we went back there, and she told PO Rivera that he did try to commit suicide before he lived with her. He called the Sergeant and out loud he said that it was prior to coming to live with her. He was like calling me a liar.

I asked the complainant if the missing person told her that two weeks after being with her, and she said that he did. Then I called the Sergeant to tell her that he had tell her that two weeks after being with her. The Sergeant became confused, so the Sergeant showed up to get all the information. When the Sergeant arrived, I made sure that the complainant told her that he had told her that two weeks after being with her. I knew that it was another scenario. It was another moment of inferno for me.

The next day, to get rid of my sadness, I decided to go with my wife to the mole. On our way there, as I was outside with my wife, she advised me to act normally, because I looked too tense, and for me to relax. But how could I with all the things that I see and hear happening around me, and if I do say something, I am afraid that they will take my gun and shield and send me to psych a unit. Now I wonder if I should allow people to treat me as if I were a perpetrator or a criminal, just because I cannot defend myself. If I voice my opinion, if I speak out, I am afraid that I may lose the good job I have. Nobody respects me.

When we went to Bob's store, there was a man who asked us that if we needed help to go to him that he will help us, because he doesn't like to be following people around. I wondered if he said it because he already knows my situation. I want to ask you. How would you feel if you enter a store and you notice that you are being followed around, because the person who is following you thinks that you might steal something? I know that nobody is ok with that. So, can you imagine being followed everywhere you go 24 hours a day to learn every move and to find out everything about you not just by an organization or an institution, but by the public? I am under public scrutiny. I wonder how many plastic bottles I have squeezed hard because of this injustice. They are trying to ruin my reputation, my record, my life and not only that, along with it, they are putting my life and the life of my loved ones in danger.

When we returned home, before getting into our apartment, we decided to go to the grocery store and when we entered, a young man who always greeted me every time I went there, this time he didn't greet me. The senior man who works there, when he saw us, he walked to the exit door and he stood there, looking at me and at my wife as if we were thieves. Only I noticed it, because my wife has no clue of what is going on. If I tell her what is happening, she will get angry at me and tell me that I need help again.

Here I am, without acquaintances and friends, for I am despised and not trusted. It has gotten to the point that I don't want to come out of the RMP (police car) unless it is to go home. Because I am concerned that they might say that here comes the most incompetent police officer. Also, it has gotten to the point that every time I walk to the 25th precinct station house, my blood pressure rises and my heart beats hard.

Chapter 16

September 2014 Events

On **Saturday, September 6, 2014**, I did the Fashion Week detail with PO Rivera at Lincoln Center. Two Sergeants there didn't want to sign my Memo-Book (Memorandum Pad/Activity Log) as a form of rejection. One officer from the 24th precinct took out his handcuff's pouch and began playing with it as a form of intimidation. Later, PO Rivera asked me if I planned to go back to John Jay College of Criminal Justice to do my master when I become an ex-cop. I wondered why he had to tell me that.

Wow, they didn't waste any time. They spread the news about me right away. It looks like they couldn't wait for this moment. They advertise me right away; right away they spread the news to people on the street, at my workplace, at church and in the gym. This is how far from the news has spread. People are looking at me with angry faces, others with sad faces, and others look like they are about to cry when they see me.

I have been so publicly humiliated. Now my question is why should I lie? There is absolutely no reason for me to lie, and it absolutely goes against my principles. Now, the big question is why I should lie when I know and I am aware of everything that is happening around me, and how they have been micromanaging my every move. But I am sorry, everybody is perfect except me.

It saddened me greatly when I went to church on **Sunday, September 7, 2014,** and I saw the bible study class half empty. It seems that even the church has been affected because of me. Brothers in Christ that used to greet me, walk away from me. Even those who sit next to me are investigating me. I responded to the shots fired job with the best intention of my heart to save lives, and gladly I gave the detective the information that I had, and suddenly, the world hated me. Even my church seems to be paying the prize dearly. Now how can I go to the police union and tell them that I have been misrepresented by someone that has been treating me as if I were a thief for a long, long time.

On **Sunday, September 7, 2014-Monday, September 8, 2014,** in the morning, Lt. Galamo didn't say a word to me. She didn't even look at me. She mentioned Detective Morales (who interviewed me for the shots fired) and how he was going to go directly somewhere. Also, I heard that one officer had GO-15 (The office in charge of investigating police misconduct) and this is where it seemed that Detective Morales was going to, to testify against me. Or is my mind failing me because of all this long-term mental and internal abuse that I have been sustaining? So, if according to them I am a liar, send me to prison, I rather be there instead of being publicly embarrassed, humiliated and be at risk of getting killed.

It is a shame for me, my family and my church congregation to be labeled a "Liar" by the public. I didn't lie; I have absolutely no reason to lie. Did I give out wrong information? It is like a history test that one studies hard for and at the time of the test, the exam is composed of various questions, and one gives the wrong answers to those questions thinking that they were the right answers. Does it mean that they lied on the test? Do those who work and study hard get the same grade as those who just study?

For I had something major than work and study. I had to deal with betrayal, distrust and false accusations, aside from the great responsibility of being not just a police officer, but a New York City Police Officer, which is a job that is well known to be stressful itself to the point that it has led many officers to attempt or had induced them to commit suicide.

Didn't Lt. Yaguchi testify that the color of the liquor found in the vehicle was clear instead of brown based on what he told me, which it was brown? Also, he told me that he had testified that the key was in the engine when the vehicle eventually functioned without a key, by the push of a button, as PO Maher had told me. According to the Bible, no liar will enter the kingdom of heaven, and I assure you that if at that instance I would have died, and gone to hell, it wouldn't be for being a liar. Am I not 100% human? Can't a human being err or make mistakes? I just pointed out two mistakes that Lt. Yaguchi made himself. But it seems that everybody is perfect, except me. Therefore, I am the government's high-value target.

On **Saturday, September 20, 2014** I was in great desperation for not knowing what to do, and seeing how those who wish me the worse, work on their evil plan to find ways to harm me, I decided to meet with the Commanding Officer of my precinct, Captain Thomas C. Harnisch, and I had NYPD Chaplain-Inspector Rev. Dr. F. Serrano as the mediator. I met with the chaplain days before and he had scheduled to meet with me and the captain in the chaplain's church in Brooklyn.

In the meeting I was told that everything was going to be confidential. I explained to them my concern and that I no longer wanted to work at the 25th precinct, because of the unusual circumstances occurring there and what I was going through. I discussed with him how I was being treated there, and how they were using the throat sound to communicate.

How one officer once told me that the metal partition that was placed at the entrance of the stationhouse was there because of me. How I was warned not to go to the station house (precinct) because there are a bunch of wolves. The other day I went to court, and I was asked by another officer if I was going back to the station house, and I said that I was going home, and how that officer told me that I was a smart kid by not going back to the station house (precinct). I told him about the time that I saw a pair of pants hanging on the outside of my locker. The paper that was attached to my locker. I told him that I didn't want to mention names, but accidentally I mentioned Lt. Gonzales. I told him that I just wanted to transfer to work somewhere else, because I just want to work in peace, and go home in peace.

The captain asked me if I wanted the day off. I told him that I had to see if we had enough manpower for the night. The Captain and the Chaplain laughed, but he ended up giving me the day off. The captain said that what they were doing to me was harassment. He mentioned something about calling E.E.O. (Equal Employment Opportunity) to report my complaint to them. I asked him if he had to, because all I wanted was to work and go home. The Chaplain told me that he was going to help me. After the meeting, I went home knowing that I had the night off.

Later that night, Sgt. Lucic called me, and he told me that I didn't get the night off, and that I had to go to work. I told him that the captain gave me the night off, and he responded as if I were lying. So, I had to go to work that night. I was assigned to a no parking detail at the 19th precinct. Cops there seemed that they didn't want to talk to me. I could hear them talking behind my back and they were mentioning the word 'fire'. The Sergeant from PSA 6 seemed to be not too happy with me. While I was on my foot post, a union PBA delegate from the Borough approached me and the least he knew was that I didn't trust him.

Unfortunately, I discovered that after the meeting, my situation worsened. PO Chiodi began making the throat sound louder and more often. They played by placing PBA cards on somebody else's locker, and they made fun of me on how the captain supposedly gave me the night off. They looked upset because one way or another, they already knew that I had a private meeting with the Captain and the Chaplain, which was supposed to be confidential. One way or the other, they seemed to have known that E.E.O. (Equal Employment Opportunity) was going to be notified in regards, but I was going to withdraw it anyway to avoid retaliation.

Trying to help, my pastor gave me the information of Inspector Luis Serrano, written by his own hand bellow, but the reunion made my situation at the 25th precinct worse. Also, he gave me the number of an attorney, but I became intimidated to get in touch with him, for if the meeting with Serrano and the Captain worsens my situation, a meeting with a lawyer would have been catastrophic, because my followers would have notified them.

On **Monday, September 22, 2014-Tuesday, September 23, 2014,** I was under tremendous amount of pressure. I did a report at Harlem hospital regarding a victim. The witness stated that at the time and place of the occurrence the victim was talking to a friend when her boyfriend, who was inside his car, told her to come over. She approached him from the front passenger side of the vehicle. He slapped her, poked her eyes, and drove away with her upper body (inside her car) hanging on the door window and when the suspect stopped his car, the door flipped open, and as the door closed, the door hit her face.

The mother told me that he had a red and blue hat (here are the colors again). Plus, the smartphone that she was using, I believe it was a secondary phone to record our conversation. At that moment I had come to realize that it was a test, which I had suspected from the beginning. I was very nervous. I asked the witness questions repeatedly to make sure that I had the story straight. Later, I went to the RMP (police car) and I began doing the DIR (Domestic Incident Report). I rushed to do it because we had spent so much time there.

Later, PO Gorman grabbed my DIR (Domestic Incident Report), he read it, and later he circled some information in my report, which he had to correct one of the questions he had circled when I began to question him about it. I made sure that he read it. Then he handed it over to me. I tried to show the copy of the DIR (Domestic Incident Report), so she may have read it to make sure that the information that I wrote on the report was correct, but she refused to look at it. So, I gave it to the mother of the victim.

I had walked in and out of the hospital several times, because I wanted everything to be done right. Later I saw Sgt. Gibbs who was at the Desk reviewing one of the reports that PO Jones had written and when he was done, he looked at mines and he told me that I did a good job, and he signed it. The Sergeant was with us at the hospital and interviewed the persons there as well.

When we went back on patrol, a man wearing orange crossed the street and he gave us the thumb up. When we got back to the station house (precinct), Lt. Galamo in a sarcastic way asked PO Gorman what type of delegate he is.

Inside the locker room, PO Gambardelli, PO Banks, and PO Morvich began talking about lying, the lockers, and the locks and they were making fun of me. At that moment, I realized that everything that was discussed at the meeting that I had with the Captain and the Chaplain, everyone already knew about it. I looked for help, and the matter grew worse. All I wanted was to get transferred, so I may work in peace, concentrate on my duties, and not to be bothered by my co-workers. Now I don't know what to do, nor where to turn to. I feel so alone.

On **Tuesday, September 23, 2014- Wednesday, September 24, 2014,** when me and PO Gorman resumed patrol, I saw that Lt. Galamo and Sgt. Williams walked out of the room that is next to the property room. They seemed to be discussing something in private. Later, Lt. Galamo told PO Gorman that she wanted to meet him in her office.

I thought that it had something to do with the paperwork I did yesterday. Before PO Gorman went upstairs to see her, I showed him the same copy of the DIR (Domestic Incident Report) that I did yesterday and that he had reviewed in case it might need correction. He looked at it, and then he gave it back to me. Then I noticed that Sgt. Williams is not treating me the same way that she used to. It seemed that she is trying to evade me.

As I walked outside, I saw people passing by me while saying the "lying" word. As I walked to my building, I heard another one saying, "…if gets fired, he will be living on public assistance." I paid a visit to Pastor N…, and when I walked out of there that I was heading to the train, I heard a person say loud enough, "He is done, he is done," and it really preoccupied me.

On one occasion that I was behind the Desk, Sgt. Gibbs, who was seating at the Desk, greeted Lt. Gonzales about something that he did. He told Lt. Gonzales, "If he wants to play dirty, we will play dirty too." I was alarmed when I heard that. The statement he made might have something to do with the grave mistake I made by mentioning Lt. Gonzales' name at the meeting. Moments later, Lt. Gonzales told Sgt. Gibbs not to be afraid to sign those 61's and from that moment on I understood that it also had something to do with the DIR report that I did when working with PO Gorman, and that he had signed after reading it, telling me that I did a good job. Wow.

I want to clarify that there are officers assigned to look at the complaint reports of every officer and they make calls back to confirm that the reports were done well. This is regular practice within the NYPD because officers do make mistakes on the reports they make. So, if I did one, why don't they come to me and tell me so?

For example, on October, I took the picture below to demonstrate that police officers can do mistakes too, because it is human to err.

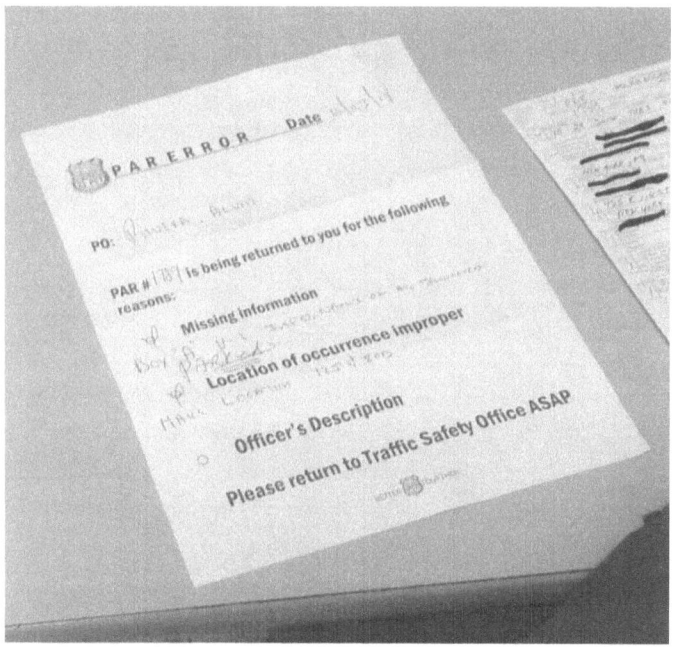

But of course, my colleagues' paperwork is all covered. They are all good. Their paperwork is double checked and if there is any error, they are told to fix it. It is like their paperwork goes through a laboratory, where every paperwork is double checked carefully, by the officer and their supervisor. But there seems to be another laboratory, but that one is just for me. To find faults and mistakes on what I do and later show it to the world instead of coming to me and telling me what I did wrong, so I could learn from my mistakes if I did any.

On **Monday, September 29, 2014, for Tuesday September 30, 2014,** Sgt. Gibbs had his RMP (police car) parked next to ours when he seriously asked me how I was doing. I told him that I was getting summonses, and he said that he won't take much of my time then. Then he looked at my partner and he told my partner that he did a good job with a smile on his face. Why did he tell him that?

On **Tuesday, September 30, 2014, for Wednesday, October 1, 2014,** at 1PP (1 Police Plaza= Police Headquarter) one of the police Headquarter security officer advised me that I should buy a used car. I knew why he said that. It is not easy to always be followed on the train and on the public bus.

While waiting to sign out at 1PP (1 Police Plaza= Police Headquarter), there I saw Sgt. Young walking by. At first, it seemed that she wanted to continue walking without greeting me, but as soon as she noticed that I was staring at her, she stopped and greeted me. I asked her what she was doing there, and she told me that she was going to the Equipment Section and that she had to do some other things after that. Meanwhile, I noticed that PO Rivera was very happy. Even on our way back to the station house (precinct), he was always smiling. He told me that when he signed out, only my name was highlighted on the list at 1PP. I didn't know what to do. I was afraid to ask why.

As we walked out of the station house (precinct), I saw someone who had an angry look on his face and as he walked pass us, he said, "Chota," which in English means, "Snitch." Why? Because I was trying to peacefully solve the problem that is affecting my life? First, I was not the one who called E.E.O. (Equal Employment Opportunity) and secondly, when they called me to follow up with the complaint, I withdrew it. Or did he say it because they are snitching on me?

When we stopped to buy something to eat, PO Rivera decided to buy something for me, and he told the woman vendor that he wanted the croissant breads in a separate bag for this guy (he meant me), and the woman corrected him by saying, "Your friend" and he kept quiet. I am so anxious about not knowing what they are going to do with me. I don't know what to do. I am all alone. Again, I meant no harm when I said the things I said in the meeting. The captain called E.E.O. (Equal Employment Opportunity) and they called me, and I told them to withdraw the complaint. What else do they want from me?

Amid all the things that are happening to me these last days, I have lost heart. It seems that every time I make a move to address the situations that are bothering me for so long, I end up getting deeper into trouble. In these couple of days, I have no more desire to do anything. All I want is to stay in bed and do nothing. Even the effort I make to type one word seems to be a lot for me at this moment. Recently, this was the third time that I went to the back of the public bus and the persons seating at the back get up and go to sit in front.

When I walk on the street, I see people spitting as I walk by them. Why? Because of the day the shots fired, they behaved as if I did something wrong? Was it because I, not knowing what else to do, addressed the Captain and the Chaplain about my concerns? The captain called E.E.O. not me. When E.E.O. (Equal Employment Opportunity) called me, I withdrew it. Now it seems that the entire city hates me. But nobody tells me what to do. The only one who could have and is supposed to at least give me words of encouragement instead of discouragement is my union PBA delegate PO Gorman, but his personal hate towards me is getting on his way of doing his PBA delegate duty and obligations. He is one of those contributing to my downfall.

Already frustrated and traumatized, one day I went to visit Pastor Nic… and I explained to him my concern. However, I being very angry told him that I wanted to sue to put an end to the harassment, but he told me, "Are you going to bite the hand that give you food?" and I felt bad for thinking that way. So yes, I withdrew the idea of suing, because I will feel bad if I bite the hand that feeds me.

Chapter 17

October 2014 Events

On **Saturday, October 4, 2014 –Sunday, October 5, 2014,** I went on patrol with PO Rivera. We went to work and inside the elevator there was a big mirror. When I looked at myself in the mirror, I couldn't believe how tired I looked. How quickly was I aging. I thought that what was going on inside of me was going to stay inside, but it is not. It is manifesting on the outside of my physical body too. It is an indication of how my health is declining.

Now I wonder, what would you do in my situation? Why am I being persecuted when I have done nothing wrong? Why are they so obsessed with me? I don't know if they have noticed it, but there is a cop that is walking among them in agony. But I do wonder why they don't come to me and ask me and tell me what they want from me? Why do they have to continue with this mysterious investigation when they can only simply walk up to me and ask me, "Hey, I would like to know you more?" I would have gladly invited them to my apartment, to my home and shown them my family's album and told them everything that they need to know about me, instead of wasting all their resources in trying to find fault in me as if I were a drug dealer, or a criminal. I am an open book, and I am as transparent as the water. One day, when there was a storm, I invited PO Rivera to my home so he could sleep there, because he lives too far, but he refused. But for how long must an innocent man pay for the sins of others.

On **Monday, October 6, 2014 – Tuesday, October 7, 2014,** I was working with PO Jones. I noticed that sector Boy went to meal at approximately 0507 hrs. or 5:07 am in the morning, and like 4 minutes before, so did another sector. It was strange to see that two sectors went to meal almost at the same time, unless they wanted me to handle a job that may require me to do a #61 (Complaint Report), so they may scrutinize it, find fault in it and share it with the general public. And as I was expecting, a job came over and PO Gomez sent me a text message letting me know that he was on meal.

I took the information from the complainant, and as I was writing the report, there was PO Jones next to me. While I was writing my report, I noticed that the report had been folded too many times, so I decided to go to the station house (precinct) and get a new one. Then when I was writing on the new one, I scratched when I was writing the narrative, so I decided to do a new one. Then when I was writing on the new one, I felt pressured to finish fast because PO Jones had approached me and he asked me if I was still writing my Complaint Report. There was PO Rivera waiting for me to go. Lt. Yaguchi was prying around like a serpent. My hand began to shake as I wrote, and as I wrote, I heard Sgt. Lucic talking about the next year, and I also heard PO Rivera say that someone had crossed the line. But probably he didn't mean me, but whoever is running the show of doing the things that are being done to me. But I still wondered if they were referring to me.

When I finished the report, I saw how messy it was, but I had to go. Then as I walked with PO Rivera towards East 125 Street, I told him that I had to go back. So, he went back with me, and I took the Complaint Report from the bin, and I added something to it for clarification, and there I saw that PO Gorman had not left the station house (precinct) yet. With so many distractions, and tension, how can I efficiently do my work and do it in a timely matter?

I am being disaccredited day in and day out, and suddenly, I am the bad guy. Are we not supposed to be united for the right reason?

On **Wednesday, October 8, 2014- Thursday, October 9, 2014** when in the precinct I approached the Desk, there was Sgt. Black with his boys, and knowing that they work for the Crime unit, I jokingly said, "Crime criminals" and immediately Sgt. Young came closer to the Desk where I was standing and she moved right next to Sgt. Gibbs. Sgt. Black said while looking at PO Rivera and at Sgt. Gibbs, that the PBA... I walked out of the station house (precinct) with PO Rivera, and we were standing by East 116 Street and Lexington Avenue. As we spoke, I told

PO Rivera how tired my body feels lately, and how I was not being transferred.

"I have taken refuge in the Lord. How can you say to me, "Escape to the mountain like a bird! For look, the wicked string the bow; they put the arrow on the bowstring to shoot from the shadows at the upright in heart. When the foundations are destroyed, what can the righteous do?" The Lord is in His holy temple; the Lord's throne is in heaven. His eyes watch; He examines everyone. The Lord examines the righteous and the wicked. He hates the lover of violence." (Psalm 11:1-5 HCSB)

While talking, I got to see the person that is handing out the newspapers. In one instance, the man distributing the newspapers faced the Aguila Mexican food establishment, and he took his right hand thumb, placed it to one corner of his throat and he sliced it to the other end, as if letting me know that they were about to slice my throat. Later, I got to see a man walking to the subway station and he stopped to talk to the newspaper man. While they spoke, the man was looking at me, and I knew that they were talking about me. Later, when me and PO Rivera departed, that I took the #4 train to 161 street in the Bronx, coming out of the train and walking to the exit, I heard someone behind me saying, "Is that your shit? Is that your shit??"and he said it more than two times. I was carrying a bag at the time.

I arrived home overly exhausted, but immediately I began typing this. Then I received a text message. It was nothing more or less than Manhattan ADA (Assistant District Attorney) Altman. I was in shock to see it was her. I became very worried, scared and concerned when I saw that she had texted me. She seemed to be up to something. Ten months have passed since that horrific moment in court. It looked like history was about to repeat itself. She texted me about the report I took the day I visited the victim in the hospital with PO Gorman. I believe that it is no coincidence that she took this case.

On **Friday, October 10, 2014,** I went to the station house (precinct) to look for the paperwork. To get there, I took a livery cab, because I am tired of the way people are reacting towards me. I went to the station house (precinct), and as soon as I entered, there was an officer who told me to report to the Desk first.

There was PO Chiodi standing. He asked me if I was going to court so we could go together. Then as I walked upstairs, I saw PO Dukas coming down the stairs with my Memo-Book (Memorandum Pad/Activity Log). He told me that he had found it. I wondered what he was doing with my Memo-Book (Memorandum Pad/Activity Log), and he handed it over to me at the precise moment that I was walking upstairs to get it.

Even to go to court, I was thinking about taking a livery cab, and when I did, the cab driver told me that I would have to pay him $35 dollars, so I refused to take it. When I arrived at court, I went to see Manhattan ADA (Assistant District Attorney) Altman. When talking to her, she asked me who gave me the boyfriend's information. At that moment, I was so nervous that I forgot, because I believed that a trap was being set for me, and that I was being recorded. When I finished talking to her, my hands were sweating. I was so nervous. Later, as I waited outside her office, a group of court staff came close to me, and two of them sat next to me. They were talking about an officer who kept forgetting things, and how he was going to get Charges and Inspect. Absolutely and without doubt, they were sent to me on purpose to mortify me. I became so heavily anxious.

Now it seems that the community, society as a whole know about my situation, and they seem to repudiate me. I never wanted to disappoint them, but their words and actions are weights that keep adding to my shoulder. I feel that every day that passes, I am dying more and more, and the closest I am to my death. I didn't sign up for this job to be treated the way that I am being treated now. This is too much. Everybody has turned their back on me. I am so tired of getting cold feet, and of my legs getting weak. I don't want to go out anymore.

I feel publicly embarrassed, humiliated, defamed, hurt, betrayed, depraved of my own privacy, unsafe, anxious, and angry and the list goes on. Where can I run for refuge? What type of job is treating their employees like this? I am not living a normal life. Until when am I going to be living like this? Why am I treated the way that I am being treated? What would you do?

Today, **Saturday, October 11, 2014,** the moment that I went to the grocery store to buy milk at approximately 12:35 pm, there they were following me. From that brief moment that I spent at the grocery store, I returned home already tired. I realized that the best thing I could do was to stay home. I don't want to go out anymore. Not even to church. I called Administrative Sick and remained home. This is the second time that I call sick in my seven years as a police officer. I received my excellent certificates of attendance almost every year for not calling out sick during the year, and for having a good attendance record.

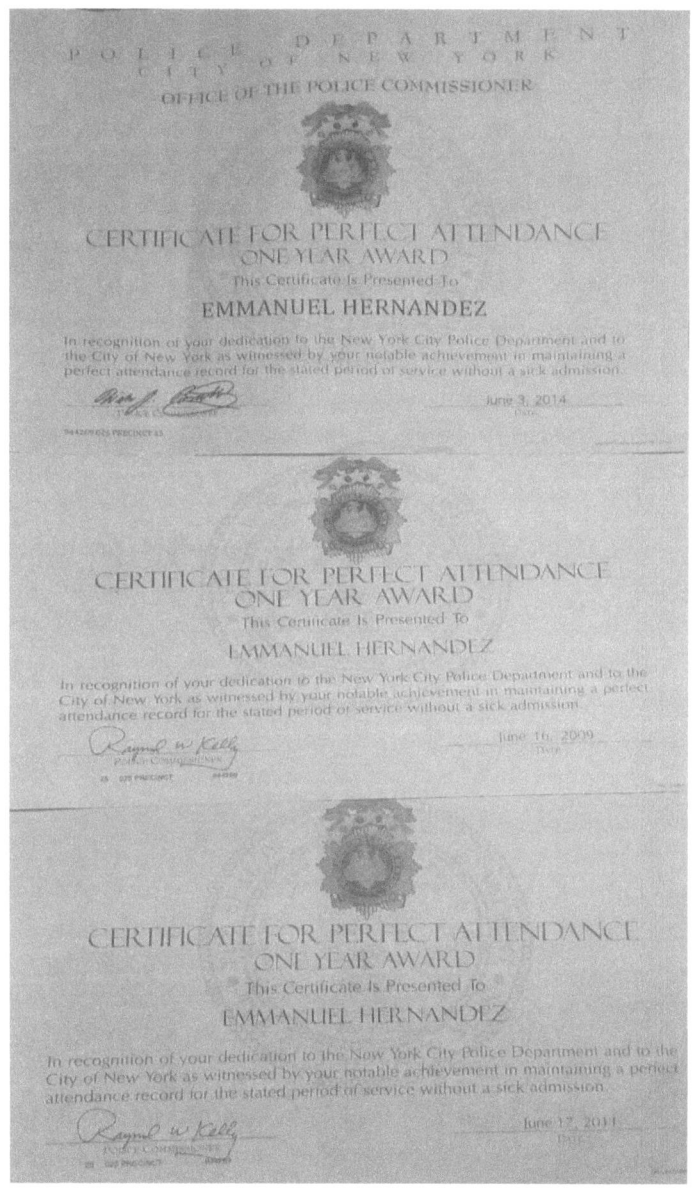

I had over four years straight without calling out sick, and my goal was to reach my five consecutive years mark without calling out sick and receive the pen that is awarded to cops who had not call sick for five consecutive years. So, I just needed one more year or less to receive mines. But unfortunately, I was made sick, yes, they made me sick, and my goal came to a drastic end.

On **Sunday, October 12, 2014**, I called Administrative Sick and remained home all day. The female spy or Confidential Informant on the apartment next to me, apartment #61, complained to her sister, who visited her, that I called sick because I had the period. She lives by herself in that apartment. Also, she keeps visiting the man who lives on the apartment underneath my apartment, apartment # 52. How do I know? I place my ear on the wall for apartment #61, and on the floor for apartment #52.

On **Monday, October 13, 2014- Tuesday, October 14, 2014,** I was laying on bed. I was assigned to do a day tour. Then I looked at my smartphone and I saw that I had a missed call. It was Sgt. Lucic, he left me a voice message stating that the captain nor the Chief of the Department gave me the day off, and that I had to go to work. But I thought that I had DMV (Department of Motor Vehicle) traffic court in the morning because I had the notification.

Well, I went to work, and I was assigned to Metropolitan hospital to be there with a hospitalized police officer. When I arrived there, there was PO Chiodi and PO Arroyo. I was relieved that they could leave, but before leaving, PO Chiodi told me to put the handcuff on the hospitalized officer. He was joking, because he was a hospitalized officer, not a prisoner. Also, he showed me a seat that was outside the room as if I shouldn't be inside the room with the officer. They left, and there I was seating outside the room.

As the medical staff walked by me, they didn't greet me, they didn't even give me a smile. They even refused to look at me, even at my direction. This seemed to be the busiest floor in the entire hospital because I saw that the medical staff were going back and forward continuously. This is how I spent the rest of my tour, outside the room, seated and being totally ignored by the medical staff. I called PO Rivera to verify for me if I had DMV traffic court, and he told me that I didn't. Later, I went to the station house (precinct) feeling the pressure, and feeling the pressure, I left the station house (precinct).

When I arrived home, I looked at the notification sheet for DMV traffic court, and I didn't think that roll call was right, unless mv court had been cancelled. I decided to take a livery cab back to the station house and I clarified it with the Administrative Lieutenant who is Lt. Yaguchi. He told me that it was just a clerical error. The case was closed, but I still went to 2 Washington to make sure. Then I went back home. I slept for like one hour or less.

On **Tuesday, October 14, 2014- Wednesday, October 15, 2014,** I went to the station house (precinct) and I took my small luggage containing my uniform to 1PP (1 Police Plaza= Police Headquarter). As I walked to the train station, at approximately 1751 hrs. or 5:52 pm, by east 119 street and Lexington Avenue, one person walked by me and he aggressively spat as he walked close to me. As I kept walking, another man walked close to me, and he spat as well. I kept on walking and as I walked, a woman walked towards me and she moved her head aggressively to the side, and she made a sound with her mouth as if she were trying to spit, but no saliva came out.

I walked down the subway station and took the train down to 1PP (1 Police Plaza= Police Headquarter). As soon as I walked inside the building, an officer that works there and with whom I had a conversation within the past, made a gesture of disappointment when he saw me and he walked away without greeting me.

"Consider my enemies; they are numerous, and they hate me violently. Guard me and deliver me; do not let me be put to shame, for I take refuge in You. May integrity and what is right watch over me, for I wait for You." (Psalm 25:19-21 HCSB)

"But I am a worm and not a man, scorned by men and despised by people. Everyone who sees me mocks me; they sneer and shake their heads: "'He relies on the Lord; let Him rescue him;

let the Lord deliver him, since He takes pleasure in him." ' (Psalm 22:6-8 HCSB)

"Do not be far from me, because distress is near and there is no one to help. Many bulls surround me; strong ones of Bashan encircle me. They open their mouths against me — lions, mauling and roaring. I am poured out like water, and all my bones are disjointed; my heart is like wax, melting within me. My strength is dried up like baked clay; my tongue sticks to the roof of my mouth. You put me into the dust of death. For dogs have surrounded me;" (Psalm 22:11-16 HCBS)

I walked to one officer who was waiting to be assigned to a post. I asked her if I could borrow her pen to sign in, and she lent it to me. When I gave it back to her, I told her something about how cute her pen looked and she said, "So nobody steals it." Then I went to my booth and there I remained meditating and thinking about my misfortune. I am tired. I have only gotten 1 hour or less of sleep. However, my anguish is keeping me more than awake. There I was trapped, inside the booth, knowing not what to do. But fear caught me by surprise, and I began to have chills on my body and my feet were very cold. My bones are hurting especially my knees. So, there I remained for more than 12 hours until I was relieved.

I signed up and when I was standing inside the train, I noticed how people were turning their backs on me. Many of them seemed to be preoccupied with me, while others seemed to hate me with passion. As a result, I felt that my legs weakened and were shaking a little bit. I walked to the station house feeling the pressure. I got change to go to DMV traffic court at the Northern Manhattan Traffic Violations Bureau, so I dragged my body to traffic court. I thank God that a Lieutenant (not Yaguchi) allowed me to take an RMP (police car) there. In front of the traffic court, quickly I began to prepare my notes, because I was running late. So, I rushed up to the traffic court and as soon as I got there, I was assigned to the court hearing room and like a minute after my arrival, I was called to testify.

At that moment I knew that I was being recorded, for there were very few chances for me not to be, and that any mistake will be shared with the public. As soon as I was done with one, another court clerk or judge went to the hearing room and called out my name so I may go to the other hearing room. There I went to testify again. I was so tired. When I was done, I went back to the station house (precinct). I felt so tired that I had to take a livery cab home.

At home, I began to toss and turn, thinking about all the things that are occurring around me, and about my court testimony.

On **Wednesday, October 15, 2014-Thursday, October 16, 2014,** I took a livery cab to go to work again. When we responded to a job, PO Morovich asked the Sergeant if he had signed the affidavit. The Sergeant said that he didn't know. Then PO Morovich told the Sergeant that he could put him in his place, for him. I was thinking that they were talking about me. Then I heard PO Rivera and PO Soto talking regarding a prisoner, and PO Soto told him that he has lied several times, while looking at me. Now I wonder what I did now. Did I say something wrong in my DMV traffic court testimony yesterday? If I did something wrong, why don't they come to me and rebuke me?

"One who rebukes a person will later find more favor than one who flatters with his tongue." (Proverb 28:23 HCSB)

Later inside of the locker room, I heard PO Morovich tell PO Gorman that he was hiding something. I wondered if he was talking about me. Then another officer walked by and said, "Zip it." Then I heard PO Maher ask PO Gambardelli if that was his gun, and PO Gambadelli told him that it was PO Quinones' gun, and PO Gambardelli began to play with it. I left the station house (precinct) and went home.

When I was getting close to my building, walking up the hill, someone said loud enough, "Fired." I am so tired of all this intimidation. I went to BJ's, and I met with my wife there. There I saw a brother in Christ and his wife. His wife was wearing red. She greeted me without saying anything and she walked away. My brother in Christ noticed and told me that I have lost weight. Then he left. Our interaction lasted probably half a minute.

On **Friday, October 17, 2014,** I woke up to have a light pain on the left side of my chest. I went to the park to run, and as I walked pass people, I heard them talking and I believed that they were talking about me. On my way back, I got to see my wife waiting at the bus stop for the bus. While I was with her, I got to see a woman who knew me since I was seven years old back then in the Dominican Republic. Her son was my best friend. She saw me grow up until I was ten years old, which by the time I came to the USA. Then I saw her like two times here in the USA.

However, this time she looked at me and I looked at her. But as soon as she saw me, she hides behind my wife and next to a man who was with her. She was trying to avoid me. She didn't want to greet me, probably because she feels embarrassed of me due to all the bad rumors that have been spreading and circulating about me where my name has become notorious. She was wearing a green T-shirt underneath her outerwear.

When we arrived home, when I tried to explain to my wife what had happened, we began to argue about that. Then we went to Red Lobster, and when we were on the train, I heard someone talking about a license. When we were eating, that my wife was talking to me, I paid absolutely no attention to what she was telling me, because all my attention was on the man who was talking to his family, which was a table away from where we were eating. He said something about a door sliding open and falling (In regard to the case in the hospital where I prepared a Domestic Incident Report), and how the person that he was referring to was going down the spiral, and how he may soon ask for an application here (at Red Lobster), and he and his family began to laugh. And he said that she has a job, in this case, referring to my wife.

I became anxious. Behind me, there were two guys seating talking about getting 'fired', and of the person having a Bachelor, which I do. After we finished eating, I tried to talk to my wife, but she didn't say anything. Later in the train, out of a group of a few young adolescents, I heard a young female say, "And who is going to hire him?" Finally, we are home.

"Lord, how my foes increase! There are many who attack me. Many say about me, "There is no help for him in God." Selah But You, Lord, are a shield around me, my glory, and the One who lifts up my head." (Psalm 3:1-3 HCSB)

"I am not afraid of the thousands of people who have taken their stand against me on every side." (Psalm 3:6 HCSB)

On **Sunday, October 19, 2014,** I went to church, and I was being completely ignored by almost all the members of the church, which made me think that I have made some big mistake at work worthy of being despised and rejected by the whole congregation.

I believe that the reason why my church membership hasn't been revoked, is because it is a Christian church and they must put into practice the mercy of God. Even my good friend brother in Christ, who used to greet me with great joy every time he saw me, this time he saw me face to face, but he didn't extend his arm to greet me. I didn't see another brother in Christ, but I saw his wife, who used to greet me every time she saw me too, but this time when she saw me, she just said to me "Excuse me" as she walked away.

When I called out another brother in Christ to greet him, he told me that he was in a rush, and he walked away. Thank God that one elderly man and another man invited me to get coffee. I went with them not for coffee, but to walk away from so much rejection.

At the bakery, I got to see many church members inside the bakery, and only one woman greeted me, and it was because I greeted her first by extending my hand to her. Back at church, I met with one church member, and he was the third one who didn't reject me. I went to eat with him downstairs since it was the pastor's day, and I left the church with him. Thank God for him. When I talked to my wife about the matter, she told me how one church member rejected her completely. How she walked after her, but she was still ignoring her.

"Now we command you, brothers, in the name of our Lord Jesus Christ, to keep away from every brother who walks irresponsibly and not according to the tradition received from us." (2 Thessalonians 3:6 HCSB)

"And if anyone does not obey our instruction in this letter, take note of that person; don't associate with him, so that he may be ashamed. Yet don't treat him as an enemy, but warn him as a brother." (2 Thessalonians 3:14-15 HCSB)

This explains why I am being ignored at church, because according to them, I am walking in disobedience.

"I am ridiculed by all my adversaries and even by my neighbors. I am dreaded by my acquaintances; those who see me in the street run from me. I am forgotten: gone from memory like a dead person — like broken pottery. I have heard the gossip of many; terror is on every side. When they conspired against me, they plotted to take my life." (Psalm 31:11-13 HCSB)

On **Sunday, October 19, 2014-Monday, October 20, 2014,** at work, my partner and I decided to back up sector Adam on a job. The ambulance EMS (Emergency Medical Service) was already there. PO Rivera was greeted by an EMT (Emergency Medical Technician). As they took the AIDED out on a bed stretcher, I opened the door for them and one of the EMT (Emergency Medical Technician) guys said, "We have no use of you …" and as soon as he said that PO Rivera who was walking ahead of us, looked back and gave him a look.

Later in the locker room, I heard PO Gorman in the locker room talking on his cellphone, "When are you taking him out," and I wondered if he was talking about me. On my way home, as I walked to the subway station, I heard a person say with an attitude "Oh God," then another one "God" as I walked past them. Then I took the train, and inside the train, nobody looked at me. Most of them were either with their eyes closed or looking down as if it angered them to see me. When I got home, I Googled the meaning of what the EMT (Emergency Medical Technician) said, so I typed, "Have no use for" and the American English Dictionary (Pioneers in dictionary publishing since 1819) gave me its definition and its meaning, which I was amazed when I read it. This is what I found to be its meaning:

1)   To have no need of.

2)   To have no wish to deal with, be impatient with.

3)   (US) To have no affection or respect for, dislike strongly.

Also, the Macmillan Dictionary defines it as follows:

1)   Use for saying that you do not want or need someone or something because they could never be helpful to you.

2)   Informal to dislike someone or something. And it gave the following example: I have no use for a liar.

So, after reading this, all I ask myself is what have I done for people to dislike me so much? My eyes are so tired of crying. My face looks so pale, and my eyes bags are so profound that they look like bruises from punches received out of a boxing match.

On **Monday, October 20, 2014-Tuesday, October 21, 2014,** since we began working together, PO Rivera has allowed me to drive all the time, because he disliked driving. From the beginning, he told me that he would do all the reports. At one point I told PO Rivera "If you are tired, can you imagine me?" I told him that because all eyes are on me. The most pressure is on me, because of the way that they are treating me by propagating my supposed incompetence. They highlight and magnify my faults, while for other officers, what they do is that they just supervise them, which is a supervisor's job, and they make corrections if needed be and hide their errors from the public. I was being told "good job" while all of this is going on. In the train, I was being ignored by the public once more.

On **Tuesday, October 21, 2014-Wenesday, October 22, 2014,** in the afternoon I went to 1PP (1 Police Plaza= Police Headquarter). There I saw PO Gloria Byrd. She spoke to me, and she told me that last week she spoke to one ADA (Assistant District Attorney) and that she was saying negative things about me. That it got to the point that due to the terrible things that the ADA (Assistant District Attorney) was saying about me, PO Byrd got so upset that PO Byrd had to stop her from continuing doing so, because she knew me well, and she told her that I was not the bad person that she was describing me to be. I asked her if it was ADA Altman, and she said, "Yes." She advised me to speak to ADA Altman's supervisor in regards.

At that moment my doubts were confirmed. This Manhattan ADA (Assistant District Attorney) has something to do with the people that are following me. I feel like Elijah who ran away from the angry woman Jezebel, in my case, ADA Altman. Later, when I was inside my booth, I came out of the booth, so the Sergeant may scratch (sign) my Memo-Book (Memorandum Pad/Activity Log), and he asked the other officer if he was 'lying' to him.

"God of my praise, do not be silent. For wicked and deceitful mouths open against me; they speak against me with lying tongues. They surround me with hateful words and attack me without cause. In return for my love they accuse me, but I continue to pray. They repay me evil for good, and hatred for my love." (Psalm 109:1-5 HCSB)

"The arrogant have smeared me with lies, but I obey Your precepts with all my heart. Their hearts are hard and insensitive, but I delight in Your instruction." (Psalm 119:69-70 HCSB)

On **Thursday, October 23, 2014,** when I entered the subway station at East 116 street and Lexington Avenue, on my way home, I heard a woman who was there close to me say, "He should get fired," and the other person responded, "I know."

On **Thursday, October 23, 2014-Friday, October 24, 2014,** when I walked out of my building, that I was walking down the hill, a woman walked across the sidewalk of the affordable housing building that is next to mines, and she spat on the floor as I walked by her.

When on patrol, PO Rivera and I went to buy coffee and some other things to eat. When he went to pay for his thing, he was short of money, and I told him that I was going to pay for him and that he could give me the money later. I insisted repeatedly, but he rather walked back and placed the items back to where he found them. He refused to borrow money from me, because I think that he believes that my hands are dirty, and so is my money.

At the end of the tour, that I was in the locker room getting change, before leaving, PO Gorman said to me, "Farewell." When I was with PO Rivera, PO Rivera began to make jokes about taking his entire locker home with him, because "…there are thieves among us." He again mentioned that "there are thieves among us." He found a lock on the floor and showed it to me.

As soon as I got home, I didn't want to go out, so I didn't go out because I am tired of listening to the negative things that are being said about me everywhere I go.

Saturday, October 25, 2014, was a beautiful day to go out, but I stayed home, because I am tired of people's gossip.

On **Sunday, October 26, 2014,** I went to church, and wishing not to go, I went. And again, many of my good brothers in Christ ignored me. I am all alone.

Every day, there is something new at work. Every day I must deal with gossip at work and outside work. There are things that I don't type down, which are directly and indirectly affecting my life, because if I would, I would have tripled the amount of information that I have already typed. I would have end up sick, or dead. The moment that I don't type, I spend them busy thinking and rethinking about what it is that I did wrong according to them.

Sunday, October 26, 2014 -Monday, October 27, 2014, I was working inside the precinct at the T/S and I saw a black smartphone charging right next to the T/S, right next to where I sat. At that moment I thought that they placed it there to see if I was going to steal it or they were recording my conversation with it. Besides, they placed a toy that looks like a rat in police uniform behind the Desk. I can imagine a camera in the toy rat's eyes.

Another thing that I noticed was that PO Martorelli and PO Gomez were being very friendly towards me. On one occasion when PO Martorelli went into the station house (precinct), he said, "Hernandez". When I was walking out of the 25th precinct from the back, that I was exiting the vestibule, PO Gomez told me to let him know if I needed something. I wondered if that smartphone belonged to PO Gomez and he was recording me.

Lt. Yaguchi arrived at the Desk, and he picked up the officers, except me, from whom he wanted copies of their Memo-Book (Memorandum Pad/Activity Log) for a certain date. Later, he changed his mind, and he wanted a copy of everybody's Memo-Book for that particular day. At that moment, I was seated at the T/S, and I was surrounded by PO Gomez, PO Martorelli, PO Chiodi, PO Arroyo, PO Mahoney, PO Dukas and Lt. Yaguchi who were by the Desk. I went upstairs to the locker room and while I was getting dressed, I saw many of the guys looking at their Memo-Book for that day. As for me, all I was thinking was to go home, to get out of there. Then I heard PO Chiodi say that they were covered. He said, "Innocent until proven guilty."

I just waited for PO Rivera who was looking at his Memo-Book. He saw that he had the day off on that day. So, he didn't make the copy. I thought that we were partners, I assumed that I had the day off too. Also, I disregarded thinking that a copy of my Memo-Book for that day wouldn't be so needed since he first picked the officers of whom he first wanted the copies from, before deciding that he wanted the copies from everyone. So, I left with PO Rivera.

Later at 0811 hrs. or 8:11 am, Lt. Yaguchi texted me, "Hey did y leave" and I texted him back, "Yes. Why?" Later I called him at 0814 hrs. Or 8:14 am and I spoke to him. I told him that I was going back to give him the copy, but he told me not to. At the same time, I noticed that he had me on the speaker because his voice sounded distant.

As I passed the turnstile of the subway station that is by the Yankee Stadium, I heard a young man who was standing there say, "Getting fire" as I walked by. Later at 0824 hrs. or 8:24 am I called him back again to make sure, but he told me not to go back there again and to go to sleep, while I could hear his voice being distant as if he had placed me on the speaker again. When I got home, I didn't know what to do, whether to get a livery cab to go back to the station house (precinct) and make the copies or just do as he told me. So not knowing what to do, I called Prestige, and I asked for a livery cab. When I was inside the livery cab, I told the driver to take me to 119 street between Lexington Avenue and Park Avenue.

As he drove me there, I wondered if I was taking a risk by going back there. First the people that are perpetually following me every day will want to know why I took the livery cab and where I was going. If I go to the station house, they will want to know why I went back there. Later, they will find out that it was to give a copy of my Memo-Book (Memorandum Pad/Activity Log) to Lt. Yaguchi. Then I will expect Lt. Yaguchi to tell them why and he might portray me as an officer who doesn't follow orders, and that I might be hiding something, and as a result, the reasonable suspicion against me will rise and I will then not be on hot water, because I am already there, but on boiling water.

So really, what would have cost me to make two copies of my Memo-Book if I had been in the middle of this dilemma, where everyone wants to get me fired? So many things went through my mind at that moment, while being in the livery cab on my way there, that I changed my mind, and I told the driver to take me back home. He took me back and I paid him eight dollars for the ride. I went to my wife to explain to her what just happened, and she completely ignored me and rejected me. But I do take responsibility for it. I should have made the copies and disregard what is happening around me.

Monday, **October 27, 2014-Tuesday, October 28, 2014,** I went to work. When I arrived that I was getting changed, as I was going to sit on the bench, and suddenly PO Arroyo pulled the bench, and I fell injuring my back. PO Arroyo, PO Chiodi, and PO Gorman were there. PO Gorman's response was for me to suck it up.

PO Rivera told me that I should report it and that people have gone sick for less things than that. But when I told him that PO Arroyo had pulled the bench when I fell, he changed his opinion and told me that he wouldn't report it, but that I don't know about tomorrow. Exactly, the amount of discomfort that I was feeling on my back at the moment could have worsened the following day. I have heard from numerous people who said that they didn't feel any pain on the day of their injuries, but that they did feel it the following day. Knowing this, I wanted a doctor to take a look, so I may follow his advice on what to do and not to do to prevent it from getting worse. Then I called PO Arroyo to ask him if it was ok with him if I went to the hospital, and he told me that it was fine with him.

Later, I saw Sgt. Lucic in the muster room and as soon as I told him that I had fallen, immediately, he walked away from me as if he had seen a ghost. He became alarmed and he mentioned some high ranks that he would have to notify them, as to prevent me from saying anything further. The polite way of saying it doesn't bother me. Again, I told Sgt. Lucic what happened, and I showed him the picture that PO Arroyo took of my injured back and that he had texted me. He responded in a way as if he felt bothered by me telling him that. He told me that it was not a line of duty, but who cares if it was a line of duty or not.

Moments later, I told him that after I finished with my obligations, I was going to take lost time and go to the hospital. As a result, he walked to me holding his smartphone to record me, and he randomly touched my back, where I didn't get hurt, like twice, and he asked me if it hurts, and I told him no, but that I felt a pressure on my back. He mentioned some remedies that I can put on my back instead. Since then, Sgt. Lucic seemed bothered, so to avoid being disliked more than what I already am, I went to PO Arroyo who was by the entrance door of the vestibule, with PO Chiodi, and PO Gorman, and I apologized to him because I feared that they may retaliate against me as a result. I apologized because I was all alone inside the mouth of the lion that was ready to chew me up and swallow me.

I wondered why the three of them gathered there only a few hours after what happened to me. I know that two officers are to be assigned to be in front of the station house (precinct), but I wondered what PO Gorman (the union PBA delegate) was doing there with them. I wondered if they were plotting something regarding my back injury. I was assigned to the T/S on that day. Moments later, PO Lolja asked me how my back was is. I told him that it was good, because at the time I was only feeling pressure on my back. Then many of the guys began to play around about me arresting PO Arroyo and doing a 61 (complaint report) against him.

When I left, I didn't go to the hospital for an x-ray because I was afraid that my followers may inform them and they may plot something else to hurt me. With everything that is being done against me, and knowing that I am very well disliked and hated, I as a human being I ask myself, did he pull the bench intentionally?

On **Tuesday, October 28, 2014 – Wednesday, October 29, 2014,** while on patrol with PO Rivera, at one point he said, "Jammed up," and I knew that it was a message for someone else. Later, we responded to a job at 117 East 115 Street. The complainant there said that the person that he was referring to had 'lied' and he said something like he is 'nut' or that he was going 'nut'. I believed that he was referring to me, because I have been listening to the word 'lie' over and over again. Again, I wonder on what I have err now (what wrong have I done?). Then there was another job in which a female complained against a group, and when we met with the group, her version and theirs were different, they had contradictory statements. Again, there was the 'lie' involved.

On **Wednesday, October 29, 2014-Thursday, October 30, 2014,** I was assigned to an arrest. I was told to take that arrest. I had no choice. I tried to make sure to do it well. PO Portero had brought the defendant to the station house, and he typed the narration on the computer. I finished processing the arrest; while still wondering why I was assigned to that arrest, while at the same time I was trying to listen to what was being said at the Desk. Sadly, I am no longer the exemplary cop I once were, motivated by hard work and good deeds.

On **Thursday, October 30, 2014 –Friday, October 31, 2014,** from home, I called the livery cab base Prestige like 9 times, but the line was busy. I walked out of the building, and I took a livery cab. I arrived at work. I got dressed and went downstairs.

As I waited in the muster room, I felt very disoriented because I heard the officers there excited talking about something or someone that is in trouble. I wondered if they were talking about me and whether I was now in trouble. I wondered if it had anything to do with the arrest that I was not asked to take, but ordered to take, even though another officer, PO Portero, was at the scene, not me, and he was the one who observed, conducted the investigation, and had apprehended the prisoner at the scene. PO Portero was the one who informed me, and he typed down the narration.

Later, PO Rivera and I got assigned to a sector and Sgt. Gibbs assigned us to RMP (police car) 5424. When I went to the Desk to pick up the key, I looked at my Memo-Book (Memorandum Pad/Activity Log) and I told Sgt. Gibbs that I was assigned to RPM # 5424, but he told me that I was assigned to RPM # 5454. Then I told him to check on the roll call, but when I looked at my Memo-Book again, further down I saw RMP # 5454, and I ended up ridiculing myself once more. I wondered what was going on with me. I felt so stressed. The stress in my life doesn't stop. I told PO Rivera what had happened.

Later, PO Rivera and I went on patrol. We headed to work. There was one woman complaining about the man that lives with her. She was accompanied by another woman. She had her things out of the building. The woman told us that she didn't care what we did with him anymore and that he was like bipolar. I suspected that it was another scenario, so I tried to remain quiet as the two of them were talking to me and Officer Rivera. Later, the man of whom she was referring to walked out of the building and he walked towards us with loose keys in his hand.

He took one key and showed it to us. One portion of the key was red, and it confirmed my suspicion. It was another test or scenario.

As PO Rivera was writing down the information on a DIR (Domestic Incident Report), the man was talking to me, but I was not paying much attention to him because I knew that it was a scenario. I was just thinking about what they have gotten me into. In addition, I was not able to understand well what he was saying because of his heavy accent. PO Rivera and I reviewed the overall account of what happened in that scenario. In the end, the man told PO Rivera that he respects him, but he didn't look at me. He told PO Rivera that he could talk about the years that he has on the job, without looking at me. So, all that complement was only given to police officer Rivera, while disregarding me. It seems that now I am the bad, and the incompetent dirty cop. I wondered what I did wrong this time.

Also, we responded to a domestic job. A man called in regards. The caller was waiting for us in front of the building. We went upstairs to the apartment realizing that it was another test, another scenario.

I spoke to the woman while PO Rivera spoke to the man. She seemed unwilling to tell me what happened, but as a cop I had to investigate the occurrence. So, I questioned her repeatedly. I asked her so many times what happened, because I wanted to do my job right. I didn't want to leave the place and later found out that he did something deadly to her. I didn't know who that man was. All I knew was that it was another scenario taking place.

The man was wearing a black t-shirt with red letters, and there was a star on the wall. I did as much questioning as I could. I don't know why I insisted on her to answer my questions. All I knew was that I was nervous because it was another test, and anyone who takes a test knows how it feels, especially when knowing that your job is on the line and your future depends on it.

Now I must admit that I was rude for insisting and demanding answers from her. I still don't know if when I told her to look at me in the eyes there was the right thing to say. I asked her if he pushed her and she fell hitting her head on the edge of the bed and she said yes. As I walked to PO Rivera, I gave PO Rivera an indication or a gesture to communicate to him that the woman had an injury on the eye. Then PO Rivera asked the man if he had strike her. Good question, so I stood there waiting for his response. But he said that he didn't hit her and that he could ask her. So, he is correct. He just pushed her and as she fell, she hit herself in the face.

Moments later, PO Rivera called me out and told me that what she said was different from what I had said. Right away, I became very anguished especially when this is a scenario and everything is being video and/or audio recorded. Then I went over to her, and I asked her again if he did push her and she hit herself on the edge of the bed and she said "yes". What else have I said that is contrary to that if I did say anything to PO Rivera? Then he asked her if he was responsible for that injury and she said "no". At that time, they were physical, he pushed her, and she felled hitting herself against the edge of the bed. As simple as that. Then I said, "But he pushed you?" because I wanted this statement to be well emphasized, loud and clear for the records. Then he said that both were shoving, but that there was no striking or hitting. I never said that he had struck her or hit her. I became so nervous when he said it that I didn't know what else to say. I was in complete shock. Even the victim had to say to stop.

I was so in shock that I had to repeat the same questions to her that when he pushed her, she had hit her head on the side of the bed, because I didn't know what else to say. I was so nervous because I knew that I couldn't afford to make mistakes. My reputation is in jeopardy. It is on the line. So, I continued with the same question of push, felled and hit, and PO Rivera continued asking her if she wanted to press charges. PO Rivera said that I sounded as if he had assaulted her. He said, "You should explain that to the officer here, because it sounded like he assaulted you." His statement was very rude.

First, I didn't want an arrest, but I thought that by him pushing her and she is hitting herself against the edge of the bed was enough probable cause for an arrest. I would have never accused someone wrongfully, because I know well how it feels and would have never commit such a great sin before God, man, and this scenario. At that time, I believed that there was a mandatory arrest to be made since domestic jobs are not taken lightly, but I was going to talk to the man also to know his side of the story. I was so pressured because of the scenario.

Only when I get home that I begin to think about what happened at work is the only time that I get the chance to think about my actions at work. The time that I should have spent resting at home, I use it to reflect on my job performance, my followers, the wrong accusations against me and this whole ordeal. "Probation", and the "fine line" are part of the things that PO Rivera keep reminding me of to intimidate me.

Then PO Rivera told the man that she saved him, and I wondered if he meant from my stupidity. PO Rivera told the man that if he had arrested him, they were going to say that the officer is a "liar." Is he calling me a liar? It seems that I have done something very bad. Then the man talked to me in Spanish too as to let me know. Then he mentioned a house and having no body to talk to. He said something about not showing up, and someone getting pissed. I wondered where I didn't show up. Was it because I missed the court on October 14, 2014, because roll call didn't show that I had court that day? I knew that I had to work a 2nd platoon in the morning because I had court, but the Sergeant gave me a call telling me that I was not given the night and that I had to go to work.

Later, when I arrived at work, I looked at the roll call and I saw that I was not assigned to court. I thought that it was cancelled. Later, when I was assigned to the hospital, that morning I called PO Rivera at the station house to verify if I had court. But he told me that I didn't, and that he had checked. Then Lt. Galamo sent me a text message to ask me to call the Desk and then PO Gomez called me and PO Rivera as well. I wondered why PO Gomez and Lt. Galamo. When I went to see Lt. Galamo she told me that she just wanted to let me know that I didn't need to wait to be relieved to return to the station house (precinct), but I didn't have an RMP (police car) to go back.

Or were they referring to the day when I missed court on June 6, 2014, because they gave me the court notification when the time to be at court had already passed. The outer part of the envelope that had the notification was handed to me and it showed that it was first sent to the wrong officer Hernandez at the 28th precinct, then to the wrong officer

Hernandez at the Court Section, and finally to the right officer Hernandez, me, at the 25th precinct.

As PO Rivera kept talking to the man, I became so frustrated that I had to ask her again and again about her being pushed, because I had nothing else to say, my mind was frozen out of the situation that PO Rivera had gotten me into. I felt so embarrassed that I didn't know what to do. If I continued going back and forward with PO Rivera to try to make myself understood, the embarrassment was going to be much greater, and we were going to look too childish. But I wondered what untrue thing I said to him to say that what I told him wasn't true. He asked the man if he had strike her, but I never told him that he had strike her or hit her. I only knew that she had admitted to me that he had pushed her and that she fell heating herself against the edge of the bed. I thought that it was enough reason to arrest a person, correct me if I am wrong. But of course, I would have interviewed him to know his side of the story.

There I saw PO Rivera in action, taking advantage of the opportunity, trying to make me look bad by portraying me as a liar in front of the man, the woman and the audience that will view, watch and hear the recordings. They so patiently watch me, and they look for ways to drag me down. Then PO Rivera offered to visit him when coming off work (off duty). Wow, what a good police man officer Rivera is. He should win an Oscar for best ….

I was so frustrated. Later, as we left the apartment, PO Rivera told me that I did a good job. But I didn't want to say anything else because I knew that he was wired and that he was recording me, and as many of us know, **"Life and death are in the power of the tongue, …"** (Proverb 18:21 HCSB)

Later, at approximately 0630 hrs. or 6:30 am in the morning, a few moments after our domestic job, as we stood outside, I noticed that he received a text message. I saw when he typed "THANKS", and I saw that it was for Lt. Yaguchi. I asked him who had texted him, and he told me that it was PO Sovulj. Why did he have to lie to me? I wondered what I did wrong, that he had to thank Lt. Yaguchi, who might have congratulated him for the job well done by ridiculing me on our domestic job. In addition, he didn't want to reveal to me the identity of who had texted him. What is the mystery?

Then we went to a 10-11 (alarm) job and there a man arrived. As soon as he did, I went back to the RMP (police car), and when I went back from the RMP (police car), there was the glass door locked with PO Rivera inside. I could see the half side of his body inside the elevator while the man was completely inside the elevator. I knocked at the glass door, but PO Rivera remained there like he was secretly talking to him, and I thought that he was just playing games, until he opened the door for me. Later, when the three of us were in the elevator, the man who was wearing a jacket with the stars on the side of his jacket, told PO Rivera that it was too premature and that he was going to pay for this one. I don't know who he was referring to, probably me, and this might mean that I have done something wrong this time. I am so tired of this. They are using the stars, besides the colors to let us know.

As soon as I arrived at the station house (precinct), I was assigned to Detail overtime for the following day. I wondered if he had assigned me to that mandatory Detail on purpose.

Chapter 18

November 2014 Events

On **Friday, October 31, 2014- Saturday, November 1, 2014,** I was awake all-night thinking about the problems that are presented to me. The young woman who is my next-door neighbor that lives in apartment #61, which I leave in apartment #62, has moved there to spy on me. The same as the person that lives underneath my apartment, apartment #52. This is another way to monitor me. They have been living there for a while now. I am not safe at my own home. I don't want to go to work. I really don't. I am so stressed out. I am not thinking right. I don't even want to take public transportation anymore.

So, I went to the station house (precinct) for the Detail. When I arrived, I saw PO Chiodi talking with the Desk Sergeant. They were talking about someone losing everything. Then PO Gambardelli came to me, and he asked me what I was doing there, and I told him that I was doing the Marathon. When he walked away, PO Quinones came to me and he asked me the same question, and so did PO Mororvich. What was their motive or intention? Then, while inside the van on our way to the Detail, the officers began to say things that had double meaning. One of them said that he should press the eject button to eject someone who was inside the van, and PO Rogozinski talked about how someone should get back from where he came from. The van was invaded by bad comments that I knew were directed at me because they didn't mention the name of the person that they were referring to.

When we arrived at Dunkin Doughnut, there were a few cops seating there from other commands or precincts and when we walked in there, one of them loud enough said, "Your presence is not welcome." I could feel the total rejection.

Later, they assigned me to a solo post at a street corner. It was raining hard, and I was watching the multitude of people running for cover. I wondered if they knew me already, while I felt a discomfort on my back. After we finished, we went back to the terror house, the 25th precinct station house, which for me is the house of terror.

On **Sunday November 2, 2014**, I am so embarrassed to go to church.

Why do I have to keep living an anxious life for not to know what is going to happen later today or tomorrow? Why does nobody approach me to tell me what is going on and what is going to be done with me? Now my future seems so dark and uncertain. I am having a crisis of self-confidence. I have been going through insomnia and irritability while trying to look for a solution to the problem I have, but the matter has worsened. I don't know what legal battle and financial disaster awaits me.

I feel that I have a social responsibility, and it is my obligation to do what I am about to do. It is my duty to do so, or I will be destined to live a dishonored life. What I am about to do will vindicate me or will fasten, rush or prompt my destruction. But I must do something about it because I have been witnessing how my life has been getting destroyed little by little. My public image is that of a man that is immoral, corrupt, and who is not to be trusted. I have been so violated, intimidated and targeted, again and again. I have been feeling forced beyond my will to go and work in that place.

I am like a boxer without a trainer, a member of a team without a coach, a student without a teacher or professor, a man that is all alone, but still, they demand high performance from me. The job by itself is stressful, plus all these things that have been added to me, will make a superman run and fly away. But it is said that the righteous will fall many times but will rise again. But there is one thing that I have to say, and it is that I shall not be called a Christian if I am not willing to die for the truth.

Today, **Thursday, November 6, 2014**, we had a pickup of a job at East 125 street and Madison Avenue. It was a dispute between the cab driver and the passenger. I knew that it was a scenario right away. I didn't

343

want to do anything anymore. In two days, I slept probably four hours. I am so hurt. And I want to apologize for not handling the job properly. My mind was not in on the job because I heard that I am going to be fired. I am afraid, but God gives me the strength.

On **Tuesday, November 11, 2014,** I asked to have the night off. As a result, I remained home all day.

On **Wednesday, November 12, 2014,** I did the 28-hub site. They knew what I was going through, but they still had me do the 28-hub site. I had to deal with fourteen prisoners, and the fourteen of them were criticizing me indirectly. One of them talked about taking off the shield and wiping his as … with it. Others were talking about how stupid he was. Another cop said to another cop loud enough so I may hear and while looking at me, that he should have left. Then all I could hear was them talking about "lies" and "lies".

Then in the afternoon, when I was taking the bus to Manhattan, I heard a woman tell another woman that he is so fired, while getting up her seat. Then I heard one MTA employee tell the bus driver that he was surprised that he was still taking this bus. Then he stepped outside as to see if I was stepping out from behind the bus, and then from outside, he looked to where I was seating, and he stepped back inside the bus and he continued talking to the bus driver.

I went to the Venezuelan place to buy food. There I was wondering if I should go to the hospital for an x-ray of my back. I wanted to make sure I was ok with working out, but I was afraid to go to the hospital, because I knew that my followers were going to inform everyone about it and I didn't know how they were going to take it. I didn't know what to do. I bought the food to go, because the workers there had the music too loud for me to stay. Probably they raised the volume on purpose so that I may not stay there. Again, I didn't know what to do. I went outside with the food thinking about whether I should go to the hospital or not.

Outside I walked back and forward not knowing what to do because I was being followed. So, I decided to give the food to a homeless man who was seating on the floor, and I walked down to the New York-Presbyterian hospital. I was afraid of going to the hospital, so I decided to stop at a Japanese restaurant. While eating the food, I still didn't know what to do. Finally, I ate the food, and I walked to the hospital. When I was there, I decided not to go any further, so I took the train back home, but then I decided to go back to the hospital. So, I took the train back to the hospital. When I got there, I went to the receptionist and I asked her where I could take an x-ray of my back, and she told me that I could go to the emergency room. I decided to leave again because I was too afraid to go there and later be retaliated against by my co-workers again.

On **Friday, November 14, 2014-Saturday, November 15, 2014,** I went to visit pastor N… When I left the place, I decided to go to Inwood Hill Park to escape from everyone, even though it was cold. But at the top end of the hill of the park or at the peak of the park, where there was no walking path, so that people wouldn't walk by, there I laid down next to a fallen tree, to hide, and there I finally rested my soul.

But out of nowhere, a man walked past me, and then an elderly man with two dogs. Then I realized that I was no longer alone. I walked down the hill, and I took a taxi home. I was so consumed and stressed out that at home, I laid down on the bed and slept for a few minutes and as soon as I opened my eyes, I felt terribly bad. I called the Desk to see if I could take the night off and go out sick, since I was not feeling well. I felt nervous, I was shaking and anxious besides my extreme exhaustion. I had an uncomfortable feeling in my stomach.

Lt. Gonzales was at the Desk, and he told me that he didn't have enough personnel, and he asked me if I was going to let the Sergeant pick up the jobs because of my absence. He was trying to touch my conscious by trying to make me feel bad if I didn't go to work. I knew that there was malice in him. He took advantage of this opportunity to retaliate against me, because I had mentioned his name at the close door meeting that I had with the Captain and the Chaplain. In addition, I want to mention that one day he asked me for a favor. He told me to go to his locker and get him his watch, which I did. How important was his watch at the time that he couldn't wait?

So, he told me to call Sgt. Gibbs, but not to let Sgt. Gibbs know that he told me to call him. I called Sgt. Gibbs, and he asked me why I always wanted to take the night off so often, and that I was the only cop doing that. He asked me who had told me to call him, and I told him that Lt. Gonzales did, and he told me to call back the Desk. He seemed to be upset. I called the Sick Desk instead and the person that I spoke to wondered why I didn't go Administrative Sick instead of Regular Sick. He found it strange because the Administrative Sick will only count for one day because it is my last day of work. For example, for Administrative Sick, I can get out sick for two consecutive days and it will count for one. But I didn't care because I needed this only day so badly. Even if it was just for this day. I was so nervous to go to work. I believed that I was going to be fired on this same day, because of all the rumors that I have been listening to. I wanted to say goodbye to everything I have. I was so scared that I wished I never existed.

So, I went back to bed. I slept for like an hour and a half or two hours, and I woke up feeling not that bad, my eyes were blood red, but as I was getting ready to go to work, I was beginning to feel much better. So, I went to work. As I was working, I could hear cops behind me saying "fire", that he is so "fired". And they kept saying that. Then I left and did the Narcotics Run to the Borough.

As soon as I got there, I could hear officers murmuring. When I went to the 28-hub site, I heard one officer say that he should have transfer back in January. Then I heard another cop say that now he was sick. Then I heard another officer say, "Now they are trying to fire Hernández," and I walked away.

Now I wonder what terrible thing have I done to deserve this? Are they claiming that I was fine when I called to get sick? Don't they know that it was on the last day of work that I called sick because I was not feeling well? It was just for one day. I could have gone sick for a week as regular sick, or I could have gone Administrative Sick in which I was entitled to go sick for two consecutive days that was going to count for one. But I just asked for one day. I have gone Administrative Sick only twice in my entire career as a police officer. The first time I called out sick

I believe was in 2010 and the second time was in this miserable year of 2014.

Now when I call for one day, because I was not feeling well, it turned out that they made a big controversy out of it. Everybody seemed upset, astonished and they seemed willing to crucify me just because of that day. I have several certificates of attendance for not getting sick during the years, because I am a hard-working person who loves to work, I like to work, but under this condition who can. Who would work? Isn't this considered a hostile work environment for God's sake? Detrimental to my health and as a result hurt the job I do as a police office.

They make a big deal out of nothing or anything I do. They keep retaliating more against me. I have no voice, no right, it seems that they can do whatever they please with me. I must confess that I am afraid of getting fired. This is why I cannot express my feelings to Pastor N..., because I believe that everything, I tell him, will be known by everyone. All I can say is that they have robbed me of my peaceful and quiet life. I have been running back and forward looking for help, and I find no one to rely on. Now it seems that I am truly helpless and all alone. When I try to talk to my wife about the matter, she curses me instead.

On **Wednesday, November 19, 2014** I was at work standing by the T/S when a detective who I had never seen before approached the training officer, PO Ramos, who was next to me and he asked her, "When are you going to get rid of the guy on your left, in six days?" and she remained quiet. But the strange thing is that on the radio, I heard something about the guy that makes the right things wrong. Also, the officers began to tell each other that it was over. I wondered what they meant by saying that it is over. I believe that the operation that they have been conducting is what is over, because they might know that I already know.

On **Thursday, November 20, 2014,** I went with PO Rivera to do a Directed at East 116 street and Lexington Avenue. We were there and we were accompanied by the transit police officers. Sgt. Gibbs met us there and he began talking with them about how he (?)is an

347

embarrassment to the Department. One of them asked for his shield to be placed inside the water with ice. They didn't mention the name of the person that they were referring to. But I have grounds to believe that the unnamed person was me.

On **Friday, November 21, 2014,** as I was in the public transportation, when I heard a person say, "He should get out of New York City. I would disappear." My God, what terrible thing have I done that I must get out of NYC?

At work I told PO Rivera that I wanted to leave the job. He asked me why. But how could I trust him with all the things that he is doing to me. In the locker room, I hear PO Gorman tell PO Rogonzinski while I was coming from the bathroom, "His days are numbered." Thank you, union PBA delegate PO Gorman, for your wordy venom. Then I walked close to them. The moment that I saw PO Gorman by himself; I asked him what he thought about me quitting. He told me that I shouldn't.

"'Lord, deliver me from lying lips and a deceitful tongue.'" What will He give you, and what will He do to you, you deceitful tongue?" (Psalm 120:2-3 HCSB)

Again, I must repeat that one night when I was at work. I was writing on the table. Suddenly, PO Sofoka Ahmed laid his hand on my shoulder, and he told me, "Hang in there." He cannot imagine how thankful I still am for that act of kindness om his behalf.

On **Saturday, November 22, 2014,** in the morning, I saw when PO Rivera told Lt. Galamo something, and she told him that it was going to be for Tuesday, and PO Rivera told her, "Please," and I wondered what it was. Am I going to be arrested or fired on Tuesday? I have become so sensitive to everything I hear.

On **Saturday, November 22, 2014 – Sunday, November 23, 2014,** we had a car stopped. I saw a person on the front passenger side holding a bottle in his right arm. It was inside a plastic bag, and I could see the top part of the bottle that was closed with its cap. Somebody had already drank from it because it was not full. He was holding it and on purpose he brought the bottle up to his mouth with the cap on to pretend that he was drinking from it and to let me know what it was, but he didn't say anything. I returned to the car, and I showed PO Rivera the charge definition. He told me that he wouldn't give him a summons.

According to him, it had to be open, not just unsealed, and that he was holding a piece of cake too. He made me look as if I was inconsiderate. But he didn't know what I had in mind, because I was afraid to speak my mind. But my intention was to approach the person one more time, see if there was a smell of alcohol coming from his breath, ask him if he could take the bottle out of the plastic bag and ask him questions pertaining to the bottle of alcohol such as if he was drinking inside the car and so on. What is it that PO Rivera wants to gain out of contradicting me? He keeps pressing the button.

PO Byrd had her RMP (police car) parked behind us. I walked to her, and I told her to follow me, which she did. In front of PO Rivera, I explained to her my position and my point of view regarding the open container and PO Rivera's opposition, and she ended up agreeing with me. I did it for the records.

"I have lived too long with those who hate peace. I am for peace; but when I speak, they are for war." (Psalm 120:6-7 HCSB)

Later, I went to church, and I saw my brother in Christ Me… who saw me, and he places his hand on my shoulder, and he told me that I looked refresh, better than before. I wondered what he meant by that. However, I am still being ignored in church. Then I saw one brother in Christ whose name in Domi …, and he was staring at something that he had on his hand and when I touched his arm, he looked at me and he whispered something while he immediately stared back at what he was staring at before. He didn't greet me as I walked by.

On **Monday, November 24, 2014,** I spent the entire day at home, worried about my job, worried about being on the news and being classified as a disgraced cop, which will be an embarrassment to friends and family.

On **Tuesday, November 25, 2014,** I remained home worried about my future, a future where everyone seems to hate me or despise me. Here I am, lamenting my position. When my wife arrived from outside, the first thing she told me was that I should find a place of my own, because she was going to hand over the apartment.

On **Tuesday, November 25, 2014-Wednesday, November 26, 2014,** I worked with PO Rivera. While walking out of the Taino towers building, he told me that he was going to call me the last time. He mentioned the last time that we spoke about the open container, and that he had a dream where Rocky was fighting with Apollo (Apollo Creed who fought Rocky) and Apollo was arrested. However, he briefly mentioned the open container and then that Apollo was arrested. I wondered what he meant by that. Does he mean that I have done something wrong? He is very sarcastic. I told him that I felt like being in the ocean all by myself. I told him that I feel safer on the street than in the precinct, and that I don't feel safe on the street, and not even in my own home.

Before leaving, I noticed that Sgt. Lucic enthusiastically gathered with PO Rivera and Sgt. Jackson. The three seemed to be talking about something, but as soon as they saw me, PO Rivera pointed at my direction, and behind me is a wall and hanging on the wall are photos of the cops of the month (Photos of cops who did a great job on a specific month). PO Rivera said something about getting rid of those photos on the wall. Later, before leaving, Sgt. Gibbs told PO Rivera to give him that arrest, so he can be the cop of the year (not just the cop of the month). PO Rivera again recommended that those photos on the wall be removed and to just place his own photo there alone on the wall as the cop of the year.

At that moment, I wondered if what Sgt. Gibbs truly meant was on PO Rivera arresting me. I am so afraid. Then since PO Rivera drove in, he offered me a ride home as Lt. Yaguchi once did. I went inside his car wondering about all this.

On **Thursday, November 27, 2014,** I told my brother and sisters that I was being followed. They thought that it was absurd. They said that I was not that important for them to have people following me. That same night, when my brother was driving home, my brother told me that he was pulled over by police officers and that the Sergeant ordered him to get out of the car for no reason. He told me that it reminded him of what I told him that night.

On **Friday, November 28, 2014,** an arrest was made for Criminal Mischief of broken window. It happened in our sector. The Impact team caught the person. Sgt. Sanchez said that the impact team was going to take the arrest. I saw that PO Anthola was going to take it. I was debating whether to take it or not. The Sergeant told me that I could take it if I wanted to. But moments later, I saw the Sergeant talking to PO Anthola and I heard him when he said to her," … jammed up." When I heard that, I definitely didn't want to take the arrest anymore.

At the end of the day, she didn't take the arrest, but my partner PO Martorelli, with whom I was working with for the night, took the arrest. I was then assigned to go to the hospital and guard a hospitalized prisoner. Already there, I heard the medical staff talking about someone calling out sick. Then I heard them say that my stomach hurts. Then I heard another one say that my back hurts. They didn't get off that topic. They kept talking about it over and over again, and one female staff began to move her upper body as if she were dancing.

On **Sunday, November 30, 2014,** I went to church and the same thing happened. I was being ignored. There I saw the church members lamenting themselves for some type of occurrence that I was not aware of, but that I think had something to do with me. I am afraid once more. It is like the weight of the whole world is on my shoulder.

Chapter 19

December 2014 Events

On **Tuesday, December 2, 2014,** I finally went for an interview at 1PP (1 Police Plaza= Police Headquarter) to be considered for a permanent position there as Headquarter Security. I was trying to escape the 25th precinct. Inside the train, I saw people shaking their heads as if they were feeling sorry for me. I don't know what to do. I don't know what is going to be of my life. I am so anxious. I am so afraid. I am so desperate. This is something so big that even my closest one is afraid to tell me anything. I am so afraid of the unknown.

They keep torturing me day in and day out. I don't want to go out. I am afraid to go out. I am afraid to talk. If I lose this job, what is going to be of me? What am I going to do since I have no trade? I spent years studying Criminal Justice in order to take what I academically learned there and apply it on my law enforcement career as a police officer.

I am so disoriented. I can go nowhere. What is the terrible thing I did that they are treating me this way? Are they going to send me to jail because I don't know what? Do I have to keep suffering? Or should I speak up? Today, in the process of washing the dishes, I began to feel pressure on my back. When I was done, I went to bed and lay there.

People are complaining that I had said that I was tired and that for that reason I wanted to go out sick. I am so tired of being the target of everything. I don't know what to do. I don't know what to say. I don't know what is right or wrong anymore. It is not only me suffering because of my condition, my family too are suffering from seeing me like this, in this condition. I made the intent to solve all this peacefully, but I see no peaceful way out of it. There is none.

Saturday, December 6, 2014 – Sunday, December 7, 2014, I received a minor violation by Lt. Gonzales because my turtleneck had a hole. I received the news that there is a group of people that want to shoot on duty cops according to SBA (Sergeant Benevolent Association). We had a job at 2026 Lexington Avenue about a family dispute on the third floor. We went there and when we entered the building, we saw a young man and a young woman walking out of the lobby. When we went up to the third floor, I saw written on one of the doors the word "lie". Then when facing the stairs to go down the stairs, I looked up and I saw the word "lie" written there too. As I proceeded to walk down the stairs, I saw that it was written on a wall the word "lie" again.

"Do not give me over to the will of my foes, for false witnesses rise up against me, breathing violence." (Psalm 27:12 HCSB)

"Vindicate me, Lord, because I have lived with integrity and have trusted in the Lord without wavering." (Psalm 26:1 HCSB)

Back at the station house, I heard when PO Gorman joyfully say to PO Gambardelli that nobody went. PO Gabandelli told him that he is no longer going to collect easy (free) money. But Gorman said, "… Welfare …." Then I heard PO Gambardelli say that he is going to work hard for his money now. But haven't I tried by giving the best of me to maintain my job without getting into conflict with anyone? I have lost heart. On this day I found out that PO Rafferty was robbed and that he was injured as a result.

When I went to church, the pastor mentioned the "lying" and the false prophets. He cited 2 Chronicles chapter 18 and the spirit of lie that should be on the false prophets. Also, how the prophet Micaiah lied at first to satisfy the king. Even in church I am admonished.

On **Sunday, December 7, 2014-Monday, December 8, 2014,** I saw PO Gambardelli stretching and he said, "My back." He had done and said the same thing on different occasions, even yesterday, and he did it right with me.

Today I was assigned to work with PO Estrada. We remained quiet almost all the time while on patrol. We were assigned to do the mail run by Sgt. Gibbs. Sgt. Gibbs told me that he forgot to send sector Boy there and that they were doing the Narco Run. As PO Estrada drove, he drove into different potholes. It appeared to me that he was doing it intentionally on purpose. We picked up and dropped the mail at four other precincts. When we were at the station house (precinct), I heard PO Gambardelli playing around with PO Estrada, and he told him, referring to an unknown person that the person was seating on his own urine. They were both joking around. It seemed that they were making fun of me.

When I arrived home, when I was laying on the bed, I received a text from Lt. Yaguchi asking me if I wanted to do overtime tomorrow at 1305 hrs. or 1:05 pm for the protest. I didn't know what to say. If I answered no, they would be accusing me of laziness and that I don't like to work when almost everyone in the precinct is doing it, and they will continue to bother me. If I answered yes, they would have less to complain about.

So, I answered, "Yes sir." Later he texted me back because he wanted to know if I was doing CRV (Another overtime assignment) and I texted him that I will do that too. Then he called me, and I knew that he would be recording me, I told him that I would be doing both. He asked me if I was good, and I told him that I was good, and then he asked me if everything was good. Was he joking? Doesn't he know that everything in my life is upside down? Why is he being so cynical about it? He thinks that I don't know what they know.

When I told him that I was good I was moved by the unbelief in how the person that I was speaking to was pretending to care for me or about me, when indeed all he wanted is to get me into trouble, ruin my career and get me fired. Now there are three things that I must not do. I must not call sick, even if I am dying, I must not ask to have a day off, and if I am asked if I want to do overtime, I must not refuse. I did what my brother in Christ Me… told me to do two weeks ago, that when people ask me how I am doing, that I should tell them that I am good.

So, besides all this tribulation, all is good in Christ who strengthens me. Every day they are making me suffer, but it is all in God's hand.

"And we know that for those who love God all things work together for good, for those who are called according to his purpose." (Roman 8:28 ESV)

On **Monday, December 8, 2014 – Tuesday, December 9, 2014,** I went to the station house to do the CRV overtime. When I was there, I could see how cops were disappointed to see me there. PO Pedrosa didn't expect me to do it. I highly suspected that she was always wired.

When we arrived at Times Square for CRV, at the muster, I could hear cops from other commands talking about faking, and one of them asked, "What is he doing here?" I wondered what was going on. PO Pedrosa and I were assigned to the Rockefeller center. There PO Pedrosa asked me if I was tired, which I didn't answer and she asked me how midnight for me was, which I was getting used to, but not at the abuse that I am receiving day in and day out. Also, she asked me about my sleeping hours. I knew that her interrogation had something to do with the day that I called out sick.

At one time when I was in the lobby, I heard the receptionist talking to another person and she was talking to him about sickness. Then PO Pedrosa arrived and another officer from the 48th precinct as well. I became so frustrated at the receptionist's comment about sickness that I furiously rushed out of the building and waited in the RMP (police car) for a break. What do they want from me? At the end of the day, PO Pedrosa told me that she saw herself getting a line of duty many times as I drove back to the 25th precinct.

When I arrived at the station house (precinct), standing by the Desk was Lt. Yaguchi, and Lt. Gonzales was in front of the Complaint room. They were both in civilian clothing. Then I saw Lt. Gonzales staring at his smartphone, which he had facing me, and I stared at the muster room. He was observing me. Then when Lt. Yaguchi walked away to go upstairs, Lt. Gonzales followed him. Moments later, I decided to go upstairs to talk to Lt. Yaguchi, and going down the stairs was PO Sovulj.

He told me that Lt. Yaguchi was talking to Lt. Gonzales in his office. From that moment, I realized that the two of them were conspiring against me. I continued walking up the stairs, and I went to the locker room. There I dropped my equipment, and as I walked a few steps down to see Lt. Yaguchi in his office, which I was going to see if Lt. Gonzales was not there, a few steps down, I saw Lt. Gonzales standing by the stairs using his smartphone. Moving by fear, I walked back upstairs to the locker room. Then I prepared myself mentally and I walked back downstairs to Lt. Yaguchi's office.

In his office, I asked him if somebody else could do the protest overtime for me. He looked upset, so I told him to forget about it. I really wanted to do this overtime, and more to come, but how can I want to spend more time at work when I see them all skimming and planning to hurt me. If I do, I can then be considered a masochist. All of this is too much for me to handle. Then I went to the muster room to rest for a few minutes.

"For my enemies talk about me, and those who spy on me plot together, saying, "God has abandoned him; chase him and catch him, for there is no one to rescue him." God, do not be far from me; my God, hurry to help me." (Psalm 71:10-12 HCSB)

Then after working for 8 hours and 35 minutes I left. I arrived home at like 9:00 am, slept for about two hours and then I went back to the station house (precinct) for the protest overtime which was going to be from 1305x0105 or from 1:05 pm till 1:05 am. 12 hours shift overtime. At the station house, my colleagues were wondering why I was doing the overtime. There our entire time was spent inside the van. I had come out of it just three times, once to get food, the other to use the bathroom and the last was to stretch for five minutes outside. While in the van, I heard PO Rogozinski talk about PO Rafferty going line of duty like four times already. Then he continued joking about PO Rafferty going out sick repeatedly. I knew that he said those things because of me.

On **Sunday, December 14, 2014 – Monday, December 15, 2014,** I was assigned to a hospitalized prisoner at Harlem hospital. I spent the entire night there listening to the medical staff talking about someone who was getting fired. 'Fired', 'fired' and 'fired', is all that I could hear from them. As a result, I became nervous, nervous and more nervous. Finally, I heard a female nurse strongly say to herself as she walked in front of me, "He is fired, and he is getting nothing." Then my reliever came, handed me over the RMP's (police car) key with a despise look on his face, and I left shaking.

When I arrived at the station house (precinct), I heard someone else say, "He is fired" and I became terribly desperate. Then I heard, "He is going downtown." I went downtown to court not knowing what to expect, but the worst, to get fired. There I spoke to ADA Hanz, and I explained to her what happened with the shots fired and I gave her the copy of my Memo-Book (Memorandum Pad/Activity Log). However, when I was talking to her, as soon as I mentioned that I saw a person dressed in black get into the apartment, I heard a great laughter coming from outside and I realized that it was them. From a private room, they were listening to the conversation that I was having with her to see how accurate I was. I know that the scenario was video recorded, and this is why I told her that she can even look at the camera, because I am sure of what I saw.

I am wondering why they laughed about it. If they consider that I was lying, then send me to jail for I have been imprisoned and tortured by them all this time. Then as soon as I walked out, I heard a man who sadly said, "Right before Christmas," and on the hallway I heard cops mentioning the cameras which I just did mentioned to ADA Hanz.

Then I went to the bathroom. While using the toilet, I heard people passing by and one of them said, "…the church guy…." What did I do now?

On **Monday, December 15, 2014,** I went home in the afternoon, and I didn't come out, I was agonizing at home thinking about

357

what I had said that has caused such an alarm, and the same on **December 16, 2014, and on December 17, 2014**.

On **Thursday, December 18- Friday, December 19, 2014,** I heard the news about a cop who committed suicide after having a dispute with his wife. It is very sad. At night I went to work after spending my last days off being mortified at home as I was lamenting by myself for everything that is happening. I am so anguished.

There was PO Rivera at the muster room and Lt. Yagushi arrived at the muster room announcing to everyone that PO Rivera is the cop of the year. He is told that Sgt. Gibbs has his award since PO Rivera didn't go to the Christmas party.

This explains why on **November 26, 2014,** PO Rivera anticipated ahead of time who was going to be the cop of the year. Who else than no other than himself. No wonder why PO Rivera didn't go to the Christmas party, where he was going to be presented to and be given an award for being the cop of the year. Award that was awarded to him, as I do believe, for his continuous and persistent contribution on their intent to bring an officer down.

He is being ten years older than I, and having more time on the job than I, has become the key participant in their mischievous scheme to take me down. They are counting on his great deal of experience which surpasses my own. He has been greatly used for their devious purpose. I believe that his conscience and guilt for putting his partner down didn't let him go to the Christmas party to celebrate my defeat. After all, if he is not with them, he is going to be against them. It is either me or them. He has no choice, especially when he has many children to feed and a sick wife to take care of.

Later, the day, PO Rivera was being congratulated again and again. It is for certain because of his contribution to the ongoing investigation of his fellow officer, who is his partner, which is me. It is obvious because many officers have been more productive than him when it comes to police activity and productivity. But none of them must deal with me for more than eight hours a day, which he has been doing, every day, tempting me, testing me, throwing me fast balls, and curves to see me strike out, and to psychologically manipulate my thoughts to inflict fear on me. Then I saw Lt. Yaguchi behind the Desk smiling. Yes, smiling, because unfortunately many people hope that something goes wrong in a person's life so they can feel better.

"How long will I store up anxious concerns within me, agony in my mind every day? How long will my enemy dominate me? Consider me and answer, Lord my God. Restore brightness to my eyes; otherwise, I will sleep in death. My enemy will say, "I have triumphed over him," and my foes will rejoice because I am shaken. But I have trusted in Your faithful love; my heart will rejoice in Your deliverance." (Psalm 13:2-5 HCSB)

It was like **Friday, December 19, 2014, or Saturday, December 20, 2014,** at approximately 2303 hrs. or 11:03 pm that I was waiting at East 125 Street and Lexington Avenue subway station for the number # 6 train. There I saw a man with the same hairstyle that the perpetrator had at those shots fired job at 1900 Lexington Avenue. He was walking by me. PO Rivera once told me that the perpetrator has a brother, and I wondered if he was his brother looking to retaliate against me. At that moment I was on high alert.

On **Saturday, December 20, 2014,** I learned that two of my NYPD fellow officers were assassinated just because the shooter wanted to kill cops in retaliation to what happened to Eric Garner.

On **Saturday, December 20, 2014 – Sunday, December 21, 2014,** I worked with PO Rivera. As we were inside of the RMP (police car), I noticed that he was coughing harder than before. He was coughing so hard that it began to annoy me. Then when we were in the RMP (police car) by Marcus Garvey Park, a young man and a woman walked by and as they were talking to each other, the man yelled at her telling her to stop "lying."

Then coming out of the RMP (police car), I heard a couple of young ladies saying out loud, "How are you going to buy food without money? No money, no money." Throughout the day I continued to hear people say, "PO Rivera cop of the year." Walking on the street, I heard people talking about "lying" again. It seems that now I am being portrayed as a great liar.

On Sunday, December 21, 2014, I read on the New York Daily News that "A **second slay attempt on NYPD officers was narrowly avoided early Sunday when a gunman's weapon jammed as he took aim at two cops outside a Bronx housing project**." On Wednesday, December 17, 2014, **an officer in the Bronx was shot in the neck with a BB gun**. On Sunday, December 21, 2014, **two officers from the 28th precinct were assaulted by a man inside of the station house (precinct)** and the worse can be expected for me for I am hated because according to them I am a liar.

On **Sunday, December 21-Monday, December 22, 2014,** as we were inside the RMP (police car), our conversation was limited. PO Rivera kept coughing hard, as if he were intentionally coughing with anger.

On **Monday, December 22, 2014- Tuesday, December 23, 2014,** my wife kept cursing at me saying that I am schizophrenic and that I need mental help. She says that I need to see a doctor because I am not well.

On **Wednesday, December 24, 2014,** I woke up early from bed because I couldn't resist the thoughts of what is happening to me. So, I left the apartment thinking about going to the location where the two cops got shot at Myrtle and Tompkins for the memorial. However, tire of being followed everywhere I go, and being harassed by my co-workers and by the Department that is doing nothing in regards, I decided to go out and eat something. Then I went to the movie theater and watched the movie, "**It is a Wonderful Life**" because there at least I could hide for a moment and escape from my cruel reality.

Inside the movie theater, a couple and what appeared to be their son and daughter, were seated right behind me. I believed that they were there to keep their eyes on me, so what I did was that I went back and sat back on the same line that they were seating. Moments later, I looked to my right, and there I saw a young man with a young woman seating together, and the two of them were wearing red colors. They were simply my dear followers. Isn't my life wonderful?

After the movie, I was so anxious that I took the train and walked over to 42 street to eat my burrito. But as I walked there, I heard people saying, "Stupid." When I finished eating in a hurry, I immediately took the train back home. Finally, I walked into my apartment wishing to never go back out again.

When I arrived home, I saw a text message that was sent to me today at 1325 hrs. or 1:25 pm. It is the photo of a document from the 79 Precinct illustrating the photos of five individuals and on top of it says, "…. **THREATS TO UMOS by Black Guerrilla Family**." UMOS stand for Uniform Member of the Service.

Then I read another text that was sent at 1326 hrs. or 1:26 pm of another photo document from the ESSEX COUNTY SHERIFF'S OFFICE P.B.A.-LOCAL 183 that says," **URGENT MESSAGE TO ALL PBA MAMBERS" Then it says," AN INCIDENT OCCURRED THIS MORNING IN PATERSON SHOTS WHERE FIRED FROM A VEHICLE AT AN OFF DUTY POLICE OFFICERS CAR WITH A PBA SHIELD DISPLAYED IN THE WINDOW. THE POSSIBILITY EXITS THAT OFF DUTY OFFICERS AND THEIR FAMILIES MAY BECOME A TARGET. EFFECTIVE IMMEDIATELY.**"

Today is Christmas day, and I stayed home by myself. I didn't go out to spend it with my family. In addition, today is my mother's birthday as well, but I didn't attend. I stayed home, by myself, because the one that is called my wife, just left to spend the day with her family without letting me know. So, because of all these threats against police officers, and their families I decided to stay away from my family on this Christmas day. What am I going to do? Everyone seems to know where I live. I have been asking for a transfer for so long. If I keep silent, and just cross my arms, I will die of anxiety. I am worried to death right now.

On **Thursday, December 25, 2014- Friday, December 26, 2014,** I went to the viewing by myself to pay my respect to Officer Rafael Ramos, so I won't have to go there with the officers from the 25th precinct (my precinct), because I am tired of being harassed by them. Even there, there were some officers in uniform that were looking at me strangely. After the viewing, I went home, and from home, I went to work. I told my co-workers that I already went to the viewing. I am tired of being overly watched by them.

Later that night, I had an RMP (police car) accident where I hit the park's bench, and as a result I got a flat tire. After my partner PO Rivera and I began to change the tire, there was PO Gomez and his partner hanging around. PO Gomez had the focus bright light of his RMP (police car) directed at us. At that moment, I was thinking that he was video recording us, because he went back to his RMP (police car) probably to do so from there. I was feeling so tense. I didn't know what to do. I was desperate.

When we were done, we went back to the station house (Precinct) to do the paperwork. When I was done with the paperwork, I could hear rumors all around. PO Gomez seemed to have gotten credit for something related to me and the accident, and PO Perez seemed to be spreading the news about my RMP (police car) accident. I was so tired. When PO Rivera and I left the station house (precinct), I saw him wearing his dark blue sneakers.

On **Friday, December 26, 2014-Satuday, December 27, 2014,** I didn't go to the funeral. I wanted to go, but I didn't go because of them. I volunteered to stay overtime to relieve another officer so that he may go to the funeral. It is so sad. So, I was with PO Bliss in the vehicle. When we were inside the RMP (police car), he took his gun out and placed it on his lap. He had it there until it was time to go back to the precinct. I wondered why he did that. Was it to intimidate me?

Saturday, December 27, 2014-Sunday, December 28, 2014, how can I deal with so much pressure? Everywhere I walk, there they are with their phones recording me. PO Rivera and his dark blue sneaker.

Sunday, **December 28, 2014-Monday, December 29, 2014,** they had me assigned as the station house (precinct) security with PO Rivera. While standing at the precinct, I was listening to a song about Mark Anthony that reminded me of 1996 and I told PO Rivera about it. He told me about El General (Reggae singer), and I told him that he also reminded back when I was ten, nine years old.

Later, when Sgt. Gibbs was at the Desk, he asked me several questions. About me going to church, and that I should begin talking about God in the precinct. But he didn't suspect that I knew that I was being recorded. I answered his questions knowing that every word that comes out of my mouth will be compromised. One of the answers that I gave him was that I have not been going to church on Wednesdays. Because before, I used to go to church every single Wednesday but not anymore. I told him that there is no excuse as to why I don't go every Wednesday. Then PO Maher walked in, and he mentioned the word 'lie' again. Then I heard Sgt. Gibbs mentioning something when he was 5 years old or remembering things since he was five years old.

At one point I was talking to PO Rivera, and he asked me about the trinity, and about Jesus being tempted by Satan by offering him the kingdoms. I said nothing, and I heard PO Chardonett in a low voice say, "No response." I know that the world is paying attention to what I say. I asked him if he didn't remember the last time that I explained it to him. Later, PO Rivera gave me an example of someone calling me a liar. Then I saw movement around, and it seemed that some people there were angry at me. Especially Lt. Yaguchi who gave me a look as if he wanted to kill me.

Then in the locker room, PO Rivera asked me, "How are you carrying?" I asked him, "Who?" and he told me, "You." Then he continued," You should ask for forgiveness." And I asked him why? And he answered, "I don't know, you don't know what you did, but maybe you, should ask for forgiveness." Then he acted as if he were plunging a sword to himself, as Samurais used to do back then when they did something dishonorable or broke their code of honor. And while doing so, he told me that only then will he (Lt. Yaguchi) be happy. He continued saying, "You are like 'You have humiliated me. Do what you must do.' The code of a Samurai, the code of a Samurai, it is a Bushido, the code of a Samurai. To know how to carry. And then all will be well. And then he remembers you as a hero. Bushido."

I asked him if I did something wrong, and he told me, "I don't know, I don't know." He continues, "You know, Yaguchi is a very private man. He doesn't say a word. He is very, vindictive." I responded, "Ah?" and he repeated, "Yaguchi is very vindictive." I asked him what he said, and he clarified, "He holds it in. He never forgets." Then I Googled the meaning of vindictive, and the meaning is, **Having or showing a strong or unreasoning desire for revenge**." Then I looked at the synonyms and it said: **Vengeful, revengeful, unforgiving, resentful, acrimonious, bitter, spiteful, mean, rancorous, venomous, malicious, malevolent, nasty, mean-spirited, cruel, unkind**. I wonder what I did to that man for him to hate me so much.

PO Rivera wanted me to give up. Ok, Lt. Yaguchi has the Bushido code, but I have done nothing wrong. And I want them all to know this, "In the warrior's code there is no surrender. Though his body says 'stop', his spirit cries, 'Never,'" from the Burning Heart-Survivor Rocky soundtrack.

Then PO Rivera told me, "And that his smile, is a thin vail. I don't trust that man." He continued, "They say, keep your friends close, but your enemies closer." I responded, "Ah?" And PO Rivera repeated, "Keep your friends close right, but keep your enemies closer. You got to watch this guy. You can't turn your back on your enemy. You have got to keep them closer than your friend. A friend you can trust, but your enemy you must keep them closer. And know everything they do. That is the … of the costa nostra."

Then we walked downstairs to see Lt. Yaguchi because he wanted to see us. When we arrived at his office I said, "Lieutenant," and he said, "Was up. How are you?" and I answered, "All right, and you how are you doing?" and he said, "I am all right." And I told him, "You gave me a strange look downstairs, and I was like, 'wait a second, what is going on'. Are you ok Lieutenant?" and he answered, "Yeah, I am all right." Then I left.

Then I left the station house (precinct) with PO Rivera, and in front of the precinct, an officer told PO Rivera that he looked like he was going to court. And PO Rivera told him, "As a defendant?" and he laughed. But before PO Rivera told the officer, "Don't get caught man." Then he told me," Don't believe the heights." I didn't understand, so he clarified to me, "The things that go around."

Then I told him that I was on vacation next week, and he laughed saying, "The first week? You did the first week. Ha, ha, ha, ha. You couldn't wait. Ha, ha, go ahead man." What he meant was that I took the first week of the New Year to go on vacation, which showed how desperate I was to get out of there. And we parted.

"God, hear my voice when I complain. Protect my life from the terror of the enemy. Hide me from the scheming of wicked people, from the mob of evildoers, who sharpen their tongues like swords and aim bitter words like arrows, shooting from concealed places at the innocent. They shoot at him suddenly and are not afraid. They encourage each other in an evil plan; they talk about hiding traps and say, "Who will see them?" They devise crimes and say, "We have perfected a secret plan." The inner man and the heart are mysterious." (Psalm 64:1-6 HCSB)

Monday, December 29, 2014-Tuesday, December 30, 2014, I worked with PO Rivera. But as I expected, when I was seated inside my police car, I saw PO Maher coming out of his police car. Then looking at me, he kicked the front bumper of my police car. Moments later, when responding to a job, PO Rivera did the same thing that PO Maher did, by kicking the front bumper with me inside. In addition, he acted as if taking the RMP (police car) by the hand and flipping it over with me inside as a form of rejection. At the end of our tour, when heading back to the station house (Precinct), I saw officers who didn't know Spanish, trying to talk in Spanish.

Later, in the locker room, I overheard PO Gorman, who is my Union PBA delegate, tell PO Rivera, "He can touch his ankle," and he walked to my aisle. Later, he told PO Rivera about something next week, and PO Rivera answered, "He is dead." I think that he was referring to me.

When we walked out of the station house (precinct), I noticed that he was wearing green paint, the same dark blue sneakers, and underneath his outer clothing, he was wearing orange clothing. Finally, I am taking a two-week vacation, and it starts now.

Chapter 20

January 2015 Events

There is one thing that I ask myself, and it is why my former partner, PO Eddie Pinero, who has eighteen years on the job, and he wanted to or already vested out (left the job) two years before his twenty-year anniversary, which after twenty years, he qualifies for retirement. If he vests out, he will not have a salary for two years, and he will not receive his Variable Supplement, which is a twelves thousand dollars annual payout that are given to police officer for the rest of their life if they retire after twenty years of service and that is besides his pension. I believe that he will also lose his health insurance benefit for two years as well.

He once told me that they (The Lt. Yaguchi Administration) failed to accommodate his schedule, because he is a pastor at a church. Then having no other option, he had to go to a higher rank outside of the precinct and only then Lt. Yaguchi was forced to accommodate him. But no, the accommodation wasn't enough, this time he vested out, giving away all his benefits. But I wonder what truly forced him to leave the job. Was there any retaliation against him being done that he didn't want to talk about, afraid of breaking the chain of command by complaining to a higher rank outside the precinct? Or was it for all the things that were taking place in the precinct where I was the main target? I wonder why one day he gave me his Speaker Microphone Vertex and along with it he gave me the receipt.

On **Wednesday, December 31, 2014-Thursday, January 1, 2015,** I didn't want to visit my parents for the New Year as result of my followers. I went to church and there I received the New Year. Moments later, I met with my wife at the bus stop. I told her that I was thinking about going to visit my parents for this New Year. We took the bus, and when we got off the bus, there I saw a suburban and on the windshield a parking permit from the City of New York, and there I wondered why the city is after me.

When we got in front of our building, we decided to take a livery cab to go and visit my parents. Suddenly, a livery cab appeared. As he was driving us there, he began to talk about race and I became disgusted at his comments, so I told him to take us back. I didn't want to ride with him anymore. Then my wife went inside the building, and I stopped another livery cab and, on my way, to visit my parents, my wife called me telling me that she didn't want to get inside the apartment, because there were people smoking on our floor. I had to tell the driver to go back to where he had picked me up, and my wife decided to go and visit my parents with me.

As we were heading there, I had the feeling that I shouldn't go to visit my parents and that I shall go back, and my indecision made my wife upset. When we got in front of the building, I saw like three people standing by the vestibule of the building. I became nervous, so I didn't want to get out of the livery cab. But I did leave my wife inside the livery cab, while I went upstairs to pick up something, and be back at the livery cab immediately. I walked inside the building, but later while in the elevator, I decided to go back down, and I took my wife with me. I told her that I was not well because I was looking at the people outside who were wearing the red colors. Then she walked with me inside the building and while we were waiting by the vestibule area, a young person walked into the vestibule wearing red. There I realized that I was not alone. It was one of my followers.

When we opened the door of the vestibule, the same person went into the elevator with us, and he pressed the same floor button that we did. The person came off on the same floor, and my wife came out with me. As soon as we came out of the elevator, I told my wife that we should leave, but she didn't want to listen to me, she kept on walking. Unfortunately, I had to raise my voice to her out of desperation, because I didn't want the person who was following me to know where my family lives. I urged her by raising my voice in the sense that a stranger had to open the door of his apartment to look out and see what was happening. Right when my wife was in front of the door's apartment, I forbidden her to knock at the door. I convinced her to walk back to the elevator with me.

When we were heading to the elevator, the person that had come out of the elevator with us appeared again from the other end of the hallway. Now he was walking towards us, and he passed us by. He kept on walking to the other end of the hallway with no other purpose. He seemed not to know where else to go, the person looked lost. Then when the door of the elevator opened, I kept the elevator's door open, pleading with my wife to please come in.

Then she came in, and as soon as she said that the door was about to close, there came the same person who had been following us, and tried to get in as the door closed, but the person forced the door open and managed to get inside the elevator. When the elevator opened the door downstairs, we came out, and I told my wife that we had to go, and at the lobby she refused to. I raised my voice again in desperation, but she still refused to leave, and she told me that she was waiting for my sister to come out of the elevator, because she had called her and told her to come.

Meanwhile, the suspicious person left the premise. My sister showed up, and we decided to take the elevator upstairs, but not before a family got into the elevator with us and told us Happy New Year, and before leaving the elevator, a woman told us to have a good day. When we reached the floor that we came out, I saw my father waiting in the hallway and he was anguished because of what happened. My dad is 82 years old, and it hurt me to see him preoccupied, so I decided to change the whole outcome. We went into the apartment and decided to forget all about what happened.

On **Saturday, January 3, 2015,** I went to PO Wenjian Liu's wake. It was a rainy day.

Today, **Sunday, January 4, 2015,** I wanted to go to PO Wenjian Liu's funeral. I woke up early to go to the station house (precinct) and wear my uniform. When I got off at the train station at 116 East Street and Lexington Avenue, I called PO Rivera to see if he was going to the funeral. He who was at the station house (precinct) told me that he was not going because he had diarrhea. I have become so sensitive to his comments that he took away from me the desire to go to the funeral, because I no longer want to be harassed, so to avoid the torture, I decided not to go.

Instead, I went to the bank, took out some cash, and I took the train to 86 Street. There I entered a bakery and while I was in the bakery, a woman entered wearing a camo pant and she was bent as if her back was hurting. She left, but another woman entered wearing black and she was holding a red smartphone. She remained there without buying anything. I finished eating what I bought, and then I decided to go to church instead.

This consistent stress which I am going through every single day because of my nonstop persistent worry is tearing me apart, I am being pulled from so many different directions, and I have nowhere to go. Overall, I don't know what to do. I feel overwhelmed, nervous and frustrated. Why do I have to suffer as if I were an evil doer by the hand of these people? As I once told PO Rivera, "If good men are against good men, what will be left in this world?" I feel life threatened, and PO Rivera confirmed to me that I should be, and that I am humiliated. I am in great pain.

On **Wednesday, January 7, 2015,** finding no solution to my problem, I went to a Civil Success class to prepare myself for the upcoming Sanitation exam. I paid $399 dollars for the course. It was far in Jamaica Queens. I had to take two trains and a taxi to get there. As I was seating inside the room closed to the door, at the entrance I heard someone say "…Hernandez…" and then the person mentioned IAB (Internal Affairs Bureau, investigate police corruption) which investigate corrupt cops.

As I was seated, I could see people wearing the colors coming in. As I was looking through the handout that they gave us, I couldn't concentrate.

I was thinking about everything that was happening around me, and looking at the handout reminded me how I am falling behind in life, going backward. I was not there because I really wanted to be a Sanitation worker, because I love my job as a New York City Police Officer, but I feel that I have no option. I am being harassed at work every single day that I go to work there, and every single day when I am out of my job.

At that moment I felt so bad that I couldn't take it anymore, I had to get up and leave the room feeling worried, desperate and anxious, because they keep playing with my life. But I guess that I have no rights at all. As pastor Ni… and PO Rivera once mentioned, "La Cosa Nostra", and if I break the rule by going to see a lawyer, they will not only break me, but they will also crush me. This is not a joke. This is scary as hell, and I am very scared for my life and my future.

On **Friday, January 9, 2015,** I went to the running track that is in front of the Yankee Stadium. I walked around it. There was plenty of snow accumulated on the ground of the baseball field. I stood around there looking at the beautiful day. Then I went to the subway station.

I walked out at 42dn Street. When I was eating my burrito at Chipotle, I heard people saying, "He is fired," "He is dead." Another man who was standing next to me said something about the person's funeral. Then another person said that everybody in his office was dead. Another one said that the person that he was referring to was soon going to be living in a shelter. Another one said that nobody is going to hire him.

I left the premises wanting to run home. I took the train, arrived home and lay on the bed. From there I am typing this now. I don't know what to do. This has been a very disturbing two-week vacation for me. I cannot go anywhere. What is going on here? My life is being so violated.

Later that night, I placed my ear on the floor to listen to the apartment below, apt. #52 and I heard a man telling my next-door neighbor who lives in apt. #61, "He knows." Then I heard a commotion as if he were packing up his belongings. Then I heard noises such as screwdriver, or some type of construction work being done on the apartment below. As if they were hiding, or concealing evidence of the work and equipment they were using to spy on me and listen to my conversations using some type of device.

On **Saturday, January 10, 2015,** I heard the same noise downstairs.

On **Sunday, January 11, 2015,** I heard the same noise. They seem to be packing up.

On **Tuesday, January 13, 2015,** I heard my neighbor on apartment #63 talking to another man regarding microphones. Then my neighbor mentioned something about unplugging. There I wondered if they had placed those microphones on the celling, my walls, or on the floor of my apartment. Many times, I heard the same type of sounds coming from those three locations, and screw drivers falling, and people like maneuvering something from these locations.

On **Wednesday, January 14, 2015,** at approximately 1330 hrs. or 1:30 pm two people knocked at my other neighbor's door, on apartment #63. When he opened the door, the person visiting introduced himself as Bruce.

Saturday, January 17, 2015, the reason why I don't keep giving description of my followers is because it happens every time I go outside. It is already obvious. It is very tiresome. I believe that everybody knows that I am being followed. If I type everything that is happening to me, I will die of exhaustion because I need to rest, but I am not resting. I just can't. But at least I have a few times to type down a few of the many things that are being done for me. At approximately 2030 hrs. or 8:30 pm, I placed my ear on my bedroom's wooden floor, and I heard my neighbor from my apartment below, apt. #..., talk to my neighbor who lives on apt. #..., next to my apartment. She paid him another visit out of her daily visits there for updates.

She told him that she needed money from the company, because she only has $40.00 dollars for food. Also, she was there complaining about being in her apartment by herself. In addition, she asked him if those two documents that he had, if he got them from the mailbox, and this is when I realized that they had been checking my mailbox too. Then it seemed that she was looking at something on the internet. He asked her why she had turned it off. Then he said that every day he learns something new. She talked to him about doing a report, but she said that she didn't know.

The other day when I placed my ear on the floor to hear, I heard the two of them talking to a third person, but that third person was heard from a speaker. I decided to turn off my smartphone in case it might ring and alert them, and as soon as I turned it off, one of them said, "He turned off the phone." Also, the person on the speaker mentioned the blue sticker that I have on my door that says, "God speaks, are you listening?" from the Bridge radio station.

I went to the Laundromat, and I saw a lot of movement in the block. There was one guy with his smartphone recording me inside the store.

On **Saturday, January 17, 2015- Sunday, January 18, 2015,** I came back to the precinct after a two-week vacation. There I learned that an off-duty police officer, PO Mirjan Lolja from my precinct, who works in my tour, and with whom I had worked with many times, assaulted an MTA Subway conductor on December 23, 2014. The Newspaper showed the picture of PO Lolja leaving the scene and later PO Lolja turned himself in. At approximately 0755 hrs. or 7:55 am I was in the locker room. They were joking, but at the same time, they were throwing some indirect statements to make me suffer more.

My partner PO Alvin Rivera and PO Chiodi said that I am a wolf in sheep clothing. Also, PO Rivera and PO Chiodi said that I am the Coyote in sheep clothing who took sixty dollars. PO Chiodi said, "I found the Coyote and his name is Hernández," naming me. Then PO Rivera said, "…But when you lose sixty dollars, it is no big deal, but it is just, it feels like a big hole. You could buy one handcuff, a new cuff key, a new belt, and all the things you could think of you should buy. I got to go to the shop, I got to get new cargo pants, a new cuff key, the long one, a new handcuff case, a new ASP holder…this is a very important stuff you know." I told PO Chiodi that he had hurt my feelings, and he said that he didn't know that I had any feelings. I said, "That I was going to take that sixty dollars." And PO Rivera answered, "Not take them, not going to, I thought you took them."

"Save me, God, for the water has risen to my neck. I have sunk in deep mud, and there is no footing; I have come into deep waters, and a flood sweeps over me. I am weary from my crying; my throat is parched. My eyes fail, looking for my God. Those who hate me without cause are more numerous than the hairs of my head; my deceitful enemies, who would destroy me, are powerful. Though I did not steal, I must repay. God, You know my foolishness, and my guilty acts are not hidden from You. Do not let those who put their hope in You be disgraced because of me, Lord God of Hosts; do not let those who seek You be humiliated because of me, God of Israel. For I have endured insults because of You, and shame has covered my face. I have become a stranger to my

brothers and a foreigner to my mother's sons because zeal for Your house has consumed me, and the insults of those who insult You have fallen on me." (Psalm 69:1-9 HCSB)

Then as I walked out of the locker room with officer PO Rivera, I forgot my earphones in my locker, and I went back to get it, and PO Rivera followed me telling me that I must sign out and that they were waiting for me downstairs. It was as if he were escorting me everywhere I went, which every day he did, and I knew it well. Then as we walked out, we met with PO Chiodi again and PO Rivera told PO Chiodi, "Yeah, I would voucher that money man." Then PO Chiodi said, "Yeah, cause," and as soon as he saw me coming, he said, "There he is, the sheep, the Coyote... the church."

Then I saw Sgt. Gibbs and he told me, "Bushytop (as he used to call me), nice jacket man." He told me that he tried to give me a **3.5** on my evaluation, but that the Lieutenant said, "No way." He gave me **3.0** out of **5**. As a result, Sgt. Gibbs said, "So you know what that means." He told me that his comments on my evaluation were good, but that he had to give me a **3.0**. I remained quiet. Of course, I know what he meant. I, being accused of I don't know what, which has affected my quality of work. As Lieutenant Trevor Allen and PO Rivera once told me, "There is a black cloud at the precinct." It was either Lt. Allen or Lt. Yaguchi the one who said, "No way."

However, last year I was given a **4.0**. But since I had spoken to the NYPD chaplain, who is an Inspector, about the matter, and as a result reunited me with the 25 precinct commander officer, Captain Thomas C. Harnisch to discuss my concern, and the Captain feeling obligated to contact E.E.O (Equal Employment Opportunity) in regards, everyone in the precinct one way or the other learned about the meeting, and as a result I was given a **3.0** on my evaluation as a form of retaliation.

Sgt. Gibbs continued, "Bushytop, you can't quit on me man. I need you. You are a man of God. I need you. I got to see what you got man." He told me that he had wished to give me **4.0**. Then PO Rivera said, "Like Rocky in the eleven rounds." PO Rivera said that because many times I have said that I feel like Rocky for the treatment that I was receiving. I noticed that Sgt. Gibbs felt sorry for me. Deep in his heart he must know that there is something wrong in the way that I am being treated, and that as a result, I was half the man I used to be. But it is simple, you want me to be the man, the gentleman, the officer I once were? Just leave me alone everybody and let me work. In a few words, people stop harassing me. What have I done to deserve this? I thought that Bullying only happened in High School.

Then Sgt. Gibbs told me, "I need you man. And don't even think about leaving the job either. Don't think about quitting or retiring or leaving early or vesting out. Don't do that or you will miss on too much money for your family. If you want to do something else there is always an option. Put just a 28 to go somewhere else or fill out an application and get off patrol and that is what I am going to do too." In a few words he was telling me to get out of there. Even PO Rivera had told me that I should transfer. But how could I transfer when they just killed my possibility of going somewhere by giving me a **3.0**, and those places require you to have at least a **4.0** or above for at least three consecutive years. And with my ruined reputation, what command will I want?

Also, it is obvious that he already knew of my intention of taking the department of Sanitation exam and of my visit to the Civil Success class on January 7, 2015 to become a Sanitation worker and pick up garbage, which I prefer than be dealing with the garbage that are being thrown at me at the 25 precinct as if I were a dirty cop. But I am not going to give up. I have done nothing wrong. And again, "In the warrior's code there is no surrender. Though his body says 'stop', his spirit cries, 'Never'" from the Burning Heart-Survivor Rocky soundtrack.

As I had mentioned before, when it comes down to my yearly evaluations, the following are my overall evaluation for four straight years. In **2011** for the rating period **(12/16/2009-12/15/2010)** I was given a **4.0**, in **2012** for the rating period **(12/15/2010-12/15/2011)** I was given a **4.0**, in **2013** for the rating period **(12/16/2011- 12/15/2012)** I was given a **4.0**, and in **2014** for the rating period **(12/16/2012-12/15/2013)** I was given a **4.0**. **So, for four straight consecutive years I was receiving a 4.0 on my evaluations, which are very good and very few cops get this consecutive rating.** And I was never a disciplinary problem. And now, for this year's 2015 evaluation I was downgraded to a **3.0**, while being told, "So you know what that means." I remember the day when Lt. Allen said that some cops come to work to pick up their welfare check, meaning receiving a check without doing their job.

Later, as me and PO Rivera walked to the subway station, PO Rivera reminded me that the yearly evaluations are only good if one plans to go somewhere. In a few words, they don't want me to go somewhere else. And he told me that the captain is the one responsible for that. Then, when we were about to depart, it seemed that he couldn't hold it and he said, "But you know how it is in life, in general, it is always the person you least suspect. It is always like that. It is the person you least suspect, on anything. 'Oh really? Hernandez? No way, wow.' You know, it is always the person you least suspect. When it comes … you see the ugliest man that they bring in, you say 'oh that guy is no good for nothing'.

You know what I am saying. You wouldn't be surprised. But it is always the guy you bring in that is sharp. Really, and that is the guy who continues doing it. And he goes around at night, and then he goes home, he goes to work, and no one suspects a thing. And that is the person, that's the person, and he continues doing it. Because if it is the person you suspect, he gets caught on the first day. The first day he gets caught. So that person that you least suspect is that person who continues doing it. And continue and continue, you know what I am saying?"

Then I confronted him by asking him," Are you referring to me?" and he answered, "No, I am not referring to you. Like for example, serious though, he hides in plain sight, I am serious too, he hides in plain sight. He could be the guy who makes your pizza. The ordinary person. The person you least suspect." I laughed aloud, and finally I told him, "You are the man," and we said goodnight to each other.

I remember the day when I went to the station house with my locks, because I thought that somebody had opened it. I told him to call the CIA, and the FBI to solve what they can't solve. I meant a lot by saying that. Lt. Yaguchi was nervous, and he told me that he didn't want to tell the captain about it, but I forced him to. Then I spoke to them in the captain's office. I left, hoping that they got my message.

On **Monday, January 19, 2015,** at night I went to the running field that is in front of the Yankee Stadium, and I was wearing my gym clothing. As I walked there, I heard people saying, "He is lying," and even young kids were saying that. I had to leave right away, and I took a cab.

What is going on? Don't I have the liberty to do what I want with my life? I became so desperate and not knowing what to do, I took a livery cab, and I gave the cab driver my sister's address so he may take me there. It was a surprise visit because my sister was not expecting me. She found it strange. Then from there I took a livery cab back home. Later, that night, I went to work, and when I got there, I heard people talking about me going to that place (the running field). It is as if they had seen me doing something improper. It is hard for me to hear people murmuring about me and not be able to defend myself.

On **Tuesday, January 20, 2015,** I went to do 1PP (1 Police Plaza= Police Headquarter). When I was there, I heard people saying, " He lost", "Oh, my back", "He is fired," "Hernandez is fired," "He is done." Due to those comments and murmurs I became so agitated, and anxious that I asked one of the people that was saying so if she was talking about me. She said that she didn't. Later, on my mealtime I went to the room that is in front of the Headquarter security office. I was there with PO Rivera.

From there I heard Sgt. Calma says that the detective should be promoted. There I thought about Detective Morales when he interviewed me for the shots fired job, and I wondered if I said something wrong. I took off my gun belt and my shield and I placed it on the table, and I told PO Rivera my concern. I demanded to know what was going on. But he said that he didn't hear anything. He denied it. When my mealtimes were over, I put on my gun belt and my shield, and I approached Sgt. Calma who was talking about the detective and probably about me, and I asked him about it, and he denied it.

"I said, ""I will guard my ways so that I may not sin with my tongue; I will guard my mouth with a muzzle as long as the

wicked are in my presence.'" I was speechless and quiet; I kept silent, even from speaking good, and my pain intensified. My heart grew hot within me; as I mused, a fire burned; then I spoke with my tongue:" (Psalms 39:1-3 HCSB)

By the time that I was inside my booth, I called my command, and I asked them if they could send a cop to relieve me early because I was not feeling well. They refused. I made other attempts, and they still refused. I have done 1PP (1 Police Plaza Headquarter Security) about **127 times** in my career, each day from 7:00 pm till 7:50 am (12 hours and 50 min.) and this is the first time that I asked to leave early. Later, Sgt. Calma came to my post, and he told me to take off my gun belt and give it to him. I did, and he told me to follow him to the office. He took my gun belt, and I walked with him to the office.

Later, he had me waiting for my command's Sergeant. When Sgt. Gibbs arrived with PO Gambardelli, I wondered why he arrived with PO Gambardelli. This is the first time that I have seen Sgt. Gibbs having PO Gambardelli as his driver. I have always believed that PO Gambardelli has something against me, but I don't know what it is. And Sgt. Gibbs, since the moment that I had the meeting with the Captain and the Chaplain, have been treating me differently. They told me that they were taking me to the hospital. I begged Sgt. Gibbs to please not send me to the hospital and Sgt. Calma, who knew me well, decided to advocate for me not to be sent there. I know this because I heard him outside of the room talking on the speaker to Lt. Reid, and Lt. Reid insisted that I be sent to the hospital while saying that I am very irresponsible. They took me to the New York Presbyterian hospital. Why there? Of course, they knew that I had visited the same hospital when I was thinking of getting an X-ray there for my back. This smells like retaliation for my intent to go there for an X-ray of my back. My despair for my lack of faith in God lead me to the hospital.

"Why are you cast down, O my soul, and why are you in turmoil within me? Hope in God; for I shall again praise him, my salvation and my God." (Psalm 42:5 ESV)

When we arrived at the hospital, at the entrance there was a hospital security police and he told Sgt. Gibbs "This is going to jinx it." I didn't know what he meant by it. Then they left me there taking with them everything that I had, including my wallet, my house keys, and my smartphone. I wondered why they didn't leave those things in the hospital. I had to change from my uniform to a backless gown.

While at the hospital's emergency unit, I begged them to let me go. I noticed that there were inpatients prying into my room. They said something like "he is fine." I heard a security guard there say, "He has the city in his packet." To this there I wonder why he said that. But it is obvious the city is also responsible for all my present troubles. Then I heard a female security guard describing to another security guard the moment that I went to the running field of the park in gym gears as if it were a big deal. I wondered what was going on. They were treating me as if I were a criminal, as if I had committed some type of crime. They didn't stop talking about it. A medical staff member inserted a needle on top of my left hand, and she withdrew blood from me.

Later they took me against my will on a wheelchair up to the nine floors to the psychiatric ward where I had to spend two weeks. During my stay there, I was suspicious of the medical staff and of the inpatients there, which were approximately ten of the number of the inpatients. I have to say that during my stay, I was highly violated. There I was asked if I had fallen and if anything was hurting by a nurse. But the first thing I told her was that I wanted to leave, I begged her to let me go, but she told me that she was going to see what she could do. Then when I was by myself, one of the female inpatients there told me not worry, that I was safe there. Safe? I wondered what she meant by that.

While in my bedroom, I could hear one of the medical staff (nurse) talking to another medical staff about me, and I heard the man cursing because of what she told him about me. How did I know it was about me? They spoke about what I had told the nurse, in private, about how I was feeling. Later during my stay, I could hear inpatients and medical staffs walking by while saying things such as, "he is fired," "he lost," "he is dead," etc. At one point in the kitchen, I could hear them talking to one another and saying, "He lied to us," continuously. Later, I asked one of the inpatients why they were saying something about a 'lie', and she warned me in Spanish not to tell that to anyone else if I didn't want them to keep me there and stay there longer.

Since day one, day in and day out, I spoke to Dr. Ryan Lawrence MB, and I begged him to please let me go, but he refused. Also, I spoke to Dr. Ravi B. Desilva and he didn't let me go either. At one point, late at night, when all the inpatients were sleeping, in my bedroom I heard a male and a female talking about me, and what surprised me the most was that they were talking about all the movement that I was making inside my bedroom. For example, as soon as I laid on bed, the man said," Now he is laying on bed." Then I heard them opening the door and walking outside, and I did the same. I stepped outside to see who it was, and I saw him, and he saw me, and I closed the door and when I looked back at him, he was no longer there. Then as I walked forward, there I saw the female with whom I believe he was talking to, and she was pretending to be getting her vital signs by a medical staff.

Another time was when I used the bathroom. As soon as I finished using the bathroom, I heard the man talking about it furiously, angry. I believe that I was not only being watched naked in the bedroom, but also when doing my necessities in the bathroom as well. I was so violated. In addition, knowing that my supervisors have access to my apartment because they have my keys and my smartphone, and to all my privacy, made me feel more anxious to leave and made me feel highly desperate 24/7 at the hospital. Again, why didn't they leave my keys, my wallet and my smartphone in the hospital? But I couldn't show them how bad I felt, because I wanted to leave the hospital as soon as possible.

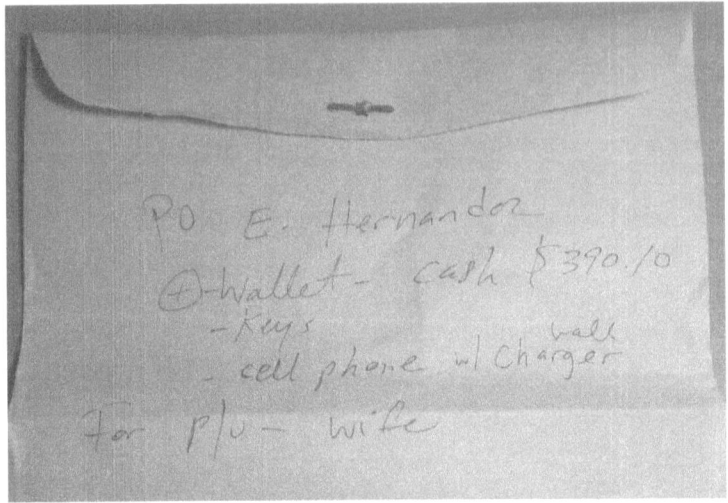

But during the time that I was there, I managed to tell my wife to please pick up my belongings in the precinct. When she went, they gave her this:

Why did they have to take my belongings and not leave them in the hospital?

About the medication, I refused to take them because I was fine, but they told me that if I didn't take it, they could bring my case to court and that a Judge order would force me to take it by injection if it needed be, and that I will remain there longer. From there I called pastor Ni... for help, and I he advised me to comply with them and take the medication, or they will keep me there. So, I was forced, obligated and intimidated to comply, and as a result, I continued taking the medication. Also, I asked the nurse if I could get a printout of the medication that I was given to have information about what I was taking. On January 25, 2015, she gave me a printout of the medication that they were giving me. It was **Fluoxetine (PROzac)**, an antidepressant.

They changed my bedroom twice. They transferred me to the bedroom that was close to the kitchen and then to the bedroom that was next to the bedroom that I first had and from where at some points were the people that I heard. Previously, I listened to people commenting about me from the inside of these two bedrooms. Incredibly, I was changed to those two bedrooms. I believe that they did it on purpose so I could see that there was nothing there.

During my visiting hours, I couldn't express how I felt to my visitors because I knew that the medical staff were listening to my conversation. They had cameras and microphones everywhere. There were times when I said something to my visitors and suddenly, many of the inpatients stood up from their seat at the same time to discuss what I had said. To see if I knew what was going on. "He is by himself," "He is dead," "He is fired," these were their comments. All this to the point that I was afraid to talk.

Two weeks passed and I was allowed to leave because they seem to have gotten what they wanted from me. I explained to Dr. R.L (for privacy reasons) what happened to me on **December 10, 2013**, and when I did, I noticed when his eyes became red and watery, and this was the last time I saw him for I was let go. So, I was there from January 21st till February 4th, for a total of 15 days. Now I am attending an outpatient program at North Bronx Healthcare Network Division of Behavioral Healthcare Services at North Central Bronx Hospital Partial Hospitalization Program. While attending there, one of the outpatients said that they had made an x-ray of her head and they found nothing, and that they should do an MRI now.

Also, one of the outpatients was talking about the E.C.T. (Electric Compulsive Therapy) that was done to her, and she ended up losing part of her memory. She explained that this was done when she refused to eat, to do anything. But I cannot say anything, I am afraid to say something, because I don't want them to send me back to the inpatient. My freedom of speech has been taken away from me. I have no rights anymore. I don't know what to do.

AS A RESULT OF THE HIGH DOSAGE OF MEDICATION, I BEGAN STUTTERING. A FEMALE DOCTOR CONDUCTED A RESEACH TO SEE IF IT WAS ANOTHER SIDE EFFECT OF THE OLANZAPINE MEDICATION, AND THE INCIDENCE DID APPEARED. SHE WAS CONSIDERING CROSS-TAPER TO RISPEDAL OR ABILIFY.

NO WONDER WHY LT. YAGUCHI PAID ME A VISIT TO THE HOSPITAL. TO DECLARE THAT I WAS NOT ON THE RIGHT MIND, INSTEAD OF CONFESSING THAT I WAS BEING HEAVILY HARASSED AT WORK AND OUT OF WORK.

2. Progress Note:

Reviewed chart and interviewed patient. Pt is a 33 year-old married Dominican male with no prior psychiatric history who was referred to PHP from NYPH following a 2 weeks hospitalization. Pt is a police officer and per her lieutenant pt had become increasingly isolative over the past years, rarely spoke to his fellow officers and had express some paranoid ideation to his partner hearing through the wall that he was being talked about negatively and was to get fired. A week prior to his admission, pt was observed win his head to the wall claiming that he could hear people talking about him through the wall. On the day that pt was admitted to the hospital he had asked nis lieutenant four times stating that he wanted to go home because he did not feel well but could not explain himself. The lieutenant spoke to the psychologist in the NYPD psychological serving who advised that pt be brought to the hospital. As per chart pt's wife and sister reported that pt had been anxious and irritable and had been sleeping only 3 to 4 hours a night over the past years and had a decrease in appetite resulting in some weight loss. . His symptoms began approximately 1 years ago following a job related court case a year ago. Pt began to have guilt and frustration over forgetting to list a specific detail in the case. He denies that the lack of this detail would have changed the outcome of the case.

Pt believes that his hospitalization was due to asking his lieutenant to leave early from work when there was not anyone to cover for him. He does report that he had marital problems over the last year. Pt and his wife work different shifts and often are not able to spend time together. He feels that they are both emotionally distant which has led to arguing and threatening each other with divorce. Pt reports that he briefly went to a psychologist and a pastor of another church for a few months and had one couple session. He stopped because he thought there was no longer a need to do so. His wife remains supportive and visited him often while he was in the hospital. He denies any other previous psychological problems but does have a brother who has been diagnosed with Bipolar Disorder. He denies any substance abuse. He denies any history of suicidal ideation or homicidal ideation. His lieutenant has his hand gun pt has no access to any other weapons.

Pt was born in the Dominican Republic and lived there with his father as his mother had already moved USA. He then came to the US at age 10. He enjoyed school and denies any problems making an adjustment to living here. He has 4 older siblings (2 brothers and 2 sisters.) He denies any history of physical or sexual abuse. He completed high school and got an associate's degree at LaGuardia Community College. He later completed a Bachelor's degree in criminal justice and John Jay College. Pt has been working as a police officer for 7 yrs. He has been married for 4 yrs and has no children. Currently he denies any mood or psychotic symptoms. His only goal he could identify was to work on saving his marriage thru counseling.

Emmanuel Hernandez

NORTH BRONX HEALTHCARE NETWORK
BEHAVIORAL HEALTHCARE SERVICES
OUTPATIENT DIVISION

○ JMC ☒ NCB

322 46 20
M 09/21/1981
HERNANDEZ, EMMANUEL
930 OGDEN AVE 62
NY 10452

INDIVIDUAL PROGRESS NOTE

Patient's Name: Emmanuel Hernandez

Date: 2/6/15   Time: 2 pm

Medical Record#: 3224620

Length of Session: 50 min

086032246209

1. **Treatment Plan Problems Addressed:**

☒ Psychiatric (1a, 1b)   ☐ Medical (2a, 2b)   ☐ Social (3)   ☒ Substance Abuse (4)
☒ Educational/Vocational/Leisure Time Use (5)   ☐ Psychoeducational (6)   ☒ Other (7): initial session

2. **Progress Note:**

Reviewed chart and interviewed patient. Pt. is a 33 year-old married Dominican male with no prior psychiatric history who was referred to PHP from NYPH following a 2 weeks hospitalization. Pt is a police officer and per her lieutenant pt had become increasingly isolative over the past years, rarely spoke to his fellow officers and had express some paranoid ideation to his partner hearing through the wall that he was being talked about negatively and was to get fired. A week prior to his admission, pt was observed with his head to the wall claiming that he could hear people talking about him through the wall. On the day that pt was admitted to the hospital he had asked his lieutenant four times stating that he wanted to go home because he did not feel well but could not explain himself. The lieutenant spoke to the psychologist in the NYPD psychological service who advised that pt be brought to the hospital. As per chart pt's wife and sister reported that pt had been anxious and irritable and had been sleeping only 3 to 4 hours a night over the past years and had a decrease in appetite resulting in some weight loss. . His symptoms began approximately 1 years ago following a job related court case a year ago. Pt began to have guilt and frustration over forgetting to list a specific detail in the case. He denies that the lack of this detail would have changed the outcome of the case.

Pt believes that his hospitalization was due to asking his lieutenant to leave early from work when there was not anyone to cover for him. He does report that he had marital problems over the last year. Pt and his wife work different shifts and often are not able to spend time together. He feels that they are both emotionally distant which has led to arguing and threatening each other with divorce. Pt reports that he briefly went to a psychologist and a pastor of another church for a few months and had one couple session. He stopped because he thought there was no longer a need to do so. His wife remains supportive and visited him often while he was in the hospital. He denies any other previous psychological problems but does have a brother who has been diagnosed with Bipolar Disorder. He denies any substance abuse. He denies any history of suicidal ideation or homicidal ideation. His lieutenant has his hand gun pt has no access to any other weapons.

Pt was born in the Dominican Republic and lived there with his father as his mother had already moved the USA. He then came to the US at age 10. He enjoyed school and denies any problems making an adjustment to living here. He has 4 older siblings (2 brothers and 2 sisters.) He denies any history of physical or sexual abuse. He completed high school and got an associate s degree at LaGuardia Community College. He later completed a Bachelor's degree in criminal justice and John Jay College. Pt has been working as a police officer for 7 yrs. He has been married for 4 yrs and has no children. Currently he denies any mood or psychotic symptoms. His only goal he could identify was to work on saving his marriage thru counseling.

Plan: monitor and decrease paranoid ideation, monitor for decreased appetite and decreased sleep, increase socialization, increase insight

Discharge Plan:. Outpatient clinic at NY Presbyterian
Patient Discussed in Treatment Team: Yes

386

I WAS FORCED TO TAKE THE MEDICATION, BECAUSE IF I WOULDN'T, MY REFUSAL WOULD HAVE LED TO A JUDGE DETERMINATION, AND THEY WOULD HAVE GET IT INTO MY SYSTEM THROUGH INJECTION.

☐ Psychoeducational   ☐ Other: ☐ Social   ☐ Educational/Vocational/Leisure Time Use

2. Progress Note:

Chart reviewed and case discussed in daily AM rounds and telephone call received from Dr. Penque, psychologist a the NYPD Psychological Center @ 718.760.7613 who was calling to ascertain if patient presented as anticipated and if he was attending. She also stated that she would need to be contacted upon his completing the program as she would needs to see him shortly aftr he is discharged. Dr. Penque asked about the length of the program and I informed her that is it a six-week Mon to Fri 9AM to 3:30PM program, but that, in general, with managed commercial insurance companies such as the patient has, we usually only get on average two weeks.

Patient is a 33yo Dominican Republic-born man, married with no children, NYPD police officer who was referred to NCR PHP by BYPH-CPMC where he was psychiatrically hospitalized for the first time as he had become increasingly isolative over the past year, rarely spoke to his fellow officers and had expressed some PMIORs to his partner—felt that he was being talked about negatively and was going to get fired and was most likely hearing voices e.g. about a week prior to his admission to NYPH-CPMC patient was observed at work in the precinct with his head to the wall claiming that he could hear people talking about him through the wall. On the day of admission, the patient had called his Lieutenant four times stating that he wanted to go home because he did not feel well but could not explain himself. The Lieutenant spoke to a psychologist in the NYPD Psychological Service who advised that patient be brought to the CPEP at CPMC. Patient was accompanied to the CPEP by his Sergeant. Patient's wife an sister reported that patient had been more anxious and irritable and had been sleeping only 3-4hours/night for the past year. He had lost interest in things which he previously enjoyed and was experiencing guilty ruminations about having forgotten to state a detail in a job-related court case a year ago. He was exhibiting a decrease in energy and had lost weight. He was very guarded and paranoid in CPEP at CPMC. He was opposed to medication and was started on botu Prozac and Zyprexa but was ultimately treated with only Zyprexa and discharged on 20mg QHS.

Dr. Penque's telephone number was provided to Mr. Cross to contact regarding discharge and disposition.

Vitamins (like vitamin C or E)
Minerals (like calcium or iron)
Herbal remedies (like ginko biloba)
It is important for you to have this medication list. It will help your health care provider in making decisions related to your health conditions. Bring your medications with you when possible.

Things you should do:

-Make a list of all medications you are taking – include the medication name and strength, amount you take, time to be taken and the reason you are taking this medication.
-Carry this medication list with you at all times in case of an emergency.
-Give this medication list to your health care provider at your next visit.
-Update this list each time when there is a change to your medication.
-If you have questions or need help updating your medication list, please ask your healthcare provider.

Take these medications at home

For any home medication listed that has medication information listed as "unknown" please call your primary healthcare provider or physician to confirm how to take the medication.

Med Name / Strength	Dose	How	How Often	Reason for Taking/ Instructions
OLANZapine 20 mg oral tablet, disintegrating Generic: OLANZapine	1 tab(s)	by mouth	once a day (at bedtime) x 14 days	1 Tablet(s) by mouth once a day (at bedtime) - Indication:Improved Thought Process

NOTIFICATION OF STATUS AND RIGHTS
INVOLUNTARY ADMISSION ON MEDICAL CERTIFICATION
(to be given to the patient at the time of admission to the hospital)

Section 9.27 Mental Hygiene Law

J797028
HERNANDEZ ENMANUEL
09/21/1981
01/21/2015
58152491

TO: Emmanuel Hernandez

Admission Date: 01 21 Mo. Day

Based upon the certificates of two examining physicians, whose findings have been confirmed by a member of the psychiatric staff of this hospital, you have been admitted as an involuntary-status patient to this hospital which provides care and treatment for persons with mental illness. You may be kept in the hospital for a period of no more than 60 days from the date of your admission, unless you have had a court hearing, or an application has been made to a court for an order authorizing your continued retention. During this 60 day period you may be released, or converted to voluntary or informal status, if you are willing to continue receiving inpatient care and treatment and are suitable for such status.

You, and anyone acting on your behalf, should feel free to ask hospital staff about your condition, your status and rights under the Mental Hygiene Law, and the rules and regulations of this hospital.

If you, or those acting on your behalf, believe that you do not need involuntary care and treatment, you or they may make a written request for a court hearing. Copies of such a request will be forwarded by the hospital director to the appropriate court and the Mental Hygiene Legal Service.

MENTAL HYGIENE LEGAL SERVICE

The Mental Hygiene Legal Service, a court agency independent of this hospital, can provide you and your family with protective legal services, advice and assistance, including representation, with regard to your hospitalization. You are entitled to be informed of your rights regarding hospitalization and treatment, and have a right to a court hearing, to be represented by a lawyer, and to seek independent medical opinion.

You, or someone acting on your behalf, may see or communicate with a representative of the Mental Hygiene Legal Service by telephoning or writing directly to the office of the Service or by requesting hospital staff to make such arrangements for you.

The Mental Hygiene Legal Service representative for this hospital may be reached at: _____

I WAS HELD, KEPT THERE INVOLUNTARILY, AGAINST MY WILL. HOSTAGE.

Now, who from my workplace went to visit me while I was hospitalized? Only two people did. Lt. Yaguchi, who went to visit me at the hospital with a package of green cookies wrapped in a paper gift, which he himself unwrapped in front of me as if he were upset to find out that the cookies were wrapped with paper gift. He visited me just to obtain information.

Also, PO Pinero, my former partner who is in the process of vesting out or already vested out of the job. He told my wife that he didn't recognize me there. He said to my wife that I was not the man he knew. He just visited me one time. Not even did my partner come to visit me. I only heard from my partner PO Rivera when I called him from the hospital where I was hospitalized to know what they did with my keys and smartphone, but besides that he was nowhere to be seen. Because again, **according to the NYPD Patrol Guide, police officers are not allowed to associate with someone "2. c. Reasonably believed to be engaged in, likely to engage in, or to have engaged in criminal activities."**

Now what should I do? I open my mouth because I wanted to know what was going on, and they ended up sending me to the hospital's psychiatric ward, where I heard one security guard or hospital police tell Sgt. Gibbs, "This will jinx it." I don't know how to spell it nor what he meant by saying that. So, I ended up being hospitalized there for two weeks as an impatient. Now there is one thing that I want to know, and it is why they didn't send me to take counseling to places such as POPA, talk to a Chaplain etc, but no, they had to send me to the emergency psychiatric room as if I posed a risk or a threat to my life or to the life of others.

Chapter 21

February 2015-March 2016 Events

On **Tuesday, February 17, 2015,** I went to the appointment for an intake to see the psychiatrist and while I was waiting there, a little kid said, "He lied," while looking at me.

I really don't know what to do now. Today, **Friday, February 20, 2015,** I went to see the NYPD's psychologist and she scheduled me back to work for Monday, February 23, 2015-Tuesday, February 24, 2015. I am restricted and I am drinking the medication, because it is helping me to relax from all this madness. What is going to be next, my death? Now I carry no firearms and no badge. They could care less about my safety. It seems that everyone knows about my condition, and that I am not carrying a weapon nor a badge. It seems that they want to destroy me completely. What can be expected of a hated cop that is without his gun? To be easily killed? In addition, there they are, the people in the mini vans following me everywhere I go.

On **Monday, February 23, 2015-Tuesday, February 24, 2015,** I began working at the 25th precinct. Now when I returned to work there, everyone there greeted me with a handshake or if a female, with a kiss. I wondered what was going on. Are they up to something? There has been a big change or a switch from the way that I was being treated before to the way that I am being treated now after I came out of the psych ward.

On **Thursday, February 26, 2015,** I did a day tour. Everyone was treating me the same way. With a handshake or with a kiss. I wonder why they are treating me with such amicability, unless again, they are up to something. Today I visited my therapist, which I do not trust at all. At this moment, I trust no one.

Lt. Yaguchi, whom PO Rivera warned me not to trust, seems not to take his eyes off me. But there is nothing I can do in regards, because he is the Administrative Lieutenant in charge of the administration in the precinct. He pretends to like me when he hates me indeed. He is totally committed to and will do all he can in his power to prevent me from transferring somewhere else, because he wants to keep me on his reach. He wants to continue to use me as his little experiment, because he is so desperate to get something out of me.

I want to know what his problem is. Why doesn't he want to let me go? Definitely, he is obsessed with me. I believe that nobody has the right to play with a human's life the way that he is doing with me. All of this is not only affecting me, but family as well. All this while he seems to be having fun destroying my life and there is no one coming out to put an end to all this madness.

"People were created to be loved.
Things were created to be used.
The reason why the world is in
chaos, is because things are being
Loved and people are being used."
By John Green, "Looking for Alaska"
On **Friday, February 27, 2015,** Lt. Gonzales was the Desk Lieutenant when I was inside as the T/S operator. There I was writing a report, and my hand was shaking because of his presence. There I was thinking about what his next move is going to be. When I gave him my report, he told me to write it over again because he couldn't understand my handwriting.

On **Tuesday, March 3, 2015-Wednesday, March 4, 2015,** I was assigned to the T/S and there was Lt. Gonzales hanging around the T/S while looking at me. I don't know why he hates me. He seems to be obsessed with me too. Now as for me, I feel nervous, and sad because I don't know what the outcome to all of this will be. But my hope is in God.

On **Thursday, March 5, 2015,** I was chosen for a random doll test. For the random doll test they take a sample of your hair and from the test they can see if you have consumed any illegal drugs so they can fire you. The day before Lt. Yaguchi told me that I had a nice haircut. The next day I had to do the doll test, what a coincidence. The man that works at the doll test told me that they wanted my sample to be taken from the hair of my head.

When I arrived home, I was inside the building walking to take the elevator, I saw two red gloves on the floor. They seemed to have planted them there to see if I was going to take them.

On March 6, 2015, I went to the Medical Division Drug Screening Hair Testing, by which I came out clean, Cleared from any illegal substance.

MEDICAL DIVISION

DRUG SCREENING QUESTIONAIRE – HAIR TESTING

DATE: 3/6/15

TIME: 0940

DRUG SCREEN NO. _____

AGENCY: NYPD COMMAND: 02?

RANK: PO LAST NAME Hamanekt FIRST Emmanuel M.I. ____

SHIELD # 2830 TAX# 941269

1. LIST ANY PRESCRIPTION MEDICATION TAKEN DURING THE PAST 3 MONTHS. IF NONE, WRITE "NOTHING TO REPORT."

OLANZAPine. + I Took one anti-depression Medicine for less than Two weeks and NOT anymore. I am Still Taking OLANZAPine daily.

==

CITY OF NEW YORK, COUNTY OF QUEENS

NAME (PRINT) Hamanekt, Emmanuel _____ BEING DULY SWORN DEPOSES AND SAYS THAT ALL OF THE FOREGOING ANSWERS ARE TRUE.

SWORN TO BEFORE ME THIS ___6___ DAY OF MARCH _____ 2015

FINGERPRINT
RIGHT INDEX

_____
OFFICER'S SIGNATURE

_____
COLLECTOR'S NAME (PRINT)

_____
COLLECTOR'S SIGNATURE

On **Friday, March 6, 2015- Saturday, March 7, 2015,** PO Portero was going to do the coffee run and he asked me if I wanted anything from outside. I told him that I wanted a coffee and a corn muffin. PO Rivera offered to pay for my muffin and my coffee. Later, when PO Portero arrived, he gave me my coffee and my corn muffin, and when he handed over the coffee to PO Rivera, he took a piece of paper and he threw it in the garbage while saying, "And there goes my dignity."

Moments later, I saw PO Portero standing by the T/S, and thru the glass part of the door, I got to see his reflection there and from there he pointed to my direction while saying to PO Rivera, "You did the right thing by buying him the coffee." I don't know what to do. I don't know why he said that to him. I have no way to defend myself. I must let them do whatever they want with me.

On **Saturday, March 7, 2015-Sunday, March 8, 2015,** when I was in the muster room, I heard PO Gorman tell PO Maher, "Now he is going to have to wait until he is 62." I wondered if he was talking about me getting fired and not being able to retire on my 20 years anniversary as a police officer. I still don't know what is going on.

Now the public seem to know that I don't have a shield or a gun, because they seem to be informed of everything that happens to me. Now how safe am I? I feel so lonely. If there is any wrongdoing on my behalf, why don't they come and tell me about it. Why don't they come forward and punish me for it. What are they waiting for? Do they want me to die of anxiety? People murmur about me, and when I ask them about it, their response is, "What are you talking about?" and that they are not talking about me.

On **Tuesday, March 10, 2015,** before I went to see my therapist, I entered a restaurant, and there I took a seat. Later, a man who doesn't speak Spanish entered the premise. He bought breakfast and he sat close to where I was seating. He seemed to be one of the people that are following me.

Later, after seeing my therapist, I took the bus back home, and I heard someone say, "It is over." Probably the person said it because I am no longer going to be followed, but there he is. It seems that they will soon cease to follow me.

At work, everyone keeps treating me well. They keep greeting me and asking me how I am doing, and how I am feeling, etc. The amicable way in which they treat me is making me feel very uncomfortable and suspicious because they overdo it. Lt. Gonzales doesn't stop looking at me. He remains by the Desk even when his tour is over, and he does it like every day. He wants to get something out of me so bad, but I don't know what.

Now here I am taking medication that helps me relax and keep me calm because I have succumbed to the strain and the stress of being followed. So, the medication that I am taking is anesthetizing my emotional and physical pain and suffering.

On **Friday, March 13, 2015,** I went to see the Department's psychologist, and she told me that I was going to be transferred to work somewhere else, and here I am desperately waiting. My co-workers are now treating me with a lot of kindness as if they were told to do so every time they see me, and they keep asking me how I feel. How am I? If I am, ok? I am tired of such treatment. I am definitely being labeled. God, until when am I going to still be working there?

Thursday, March 19, 2015, I have several days without typing anything because I lack the energy, and the desire to do so. Probably it is the medication that I am taking. I believe that the more I type, the more I will get myself into trouble. I am not allowed to communicate my feelings, and if I do, the more I will get myself closer to the mouth of the lion. **"Life and death are in the power of the tongue ...."** (Proverb 18:21 HCSB) This has been preventing me from expressing myself openly to the social worker, the psychologist, the therapist and the psychiatrist. I have spent most of my time in bed, thinking about my problems. I really don't want to go to work, but I must.

Today, **Friday, March 20, 2015,** I received the notification. I have been transferred to the Bronx Viper Unit. I am so happy, I am so exuberant to be out of there.

"He reached down from heaven and took hold of me; He pulled me out of deep waters. He rescued me from my powerful enemy and from those who hated me, for they were too strong for me. They confronted me in the day of my distress, but the Lord was my support. He brought me out to a spacious place; He rescued me because He delighted in me. The Lord rewarded me according to my righteousness; He repaid me according to the cleanness of my hands." (Psalm 18:16-20 HCSB)

"God — His way is perfect; the word of the Lord is pure. He is a shield to all who take refuge in Him." (Psalm 18:30 HCSB)

It is **Wednesday, March 25, 2015**. I am home. I will begin working at that new place on Saturday night. How angry and upset PO Maher became when I told him that I was being transferred. When he talked to PO Gorman in regards, he referred to me as the "Fu…g guy." PO Gambardelly reacted angrily to the news too.

I am in bed, not knowing what to do. I don't want to go outside. Luckily, I am typing this now that I am in bed. I can't wait to start working in that new place. But as for now, all I want to do is to remain in bed all day long, and let time pass by.

Wow, I feel so bad. I cannot express myself to anyone. I don't know who to trust. It is too much for me to bear.

Thursday, **March 26, 2015,** I didn't go out yesterday. I am afraid of whatever it is that they are planning against me. I am afraid to go out of my apartment. Who can live this way?

APRIL 2015

On **Thursday, April 2, 2015,** I finished my week of work at the new place. There I gave too many thoughts about what my future holds. There I was anxious to give thoughts to my situation, and to all that is happening to me. But I feel great relief by working in this new place. There I don't feel that I am being persecuted by my co-workers, even though I suspect that they are there to report on me.

On **Saturday, April 11, 2015,** I went outside for a walk with my wife, and I noticed that I was no longer being followed. Finally, after so long. After they made my life a living hell. After having me go through such misery. After getting me hospitalized, and being labeled as being psychotic with major depression, and having me on medication, they have finally decided to dump me. They have stopped micromanaging my life. Now they see no need to follow me anymore after getting me ill. And my question is, what will be of my life now?

Thursday, April 16, 2015, I am tired. All this time I have been feeling as if I were under house arrest because I don't want to come out of my apartment. I don't want to come out for anything. I don't want to do anything. I feel all alone.

On **Wednesday, April 22, 2015,** when I arrive to the Viper unit, a detective there asked me how I was doing and if I needed a hug. He seemed to be aware of my situation and seemed to know of the reason why I am working there. Besides, now that I am working in Viper, there is not much going on there. I am there just looking at the cameras. Nobody bothers me and I bother no one.

When I went home, all I wanted was to stay in bed. I don't want to get up. I don't want to do anything. And the medication is a factor as well. Also, I have been stuttering for the past few weeks due to the side effects of the medication.

MAY 2015
Friday, May 15, 2015, Since I have been transferred, I have not much to say. Nothing else has happened. There are no more gossip nor

people murmuring. It is like my life has been back to normal. I haven't gone back to work out because I am afraid of the unknown. All I want to do is to work and go straight back home. So, this is what I have been doing for the pass days. I have nothing else to type. But there is one thing that I have to say, and that is that since I have been transferred, I finally feel at peace.

September 2015

After a long time without typing, on Thursday, September 3, 2015, my neighbor, or lets say, my female spy, who lives on the apartment that is next to mines (Apt.61), is moving out. I believe that since they haven't gotten anything or any evidence against me, they finally gave up.

I spent most of my time in bed thinking and rethinking about what I am going through. I haven't stopped thinking about my condition for a single moment. Condition that I call, my daily nightmare. When I went to my therapist, I didn't want to mention to her that I was or that I am being followed, because she will think that I am going crazy, and I will be given a higher dosage of my medication. Or she might be collaborating with them, with those that are making my life a living hell, because there is no privacy in my life. As time passes, the more deteriorated I become.

October 2015

Tuesday, October 27, 2015, I couldn't keep it to myself anymore. I had to confess to my psychiatric Dr. Fox that at one point in the past I was being followed and that sometimes I wonder if I am still being followed. As a result, he increased the dosage of my medication **(Olanzapine)** from **10 MG** to **15 MG.** Now I must deal with the side effects of that high dosage, which includes a bloody and painful constipation, difficulty talking and stuttering all the time. I have gained a massive amount of weight, and I am not able to think right. I feel like a zombie. But it helps me sleep almost all day. After I go home from work, I sleep all day until I wake up again to go to work. I sleep 12 hours or more a day. Dr. Fox doesn't believe that I was being followed indeed. No one has come forward. No one has claim responsibility. So, my diagnosis, according to the doctor, is schizophreniform. Why wasn't I told that before?

I went home regretting the moment that I told him that I was being followed in the past. I went home thinking again about my unfortunate life. At home, I don't spend most, but all the time on bed, turning and tossing thinking about what is going on in my life. At work I cannot stop thinking about everything. Every day when I am at work, I stare at the computer monitor, but I am not paying attention to whatever is going on in the monitor, because I am thinking about my past, present and future. I just can't stop thinking about it.

November 2015

On **Sunday, November 8, 2015,** I went to church, and I noticed how some of the church members tried to ignore me. They either turned their back on me or tried not to greet me. They might know what is going on, but they don't tell. Meanwhile, my family is suffering by seeing me like this. To see what has become of my life. They believe the same thing my doctor believes that I am not mentally well.

March 2016

Months have gone by, and my preoccupation doesn't stop. I cannot catch a break. On **Thursday, March 17, 2016,** I went before the Medical Board (article 2), and they determined that I was not mentally fit to be a police officer. They approved that I should retire. I cannot believe it. I am mentally fit. But nobody has come forward. They give me two more chances to fight the Medical Board's decision. So, I refused to let them retire me and decided to fight their decision two more times.

Chapter 22

May 2016 Events

On **Friday, May 27, 2016,** after hearing from no one from the 25th precinct, my old command, a year and two months later, after being transferred, I received a text message from PO Rivera, my partner.

He who never visited me during the two weeks that I was in the hospital, and who hadn't communicated with me for so long, now wanted to know how I was doing. As soon as I read the text message, I imagined a red flag. And what is sad is that after having worked for more than six years in the 25 precinct, none of my colleagues from work visited me at the hospital, except Lt. Yaguchi, who went to see me at the hospital just to obtain information, and also my former partner PO Pinero, who had decided to vested out of the job, and who had told my wife that he didn't recognize me there. So besides them two, none of my colleagues have called me to know how I am doing after I got transferred.

One night when I was at work at the 25precinct, I learned that one police officer from my command got into trouble, and I asked why they didn't call him to see how he was doing, and I was told that they didn't call him because IAB (Internal Affairs Bureau, investigate police corruption) was wiretapping his phone. When I think about it, I wonder if that is the reason why they don't communicate with me, because IAB (Internal Affairs Bureau, investigate police corruption) is maliciously wiretapping my smartphone, because they want to know everything about me. Because they believe that I am truly a wolf in sheep clothing. **Also, another reason is that according to the NYPD Patrol Guide, police officers are not allowed to associate with someone "2. c. Reasonably believed to be engaged in, likely to engage in, or to have engaged in criminal activities."**

My Beyond Human Capacity Effort to Stay on the Job: A Decision of Life and Death

I wanted to be so bad and tried so hard to stay on the job that the following happened. On December 2015 I was transferred to another psychiatrist, because I no longer needed therapy. This new psychiatrist agreed with me to taper down the doses of the medication until I finally came off it, with the intention to increase the chance to stay on the job. So, in the summer of 2016, after beginning my medication at **20 mg**, it took me months to come down to or lets say to taper down to **5 mg**. Finally, from **5 mg** of the medication, I went completely off the medication, with the doctor's consent, direction and supervision, just to try to go back full duty as a police officer again. What happened next was a total nightmare. **2.5** MG, **5** MG, **7.5** MG, **10** MG, **12.5** MG, **15** MG, **17.5** MG, and **20** MG are the milligrams for this medication called Olanzapine. So, I got off at 5 MG and it was hell on earth.

Patient Name: Emmanuel Hernandez
Date of Birth : 09/21/1981

TO WHOM IT MAY CONCERN

Patient is a 34 years old Hispanic man with a psychiatric history of psychotic illness who has been in treatment for over a year and 2 months, he was treated at Jewish board x 8 months where completed psychotherapy treatment, and he was referred to this clinic for continuity of psychopharmacological treatment.
He was initially treated with Zyprexa 20 mg qd which was tapered off to 15 mg while in treatment at The Jewish Board and he was continued on this dose x about 8 months. On 2/15 his medication was again decreased to 10 mg at bedtime. He continues to be stable despite decreasing on medication. No acute psychotic, mood and any other psychiatric symptoms.
Patient will like to be off medication and he has been advice to continue present regimen for few months until his medication could be safely discontinued. Thereafter he will be observed off medication and if symptoms recurred his medication will be resume.
He is presently stable, no a danger to self or others.

If you need further information, please contact this office with patients written consent.

Finally, from **5 mg** of the medication, I went completely off the medication, with the doctor's consent, direction and supervision, just to try to go back full duty as a police officer again. What happened next was a total nightmare. **2.5** MG, **5** MG, **7.5** MG, **10** MG, **12.5** MG, **15** MG, **17.5** MG, and **20** MG are the milligrams for this medication called Olanzapine. So, I got off it at **5 MG** and it was hell on earth.

The results of my coming off the medication were total insomnia that lasted for around two Months and a half and during that time I slept zero hours. During this time, I decided to do research on the high dose

TO WHOM IT MAY CONCERN

EMMANUEL HERNANDEZ, is a 34 years old   male patient, he is under my care, for his diagnosis of Schizophreniform Disorder - F20.81. he has been following treatment for his condition with psychotherapy and Medication Management. He was evaluated today, his medication has been tapered off slowly for the last 3 months, and he is currently off medications for 3 weeks. He continues to deny all symptoms, including Psychotic, mood, anxiety and/or any other psychotic symptoms. Mr. Hernandez will be observed off medication and if symptoms relapse, he agrees to resume treatment with medication.

If you need further information, please contact this office.

medication that I was taking for more than a year and a half, which I religiously took every single day. When I did the research on the medication, which is the generic Olanzapine (Zyprexa), I became astonished. I was without words. I was appalled. I opened my mouth wide open, and my jaw dropped after learning how many lives have been destroyed using such medication. The side effects are devastating, and the withdrawal process is even worse.

I looked at the Olanzapine withdrawal symptoms and my findings terrorized me, especially when I read about the number of people that have fallen victim to it. One of the many testimonies is that of Sally's story whose doctor told her to get out of that stuff before it killed her. Her story can be found when you Google Olanzapine withdrawal and click on the link that says RX, and Sally's Story which has part two as well. This is one of the link: **https://rxisk.org/olanzapine-withdrawal-sallys-story/**

Also, I read this information:

Medication Guide
OLANZAPINE
(oh-LAN-za-peen)
Tablet

Read the Medication Guide that comes with olanzapine tablet before you start taking it and each time you get a refill. There may be new information. This Medication Guide does not take the place of talking to your doctor about your medical condition or treatment. Talk with your doctor or pharmacist if there is something you do not understand or you want to learn more about olanzapine.

What is the most important information I should know about olanzapine?

Olanzapine may cause serious side effects, including:
1. Increased risk of death in elderly people who are confused, have memory loss and have lost touch with reality (dementia-related psychosis).
2. High blood sugar (hyperglycemia).
3. High fat levels in your blood (increased cholesterol and triglycerides), especially in teenagers age 13 to 17 or when used in combination with fluoxetine in children age 10 to 17.
4. Weight gain, especially in teenagers age 13 to 17 or when used in combination with fluoxetine in children age 10 to 17.

These serious side effects are described below.

1. Increased risk of death in elderly people who are confused, have memory loss and have lost touch with reality (dementia-related psychosis). Olanzapine is not approved for treating psychosis in elderly people with dementia.

2. High blood sugar (hyperglycemia). High blood sugar can happen if you have diabetes already or if you have never had diabetes. High blood sugar could lead to:
* a build up of acid in your blood due to ketones (ketoacidosis)
* coma
* death

After being informed, there was no way that I was going to take that drug again. At first, I thought that it was just a harmless tranquilizer, or a relaxer that I could stop taking at any time. The last thing I knew was that it was an antipsychotic, a psychotropic drug, or lets say a neuroleptic drug. All this time I thought that it was less toxic than an antidepressant. I was told in the hospital that I was taking an antidepressant based on the handout that they gave me. And when I looked at the handout at home to compare the name of the medication, I was surprised that the medication was a different beast. I was given **Fluoxetine** in the hospital which is an antidepressant.

However, out of the hospital I was prescribed **20 MG** of **Olanzapine** without knowing that it was a dangerous antipsychotic. My reaction was, "My God, what have they done to me." So, during the two and a half months without sleeping not even for an hour, after I stopped taking this dangerous drug, my muscles all over my body were moving by its own, my hands and foot fingers too. I began to have a ringing on my ears and began to see black floaters on my sight. My body was moving involuntarily, especially my fingers, both hand and foot, and I was stuttering like never before. During these two and a half months, I had dropped more than 20 pounds, to the point that at my workplace everybody began to notice it and my coworkers were telling me that I looked different and that I was losing a lot of weight. My blood pressure rose to the top, and I went to see my general Doctor in regards.

The last time I visited my general Doctor was on **April 23, 2010**. My pulse was **60**, my blood pressure was **120/70**. On **August 5, 2014**, I went to Cobra training, and they measured my blood pressure, and it was **130/74**. The reason why on this date it was a little high was because of the enormous amount of pressure and the stress that I was enduring by the constant harassment received at work and off work which was way beyond human capacity. I had no medical issues. So besides resisting who is against me, now I had to fight a different animal, called Olanzapine.

But now, on **September 19, 2016**, I went to see my doctor because I was not feeling well and when he checked my vital signs, my pulse was on **110**, and my blood pressure was **170/110**. The Dr. was shocked. Immediately, and for the first time in my life, he prescribed me high blood pressure medication. He prescribed me **100 mg of Metoprolol Succinate ER** which is a beta-blocker used to treat chest pain (angina), heart failure, and high blood pressure. So instead of starting with the lowest dose of **25 mg**, my blood pressure was so high that he had to give me **100 mg**.

Vitals Report

Emmanuel Hernandez
Patient #: 38736
Birth Date: 9/21/1981
Medical Sex: Male

Date/Time	Temperature	Pulse	Respiration	Peak Flow	P.Ox	BP	Weight	Height	Waist	Neck
5/22/2018 2:15 PM	98.1° F	85	16		98%	120/74	221 lb	72 in		
4/16/2018 12:51 PM		77	16		99%	124/80	218 lb	72 in		
1/9/2018 3:37 PM		81	16		99%	130/78	218 lb	72 in		
9/13/2017 11:44 AM		80	16		97%	139/74	213 lb	72 in		
6/21/2017 11:44 AM		80	16		98%	140/90	215 lb	72 in		
4/26/2017 1:16 PM		77	16		98%	130/75	224 lb	72 in		
4/26/2017 1:14 PM	98.1° F	77	16		98%	130/75	224 lb	72 in		
3/20/2017 10:50 AM		78	16		98%	128/72	220 lb	72 in		
3/20/2017 10:04 AM	98.1° F	78	16		98%	128/72	220 lb	72 in		
10/4/2016 12:46 PM		80	16		96%	127/76	200 lb	72 in		
9/19/2016 5:05 PM		110	14		98%	170/110	200 lb	72 in		
5/10/2011 10:45 AM		72	14		97%	137/78	204 lb	72 in		
4/23/2010 1:37 PM	97° F	65	14			122/72				
4/9/2010 11:45 AM	98° F	60	14			120/70	190 lb	72 in		

AND THIS WAS MY BLOOD PRESSURE IN 2014, BESIDES ALL THE PRESSURE PLACE ON ME.

CBRN/HAZMAT OPERATIONS LEVEL STATUS FORM
PD 467-060 (08-07)

INSTRUCTIONS: PART A – Prepared by the member attending CBRN/HazMat Operations Level Training.
PART B – Prepared by the police surgeon assigned to the CBRN/HazMat Operations Level Training site.
PART C – Prepared by a member of the Police Academy's CBRN/HazMat Operations Level Training staff.

DISTRIBUTION:

ORIGINAL – To be Returned to Member's Commanding Officer by Member Concerned.
FIRST COPY – Medical Division's CBRN/HazMat Operations Level Coordinator, One Lefrak City Plaza, Room 1637 (Via Messenger)
SECOND COPY – Police Academy's CBRN/HazMat Operations Level Supervisor, C/O Specialized Training Section
THIRD COPY – Member Concerned

Signature _____ Date 2/5/20__

DO NOT WRITE BELOW THIS LINE

BLOOD PRESSURE: _____130/74_____ MEDICALLY CLEARED: ☑ Yes ☐ No

Title _____ Name (Print) __EUCID__ Signature _____ Date __

DISTRIBUTION:
ORIGINAL – Medical Division's CBRN/HazMat Operations Level Coordinator, One Lefrak City Plaza, Room 1637 (Via Messenger)
BUFF – Member Concerned

Adding to my surprise, it is to know that the highest dose of Olanzapine prescribed to a patient is **20** MG. So, the highest dose prescribed to a mentally ill person is **20** MG. The medication Milligrams go as follows: **2.5** MG, **5** MG, **7.5** MG, **10** MG, **12.5** MG, **15** MG, **17.5** MG, and **20** MG. Now using common sense, and using logic, if a patient has an illness, that illness should be treated, if needs to be, with medication beginning with the lowest dose. Now my question is why, after being released from the New York Presbyterian Hospital, Milstein Building 9 Garden North, of the 9th floor, and being treated by **Dr. Ryan**

Lawrence, why this same Doctor, on 2/4/2017 prescribed me to take **two** tablets of Olanzapine of **10 MG** each, as the prescription bottle said, **"DISSOLVE 2 TABLETS MY MOUTH SUBLINGUALLY EVERY NIGHT AT BEDTIME,"** in total, **20** MG of Olanzapine daily.

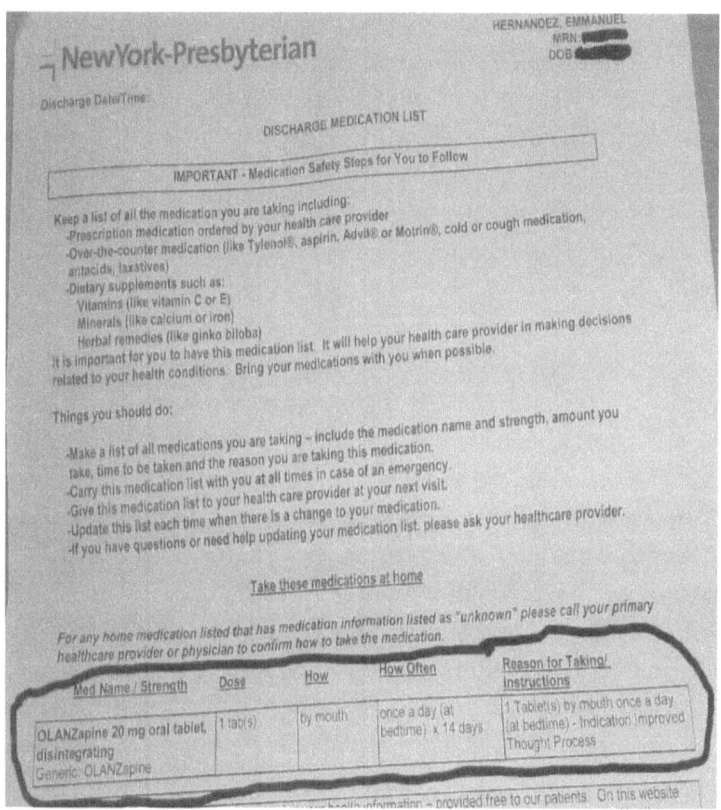

How and why in the world was I prescribed the highest dose of such a dangerous drug or let's say antipsychotic? How many times, while in the hospital, I told them that I was fine. I begged them to please let me go because there was nothing wrong with me, but they refused to let me go. Many times, I told them that I refused to take the medication that they were giving me, but they threatened me by saying that if I refused to take them, and didn't comply with them, they would have a Judge's authorization to force me to take them by injection. I had no other choice.

But why did I have to take an antipsychotic drug that I didn't need? Was I at any time a violent person? Did I hurt anybody? Did I try to hurt myself at any point? So why in the world was I forcibly kept there against my will? But one of the interns who was assisting Dr. Lawrence told me that they had to diagnose me with something. He told me that I had mild psychosis with mayor depression, unbelievable.

My question is: I was I supposed to feel normal when I was being locked up in a psych ward for the first time in my life? I have never been hospitalized before and they expected my emotions to remain neutral when I am placed in a mental institution, forbidden to go out. Are we as human beings forbidden to have feelings or emotions especially when you are being locked up against your own will? And if you do, they want to diagnose you with something. But there might be one factor of many that are unknown to me, of why he prescribed me the high dosage.

The day before I was discharged, I told the doctor how the court case of **December 10, 2013,** had affected me, and as I explained to him what happened on that day, I observed how his eyes turned watery and red. He looked like upset. This was the last time I saw him. The next day, I was let go, and I was prescribed that poison probably because he took what I told him personally. He simply disliked me. So, after two weeks of being there, from **01/21/2015-02/04/2015,** I was discharged. I went to the pharmacy to pick up my prescription drug and having faith in the Doctor that he was not going to prescribe me something harmful, I followed his instructions, and day by day I ingested **two tablets** of **Olanzapine 10 MG** each, that melted in my mouth as a candy, but made me sleepy all the time, and made me sleep for more than twelve hours a day.

It helped me to sleep off the daily idea of being followed. The bloody constipation, the daily stuttering, the weight gain, and feeling like a Zombie, were side effects that I tolerated for the sake of complying with the psychiatrist, and to sleep away from my daily struggle. The following picture is a picture of my face that shows how much weight I gained while on medication and before the medication. I didn't notice it before until I saw my unrecognizable face on the picture. I was told that I was not fat but swollen.

On Medication | **Before Medication**

So, as I previously mentioned, the withdrawal from that poison has been my worse battle. In desperation for not being able to sleep, on Sunday, **August 14, 2016,** I went to New York Presbyterian emergency room to see if a doctor could prescribe me something just to put me to sleep, because it was all I needed, to sleep, which I hadn't for weeks, not even for an hour. When I saw the psychiatrist there, he told me that if I had been inside the emergency room, I would have been forced to stay against my will. I told him that I just wanted something to sleep, but he told me that I was being manic, and he advised me to go back on my medication. As a result, I walked away. I had called my sister to tell her that I loved them because I was sure that I was going to soon die in the process.

Then I went to visit a health food center, and I spoke to a person who besides being a health nutritionist expert, he is a psychologist. I explained to him my situation. I told him that I was hospitalized once, and I told him of the medication that I was taking and much more. He moved his head as if showing pity for me. He told me that I was a victim of the system. He said that each hospital has a budget, and that each department within a hospital must mandatorily generate or produce a certain amount of money to keep afloat.

He said that it is a big business and not a charity institution. He explained to me that there are people who can just solve their problems with just talking to a professional, but that the psychiatrists don't want to do that because part of their income come from prescribing them those drugs, or by drugging them, so they can become dependent or hooked on those drugs. For example, he told me to look at what happened to me when I stopped taking it. Doctors swear under oath to save lives, but it seems that they also have the license to destroy a person's life.

So, I tried all sorts of alternatives and researched trying to find myself a way to fall sleep except, going back to that drug again.

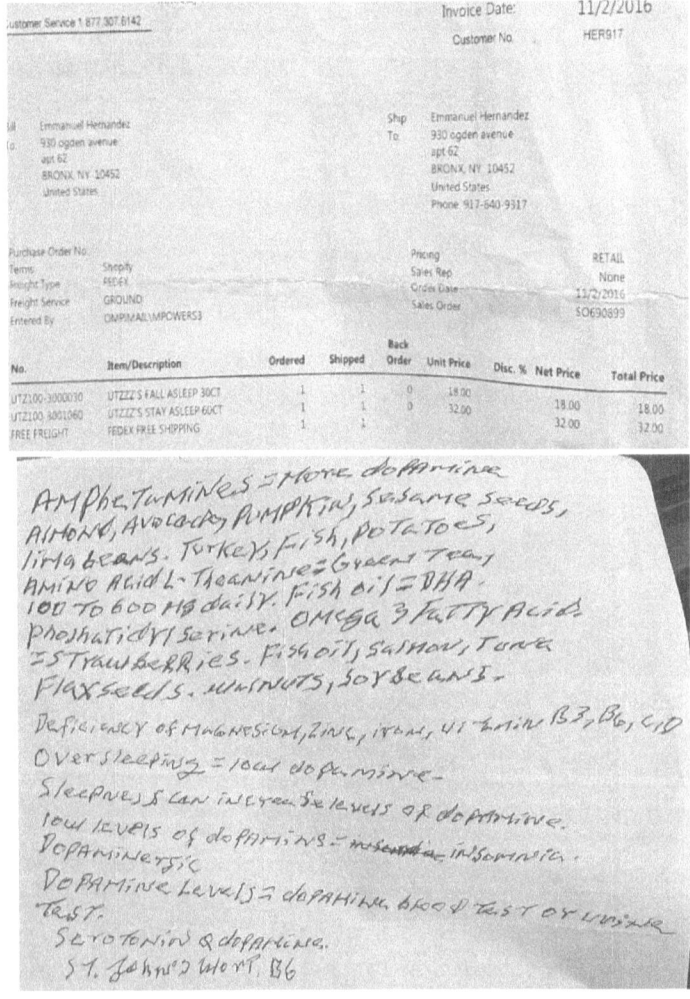

AT THE END THE DOCTOR DECIDED TO Prescribe me Lunesta and or Ambien to make me fall sleep and nothing worked.

he officer has been diagnosed with schizophr[
not otherwise specified. His last epis[
asted more than six months. His treating physic
:ophreniform or schizophrenic symptomatolo
anzapine and Lunesta or Ambien for sleepin[
1e relapse rate for schizophrenia is significan
on the schizophreniform course was the up[
impending divorce.

:view of the history, the medical records, tl
:he clinical findings, the symptomatology and
edical Board finds that the off

FINALY, I HAD TO GO BACK TO OLANZAPINE ON 2.5 MG, AFTER 2 AND HALF A MONTH WITHOUT SLEEPING. BUT SLOWLY I TRIED TO CUT IT DOWN, FOR MANY MONTHS TO COME, UNTIL FINALLY COMING OFF IT.

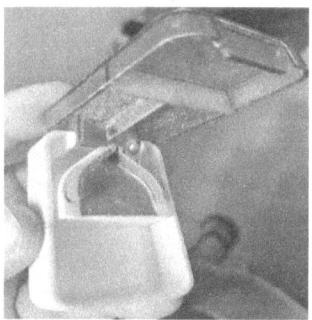

It seems that Doctors such as Dr. Lawrence wishes people to get sick to generate more money. Why didn't he explain to me the pros and cons, the advantages and disadvantages of taking such medication? For instance, what will happen the moment that I stop taking it? Neither he nor Doctor Fox did. They lack respect for medical practice, because of their disregard for the health of others. Kurt Vonnegut said, "If you can do no good, at least do no harm."

No wonder I was kept hospitalized in a psych ward for two weeks against my will. When I received my bill statements for my stay in the hospital from **01/21/15-2/4/15**, for exactly **15** days, one of my bills was for the amount of **$95,065.29** and the other one was for **$4,850.00**. So, for staying in the hospital for 15 days against my will, they charged me a total of **$99,915.29**. WHAT A BIG, HUGE BUSINESS THIS IS. Below are two copies of my bill statements.

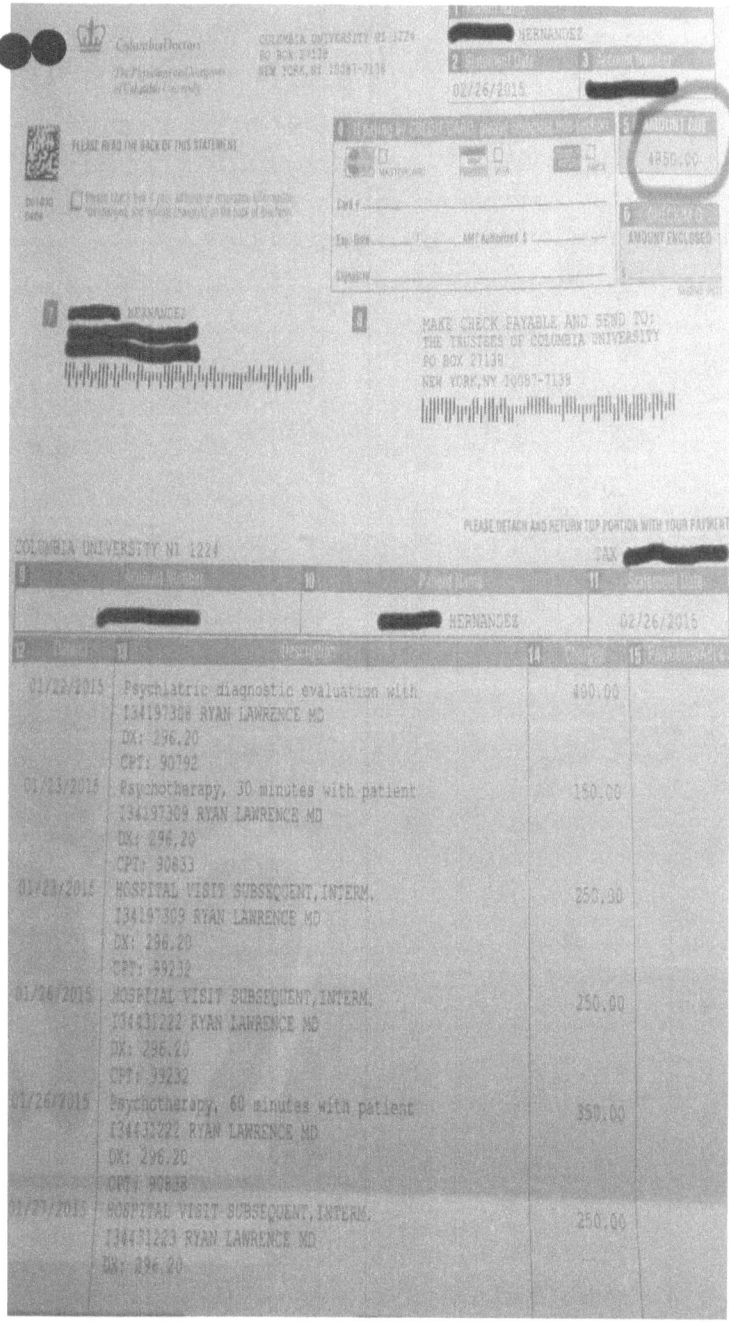

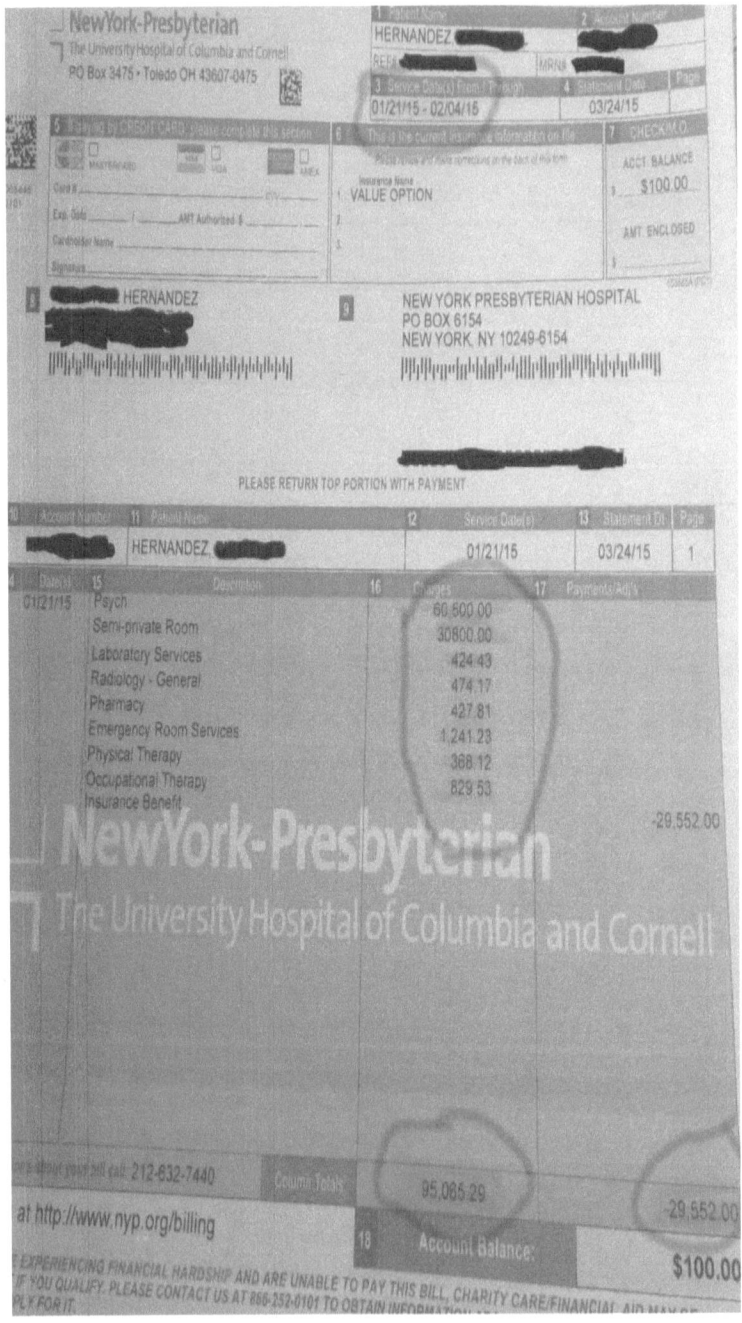

Chapter 23

September 2016—March 2017 Events

Then on **Monday, September 19, 2016,** after visiting my general doctor who had just prescribed me high blood pressure medication, and because of the pressure I felt on my eyes, I called out sick at my job, and as soon as I did, history began to repeat itself again.

Because of the gravity of my condition, I went to spend the night somewhere else, not at home, because I needed support. The moment I visited the apartment of the person that I went to visit that I sat on the sofa, their dog walked towards me, and the dog began to lick my forearm continuously, non-stop, like for more than 25 minutes. Then when the dog stopped liking my forearm, it was because the dog was tired of licking my forearm, and the dog looked agitated, but half a minute later, the dog began to do it again. It caught the attention of the people I visited, and he began to record it because the dog had never done that before. It got to the point that they had to take the dog and bring the dog inside the cage, because the dog didn't want to stop doing it.

This is my SICK RECORD. From 2007 till 2013, For 6 years straight, I only called out sick 1 time. Then, on 2014 I called out sick 1 time, and it was based on their constant harassment. On

SICK RECORD
(LAST 3 YEARS)

| # OF TIMES SICK LOD | 0 | # OF DAYS | 0 |
| # OF TIMES SICK NON-LOD | 2 | # OF DAYS | 24 |

WERE YOU EVER CATEGORIZED AS CHRONIC A/B SICK? 24

IF YES, EXPLAIN _____

ATTACH COPIES OF LAST 3 EVALUATIONS
CO'S RECOMMENDATION (UPON REQUEST)
APPLICATION MUST BE TYPED

2013   0 sick
   ADMIN sick
2014 Oct 12/13
2015   22 Day
   Jan 21 - Feb 21

2015, I was placed on sick, and it was a disaster.

So, on **September 23, 2016,** at 1:10 pm when I was in front of the building I visited, I received a text message from PO Flores, "Hey is FloresJay. Is that you in front of ....?", "There is a guy that looks like u from far but my eyesight sucks." I crossed the street and greeted her. She was in uniform, and she was with her partner. We spoke for a while and then we departed. After that moment, I began to be followed again. At my workplace my co-workers began to talk about me and behind my back, and people on the street and everywhere I went to were talking about me. One of my co-workers, PO Almonte told me, "Things are going to happen in the job and outside of the job and people will say that you are schizophrenic."

One afternoon, I saw Lt. Allen at PSA where my Viper Unit office is. I wondered what he was doing there. I went downstairs

and greeted him. Another night I saw Sgt. Gibbs there. I greeted him also. What were my 25 precinct bosses doing there?

Suddenly, Sergeant John Fischetti, began to ask me if I had seen "The 75" movie. "The 75" movie is a real-life documentary about the most corrupted NYPD Police Officer, Michael Dowd. When I watched the trailer, I was more than surprised to see how dirty and corrupted a person can be. Then I noticed that Sgt. Fischetti kept asking me if I had seen it and he kept advising me that I should watch it. I wondered why he asked me specifically, and not to the other officers that were around? What is he insinuating? That I am a corrupt dirty cop? I shall LOL, or lets say Laugh Out Loud. Now no wonder why when he did my yearly Performance Evaluation, on the Police Ethics/ Integrity caption he graded me **3.0** out of **5**. In my entire career as a police officer, the only time I received **3.0** on this category was when I was evaluated for my first six month as a Police Officer in 2008. Never again until now, in 2017 that he gives me a **3.0** which truly rings the bell.

Now no wonder why I am now being scrutinized and harassed at the Viper Unit. They suspect that I am dirty, and the worst thing is that they are treating me as if I were. Before PO Almonte used to wait for me to give me a ride home, but he no longer waits for me to give me a ride. Now he leaves without waiting for me. When I call him, he never answers, and he doesn't call me back. The reason why is simple, **according to the NYPD Patrol Guide, police officers are not allowed to associate with someone "2. c. Reasonably believed to be engaged in, likely to engage in, or to have engaged in criminal activities."**

No wonder why one day when I was looking for the phone number of PO Almonte, which he had previously given to me, and I was going to check on the list that have the names of the officers and their phone numbers, Lieutenant Glenn furiously yelled at me in front of everyone there telling me that I am not going to look at the phone number of the officers. When I tried to explain to him, he yelled out at me, "Are you going to go back and forward with me?" I said, "Good night, everybody," and I left. This is how I am being treated. The next time I went to work, he was suspended and transferred. The reason was because he was caught sleeping. Or was it for the way that he spoke to me, which interfered with or jeopardized the ongoing investigation that is taking place against Police Officer Emmanuel Hernandez?

One day I was on the bus BX 13 when someone yells out, "Lying under oath." Also, on the public transportation and the public places I visit now, I see people turning their back on me, making sounds with their throat, and saying things such as, "You are lying," "That's a lie," and so on. To avoid all this, I have stopped going to the gym, and I have avoided going to public places by staying home. The only thing I do is to go to church and go to work, and the transportation I use is liveries, taxi, or if someone give me a ride. I had to go back to Olanzapine to sleep, this time the lowest dosage, 2.5 mg. I still wonder why Dr. Ryan Lawrence first prescribed me **20** MG of Olanzapine which I took trusting him and thinking that it was not a big deal. As I took those high doses, it gave me side effects that I thought was going to go away with time. But when I stopped taking it, I couldn't sleep, and when I decided to find out about this medication withdrawal symptoms, and when reading from the testimonies of others that had gone through the withdrawal process, and their suffering, I didn't know what to do. This is when I found out that what I was taking was an antipsychotic, a psychotropic drug that is highly detrimental to my health.

Why was I prescribed this in the first place, and in the highest dose prescribed to a patient? Again, I wasn't a violent person. But there is one thing, they expect you not to have feelings or emotions, and psychiatrists such as Dr. **Ryan Lawrence** have the License and legal authority to kill the mind and the life of others. They do as they please.

Now I am fighting two fronts. The medication which has hurt my physical body, which as a result, I now need to take high blood pressure medication, and my tormentors who have begun to persecute me again since the day that I called out sick.

My God, I am so tired of all this. Every single day I am at work, I am being harassed. They keep making sound with their throat, and they keep saying the words "Lying." Lying here and lying there, it is nonstop. I heard PO Accoster say, "Freddy (PO Ipince) has everyone wired here."

Detective Dellomo said to PO Freddy Ipince who was seating right next to me "Freddy you destroyed his life, Freddy." PO Freddy Ipince remained quiet. Then days later, I overheard Detective Dellomo tell PO Ipince," Freddy, every time you point a finger, there is more money back into you, you know," and PO Ipince tried to blame Detective Mejia for it. Now I understand why Detective Mejia, after being in the Viper Unit for more than six years as a form of punishment, while his case was being investigated, was exonerated, given back his gun and shield, and given the option of where to go.

Now I understand why I heard Det. Mejia say that the city knows everything about you. Now I understand why PO Almonte one day told me not to trust Sgt. Rich. Now I understand why Sgt. Rich said in my presence that the moment that one signs up for this job, one's privacy is taken away. He said that one has no rights. After being in Viper for a long time, because his gun and shield were taken away for an alleged wrongdoing, Sgt. Rich received his long-awaited notification, for his case to be dealt with on a certain day, so he can be restored back to his old status, and be given back his gun and shield, and be full duty again. It looks like many are benefitting from my hardship.

One day when suddenly, I entered the Viper Unit room, Det. Dellomo said, "Here is Hernandez," as to alert PO Ipince of my arrival and to stop talking about me. Yes, I confirmed it, you PO Ipince, the man I trusted for more than a year and a half, have pointed his accusatory finger at me, and in return, he was compensated for it. He knows well what I am going through, but he doesn't care. Also, I remember the second day after having met Detective Dellomo that he told me, "You have a heavy accent. Just because you have a heavy accent doesn't mean that you are a bad guy." His comment was rude, but I wondered if what he was trying to do was to send me a message.

Then I heard PO Jessica Nieves who doesn't stop making sound with her throat say, "Fired, suspended, fire, suspended...." and others were saying that good people have been fired from the job. Police Officer Martinez looked at me and acting as if he were playing, he told me that someone is out to modify me and to have me back as a civilian again. I know that they are being wired to see if I say something wrong to hang me. Who wants to work in such a hostile work environment? They are retaliating against me again. This is never ending. This is every day. I must go through all this every single day, but if I say something, they will say that I have psych problem, but God is my witness. Now outside my job, there are people making sound with their throat when they are near me. It is like the whole world knows me.

PO Freddy Ipince keep telling me to sell him my tablet which is the instrument I use to type these words. But I believe that the reason why he wants my tablet is to see if he or they can find something incriminating in it to use it against me. Once I heard him talking on his smartphone and telling someone that he does it for money. One day in the morning, after I finished changing that I entered the Viper Unit office, I saw PO Ipince talking to another officer and when he saw me, he played the following song out loud by Amanda Miguel that is titled, "El Me Mintio," which translated into English is "He Lied to Me," and he played it over and over again in my presence.

Recently, every time I open my bible randomly, it automatically opens on Psalms 54, 55, and 56 and I read:

54 "O God, save me by your name, and vindicate me by your might. 2O God, hear my prayer; give ear to the words of my mouth. 3For strangers have risen against me; ruthless men seek my life; they do not set God before themselves. Selah 4Behold, God is my helper; the Lord is the upholder of my life. 6...I will give thanks to your name, O LORD, for it is good. 7For he has delivered me from every trouble, and my eye has looked in triumph on my enemies." (Psalm 54 ESV)

55 "Give ear to my prayer, O God, and hide not yourself from my plea for mercy! 2Attend to me, and answer me; I am restless in my complaint and I moan, 3because of the noise of the enemy, because of the oppression of the wicked. For they drop trouble upon me, and in anger they bear a grudge against me. 4My heart is in anguish within me; the terrors of death have fallen upon

me. 5Fear and trembling come upon me, and horror overwhelms me.

6And I say, "Oh, that I had wings like a dove! I would fly away and be at rest; 7yes, I would wander far away; I would lodge in the wilderness; Selah 8I would hurry to find a shelter from the raging wind and tempest." 9Destroy, O Lord, divide their tongues; 12For it is not an enemy who taunts me— then I could bear it; it is not an adversary who deals insolently with me—then I could hide from him. 13But it is you, a man, my equal, my companion, my familiar friend. 14We used to take sweet counsel together; within God's house we walked in the throng... 16But I call to God, and the LORD will save me. 17Evening and morning and at noon I utter my complaint and moan, and he hears my voice. 18He redeems my soul in safety from the battle that I wage, for many are arrayed against me... 20My companion stretched out his hand against his friends; he violated his covenant. 21His speech was smooth as butter, yet war was in his heart; his words were softer than oil, yet they were drawn swords. 22Cast your burden on the LORD, and he will sustain you; he will never permit the righteous to be moved... 23...But I will trust in you." (Psalm 55 ESV)

56"Be gracious to me, O God, for man tramples on me; all day long an attacker oppresses me; 2my enemies trample on me all day long, for many attack me proudly. 3When I am afraid, I put my trust in you. 4In God, whose word I praise, in God I trust; I shall not be afraid. What can flesh do to me? 5All day long they injure my cause; all their thoughts are against me for evil. 6They stir up strife, they lurk; they watch my steps, as they have waited for my life... 8You have kept count of my tossings; put my tears in your bottle... 10In God, whose word I praise, in the LORD, whose word I praise, 11in God I trust; I shall not be afraid. What can man do to me?" (Psalm 56 ESV).

February 2017

On **Tuesday, February 7, 2017,** in an act of desperation, I made clear to PBA Attorney Chris McGrath that I wanted to leave things as they are, to just let them retire me. I told him that I won't fight it anymore. McGrath asked me if things were well at work. I told him yes. But not everything is well. I have no problem with being in Viper, but the people that are working there are very sarcastic with their comments, which of course, are directed at me.

From its windows, I can hear people walking by talking about what I believe to be about me, because they are talking loud enough for me to hear. They were saying the 'lying' word. When I finished talking to McGrath, when I was waiting for the elevator, I heard someone say, "He doesn't want to work." The comment made me think about how unjust people are. My question is, are you in my place? Are you going through the same nightmare that I am being forced to endure? It is a great feeling when you are told by your boss "Good job" as I was told once by Sgt. Rich on an assignment I did.

On **Wednesday, February 8, 2017,** McGrath adjourned (postponed) my Board meeting for retirement for next month.

On **Thursday, February 9, 2017,** the harassment continued at work. Detective Dellomo showed a picture that he had on his smartphone to PO Duke and to PO Harty telling them that it is him on the picture. They denied it was him. They said that it was not him. But then Det. Dellomo began saying that he was not lying that it was him. He said that he was not pretending to be someone else. He kept saying that. One thing I noticed is that Det. Dellomo talks to everybody except me.

At this point in my life, I know not what to do. I try to talk to my wife about the matter and all she says is that I need help, that the psych medication that I am taking is not helping me, because I am still thinking that people are talking about me. This situation has become the main factor for our divorce in progress. I am so mentally drained that I am physically whipped out. I am so fatigued.

Many times, I wonder if it is worth it to keep typing what I am going thru, but I believe that God keeps encouraging me to do so. One day, when I looked up at the television, on Daystar, I read the following on the screen, **"Your story matters."** On the same channel, I listened to preachers talk about giving up what you got, to get what you really want. To lose to gain. Joyce Meyer said that God will raise you up and make them watch. But I love my job as a Police Officer. I don't want to let it go. But to prevent them from inflicting more psychological damage on me, I must take a different path. My emotional distress and the slander against me remain vivid, active, and alive, so for my well-being, I must desist. And with my face high up, I must walk away.

But there is one last thing that I want to say, and it is that they knew well on whom they were picking on. They picked on a defenseless individual. Someone that couldn't defend himself and had no one to defend him. Someone who comes from a humble family without malice. I was like a lamb among wolves. A lamb who blindly believed in his neighbor, but who at the end was stabbed multiple times behind his back. In a few words, they prayed on the vulnerable. PO Rivera once said to me that PO Ahmed was like a fish out of the water every time his partner PO Banks didn't come to walk. But it applies to me as well. All this time I have been feeling like a fish out of the water, having no one to lean on.

March 2017

Finally, on **Monday, March 6, 2017,** I told McGrath that I will not fight it anymore. To let them retire, and he accepted my decision.

On **Wednesday, March 8, 2017,** I was told that the Board had approved me, and that today I could report to work for the last time. It was sad news for me. I went to my workplace and said goodbye, but before leaving, I asked my good boss Lt. Hawkins how many years he has on the job, and he told me that he has 31 years on the job and more to come. The contrast of me who has 9 years and 8 months on the job, almost 10 years, plus 6 years as a police cadet and now retire this soon. When I left the office, from the glass wall of the second floor, I looked down to the 1st floor where I saw officers gathered there behind the Desk. I used to stand on the same spot there every night I went to work at Viper, to look down at the Desk. From there, I sadly looked at them gathered as brothers and sisters in blue. Talking, hugging, kissing, and laughing like there is no tomorrow. The fellowship they have is something that I didn't get back at the 25th precinct. I felt nostalgic. Then I left, leaving everything behind on typed words.

I paid a visit to the 25th precinct to pick up part of my belongings. When I got there, I knew none of the officers that were there. I wondered how come that after two years of leaving the place, the precinct has so drastically changed of personnel. Did the change have anything to do with me?

On **Monday, March 27, 2017,** my wife received another letter from Optimum stating that she has violated some copyrights by illegally downloading videos such as the Game of Thrones. She had disconnected everything, and while she was talking to the representative, they said that it was still connected to an Apple device, and as soon as the representative said that the representative said that it got disconnected just now, as if those who were using it, heard the conversation. We have never used Apple devices. After knowing that, immediately, I went to conclude my retirement. Finally, I will not be followed anymore. After I retired, I thought of the following song:

"… Libre, como el sol cuando amanece yo soy libre, como el mar. Libre, como el ave que escapo de su prisión y puede al fin volar. Libre, como el viento que recoge mi lamento y pesar, camino sin cesar, detrás de la verdad y sabre lo que es al fin la libertad…" from a song by Nino Bravo.

Translated into English:

" … Free, as when the sun rises I am free, as the sea. Free, as the bird that escaped its prison and can finally fly. Free, as the wind that takes away my lament and grief, none stop I walk, after the truth, and I will know what freedom finally is…" song by Nino Bravo.

"The Lord helps and delivers them; He will deliver them from the wicked and will save them because they take refuge in Him." (Psalm 37:40 HCSB)

On **Wednesday, March 29, or Thursday, March 30**, at around 1330 hrs. or 1:30 pm I took the elevator, and it stopped on the next floor. A guy wearing red entered the elevator. We came out of the building, and then he hung around where I was standing at waited for the bus.

On **Friday, March 31, 2017,** I went to the grocery store, bought myself an almond milk, and at 8:12 pm, entered a guy wearing a red sweater, with no legitimate purpose of buying anything. He just stood there, looking at his smartphone. He was just spying on me. At 9:50pm, two males came out of apartment # …, and took the elevator. They are the same people that keep going to Apt. …. I think that they are spying on me.

Chapter 24

Finally Decided to take the Risk of taking Pictures

I finally decided to take the risk and take some pictures so you may see. I am putting myself in harm's way by doing so.

On **Saturday, April 1, 2017, I** came out of the building, and I saw a group of people in the block. As I walked to Rite Aid to pick up my medication, I got to see people wearing red and the Camo colors as I walked pass them.

As I continued to walk to Rite Aid, I saw two people across the street looking at me as I walked. See the pictures below.

I was putting my life in danger by taking these pictures, but I had to at least take a picture to show you an example of what I am going through. Before I didn't take pictures because they were monitoring my smartphone and they knew everything I did with it, also, to avoid being assaulted. In addition, I don't know if it is legal to take pictures of my followers.

Then I saw when the two of them got into Rite Aid (look at the above pictures). When I went into Rite Aid to pick up my medication, at the entrance they were there waiting for me. They faced me and one of them asked me why I was following them. I told them that I went to the store to pick up something. The security guard got involved and they left.

This is why I don't take pictures of my followers. I don't know how dangerous they are. Moreover, people don't like strangers to take pictures of them, and I am one of them who doesn't like it. To do so is to look for trouble. It happened at 1539 hrs. or 5:39 pm. I thought that by retiring they were going to stop following me, but no, they are being more aggressive about it. They just cannot stop following me because they are trying to make out of my life a living hell. They want to drive me to suicide. When I went to the park, I saw people wearing the same red colors.

Then I went to visit someone at 760 Melrose Avenue, and when I came out of the building, right in front of the building, I saw a guy leaning on the wall wearing a red hat. See the picture below.

On Wednesday, April 5, 2017, I went outside, and I saw people standing in different corners. See the picture below.

I went to the gym and when I used the treadmill, a young woman wearing red walked to the treadmill, and she used the treadmill that was close to me. Then I walked downstairs, and when coming up the stairs, I saw and heard a Blink employee tell a young guy that they had enough proof that he was going to get fired, and I walked out of the door. At 1420 hrs. or 2:20 pm, I was at the Subway eating a sandwich, and I saw two people wearing red seating eating. See the picture below.

431

Then a young man and a young woman walked inside, bought their sandwiches and they seated in a corner. She told him that the other seats were too bright and that it causes her mild headaches and she jokingly said, "I am disabled". I left.

As I walked to my building, walking up the hill, I saw the same person that I saw standing at another corner previously. He was sitting

down. See the picture below.

I entered the building, and I took the elevator with the super. The super told to two women that were in the elevator with us that the people that lives in the building are working people and that 5% of them are retired.

Then I went to do the laundry, and before I came out of the building, across the street of my building, I saw a man there standing wearing a red hat. See the picture below.

Then I left and went to do the laundry. After I did the laundry that I went back to my building, right at the door entrance, I saw two males, and one of them was wearing red sneakers. All this in just one day. See the picture below.

On **Thursday, April 6, 2017,** I stood home. I went nowhere.

On **Friday, April 7, 2017,** I only went out to go to the bodega. When I was paying for my products over the counter, I saw a young man walk in with the American flag drawn on his pant which of course, it had red. It happened around six something. I went home. See the picture below.

Now to make it short, I will just show pictures with dates, and look at how close the dates are:

4/05/2017

4/8/2017

4/10/2017

4/17/2017

4/20/2

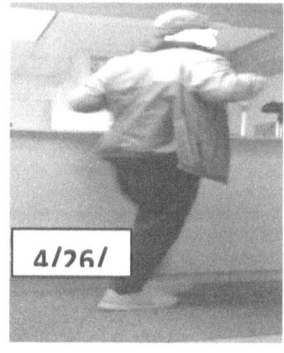

4/26/

5/11/20

5/12/201

5/12/20

5/12/201

5/16/2017

5/16/2017

5/16/2017

August 2017

Now if I had been typing down everything that happens to me every day, it would have been an additional hundreds of pages. Those behaviors and patterns keep repeating. Now **Thursday, August 31, 2017**, I decided to continue typing.

On **Thursday, August 31, 2017**, I arrived at John Jay College of Criminal Justice at 1600 hrs. or 4:00 pm. There was a guard standing and there was a female security guard seated. I gave her my mini-diploma card, and she asked me for my I.D card. When she does, I looked for my I.D and the guard that was next to her told her, "You don't need I.D." She answered, "You are crazy. You are a psycho." Now, how can I interpret this? He might have told her that she needed no I.D because she already knows who I am, since everyone knows about me, and by saying the words "crazy," and "psycho," you can imagine for whom were those words directed to indeed.

I read an article for **August 14, 2017,** from Livestrong.com by Nancy Clarke which stated, "The American Chiropractic Association lists restricted memory, judgement, attention and patience among the mental

441

limitations brought on by inadequate sleep quality and quantity." I wonder if my sleep deprivation, the constant stress and harassment at work contributed to my memory loss on the case of **December 10, 2013,** that I couldn't remember the details of the events well.

September 2017

On **Friday, September 29, 2017,** I went outside to take the bus to go to the park, which I do every Friday and at the same time. At the bus stop, I saw a woman standing with a NYC ID hanging on her chest. It is obvious that she works for the city. I wondered what the city wants from me. When I arrived at the park, there they were, my followers.

October 2017

On **Monday, October 2, 2017,** I arrived at the swimming pool of John Jay College of Criminal Justice. There I saw an individual that I hadn't seen before. When I handed over my card to the person in charge, he said loud enough, "He is a healthy and strong man." He looked at me several times while I was swimming.

His presence there was obvious since yesterday, this past Sunday, I told one member of my church congregation whom I going to call XXX to hide his identity, that I go swimming many times. He asked me where, and I told him where, and that same Sunday, I went to visit his family for the first time, and I felt so unwelcome there. This is the same person with whom I share time with inside church and outside church. However, every time the church service ends, he waits for me outside.

Every time we speak, I feel that he is interviewing me, as if he is trying to obtain information from me and about me for a certain purpose. But to him I quote Psalm 55:12-14 HCSB which says, **"Now it is not an enemy who insults me — otherwise I could bear it; it is not a foe who rises up against me — otherwise I could hide from him. But it is you, a man who is my peer, my companion and good friend! We used to have close fellowship; we walked with the crowd into the house of God."**

On **Friday, October 6, 2017,** I went to the grocery store and the woman that works there said," He is crazy, and without money." How much can a human take after being humiliated, harassed and being pushed against the wall. The pressure of constantly being in the public eyes, being scrutinized and being put in harm's way is enormous. All because of malicious suspicion.

But I want to ask all of you some questions. Throughout your investigation, and as a result of your investigation, can you name me one person that I may have wronged, insulted or disrespected? Can anyone, with whom I have worked with in the past or in the present, even since I was a police cadet or even before that, come forward and say that I have ever used a cursing word or at any time swear? Has anyone that I have arrested said anything negative about me? Has anyone in the community done so? And if you haven't found anything to blame me for, what is your obsession with me?

It was like on **June/2014** that as I walked with one of the ADAs to the elevator she said, "This f...ng guy," probably referring to me, and I was surprised because I thought they didn't curse, because they are held to a higher standard, and that is something that I don't even dare to say. But as I once told PO Rivera, "If good people are against good people, what is going to be left?" You think that I am going to risk my salvation for doing the wrong thing?

On **Wednesday, October 11, 2017,** I was in the gym at John Jay College of Criminal Justice. I was using one of the machines. There a woman used the machine that was next to me. Then she began to talk to someone on the smartphone. She asked the person with whom she was talking to if he was working. Then she asked him if he was sick. Then she told him that she was going to work.

After the gym, I went to the swimming pool. There I saw the same strange individual at the swimming pool. Also, there were a total of six individuals, excluding the person who works there, seated surrounding a table. Then the stranger, who was standing, began to record with his smartphone the swimming pool from one end to the other end. When he pointed his smartphone at me, I lifted my right arm and waved my hand at him. Then I began swimming again and at one point we made eyes contact. He stared at me. About three minutes later, the six of them, and the stranger left, leaving the person who works there by himself. But before leaving, the stranger gave the thumb up to the man who works there. They all left because they got my message when I waved my hand to the stranger.

Normally, a person feels aggravated for something as simple as being stared at. A person may simply tell the person that is staring at him, "What are you looking at." It also bothers a person when another person is being nosy and as a result, he or she may tell he or she, "It is none of your business." If those responses are just given to people because for a brief moment, they stare at them or because someone becomes nosy, can you imagine when you are constantly on a daily basis and for years being followed, and watched? What would be your response?

If one day you decided to go to the store and in the store you see that the staff of the store follows you everywhere in the store and ask you if you need help, and you tell he or she that you don't need any, but still, that person keeps following you because that person thinks that you might steal something from the store because of your look. How would you feel? I know that many of you need anger management classes to deal with such a situation.

So how do you expect me to react? My question is, have I been pre-judged? Or there have been some type of prejudice against me, because I am a Hispanic man whose color of the skin is olive because of interracial marriage between a white woman and a black man? At this stage of my life, I think that everything is possible.

Sunday, October 15, 2017, was a very sad day for me. I went to church, and I sat down on the chair that was next to a book bag, which meant that someone was seated there. I kneeled to pray. Then I noticed that the owner of the book bag took the bag, and when I looked up to see who he or she was, it was nothing more than a good friend of mines, a brother in Christ. He didn't greet me. He just grabbed his book bag and walked away.

When I finished praying, I looked back, and I saw him looking for another seat. But there was a seat next to me, but why didn't he want to sit next to me? He went to the other side, and he sat there. Then I saw that someone approached him probably claiming the seat where he sat on, and he got up and moved back. There he stood looking for a seat, but the seat that was next to me was still available, but it was obvious that he didn't want to sit next to me. At one point, someone pointed out to him that there was a seat which was closer to me, but he refused to take it. He preferred to take the one that was very tight between two people. It broke my heart.

On **Friday, October 20, 2017,** I went to the park at Fort Tryon Park, and they keep sending people there to watch me. They keep making scenarios, because they already know the day and time that I go there every Friday. This time I saw two Hispanics men with their heads shaved, which most cops do, looking at me. I looked at one of them and greeted him with my head. Then I saw a man who asked me for money, and he talked to me as if he were an emotionally disturbed person. And I saw people around pointing their smartphones at me and it is obvious that the city is after me. They want to know my every move. I am tired of this nonsense.

Chapter 25

Harassment Intensifies Pictures Taking
November 2017

Friday, November 3, 2017, was a very unusual day at the park as I did my jogging. Before I started jogging, I saw a man seated on the bench where I am used to seat every Friday when I go to the park. He had hanging on his neck, a professional camera. As I jogged, I saw another man taking selfies with the people that he was with and as jogged by him said, "Taking more pictures of this guy."

As I continued, at the other end I saw another man taking pictures of the woman that he was with while pointing his phone at my direction. As I continued jogging up the park, I saw like three men with professional cameras, and one of them bent down to take pictures at a woman who was on top of a bottle in a ballet position, but she was in front of me, so they were taking pictures of her with me while I was jogging by. When I turned the corner, there I saw another man with a professional camera taking pictures at my direction and further up there was a woman pointing her phone at me while I was jogging up.

When I was reaching the end, there I saw another man with a professional camera taking pictures and another woman pointing her smartphone at me. It looked like the paparazzi were busy at the park.

On **Sunday, November 5, 2017,** I found out that one relative of my brother-in-law who worked for the post office, was sent to a psych ward because he had a heated dispute with someone there. Then he explained how there were people following him. I have decided to travel to Dominican Republic to escape all this madness.

I saw a video on YouTube titled, "THE VIDEO THE DEVIL NEVER WANTED YOU TO SEE!!" published on October 9, 2017, where Priscilla Shirer stated, "There is an invisible enemy, and he is breaking on the fact that you will forget that he is there. He so wants to disguise himself behind the tangible physical problem of your life that you will forget. He is often the one that is influencing some of the most difficult circumstances not only in our nation but in our homes. That there is always something you cannot see controlling what you can't. The enemy is scheming against you.

Listen, if I find out that somebody has done wrong. I mean, I am upset but I can get over that. But if I find out somebody has been planning to do me wrong, that's another new story. I find out you have been scheming against me. Meaning you have been sitting back studying my tendencies and my patterns. You have been watching where I come from and where I go. You have been trying to take advantage of the weaknesses of my flesh. You have been looking into my personality to figure out what will be the best way to throw me off course. When I find out that not only have you been studying me, but you have been studying my husband, trying to investigate his history, so you can figure out given my history and his history the best way to make explosions of anger happen in our family.

When I find out you been trying to explore his weaknesses so you can tempt him away of his heart and his emotions being at home with me… When I find out that you have been studying me and the people that I love, you got to believe that now a holy indignation rises inside of me… If it is a war the enemy wants, it is a war he will have. Not by our strength and not in our power, but by the power of God's own spirit…"

It is as if she were talking to me, what is happening to me, and what is being done against me.

This is **Monday, November 27, 2017,** and I am in a farm in the Dominican Republic hoping to escape from my persecutors. Like three days ago, I read an article from the New York Daily News explaining how the NYPD can track where you are through your smartphone. I use my smartphone hoping that they don't continue violating my privacy.

However, while I was home, at approximately 12:00 pm, I saw a Policia Nacional (National Police) marked white vehicle parked inside of my property, and in front of the house. When I walked out to see, there

I saw a National Police accompanied by his Sergeant (Sargento Mayor). They were seated talking to my father. They introduced themselves to me and about thirty minutes later, they left. I suspect that somehow, they found out about my whereabouts, and they sent those officers to inquire about me or to intentionally plant psychological fear on me, by stealing my peace and letting me know that they know where I am at, and that they are watching me.

One day I was riding in a car with a friend, and he pointed to a woman who was wearing a red sneaker, and he said that here were imitating the same fashion of New York. He said it because of the color of the sneakers that she was wearing.

Back in New York, **On Saturday, December 2, 2017,** I was in the bathroom with my wife. She hugged me while smiling at me. But suddenly, her face turned sad, and she stopped hugging me. I asked her what happened. She said, "It just came to my mind when I saw you in the hospital."

On **Tuesday, December 5, 2017,** I met with a person regarding a short sale. He introduced himself to me. He told me that my face looked familiar. He asked me if I was arrested before. He told me that he had been a private investigator for ten years and that he had left it. What a coincidence, because I served for almost ten years as a police officer. I told him that I am retired, and he said that he knows. How does he know?

On **Saturday, December 9, 2017,** I went to the movie theater. There, when I paid for my movie ticket, a woman at the register congratulated one of the customers for obtaining his bachelor's degree. I mention this because I have a bachelor's degree, and I do mention it on my manuscript of my book, "The 777" and I wondered if she already read my manuscript that I sent to a publishing house. From there I walked to the elevator where I saw a man of about 6'7 feet tall and I said, "They already know that?" and he looked at me and he shook his head slowly as if showing disapproval for the treatment that I am receiving.

The day before, I went to watch another movie in Queens. Then I went to Wendy's, and at Wendy's, there were two women talking as they waited on the line, and one of them said to the other, "I don't know why he had to lie."

Today, Sunday, **December 10, 2017,** marks the Fourth Year Anniversary of a day that I should forget, but that I can't forget.

On **Wednesday, December 13, 2017,** I spoke with my mother to see how they were doing, and she told me that they were fine. Also, she told me that the police went to visit them again.

On **Sunday, December 17, 2017,** I spoke to the brother in Christ XXX about going to the precinct, at the 25th precinct, and empty up my two lockers. He told me that he couldn't because he had to do something. I wondered what he might be thinking since I told him that. Does he think that I want to go there to steal? When indeed, the reason why I want to empty my two lockers is because I don't want them to open it, plant something illegal in them, and then blame me for it. As you can see, I am in a very dangerous position right now.

On **Saturday, December 30, 2017,** at 5:30 pm, I was filling out my Retro fitness membership information, and while I was doing that, two of the gym staff were talking. One of them asked about the phone charger and one of them said that he was not a thief. One of them mentioned retirement. They were very unprofessional.

On **Wednesday, January 3, 2018,** I went to Retro Fitness for the second time. There I saw a brother in Christ who attends the same church that I attend. He asked me about my job and about the time that I plan to go to the gym. I told him that I like to use the punching bag that is in the corner.

On **Thursday, January 4, 2018,** at approximately 8:40 pm, my wife and I used the livery service provided by Lyft to get a livery cab.

When the Toyota livery arrived, my wife who first entered the livery said, "Hi Jonathan," to the driver.

When I looked at the driver, it was no other than ex-cop Jonathan Wally. He was the cop who was arrested once and who I knew, and who I had seen in the gym back on April 8, 2014, which was the time when I was intensely being followed. To see him again, I don't know if it was pure or mere coincidence or was its part of their plan?

On **Friday, January 5, 2018,** I saw the same brother in Christ who just arrived at the gym at the same time that I did. Later in the gym, I went to use the punching bag and there I saw an unattended black gym belt. Wow, they are still playing games with me to see if I steal it. I am back to my past misery.

On **Monday, January 8, 2018,** when I arrived at Retro Fitness that I opened the last locker at the end, which I have been using lately, it was unlocked, and it had things inside. It was laughable.

At approximately 6:50 pm, I walked out of Retro Fitness and when I began walking up the very long stairs that goes up and connects Jerome Avenue with Anderson Avenue at 167 street, right at the corner end of the stairs, there was a man and a woman looking at me. I knew that they were my followers, and when I was walking by them, I laughed out loud, and the man said something to me, but I couldn't hear what he said, because I had my earphones on and I was listening to something.

As I walked, there was a young guy wearing red standing at 1070 Anderson Avenue and another one at 964 Anderson Avenue, and so on. When I got close to Woodycrest Avenue, one man yelled out at me, "That white girl," and I wondered if he was referring to ADA (Assistant District Attorney) Altman. This is the first time that I laughed at them. But it was a way to defuse my anger.

The following day, on **Tuesday, January 9, 2018,** I went to the Gym. I used a machine and at 6:05 pm, I went into the dark
room where there is a big screen, and a movie was being shown. As I did my work out, a few minutes later, there was a scene in the movie

where it shows a woman with actor Jim Carry, and then the father of the woman comes by, and he tell Jim Carry that she is Schizophrenic. This is my fifth day in the gym, and I look at the coincidence. The name of the movie is ….. At 6:07 pm, I began taking the pictures below of the movie.

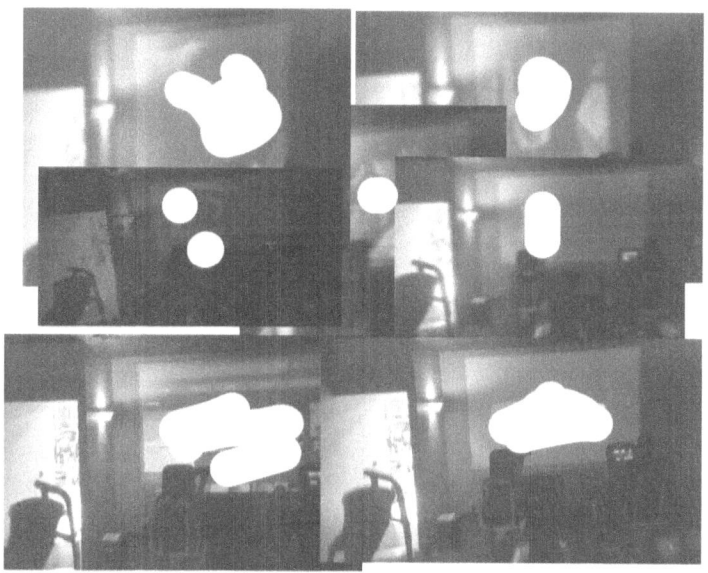

As soon as I began taking the pictures, at 6:10 pm, they stopped playing the movie as you can see below.

Then I looked at the camera that is in the corner of the room, and I began to make gestures as to let them know to put back the movie. I believe that they got my message. To my right there was a guy wearing blue running on the treadmill and he left. Then came who I was expecting, a guy wearing a red sweater and he used the treadmill next to me on my left. When I was leaving at 6:32 pm, I took a picture from behind of the person that was to my left wearing a red sweater. As you can see in the picture below.

Also, I took a quick picture of the camera that is at the corner.

Then when I went to the corner where I usually go to work out, I found the guy wearing blue who was running on the treadmill next to me. See the picture below.

Then when I walked out of the gym, that I went to take the same stairs that I took yesterday, where I found the woman and the man at the corner of the stair, and where I laughed out loud, at the same corner today, at 7:09 pm, I saw just the man standing at the same corner with a loud music. As I walked past him, from the side, I looked at his smartphone and its cover were red. I took a risk by taking a quick

 picture and it is

the picture below.

On **Wednesday, January 10, 2018,** I received an e-mail from a publisher about the Page Design of the book that I sent to be published titled, "The 777." When I went to the gym at Retro Fitness, as I sat and did my work out at 3:24 pm, someone wearing a red T-shirt stood almost in front of me wearing the number 7.

At that moment, besides the red colors of my followers, I wonder if they have read my email regarding the "The 777" book and they sent this kid wearing the number 7 to let me know that they know. Then a woman came and used the machine next to me on to my right. The cover of her smartphone was red, and she was using the machine on the lowest level which is 1. Meaning that she was not using it to exercise indeed, but to wonder about me.

Later I went to the dark room that has a big screen to show the movies. This time the movie was "Batman ..." And what was this Batman movie about? The movie had to do with the Assistant District Attorney, the Police, Batman etc.

Then when I went to the corner that I always go to do my work out, there I saw a woman occupying my space. Then as I continued with my work out, I heard a man say, "He is crazy, but he is fine." Then I left the gym, and when I arrived at 162 street and Ogden Avenue, at approximately 5:25 pm, there was a man yelling out incoherent sounds with his mouth. What an act. They did it on purpose because the day before, I yelled out a sound as I walked home.

At home, while I was typing this at approximately 7:16 pm, I felt movement under my feet, from the apartment below.

On **Thursday, January 11, 2018,** at approximately 2:40 pm, I walked out to go to the gym, and across the street of my building there was a NYPD vehicle parked. When I went to the grocery store, at the door, there was a group of people and one of them said, "That n… is in trouble." When I came down the stairs that I always take, at the end, there was a man seated wearing a Camo pant.

I arrived at the gym, and I began using one of the machines. While using it, at 3:22 pm, in front of me, there were a few guys working out. One of them was wearing a white T-shirt with a red sweater underneath. The white t-shirt had the Dominican flag at the back. The other guy that was with him was wearing a black Yankee hat that had the Dominican flag on the side. The reason why I mention the flag is because yesterday I was checking for the price of a flight to go to the Dominican Republic at Jet Blue. I used my smartphone. Isn't this quite a coincidence? Or does this confirm that they have access to my smartphone? In addition; as they spoke, they mentioned the word 'crazy' like three time. I was just giving a cynical smile to them, the way that PO Gorman used to do to me. I didn't take pictures because it was going to be very risky. I knew that there is a camera facing me in the gym, and they can look at my behavior through it. If I take my smartphone to take pictures, they will notice, and I can't alert them. Hey, I used to work at the Viper Unit looking at cameras and I know what the cameras are capable of doing.

Then I went to use the treadmill in the dark room. When I arrived, there was loud music, which they turned off the moment I entered. This time, there was no movie shown. There was a woman using the last treadmill. I took the first treadmill and bingo; there was a set of keys in the treadmill. I continued my jogging, and a young guy came in. He used the treadmill that was next to her, not the one that was next to me, strange. Then when she finished, she walked to my machine and with an attitude she asked me if there was a set of keys, I took it from the machine and gave it to her. As I walked, there were people doing double cough.

I believe that whoever is responsible for all this needs counseling. This person needs to learn to let go.

On **Saturday, January 13, 2018,** at 5:56 pm, I was in the Laundromat doing my laundry and one man arrived with two kids, and

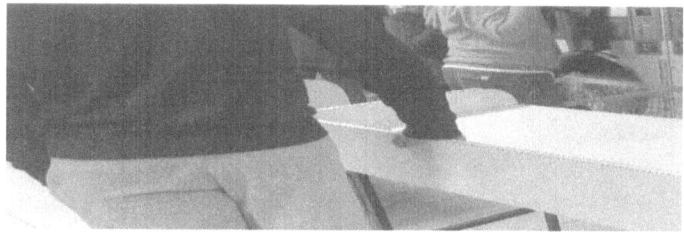

the kids were around the ages of ten. The photo below shows the man standing and the two kids in front of him.

I was next to them. The kid who was wearing the red sweater said, "Ta loco," which translated into English is "Is crazy," and he said it so loud that the other kid told him, "Baja la voz," which translated into English is, "Lower your voice," and the man just stood there quiet observing. I cannot take it anymore, so that same night, I bought my plane ticket to Dominican Republic.

On **Sunday, January 14, 2018,** I went to church. After the bible study class I went upstairs and I met with the brother in Christ XXX with whom I, must of the time, go to eat before the church's devotional. He was wearing his red coat.

While we were eating, he told me that the super, with whom he was doing some type of construction work, was asking him for I believe it was his drill. He told me that he had told the supper that he didn't have his drill. In a few words, he believed that the supper was accusing him of stealing the drill. Later, he asked me how much I pay for my smartphone service provider, and I told him that I am in Metro pcs and that I pay $61 dollars every month. He told me that we could share a line from his T-Mobile contract and that I will just need to pay him $50 dollars a month. In a few words, he or them want to monitor what I do on my smartphone.

Later in church, again, he told me that the supper was still calling him regarding the drill. He showed me on his smartphone multiple times that the supper had called him. I told him, "Peace." What he is insinuating is that he is being wrongfully accused of stealing something the same way that I was and probably am. Later, while seated at the church service, my

457

pastor saw me and he greeted me saying, "The police," and the same brother in Christ, XXX, with a cynical smile on his face and loud enough for everyone around to hear, told the pastor, "He is no longer a police," and the pastor answered, "But for me he is still a police." I felt so bad.

I told him that I was traveling to the Dominican Republic the following day. He was pleased to know because he finally had something new to report to those that oversee scrutinizing me. He showed a lot of interest. He asked for how long I was going there, at what time I was leaving, and at what airport. Also, he recommended to me someone who could take me to the airport.

At home I saw my wife sitting on the bed. There I told her of what the supposed brother in Christ told the pastor about me not being a cop anymore, and angrily she punched the bed and said," Can't you see that he is humiliating you!" I was speechless.

"Now it is not an enemy who insults me — otherwise I could bear it; it is not a foe who rises up against me — otherwise I could hide from him. But it is you, a man who is my peer, my companion and good friend! We used to have close fellowship; we walked with the crowd into the house of God." (Psalm 55:12-14 HCSB)

Later that night, I made 25 copies of pages from the book, "The Best of Me" and placed them on top of my printout diary to disguise it, in case I get stopped and someone forcibly takes it from me. So, if they get to read the first few pages, they might get discouraged to continue reading before they get to this diary.

Chapter 26

Escape to the Dominican Republic

Finally, **Monday, January 15, 2018,** arrived. I went to the JFK airport feeling like a fugitive who is escaping to another country. There I waited for the plane on departure number 28. I was seated. There I asked a man and a woman where they bought the bottle of water, and they told me where, but not before the man asking me for how long I was going to the Dominican Republic. Also, he asked me where I work. Amazing.

When I got back from getting food and water that I was seated, at 3:22 pm, a woman who was accompanied by a girl whose age was like nine or ten, walked to me and she seated in front of me. She was like in her late forties. She didn't stop talking on her smartphone. At one point she said twice, "I am crazy, I am crazy." When I looked at her smartphone's cover, it was red. Then we walked to the plane. My seat was 25 F, on row 25, by the window. I felt relieved, but not until I heard the same woman talking on her smartphone and when I looked back behind me, it was the same woman seated on row 26, to my left, and from there she could watch my every move. Then twice she said, "I am getting crazy, I am getting crazy." Wow.

When the plane landed, I waited for everyone to come out first. Then I stood, but before walking away, the same woman who had walked away, returned and she sent the girl to revise the seat because it seemed that she had left something there and she said, "I think I left it there." Wow, this is absurd. Later, I waited for my driver, and he drove me away. When I saw him, he was wearing a red hat and a T-shirt of red and white stripes. At that moment I realized that he was an accomplice or lets say, a Confidential Informant. But finally, I was going away, away from people, away from human malice, away to the farm.

A farm that very few people know of and which road to get there is kind of difficult, because of its many potholes and stones. Those who take me there always complain about the road. One day a taxi driver was taking me there and when we were halfway there or midway there, he gave up and stopped his vehicle. He made a U-turn and decided to go back, and he gave me back my money. But at this stage of my life, I love the farm, because there only lives a hand full of people. I will no longer hear my critics and finally there I will find tranquility, peace, and quiet. Finally, after four years, I found my right to privacy on the farm, something that I have longed for. But for how long was this going to last.

On **Tuesday, January 16, 2018**, the following day after arriving from New York, something horrendous happened, as if taken out of a horror movie.

In the afternoon, I went to the supermarket to do my groceries. There I was talking to my driver who was wearing the same reddish clothing he wore yesterday. As we spoke, one of the employees who was carrying out a milk quake looked angry and he threw the milk quake on the floor next to me, and it sounded very loud. He didn't apologize. At one point I saw the driver talking to a woman in close proximity so I may not hear what they were talking about. I noticed how strange people were coming close to me. I felt not welcomed.

When I arrived home, I noticed that my father was very upset. I asked him why? He told me that he was seating in the balcony when he saw a flying object close to him, in front of him and facing him. Then that the flying object was flying around the house. Then I was told that the flying object, the drone, belonged to the husband of the nephew of my cousin's wife who had come from New York. What a coincidence, this is the first time it happened, and it happened the day after I came from New York, from someone who came from New York, who doesn't live on the farm and who is now leaving for New York. I don't know him, and I have not seen him. When he was asked about the drone, his response was that he was going to send us the pictures he took with the drone. Again, my privacy continues to be highly violated, no matter where I go.

On **Wednesday, January 17, 2018**, my driver arrived to take me to the swimming pool. When I saw him, he was wearing a red hat and something red on his left arm as you can see in the following picture:

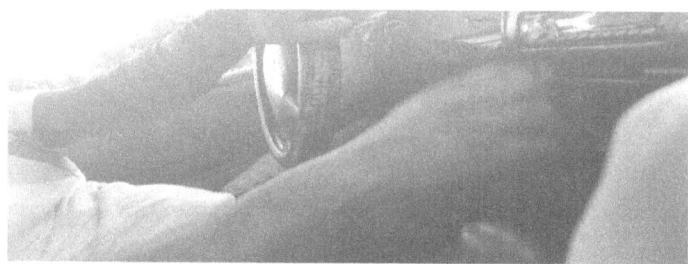

Now I never wanted nor wanted to be famous because I don't want people to know my business, and much worse, to be infamous, which is what they have done with me, they have made me infamous by spreading falsehoods about me everywhere I go. When I think of it, it gives me stomach ulcers.

On **Sunday, January 21, 2018,** a 35-year (I will call this person, 35 years man) man took me on a motorcycle to the zoo. When we got there, a man of around my age followed us everywhere we went. After the zoo, on our way home, the person I was with slowed down the motorcycle and he asked me, "Did you see that bag of marijuana on the floor? Someone might have dropped it. Would you like to take a look?" Isn't this funny? Of course, we didn't go back to look at the bag.

I believe that it was part of the same set up. They want to know how I was going to react. This was a review of the day when ADA (Assistant District Attorney) Altman told me not to mention the zip lock of marijuana that I found in the defendant's packet, and where Lt. Yaguchi, not letting the ADA know or on the ADA's back, maliciously gave me the marijuana lab test document results for me to mention it in the grand jury, which I did and it displeased ADA Altman. It was Lt. Yaguchi's intention to have her against me. But on this day, five years after the occurrence, I thought about it. What was the whole issue with marijuana? Did they think that I had planted the zip lock of marijuana on the defendant? Why didn't they test him for marijuana then?

Oh my God, was it because Lt. Yaguchi and PO Maher questioned the fact that they had searched the perpetrator at the scene and didn't find the zip lock of marijuana on him, but later I did? Just in case, I took the perpetrator to the 28 precinct, and there I searched for him again, and I found the zip lock of marijuana in the small packet that the front packet had. PO Quinones was there when I was searching for him and when I found it, which was right away, I lifted it up for him to see, because I knew that there was something fishy going on. I am 100% sure that they didn't search for the small bag that looks like the secret bag that **must pants have.** I am so angry right now. Bunch of idiots. I do really want to curse right now as I am typing this.

Then the 35 years man told me that he was going to pick up some money first from a woman that he knows. We went to the place to meet with the woman. There was a party going on. I waited outside. While I waited outside, the mother of the woman who had come from New York, stepped out too accompanied by a young woman.

Then the person I was with came back and he told me that the woman who I saw seated with another young woman is the mother of the woman who has the money. He wanted to introduce her to me. I said no problem. When he did, she completely ignored him, and she looked the other way. The young woman who was with the woman was so embarrassed that she hurriedly greeted me. We left without her saying a word to us. Hey, she came from New York, and she surely heard all the bad rumors about me.

On **Wednesday, January 31, 2018,** at approximately 6:03 pm, while I was working out, I saw a white or grey suburban vehicle parked in front of me. In the driver's side, there was a white man wearing dark glasses, and he was wearing like a white shirt. Why do those who do undercover work like to wear black glasses? In addition, I noticed that there was a triangle on the front plate. If you read the book, I wrote titled, "The 777" by Emmanuel, you will read that in one of my dreams I dreamt that I had three triangles in two of my fingers. The following continues. See the picture below.

On **Sunday, February 4, 2018,** I was in the kitchen with two kids, one is like 12 years old, and the other one is like 14 years old, and there was the 35 years old man too. The 14 years old kid said," … the least you suspect is a thief," and as soon as he said that the 12 years old kid moved his lips back and forward to point at me, and when he saw that I noticed that he was doing that, he said that the 35 years old man is the one. The 35 years old man replied, "What are you insinuating?"

Later that night, I was talking to the 35 years old man and in the middle of our conversation I told him that the bad things he does in his town, not to do them here. He asked me why I said that, but I managed to deviate the conversation. In the morning, I saw him again, but it wasn't until we went out together that he asked me why I had said that last night. He said that he couldn't stop thinking about its last night. If I had seen him doing something wrong. I said to him, "Now you see how it feels." He told me that there are people who see someone doing something wrong but don't tell him or her about it. Instead, those people go and tell others about it, rather than confront the person who did it, which is wrong. If he would have been a police officer, and would have said such a thing, he would have been sent to a psych unit for evaluation.

Later, before going to the gym, I took the black folder that I always carry around containing this diary, took out my diary, and I replaced it with copied pages of the popular novel titled, "The Best of Me." Then I took the black folder and placed it on the dining room table and then I went to the gym. When I returned, immediately I was told by the house's female employee that I left my black folder on the table. I did it on purpose because I know well that they are wondering what I have inside my black folder. Now they are not going to be so intrigued to know. This is temporary useful information for my followers. I know that whoever submitted this information will be one way or the other rewarded or compensated for it.

The next morning, I saw the cat of the house playing with a mouth and later kill it. As I observed the two of them, I realized that I am the mouse, and they are the cat.

On **Tuesday, February 6, 2018,** I went to the gym. There I was on the pedal exercise bike machine when there I saw two young black American man. One of them was seated on the machine that was next to me to my right. He had a camo hat, and he wore tattoos on his body. You know what I mean. Very few people in the Dominican Republic have tattoos and one of the motives is that it is expensive or many just don't like them. But in New York, it is a fashion. So here we go again.

On **Wednesday, February 7, 2018,** I went to the kitchen and there I saw the 35 years old man talking to the woman who cooks and as soon as they saw me, they stopped talking. Later at night, the 35 years old man told the female employee that he needed to tell her something, but she said, "Not now because Emmanuel is in the kitchen." I heard that loud and clear. Again, later that night, the 35 years old man went silently to where I was seated typing this, and before he got close to see what I was doing, I grabbed and closed my black folder, and changed the tablet's monitor screen from Microsoft word, to an electronic bible, so he may see that I was just reading the bible. Then in front of him I opened the black folder, and I took out copies from the book, "The Best of Me." I asked him where I could make copies of it, and he became very excited. He told me that he knows well where to make them, and that we could go there in the morning.

The next day, on **Thursday, February 8, 2018**, I was on the second-floor typing, and the 35 years old man silently approached me from behind, again, but I turned before he got to see what I was doing. When I faced him, he told me that he wanted to show me something, while looking behind me, at my tablet, wondering what I was doing. I followed him to the first floor and into the kitchen, and there was the female employee standing with the woman that cooks, and she was looking at us as we walked away.

He showed me what he wanted me to see, and he reminded me of the copies that I wanted to make, and like fifteen seconds later, I decided to go back, and as I was walking away, he was still talking to me as to prevent me from going back. As soon as I went to the kitchen, I didn't see the female employee there, only the woman that cooks. As I was heading to the second floor, the woman that cooks, began to tell me something as to prevent me from going to the second floor. But at the same time, she was trying to alert the female employee that I was around and, on my way, there. When I was about to take the stair up, I saw the female employee coming down the stairs, and she was staring at me as she was coming down, and as she did, I was staring at her as well, as I began to walk up the stairs.

They so badly want to know what I am doing. During the day and during the night, the 35 years old man reminded me two more times about the copies that I want to make of those pages.

On **Saturday, February 10, 2018,** I went out to eat pizza at Pizza Hut with my dear cousin C.... On our way there, and when returning home in his car, he told me how people who commit crimes, for example thieves, behave in a certain way and that based on their behavior we can determine that they have committed the crime.

But I told him that it wasn't always the case. I told him that we are spiritual beings that can sense when there is something wrong. For example, a person can be eating an ice cream cone, and many times when the ice cream falls, it is because there was somebody staring at you eating it. There are times when one senses that somebody is looking at you and you turn around and look directly at the eyes of the person that was looking at you. Also, when you see a person yawn, you tend to yawn also. How many times have we told someone that we had the same thought, or that I was about to tell you the same thing, or that you took the word from my mouth, and the list goes on.

465

I told him that a person that is very spiritual can sense when he is in trouble and may act accordingly, and that the psychologist might give it a name, because they don't know that it is something spiritual. And my cousin said, "...they may say that the person is schizophrenic...." There I realized that he is already informed of my situation. Also, we spoke about a person we know, and he told me that he is not to be trusted because of the way he looks at us. How he doesn't make eyes contact as he speaks, and how he lowers his face or head down and then looks up at one while talking.

I told him that I was able to notice the same behavior coming from my ex-supervisor (Lt. Yaguchi) at work that when I kept making eyes contact with him, he couldn't keep his eyes looking at me, and how he most of the time that he communicated with me, he had his face down while looking up at me. But then he said something that sounded like a confession. Right after I told him about my ex-supervisor's behavior, he told me that there are people who little by little inserts the knife (stab) on your back and try to record you to get something to later cut your head off. Yes, he knows.

On **Sunday, February 11, 2018,** at exactly 8:45 am, the 35 years old man approached me, and he showed me a number on his cellular. It began with area code (646 ... ...) and he asked me from where this phone number was. I told him that it was from New York. Isn't this funny?

On **Monday, February 12, 2018,** I was showing a video that I recorded to the 35 years man of the dog of the house who did something, and after he watched the video, he told me, "I believe you, because you showed me the video." What did he mean by saying that? That I am a liar?

On **Wednesday, February 14, 2018,** I went out of the house with the 35 years man, and in front of the house there were many chickens. He told me that someone who had driven by a truck dropped the chickens there without knowing and left. He told me that somebody had told him to take them. I told him that he is not a thief to take them, and that the person who suggested that he should take them is truly a thief for taking what doesn't belong to him. I knew that this was just another test. Good healthy-looking chickens in front of one's house, where do you see that? Then on the same street half a block away, there were loose horses. I believe that the horses and the chickens were intentionally planted there to see if I was going to take them.

Also, on **Thursday, February 22, 2018,** the 35 years man was wearing a red long sleeves shirt and a brand-new hat that said, "NY".

Tuesday, February 27, 2018, has been the most painful day in my entire life. Never have I felt so much pain. It was indescribable. It was the day of the Independence Day in the Dominican Republic. In the morning, my 42 years old great cousin C…, felt a massive amount of pain in his chest, and he called his other cousin to take him to the hospital. On the same morning, I was told that he was in the hospital. I hurried and got dressed to go out and see him. Until I heard a loud scream coming from his house, which I heard in my house. Immediately, I stopped everything that I was doing and slowly headed to his house.

As I walked there, I saw a neighbor walking out of C…'s house. I asked her, "What happened?" She told me that he died. As I type this tear accumulates on my eyes and drops. My great good, best cousin C… has passed away.

His uncle had died on the same month and day of the Independence Day of the Dominican Republic. C… was considered a hero in his community. His departure broke my heart and the heart of many others. The day before, I saw him on the ceiling of his house fixing it. The next day he died of a massive heart attack. It was said that days before, he was vomiting blood, but that he had told the people whom he saw not to tell anyone. Many said that he had terminal cancer besides having heart problems. He refused to take medications and refused to see his family suffer for his condition, therefore, he bears it alone, he didn't let anyone know of his suffering. He kept it to himself until his death. What a brave soul. I salute you C…. May the lord have you in his glory my good, best man. I know where you are, it has already revealed to you who I am, and I am glad to know that you do.

467

Since the death of my cousin C…, I stopped typing. I was crying every day and every night. From my house, I could see his house. Having him so close to me, he didn't tell me anything. Having him so close to me, I was helpless. Having gone to Pizza Hut with him, he was so happy. The last time I saw him; he was on top of his house fixing his ceiling. I am sorry, but I just can't keep typing about him, because it hurts. I am too silencing my pain, and I hope not to die from it. But by typing my suffering has helped me cope with it.

But what truly hurt me, indeed my brothers and sisters, is that I thought that he too was following me, because one day I saw him wearing a red shirt. Therefore, I maintained a certain distance from him. If it had been the case, I would have spent more time with him and the outcome would have been different. Thank you, New York City, for putting a weight on me that I don't deserve, and for putting a barrier between me and my cousin C…, at a time when he needed me the most. To know that I didn't reach out to him the way that I wanted to because of the red sign, is truly painful.

On **February 28, 2018, on** my way back from the Microsoft store, on the street, I began yelling and cursing. I entered the train and there I continued yelling and stating how disgusted I felt at their action of stealing from me, and how it wanted to make me vomit. Someone who was seating on the train gave a nasty look and I walked to him, and I stood in front of him. We stared at each other straight on the eye for over five minutes until he surrendered.

On **Saturday, March 31, 2018,** at 8:45 pm, the 35 years man told me that today he met friends that he had not seen for fifteen years, and that he saw them today. They are from New York. Is this a mere coincidence? Today marks my 76th days in the Dominican Republic. Two and a half months. I am afraid to return. If it wasn't because of my wife, I don't know for how long I would remain here. Again, I am afraid to go back to New York.

On **Thursday, April 5, 2018,** after six days without visiting the gym, I finally went. I think he is the owner of the gym, didn't greet me when he saw me. He looked the other way. He made an above face. As I was working out, the music in the gym was very loud. I asked the person in charge if she could lower the music because it sounded like a disco in there. She agreed to lower it. When I began to work out again, she raised the volume even higher, and she played disco music. She did it on purpose.

When I went into the aerobic room where the music was not so loud, there were three women close to the corner where I always do my work out. They began talking and one of them said that she had no problem working, because she didn't want to be a parasite who does nothing. When I went to use the other machine, I decided to take pictures of those who joined the list of followers. Almost all the time that I have been in the gym, I have seen the same man with the blue tank top, seated waiting not inside the gym, but outside where the woman in charge always is. But today I saw him working out there. He was accompanied by a young man wearing

a red short, as you can see below.

Also, there was a woman waking close to him who had a tattoo on her thigh. Also, he has a tattoo on his right arm that has a triangle and an eye in the certain (The All-Seeing Eye). See the picture below.

Later came another young woman in a luxurious suburban and she walked into the gym. She had tattoos on her arm as well.

When leaving the gym, I saw that the man with the blue tank top, and the woman with the tattoo on her arm, were together talking to the woman in charge of the gym. They were having a little meeting, and it explained why the woman in charge of the gym, raised the volume when I told her to please lower it. Before leaving, I told them, "What a good overtime. From New York to the Dominican Republic. Who are paying you?" and I walked away.

When I arrived home, hours later, a blackout occurred at 10:03 pm. It had never happened at this time of the hour, because it always comes at 10:03 pm. I told the 35 years man that it happened because of what I told to those who are following me. It came back at 11:35 pm. It is very strange. Later, when I woke up, the blackout was still going on. It is 11:20 am and nothing yet. It seems that they don't want me to have electrical service so I may return to New York sooner. Right now, my tablet's battery life is 62% and my smartphone is on 13%. They really want to get on my nerves. But later I found out that something had happened to an electric transformer, which caused the blackout. I suspect of anything now.

On **Wednesday, April 11, 2018,** I went to the Associacion Cibao bank in the Dominican Republic. As I was talking to one of the representatives by the name of Julissa regarding a loan, she told me that since I was disabled…, and I said to her that I never told her that I was disabled, and she said that she thought I had told her that.

First, ordinary disability and the disability that impairs you working are two different things. At that moment, I realized that she already knew everything about me. The news spreads so fast. At that moment I cut short our conversation, and l left knowing that everybody knows me, and I walked away disappointed at the system.

Chapter 27

Back to New York

On **Friday, April 13, 2018,** I was on my way to Santiago airport for it was the day of my departure from the Dominican Republic to New York. One of the workers there, when she looked at my passport, she placed a red sticker at the back of my passport that said, "Delta Security," and let me walk away.

When I showed my passport to the other women in immigration whose last name was Hernandez, she told me to go to a small room. There I was seen by another woman who said that she had to investigate me, because there was another man who had the same first name and last name that I have and that the person had an "Impedimento de Salida," a travel impediment, meaning that he was being forbidden to travel. After a long waiting period there, when I had to call my mother for information, and thinking that I was going to miss the flight, she found out that it wasn't me, and she let me go.

When I went through security that they checked me, I went upstairs, and I waited there until they began to take people into the plane. I went to use the bathroom and when I was using the toilet, I heard on the speaker that they were calling out many names and among them was my name. I finished what I was doing and headed there. When I got there, I told the woman that they had called me and she asked me," Are you Emmanuel?" I told her that I was. But my question is, how did she know who I was when she had called many names?

Later, the woman next to her looked at the red sticker behind my passport and she told me that I had to go back down and see security again so they may put a stamp on the piece of paper I had. I did go back downstairs and when I explained to the security guy that I had to see him because of the red sticker on my passport, and for the piece of paper to be stamped, he asked me, "Why did she sent you here?" as if there were no reason to do so, and I told him, "She is just being capricious." He grabbed something and he passed it through my hand and my clothing and then he placed it on a machine, to see if it comes positive for drug, cocaine. I was negative and I was allowed to board the plane.

My flight was DL 382. This was my day at the airport. This is the first time that I have been treated like this at an airport. Finally, when I arrived at New York, where I took an Uber, the driver gave me a look as if he hated me, and he only said like four words throughout the trip.

On **Saturday, April 14, 2018,** I went to BJs and at 1:14 pm a guy who was with a woman was acting as if he were mentally impaired, but then he stopped behaving like that. I guess you know why he acted that way.

On **Sunday, April 15, 2018,** I took the train to Brooklyn, and as I was seating, to my left, there were two individuals talking and one of them said that the person who she knew went to see a psychiatrist. Isn't this a mere coincidence or are they mocking me?

When I took the A train back to Manhattan from Brooklyn Tabernacle church, a woman entered with two of her daughters. One of them sat down and the other looked desperate for a seat. I stood up and told her to take mines. She thought of taking it, but her mother told her to take it. When she sat down, she told her daughter something and being half a feet away from me, and in front of me, she told her, "…because of my Mental Health…."

On **Tuesday, April 17, 2018,** at 11:27 am I received the following voice message, "For you there, there is a lawsuit has been filed against you and on available risk a warrant has been issued on your name by the Internal Revenue Service. So, before we move forward with the lawsuit, call us back as soon as possible on the number 509-203-4850 I repeat the number is 509-203-4850 thank you."

Isn't this great? Do they want me to lose my head?

On **Tuesday, April 17, 2018,** on the website BuzzFeed I read a list of NYPD police misconducts and in one of them was my former 25 precinct companion **PO Damien Banks** who on **1/24/2012** was found guilty of making **inaccurate statements in a supporting disposition** and of making **inaccurate statement in a supplemental fact sheet**.

The Department punished him by taking 30 vacation days away from him.

I would have wished they did the same thing with me at the time, if they considered that I did something wrong, which I didn't. But it wasn't my case. My punishment was far way worse. My punishment was and still is cruel and unusual. They went after my mind, my sanity, and by manipulating it, they destroyed my career, my mental health and my physical body. It has been worse than cruel and unusual punishment. It was simply, daily torture. No wonder why on this same day I watched on YouTube "**The video that will change your future**." Published on February 5, 2018, 7:16min.-8:00min. where Bishop TD Jakes said:

"…Neurologists tell us has so affected your frontal lope that your brain swells with stress taking away memory and functionality because your fight or flight instincts are activated by the negativity of the words that have been told to you that's why even when you are laying down at night, you can't rest cause your body is still playing repeat of a narrative of things that are not even there anymore, but your body's reacting because it is still going on in your head…"

This explains why my memory failed on **December 10, 2013**.

On **Wednesday, April 18, 2018,** I went to Retro fitness gym. At 5:30 pm when I went to the small dark room to work out this is what I found on the movie screen:

The movie of 'Scarface". Within the 25 minutes that I ran, they showed the scene where a cop was talking to Scarface about the Supreme Court's decision that a man's privacy can be violated. And as you can see above, the scene where the filthy corrupt cop was being shot. Isn't this funny that on my first day back at the gym they had me watch that scene.

As I was heading to the exit door, the aerobic room was full of people working out following their instructor. Suddenly, all of them faced me, their instructor solute me and so did his students as I was leaving. I didn't know where to hide my face.

On **Thursday, April 19, 2018,** I went to see my psychiatrist, and at 11:52 am, I was waiting to see her. The woman that was seating next to me, who was going to see a regular doctor said, "Everywhere there is a crazy man now." How did she know that I was going to see the psychiatrist? But before her saying that, the people in the waiting room didn't stop talking about people that are crazy. In the few minutes that I waited there, I heard the word, "crazy" like ten times.

When I arrived home, the brother of my wife sent a funny video to my wife about two crazy man that were admitted in a mental institution or psych ward and they say, "… Many say yes, many say no, but for me yes…" for the answers that the two crazy men gave to the psychiatrist. Then a co-worker of hers sent her the same video. Is it just a coincidence?

On **Friday, April 20, 2018,** I went to the gym. Again, I entered the small dark room where they had the big movie screen. As soon as I got in, the movie started. It was the "Bad Boys" movie. In the movie they also sang the song, "Bad boys, bad boys what you goanna do, when they come for you." A movie about good cops, and bad, corrupt cops or ex-cops. Isn't this quite a coincidence for them to be giving another cop movie? See the picture below.

Then when I went to work out at the corner of the gym where I always go, there I saw through the glass wall a NYPD vehicle parked for a while as I did my workout. Look at the picture below.

I spent like approximately an hour and a half in the gym, and during the time that I was there, I heard the word 'crazy' like five time.

At 5:55 pm I entered Rite Aid, and I began to look for scissors, and as I was looking, immediately a man who was wearing a grey hoodie sweater and who had his head covered with the hoodie got close to me. I was on the woman area looking for the scissors. What was he doing there? The security guard came close to me, and I asked him about the scissors. The man with the hoodie began to have a conversation with the security guard, and in the approximately 20 seconds conversation that he had with the security guard, he mentioned the word 'crazy' four times. Then, knowing not what else to do, he stood by the cashier with no legitimate purpose. As you can see in the picture below, he was just standing there.

On **Saturday, April 21, 2018,** at 7:50 am my wife arrived from work. She told me that today a CNA (Certified Nurse Assistant) at work told her that she needed to find a good hardworking man. Not a man who does nothing. Not a sh..t eater man that expects her to do everything. She said that she needs no find a hardworking man like herself who is a woman of iron. For her not to allow such a man to take advantage of her. Then my wife said, "Wow, she spoke as if she knew my whole life." If my wife knew that it was not just her who knew our life, but all of them.

Later, at 10:02 am I received a call from 202-622-5059 where the machine said that I am being accused of tax evasion. The machine said that, but when I called back a man picked up the phone, and when I said hi, he hanged the phone. I called back again and nobody answered. They are so hungry to charge me with something, because for them I am such a high-value target, but since they can't find anything, at least they want to play with my mind. Then I received a missed call at 12:04 pm from phone number (212) 244-6058, and when I called back, the machine said that the number that I dialed was not in service. They want to intimidate me more than I already am.

Today I read the New York Daily News, and I learned that another NYPD officer took his own life. So far this year, four NYPD officers have committed suicide.

On **Sunday, April 22, 2018,** I received a WhatsApp video sent to me by the church guy. It is a video where a woman or a man is acting crazy in church.

(BLANK IT NOT TO VIOLATE COPYRIGHT)

When I tapped at the link, it showed a person's comment in regard to the video. As you can see on the picture below, the person's comment which is in Spanish contain the word 'crazy' two times, and 'craziness' one time. They do want me to go crazy.

(BLANK IT NOT TO VIOLATE COPYRIGHT)

On **Monday, April 23, 2018,** I went to the gym. In the gym, as I went to use one of the works out machine, a woman walked by me and she said the word 'crazy.' After I finished my work out in that machine, at 5: … pm, I went to the dark room to run, and there I noticed that the first machine was being used by a young woman, the second one was empty, the third one was used by another young woman, and the fourth one was being used by another woman. I went to use the second machine. I stood there but the machine wasn't working. When the young woman on the third machine saw that mines wasn't working, she stopped working out, came off the machine, and she stood in front of the fourth machine to talk to her friend. Her friend was just walking slowly on the machine as she was talking to her.

They spent approximately sixteen minutes talking, and all their talking had to do with me. I was listening to a video on YouTube, but I managed to listen to some points they made as they spoke. They mentioned the words, 'crazy' and 'lies and the most absurd thing she said was when she mentioned someone who had come out of a 'mental institution'. Sixteen minutes of poisonous talking. They were spitting venom out of their mouth to affect my emotion or to see how I was going to respond. When they were leaving, they gave a high five to each other.

Later, I went to work out at the corner where I always finish my workout. There I saw the man that I saw the last time that I went to the gym. He was training two women at my spot. He mentioned the word 'crazy', and he told the woman, "Three weeks in the Dominican Republic...are you from Santiago?" and the woman said that she is. Bingo, I spent three months in the Dominican Republic, and I was in Santiago, what other proof do I need that they were talking about me. In addition, as he did the throat sound, a second later she did the same throat sound. This happened on two occasions. What do they want from me?

When I was walking home, a guy passing by me said, "If you don't want to work, that is not the right place to be."

Today, **Wednesday, April 25, 2018,** I prepared to go to the gym. At 3:56 pm I walked out of the building and entered the grocery store. As soon as I entered the grocery store, two persons that work there played out loud the same video of the two crazy man that was sent to my wife on April 19, which I explained above. I told them that I saw that video too. I said that it was very funny. The employee then repeated the same exact words to me that are said on the video by the two crazy man, "...Many say yes, many say no, but for me yes."

At 4:26 pm, as I began to work out, in the gym they played a music where the word 'crazy' is mentioned many times and it went like this, "...go crazy, go crazy...go crazy, crazy, go crazy..." Then on my way to the dark room, I heard the word 'crazy' like two times by a man and a woman who were working out. One of the women said, "...and he is so young..." On my way home, going up the steps of stairs that lead to another avenue, I saw my old friend and his brother. What a coincidence. Later, as I was walking home, I saw a guy and as he walked past me, he said, "Hey crazy."

All I just wanted was to go to the gym, and all of this happened. If I say something about it, there is the possibility that they will send me to a mental institution or a psych ward again. If I tell my psychiatrist this, she will absolutely raise the doses of my medication to higher milligrams.

It seems that they had forgotten that they were the ones responsible for the day that I was sent to a mental institution or psych ward for two weeks, and they didn't do anything to prevent me from going there. But they continue doing it. What do they want with me?

The harassment continued today **Friday, April 27, 2018**. At 4:47 pm, I went to the dark room and when I was preparing to run, I looked at the movie screen and they were showing a movie with actor Will Smith. He was seating down with a woman talking about IRS (Internal Revenue Service) and how IRS was going after her, and that he worked for IRS etc. You can see the picture. Are you kidding me? First, the terrorizing phone call telling me that IRS was coming after me, and now they have me watch this movie?

At 5:13 pm I went to the corner where I always go to finish my work out. Suddenly, a young woman came to where I was working out, with a pink speaker, she laid it on the floor, and she played a song that goes, "...you make me 'crazy'...." and she sang along the song.

At 5:23 pm, I was in the locker room when a young man mentioned the word 'crazy' as he was talking on the phone. At 5:25 pm,

when leaving the locker room, the same young man mentioned the word 'crazy' again. Walking out of the gym another man yelled out the word 'crazy'.

At 5:30 pm, I went to see my old friend whose brother has a grocery store at 166 or 167 street and Anderson, and when I entered, his brother had two orange prescription drug bottles that are used for prescribed medications, and he was tapping one on the other one as for me to see. I asked him for his brother, and he said, "That crazy, he is not here."

I just spent two hours outside, and this is what I encountered. They don't care for my well-being, and they don't consider the fact that I am drinking two high blood medications and an antipsychotic drug because of them. What they are doing to me is making my condition worse. Who can put an end to this? Who?

On **Saturday, April 28, 2018,** at 10:50 am, I entered a pharmacy at 905 Gerard, and the woman that was working in the pharmacy told the other pharmacy staff to listen to the music. She told him that three times. Then she grabbed the remote control to raise the volume of the music that was being played. It was the same song that the woman at the gym played on the speaker when I was working out, which lyric says, "...you make me 'crazy'..."

On **Sunday, April 29, 2018,** on my way to church, I took an UBER cab and the two women at the back began talking about working.

At 11:24 am the driver began talking about work too on his smartphone and he said, "I will leave nothing to my children, tell them to go to work."

In church, when I was at the Bible study class, the man teaching the class stopped reading on 2 Corinthians 5:7 that says "For we walk by faith, not by sight," and when he read it, he said that he has been saying many times the things that he is about to say, but that he was going to repeat it again **"… we need to work…if you are healthy and there is no disability in you, you must work, and stop being a burden to the system,"** he said. He continued talking about people needing to work, but someone behind me said that the bible was referring to the spiritual, and not on the physical work. The teacher, without words to say, returned to the topic. The word 'work' was mentioned over ten times during the hour and a half that I was there.

Later, I went to the devotional and at 2:23 pm, and the woman that was preaching said, "… and they thought that I was crazy, and they said poor her, she became crazy, after being proud and so many vanities she became crazy…" She also said that she had two months without sleeping. There is no doubt that they were referring to me when they mentioned 'work', 'crazy' and the sleepless hours.

This is the support that I find in church. None of them reached out to me when I needed them the most. They keep pressing their fingers on my open wound. Where is the love that Jesus taught? Instead of healing the broken, they judge the broken. Aren't already enough people pushing me down? Then at home I hear my wife say, "A lazy guy on the house,'"" "A parasite in the house," "I am tired of seeing you seven days a week seating there writing. You are going to repent, you will see."

On **Monday, April 30, 2018,** I went to the gym to ease my emotional pain. When I went to the dark room to do my running, a man in his 70s dressed in casual attires entered the dark room, looked at me, then looked at the movie screen like for two seconds and then he left. I went to the bathroom and there he was. When I finished my work out at 5:57 pm, at the exit door, there he was seating, staring at me as I left. He looked like the person who works for the NYPD's Medical Board who found me not fit to be a police officer. Wow, they really don't know what to do with me. But I must be strong.

On **Monday, May 7, 2018,** I went to the gym, and there I saw the same old man that I saw the last time. He was not wearing gym clothes; he was just sitting there. He seemed to be there to check on me. Then as I was using one of the machines, I lifted my head up and smiled at them nonstop to hide my hurt. So, they won't think that they have defeated me. Because what they expect of me is to overreact, they can then send me to a psych ward again, yes again, the same way that they did on **January 21, 2015**.

Then at 6:57 pm I went to the same corner that I always go to do my final work out and there I found a woman working out. It was just me and her there when she said, "Stupid shit." She couldn't keep it to herself. Also, she had a red pen on the floor to let me know what was going on.

On **Wednesday, May 9, 2018,** I went to the gym, and when I entered the dark room, a movie was showing a psychopath, and the movie had to do with cops, court, the judge and the Assistant District Attorney. Here we go again. Moments later, a man wearing a black t-shirt went in. Then he went to the corner where I finished my workout to see what I was doing there. Then from a distance he began to look at me. It is the man on the picture below. As you can see, he is looking at me.

On **Wednesday, May 10, 2018,** I read a New York Daily News article by Shayna Jacobs titled, "Trial tale of drug cop's 'protection' brag"

about Police Officer Nysia Stroud that according to her attorney, "…the department's Internal Affairs Bureau followed Stroud for two years without finding dirt on her." Also, her lawyer stated that the officers, "'They fabricated the crime. Created the crime –a pretend crime.'"

This article confirms what they have been unjustly doing to me. My wife is now packing up to move with her mother, because she can't stand seeing me without working, but how can I look for a job when I am afraid of history to repeat itself, which part of it is repeating again already. She has already filed for divorce. Thank you, NYPD, thank you Manhattan District Attorney's office for all the things that you guys are doing to me.

On **Friday, May 11, 2018,** I went to the New York Philharmonic at 10 Lincoln Center Plaza, which is by 62nd street.

It is **Saturday, May 12, 2018**. It is 10:59 am, and my wife just calls me to tell me that she is scared for her life because an Emotionally Disturbed Person, a man with mental issues has approach her and he is talking strange things to her. She says that he is staring at her now. I tell her to record him, but she says, "So he may kill me!" She hung up the phone to call her mother. When she came home, she was feeling afraid, because that stranger approached her talking nonsense. She feared for her life. Also, this reminded me of the day that someone grabbed her butt.

She was angry at me because when she called me, I told her to record it. When she arrived home, she asked me why I told her to record it. **This is how far they are going, therefore, I must seek an attorney, for my life and the life of my loved ones is in danger. It is a duty, it is a must, it is my obligation to publish this diary and find myself an attorney. Nobody has read my diary, just me. Years ago, pastor Ni… asked me if I was going to bite the hand that give me food and such statement held me back from seeking justice, because I didn't want to be ungrateful. I have been loyal to my wife; I have been loyal to the NYPD and the community I served even though they mistreated me. But after what they did to my wife this morning, I must act now.**

Later, I went to the gym and right at the entrance, at 4:14 pm, one of the guys said, "… and they moved everyone to 62nd street…" Isn't this terrible? They know that I went to the New York Philharmonic yesterday, because it is by 62nd Street. When I was doing my running on the treadmill inside the dark room, after a while, one of the staff entered and he asked me if I wanted to watch something in particular. I told him that he could put anything, and he put Lethal Weapon 3, where there is a

crazy cop, and a cop that is about to retire.

As I walked to the locker room, I heard a man say, "She did a good job during those four years," and guess what? They have four years or more following me. But there is one thing I noticed, they haven't mentioned the word, "crazy" nor "lie" because they must have heard when I told my wife to record him. However, I heard a man say, "This sh…t is dead."

On **Tuesday, May 15, 2018,** I went to the Retro fitness gym. When I began using one of the machines, I noticed that I didn't have Wi-Fi, nor was I having signal on my smartphone. I went downstairs and I asked the person in charge if there was a problem with the WI-FI and he told me that their WI-FI was not good now. So, I went upstairs. It was 4:13 pm. I suspect that they don't want to give me access to Wi-Fi, so I won't listen to my YouTube videos and then be able to listen to what my followers say.

At 4:33 pm a woman and her friend began using the machine next to me to my right. They were talking about work. Later I went to the small dark room, and they were showing the ending of the Scarface movie. Then, at the end, the following remained on the screen.

As you can see, on the screen there are three lines of cocaine then to the right peels and a gun next to it. Earlier in the afternoon, I called my pharmacist to ask them if I could pick up my medication and the person that I spoke to said that I could pick it up in an hour. I went to the gym, and this is what I had to stare at as I did my running. And the end of the Scarface movie had to do with cocaine consumption.

Then I went to the locker room and two people entered and they began talking. "…because I suffer from that I am crazy." Then the other guy turned on a device he had, like a speaker and he began to play a merengue song that mentions the word 'crazy'. Then the man began to break his lock because he forgot where he dropped his key. Then he said, "… because I am crazy.", and he continued, "Yes, close the lock, I am crazy."

Later, I went to my corner where I always finish my work out, and there I found the same person that I saw looking at me the last time I went to the gym. And he was using the same position that I always take. Then they began mentioning the word 'crazy'. See the picture below.

Then I went to the locker room, and next to my locker I found this:

At approximately 5 minutes later, he showed up in the locker room.

I left and I walked up the stairs leading to the next avenue, Anderson Avenue and 167 Street. There I entered the grocery store and greeted my old friend, but he just said hi to me as he was staring at his phone. His brother did the same. I bought two oranges there and his brother refused to charge me for them. Probably he was doing the same thing that PO Rivera did to me every time that I offered him coffee, but he refused to have it, because he probably thought that my money was dirty. I greeted them joyfully and I told my old friend to stop being lazy and to begin to work out. I just made a joke, because I know that they believe that I am the lazy one, because I am not working. I had to defuse the situation. I had to show a happy face even though I am dying inside.

On **Wednesday, May 16, 2018,** I took UBER and the driver from 4.71 rating that I had, he gave me a very low rating, which lowered my rating to 4.67 I wonder why when I was on time, and I only greeted him.

I went to the bank and took out about $6500 dollars and then I went to the dentist. At the dentist, one of the patients there began talking about how she spent $6500 dollars fixing her teeth. It seems that they already know that I took that amount of money out of my bank account. When I walked out of the building, there was a man wearing red waiting outside.

Today, **Thursday, May 17, 2018,** I went to the gym and as I walked, I heard a man talking about stealing, and when I went to the dark room, in front of the machine that I used, there was a $1 dollar bill on the floor. Behind me was the guy that keeps following me in the gym, and to my left there was a young woman working out. Then the guy, at approximately 4:… pm, walked from behind me and he stood in front of the dollar bill as you can see below:

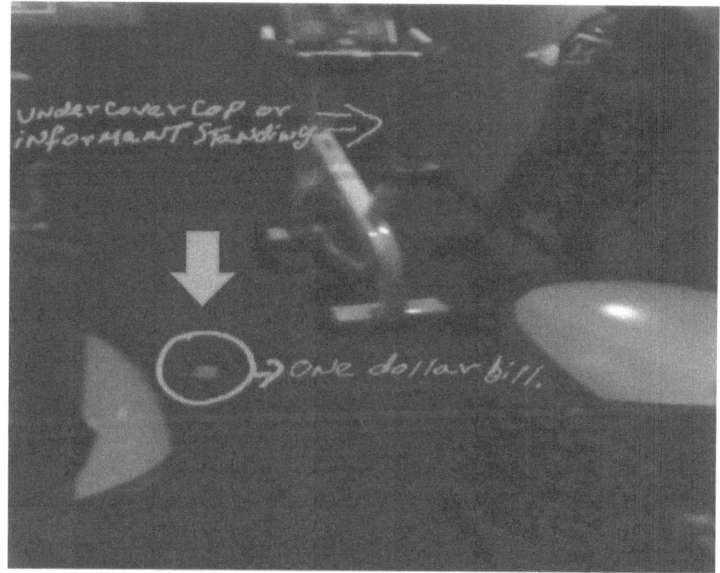

Then he stepped outside, and after a while the woman to my left, left the place and then returned and left again. And there was the dollar bill there. Then a young guy wearing red came in and he used the machine behind me. Later, I was by myself and then I left. As I was using the machine outside, I noticed how a white man entered the dark room and the woman that was to my left, returned to the dark room, and the guy too. It seemed that they had a small meeting there. Also, in front of the dark room was a white man working out and he was wearing red sneakers.

Then something very unusual happened. When I was using YouTube, some type of device tried to connect to my smartphone.

This never happened to me before. Then I heard the video that I was listening to on the gym's speaker where everyone heard what I was listening to. I was appalled. It happened at 5:30 pm.

Then I went to my corner where I saw a man that I met many years ago and he was talking to a woman and in their conversation, they spoke about work, pension, and mentioned the word, 'true' several times.

As I walked on the street, I heard a group of man talking about stealing. Then I went to visit my old friend at the grocery store and the person that was there told me that he had been arrested for violating an underage girl. Then my old friend came, and I made a joke by saying, "I knew it," and we both laughed. Then my old friend told me how a good man went to prison for fifteen years. It is ridiculous.

Within the time that I spent in the gym and with my old friend, I had to smile at them even though I was dying inside.

On **Friday, May 18, 2018,** I went to the pharmacy and on my way back, I heard people saying the "crazy" word more than five times. If I tell my wife, she will leave me. My next-door neighbors and my neighbor below my apartment will not definitely hear from me that I am being followed.

On **Saturday, May 19, 2018,** the guy doing the pullups saw me in the locker room and he just couldn't pretend that he was not looking for me. Then he went to do the pullups close to where I was. He had his legs covered by a camo outwear.

Then I looked outside the window, and I saw a vehicle with the NYPD parking plate on the windshield.

On **May 21, 2018,** I received four missed calls from no other than retired PO Freddy Ipince, who called just to know about me and to meet with me. Wow. The man who seems to have initiated again my persecution since the time that I was working in Viper, now wants to obtain some information from me.

On **Wednesday, May 23, 2018,** I went to the gym and the same happened. I was first working on a machine. Then I decided to walk to the dark room, and when I entered, I looked at the movie screen and

491

there I found out that the video that I was playing on YouTube on my smartphone at the moment, was being played on the movie screen of the dark room, as you can see below.

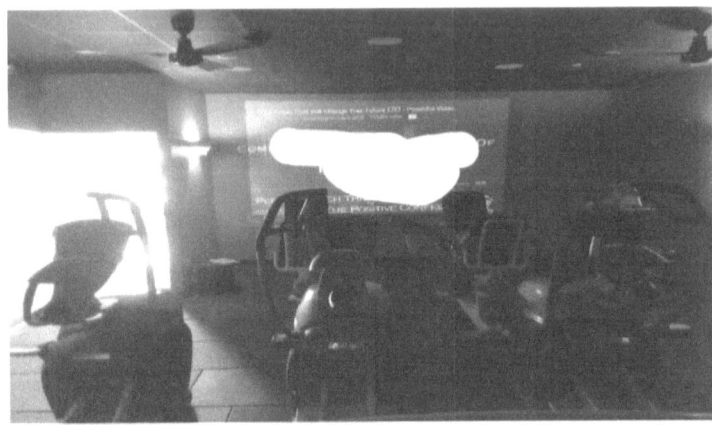

As you can see, the video was loading, and the same video was loading on my smartphone and on the same minutes and seconds. I took screenshots of my smartphone, and this is what I found.

(BLANK IT NOT TO VIOLATE COPYRIGHT)

It said that it was connected to (BD)J5100 which I cancelled right away. This means that everyone was watching what I was watching on my smartphone. There were two guys to my right using the treadmill and one to my left. Then two women came into the room, and two more, one was wearing a red t-shirt, and the other one a green t-shirt.

On **Thursday, May 24, 2018,** I met with retired PO Freddy Ipince in Central Park. He wanted to walk with me through the park. He wanted to exhibit me, as we walked, to everyone in the park, who were for sure, observing me. I had to be strong and not faint.

On **Wednesday, June 6, 2018,** I came out of my building, went to the grocery store and a block away from the grocery store, on my way to the gym, I saw a white man in business attire that as soon as he saw me, he looked the other way. When I walked next to him, I said, **"Nobody is above the law"** hoping that he heard it, and with this statement, I will end typing my daily agony, because if I continue doing so, I will go crazy, and the pages will go to the thousands.

On **Wednesday, June 13, 2018,** I rode my bicycle to the gym. I parked it in front of the gym. There I met a brother in Christ. When I came out of the gym, the front tire of my bicycle was flat. Right away I suspected that somebody did it. I went to a place near a gas station, and I put some air on my tire, which was enough to take me home. The next day in the morning, my tire was flat. I went outside to a nearby gas station and pumped some air in the tire and then headed to a bicycle shop. The person there told me that I needed a new tube for my tire. So, I had to pay for a new one.

Wow, I thought that I could end the typing with the above statement, but it doesn't end there. On **Saturday, June 16, 2018,** my wife received a voice message from a suspected thief at work. My wife took the opportunity to explain to me that at work they posted pictures on the third floor of two lockers with stolen items. Some employees have been stealing them. They are blaming one employee, but they are not letting the employee know that he is the suspect. The two lockers resonate with the two lockers I had at work. When I allowed Lt. Yaguchi to search my lockers. Also, one of my wife's co-workers said to my wife, "Your people (Dominicans) are thieves." I guess that we are going Back to the Past.

Chapter 28

I See No End to This PBA Visit

On **Friday, June 29, 2018,** I went to visit union (PBA) attorney Chris McGrath. At 2:48 pm I spoke with him for approximately 7 ½ minutes and I gave him a copy of the following letter, SIGNED AT THE BOTTOM.

Dear representative or member

I am writing this letter to inform you why I should be compensated to receive a ¾ pension.

I was a young healthy New York City police officer. I performed my duties with courtesy, professionalism and respect towards everyone that I came in contact with. I was never a disciplinary problem to the department. I was mentally and physically healthy and had not visited a doctor for years because I didn't need to. I was a healthy young man with a lot of goals and plans within the NYPD. But then the unexpected happened.

We all know that the job of a police officer can be stressful itself, but when more is asked than the job that is to be performed, and when internal and external factors begins to influence and to alter the officer's life, it can be destructive, and it was to the point that I burned out.

I was a police cadet for six years and then a police officer for many years. But after living a normal life as a police officer, all of the sudden, I began to receive Cruel and Unusual treatment unparalleled to any other ever received by a Uniform Member of the Service in the history of the NYPD. As a result, such treatments affected my physical and mental health to the point that I am still taking medication. Therefore; since the job was 100 percent responsible for all of my hardship, I am applying to receive a ¾ pension.

If you deem necessary, walk over the blue line of secrecy, or conduct your own investigation and you will be surprise that I am still alive today.

In the hostile work environment I was in, I endured ongoing harassment and retaliation. When I tried to look for remedy, the harassment intensified. All of them were united against one officer. Such malicious and malevolent treatment towards me was highly detrimental to my health and my well-being. I was and I am under a so strict and high level of scrutiny that is without precedent. It surpassed and surpasses the bar set for politicians, public officials, and the list goes on.

The horrendous harassment, the tension, and the stress was way beyond human capacity to the point that they disregarded my safety by putting me on harm's way. As a result, I feared and still fear for my own life and for the lives and safety of my love ones. All to obtain what purpose? Amusement? I know that what they did and still do to me was and still is arbitrary and capricious. I know that no other officer have gone thru the same series of extraordinary circumstances that they put me on and I know that it is without precedent. This is the situation where all odds are against one man.

The City, the NYPD, and the Manhattan District Attorney's office wronged me big time. Therefore, I should be compensated accordingly. So far nobody have come forward to claim responsibility for their actions or have come forward to apologize for their misdeeds and abuse of power.

Notary Publi   rk
No. 01RI0014211
Qualified
Commission

Dear representative or member

I am writing this letter to inform you why I should be compensated to receive a ¾ pension.

I was a young healthy New York City police officer. I performed my duties with courtesy, professionalism and respect towards everyone that I came in contact with. I was never a disciplinary problem to the department. I was mentally and physically healthy and had not visited a doctor for years because I didn't need to. I was a healthy young man with a lot of goals and plans within the NYPD. But then the unexpected happened.

We all know that the job of a police officer can be stressful itself, but when more is asked than the job that is to be performed, and when internal and external factors begins to influence and to alter the officer's life, it can be destructive, and it was to the point that I burned out.

I was a police cadet for six years and then a police officer for many years. But after living a normal life as a police officer, all of the sudden, I began to receive Cruel and Unusual treatment unparalleled to any other ever received by a Uniform Member of the Service in the history of the NYPD. As a result, such treatments affected my physical and mental health to the point that I am still taking medication. Therefore; since the job was 100 percent responsible for all of my hardship, I am applying to receive a ¾ pension.

If you deem necessary, walk over the blue line of secrecy, or conduct your own investigation and you will be surprise that I am still alive today.

In the hostile work environment I was in, I endured ongoing harassment and retaliation. When I tried to look for remedy, the harassment intensified. All of them were united against one officer. Such malicious and malevolent treatment towards me was highly detrimental to my health and my well-being. I was and I am under a so strict and high level of scrutiny that is without precedent. It surpassed and surpasses the bar set for politicians, public officials, and the list goes on.

In the hostile work environment I was in, I endured ongoing harassment and retaliation. When I tried to look for remedy, the harassment intensified. All of them were united against one officer. Such malicious and malevolent treatment towards me was highly detrimental to my health and my well-being. I was and I am under a so strict and high level of scrutiny that is without precedent. It surpassed and surpasses the bar set for politicians, public officials, and the list goes on.

The horrendous harassment, the tension, and the stress was way beyond human capacity to the point that they disregarded my safety by putting me on harm's way. As a result, I feared and still fear for my own life and for the lives and safety of my love ones. All to obtain what purpose? Amusement? I know that what they did and still do to me was and still is arbitrary and capricious. I know that no other officer have gone thru the same series of extraordinary circumstances that they put me on and I know that it is without precedent. This is the situation where all odds are against one man.

The City, the NYPD, and the Manhattan District Attorney's office wronged me big time. Therefore, I should be compensated accordingly. So far nobody have come forward to claim responsibility for their actions or have come forward to apologize for their misdeeds and abuse of power.

ate of New York

No.

Qualified in Westchester County

Com. Expires October 05, 20_8

He told me that there was nothing he could. That I didn't qualify for a ¾. When he finished reading the letter, he asked me, "What can I do for you?" At the end I told him that God is in control of everything and that I hope that the letter touch somebody's heart.

They have left me taking medications, suffering from high blood pressure, tinnitus on my ears, floaters on my eyes, swelling on my feet and legs feeling unwell. My sense of smell has diminished, and as a result I must touch the flowers and roses with my nose to smell them, and the floaters and the white moving dots on my eyes that prevent me from viewing and enjoy the clear blue beautiful sky. In addition, I have developed astigmatism, where I slightly see the letters double. Also, I am not producing as many saliva as I once did, which of course will affect my denture, and my ears are no longer producing wax, probably because of the tinnitus.

On **July 2, 2018,** I read an article on the New York Daily News titled, "Prosecutors need oversight now" by Nick Encalada-Malinowski and Roger Clark. It refers to the unlimited power the prosecutors must do what they please. The article states, "Currently in New York State there is no independent oversight body to investigate wrongdoing in the offices of local prosecutors, despite prosecutors having unparalleled authority and discretion in the criminal justice system and a growing list of people of color—almost all people of color—who have been exonerated after decades in prison due to misconduct on the part of either prosecutors or police."

No wonder they are so bold about doing what they did and are still doing it to me. Because there is no limit on what they can do to me.

On **Monday, July 2, 2018,** I was riding my bicycle to the gym, but when I was at 1105 Jerome Avenue, I heard a strange sound and air was coming out of my back tire. My back tire was flat. I went to the gym, parked the bicycle in front of the gym and I took the tire out. I ordered an UBER, and I took the tire to the bicycle shop. There the person told me that I had to change the tube and the tire. When I took a close look at my tire, I found out that it was knifed twice.

When I returned to the gym, that I was putting my tire on my bicycle, there was in front of me a car parked that had an NYPD plate on the windshield. There was a person inside. I knocked on his window and when he opened the door of his car to talk to me, and I told him, "IAB" and he said, "Hi". I explained to him what happened to my tire. He told me that he cannot wait to retire and move out of the city. In a few words, he was advising me what I should do.

I did my work out, and I explained to the people in the locker room that what was done to my bicycle was a crime. Then went to the 44th precinct to report it. PO Ruso told me that it wasn't enough to make a report. I went home having the tube of my bicycle hanging on my neck as I was holding my damaged tire with my left hand as I was riding my bicycle. I did it on purpose, because I wanted to show everyone how far they have gone. At home I took the following picture of my tire.

They did it to two of my tires, next time, who is going to be? Me? It is no coincidence that all of this began within the week that I began using my bicycle. It reflects people's sentiment towards me. I was so upset that I had planned to go to court the next day with my damaged tire, and see ADA (Assistant District Attorney) Altman and ask her as I show her my damage tire, the same unforgettable question she asked me on December 10, 2013 when I finished testifying, "Do you want to tell me something?" And ask her the same question she asked me the following day, "Are you glad?" Then I was thinking of leaving her office expecting an answer from her, and then asked to speak with her supervisor, which PO Gloria Byrd once advised me to do, but I was too afraid. And finally demand an answer. But I didn't dare.

Days later, I began to ride my bicycle again, and when I entered the gym, I told the gym staff that I expected them to keep an eye on my bike, having in mind that they realized what I meant by that. When I was leaving, I explained to one of the employees there what happened to my bicycle.

On July 8, 2018, I read an article titled, "If job stress is killing you, it's time to leave," by Virginia Backitis. She said, "It may sound a bit dramatic, but Jeffery Pfeffer, a Stanford professor and author of **"Dying for a Paycheck" (Harper Business), says that toxic workplace prac**tices — micromanagement, fear of layoffs, long or unpredictable working hours and making people feel as if they are not good enough — is the fifth leading cause of death, in front of Alzheimer's and kidney disease.

"'People stay in jobs that are unhealthy for them, which cause stress.,'" he says. "'That often leads to smoking, drinking, overeating, not sleeping and dying.'"

Today, **Wednesday, July 11, 2018,** I went downtown a few blocks away from the courthouse in Manhattan where ADA Altman's office is. There I ate two pizzas and then I went for a walk by the courthouse, and across the street from the court where ADA Altman's office is, there I sat for a few minutes. I was tempted to pay her a visit, but I didn't. I was there because the city was going to auction an empty lot, but it was cancelled because it appeared that the city decided to do something unfavorable to me. An outcome that I didn't want, and I wonder if it was the city's purpose to have it cancelled. Probably so the theft could expand more, and so that they won't have to pay me much if I sue them. No wonder why the Corporation Counsel of the City of New York was notified.

On **Friday, July 13, 2018,** I looked at my publisher's Portal to view my book information before it gets print out and then be ready to be published. I used my smartphone Wi-Fi to do it on my tablet. When I did so, I noticed a commotion from my neighbor's apartment, apartment # 63. There was someone reacting to it.

On **Saturday, July 14, 2018,** I went to the gym Retro fitness, and as soon as I went to scan my card in, I heard a guy talking to the employee there and I heard him say, "The Wi-Fi, and he was like where is my body?" and what he said is on my book. They were talking about my book. They stole my file.

Then a man got into a conversation with me, and we spoke for many minutes. But then he told me that if they can't get through to me, they will try to get through me by my family.

On **Sunday, July 15, 2018,** I went to church, and they discussed some points that were in my book. On my book, I decided to use a mononym name by just using my first name on the book, because I didn't want the public to know who the writer was, that's how I value my privacy. And now they did this to me? How should I feel?

On **Monday, July 16, 2018,** I couldn't stop thinking about it to the point that I couldn't remain steady. So, I grabbed my slashed tire and headed to the Manhattan District Attorney's office. On my way there, I was exhibiting my knifed tire to everyone as I walked there. When I entered the building, I was questioned by an NYPD officer and his Sergeant for my reason to be there. I told them that I wanted to talk to the ADA's (Assistant District Attorney) supervisor about my knifed tire or to talk to any ADA. The Sergeant told me that I couldn't, unless I had an appointment. I walked away. I didn't know whether to thank him or not for not allowing me in. Probably he prevented me from doing stupidity, because I was ready to vomit out many things, especially to discuss my hacked and wiretapped smartphone, and hacked tablet, from where they stole my file.

So, I walked away and sat on the stairwell of the District Attorney's office, at the entrance of the building, holding my tire. Suddenly, I black man wearing a camo pant stood to my right and he began to take pictures of me with his professional camera.

As I walked to take the train, I heard a man say, "All that energy. He is lit." I don't know what he meant by that. Then I met with my wife to go and see an eye doctor. When we were in front of the building, there was a man talking about what I saw in my book.

When I returned home, I grabbed a white t-shirt and I wrote on the back of it, "High Value Target". I put it on and then went to the gym. When I arrived, the one in charge there said, "What are you doing here?" but she was not looking at me when she said so.

Also, today I texted my book publisher about what happened and a copy of what one of my printed b

ooks says which is the following:

Her response was that it needs to be reported by me to the authorities because I am the author. And when I was going to shut down the computer, the following happened:

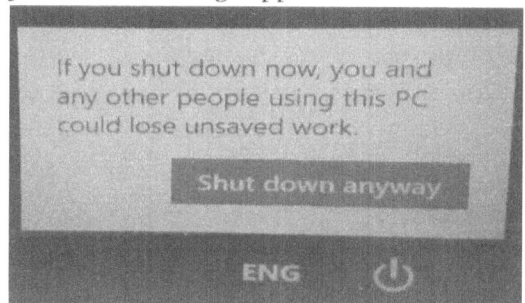

What are other people? Also, three days later, I found this on my smartphone screen: (HAD TO DELETE IMAGE DUE TO COPYRIGHT RESTRICTION)

Chapter 25

On **Wednesday, July 18, 2017**, I went to the gym. There I did my work out all the way, smiling. If they knew that when they saw a smiling face, it doesn't mean that he or she is smiling. I learned that back at the 25th precinct.

Back home, my wife told me to read her text message because she had done something to her eyes. When I looked at it, I had to take a picture of the text message

He spoke to her a long time ago and now he is texting her this. This is because of the book I wrote in which the mysterious hacker made it public for everyone to see.

Amazing, they have even hired Hackers to come after me. This reminds me of the day when we were accused by Optimum of illegally downloading Game of

Thrones movie through the internet, which forced me to immediately finish my retirement papers. **(BLANK IT NOT TO VIOLATE COPYRIGHT)**

On **Thursday, July 19, 2018,** I went to visit my psychiatrist. I told her how my smartphone and tablet were hacked. When I went to make my appointment for another three months, one of the staff said that it was fast. I saw one of the staff there blowing on a pen that she was holding with both of her hands from one end to the other end. Her co-worker asked her for the sound that she was making by blowing on the pen, and I told her, "You seem to be playing the flute," and the three of them laughed. And the other one said, "No, the thing is that they didn't know that we were crazy before hiring us." I left smiling. Then as I was waiting for the elevator, I heard my psychiatrist say, "He knows."

Later at night, I told my wife about it, and she became upset. She told me that they were making fun of me. And the reason why she used the pen to do that was because in my book, which they stole, and hacked, I wrote about pens.

I went to a Mexican restaurant with my wife and her mom. There, I showed her a video from the New York Post where a man wearing red grabbed the butt of a woman and the woman grabbed him and threw him on a chair. When my wife looked at it, she said that it reminded her of the day the man grabbed her butt. I guess you still remember which day she is referring to.

Also, I want to emphasize something else. My wife and I are moving out. She is going somewhere, and I was searching for a room. The church guy learned about it, and suddenly, a position was offered to him to be the superintendent of a building. He asked me to lend him $3000, so he could have the position.

Days later, he went to see the apartment that was going to be given to him rent free and he told me that it has three bedrooms. Also, he told me that I could have one of the bedrooms and that I can live there for rent for free until I find a place of my own.

Today I went to visit the place for the second time. When I arrived at the building, I found a set of keys hanging at the entrance of one of the doors. I called the church guy and told him about the keys, and he told me not to worry about it. I told him to leave a note at the door, but he told me that the person would come to him and ask for the keys.

The apartment is big, it has birds, it has a playing pool, it has a big patio, two basketball baskets and it is not far from the gym. I helped him clean the place. Then he told me, "If feels like in the Dominican Republic here." In few words, they want to accommodate me, so I won't go back to the Dominican Republic. There is no doubt that they have cameras everywhere there. And about the key sets, they were trying to see if I was going to take them.

On **Sunday, July 22, 2018,** I went to visit my sister. My brother-in-law showed me a text message of the person who is working on buying the lot from the bank. He texted the following to my brother-in-law as the reason why the lot wasn't put on sale at the auction, "The process stopped the bank." So, it seems that they want the debt to keep on rising so they may hang me or drown me. This could be the reason why they might have hired this retired investigator, to delay, delay, delay the process so I may never come out of debt.

Today, **Friday, July 20, 2018**, I gave a call to my mother. As I spoke to her, I asked her about my father. She told me that the same National Police that always go to visit them there took my father for a ride. And that they have been doing that. No wonder why the man in the gym told me that if they cannot get to me thru me, they will get to me thru my family. No wonder why they didn't want food when my mother offered them food, she told me. Because what they want is information.

On **Tuesday, July 24, 2018** at around 9:... am, I was helping my wife move her belongings out of our apartment, and when I was by the elevator, a young black man came down the stairs wearing a red hat and as he was walking away, I heard him say loud enough, "They have to shut it down now."

Later, I went to the laundromat to wash my police uniforms to keep two of them for myself as a reminder and the rest to bring it to the precinct for officers to use, in addition; I cannot throw away the uniform in the garbage without taking away the patches.

So, I went to the precinct with the uniforms and some other police equipment to give it away there. When I arrived at the precinct, the PAA there was glad to see me. However, I didn't know Desk Sergeant. I explained to him the reason why I was there, and he told me not to leave the things that I brought there. To give it to some officer that I may know, but not to leave it there. There I saw Sergeant Jackson who was not happy to see me, but she greeted me with a serious face, and she couldn't talk to me because she was supposedly in a hurry. Then I saw another officer who greeted me with a serious face also. It was as if they had seen a ghost. But there was an old timer whom I love, and he has over 30 years of service in the police department.

Then as I was talking to the Desk Sergeant about what to do with the things I brought, that I told him that I didn't want to throw them in the garbage, he finally told me that I could leave them at the back, in the cell room where they kept all the unwanted police property. But then I saw PO Rogozinski or Roginsky, I don't know how to spell his name right, and he looked at me despitefully and he didn't greet me. He gave me a hateful look. As soon as he walked by, the Desk Sergeant changed his mind. He wanted me to take all my stuff with me and not leave them there. But after going back and forward, he told me to wait there, and he went upstairs to talk to someone.

As I waited, I stood there talking to the PAA. I asked about PO Sovulj, and I was told that he was transferred to the Shooting Range. So, he got what he wanted. He got accommodated, as well as many of the officers that I no longer see there. They were transferred probably because of what they did to me. So many officers were transferred in a very short time. I wonder if this has been the highest quantity of officers ever transferred in a short period of time in a precinct command. All because of one officer, me.

So, the Desk Sergeant came back, and he gave me permission to leave my stuff at the back. Wow, I was so unwelcomed.

So, on Wednesday, July 25, 2018, as a form of peaceful, and silent protest for what they did by stealing my file, and for illegally spreading and illegally distributing what I wrote on my book, I went to Meadville, Pennsylvania, directly to the publisher. I was planning to meet with the publication specialist Ta... By..., who is with whom I have been communicating regarding my book. So, after spending $301 on my flight ticket, and paying $300 for a taxi to take me from the airport to there, when I arrived, she had left the office. I went to the Hotel nearby and paid $78 for the night. On the same night, I went to Applebee's for dinner. In front of me, there was a family. When they were leaving at approximately 8: ... pm, one of them said to make sure that they don't leave anything behind. And one kid ironically said, "Yes, I have my keys with me."

In the morning, I stayed at the EconoLodge hotel. In the morning, at approximately 8:44 am, as I was serving my breakfast, one of the staff there said loud enough, plain and simple, "You are a thief." She didn't say anything further. I continued serving my breakfast. It hurts, but there is nothing I can do. So, when I went to the Christian Faith Publishing to talk to Ta... By..., she didn't receive me. Instead, two men escorted me inside to talk about my concern. I spoke to them, and they gave me a RED flash drive that contained the corrections they made, and for me to review. I asked them if I could do it right away, but they told me that I shouldn't. That I should take a week to revise it. One of them was wearing a red T-shirt.

I walked away and sat outside for a moment to do a little revision. When I did, I asked them to see them again. The secretary told me that they couldn't see me again because they were in a meeting. Thank you, Christian Faith Publishing, for being so hospitable to a brother in Christ. What a disappointment. I paid $200 for the flight ticket to return to New York. Plus, $61 for the taxi.

After such a long trip, why didn't she want to see me? Why did I have to be received by these two strangers? And then these strangers didn't want to see me again. So, I went to Burger King and there I heard people mentioning the word, "Lie" many times as they laughed.

Today's day is **September 23, 2018**. The last time I typed was like almost two months ago, in the month of July. The reason why I didn't continue typing was because on July 30, 2018, my wife and I moved out of the apartment. We went separately. I went to live with the brother in Christ, who a week or two weeks before I moved out, he was offered the job as Superintendent of a building. He told me to go and live with him there until I find a place of my own. He told me that I could stay there as long as I want. And that I didn't need to pay him anything. That I could be there for free. That it is a three-bedroom apartment, and that it will be just him and his wife leaving there.

When I moved out there, it was too good to be true. I have two bedrooms because I have too much stuff with me. At the end of the day, I ended up paying him one hundred dollars a week. Still, it is too cheap for all the space that I am occupying. Again, too good to be true, and therefore, I decided not to type if I remained there, because I don't know who is watching me from my own room.

One day, a person who always helps my brother in Christ, XXX, pick up the garbage, secretly told me that he felt bad about him because it is a trap, and that he didn't want to see it happen because he is a nice guy. I wondered if he was referring to me. Of course, the place has three basketball baskets, a pool, and it is very spacious. One day that we were seating outside, he told me, "You see, it feels like Santo Domingo" as if he were letting me know that I need not to go to the Dominican Republic, so I could be close to him and execute whatever is already planned to be done against me.

On **August 10, 2018,** I hurried and went to the Dominican Republic. There I thought that I could continue typing. But unfortunately, I left my tablet's charger back home. I returned home on **September 07, 2018**, mainly because I needed my charger for my tablet, because without it, I can't type. So, during my stay in the Dominican Republic, I was unable to type a word. Back to the Bronx, in that strange apartment, I believe that all my movement is being monitored and studied.

For example, the other day I went to eat something, and as I was eating, I asked a lady if she could pass me a straw, and she said to me, "I will pass it to you because I know who you are." Also, on another day, in a different establishment, I told the woman who work there to charge me for the orange juice, and she said, "Yes Emmanuel." How in the world does she know my name? One thing I have to say is that I went to many places, especially places downtown, near the courthouse, because I was trying to pacifically provoke them. Including, I went to the movie theater to watch part 2 of the movie Unbroken, which was Unbroken: Path to Redemption.

I went to the movie theater twice to watch the same movie one day, and on the next day I went to see it again. I did so to send a message on how brutally I was being treated back then at the 25th precinct station house by the hand of who was back then Lieutenant Naoki Yaguchi. He was the mastermind of my suffering there. It was pure evil. Pure emotional torture. The main character of the movie suffered physical and mental injuries by the hand of a Japanese soldier. However, I suffered mental and then physical harm by Lt. Yaguchi ruthless treatment towards me.

I felt so uncomfortable living in New York because I saw that nothing had changed. Therefore, on **September 19, 2018**, I took a plane back to the Dominican Republic. In the Dominican Republic people keep using the "crazy" word, but here I find less tension. Here I can continue typing without worrying that I am being recorded in my own apartment.

On September 26, 2018, I went to my nephew's apartment. We have been working on the cover of this diary where I have a picture of who was then Lt. Yaguchi and me shaking hands in front of the 25th precinct. My nephew, who is going to travel to New York for the first time, gave me the address of where he is going to stay there. I was astonished to learn that his address there is at 115 east 119 street between Park Avenue and Lexington Avenue. Right in front of the 25th precinct, where I worked, and right in front of the location where I took the picture of me and Lt. Yaguchi. Is this a mere coincidence?

On October 13, 2018, I went with the 35 years old man to see two witnesses in regard to a lot that belongs to my father but was invaded by people who illegally made a house there. When we were inside the house of one of the witnesses, he offered some kind of herb to the other witness in front of me and the 35 years old man. I asked him what it was, and he told me that it was marijuana. Are they kidding me? Haven't they still put an end to the scenarios?

-------------------------- I left the gym I was going to for good because of the pressure that everyone there was putting on me. So, I joined the Exercise Metropolitan Club gym. There, most of the members don't put locks on their lockers. It seems that they have intentionally left their belongings there without a lock in mind.

But on **Wednesday, November 14, 2018**, after many days of attending this new gym and being harassed there, again, something happened there that made me feel indignant. The gym has three-bathroom showers. When I finished my workout, I went to take a shower in the last shower room that I always use, that I entered, there I found unattended properties inside the shower room. Then I went to the other shower room and there were more unattended properties or lets say clothing. It made me angry. First, the gym members leave their belongings in the locker without a lock, and now they place items and clothing inside the shower rooms. Then, when I began to dress myself one of the members asked me if the things that were inside the shower rooms belonged to me. I told him it didn't and that it should be thrown in the garbage.

The next day on **Thursday, November 15, 2018,** my level of distress in the gym was very intense. To the point that I accidentally stepped on one of the small plastic cones that were on the floor and one of the trainers with an attitude told me about the cones, and as soon as he said that to me, I yelled out at him, "…coño?…" as if he had said "coño" instead of "cones". The word "coño" is a cursing word in Spanish which means "dam it" in English. I continued yelling out at him that people are not allowed to be saying cursing words in the place, and then I furiously delivered several hard punches on the punching bag.

On **Saturday, November 24, 2018,** I went to the gym. In the boxing class that I was taking, a lady (one of the persons taking the boxing class) in class told two other guys that look like the professor in the television series, "Casa de Papel," which translated to English means, "House of Paper." She said it because of the beard that I have allowed myself to grow, and that I just needed the eyeglasses he wears to look just like him. However, when I arrived home, I used YouTube to search for that series, at least to watch a trailer. When I did, I wasn't surprised to see what the series was about. The professor that she claims looks like me, is the mastermind behind a robbery. There you go, plain and simple. Here we go again.

On **Wednesday, November 28, 2018,** my cousin was accused of stealing chicken. The accuser said that she had seen him feeding, treating the chickens and that the sons of one of the neighbors saw him with a sack/bag, which is believed to be used to steal the chickens. In the end, on the same day, it was proven that it was a falsehood. The sons of the neighbor didn't say anything to her, and the chickens that were thought to be missing seemed to be not missing at all. The accuser apologized. I do believe that it was nothing more than another scenario, from New York, to the Dominican Republic.

Chapter 29

My Great Desperation

Wow, today's date is Monday, **December 10, 2018**. Right now, it is 2:04 pm. Wow, today marks my fifth anniversary from that disastrous day of **December 10, 2013**. It has been five long, intense and miserable years. They intentionally and violently threw a so delicate and fragile glass on concrete, but what they intended to achieve didn't come to pass, for even though irreparable harm was done to it, it didn't break, for my hope is in God, not in man. Therefore, I am still standing today, for God has given me the strength and fortitude to endure all the hardships that only a few selected people can resist. And now, after more than five years of torture, I am ready to speak out through my writing and if it needs to be, through my own voice.

ON FEBRUARY 26, 2019, I WENT TO SEEK AN ATTORNEY ADVISE, AND IN A FEW WORDS, I NEEDED TO SPEND A SIGNIFICANT AMOUNT OF MONEY TO OPEN A CASE, AND IT IS THE LESS I HAVE. I WALKED OUT HOPELESS FOR I HAVE NO ONE'S SUPPORT.

They disabled my right to sue. They disabled me, so I won't sue them. It clouds anyone's judgement. Typifies the violation of my rights of human dignity, respect to the integrity of my psych and moral, and personal honor. For sure they have formed a movement, a powerful, and mass campaign against me. I am going to the gym to treat my body according to the enormous pain it is going to endure on my last walk of life. It is going to be my last type of earthly pain. I know that the process is going to be excruciating painful, but my last pain is going to be my last. I will see how this body of mine is going to deteriorate little by little, and how it will begin its process of decomposition. I will see part of it rote, for I will no longer be in this body by the time that all organ of this body stops functioning. My corpse will be eaten by the flying birds of the brightest sun. This will be my final countdown. For this end I go to the gym. Where I go, they can't come.

They judge me without asking me. Did the punishment fit the crime? The pressure is intense. I no longer want to be part of human affairs. I should move aside and observe but not interfere. Remaster my manifesto. My whole confession under God and before God as my witness.

They rather not investigate, because that will imply, demonstrate and confirm my innocence, and as a result, they will find themselves swimming in the ocean and be down deep in trouble. This is my end because I have nothing else to do. The end. Fin. Finito. Now death can come and get me. I am not leaving the dream. Instead, I am living in a reality where I don't want to be. I just want to wake up from this nightmare. Ignorance of your rights doesn't mean you have no rights. They taking my stuff really hurt me, but what really hurt me the most is that after they read my stolen written words, they increased and intensified their attack upon me. It is the most powerful country in the world fighting against one man. The greatest problem is that I don't know whom to blame, but NYPD Naoki Yaguchi.

The Great Disappointment, Disenchantment, Disillusion, and Deception.

Introduction

March 1, 2019 -I do not understand what happened. Probably God is angry at me because he dislikes my prayers. Probably him seeing me tithe makes him angry. Probably to give him thanks for everything makes him irritated. Probably he has never been with me and the enemy had made me believe that he was when he wasn't. Probably I have been on this journey all alone without knowing it. Everything I thought was good was a deceit. There is no good nor bad. In vain I have tried to live my life with dignity. In vain I have tried to make others believe the good truly exists. In vain I have lived my days. In vain have I forbidden my body from enjoying all the garbage that life has to offer. For me, there is no longer a reason to be or become. There is only the hope that death will soon catch us all.

I am so angry. My heart is filled with anger and hate. I hate everyone, except my blood family line, my cat and dog. I hate them because they hated me first. Every eye that sees me, wishes the worst for me. They can't stand me, but I can't stand them either, again, except my blood family line, my cat and dog. I can no longer be in New York. The number one city in the world and its inhabitants hate me. For the sake of my wellbeing, I must leave the state, probably the country. Go back from where I came from, when from the country that I came from, no longer welcomes me either. I am like a bird who is trying to form a net in the middle of the ocean. I am damned if I do, and damned if I don't. It is as if I am forbidden to exist.

After so much sacrifice and years of hard work, this is how everything ended. Victory, fame and money for the wrongdoers, and shame, defeat and humiliation to the person who is trying to be good. But the cruelest and saddest part of all is when they not only steal and destroy your dream, but what they do with your dream. On my behalf, I have to say that the closest thing to my heart was taken from me, and that from that moment, my life has become meaningless. And what they have done with it is pure cruelty. All I have to say now is that I am ready to die. I will consider it an act of mercy, if my life ends today.

Now this is me, writing in desperation for in my empty mind is navigating the idea of what I should do now with my life. This is **March 1, 2019,** and I have just finished watching the Netflix original documentary, "Losers" just to appease not tranquil mind. Wow, my way of leaving is tough, but I must endure it till the end. Now I will release my anger not by hitting someone, for desire I do have to do so, but that's what they want me to do, so they may later say, "I told you that he is a criminal," just to justify their criminal activity and treatment towards me. Now I will share with you what my goals, my incentives, my hopes and dreams that were under attack by dark clouds, and under so much darkness, no one have stood next to me. This is retired NYPD police officer Emmanuel Hernandez shield #2830, and this is the account of a young man that is trying to be a decent human being.

On **March, Monday 4, 2019** I was on the train. While I was waiting for the train to go home, a tall guy looked at me and he yelled at me, "What are you looking at N…?" I didn't respond. I just walked to him, and stood at the edge of the platform, where the train comes through. When he saw that I did that, he said to himself, "I have to back up" as if he were talking to someone, and he put his hood over his head.

AN UPDATE, AND WHY I WAITED FOR SO LONG?

I had moved to the Dominican Republic. On December 2019, I went to the gym, and I believe that one of my memories was stolen. They had this diary in their possession. I waited for their response. My followers were talking about what I had written. As a result, I began yelling out to the crowd the injustices committed against me, in Spanish, daily, every single day. People are still following me everywhere, by car, and on foot. They are everywhere. So, out of anger, I travel to New York City to face the one responsible for all my calamity. I went to the heart of

New York City, and I did my peaceful protest, with Zero Result. It was useless.

The Passion to Write

The book that I wrote titled, "The 777- El 777" by Emmanuel, explains the moment when I developed an interest in reading and writing. I hated to read and write, but all a sudden, I ended up loving it. In the book, I explain how one night, knowing not what to do with my life, I kneeled by my bedside, and I prayed to God as to what he wanted me to do with my life. What was my purpose in life? That night I had a dream. In the dream I saw myself seated and writing on a desk. I was writing with my left hand, when I was right-handed, and I was using a quill to write.

I noticed that the hand with what I was writing had three rings. Two of them were triangles that had an eye in the center, while the other was a rectangle that had something written on it. Later, in the morning, on the blue curtain of my bedroom, I saw the shadow of a man kneeling, and he was holding what appears to be the two stones of Moises, where God wrote the ten commandments. The dream had to do with me writing, and the curtain, the written stones of God's law: the two had to do with writing. After this day, a mysterious desire to write and read emerged in me. My initiation or let say, my inauguration was on the train. One day I was riding the train when all a sudden, a poem popped into my head, and immediately I felt the urge to write it down on paper.

I can't beg them to believe me, for they believe what they want to believe. They feel better at the idea of me being guilty than being innocent. I can't help that. No matter how much I try to reason with them, they will try hard to advocate that they are right and I am wrong. **Already, they read my two stolen manuscripts, and they have become hard on me**.

I think that the DA's office can't leave trace of their wrongdoing. They cannot take anything with them but take pictures. And that's what they did with my memory. They acquired my information without stealing my memory card, but they extracted the information that my memory had, which is the same thing as stealing.

If my writings have not made them reason, my words of mouth will do less. I spoke and poured my heart to a counselor who is a pastor, and nothing came out of it. I spoke with the church guy who rented me a room, and told him everything that I am going through, and nothing. I spoke to a lawyer about the matter, and he told me that he will have to hire private investigators (Probably those who are following me), for there is no proof to what I am talking about. And that was going to be too expensive.

I tried to get in touch with other attorneys, but their secretaries have tried their best to interfere by wanting to know what the case is about (Hello, isn't it confidential?). I haven't been able to talk to any other aside from the first one I talked to. I tried to talk to a reporter, but unfortunately, they haven't called me back. I went to court like on four occasions carrying four big signs that states:

These four posters say the following:
The 1st said:
**OUR LIVES BEGIN TO END
THE DAY WE BECOME SILENT
ABOUT THINGS THAT MATTER.
MARTIN LUTHER KING JR.**

The 2nd said:
"The grief that does not speak, moans in the heart until it breaks it" or straight from Shakespeare, "Give sorrow words; the grief that does not speak knits up the o-er wrought heart and bids it break." William Shakespeare.

The 3rd said:
"Good name in man and woman, dear my lord,
Is the immediate jewel of their souls:
Who steals my purse steals trash; 'tis something, nothing
But he that filches from me my good name

Robs me of that which not enriches him,
And makes me poor indeed." William Shakespeare

And the 4th, with a **drawn arrow pointed at me, said:**

HE IS A LIAR
HE IS A THIEF
HE IS A LYING THIEF
COME FORWARD YOU BIG PROMOTER OF LIES, FALSEHOOD AND DECEPTION. SHAME ON YOU.

Also, I went to IAB (Internal Affairs Bureau, investigate cops), and spoke to Detective Duncan. On a recorder he had, I explained to him my concern about the Copwatch groups that are following officers, the watchdogs. He told me that there is nothing they could do about it. He asked me if I feared my life, because if I did, he would have to call 911. This might mean sending me to a psych ward. I became afraid, and I wanted to run away from there. This means that if I continue pushing the button, I will end up in a psychiatric unit again.

Therefore, it is no longer up to me. There is nothing, absolutely nothing I can do. I must fly to the Dominican Republic and leave all this behind. I must go because I can't continue feeding my hate. I must go away defeated. They have won over me. Now, I must live this life with a ruined reputation. I must let others say whatever they want of me, and I must say nothing. I must not defend myself. What needed to be said and written they already heard and read. There is absolutely nothing else for me to do other than to pack my stuff and leave.

I went to the Internal Affairs Bureau looking for an answer, and I had none. The Detective Duncan, followed by a second other, attended me. It was just a waste of time.

After my protest, nothing was done. I went back to the Dominican Republic. People continued to follow me, and I continued to cry out to the crowd, the injustice committed against me, day in and day out. In 2020, I met someone who gave me a child in 2021, and in 2021 we had the Corona Virus pandemic. As the mother of my child remained leaving with her mother, when I was not with her, my followers kept putting music and saying things that made me think that she was cheating on me. So, we argued a lot based on that until she moved with me in 2023. In 2022, my dear mother passed away. The doctor who attended her was dressed in red. People kept harassing me until now, in Feb. 2025, I decided to look at this diary. I had not touched my diary after 2019, since it was stolen, in December 2018, as I think.

By Craig McCarthy and Bruce Golding on **April 22, 2019,** by the New York Post.

"Prosecutors across the city are using secrete spreadsheets to identify cops who could have trouble on the witness stand because they have been sued, arrested, accused of misconduct or testified suspiciously in the past, sources told the post on Monday"

According to the article, the Manhattan District Attorney's office has kept record of these officers in an internal database for several years. The Brooklyn and the Bronx District Attorneys have done the same, along with the Queens DA who began doing the same last year. Staten Island is planning to do the same.

On Wednesday, May 15, 2019, I spoke to my wife, and she told me that her newly obtained car was punched, according to her brother who is a mechanic, resulting in a dent on her car.

Chapter 30

The News Articles

I read news articles of events that happened within the District Attorney's office and the NYPD just from March, 27 2017 till April 6, 2018 in just one-year span, that confirmed my suspicion as to how far the District Attorney's office and the NYPD can go by violating someone else's privacy and the power they are able to exercise and conditions that they are able to manipulate in order to find a person guilty even when there is a chance that they might be innocent.

Also, these articles talk about police misconduct and the punishment that the officers received based on their misconduct. Moreover, the articles talk about misconduct committed by Assistant District Attorneys. And to this day, I ask myself and still wonder why the police officers mentioned in these articles received a slap on their wrist because of their misdeed, while I received and I am still receiving a Cruel and Unusual Punishment, still not knowing why. As you read along these articles, you will realize how unfairly I was treated.

Going back to previous pages:

"On **Tuesday, April 17, 2018,** on the website BuzzFeed I read a list of NYPD police misconducts and in one of them was my former **25 precinct companion PO Damien Banks** who on **1/24/2012** was found guilty of making **inaccurate statements in a supporting disposition** and of making **inaccurate statement in a supplemental fact sheet**. The Department punished him by taking away from **him 30 vacation days**."

I would have wished they did the same thing with me at the time, if they considered that I did something wrong, which I didn't. But it wasn't my case. My punishment was far way worse. My punishment was and still is cruel and unusual. They went after my mind, my sanity, and by manipulating it, they destroyed my career, my mental health and my physical body. It has been worse than cruel and unusual punishment. It was simply, daily torture.

Now, back to the articles:

On **Monday, March 27, 2017,** I read an article on the New York Post titled, "**Brooklyn Prosecutor Accused of Forging Wiretap Faces Federal Char.**" by Christina Carrega, and Andrew Keshner. They reported Assistant District Attorney Tara Lenich, a former high-ranking Brooklyn prosecutor who is accused of forging Judges' signatures in order to obtain wiretaps to listen to calls conversation of a married police detective, and now she is being indicted by a Brooklyn federal prosecutor for illegal wiretapping, and for wrongfully obtaining fake search warrant in order to gain access to the test messages. She copied and pasted Judges' signatures and placed them on the warrants without the Judges' consent. She was also charged by the state for possession of a forged instrument and for eavesdropping, which is the act of secretly listening to the private conversation of others without their consent.

This article made me think twice about whether there have been some type of mishandling or manipulation on behalf of the Manhattan District Attorney's office in their effort to violate my civil rights to obtain evidence against me. They are so desperate to find something incriminating against me.

On **Tuesday, October 10, 2017,** I read an article on the New York Daily News titled, "**Let Prosecutors Face Justice**." by Errol Louis that explains that lawmakers in Albany should hold prosecutors accountable for their misconduct that send innocent people to prison. He states, "**Current laws in New York allow a prosecutor to withhold evidence and even lie about it with few consequences... they should pass a law punishing prosecutors who use deception and shady tactics to slant the scales of justice.**" He explains how Kenneth Thomson won over District Attorney Charles Hynes and decided to correct past injustices committed during Hynes' leadership, and for the last three years after Thomson took over, **22 convictions were overturned**.

Past Injustice? For God's sake, there should be no room for injustice. Things are what they are, and any addition or subtractions from what they are, is unlawful, wrong and should be penalized. Louis gives an example of a case where a man served **16 years in prison of a 34 years to life sentence** because, "… **prosecutors suppressed the fact that they had threatened, jailed and badgered witnesses into testifying against…**" the defendant, something that the Judge nor the Jury knew about. So, after obtaining enough evidence from his lawyer while he was incarcerated, his conviction was reversed.

Another man **served 20 years in prison because that District Attorney's office wrongfully kept and didn't present evidence that would have helped his case, and how the prosecutor punished and harassed the witness to compel him to testify against the defendant**. Also, Louis emphasizes, "**Prosecutors in Chicago, Cleveland, Tampa and Houston all lost their jobs amid charges of misconduct.**" However, they are allowed to practice law, and they are not charged.

I was frightened after I read this article, which informed me and demonstrated to me how evil a prosecutor can be. What they are capable of doing in order to make a case and win it.

On **Wednesday, October 18, 2017,** I read an article titled, "**Blue lies on trial: Fed hearing eyes if cop falsehoods 'widespread'**" by Andrew Keshner and Graham Rayman. The article states," A FEDERA JUDGE in Brooklyn has ordered a special hearing **to examine how commonly police officers lie and whether the NYPD does enough to stop it**." The Judge decided on the hearing after someone is suing the city for "false arrest" and "malicious prosecution" claims. The hearing will take place if the Jury find the cops liable, and if so, they will investigate if there is, "'widespread lying by police officers.'" According to the article, the NYPD's top lawyer, Lawrence Byrne said that "…cops don't lie on the stand any more than any other type of witness."

Unbelievable, there must be zero lies, PERIOD. The judge was also influenced by many other news articles with cases such as this one.

Police officers lying to justify false arrest. It states that one officer falsified overtime and has been sued many times for false arrest. Also, the article mentions that the judge, "…said prominent civil rights advocate Michelle Alexander has written that some experts on police practices treat lying by police as " 'commonplace.' "

When I read this article, I couldn't believe that cops were so able to lie, and that it was a common practice. How could they? And how come that they are so severely after me for my confusion of December 10, 2013, by which as a result, everywhere I go people keep adding in their conversations the word, "Lie," as if I were a liar, when others have truly and intentionally lied, and they don't go thru the same hell that I am going thru.

On **Tuesday, November 21, 2017,** I read an article from the New York Daily News titled, "**J. Edgar Hoover's Name Lives in Infamy**," by Richard Cohen. The author explained how J. Edgar Hoover wanted to destroy Martin Luther King Jr. by using all means necessary.

Hoover's persistence to take down King led him to even bug a room where Dr. King stood. And so much was Hoover's insistence to hurt Dr. King, that according to the author, "**King sensed that Hoover wanted to drive him to suicide**."

I am appalled to learn of Dr. King's struggle and desperation when he expressed, "**They are out to break me, harass me, break my spirit.**'" Also, Cohen explained, "The unlawful and totally outrageous attempt to undermine and / or destroy King was Hoover at his most egregious … the FBI engaged in **illegal wiretaps, spread false rumors, forged documents and …**'" Yes, Hoover's main goal was to destroy Dr. King's reputation.

In today's day a psychiatrist will label Dr. King as being schizophrenic and suffering from delirium of persecution. I can relate to Dr. King's experience, but of course, it wasn't the same, but when I wanted to speak up, they silenced me by throwing me into a psych ward. For me it seems that I have been the target of an NYPD-FBI investigation, headed by the Manhattan District Attorney.

On **Saturday, December 9,** 2017, I read a New York Daily News article titled, "**$9.5 M Bad Rap**: **Settles with city after 24 yrs. falsely imprisoned,**" by Andrew Keshner. The article talks about a man who was **imprisoned for 24 years for a crime he didn't commit**.

According to Keshner, "During the trial, **prosecutors withheld the details** of Salcedo's secret overnight stay," which was a **vital information to prove his innocence**, and how the **prosecutor lied as the author wrote** in regard to the District Attorney's office "Thompson's office uncovered a 2004 email that confirmed an appeals prosecutor knew about Salcedo being stashed away at a hotel." He continued, "The prosecutor previously said she didn't know anything about the witness warrant."

Isn't this scary? And you may wonder why I am still traumatized and disturbed by the mistake I made in court on December 10, 2013. You can read about what prosecutors are capable of if they come to dislike you. I think that some of them might have made a pact with evil to reach their ambitious goal.

On **Saturday, December 16, 2017,** I read a New York Daily News article titled, "**Prosecutor's hell: Co-worker's tryst lies ruined my life: suit**" by Andrew Keshner. According to the article former Assistant District Attorney Stephanie Rosenfeld had no option, but to resign from her job after, "… **becoming a target of ridicule and scorn around the District Attorney's office** …."

All this came about after she denounced former Assistant District Attorney Tara Lenich's misconduct of forging court documents to bug phones or lets say, to obtain illegal wiretaps. The author quoted the following in regard to Rosenfeld who, " ', **endured months of humiliating looks and behind-the back comments from supervisors and colleagues at the King County DA, defense attorneys in the courthouse, and even Judges and court staff**'" so she couldn't take it anymore and as a result she resigned. Also, as a result, she was diagnosed with Post-Traumatic Stress Disorder.

Why didn't they diagnose her with being schizophrenic? She was treated the same way that they are treating me, but worse, because I am being followed and much more.

On **Tuesday, December 19, 2017,** I read a New York Daily News article titled, "**Cop hit-and-'lie'**: Hurt pedestrian will sue over "faked" report"" by Stephen Rex Brown. It stated that a pedestrian was struck by an unmarked NYPD SUV and when the police report was made that the victim read the report, he discovered that in the report, the officer blamed him for the accident, which wasn't the case. There was another article about a NYPD cop sexting a 16 year old girl. **Later, at 7:50 pm, a detective from the Detective Squad knocked at my door. He asked me if I heard something from downstairs, because somebody broke into the apartment below me. Great. Is this another scenario?**

On **Monday, January 8, 2018,** I read a New York Post article titled, "**Lawyer of cop accused of raping teen blasts prosecutors**," by Emily Saul where according to Saul, the defense attorney for one of the NYPD Detectives accused of rape,"… blasted prosecutors in new court fillings, claiming they **knowingly allowed the accuser to lie to the grand jury.**"

What a game this is. Playing around with people's lives. I also wonder why ADA (Assistant District Attorney) Altman had me testify on December 10, 2013, when she knew well that I was not ready to do so.

On **Thursday, January 11, 2018,** I read the New York Daily News article titled, " **Shot down: DA eyes precinct for wrongdoing in gun bust rise,**" by Rocco Parascandola and he explained, "Some cops could be indicted for perjury and official misconduct, police sources said. The NYPD may transfer others or bring them up on departmental charges, the sources said." Well, they intentionally lied to arrest people for possession of a firearm. There is a possibility that they might be indicted for it.

They 'could', interesting. If they think that I am a liar, why didn't they indict me? It is because deep in their heart they know well that I am innocent, and that my case was going to be dismissed because I am no liar. The NYPD plan to transfer some of them or bring them on departmental charges. Why wasn't I transferred the moment I began to be followed, and why didn't they bring departmental charges to me? It is simple, because they will have to stop following me then, and I will have been cleared. But they needed a reason to do what they are doing to me. It is simply malicious and capricious.

On **Monday, January 22, 2018,** I read a New York Daily News article titled, "**7 Yrs. AT RIKERS WITH NO SENTENCE: Convicted of attempted murder, inmate expected to finally learn fate this week**," by Stephen Rex Brown. The article states that Assistant District Attorney David Slott, "…along with cops from the 42nd precinct, has been accused of intimidating witnesses in the Hernandez case and demanding they lie."

On **Sunday January 28, 2018,** I found an article on the New York Daily News titled "**CITY'S WORST COP**" by Esha Ray, Chelsia Rose Marcius and Graham Rayman and it talks about New York City Detective Thomas Rice who closed cases that needed to be investigated by claiming that he did work on them when he didn't.

He provided **fake** witnesses, **fake** addresses, and documented places that he didn't visit on the police report, and he claimed that he exhausted all investigative resources to close the cases that were assigned to him. In addition, he copied and pasted the statements that he supposedly received from the fake witnesses. He committed official misconduct, falsified reports and lied on official documents. According to the authors, "In all, he entered 47 fake addresses in the reports. Out of 100 witnesses mentioned in Rice's reports, 94 people were nonexistent, an internal investigation found. Just six were actual people."

On **Monday January 29, 2018** I read another article in regards to the same article above on the New York Daily News by Graham

Rayman titled, "**BIG FAKERY, TINY SLAP: Shroud of secrecy helped protect cop**," and he stated that Detective Thomas Rice and other cops were sued because, "…the cops lied to the Brooklyn district attorney to justify the false arrest."

On **Tuesday, January 30, 2018,** I read the continuation of the article above of the New York Daily News by Erin Durkin, Rocco Parascandola and Graham Rayman titled "**COP UNDER FIRE: Why wasn't he axed, pol asks**." According to the writers, "Berger noted that he sees the phenomenon in cases where **officers commit perjury**." Also, the writers quoted, "'**It happens very frequently that when an (assistant district attorney) suspects or knows a cop is lying, that gets swept under the rug**,'" As a result of all this detective's misconducts, the **Department punished him by taking away 20 vacation days from him, and he remains a Detective.**

This Detective lied multiple times openly, and his punishment was 20 vacation days taken from him. So why wasn't I treated the same way for the honest mistake I made on December 10, 2013? If I did wrong, why didn't they just punish me and it was going to be the end of the story. But no, they just keep harassing me until this day, as if they wish me to die of a heart attack or stroke. They keep tirelessly pressuring me until they reach their goal of getting Hernandez annihilated.

According to the authors, when the Detective saw the media, "'Oh my God' he said, freezing when he spotted a photographer from The News. He turned and ran back into his house like he had seen a ghost.'" He freaked out by just seeing a photographer. Can you imagine what he would have done then if he had tasted a little bit of the same poison that was and is still being administered to me by the law enforcement (NYPD) and the judicial system (Manhattan District Attorney)?

On this same day of **Sunday, January 28, 2018,** I read another New York Daily News article by Thomas Tracy titled, "**Blue Wall of Lies: Attacked by fellow cop, told to say I slipped, says officer**." According to Tracy, "WHEN YOU'RE surrounded by a **Blue Wall of**

Silence, no one can hear you scream in pain." It talks about a New York City police officer who was attacked and injured by his fellow officer and needed two surgeries on his knee. His **supervisors**, such as his **Lieutenant**, his **Sergeant**, and his **Union Delegate,** were forcing him to lie on the report, to say that he slipped instead. **Two other officers, including the officer's partner and the partner of the aggressor said that they didn't see anything even though they were closed.** However, in the end, the officer that was the aggressor admitted that he fought the officer.

This article reminds me of how everyone in the precinct conspired against me.

On **Monday, February 12, 2018,** I read an article on the New York Post titled, "**NYPD cop accused of mugging stranger wants $50 M from city**" by Emily Saul. It stated that Police Officer Anthony Delacruz has been accused of robbery and now he is suing the city for $50 million because, "…he was **framed** because the NYPD and the Office of the District Attorney County of Kings have a **history of falsely arresting officers of color based upon racial stereotyping** i.e officers of color are drug dealers, 'perps' and other derogatory terms based upon 'looks' and 'flashy' lifestyle.'"

Now my question is, did they frame me because I am a poor Hispanic man who has a heavy accent? The son of a black man and a white woman? Of course they will deny it, but their actions do the talking. I also want to make clear that not only do whites discriminate against minorities, but there are also minorities that discriminate against minorities.

On **Tuesday, February 27, 2018,** I read an article in the New York Daily News written by Molly Crane-Newman, Thomas Tracy and Graham Rayman. They explain the testimony of an old-time employee at the Bronx district attorney 's office where the prosecutors get involved with one another into performing sexual acts by sleeping with each other and with officers, not minding whether they are married or not, and consuming alcohol, all while on duty and in their office. And after drinking, they go into court.

On **Sunday, March 4, 2018,** I read the following New York Daily News article by Police Commissioner James O'Neill:

This isn't a new challenge for

JAMES O'NEILL

Police departments, just like other segments of society, are staffed by human beings who are fallible, make mistakes, and yes, on rare occasion, lie. But a police officer who intentionally lies under oath has no place in law enforcement. Officers who err in good faith are a different story.

Our members have the capability to arrest people and, because of that power, we also have the utmost responsibility to hold ourselves accountable to the highest standards of ethics and integrity.

O'Neill is the commissioner of the NYPD.

In general, an adverse credibility ruling is not the same as a finding that an officer lied or committed perjury. It is usually not a criminal offense, although it too may damage the prosecution's case in a given trial. It is clear from transcripts that the officers in some cases failed to prepare adequately, to review their notes, or to remember accurately the particulars of a respective case. And those find-

So, if they do know that we police officers are human being that do mistakes, why do they come after me with all their might and fury for the honest mistake I made on 12/10/2013 that still haunts me?

On **March 5, 2018**, there was a New York Post article written by Ruth Brown: **NYPD cops lie and steal get slap on the wrist, report reveals**. She explains how dozens of NYPD workers, between the year 2011-2015, who lied under oath, and used physical force beyond measure, were disciplined by just taking away vacation days and placed for dismissal probation for one year. Brown used the Buzzfeed report to bring the following data of those who were placed on dismissal probation as result of the following offenses: From a total of 319 officers, 75 were for ticket fixing, 50 for lying about the cases, and their investigators, 38 for using force beyond measure, for sexual harassment, theft, and drug use.

Now I do wonder why those officers who committed serious infractions were not treated the same way that I am being treated?

On **Wednesday, March 14, 2018,** I read a New York Daily News article titled," Secrets of the Blue Line: **Public kept In The Dark**," by Graham Rayman, John Annese, and Thomas Tracy. They explain the severe misconduct done by police officers and how soft their punishments were.

Such as in the case of a rookie cop by the name of Asar Sanad which the article explains, "Sanad, then 29, claimed she witnessed a man hitting his girlfriend on Feb. 15, 2013, but the suspect beat the rap after Sanad **admitted she lied about seeing the assault herself**. In fact, the suspect was already under arrest when she arrived on the scene. She didn't make that distinction in a sworn statement and wound up criminally charged in a case that has since been sealed. Her internal discipline was likewise secret-until The News got her case orders. On Sept. 22, the department hit her with a **32-days suspension and placed her on dismissal probation** for a year.

Now I demand answers. Look at how this officer who intentionally lied in a sworn statement was given a slap on the wrist compared to the long-term treatment I received and am still receiving for the December 10, 2013 incident, for I see no other reason why they are treating me the way that they are treating me.

On **Thursday, March 15, 2018,** I read the following New York Daily News article written by Esha Ray, Shayna Jacobs, Victoria Bekiempis and Graham Rayman: **Secrets of the Blue Line**. They address how Lt. Adam Lamboy, had lied to his working hours. Stole 200 working hours, and $15,000 worth of overtime. How he forged documents and lied on official documents, and all this happened in 2013 besides having something aside with a young woman, unknown to me. The larceny was kept secret by department officials. He lied about his whereabouts during his police working hours and on official documents. He retired

In the end, he retired with an $87,310 a year lifetime pension after all he did. Did he receive the same treatment I am receiving?

On **Friday, April 6, 2018,** I read a New York Daily News article titled, "$75G RIP IN SPYING" by Laura Dimon and Thomas Tracy and they wrote, "The monitoring included video surveillance, photographing license plates, community mapping, and infiltration by undercover officers and informants."

And everyone that I say that they do this to me finds it impossible to believe because I have nothing to hide.

On **Tuesday, May 29, 2018,** I read a New York Daily News article titled, "**NYPD Pains in the Brass,**" by Graham Rayman. The article talks about Warner Frey, who was the head of the Detective Bureau investigation unit. Frey explains how cops who knew high ranking cops were treated differently than those cops who didn't have any connection.

In addition, Frey explains how they treated cops they didn't like. According to Rayman, "**At the same time, they didn't hesitate to try to damage careers of cops they didn't like, Frey said – often because the cop had a run of high crime numbers or there was an old grudge.**" Rayman quoted Frey who said, "'They would say, '**This guy is no good,**'" he said. "'**Get as much as you can on this guy. I want to really hammer this guy.**' O, yeah, completely, it happened all the time.'" According to Frey, "'…the system was an arbitrary and capricious beast."

Since Lieutenant, who is now a Captain, Yaguchi disliked me, no wonder they did what they possibly could to destroy my career.

On **Thursday, February 15, 2018**, I read the following article on The New York Daily News: **Capt. Indicted in cop-probe delay,** by Rocco Parascandola, John Annese, Thomas Tracy and Graham Rayman. Yes, Captain Naoki Yaguchi was indicted for official misconduct, for supposedly delaying a drunk and driving text from another officer.

The next day in the morning, as I prayed with tears going down my cheek, I asked God why this man, Lt. Yaguchi, hated me so much, when all I did was to do everything, he told me to do with love. I even went the extra mile to do for him the quality of work that he expected of me. Just look at my yearly evaluations. But I never knew his motives, as to why he insistently, and persistently was he so bucked down to destroy me and my career.

To the extent of allowing me to fail on that unfortunate day of December 10, 2013, which was the day that I needed him the most, he turned his back on me, and made my other colleagues do the same. I read the following quotes in Spanish that says that somebody had asked Aristotle: "What can be gain out of lies?" and that he answered, "For them not to believe you when you tell the truth." The quotes clearly explain why Lt. Yaguchi, my ex-colleagues, and ADA (Assistant District Attorney) Altman framed me, because the moment I gave out the wrong information in court, which I thought them to be right, they were going to be able to justify their abuses, and that by the time I reported their wrong doing, nobody would then believe me because of what happened on December 10, 2013.

And on **Wednesday, February 21, 2018** another article came on a different newspapers, the New York Post, pertaining to Lt. Yaguchi: **NYPD captain intentionally botched DWI case against detective: prosecutors** by Shawn Cohen and Chris Perez at 7:39 pm

"An NYPD captain is facing up to a year behind bars for intentionally botching a drunk driving case against an off-duty detective".

And on **Thursday, February 22, 2018**, I read in the New York Daily News another article regarding him: **NYPD captain surrenders in DWI coverup**. (BLANK IT NOT TO VIOLATE
COPYRIGHT)

The photo at the bottom is unknown to me from what source comes, all I know is that he is there seated facing trial. **(BLANK IT NOT TO VIOLATE**

COPYRIGHT)

When reading this article, I was drinking coffee and thinking of all the harm that this man has caused me. When I got up my seat, two drops of coffee felled on my bible. When I was cleaning the page where the coffee dropped on my bible, one of the drops felled on the following verses on the bible.

"Do not rejoice over me, O my enemy. Though I have fallen, I shall rise; when I sit in darkness, the Lord will be my light. Because I have sinned against Him, I will bear the indignation of the Lord until He argues my case and establishes justice for me. He will bring me out to the light; I shall look upon his vindication. Then my enemy will see, and she will be covered with shame, the one who said to me, "'Where is the Lord your God?'" My eyes will look at her in triumph; at that time, she will be trampled like mud in the streets." (Micah 7:8-10 HCSB, ESV)

I believe that deep inside of him remains some guilt for what he did to me. He might want to amend what he did to me in the past by helping this detective, and to avoid the image of having destroyed another officer career, which in this case the drunk detective did it to himself, and in my case, Lt. Yaguchi did it to me.

On **Saturday, December 1, 2018**, I read an article from the New York Daily News titled, " **Pols: Which Finest are known liars**?" by Janon Fisher who stated, "A group of Manhattan lawmakers want District Attorney Cy Vance Jr. to stop shielding lying cops." The author stressed that these groups are "… demanding the prosecutor release his secret list of officers with credibility problems that make them liabilities on the witness stand." Also, he explains, "Release of the list will likely encounter resistance not only from Vance, but from the NYPD, which has interpreted all police personnel records as confidential including disciplinary cases."

After reading the article, I realized that police officers are prone to do mistakes at the stand. I call it mistake, because the article made the mistake of using the word "lie" instead of "mistake." They should replace the word "lie" with the word

"mistakes" because it is human to err. And I don't believe that an officer will have the guts to intentionally lie, and those who do so, should no longer be a police officer. I made an honest mistake at the stand, which turned into a lie, because they found it convenient for them because they needed a reason to do what they did and are still doing to me. Now, the golden question is why didn't they keep my personal record confidential the same way that all the officers, except me, are kept?

On **Sunday, January 13, 2019,** I read a New York Daily News article titled, "The NYPD is goin' Crazy on me: cop. Payback for 'panties' hit on his boss" by Kerry Burke and Thomas Tracy." According to **Detective Victor Fallon**, " 'They want to send me to a **psychiatric facility** for **30 days**.' " " ' This is because of the complaint I made. **They do this to discredit cops.'**" " '**They're trying to do an Adrian Schoolcraft on me'** " '**When I get out, I'll have nothing**.'"

They are trying to do with him the same thing they did with me and Schoolcraft.

On **Sunday, January 20, 2019,** I read a New York Daily News article titled, "Cop is arrested in pot sale," by Thomas Tracy. It talks about how NYPD officer, Gilberto Mercedes, a 14-year veteran was caught and arrested for selling marijuana and was also charged for criminal possession of a weapon. Tracy quoted, "A law enforcement source said Mercedes had been in trouble with the department before and was disciplined after he was accused of stealing department property several years ago."

On **Monday, July 29, 2019,** there was a NY Daily News article titled, 'Latest cop to take own life was a transit unit sarge' By Thomas Tracy, Trevor Boyer and Clayton Guse. "He is the seventh NYPD officer to take his life this year. Four officers killed themselves just last month."

It is weird that he was disciplined and not fired for stealing department property. While I must go through a hellish pandemonium doing nothing wrong.

ABOUT THE UNIQUE POWER OF THE NYPD

541

Also, about the powerful organization that I worked for, the NYPD, I read an article titled, "9 Frightening Things About America's Biggest Police Force" by Tana Ganeva, Laura Gottesdiener/ AlterNet and I want to address the might of the NYPD based on this article: **First**, that the influence of the NYPD is in the entire world, and that they are highly equipped as the military. **Secondly**, the FBI are surprised at the way that the NYPD is able and capable of violating people's civil liberties. **Thirdly**, in regard to a NYPD unit, a detective said, "'We are in the business of scaring people—**we just want to scare the right people**.'" And **fourth**, monitor people and communities and keep them under surveillance, a practice, that the FBI disagree.

Also, on a report by The New York Times, states that the New York City police recruited immigrants to act as Confidential Informants eavesdropping in café, restaurants etc.

Overall, I was stunned after I read these articles. Before it was something unconceivable for me to think that the District Attorney's Office and the NYPD were so corrupt. It is scary. It made me wonder if the Manhattan District Attorney's office and its Assistant District Attorneys are motivated by a quota the same way that the NYPD does. I heard from someone that the goal of many Assistant District Attorneys is to become a judge one day, and that the more cases they win, the closer they get to that goal, but if they lose cases, it affects their career advancement.

Also, it is not based on quantity but in quality, and **it will be a golden opportunity for them if they can find a reason to charge a so high-value target as myself, for I was and am a retired police officer**. Especially a defenseless individual like me. **And the golden question is why do they still seek to crucify me for an honest mistake I made many years ago when according to these articles, many cops had intentionally lie and their punishment was a slap on the wrist?**

For a long time, I have been aware of their capacity to infringe on a person's civil rights and privacy. Also, I was trained to observe, and as a result, I was able to identify all the things that were taking place around me. So, can you imagine when both the hungry Manhattan District Attorney's office and the NYPD come after this fresh meat? Sincerely, I shouldn't be afraid because I have done nothing wrong, but what really concerns me are the rules that they are able to bend and break to get to me. So far, my mental and physical health have been deteriorating to the extent that now I am taking three different medications, all because of them.

I don't hear from apartment # 61. It is always in total silence. No one is visiting. I only saw two different people like on three different occasions. I have grown very suspicious of apartment # 61. Do they have their ears on the wall to hear what I say or do? At this stage, everything is possible.

Wow, after I finished typing this that I stepped outside and waited for the elevator, I saw the two of them coming out of apartment #61. After a long time without seeing them, now I see them. Did they stepped out because they knew what I was typing?

The NYPD Tapes Book

One day in October of 2017, I decided to buy the book, "**THE NYPD TAPES: A SHOCKING STORY OF COPS, COVER-UPS, AND COURAGE**" by Graham A. Rayman. The book is about former New York City police officer Adrian Schoolcraft **who secretly recorded misconducts committed by his supervisors and fellow officers by illegally misclassifying and downgrading crimes by fudging reports, by not taking police reports, and by forcing quotas on officers.**

Also, the author mentions how one of the high ranks **had more than twenty allegations of misconduct against him and nothing was done about it**. And **how they lied in order to cover themselves**. Even a **Detective's signature was forged on a report he had not taken, testified the detective himself**. I never knew of the downgrading of crimes until I read this book.

When I read the book, I was astonished. I never knew that what happened, according to the book, in the life of PO Schoolcraft by his supervisors, was so common within the NYPD. I read that even 32 officers denied that there were quota numbers. It is laughable. There has been a very lack of sincerity and honesty in the brief existence of their lives, which they will take with them to the grave where they will be judged accordingly. Everyone should know that with the same rule you use to measure others, you will be measured too. I thought that everyone in the job was adults who knew how to distinguish between what is right and what is wrong. It is common sense that to do the right thing is the obligation of everyone.

Throughout the investigation, his superiors and police officers openly lied to investigators, and they went as far as, and to the extent of sending PO Schoolcraft to a psych ward in a form of retaliation against him. There he was involuntarily admitted, and Jamaica hospital, became an accomplice of the scheme done against him. It all started when he left work early, because he didn't feel well.

The author explains that PO Schoolcraft had a right to refuse medical treatment, and that at the time he behaved rational as he emphasized, "Schoolcraft had jousted with Marino, but he didn't raise his voice, cursed, or shown any violent tendencies." But still he was forced to go to the hospital. **Now I still wonder why**

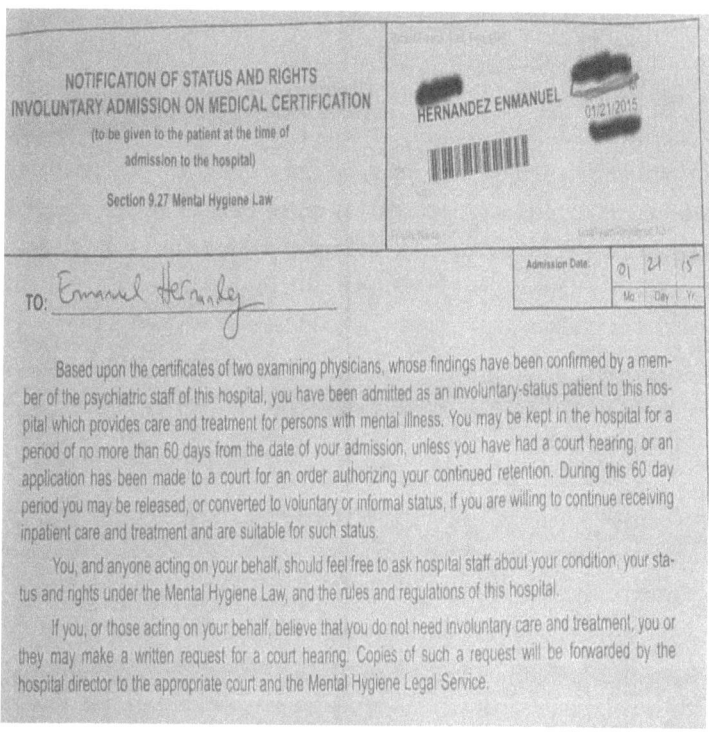

I was involuntarily taken to the hospital when I never raised my voice, cursed or showed any violent tendencies.

If I were a threat, why did they allow me to ride to the hospital on the back seat of the police car without being handcuffed? I at all-time obeyed their command. However, the medical staff seemed to be highly influenced by the NYPD. The day I was brought to the hospital I was left by myself. No police officer accompanies me because obviously, I posed no risk. Not even my union PBA delegate went to visit me. But they needed to find ways to discredit me.

The author quotes The New York Mental Hygiene Law section 9, subsections 39 and 41, which give the reasons as to when a person can be involuntarily admitted and it is when " ' **a substantial risk of physical harm to himself as manifested by threats of or attempts at suicide or serious bodily harm' and/or 'a substantial risk of physical harm to other persons as manifested by homicidal or other violent behavior.**'" And Subsection 41 which says, "'Any **peace officer, when acting pursuant to his or her special duties, or police officer…may take into custody any person who appears to be mentally ill and is conducting himself or herself in a manner which is likely to result in serious harm to the person or others**." None of these applied in my case for them to take me to the hospital involuntarily. I was never violent, nor did I show them any sign of wanting to hurt myself. And according to Graham A. Rayman, under police procedure a person "'**May refuse medical attention.**'"

Also, he cited the 1914 court case of Schloendorff V. Society of New York Hospital which the court declared, "'**every human being adult years and sound mind has a right to determine what should be done with his own body.**'" The only reasons where consent is not needed is in " ' **cases of emergency, where the patient is unconscious and where it is necessary to operate before consent can be obtained.**'" Also, Rayman quoted justice John Paul Stevens of the US Supreme Court who wrote, "'**There is no doubt…that a competent individual's right to refuse medication is a fundamental liberty interest deserving the highest order of protection.**'"

While PO Schoolcraft was in the hospital, they wanted him to take **Risperdal which is an antipsychotic**. He should thank God; he didn't take it. But in my case, I wasn't that fortunate. I remember when I was in the hospital that I refused to take the medication and I told them that I didn't want to, but they said that I must, and that if I refused they were going to get a permission from a judge to force me to take it, and that as a result, I will spend more time in the hospital. Also, I remember when one of the psychiatrists told me that they had to diagnose me with something.

I just moved my head in disbelief when I read a quote from Rayman who quoted retired Lt. Anthony Miranda who said, "'**If you, as a cop, file complaints, there's more of a tendency to refer you to**

psych services. If you are not hitting the quota, that becomes part of it. And that ruins a person's career.'" I wonder if the day that I complained to my commanding officer in front of the NYPD chaplain, which as a result, the commanding officer called and referred me to the Equal Employment Opportunity, was a contributing factor of sending me to the hospital, in addition to my police activity numbers being low. Also, by being brought to the hospital by the same Sergeant (Gibbs), who one day told me because my activity was low, "So you know what that means?" This explains everything.

The author quotes what Deputy Chief Michael Marino said, "'When I came on the job a cop would never do any damage to another cop, not for all the money in the world. Things change.'" And I never thought and could have never imagined that my colleagues, with whom I have worked for many years, and loved, could throw me down the pit.

POLICE DEPARTMENT
CITY OF NEW YORK

March 27, 2017

From: PO Hernández, Emmanuel Tax # 944269

To: Retirement Counseling Unit, Steven Welsome

Subject: **REQUESTING A CHANGE OF RETIREMENT DATE.**

1.   The undersigned respectfully request for my retirement date to be changed from 4/30/2017 to 3/27/2017.

2.   For your **CONSIDERATION**.

Emmanuel Hernandez
Police Officer

Chapter 31

What Uncertainty Awaits Me

I HURRIED MY RETIREMENT. I ASKED IT TO BE RETIRED A MONTH EARLIER, FOR I THOUGHT THAT IT WAS GOING TO END MY PERSECUTION, BUT IT WASN'T. IT IS March 27, 2025, AND I HAVE NOT WORKED EVER SINCE. IT IS 8 LONG YEARS, AND PEOPLE STILL FOLLOW ME TO THIS DATE. **I OBTAINED MY BACHELOR DEGREE IN CRIMINAL JUSTICE, MAINLY TO WORK IN LAW ENFORCEMENT, BUT WHO WILL HIRE ME NOW THAT MY MEDICAL RECORD HAS BEEN RUINED AND THE MUD THROWN AT ME BY THE DEFAMATORY ACT TAKEN AGAINST ME BY BEING CONSIDERED A THIEF, ALL BECAUSE ONE MAN THINKS I AM SO. SO MUCH WORK FOR NOTHING.**

EVERYWHERE I GO, EVERYWHERE I WORK, I WILL ENDURE THE SAME TREATMENT, THEREFORE, MY DAYS OF WORKING HAS ENDED UNLESS MY ACCUSERS RETRACT FROM WHATEVER IT IS THAT THEY ARE ACCUSING ME OF. UNLESS THEY CLEAR MY NAME. **A PERFECT EXAMPLE HAPPENED ON APRIL 10, 2025, A DAY AFTER I TRAVELED FROM DOMINICAN REPUBLIC TO NEW YORK CITY, THAT I WAS INSIDE SOMEONE'S BUSINESS STORE, AND THERE WAS MONEY IN SOME ESPECIFIC PLACES. I WAS SEATED THERE, AND THERE WERE TWO CASHIERS COUNTING MONEY. ONE OF THEM WENT TO LOOK FOR A BAG OR ENVELOPE THAT HAD MONEY IN IT.**

IN LESS THAN 30 SECONDS SHE COULDN'T FIND IT. THE OFFICE BECAME TENSE. SHE BEGAN MAKING THE THROUGHT SOUND OF SUSPICION, BECAUSE

OBVIOULY, SHE THOUGHT I HAD TAKEN IT, BUT THANK GOD, SHE FOUND IT RIGHT AWAY.

IN ADDITION TO THE IMPOSSIBILITY OF WORKING FOR OTHERS, I CANNOT WORK ON MY OWN ENTREPRENEURSHIP, FOR IF I PUT BUSINESS OF MY OWN, IT WON'T SUCCEED BECAUSE OF MY RUINED REPUTATION.

IN AN ACT OF DEFIANCE TO PROVOKE MY ACCUSERS TO TALK, I MADE MYSELF PUBLIC, BY RUNNING FOR CONGRESS IN THE DOMINICAN REPUBLIC, BUT NO

ACCUSER CONFRONTED ME. **I ONLY RECEIVED 100 VOTES. MY ACCUSERS ARE TRULLY BLOCKING MY SUCCESS.** NOT ONLY THAT, MONTHS AFTER MY DEFEAT IN THE ELECTIONS, I WENT TO FIX MY WHITE TOYOTA HIGHLANDER BENEATH, AND THEY KEPT MY VEHICLE AT THE MECHANIC FOR TWO MONTHS AND THEY WORSEN THE CONDITION OF MY VEHICLE, FORCING ME TO TAKE IT TO ANOTHER MECHANIC, WHO DEALT SUCCESSFULLY WITH THE ISSUE, BUT I HAD TO WAIT ANOTHER MONTH, SPENDING OVERALL OVER $3000 DOLLARS ON FIXING IT. IN THE PROCESS, I HAD TO FINANCE ANOTHER VEHICLE. **MY ACCUSERS ARE TRULLY BLOCKING MY SUCCESS.**

IN 2024, I RENTED THIS COMMERCIAL ESTABLISHMENT AND ESTABLISHED A SPA WITH NO SUCCESS. I MADE A BIG INVESTMENT IN WALL PARTITIONS, AIR CONDITIONER, SEATS, CHAIR, OFFICE DESK, DECORATIONS AND LIGHTINGS. IT HAS BEEN THERE FOR MONTHS AND NO SUCCESS. ONLY ONE CLIENT. **MY ACCUSERS ARE TRULLY BLOCKING MY SUCCESS.**

BY THE END OF OCTOBER 2024, WHEN CLOSING THE SPA FOR GOOD, AND HANDING OVER BACK THE KEY TO THE OWNER OF THE COMMERCIAL ESTABLISHMENT, I WAS TOLD THAT I HAD TO GET RID OF THE WALL PARTITIONS I MADE IN THE ROOM. SO, I, BY MYSELF, WITH MY OWN HANDS, BEGAN TO RIP OFF THE WALL

PARTITIONS I MADE. **MY ACCUSERS ARE TRULLY BLOCKING MY SUCCESS.**

MY ACCUSERS ARE TRULLY BLOCKING MY SUCCESS.

I AM EXHAUTED, AND IF THERE IS ANYTHING I CAN DO, TO HELP THEM FIND OUT THE TRUTH. I WILL DO MY PART. FIRST OF ALL, THERE IS NO POSSIBLE WAY THAT I WILL LIE, ESPECIALLY IN OFFICIAL DOCUMENTS AND INCREDIBLY NO WAY, NEVER, MUCH LESS IN COURT.

NOW, ON WHETHER I AM A THIEF, THAT SHOULD HAVE NEVER CROSS YOUR MIND IN FIRST PLACE. BUT TO APPEASE YOUR DISTRUST HEART, I WILL INTRODUCE A NEW DISCOVERY EVIDENCE OF WHATEVER IT IS THAT I CAN FIND OR GATHER, TO ILLUSTRATE TO ALL OF YOU, AND TO PLEASE STOP HARASSING ME FOR STUPID THINGS THAT I DIDN'T DO, SO HELP ME GOD.

IN 2011, I WAS tired OF WORKING NIGHTSHIFT. I WAS LEAVING FROM NIGHT TOUR TO DAY TOUR. UNTIL ONE DAY PO BLISS TOLD ME THAT PO EDDY PINERO WAS COMING TO WORK MIDNIGHT, I THAT I SHOULD STAY TO BE HIS PARTNER. I HAPPILY ACCEPTED, BECAUSE AT LEAST I WILL BE WORKING WITH A PASTOR, WHAT BETTER THAN THAT. SO, WHAT I DID WAS TO CHANGE FROM SQUAD. SO, I SUBMITTED THIS FORM TO GO FROM MY SQUAD TO HIS SQUAD.

**POLICE DEPARTMENT
CITY OF NEW YORK**

From: Police Officer, 25th Precinct   April 14, 2011

To: Commanding Officer, 25th Precinct

Subject: **REQUEST FOR SQUAD CHANGE**

1. The undersigned respectfully requests to be considered for a squad change from A-2 to A-1.

2. For your **CONSIDERATION**.

Emmanuel Hernandez
Police Officer

DURING THE TIME THAT WE WERE PARTNERS, IT WAS A BEAUTIFUL THING TO GO TO WORK AND BE AT WORK, BUT AS WE ALL KNOW, GOOD THINGS CAN'T LAST. LT. NAOKI YAGUCHI WAS TRANSFERRED TO OUR PRECINT AND THE REST IS HISTORY. THEY SEPARATED US, AND THIS IS WHEN EVERYTHING CAME DOWN THE HILL. IN 2014, HE DECIDED TO RETIRE, 2 YEARS PRIOR HIS RETIREMENT DATE. HE DID SO, EVENTHOUGH HE WAS GOING TO LOSE

553

HIS BENEFITS FOR TWO YEARS, UNTIL HIS 20 YEARS ANNIVERSARY COMES.

BUT BEFORE LEAVING, HE LEFT ME HIS LOCKER, AND HE GAVE ME HIS SPEAKER MICROPHONE VERTEX, AND TOGETHER WITH IT, THE RECEIPT AT THE BOTTOM. YES, I KNOW WHY THE RECEIPT. BECAUSE THEY MIGHT THINK THAT I STOLE IT, SO HE LEFT ME THIS AS PROOF THAT IT WASN'T. IT IS SAD TO SEE THE DATE IN THE RECEIPT. 04/05/12. HE PAID $79 DOLLARS FOR IT THINKING THAT HE WAS GOING TO FINISH HIS 20 YEARS' CAREER, WE HAVE TOGETHER AS PARTNERS.

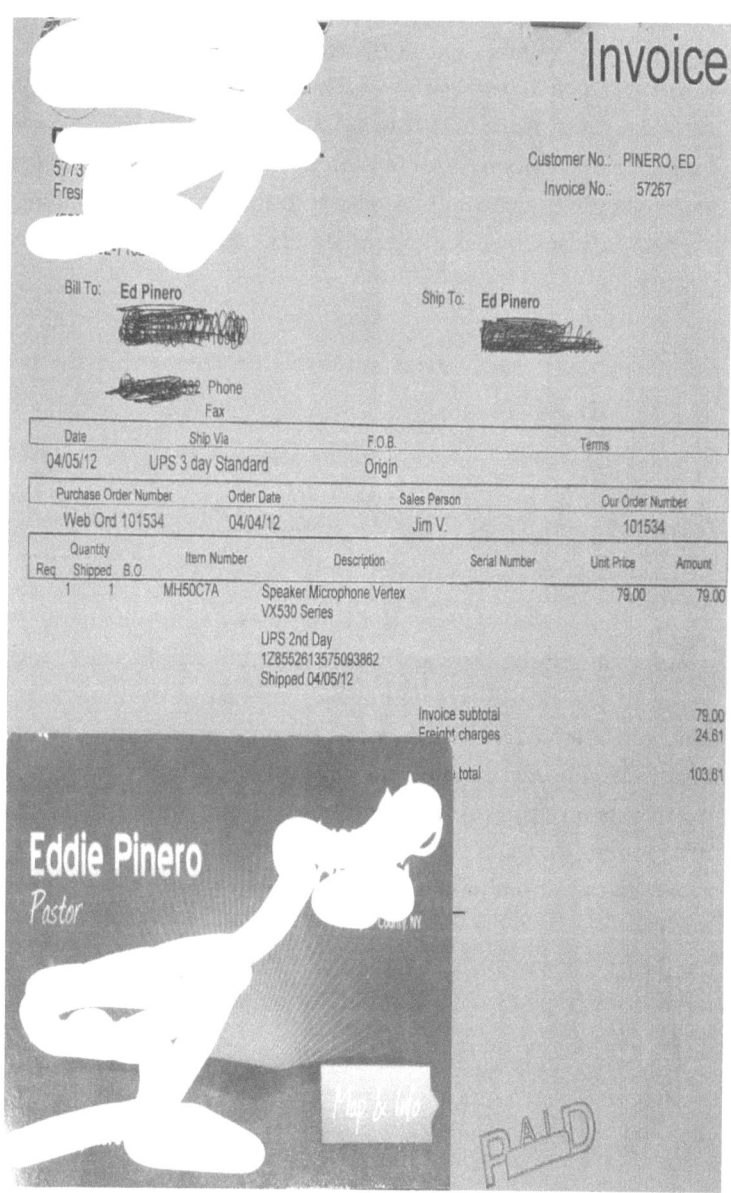

Yes, I believed it to be true that there was a thief in the precinct, for I have lost stuff, but I didn't go out to tell everyone about it, for it is too embarrassing to even think that there might exist the possibility that among us, crime fighters, is a criminal. So, I simply convinced myself that I missed placed it or lost it. But when they began to accuse me of being a thief, I realized that by property didn't just disappear by art of magic. There is a thief in the house.

One of the items that I lost was my department issued and official flashlight by the brand of MAG-LITE. The one that are given to police officers when they are out of the police academy. I lost, but after what I know now, someone stole my flashlight. So, I bought a second one, and the second once again, was stolen. At the bottom is a picture of the receipt of the last one I bought, but time after, was stolen too. And this is when I saw myself without a flashlight and had asked PO Pinero to lend me his, since he had an additional, tactical, smaller and more powerful flashlight. The MAG-LITE was more to have as requirement. The only thing left of that flashlight is the manual shown at the bottom as well.

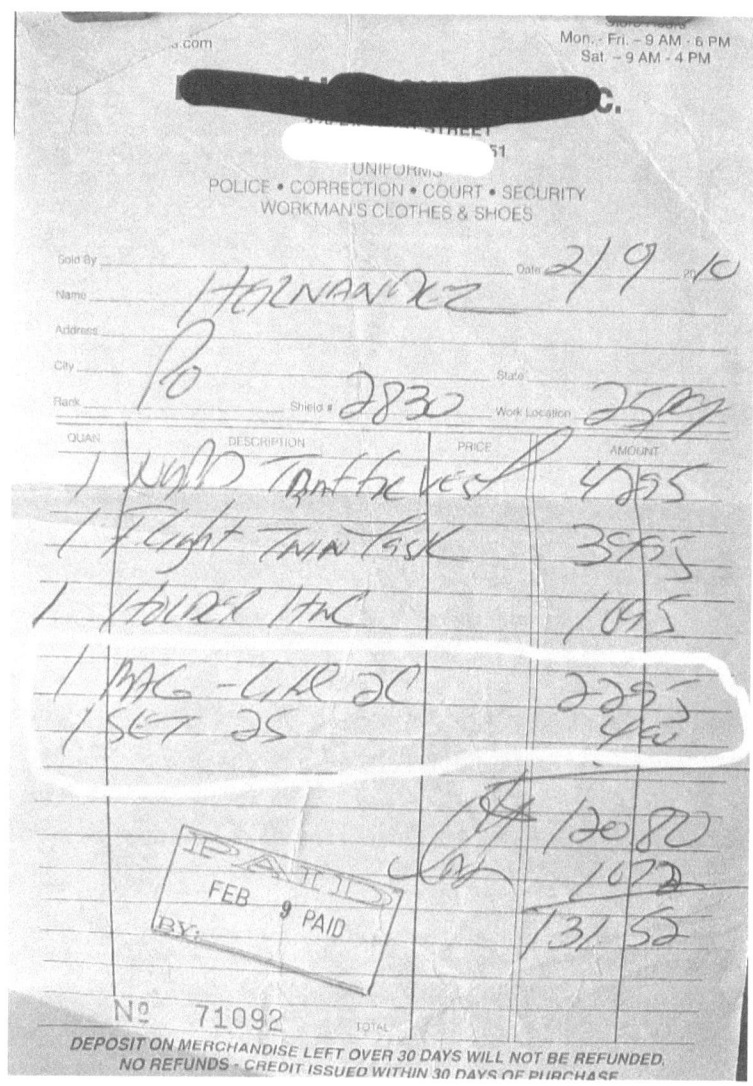

Emmanuel Hernandez

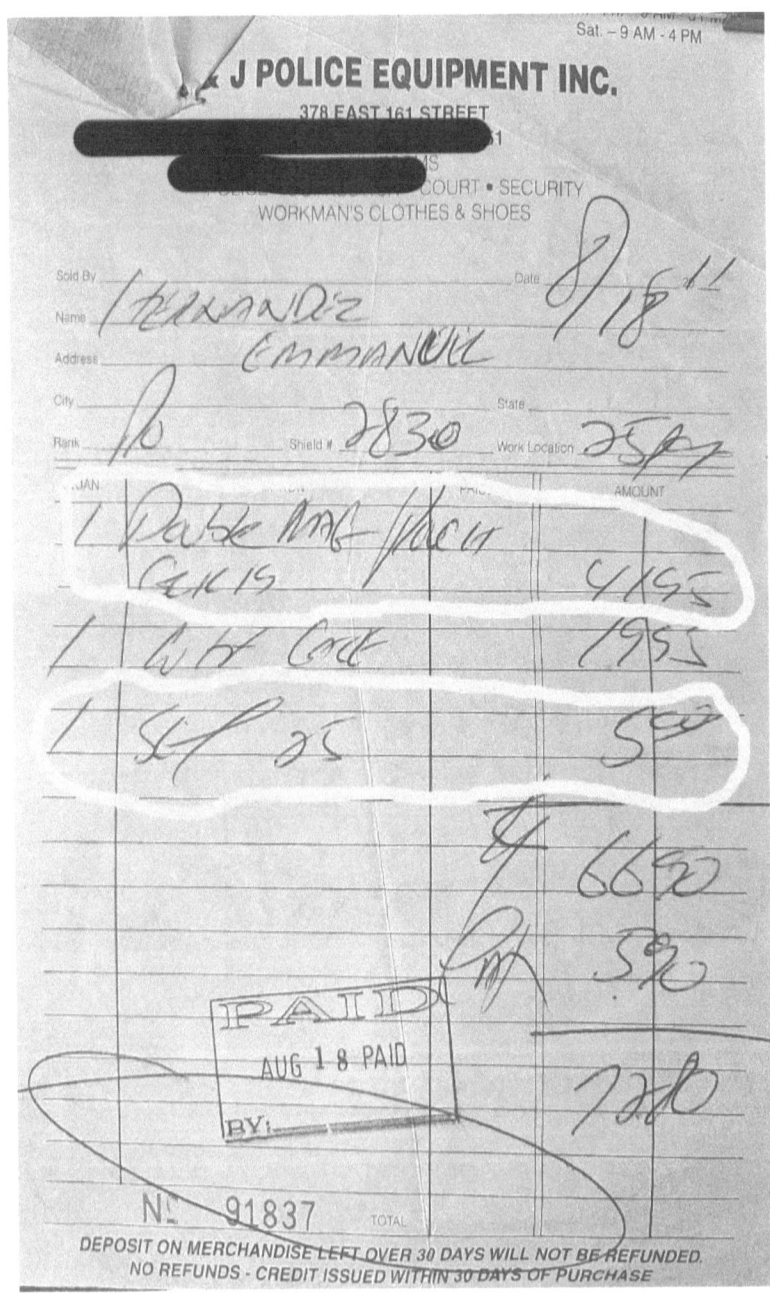

558

PO Pinero, my partner, has his flashlight engraved, as shown at the bottom, with his name and shield number. He did it because things got stolen. But this is when all this stupid chaos started. Then one night, I found myself without a flashlight, and I asked him to lend me his, which he did. And with all the attacks, harassment and turmoil inside and out of the precinct.

My locker that was upside down, full of nonsense everywhere, I forgot to return his flashlight, the last day that I saw him that he gave me his speaker. When I began to organize my stuff, it was when I found that I still had his flashlight. I was waiting for this moment to return it to him. Because if I did it earlier, the wolves of the 25th precinct will use this to support and exploit the idea that I am the thief and use it as proof and weaponized it to confirm that they finally found the thief.

In addition, I bought a tactical flashlight myself, STREAMLIGHT STRION LED that cost me $163.25. The first one I had was stolen. So, I had to buy a second one. The last one I bought, I still have, as shown in the picture below. I remember when one of the officers asked me to let him see my STREAMLIGHT flashlight, I took it out and gave it to him. He looked at it carefully, prying around it and then he gave it back to me without altering a word. It seems that he too lost his. But here I show you a picture of my tactical flashlight and two of my receipts of purchase of my two flashlights, on different date and different times.

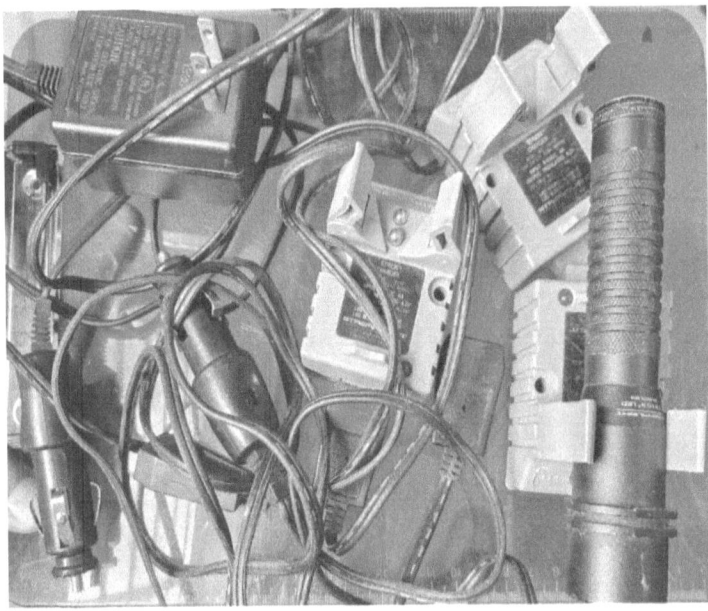

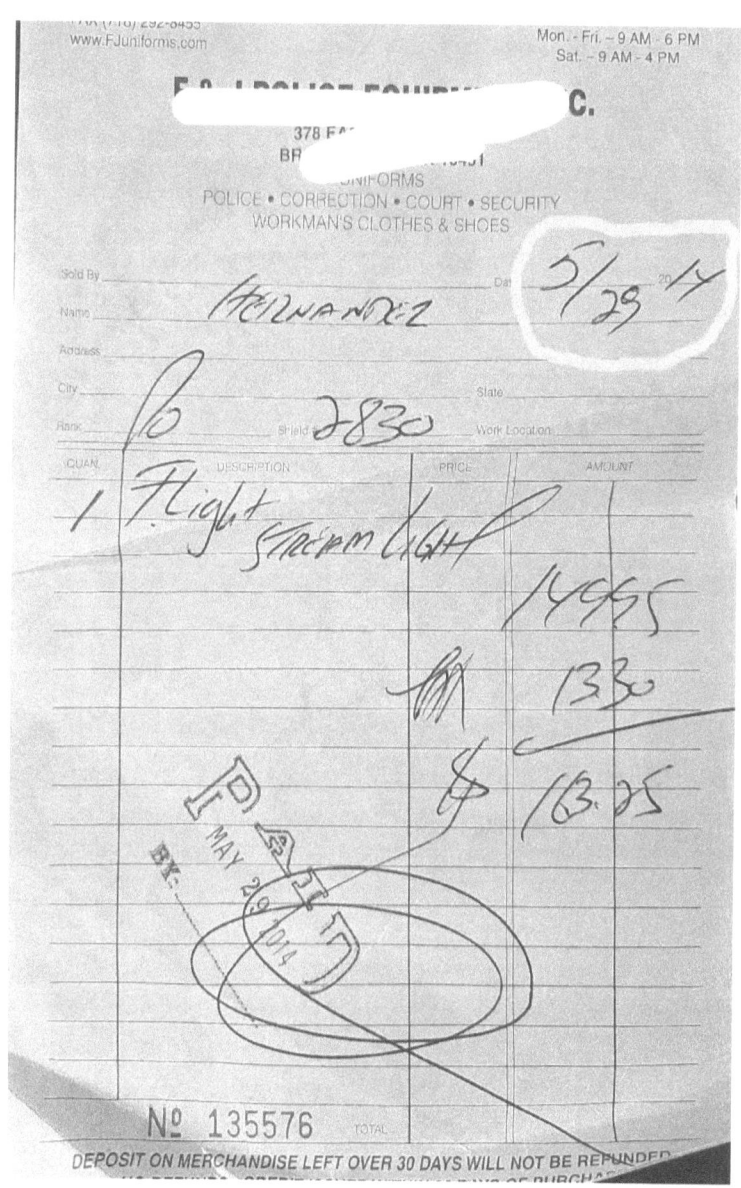

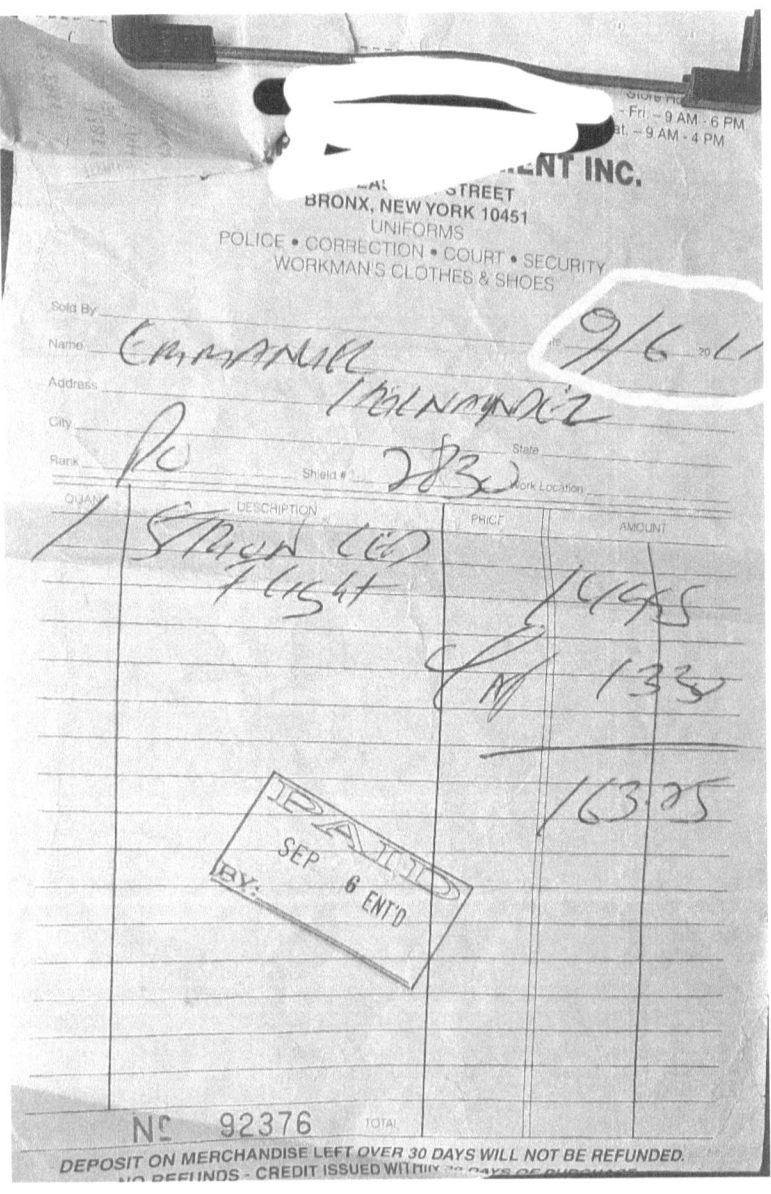

THE BOTTOM LINE IS THAT THEY ARE SO GOOD AT THEIR INVESTIGATIVE WORK, THAT THEY DIDN'T GO TO THE EQUIPMENT SECTIONS TO LOOK AT MY PURCHASES AND FROM THERE DETERMINE IF I TOO HAVE FALL VICTIM OF THEFT CRIME AT THE 25 PCT, BASED ON MY PURCHASES RECORD. I LEAVE YOU WITH THIS RECEIPT TO SEE IF YOU FIND IT USEFULL, FOR IF I HAVE ANY OTHER, I HAVE LOST IT.

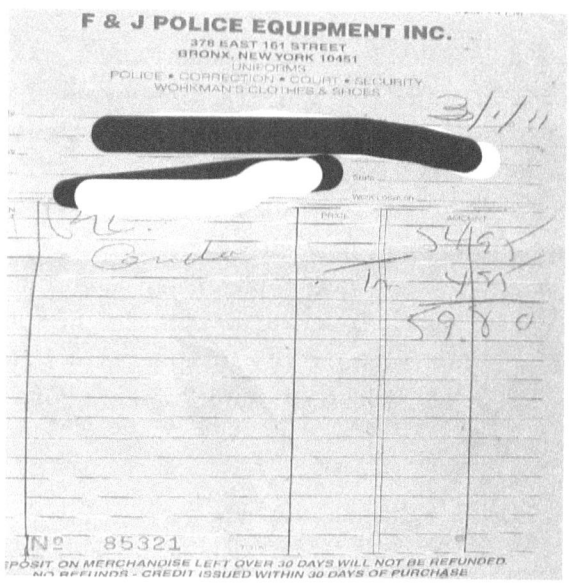

NKJV Malachi 3: 8-11
"'Will a man rob God?
Yet you have robbed Me!
But you say,
'In what way have we robbed You?'
In tithe and offerings.
9 You are cursed with a curse,
For you have robbed Me,

Even this whole nation.
10 Bring all the tithes into the storehouse,
That there may be food in My house,
And try Me now in this',"
Says the Lord of hosts,
"'If I will not open for you the windows of heaven
And pour out for you such blessing
That there will not be room enough to receive it.'"

Logic and common sense tell us that there is no way that you may not steal from God, but yet, steal from mankind, and still go to heaven. No Sir. You will inherit hell for sure. Logic speaks for itself or by his own. Therefore, there is no way whatsoever, that giving my tithe to the Lord, I will steal men, for if I do so, I will have given my tithe in vain, for God will never accepted things, sacrifice, or money, out of corrupted, dirty, bloody and sinful hands. Such practice, he will condemn for it irritates him. It will be best to give nothing to the Lord, if you are a man who steal things from other people. But he will accept it if it comes out of a sincere, honest and pure heart.

AND THESE WERE MY TITHES.

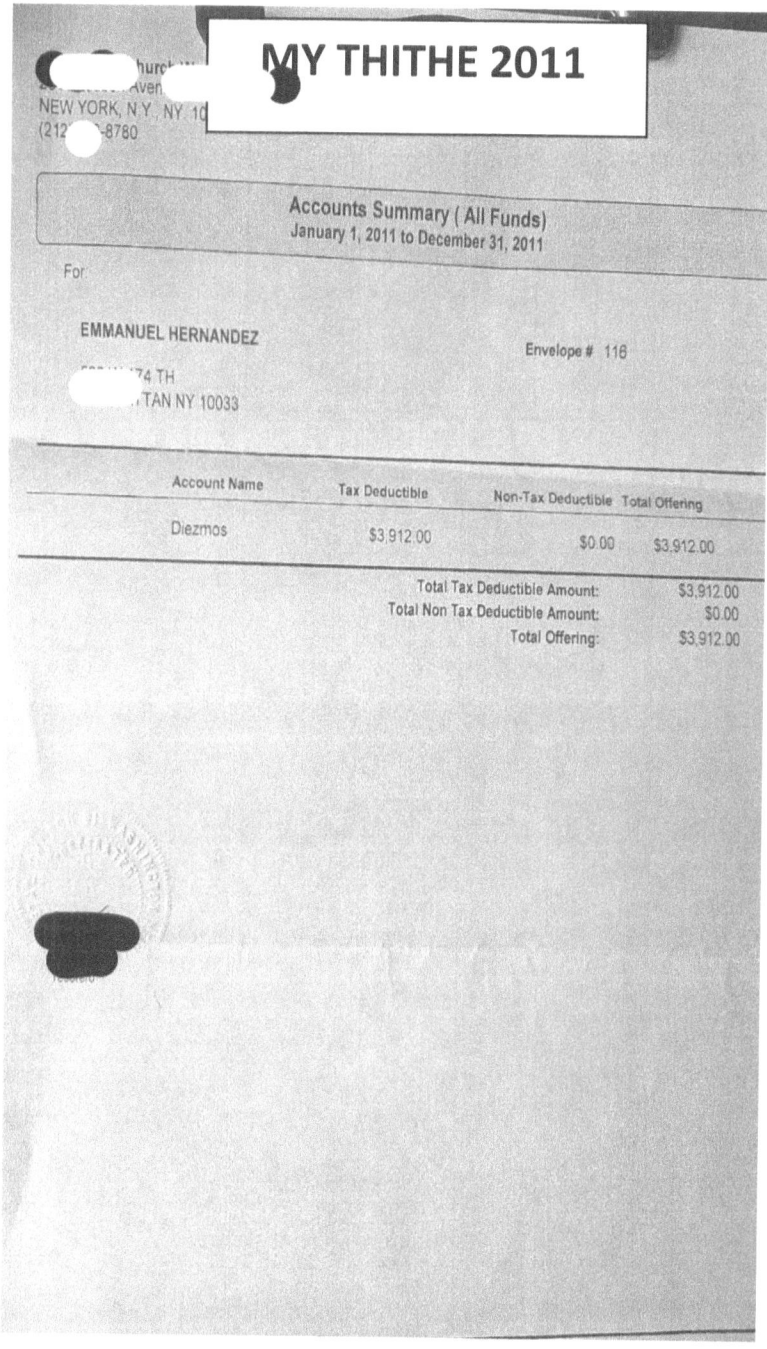

MY THITHE 2011

NEW YORK, N.Y., NY. 10
(212) -8780

Accounts Summary (All Funds)
January 1, 2011 to December 31, 2011

For

EMMANUEL HERNANDEZ

Envelope # 116

74 TH
TAN NY 10033

Account Name	Tax Deductible	Non-Tax Deductible	Total Offering
Diezmos	$3,912.00	$0.00	$3,912.00

Total Tax Deductible Amount:	$3,912.00
Total Non Tax Deductible Amount:	$0.00
Total Offering:	$3,912.00

Emmanuel Hernandez

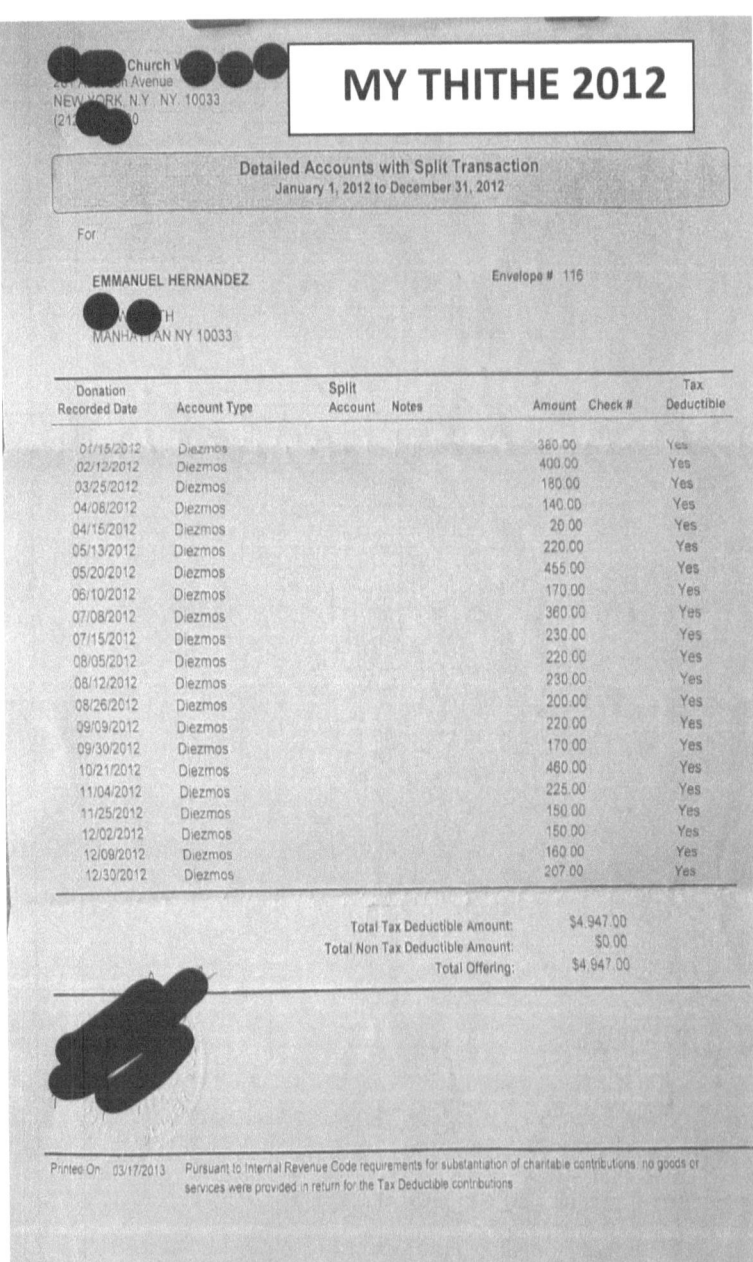

MY THITHE 2012

Detailed Accounts with Split Transaction
January 1, 2012 to December 31, 2012

For

EMMANUEL HERNANDEZ

Envelope # 116

MANHATTAN NY 10033

Donation Recorded Date	Account Type	Split Account	Notes	Amount	Check #	Tax Deductible
01/15/2012	Diezmos			360.00		Yes
02/12/2012	Diezmos			400.00		Yes
03/25/2012	Diezmos			180.00		Yes
04/08/2012	Diezmos			140.00		Yes
04/15/2012	Diezmos			20.00		Yes
05/13/2012	Diezmos			220.00		Yes
05/20/2012	Diezmos			455.00		Yes
06/10/2012	Diezmos			170.00		Yes
07/08/2012	Diezmos			360.00		Yes
07/15/2012	Diezmos			230.00		Yes
08/05/2012	Diezmos			220.00		Yes
08/12/2012	Diezmos			230.00		Yes
08/26/2012	Diezmos			200.00		Yes
09/09/2012	Diezmos			220.00		Yes
09/30/2012	Diezmos			170.00		Yes
10/21/2012	Diezmos			460.00		Yes
11/04/2012	Diezmos			225.00		Yes
11/25/2012	Diezmos			150.00		Yes
12/02/2012	Diezmos			150.00		Yes
12/09/2012	Diezmos			160.00		Yes
12/30/2012	Diezmos			207.00		Yes

Total Tax Deductible Amount: $4,947.00
Total Non Tax Deductible Amount: $0.00
Total Offering: $4,947.00

Printed On 03/17/2013   Pursuant to Internal Revenue Code requirements for substantiation of charitable contributions, no goods or services were provided in return for the Tax Deductible contributions

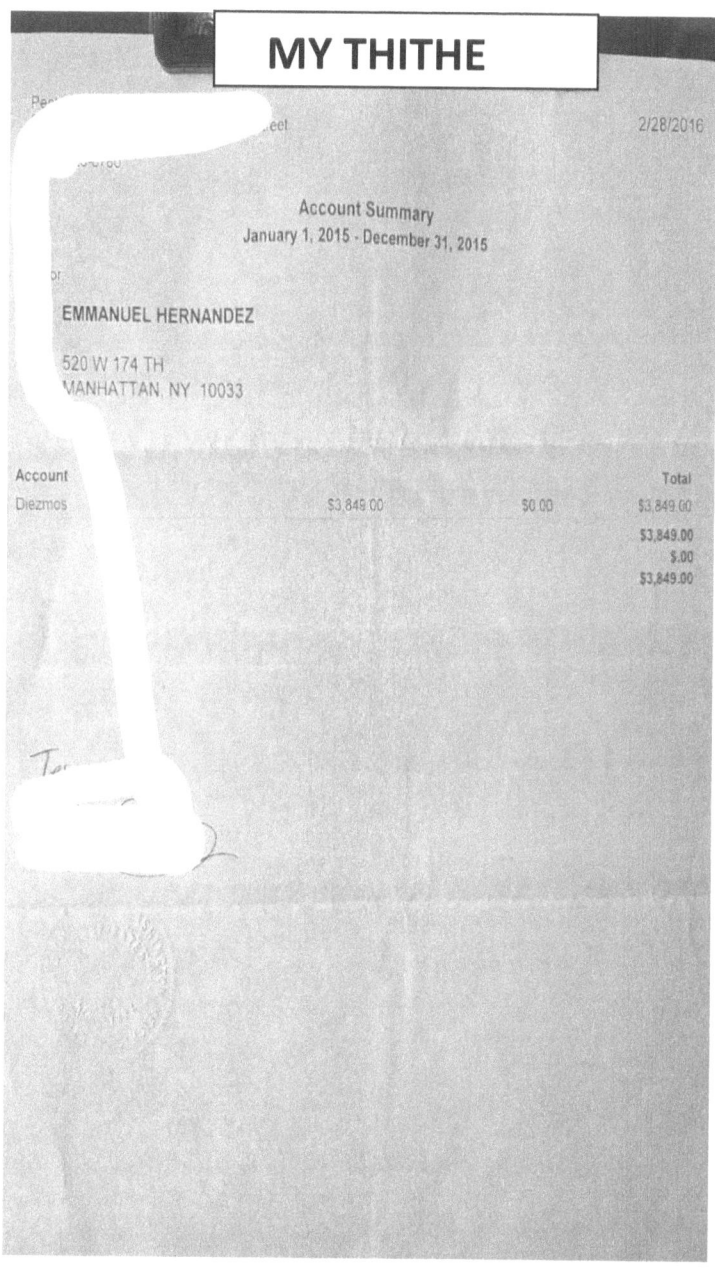

MY THITHE

2/28/2016

Account Summary
January 1, 2015 - December 31, 2015

EMMANUEL HERNANDEZ

520 W 174 TH
MANHATTAN, NY 10033

Account			Total
Diezmos	$3,849.00	$0.00	$3,849.00
			$3,849.00
			$.00
			$3,849.00

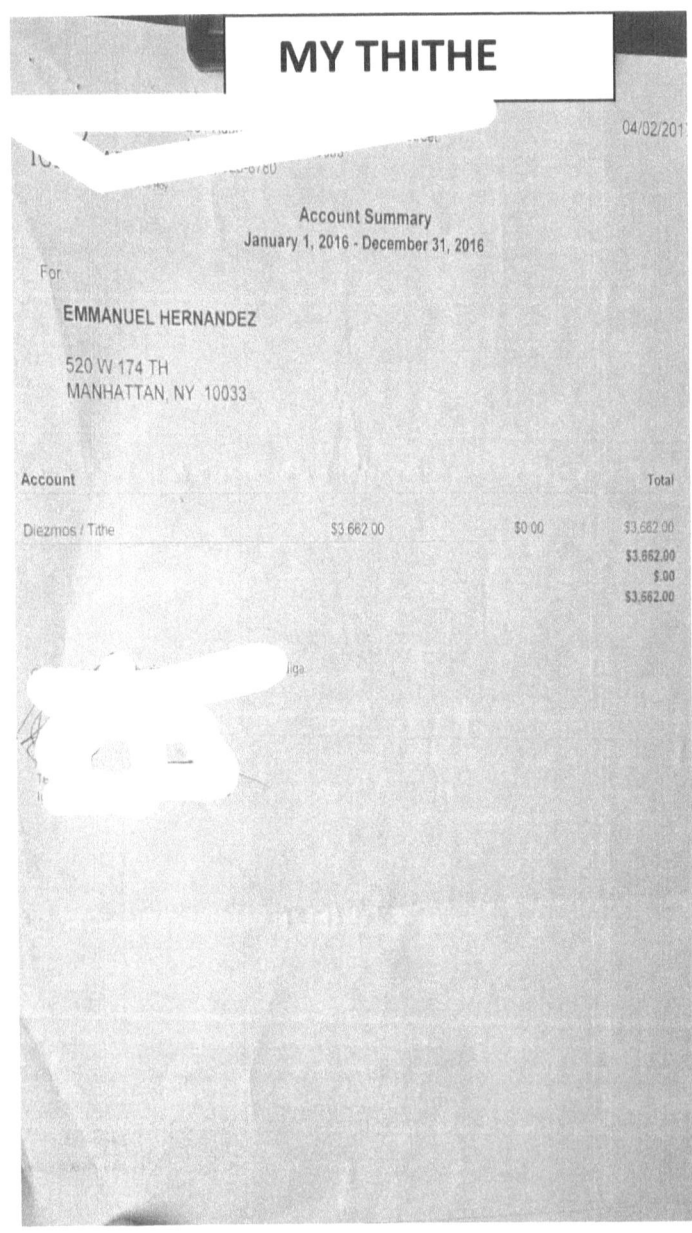

MY THITHE

04/02/201

Account Summary
January 1, 2016 - December 31, 2016

For

EMMANUEL HERNANDEZ

520 W 174 TH
MANHATTAN, NY 10033

Account			Total
Diezmos / Tithe	$3,662.00	$0.00	$3,662.00
			$3,662.00
			$.00
			$3,662.00

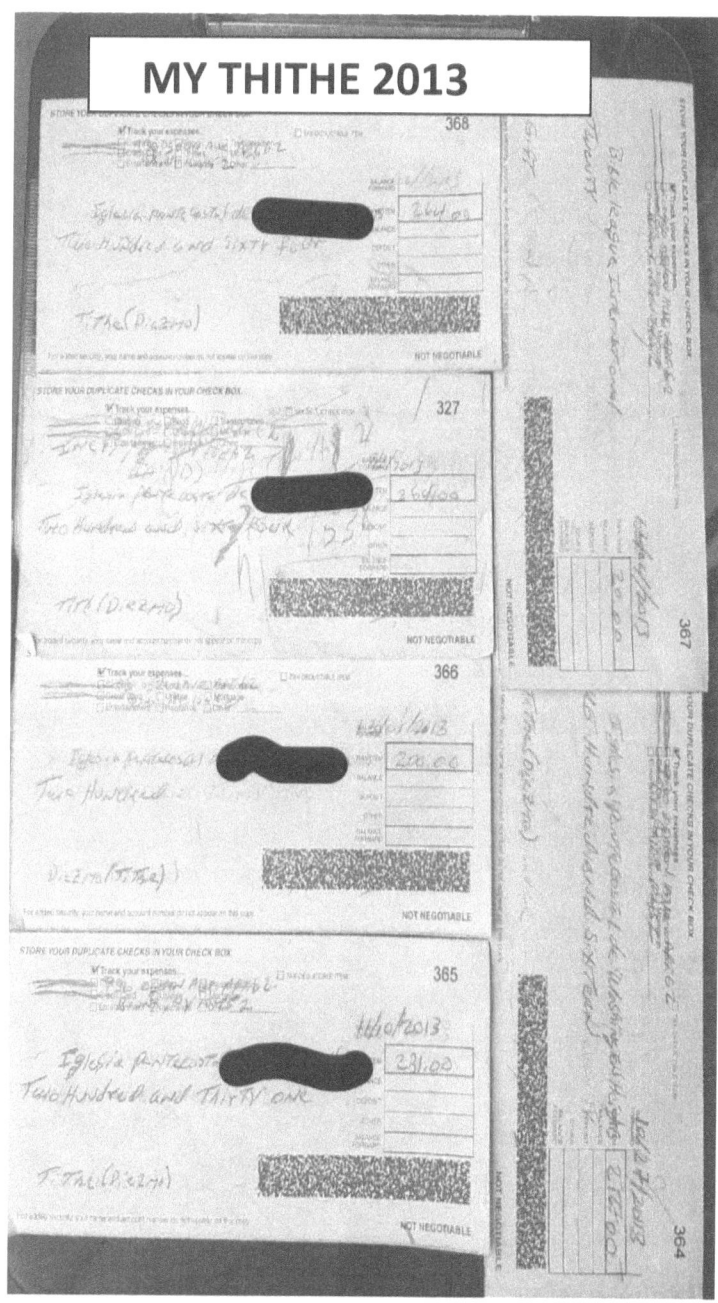

MY THITHE 2013

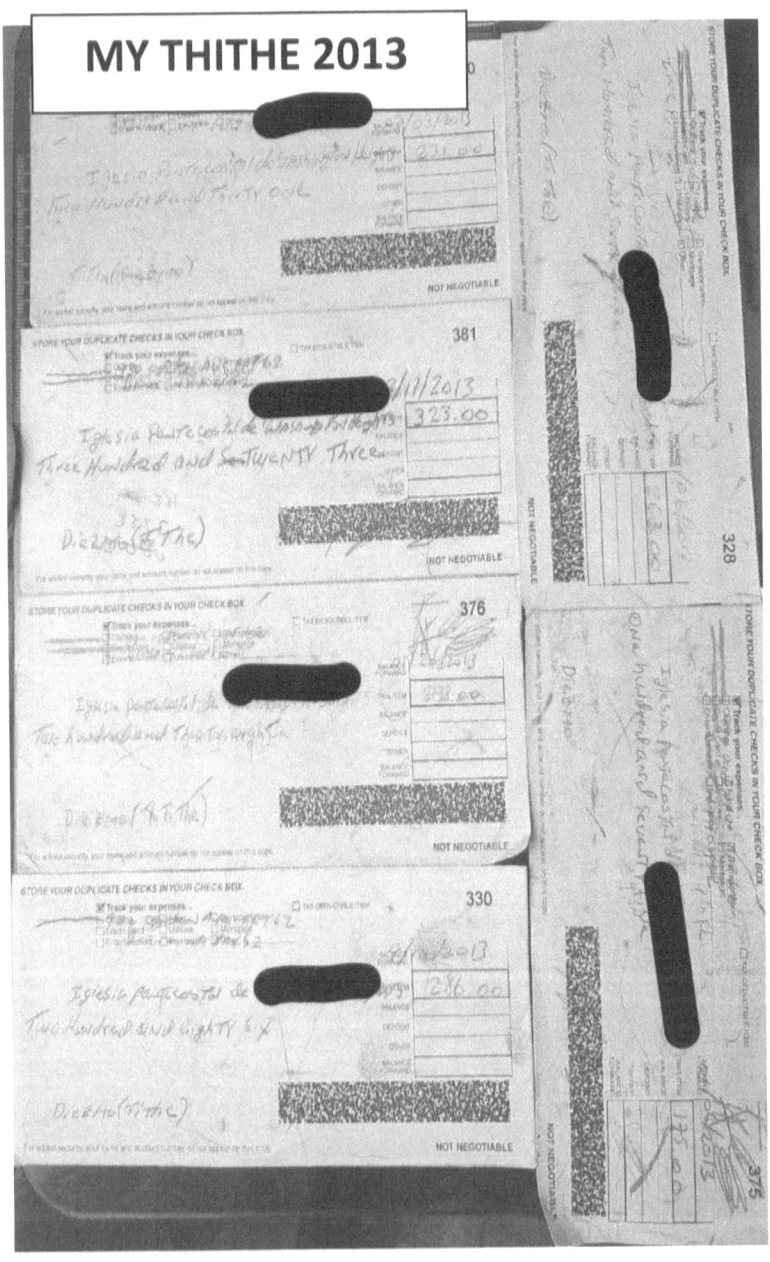

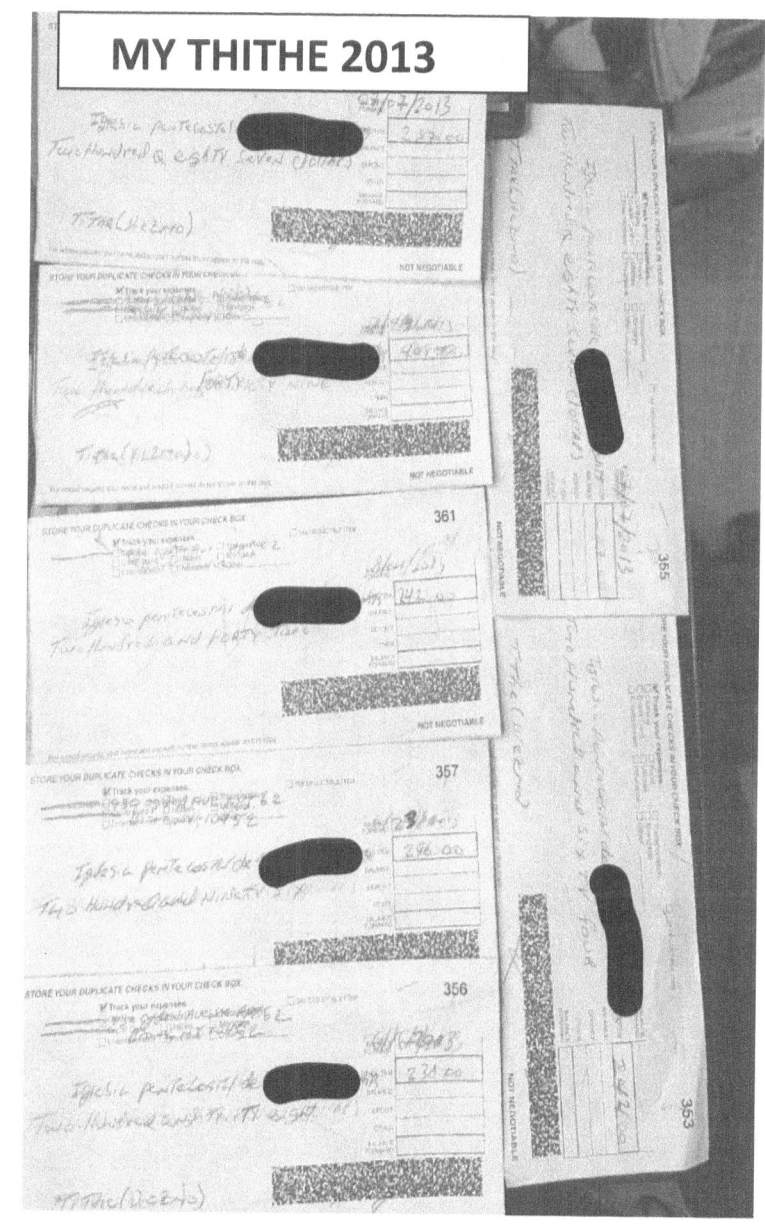

Emmanuel Hernandez

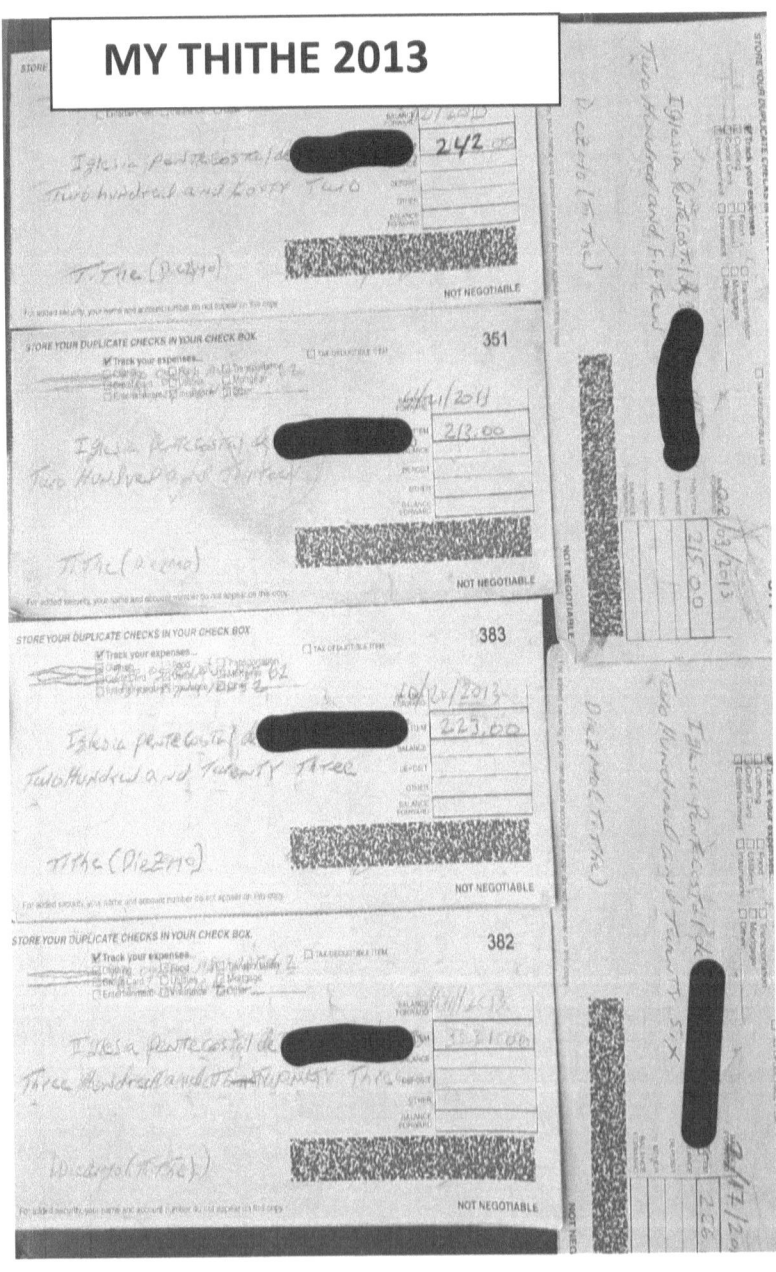

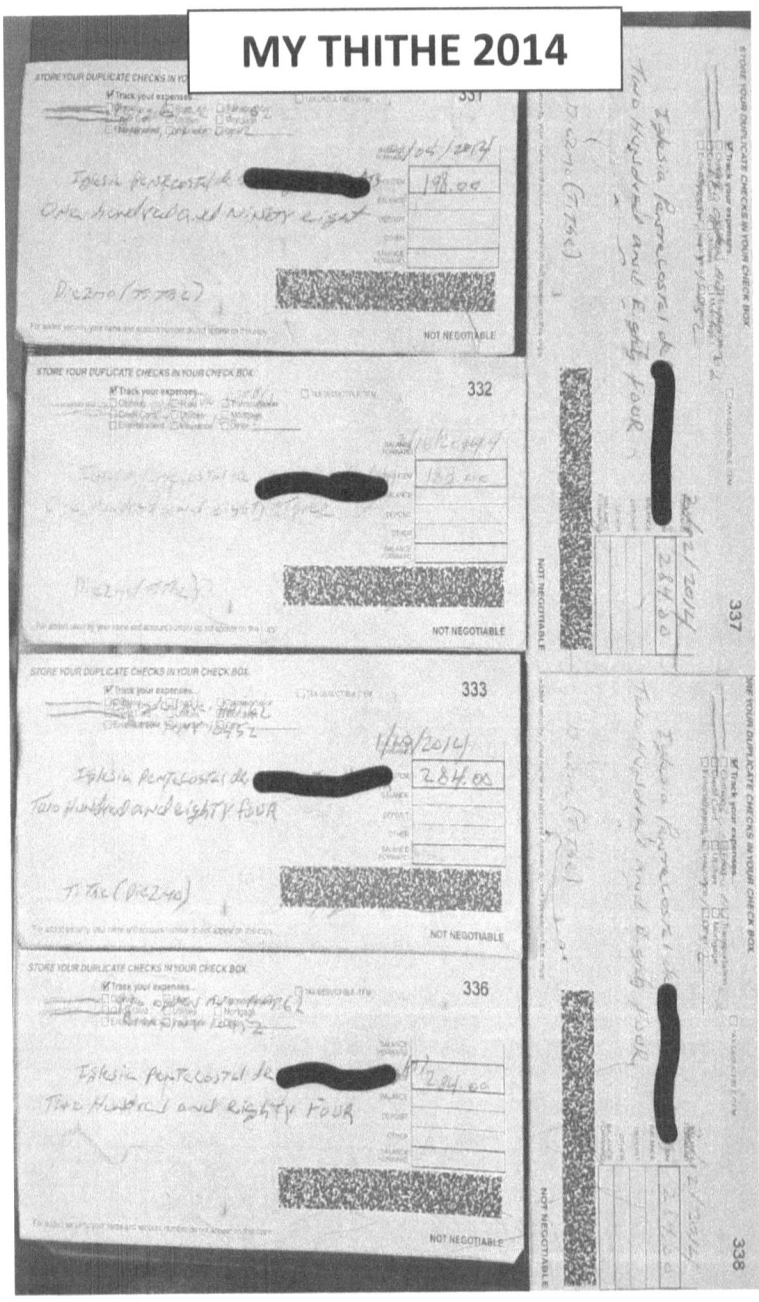

MY THITHE 2014

Emmanuel Hernandez

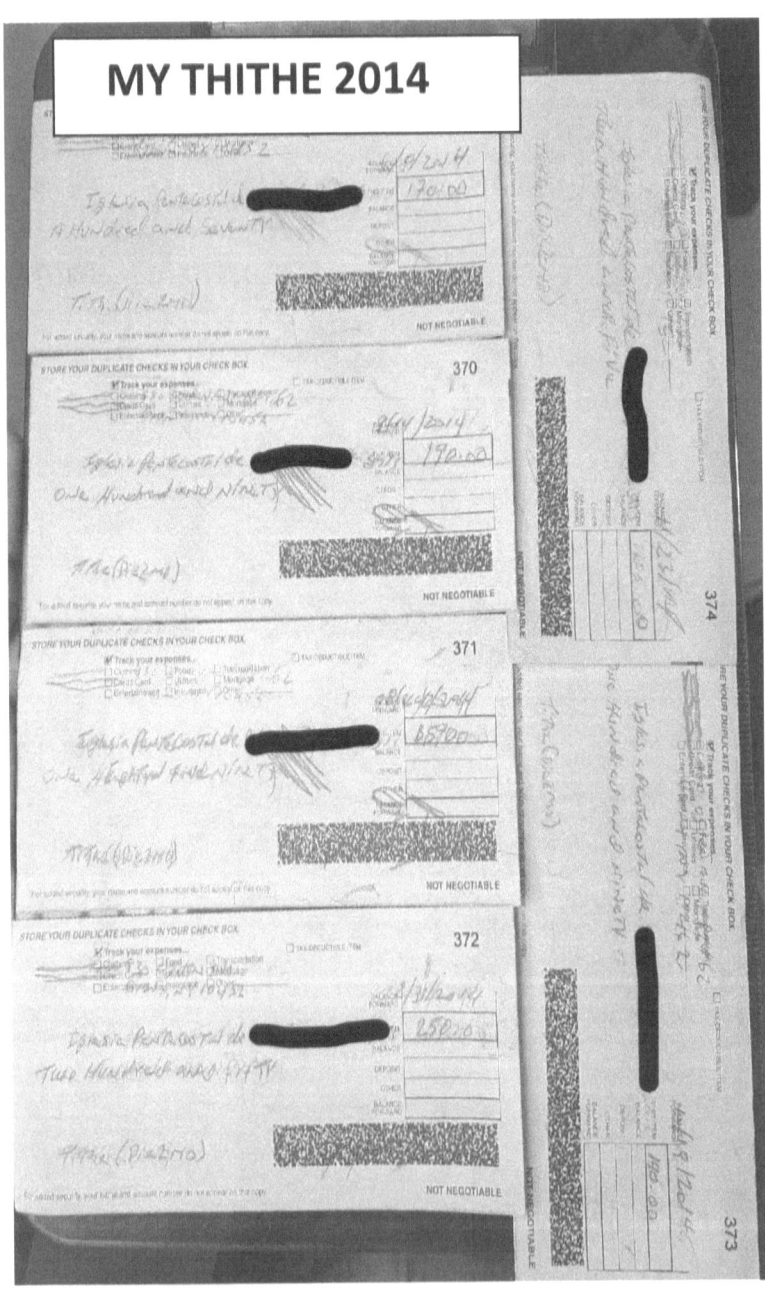

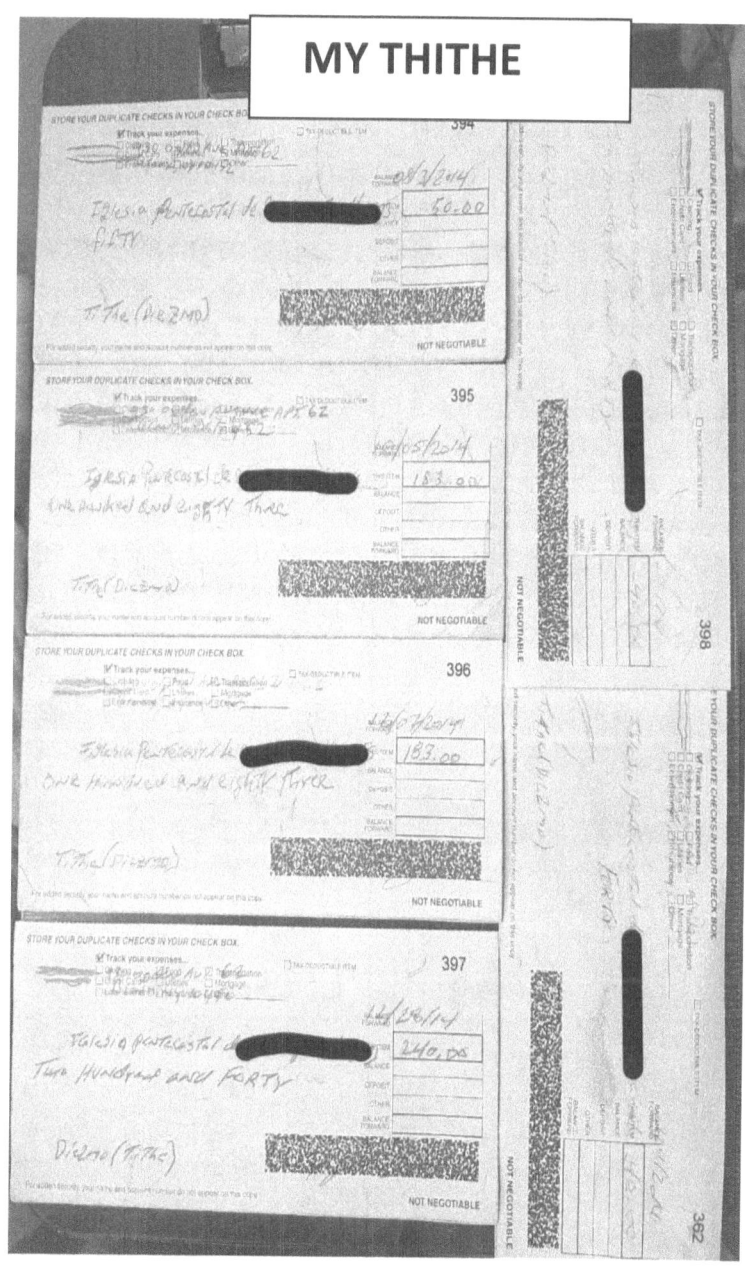

MY THITHE CONTRIBUTION WAS OVER $28,000 THOUSAND DOOLARS BEFORE THE COVID PANDEMIC, WHICH IN TODAY'S VALUE MIGHT BE $40,000.

NOW, TO ALL THE BRILLIANT MINDS, I WANT TO ASK THEM THE FOLLOWING QUESTIONS?

HOW IN THE WORLD, THEY DIDN'T GO TO THE EQUIPMENT SECTIONS STORES TO FIND OUT IF I HAVE BEEN BUYING STUFF, AND FROM THERE DETERMINE WHETHER I TOO HAVE BEEN MISSING STUFF, AND LATER FIND OUT THAT I WAS BEING ROBBED TOO?

NOW, WHAT IS THE USE TO NOT STEAL GOD, BUT YES, STEAL TO PEOPLE? WHAT MAKES YOU THINK THAT I WILL NOT STEAL GOD, BY GIVING MY TITHE OUT OF MY EVERY PAYCHECK, MY 10% OF ALL MY INCOME, BUT YET, I WILL ROB MY FELLOW MEN AND WOMEN? IT MAKES NO SENSE AT ALL.

Why?

Ever since I began working for the NYPD, since I was a police cadet, I openly spoke about the love of God to my colleagues. But I never knew that it was going to produce and provoke such a cruel outcome. I never thought that it was going to come back to bite me, and all this is because on John 15: 19-20 Jesus said, "If you were of the world, the world would love you as its own; but because you are not of the world, but I chose you out of the world, therefore the world hates you. 20Remember the word that I said to you: 'A servant is not greater than his master.' If they persecuted me, they will also persecute you...." Oh my God, I preached your word, and it was as if everyone around me turned against me at my workplace, and they all falsely accused me of something that till this day I don't know why. This is how effective your word is.

But I heard a preacher who taught, "Jesus said that we are in a planet of wolves. And that we were like sheep and that if we study the life of the sheep, we will discover that sheep are the most defenseless animals that exist in the creation. **In a few words, the rabbit, the squirrel, the**

deer all defend themselves, the claws, the speed, the hoofs, but the sheep are the stupidest, the dumbest, semi blinded, and most defenseless of all animals that exist. In few words, when Jesus says that you are going to dwell in a world of wolves, in a planet of wolves where everyone around you would like to deceive you, everyone would like to take advantage of your life and use you like an object." It is more than clear. At the beginning my faith was strong, but it weakened as the persecution against me intensified. If I had kept a strong faith, I would have been triumphant today.

Are not police officers normally told when they are placed on some type of monitoring? If so, why wasn't I told about it, so at least I may know what was for and what is going on? If there was any problem, why didn't they consult me in regards? Why didn't they simply ask? Why all this odyssey? Did I at any given time disrespect or have any argument with my colleagues, bosses, or superiors? Was I a disciplinary problem? Did I give them a motive not to trust me? Or am I too good to be true in this corrupt world, and therefore they need to put dirt on me so they can feel good about it? Can someone take the stand and dare to look at the background and the habits of whoever is investigating me? I consider all their informal investigation to be nothing more than a demonic activity. I wonder who is profiting from all of this. Who is benefiting from my suffering.

Overall, I always wondered why they didn't take any disciplinary action against me if they thought that I did something wrong, but they didn't. Why? Because if they had corrected me for some wrongdoing that would have been the end of it. I would have been accused; I would have had the chance to know what was going on and would have the opportunity to advocate on my behalf. I would have been disciplined and that would be it. But no. The degree of the punishment wouldn't be enough for them. They wanted more than that. So, they realized that if they had disciplined me for whatever wrongdoing they think I did at the time, they wouldn't have been able to justify why they are following me today.

They so bad want me to commit a crime, so they can say to each other "good job", "I told you that he was a criminal," and then have a party to celebrate their victory. Today I still remember the day when I was in the front passenger seat of the police car that PO Clement was driving. Then suddenly, she said to herself, "Accusing people of sh…t." But I remained quiet. You think that I, who offer 10% of all my earnings to the Lord, my God, am going to risk my salvation by doing the wrong thing?

The day that Lieutenant Yaguchi maliciously asked me for the combination of my locker that I gave him not one, but the combination of my two lockers, so he may go and search for them, why didn't he ask me for the key to my apartment as well, so he could go and search for it too. Why didn't he ask for it? I would have allowed him to search my apartment if that would have helped him with something, and at the same time I would have called my wife to prepare dinner for him and others that might have accompanied him. Why all this worthless drama? I regret not having proposed that. But during the storm, didn't I invite PO Rivera to go to my apartment and sleep there, so he won't have to travel far away in such terrible weather conditions? Also, I offered to visit my home to show him and them that I have nothing to hide.

This is what I have deduced and have come to conclude as a former New York City Police Officer who had been trained to observe and analyze situations and to think out of the box. However, I have been punished for being too observant, which as a result led me to know too much, and sometimes knowing too much could be like eating from the fruits of the forbidden tree that give the knowledge of good and evil. If I wouldn't have been aware of what was going on, now I would have been a healthy cop. I would have been an exemplary young man because I have always lived a decent life, and I would have continue leaving a normal life.

In my background, there is no record of wrongdoing. On the other hand, I believe that they wanted to help me by making sounds with their throat, and by saying things pertaining to my situation so I may know that I am being watched, and by them being cynical about it. Also, by wearing or carrying colors so that I may know that I am being cornered. I don't know if their intentions were good or bad, but what I know is that it didn't help me at all. It got me to where I am now.

There has been a breach of good investigational practice. It wasn't an honest investigation. Who are my witnesses? God is my witness. And all of you are my witnesses. Every Police Officer, undercover cop, Confidential Informant, every Sergeant, Lieutenant, Captain, Chaplain, private eyes and civilians that I have encountered, are my witnesses. And if you believe in God, or in Buddha, or in Bushido or have other beliefs, or don't believe in anything, there is a universal moral law that applies to every single one of us. And to tell the Truth is one of the most sacred possessions that a human being has and it defines who they are. So please, don't put a price on your dignity, and integrity. And if asked about the investigation, be honest. Be an example for others to follow.

Many people have died, and are dying, and many were and are being persecuted for the truth, because they value more their principles than their own lives. So, don't silence your truth. Tell the truth even if it hurts, and the truth will set you free, as Jesus said. May this moment define who you are.

Like fifteen years ago, I was playing basketball. I wanted to win the game so badly because my opponent was a very rude and mean individual. On one occasion I went for a rebound, and as I was suspended on the air, my opponent pushed me hard, I lost my balance and I fell on the floor, left arm first, and as a result I dislocated my left shoulder. As I laid there with the bone out its place, I hit my shoulder against the ground several times until I felt that the bone on my shoulder rotated back to its former place. Then I got up, and with my injured shoulder I kept on playing until I lost the game. I endured all this public humiliation because that is who I am. I hate confrontation. I had and had to stand tall, with my hands on my waist, which is a posture that have become part of me, which I acquired when I was in full uniform, when I used to place my hands on my gun belt.

Now it is clear that perpetrators don't like me, because I was a cop, a member of the New York Police Department and don't like me because they thought or think that I was or am a perpetrator. The District

Attorney's office seems to hate me likewise or alike. And the general public's perception of me seems to be highly negative. My wife wants a divorce and those whom I considered my friends have disappeared from my sight. My family are wholly innocent and completely ignorant of my dilemma. I could have faced Lt. Yaguchi, and the officers in my platoon, even the entire department if it needed to be. But to face the NYPD, the District Attorney's office, the public, the private eyes and my closest ones, is way too much for an inexperienced 32-year-old who is now 36 years old, to face and bear alone. I wonder if more than ninety percent of NYPD officers would have put an end to their own lives if the same rule were applied to them.

Not one word of encouragement I heard or received from anybody, and if anyone ever did, they were nothing more than empty words. Except that day that PO Sofoka Ahmed told me by placing his hand on my shoulder to hang in there. Words from a Muslim to a Christian, and he cannot imagine how much I thanked him for that supportive act of kindness, which I didn't find in any of my brothers and sisters in Christ.

"Don't hide Your face from Your servant, for I am in distress. Answer me quickly! Draw near to me and redeem me; ransom me because of my enemies. You know the insults I endure — my shame and disgrace. You are aware of all my adversaries. Insults have broken my heart, and I am in despair. I waited for sympathy, but there was none; for comforters, but found no one. Instead, they gave me gall for my food, and for my thirst they gave me vinegar to drink." (Psalm 69:17-21 HCSB)

One day my mother called me, and having the phone on my ears, I begin to type what she was telling me, "… yo me siento mal, porque veo que tú no eres el hombre alegre que era ante. Si a ti te pasa algo yo paso después de ti. Yo me iría también. Piensa en tu madre. Pon de tu parte. Usted nunca ha hecho una maldad. Piensa en tu vieja. Tu eres una flor porque solo tienes 33 años. Hay que tener un amigo para desahogarte. Dame esa alegría. A lo por Dios y tu madre".

My mother's statement Translated, "… I feel bad because I see that you are not the same happy man you were before. If something happens to you, I will pass after you. I will leave as well. Think of your mother. You have never done bad to anyone. Think of your old lady. You are a flower because you are only 33 years. One needs a friend with whom to talk to. Give me that happiness. **Do it for God and your mother**".

Final Chapter

BUT WHAT WOULD YOU DO?

My constant stress has greatly impacted my health. It has been like repetitive blows to my body, and mind. I see no end to this. But all I can in Christ who strengthens me. You cannot imagine how much I hate conflict. I have always tried to avoid it, but it seems to be inevitable. I dislike bringing attention, but it has come to me. After all that I have been through, nobody has claimed responsibility for what they did to me. Nobody has come forward. I don't understand all this animosity towards me.

Who am I to receive all this attention? The only solution that I see to this is to make this public. Let my voice be heard and yell it out, yell out the words that I have fettered and kept enchained because I was afraid of the unknown. William Shakespeare wrote, "El dolor que no habla, gime en el corazón hasta que lo rompe," which translated to English means, "The grief that does not speak, moans in the heart until it breaks it" or straight from Shakespeare, "Give sorrow words; the grief that does not speak knits up the o-er wrought heart and bids it break."

No wonder why when I checked my heart with the doctor that he made me an echocardiogram, the study found that I had a mild regurgitation on my tricuspid valve of my heart and a mild septal asymmetric hypertrophy of the left ventricle of my heart. Besides causing me high blood pressure, and suffering from other conditions, they are really breaking my heart.

They have robbed me of my good name. But as Booker T. Washington once said, "I shall allow no man to belittle my soul by making me hate him." Thank God, I don't hate those who have harm me. But I am hurt, deeply hurt because of them. Neither have I held resentment for those who saw what I was going through, but didn't do anything to stop it. But God is good, all the time, God is good. And as Jeremiah said, I say that **God** is my portion, and nobody will take him away from me. Also, Jeremiah 17:18 said, "Let those be put to shame who persecute me, but let me not be put to shame…." However, I learned that Lieutenant Naoki

Yaguchi was honored for becoming the 1st Japanese Captain. Yes, he is now Captain Naoki Yaguchi. On the other hand, I have become the most persecuted, mistreated, humiliated, and harassed police officer in the history of the NYPD.

AN IMPORTANT UPDATE:

In January 2023, Inspector Naoki Yaguchi announced his retirement without his full pension since he almost completed 18 years of service in the department, and not fulfilling his 20 years career as is required in order to receive full pension benefits. The reason for his early retirement is unknown. But I can speculate that the reason behind his early retirement has to do with one man: EMMANUEL HERNANDEZ

FINALLY

Before closing, I do want to honor my sister Olga. When we first arrived from the Dominican Republic, she was already engaged in the Dominican Republic to a man of a humble and poor family. However, as days went by, at the building where we lived in Manhattan at 506 West 171 street, New York, N.Y 10032 (A building of 5 floors and 20-24 apartments), the landlord of the building used to collect his rent in person at our apartment. I believe that his name was Rabon, and I was ten years old at the time. This landlord was the owner of several buildings. After several visits to my apartment, the landlord confessed to my mother that he wanted to marry her daughter, but my sister told him that she was engaged. After that, he kept visiting our apartment to collect the rent himself or to see my sister.

However, my sister went to the Dominican Republic, and she married the man with whom she was engaged to. She honored her engagement. She took a big picture of her with her husband on the wedding night, she framed the picture, and she hung it on the wall of the living room. On day, our landlord visited our apartment, and he saw the framed picture hanging on the wall and he said, "Oh, so she got married?" This was the last time we saw him. My sister, a factory worker, valued love over money by marrying a poor man instead of an over 6-foot-high Anglo-Saxon millionaire.

Later, we found out that our landlord died of a heart attack or stroke. It seemed that he wanted to leave his fortune to someone, but my sister rejected it. This is why I am proud of her integrity and dignity. She was never touched by a man until the day that she married him. This is why I solute her.

I have always tried to be in good term with God and man, but it has been difficult with men, because evil hate good naturally. There is a difference between getting sick and being made sick. In my case, I was made sick because of a terrorist act committed against me. There is no way that a human being can do a good job while receiving strange interferences constantly. This is a critical and crucial time in life where there is a desperate man who need clarification my dear brothers and sisters. Many already have, whether consciously or unconsciously, blood in their hands. Don't take this secret with you to your grave.

So far, nobody has stood for me. I wouldn't have felt bad if I had done something wrong, and would have been punished for it, because I would have deserved it. But to know that I did nothing wrong to be treated the way that I am being treated is what angers me. I would have felt the same way if it had been done to you or to any other human being unknown to me. But I have one question. **Who got away from the thing or things that he or she did and that I am being blamed for?** This experience has taught me that what something appears to be, isn't always the case. And that many people treat them I think' as if it were. They make their 'I think' a reality even when that reality doesn't exist. I have a deep and profound thirst for justice.

In addition, to this day I wonder why I wasn't, and I am not protected by the **New York State Civil Rights Law Section 50-a?** When will their perennial cruelty towards me come to an end? When am I dead? This has been absolutely a **'"rare and exceptional circumstances,"'** which is a term used by District Attorney Cy Vance Jr. himself which appeared on the New York Daily News article, " Cy hands susps to Ice for deport," by Steven Rex Brown, where he explains why he is turning some suspects over to ICE.

Thank you for reading my diary. May God bless you, keep you safe, and may the peace of God be always with you.

So please, stretch an arm towards me and take me out of the mouth of this lion by giving your opinion and by providing me with information pertaining to all of this, because that is all I need. No matter how small or big, any information is highly appreciated. For all I need is for you to tell the truth, my truth.

You can write me your feedback at: Emmalher71@gmail.com

IF YOU WANT ME TO INQUIRE AND FIND OUT WHAT REALLY LEAD TO MY PERSECUTION THRU ANY MEAN NECESSARY, I NEED FINANCIAL SUPPORT TO MOVILIZE. THEREFORE, ANY FINANCIAL CONTRIBUTION WILL BE HIGHLY APPRECIATED, AT:

EMMANUEL HERNANDEZ
CAPITAL ONE BANK
ACCOUNT NUMBER: 36056798488
ROUTING: 031176110

Again, thank you for reading my diary. May God bless you, keep you safe, and may the peace of God be always with you.

"You pushed me hard to make me fall, but the Lord helped me. The Lord is my strength and my song; He has become my salvation." (Psalm 118:13-14 HCSB)

AS FOR NOW, I FINISH, CLOSE THIS DIARY WITH THESE FINAL WORDS. THANK YOU, LORD, THANK YOU GOD FOR EVERYTHING, FOR THE GOOD AND THE BAD THAT HAPPENS IN MY LIFE. I PRAISE YOU AND WORSHIP YOU IN THE MIDDLE OF MY CAOS. THANK YOU FOR BEING MY TRUE COMPANION AND MY TRUTHFUL FRIEND. THANK YOU FOR BEING MY STRENGHT AND HOPE, FOR BECAUSE OF YOU, I STILL LIVE. THANK YOU. EMMANUEL HERNANDEZ

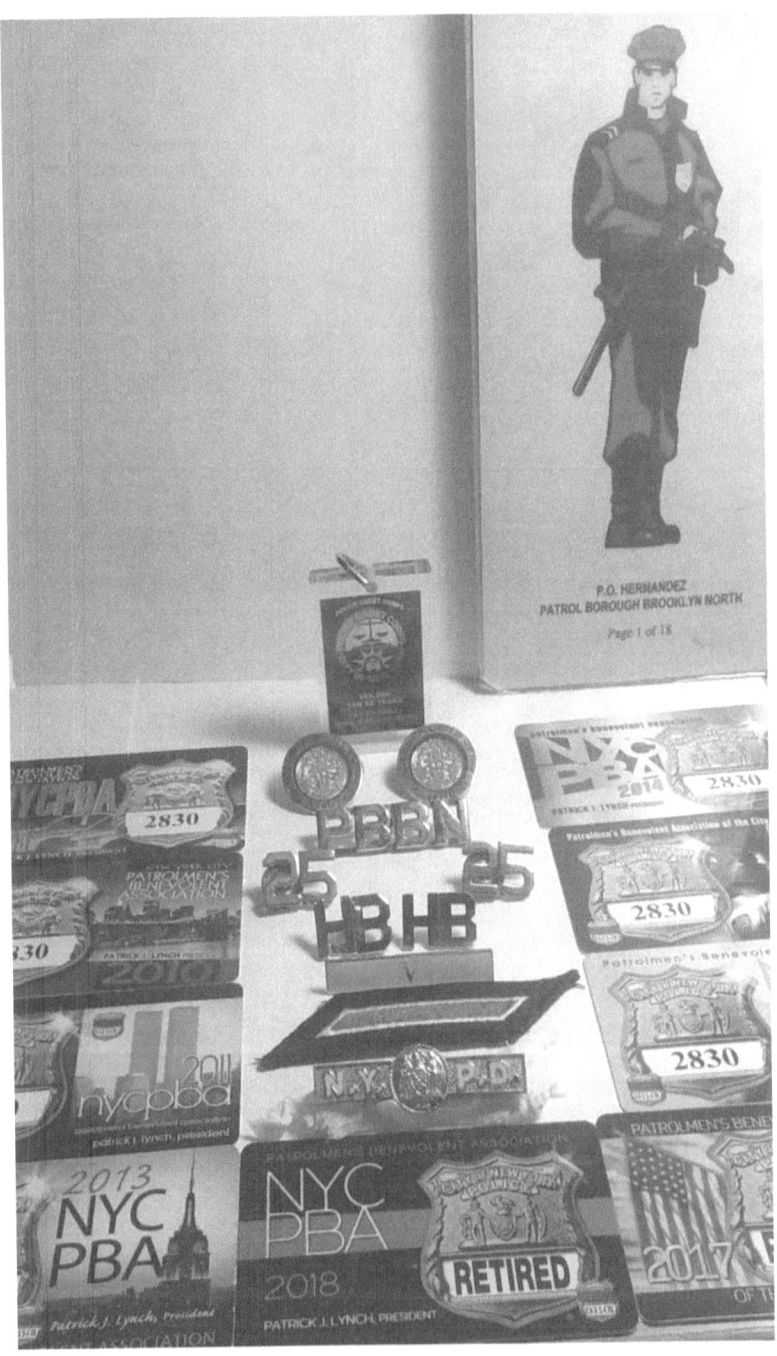

P.O. HERNANDEZ
PATROL BOROUGH BROOKLYN NORTH

THE END OF A SO HARD-FOUGHT DREAM.

RESOURCES

By McCarthy, Craig and Bruce Golding on **April 22, 2019** by the New York Post.

"**Prosecutors across the city are using secrete spreadsheets to identify cops who could have trouble on the witness stand because they have been sued, arrested, accused of misconduct or testified suspiciously in the past, sources told the post on Monday**" 701

Tuesday, April 17, 2018 on the website BuzzFeed I read a list of NYPD police misconducts and in one of them was my former **25th precinct companion PO Damien Banks** who on **1/24/2012 (702)**

Monday, March 27, 2017 I read an article on the New York Post titled, "**Brooklyn Prosecutor Accused of Forging Wiretap Faces Federal Char**" by Carrega, Christina, and Andrew Keshner.

On **Tuesday, October 10, 2017** I read an article on the New York Daily News titled, "**Let Prosecutors Face Justice**" by Louis, Errol.

On **Wednesday, October 18, 2017** I read an article titled, "**Blue lies on trial: Fed hearing eyes if cop falsehoods 'widespread'**" by Andrew Keshner and Graham Rayman.

On **Tuesday, November 21, 2017** I read an article from the New York Daily News titled, "**J. Edgar Hoover's Name Lives in Infamy**," by Richard Cohen.

On **Saturday, December 9, 2017** I read a New York Daily News article titled, "**$ 9.5 M Bad Rap: Settles with city after 24 yrs. falsely imprisoned**" by Andrew Keshner.

On **Saturday, December 16, 2017** I read a New York Daily News article titled, "**Prosecutor's hell: Co-worker's tryst lies ruined my life: suit**" by Andrew Keshner.

On **Tuesday, December 19, 2017**, I read a New York Daily News article titled, "**Cop hit-and-'lie': Hurt pedestrian will sue over "faked" report**" " by Stephen Rex Brown.

On **Monday, January 8, 2018** I read a New York Post article titled, "**Lawyer of cop accused of raping teen blasts prosecutors**," by Emily Saul

On **Thursday, January 11, 2018** I read the New York Daily News article titled, " **Shot down: DA eyes precinct for wrongdoing in gun bust rise**" by Rocco Parascandola.

On **Monday, January 22, 2018** I read a New York Daily News article titled, "**7 Yrs. AT RIKERS WITH NO SENTENCE: Convicted of attempted murder, inmate expected to finally learn fate this week**," by Stephen Rex Brown.

On **Sunday January 28, 2018** I found an article on the New York Daily News titled, "**CITY'S WORST COP**" by Esha Ray, Chelsia Rose Marcius and Graham Rayman

On **Monday January 29, 2018** I read another article in regards to the same article above on the New York Daily News by Graham Rayman titled, "**BIG FAKERY, TINY SLAP: Shroud of secrecy helped protect cop**".

On **Tuesday, January 30, 2018** I read the continuation of the article above of the New York Daily News by Erin Durkin, Rocco Parascandola and Graham Rayman titled "**COP UNDER FIRE: Why wasn't he axed, pol asks**."

On this same day of **Sunday, January 28, 2018** I read another New York Daily News article by Thomas Tracy titled, "**Blue Wall of Lies: Attacked by fellow cop, told to say I slipped, says officer**."

On **Monday, February 12, 2018** I read an article on the New York Post titled, "**NYPD cop accused of mugging stranger wants $50 M from city**" by Emily Saul.

On **Tuesday, February 27, 2018** I read an article on the New York Daily News written by Molly Crane-Newman, Thomas Tracy and Graham Rayman.

On **Sunday, March 4, 2018** I read the following New York Daily News article by Police Commissioner James O'Neill: **Battle VS Lying cops**: **Commish: NYPD is ever vigilant**.

On **March 5, 2018**, there was a New York Post article written by Ruth Brown: **NYPD cops lie and steal get slap on the wrist, report reveals**.

Wednesday, March 14, 2018 I read a New York Daily News article titled, "**Secrets of the Blue Line: Public kept In The Dark**," by Graham Rayman, John Annese, and Thomas Tracy.

On **Thursday, March 15, 2018** I read the following New York Daily News article written by Esha Ray, Shayna Jacobs, Victoria Bekiempis and Graham Rayman: **Secrets of the Blue Line**.

On **Friday, April 6, 2018** I read a New York Daily News article titled, "**$75G RIP IN SPYING**" by Laura Dimon and Thomas Tracy.

On **Tuesday, May 29, 2018** I read a New York Daily News article titled, "**NYPD Pains in the Brass**" by Graham Rayman.

On Thursday, February 15, 2018, I read the following article on The New York Daily News: **Capt. Indicted in cop-probe delay,** by Rocco Parascandola, John Annese, Thomas Tracy and Graham Rayman.

On **Wednesday, February 21, 2018** another article came on a different newspapers, the New York Post, pertaining to Lt. Yaguchi: **NYPD captain intentionally botched DWI case against detective: prosecutors** by Shawn Cohen and Chris Perez at 7:39 pm

On **Thursday, February 22, 2018**, I read on the New York Daily News another article in regards to him: **NYPD captain surrenders in DWI coverup**.

On **Saturday, December 1, 2018**, I read an article from the New York Daily News titled, "**Pols: Which Finest are known liars?**" by Janon Fisher.

On **Sunday, January 13, 2019** I read a New York Daily News article titled, "**The NYPD is goin' Crazy on me: cop. Payback for 'panties' hit on his boss**" by Kerry Burke and Thomas Tracy."

On **Sunday, January 20, 2019** I read a New York Daily News article titled, "**Cop is arrested in pot sale**," by Thomas Tracy.

On **Monday, July 29, 2019** there was a NY Daily News article titled, '**Latest cop to take own life was a transit unit sarge**' By Thomas Tracy, Trevor Boyer and Clayton Guse.

"**9 Frightening Things About America's Biggest Police Force**" by Tana Ganeva, Laura Gottesdiener/ AlterNet.

The book, "**THE NYPD TAPES: A SHOCKING STORY OF COPS, COVER-UPS, AND COURAGE**" by Graham A. Rayman.

on YouTube "**The video that will change your future**." Published on February 5, 2018, 7:16min.-8:00min

www.ingramcontent.com/pod-product-compliance
Lightning Source LLC
Chambersburg PA
CBHW021656120626
46545CB00004B/1259